ÉTIENNE GILSON

Étienne Gilson

An Intellectual and Political Biography

Florian Michel

Translated by James G. Colbert

The Catholic University of America Press
Washington, D.C.

Originally published as:
Florian Michel, Étienne Gilson,
Une Biographie Intellectuelle et politique.
Paris: Librairie Philosophique J. Vrin, 2018

The paper used in this publication meets the minimum requirements of
American National Standards for Information Science—Permanence of
Paper for Printed Library Materials, ANSI Z39.48-1992.
[infinity symbol here]

Cataloging-in-Publication Data is available
from the Library of Congress

ISBN: 978-0-8132-3673-5 | eISBN: 978-0-8132-3674-2

Book design by Burt&Burt
Interior set with Minion Pro and Meta Pro

To Jacques Prévotat and Fr. Thierry-Dominique Humbrecht, O.P.
extraordinary Gilsonian companions,

To Étienne Fouilloux,
In friendship and gratitude for shared insights

"It is not true that the progress of humanity must take place inevitably and by necessary laws. To the contrary, it is to be feared that this labor is always threatened by the best among men, that what has been done can always be undone, and that what could be done, may never be done. If this is the case, every error has its price."

Étienne Gilson, "L'humanisme de saint Thomas," *Atti del quinto Congresso Internazionale di filosofia*, Naples, May 5–9, 1924, 989.

"Malebranche can be explained by Marcel Proust."

"I love my time. I love it with such a love that, even after having seen my comrades fall at Verdun and little children die of hunger in the name of progress at Odessa and Saratov, I cannot bring myself to despair of it."

"An hour with Étienne Gilson," *Les nouvelles littéraires*,
Paris, January 3, 1925, 1–2.

"St. Bonaventure was taken prisoner at Verdun at the same time that I was."

Sketches of Étienne Gilson, *Les nouvelles littéraires*, Paris, January 3, 1925, 1–2.

Contents

Translator's Preface

Very briefly, I want to thank the Catholic University of America Press for the honor of permitting me to help introduce Florian Michel to the English-speaking world. Professor Michel is the editor of volumes I and II of Étienne Gilson's complete works (*Un philosophe dans la cité, 1908–1943*, Paris: Vrin, 2019; *Un philosophe dans la cité 1944–1973*, Paris: Vrin, 2023). He has done an invaluable service in situating this great personality, historian of ideas, Christian philosopher, and theoretician of art in his country and time. My thanks for Professor Michel's friendship and assistance.

The Catholic University of America Press has painstakingly helped to keep the project to the highest standards.

Finally and always, I would not be able to do this work without the tireless assistance of Ana Goicoa Colbert.

Author's Acknowledgments

This book would have never seen the light of day without a great deal of help; to begin with, the enormous good will, patience, and generous dedication of archivists and conservators:

Dominique Parcollet of the Centre d'Histoire de Sciences-Po; Brother Jean-Michel Potin of the Archives Provinciales Dominicaines de France; Brother Damase, archivist of the Benedictine Abbey of Sainte-Marie de la-Pierre-Qui-Vire; Jessica Barr of the Archives of Saint Michael's College of Toronto, Fr. Philippe Ploix and Vincent Thauzies of the Archives Historiques de l'Archevêché de Paris; Catherine Faivre d'Arcier, Marie-Odile Germain, Anne Verdure-Mary, and Guillaume Fau de la Bibliothèque Nationale de France; Julie Le Men of l'IMEC in Normandie; Claire Guttinger of the Archives of the Collège de France; Nicolas Barbey of the Bibliothèque Municipale of Bordeaux; Patricia Reymond of the Centre d'Études and Musée Edmond-Michelet de Brive; Paul Pearson of the Thomas Merton Center of Louisville, Kentucky; Anabel Vasquez of the Centre Alexandre Koyré in Paris; Gabrielle Montarnal of the Archives Départementales des Yvelines and of the Musée Maurice Denis de Saint-Germain-en-Laye; Leslie Choquette of Assumption College in Worcester, Massachusetts;

Vincent Laloy, who has informed me of Gilson's correspondence with his father Jean Laloy; Juan Miguel Palacios of the Universidad Complutense in Madrid, who likewise shared the letters sent by Gilson to his father Leopoldo Eulogio Palacios; Margot Georges and Jacques Berchon of the Archives de l'École Pratique des Hautes Études; Julie Kieffer of the Maison de Robert Schuman at

Scy-Chazelles; Anicette Sangnier and Jean-Michel Cadiot of the Institut Marc Sangnier; Jean Leclercq and Thierry Scaillet of the Archives Maurice Blondel at the Université Catholique of Louvain; and Béatrice Gervis, trustee of the Fonds Laberthonnière at the BNF.

Likewise, I want to thank the group at Librairie Vrin that is working on the preparation of the complete works of Étienne Gilson: Anne-Marie Arnaud Paulhac, Denis Arnaud, Gaël Kervoas, Jean-François Courtine, Alain de Libera, Ruedi Imbach, Fr. Thierry-Dominique Humbrecht, as well as Fr. James K. Farge of Toronto for his customary extraordinarily gracious reception at the Pontifical Institute of Mediaeval Studies and on the campus of Saint Michael's College.

My debt to my historian friends and colleagues is ever greater: Dominique Avon, Étienne Fouilloux, Michel Fourcade, Friar Augustin Laffay, René Mougel, Charles Personnaz, Jacques Prévotat.

Finally, my immense and profound gratitude to Séverine, who has bravely reread everything, and to our dear children Clément, Claire, Étienne, and Jacques, whose creative intuition, never failing, has added color and poetry to these pages.

Abbreviations

ACCE	Archives of the Congregation for Catholic Education (Rome)
AF	Action française
AHAP	Archives de l'Archevêché de Paris
AM	Archives Maritain (Bibliothèque nationale et universitaire de Strasbourg)
AMAE	Archives du Ministère des Affaires étrangères (La Courneuve)
AN	Archives nationales
APDF	Archives de la Province Dominicaine de France (Paris)
APQV	Archives de l'abbaye de la-Pierre-qui-Vire (Yonne)
AUM	Archives of the University of Montreal
BIS	Bibliothèque interuniversitaire de la Sorbonne
BNF	Bibliothèque nationale de France
BNUS	Bibliothèque nationale et universitaire de Strasbourg
CHSP	Centre d'Histoire de Sciences Po (Paris)
FG	Fonds Étienne Gilson (Saint Michael's College Archives, Toronto)

GABF	General Archives of the Basilian Fathers
IMEC	Institut Mémoires de l'Édition Contemporaine
ISFC	Institut Scientifique Franco-Canadien
MRP	Mouvement Républicain Populaire
NAF	Nouvelles acquisitions françaises (BNF)
PIMS	Pontifical Institute of Mediaeval Studies (Toronto)
SMCA	Saint Michael's College Archives (Toronto)
UCA	University of Chicago Archives
UNDA	University of Notre Dame Archives (Indiana)

Introduction

How can one tell that he is not fabricating the history he believes he narrates?[1]

Étienne Gilson (1884–1974) was not only the learned professor of medieval philosophy at the Sorbonne and the Collège de France who left us scholarly tomes on Thomas Aquinas, Augustine of Hippo, Duns Scotus, Bonaventure, and Bernard of Clairvaux. In the obituary note Étienne Borne wrote for *La Croix*, he rightly emphasized Gilson's political allegiances, citizen of the City of God and of the City of Men, who "did not evade the problems of humanity through metaphysical abstractions, either in the Middle Ages or in our own century."[2] Even if he deemed himself a "bad politician,"[3] part of his output and of his existence was vigorously involved in the socio-political realm under the great banner of "integral humanism" from 1924 or 1925[4] onward, and of the "common

1 Letter from Étienne Gilson to Jacques Maritain, April 6, 1953, *Correspondance 1923–1971: Deux approches de l'être*, ed. Géry Prouvost (Paris, Vrin, 1991), 188.

2 Étienne Borne, "Stature d'Étienne Gilson," *La Croix*, September 22, 1978, 10.

3 Letter from Étienne Gilson to Augusto Del Noce, May 8, 1968, *Caro collega ed amico: Lettere di Étienne Gilson ad Augusto Del Noce (1964–1969)*, ed. Massimo Borghesi (Sienna: Cantagalli, 2008), 163.

4 The paternity of the phrase "integral humanism" in Thomist circles belongs to Gilson, ten years before the lectures and book by Maritain bearing this title. See

good," after February 6, 1934.[5] He placed himself under the double rejection, no to communism, no to fascism, neither subordination of politics to economics, nor renunciation of the subordination of the political to the ethical, to the "spiritual" and the "universal."

This neglected or unappreciated part of Gilson's activity affects the majority of the great debates of his time: the Church's place in society and laicism, but also the political parties, educational concerns, the construction of Europe, international relations, the occupation, the extreme right, Atlantic problems. More deeply, it involves thinking through the "universal society" in gestation, the "world republic" less defined than hoped for by philosophers and theologians since Tertullian and Augustine. The issue of political, religious, and philosophical "liberalism" poses itself fully for someone like Gilson who grew up in the wake of Modernism and of Le Sillon, the movement led by Marc Sangnier. The philosopher argued on behalf of a liberal conception of secularism in the nineteen-thirties, that is to say, in favor of a genuine state *neutrality*.[6] In the MRP [Translator: Mouvement Républicaine Populaire, the Christian Democratic Party of the Fourth Republic] after World War II, Gilson intended to promote a "concept of democracy" that was neither "an anarchist liberalism, nor a totalitarian statism, but the conscious and reflective placing of the State at the services of all freedoms."[7] Likewise a liberal Thomist, Gilson was under heavy fire from the intransigents, recalling the legitimate pluralism of Christian theologies and philosophies, and willingly emphasizing the "radical contingency of Catholic philosophies and theologies in relation to faith."[8]

Étienne Gilson, "L'humanisme de saint Thomas," in *Atti del quinto Congresso Internazionale di Filosofia, Napoli, 5–9 Maggio 1924* (Naples: 1925), 976–89: "The humanism of Saint Thomas consists in a conscious will to do justice to the beauty of human beings and to assure the integral development of their nature."—See likewise Étienne Gilson, *Saint Thomas: Textes sur la morale* (Paris: Vrin, 1998), 10: "Thomist ethics . . . is a Christian humanism. . . . It bears witness to the fundamental identity of a Christianity in which complete humanism is included and an integral humanism that finds its full satisfaction only in Christianity." (Originally, *Saint Thomas d'Aquin* (Paris: Gabalda, 1925.)

5 In March 1934, Étienne Gilson signed the manifesto entitled "Pour le bien commun [For the common good: The responsibilities of the Christian and the present moment]." See Jacques Maritain, *Oeuvres Complètes*, vol. 5, *1932–1935* (Fribourg, Switzerland: Éditions Universitaires; and Paris: Éditions Saint-Paul, 1932), 1022–41.

6 Étienne Gilson, "Libéralisme et neutralité," *Sept*, November 9, 1934.

7 Étienne Gilson, *Notre démocratie* (Paris: S.E.R.P., 1947).

8 Letter from Étienne Gilson to Fr. Irénée, June 10, 1942, Archives de l'abbaye de la-Pierre-qui-Vire (Yonne) [APQV]: "With the same faith, Catholics are equally saved, although they may be

Gilson's positions are sometimes summarily identified with those of Jacques Maritain. They are not very accessible today because of the medium in which they were transmitted. Sometimes they are reduced to their polemical value—against Blondel, against Teilhard de Chardin, against the liturgical translations in the postconciliar period, and so on. These positions are scattered throughout volumes, publishers, courses, lectures, or correspondence, written during seven decades of intellectual activity. They were sometimes set out on the first page of daily newspapers. An archived letter reveals that in March 1933 Gilson had signed the manifesto issued by the Collège de France on behalf of German Jewish intellectuals threatened by Nazism.[9] In a letter that appeared in the British press, we discover that Gilson was ephemerally the vice-president of the Catholic Action movement *Ad Lucem*, Association de Laïcs Universitaires Catholiques et Missionnaires.[10] A chance discovery in a catalogue of the sale of archives brings to light Gilson's role in saving intellectuals threatened by the disaster of June 1940; in this case he recommended Alexandre Koyré to American universities.[11] By reading the report of an English diplomat we learn that in 1946 Gilson articulated the well-known formula about "the fertile diversity of cultures" that appears in the founding document of UNESCO.[12] Through correspondence between Maritain and Journet, we see Gilson in political discussion with an anxious Pope Pius XII

Thomists, Scotists, Bonaventurians, or Augustinians. Accordingly, there is a contingency of Catholic philosophies and theologies in relation to the faith. That is a fact." Gilson gave a lecture in June 1942 in the Abbey of la-Pierre-qui-Vire. There, he evoked the "radical contingency" of philosophy in regard to the faith. The lecture was very badly received, notably by the [translator: contemporary] Reverend Father Thomas Aquinas, educated in the French Seminary of the 1920s, who brandished conciliar decrees and passages from Denzinger against Gilson.

9 Letter from Étienne Gilson to Ralph Barton Perry, May 27, 1933, Harvard University Archives. Gilson explained: "I myself cannot enter Germany because I am a pacifist and signed the French protest against the persecution of the Jewish intellectuals in Germany." The text of the position appears in the publication *Paix et droit, organe de l'alliance israélite universelle*, Paris, March 1933, 7.

10 The Association was founded in 1931. See Étienne Gilson, "The Layman and Society," *New Blackfriars* 16, no. 182 (May 1935): 377. On this point, see the letter from Fr. Robert Prévost to Étienne Gilson, August 28, 1965, FG, SMCA [Fonds Gilson, Saint Michael's College Archives, Toronto]: Gilson became vice-president of the movement in 1932 with Fr. Thomas Delos, and seems to have left this position in the second half of the 1930s.

11 Letter from Étienne Gilson to Alexandre Koyré, 1940, sales catalogue of Librairie Vignes.

12 Frank R. Cowell, "Planning the Organisation of UNESCO, 1942–1946: A Personal Record," *Cahiers d'histoire mondiale, Journal of World History, Cuadernos de Historia Mundial* 10, no. 1 (1966): 225.

on the eve of the Cold War; amazingly, he encouraged the Sovereign Pontiff to "build on the Church's supernatural character."[13]

A historian of medieval philosophy and a philosopher, Gilson was successively professor at the Universities of Lille, Strasbourg, the Sorbonne, the École pratique des hautes études, Harvard, the University of Toronto, and the Collège de France. He was a member of the Académie française and a Christian-Democratic Counselor of the Republic (March 1947 to November 1948). Étienne Gilson lets us examine a *political* theory and action, rooted as will be seen, in the long history of the Church that goes back to the author of the *Epistle to Diognetus* and St. Augustine, but at the same time take into account the upheavals of the twentieth century. According to Étienne Borne's frequently repeated expression, Jacques Maritain was a "Christian philosopher of democracy." Without reducing himself to that, Étienne Gilson, along with others, was perhaps one of the Christian philosophers *critical* of Christian democracy.

In English, there is a biography of Étienne Gilson written by Fr. Laurence Shook (Toronto: Pontifical Institute of Mediaeval Studies [PIMS], 1984), based on a compilation of sources and of interviews with Gilson himself. This work, not yet translated into French, continues to be authoritative. Our biographical essay here in no way attempts to replace Fr. Shook's well-founded work. However, recent decades have seen the publication of Gilson's correspondence, notably with Jacques Maritain, Fr. Marie-Dominique Chenu, Augusto Del Noce, Henri Gouhier, Fr. Henri de Lubac, and Fr. Michel Labourdette of the *Revue thomiste*.[14] They permit us to refine our analyses and call for a new synthesis, this time freed from the necessity to establish all the actions and accomplishments of Gilson's life. In 2013, Jacques Prévotat published a nuanced political portrait of our philosopher.[15]

13 Pius XII received Étienne and Thérèse Gilson in a private audience in 1947. For echoes of the encounter see the letter of March 29, 1952, from Charles Journet to Jacques Maritain, *Correspondance Journet—Maritain*, vol. 4, *1950–1957* (Fribourg: Saint-Augustin, 2005), 192: "You recall that Gilson had found the Pope quite anxious about political events, and he had directly reminded him—at least so they told us at Rome—that there was only one issue: to rest upon the Church's supernatural character; nothing but that would win more souls to Jesus than were being lost to him."

14 See the bibliography of published sources at the end of the present volume.

15 Jacques Prévotat, "Étienne Gilson est-il un chrétien modéré?," in *Les "Chrétiens modérés" en France et en Europe (1870–1960)*, ed. Jacques Prévotat and Jean Vavasseur-Desperriers (Villeneuve d'Ascq: Presses Universitaires du Septentrion, 2013), 433–53.

Fr. Thierry-Dominique Humbrecht composed an introduction for the 2013 re-edition of Gilson's *Pour un ordre catholique* and published as an appendix a collection of reactions provoked by Gilson.[16] In 2014, Fr. Humbrecht also published a remarkable article in *Revue thomiste* titled "Étienne Gilson et la politique."[17] In it, he presented a vast panorama to clarify "certain little-known aspects of Gilson the political philosopher," and told us, "Gilson's political approach seems to be dead."[18] The observation is perfectly justified.

With the exception of scattered recent studies, it must be acknowledged that the figure of Gilson has been forgotten in French cultural history. The remoteness of his personal archives, lodged in Toronto, is probably one cause of this, but the archives in France have not been used much more. The lack of institutional posterity, the apparent expiration of Gilson's intellectual position, the disappearance of his influence in university and Church, the rather unjustified discredit of the great Catholic intellectual personalities, as well as the lack of an institution devoted to their memory, are all likely causes of this state of affairs.

THOMISM, POLITICAL PASSION, AND CONTROVERSIES

The relations between Thomism and French politics are a complex historical matter. Henri de Lubac has depicted "a kind of Thomism mixed with Action française in the first third of the twentieth that could count on the support of well-known persons."[19] In 1941, Yves Simon, who defined himself as a "sans-culotte Thomist" wrote to Jacques Maritain: "If St. Thomas were alive today, he would be for Franco, for Tizo, for Pétain. It is obvious."[20] In 1945 Maritain did not hesitate to declare that "intelligences are scandalized,

16 Étienne Gilson, *Pour un ordre catholique* (Paris: Desclée de Brouwer, 1934; new edition, Paris: Parole et Silence, 2013, with Thierry-Dominique Humbrecht's introduction and appendixes).

17 Thierry-Dominique Humbrecht, "Étienne Gilson et la politique," *Revue thomiste* 104, no. 2 (2014): 227–87.

18 Humbrecht, "Étienne Gilson et la politique," 229.

19 Henri de Lubac, *Lettres de M. Étienne Gilson adressées au P. de Lubac et commentées par celui-ci*, rev. ed. (Paris: Cerf, 2013), 224. [Published in English as *Letters of Étienne Gilson to Henri de Lubac, with Commentary by Henri de Lubac*, trans. Mary Emily Hamilton (San Francisco: Ignatius Press, 1988); for a sense of the period, see 47, 51.]

20 Letter from Yves Simon to Jacques Maritain, *Correspondance Jacques Maritain—Yves Simon*, vol. 2, *Les années américaines (1941–1961)*, ed. Florian Michel (Paris: CLD, 2012), 65.

they have heard too many Thomists sing the litanies of Mashal."[21] Likewise, Maritain denounced "the Thomists who are reactionaries in politics."[22] Simon's phrase clearly indicated the philosophical work he planned to undertake: to draw out St. Thomas's political intuitions in order to find a new basis for Catholic political thought about democracy. "Subsequently, the ambiguities caused by a sector of the Maurassian or Petainist clergy were described precisely in historical studies of 'neo-Thomism' in the context of the condemnation of Modernism[23] or of the National Revolution.[24] They were however eradicated by philosophers, even if historians, for good reasons, could not always understand the arguments."

The two greatest figures of Thomist philosophy in the twentieth century, Jacques Maritain and Étienne Gilson, were both republicans by family tradition. Both sought to show the deep bonds between Thomas Aquinas and a "genuine philosophy of democracy,"[25] sometimes at the cost of violent criticism. They were regularly taken to task by the most intransigent wing of the Church. In 1951, an anonymous lampoon traced a direct connection between Gilson and the liberal Catholic currents condemned in the nineteenth century: "Gilson deserved all the loathing expressed in other times by Gregory XVI and Pius IX against his ancestor Lamennais. The disciple reproduced all the errors of his teacher with deliberate cynicism."[26]

21 Letter from Jacques Maritain to Charles Journet, June 24, 1945, *Correspondance Journet—Maritain*, vol. 3, *1940–1949* (Paris: Saint-Augustin, 1998), 324.

22 Jacques Maritain, letter of July 24, 1965, *Œuvres complètes*, vol. 12, *1968–1973* (Fribourg: Éditions Universitaires, 1993), 1236.

23 Jacques Prévotat, *Les catholiques et l'Action Française: Histoire d'une condamnation* (Paris: Fayard, 2001), 71–75.

24 Ruedi Imbach, "Démocratie ou monarchie? La discussion sur le meilleur régime politique chez quelques interprètes français de Thomas d'Aquin (1893–1928)," in *Saint Thomas au XXe siècle: Acts du colloque du centenaire de la Revue Thomiste*, ed. Serge-Thomas Bonino (Paris: Saint-Paul, 1994), 335–50: "The recollection of certain passages in Thomas lets us affirm that it is undeniable that there are strong democratic elements in St. Thomas Aquinas's thinking. In this sense, Fr. Schwalm and Jacques Maritain express a real authentic aspect of Thomas Aquinas's thinking. Still, these elements are only sketched in Thomas Aquinas, who expresses them on the level of general principles."

25 Jacques Maritain, *Christianisme et démocratie* (New York: Éditions de la Maison française, 1943); Étienne Gilson, *Notre démocratie*; *L'Aube*, April 26, 27, 28, 29, and 30, and May 2–3, 4, and 5, 1948.

26 Mimeographed pamphlet, 1951, Archives Maritain [AM], at Bibliothèque nationale et universitaire de Strasbourg [BNUS]. The document is reproduced with an introduction in the *Correspondence Journet—Maritain*, 4:869–84. The passage quoted is on p. 873. See likewise the pages titled "Jacques Maritain is no longer a Catholic, Thomist Philosopher," no date, circa 1951,

The politico-religious issues at stake in Maritain's work have been analyzed by historians and philosophers. The basic lines of Maritain's path have been traced from his being a follower of Juarès in his youth to his conversion to Catholicism in the line of Léon Bloy, from his dispute with Action Française to *Primauté du spiritual* (1927) [*The Things That Are Not Caesar's*, 1930], *Humanisme intégrale* (1934–36) [*True Humanism*, 1938, and *Integral Humanism*, 1968], to *L'Homme et l'État* (1949–1951) [*Man and the State*, 1951].[27] Gilson was "born Catholic, and affirmed his religious commitment loud and clear," as he wrote in *Vie Catholique* in 1924.[28] At the other end of the twentieth century, de Lubac commented that one of Gilson's principal contributions was his "simple, robust faith,"[29] with, let us stress, an assertive, apologetic, and sometimes dogmatic side. "Genuine agreement always consists in defining oneself and not being confused," he wrote to Léon Brunschvicg in 1925. "[It is necessary] to accept oneself as one is in order to direct oneself wholly toward that which one serves."[30] In 1925, Gilson did not hesitate to deplore the "lack of pride" of French Catholics. He is one of those who boldly write that Catholic thinkers are "taken seriously by nonbelievers" only in the measure in which they put the person of Jesus and the grace of God in the foreground of their reflections.[31] "My personal dogmatism

4 pages, AM. Maritain's anonymous enemies, in the fundamentalist movement of Fr. Messineo and Charles De Koninck, also attack the "absurd flattery" that Gilson directs to Maritain.

27 Étienne Fouilloux, *Une Église en quête de liberté: La pensée catholique française entre Modernisme et Vatican II (1914–1962)* (Paris: Desclée de Brouwer, 1998); Philippe Chenaux, *Entre Maurras et Maritain: Une génération intellectuelle catholique (1920–1930)* (Paris: Cerf, 1999); Michel Fourcade, "Feu la modernité? Maritain et les maritainismes," PhD diss., Université Paul Valéry-Montpellier III, 2000.

28 Étienne Gilson, Letter to the editor, "Pour travailler tranquille," *La Vie catholique en France et à l'étranger*, November 1, 1924, 2.

29 Cardinal Henri de Lubac to Étienne Gilson, *Lettres de M. Étienne Gilson adressées au P. de Lubac*, 253.

30 Letter from Étienne Gilson to Léon Brunschvicg, January 5, 1925, Institut Mémoires de l'Édition Contemporaine [IMEC].

31 Étienne Gilson, *Christianity and Philosophy*, translated by Ralph McDonald, CSB (New York: Sheed & Ward, 1939) (published for the Institute of Mediaeval Studies). See chapter 5, "The Intelligence in the Service of Christ the King," 103–25; in particular, 117, 119: "I believe, therefore, that I ought to say, first of all, that one of the gravest evils from which Catholicism suffers today is that Catholics are not proud enough of their faith. . . . Run through the history of French philosophy in these latter years; you will see that Catholic thinkers have been taken seriously by unbelievers In the exact measure in which they put in the first place what, for them, is truly first: the person of Jesus Christ and his grace."

requires the understanding of that of others and the complete respect for their freedom."[32]

Being a democrat and a republican was a constant in Gilson's life. In contrast with Maritain, we find no denunciation of the "Masonic Republic" at the moment of the expulsion of the religious congregations, even though Gilson was horrified by "the hideous policies of Combism" [translator: Émile Combes, leftist, Freemason, Prime Minister from June 1902 to January 1905].[33] As a young man, he was "deeply affected by the condemnation of Le Sillon in 1910," even though he was not politically involved at the time.[34] He had no ties intellectually or of friendship with Action Française. Again, unlike Maritain, the year of the publication of the first edition of *Thomisme* (1919), he did not sign the "Manifesto for a Party of Intelligence." A "solid republican" according to Henri de Lubac's expression,[35] Gilson was very measured in political matters. The first and last goal of good government is peace, he often noted: "close up, the situation of France does not seem very pretty. From far away, it is frightful. . . . I am always for the cabinet in power," he wrote after the victory of the Popular Front. "At this moment, I am for those who try to avoid a civil war, and I will always be for them, whoever they are."[36] Gilson sometimes had the lack of charm of someone with the annoying certainty of never being mistaken and always occupying the middle high ground. He wrote to a philosopher friend at Harvard in 1938 that he was neither *communist* nor *fascist*, because he *knew* that those two doctrines were *false*. The friend knew it too. In the spirit of healthy dogmatism, why not say so?[37] "The revolution will be done by the law, or it will not be done," he again explained to one of his MRP colleagues in April 1948.[38]

32 Letter from Étienne Gilson to Louis Pasteur Vallery-Radot, quoted in "Réponse au discours de réception d'Étienne Gilson" (reply to the reception speech by Étienne Gilson), May 29, 1947, complete text available on the Académie française website: https://www.academie-francaise.fr/reponse-au-discours-de-reception-detienne-gilson.

33 Étienne Gilson, *The Philosopher and Theology*, trans. Cécile Gilson (New York: Random House, 1962), 58.

34 Étienne Gilson, *The Philosopher and Theology*, 56.

35 *Lettres de M. Étienne Gilson adressées au P. de Lubac*, 224.

36 Letter from Étienne Gilson to Henri Gouhier, October 30, 1936, Archives Gouhier (part of National Archives, not to be confused with Archives Madame Gouhier).

37 Letter from Étienne Gilson to Ralph Barton Perry, August 15, 1938, Harvard Archives.

38 Étienne Gilson, *Notre démocratie*.

Gilson's many interventions in politics may have seemed doubly paradoxical: a medievalist philosopher involved in the present and a friend of the New World to the point of crossing the Atlantic for a semester each year during fifty years is an unusual and, in principle, surprising picture. Mauriac and many others along with him, on occasion, did not refrain from reproaching Gilson for "dabbling in journalism."[39] Gilson himself was aware of "usurping a role" and of "going beyond his trade," "under I know not what inner pressure, with no pleasure in doing it."[40] In the long term, Gilson's numerous socio-political actions escape any rigid classification.

Cautiously approved in the newspaper *La Croix*,[41] those interventions provoked "intense astonishment in *secularist* university sectors," according to Paul Vignaux's euphemistic expression,[42] and even gave offense to some of his colleagues within the "Republic of professors linked to secularist militancy."[43] Marc Bloch, whose candidacy to the Collège de France Gilson had unsuccessfully supported in 1933,[44] found the volume *Pour un ordre catholique* published by Gilson in 1933 "curious, lively, and singularly frightful"; he privately wondered where the "solder" was between Gilson's "religious mentality" and his "image of the world," between the honorable university man and the Catholic militant.[45] Maurice Halbwachs, an old colleague given

39 François Mauriac, "Les amarres rompues," *Le Figaro*, February 20–21, 1951.

40 Letter from Étienne Gilson to Fr. Marie-Dominique Chenu, May 6, 1934, Fond Chenu, Archives de la Province Dominicaine de France (Paris) [APDF].

41 See, for example, the editorial by Jean Guiraud, *La Croix*, January 23, 1935, 1–2: "The most fundamental problem has been posed by M. Gilson with a logic and frankness that leave nothing to be desired."

42 Paul Vignaux, "Étienne Gilson," in *Encyclopedia Universalis* (Paris: CFL-Encyclopaedia Britannica, 1979), 591, col. 3.

43 Paul Vignaux, in "Étienne Gilson," *Annuaire de l'École pratique des hautes études* 77 (1978–79): 28, speaks for himself, a member of the SGEN [Syndicat général de l'éducation nationale], dissatisfied with social Catholicism, and Christian democracy, concerned about freeing France from a "social Christian order" and about secularizing society.

44 Letter from Marc Bloch to Étienne Gilson, December 28, 1933, FG, SMCA. Similarly on March 20, 1934: "I am proud of having you as my advocate."

45 Letter from Marc Bloch to Lucien Febvre, February 11, 1935, *Correspondance Marc Bloch—Lucien Febvre*, vol. 2 (Paris: Fayard, 2003), 209: "Have you had the chance to leaf through Gilson's *L'Ordre Catholique*? It is curious, lively, and singularly frightful. A historian ought to understand everything. I admit that I understand badly. Take Saint Louis. Yes, I understand how his religious mentality is connected with his picture of the world. I can't see what the solder is in a Gilson. Nevertheless, it would be too facile to say there is no solder. Surely, we must make room for a kind of voluntary ignorance, ignorance about everything that is both physical sciences and critical disciplines. Along with that, some passages on teaching and his lack of a grasp of youth are worth meditating upon for the most secular among us."

to harsh judgements, also, mistakenly, reproached Gilson "for preaching *immigration to the interior* to Catholics."[46] By contrast, Maritain emphasized that Gilson stressed "very clearly that [his] intention was not to invite Catholics to secession."[47] Emmanuel Mounier, to express his reverence for his professor—"who guided a whole period of our youth"—and at the same time to underline their separation in the political arena, wrote that he himself was one of the "critics" motivated by a "demanding friendship."[48]

It must be acknowledged that Gilson had a real talent for stirring up controversies and exasperating certain of his readers. "I would be nourishing the most naive illusions," he wrote in 1936, "if I thought I were now setting forth popular opinions."[49] "Naturally, this is a provocation, both for the public and in my framework," Hubert Beuve-Méry indicated in May 1950.[50] In July 1950, after the North Atlantic Treaty was signed, Alexander Koyré wondered in a letter to Raymond Aron, on the subject of this "stupid balloon of neutralism," whether "our teacher Gilson" has not become a "progressive Christian."[51] Approved this time by Emmanuel Mounier,[52] Gilson went down

46 Maurice Halbwachs, "Ma campagne au Collège de France," *Revue d'histoire des sciences humaines* 1 (1991): 194. The original is found in the Fonds Maurice Halbwachs, IMEC, Journal, notebook 4, p. 197: "I knew that Gilson was active on the side of the Dominicans, that he demanded not only that Catholics have their own schools, but almost the possibility of living apart from non-Catholics during their whole lives, in a word, 'immigration to the interior'." In his diary Halbwachs refers to Lucien Febvre's "obscure peasant origins" to explain his "harshness" and his "group spirit" (Journal, notebook 4, p. 201). Jean Baruzi is labeled "a completely puffed up puppet," and a "cute lecher, leaden, soft, sly, rouged, larded, sad," and so on for two pages (211–12). Paul Hazard is only a "a little man" and a "counterfeit token" (221). André Siegfried is a "big bourgeois," "a rather minor talent" (222). Only the Durkheimian sociologists are spared in the human sciences.

47 Letter from Jacques Maritain to Étienne Gilson, January 4, 1935, *Correspondance 1923–1971*, ed. Prouvost, 123.

48 Emmanuel Mounier, review of *Pour un ordre catholique*, by Étienne Gilson, *Esprit*, March 1935, 959–64.

49 Étienne Gilson, *Christianity and Philosophy*, 123.

50 Letter from Hubert Beuve-Méry to Étienne Gilson, May 12, 1950, FG, SMCA. The Beuve-Méry Archive contains some sixty letters from readers about neutralism and the "Gilson Affair" (Centre d'Histoire de Sciences Po [CHSP], Fonds Beuve-Méry, 133).

51 Letter from Alexander Koyré to Raymond Aron, July 15, 1950, published in Raymond Aron, *Mémoires* (Paris: Robert Laffont, 2010), 357.

52 Emmanuel Mounier, "Le pacte atlantique," in *Carnets de Route*, vol. 2, *Les certitudes difficiles* (Paris: Seuil, 1951), 341: "Accordingly, the Atlantic Treaty does not provide any serious guarantee, does not commit America to any measure that its interest would not have automatically dictated to it in case of aggression. The mentality of protection and security, as Gilson has shown in a resounding article in *Monde*, is once more duped. If it were merely inoffensive, it would be a lesser evil, but the Treaty's vanity is bristling with dangers."

like an arrow in *Aspects de la France* by Pierre Boutang, speaking for the Pétainist Party. "Hidden in Canada," "voluntary exile,"[53] In April 1951, Gilson was brought to the stage in a play by Gabriel Marcel, *Rome n'est plus dans Rome* (Rome is no longer in Rome), with the characteristics of an erratic person.[54] Marcel takes advantage of the rhyme of "neutre" [neutral] with "pleutre" [coward]. Subsequently, he was denounced in 1953 by the Association of anti-Totalitarian Intellectuals. Taken to task on page one of the *Canard enchaîné* of January 31, 1951, Gilson was described as an "elitist rat trying to flee the European raft on the point of sinking."

In Jean Madiran's debatable opinion, Gilson was "a man of the left, although of wonderful health; his left was not the nasty, poisonous ideological left, as in Maritain's case; it was the left of the poor who distrust the rich."[55] According to the Action Française of the 1930s, Gilson was "a man with principles of the right" and friendships that inclined him leftwards—an analysis Gilson found insane.[56] "The formula of Catholic order does not seem to lean leftwards," Étienne Borne explained in regard to Gilson in *La Croix* in 1978, while Paul Vignaux insisted that Gilson in character was "very much a non-conformist."[57]

With good reason it could be said that Gilson's political thinking was "often disconcerting." Sometimes he seemed to situate himself in the intransigent Catholic camp, preaching unconditional submission to the hierarchy, and setting up the plans for a Catholic civilization, whereas at other moments he seemed to be an *avant-garde* Catholic, critical toward the hierarchy and favoring bold political action.[58] On occasion he did not hesitate to educate certain bishops. A rapid survey of his reception in the political and ecclesial

53 *Aspects de la France*, February 16, 1951, 4.

54 Geneviève Latour, *Le Théâtre, reflet de la IVe République: Evénements, politique, société, idées* (Paris: Bibliothèque Historique de la Ville de Paris and the Association de la régie théâtrale, 1995), 229–32. Gabriel Marcel wrote in *Combat*, April 18, 1951; "This is the theme of people who leave, who abandon their country driven by a fear that they cannot keep from growing, dominating them, and driving them to anguish," *Nouvelles littéraires* of April 12, 1951, Marcel insists that he is not dealing with the Gilson case. At any rate, the critics perceive "Gilson's silhouette" and point to "behavior that resembles gossip and has its spinelessness." (J.-H. Rey, *Les temps modernes*, 1951).

55 Jean Madiran, "Pour saluer Gilson," in *Gilson, Chroniques philosophiques* (Paris: Difralivre, 1992), 15.

56 On this point see Étienne Gilson, "Pour éclairer *La nouvelle lanterne*," *Sept* 69, June 14, 1935, 4.

57 Vignaux, "Étienne Gilson," in *Encyclopedia Universalis*, 591, col. 3.

58 Aline Coutrot, *Un courant de pensée catholique: L'hebdomadaire Sept (mars 1934–août 1937)* (Paris: Cerf, 1961), 95.

spheres invites us to take the measure of the variety of critiques that he stirred up and the debates in which he engaged with Aron, Bloch, Borne, Boutang, Halbwachs, Koyré, Marcel, Maritain, Mounier, Vignaux, and so on.

Marc Bloch's comment to Lucien Febvre in 1935 is perfectly legitimate. Where, indeed, is the solder holding Gilson's opus together? To say there was none would indeed be "too facile."[59] What did Gilson's political thinking owe to Thomas Aquinas's philosophy? How did Gilson's political activity fit into modernity or rather, to use an endogenous category, into the present time? What was Gilson's personal evolution and what were its turning points? Were his political positions comparable to those developed by Jacques Maritain (1882–1973) in *Integral Humanism* or *Man and the State*? How did Gilson interpret the major ideologies of the twentieth century? What was his perception of the totalitarianisms, anti-Semitism, cultural pluralism, secularizations, or of the Catholic crisis? What did he think about war, peace, or international relations? What was the perception of this "committed Gilson" in the university and the Church? What is his influence on the intellectuals of the following generation?

SIC TRANSIT GLORIA MUNDI?

In his description of his student days, Paul Vignaux recalled the decisive influence upon a generation of young scholars of *The Philosophy of Saint Bonaventure*, the product of Gilson's reading during World War I that he published in 1924.[60] "One day Étienne Gilson came and made us re-read a work that nobody read any more. It was St. Bonaventure's *De Mysterio Trinitatis*," reported Marrou, for whom the paradigmatic modern sin is the "canonization of ingratitude." Marrou acknowledges a debt to Gilson for "an abrupt amplification of perspective and the emancipation from a kind of rigidity of the spirit of orthodoxy." Thanks to Gilson, Marrou learned that the choir of the blessed does not sing "in unison but in a delicious polyphony."[61] Marrou sent Gilson a copy of his classic work *De la connaissance*

59 Letter from Marc Bloch to Lucien Febvre, February 11, 1935, in *Correspondance Bloch—Febvre*, 2:209.

60 Paul Vignaux, "Témoignage sur une jeunesse étudiante (1925–1932)," in *Crise de notre temps et réflexion chrétienne (de 1930 à 1975)*, by Henri-Irénée Marrou (Paris: Beauchesne, 1978), 107–8.

61 Henri-Irénée Marrou, "De la philosophie à l'histoire," in *Étienne Gilson, Philosophe de la Chrétienté*, by Jacques Maritain et al. (Paris: Cerf, 1949), 75–79.

historique with the following inscription: "To Étienne Gilson, a teacher to whom I owe having understood what history is—and what the historian is" (Gilson Library, PIMS). For Paul Vignaux, "Gilson is a teacher in the full sense that a person can be one: as an example and suggestion of research."[62] Cardinal Henri de Lubac expressed his gratitude toward Gilson: "You were beginning the publication of your writings at the moment of my first formation. I read them all, one by one, and very often went back to them,"[63] something to which *Le mystère du surnaturel* bears ample witness.[64] The works of both Fr. Marie-Dominique Chenu and Fr. Yves Congar, who as a young student participated in Gilson's seminars at the École pratique des hautes études, illustrate this role, perhaps more as a point of reference than as an original influence. In 1928, Claudel dissected *Saint Bonaventure* meticulously.[65] Mounier most attentively read *Le Thomisme* published by Vrin in 1922.[66] Cardinal Jean-Marie Lustiger wrote that at the end of World War II the universe of his teachers was "dominated by Maritain and Gilson,"[67] which, by the way, hardly seemed to make the future cardinal enthusiastic. The publication of the French edition of *The Mystical Theology of Saint Bernard* in 1934 was deemed "a major event in the history of spirituality" by Brother Irénée Vallery-Radot, Bernard of Clairvaux's biographer, who discovered his Cistercian vocation in the pages of Gilson.[68]

62 Vignaux, "Étienne Gilson," *Annuaire de l'École pratique des hautes études* 77 (1978–1979): 37.

63 Letter from Henri de Lubac to Étienne Gilson, July 20, 1956, in *Lettres de M. Étienne Gilson adressées au P. de Lubac*, 70.

64 [Translator's note: Henri de Lubac, Le mystère du surnaturel (Paris: Aubier, 1965); English translation, *The Mystery of the Supernatural* (New York: Herder, 1998).]

65 Paul Vignaux, "Témoignage sur une jeunesse étudiante (1925–1932)," in *Crise de notre temps et réflexion chrétienne (de 1930 à 1975)*, by Henri-Irénée Marrou (Paris: Beauchesne, 1978), 107–8.

66 Emmanuel Mounier, manuscript of an index card from his reading, entitled "Étienne Gilson, *Le Thomisme*, Vrin, 1923," IMEC, Fonds Mounier (MNR 2.D5-04-02, no date, two handwritten pages of reading notes). Mounier takes notes on the first three chapters of Gilson's work: "The Thomist Problem," "Faith and Reason: the Object of Philosophy," and "The Alleged Evidence for the Existence of God."

67 Jean-Marie Lustiger, *Le choix de Dieu: Entretiens avec Jean-Louis Missika et Dominique Wolton* (Paris: De Fallois, 1987), 157.

68 Irénée Vallery-Radot, *Bernard de Fontaines, abbé de Clairvaux: Les noces de la grâce et de la nature*, vol. 1 (Paris: Desclée de Brouwer, 1963), 7–9. In the foreword, the author tells how in March 1943 his glance was "attracted" in the Vrin bookstore by Gilson's book, which allowed him to discover "the master of interior life that I had been seeking for so many years." "Passages that were as splendid as they were abundant, beautifully translated, commented with penetrating intelligence, revealed to me one of the greatest poets of all times."

Similarly, there is testimony about Gilson's influence upon the atmosphere of Rue d'Ulm on the threshold of the nineteen thirties. "That man's influence is growing. Célestin Boude [at the time director of the Higher Normal School at Rue d'Ulm] told me the other day that when Gilson came last year to question the applicants to the Normal School, a circle gathered to listen to him. Here is someone who belongs to the encouraging side of our period."[69] After the Liberation, a young Louis Althusser (1919–1990) attentively read the second edition of *Saint Augustin*,[70] even if the old "Prince Tala," who soon became a Marxist, did not seem to have absorbed much. In 1951 Albert Camus, who met Gilson several times, dedicated his *Homme révolté* to him: "To M. Étienne Gilson, as a sign of appreciation for himself and his work" (Gilson Library, PIMS).

In Catholic circles and beyond, from the nineteen thirties to the nineteen fifties, and notably during his two decades as professor at the Collège de France (1932–1951), Gilson loomed large in the world of French letters and philosophy, holding a sort of middle ground between two spheres that seldom came in contact. "I hope that you become habituated to loving souls who do not love themselves," he wrote to Charles Du Bos one day. "You told me that you suffered because of this. For me, who does nothing else after twenty long years, I am convinced that we end by bringing them closer to each other by bringing each soul closer to itself, and I insist on it."[71]

Gilson's election to the Académie française in 1947, the glorious year, enhanced his prestige. At the same time, he entered under the Cupola and also into the Luxembourg Palace as Counsellor of the Republic in the Christian Democrat ranks. The opposite camp expressed its rage in *Aspects de la France* at seeing Gilson vaunted as "the thinker of the new MRP in France."[72]

---

69 Letter from Yves Simon to Jacques Maritain, March 15, 1931. In *Correspondance Jacques Maritain—Yves Simon*, vol. 1, *Les années françaises (1927–1940)* (Paris: CLD, 2008), 69. Gilson was a member of the admission committee for l'École normal [ENS] in 1930.

70 See Althusser's copy of the second edition of *L'introduction à l'étude de saint Augustin* (Paris: Vrin, 1943), in the Bibliothèque Althusser, IMEC. There are many notes in the margins and underlined phrases, notably in part 2, chapter 4, "The Christian Life." Althusser copies the phrase "Virtue = *ordo amoris*." He underlines *Solo Deo fruendum*; "one must enjoy God alone" (228). He underlines passages on peace as "tranquility of order" (228); on the relations of the two cities, on property, and so forth.

71 Letter from Étienne Gilson to Charles Du Bos, May 23, 1930, Archive littéraire Jacques Doucet, Paris.

72 Daniel Halévy, "La réponse de M. Daniel Halévy," *Aspects de la France*, February 9, 1951, 6: "My dear Boutang, it is very good of you to invite your friends to execute the miserable Gilson.

Exalted by Cardinal Suhard, archbishop of Paris, he was cited in the pastoral letter entitled *Rise or Fall of the Church* (1947). The Thomism of Jacques Maritain and Étienne Gilson appeared as a doctrinal middle path between "the two options to be excluded," namely modernism and fundamentalism. In the political sphere, Gilson's influence was found in the European network of Christian Democracy; in Italy with Giorgio La Pira and in Germany with Heinrich Lübke, President of the German Federal Republic.[73] It even reached India, if we believe the testimony of Wladimir d'Ormesson. Pope Paul VI, after his meeting with Nehru's successor at Bombay in December 1964, recalled Maritain and Gilson's work.[74] General de Gaulle read the philosopher's books and was careful to express his appreciation for them: "Thanks for your faith, your intelligence, and your talent," de Gaulle wrote him regarding *Introduction à la philosophie chrétienne*.[75] And again, "Your book, *The Arts of the Beautiful* is a great work, because you open paths of clarity scorning all mystification. On this occasion, let me pay tribute once more to you magisterial talent."[76]

Foreign students also left very valuable testimonies about the international reception of this Gilson moment. In a letter of Joseph Ratzinger, we read: "As a student I had already read your works with the greatest enthusiasm; they were a source of knowledge and joy."[77] The semiologist and novelist Umberto Eco (1932–2016), author of a thesis on aesthetics in Thomas Aquinas, directed a thank you letter to Gilson in 1957. "In you, I acknowledge

---

After having led and made a success of the prudent life of a Catholic university man, he believed he risked nothing by rising to unexpected heights in 1946. Academician and senator, all that came to pass in a year. He was the thinker of the new MRP France."

73 See Heinrich Lübke's telegram to Étienne Gilson, June 13, 1969, SMCA. La Pira sent several letters to Gilson between 1952 and 1963 [Giorgio La Pira, Christian Democrat, Mayor of Florence and member of the Italian Chamber of Deputies].

74 Letter from Wladimir d'Ormesson to Étienne Gilson, December 15, 1964, SMCA: "Yesterday, I was received by the pope. He spoke warmly of his trip to India, with the strongest praise of Nehru's successor [Lal Bahadur Shastri], whose profound culture and noble sentiments he praised, and told me: 'He [the Indian Minister] spoke to me of Maritain and of Étienne Gilson. . . . Gilson's name came up twice in an interview at Bombay.' I thought that you would be happy to learn that your thinking and your work have been brought up during the furthest trip that a pope has undertaken in twenty centuries."

75 Letter from Charles de Gaulle to Étienne Gilson, June 27, 1960, SMCA, and copy in AG 5(1)/1177, at Archives nationales, Pierrefitte-sur-Seine [AN].

76 Letter from Charles de Gaulle to Étienne Gilson, April 14, 1963, AG 5(1)/1177, AN.

77 Letter from Joseph Ratzinger, September 13, 1959, SMCA.

a teacher who has greatly influenced my aesthetic formation."[78] In *L'oeuvre ouverte* (Seuil, 1965), Eco connected the aesthetics of Joyce's pun in *Finnegans Wake* (1939) with Gilson's *Les idées et les lettres* (Vrin, 1932).[79] The preface to the novel *The Name of the Rose* (1980), which traces the imaginary origin of Adso de Melk's manuscripts, opens with a beautiful tribute to the "dear, unforgettable" Gilson, who had died two years earlier.[80] In his famous spiritual autobiography, *The Seven Storey Mountain*, the American Trappist Thomas Merton narrates how much he owes to the author of *The Spirit of Mediaeval Philosophy*, where Gilson develops the concept of divine *aseitas*, which was to "revolutionize" Merton's life and make him understand the meaning of *God*.[81] Merton wrote in 1951:

> I want at last to do what I should have done long ago—write you a line to assure you of my recognition of a spiritual debt to you which I too sketchily indicated in the pages of *The Seven Storey Mountain*—in a rather badly constructed section of the book, at that. To you and to Jacques Maritain, among others, I owe the Catholic faith. That is to say I owe you my life. This is no small debt. Can you feel as abandoned as you do when you are handing out to other people as great a gift as is the kingdom of Heaven?[82]

Likewise, we encounter the testimony of the Romanian Mircea Eliade in a letter of 1953. "I remember all that my youth owes to your books. Above all, I recall the discovery of your little history of medieval philosophy, which

78 Letter from Umberto Eco to Étienne Gilson, February 25, 1957, SMCA. On this point, see Umberto Eco, *Écrits sur la pensée au Moyen Âge: Essais* (Paris: Grasset, 2016); originally published in Italian, *Scritti sul pensiero medievale* (Milan: Bompiano, 2012).

79 Umberto Eco, *L'Oeuvre ouverte* (Paris: Seuil, 1965), 283–302; originally published in Italian, *Opera Aperta* (Milan: Bompiano, 1962); available in English as *The Open Work* (Cambridge, MA: Harvard University Press, 1989).

80 Umberto Eco, "Un manuscrit, naturellement," preface to the novel *Le nom de la rose*, dated January 5, 1980 (Paris: Grasset, 1982), 11; in English, *The Name of the Rose* (San Diego: Harcourt Brace Jovanovich, 1983).

81 Thomas Merton, *The Seven Storey Mountain* (New York: Harcourt Brace, 1948). See particularly part 2, chapter 1, "With a Great Price," which starts with Merton reading Gilson's *The Spirit of Medieval Philosophy*: "And the one big concept that I got out of its pages was something that was to revolutionize my whole life" (172).

82 Letter from Thomas Merton to Étienne Gilson, November 12, 1951, SMCA. See the letter in *Nunc* magazine, November 2004, 31–32. Gilson had read *The Seven Storey Mountain* in 1949. See Gilson's letter to Dan Walsh, November 30, 1949, The Thomas Merton Center, Louisville. "*The Seven Storey* will remain the first "classic" in the history of American Catholic spirituality. As to the part which I happen to play in it, I like it very much, because I have nothing to do with it."

revealed an unsuspected world to me."[83] Also, there is the University of Madrid professor Leopoldo Eulogio Palacios, who translated Gilson into Spanish in the years 1948–1950, and introduced him to the Spanish speaking world.[84] Again, we have Leo Strauss's slightly enigmatic remark in a 1933 letter, when he was in the process of writing a book about Hobbes, that Gilson's objections had been very useful in making him better understand the difficulties he would have to overcome.[85] Among French scholars other than Marrou and Vignaux, there are the testimonies of Maurice Schumann,[86] Jean Guitton,[87] Claude Tresmontant,[88] Henri Gouhier, Alexandre Koyré, Jean de Fabrègues, Henry Corbin, or the still Protestant student Louis Bouyer, the future Oratorian scholar, who narrated in his memoirs Gilson's attraction for the students of Protestant theology at Arrago Boulevard.[89]

Gilson's position of influence inside and outside the Church, based on the fourfold acknowledgment by students, political activists, persons dedicated to the humanities, and ecclesiastics, crumbled three decades later. From the second half of the nineteen fifties onward, for political reasons that are connected to the war in Algeria and the growth of Gaullism, the MRP disintegrated.

83 Letter from Mircea Eliade to Étienne Gilson, June 25, 1953, SMCA.

84 Letter from Étienne Gilson to Leopoldo Eulogio Palacios, August 25, 1950. Palacios Archives: "I have just received *El Realismo Metódico*, much more handsome than in French. The translation seems excellent. . . . I can appreciate the content of your introduction, which, along with an American article, is truly by far the most accurate, penetrating, and complete thing that has been written about my epistemological positions."

85 Letter from Leo Strauss to Étienne Gilson, May 11, 1933, SMCA.

86 Speech of Maurice Schumann, "Discours prononcé à l'occasion de la mort de MM. Étienne Gilson et Jean Guéhenno," session of the Académie française, September 28, 1978 (Paris: Firmin-Didot, 1978).

87 Jean Guitton, "Étienne Gilson est mort, une sorte de lion de la pensée," *Le Figaro*, Thursday, September 21, 1978: "Tuesday mornings in 1928, I avidly attended his two courses at the Sorbonne."

88 Letter from Claude Tresmontant to Étienne Gilson, January 31, 1962, SMCA: "I have spent a great deal of time on your books, and I owe you a great deal."

89 Louis Bouyer, *Mémoires*, afterword and notes by Jean Duchesne (Paris: Cerf, 2014). See chapter 4: "Malbert was the first to drag me to the Sorbonne attic when Gilson was still relegated there. He explained with dazzling lucidity the most intricate theses of St. Thomas."

In the ecclesiastical sphere, the nuncio Roncalli, the future Pope John XXIII, described Gilson in 1948 as very "papal."[90] In December 1960, he received Gilson in the Vatican during a very friendly audience.[91] The Second Vatican Council, and still more the postconciliar period, pushed Thomism into the margins of ecclesiastical culture. "Shares in Thomism," Gilson noted lucidly, "are at the bottom of the ecclesiastical stock exchange."[92] From his leadership position, Gilson observed that, at the age of more than eighty, he had no successor and, to his surprise, had adopted a dissident appearance, "wandering among the ruins,"[93] and wondering whether he had not become a schismatic in spite of himself.[94]

At the Sorbonne, the École pratique, the Collège de France, and the Académie française, time carried out its work of erosion. Certainly, a chair of medieval philosophy still exists at the Sorbonne. There is also an Étienne Gilson chair of metaphysics created in 1995 at the Catholic Institute of Paris. At Place de la Sorbonne, Vrin continues to publish the works of the man who was one of the pillars of the house. As Malebranche came after the masters of the Middle Ages, Henri Gouhier succeeded his teacher and friend Gilson under the cupola of the Académie. In *Le Monde*, October 1978, Jean-Luc Marion rendered an energetic tribute to Gilson, "the discoverer of a continent," "the silently indicative monument that absolutely cannot be ignored."[95] In 2014, the Collège de France reopened a chair of the history of medieval thought, closed in 1951 after Gilson's retirement. Its occupant, Alan de Libera, paid homage to the philosopher in the inaugural lecture, February 13, 2014, proposing what in a sense was the very Gilsonian project of showing the

90 Angelo G. Roncalli, *Journal de France, I, 1945–1948*, introduction and notes by Étienne Fouilloux (Paris: Cerf, 2006), 492. On April 18, 1948, the Nuncio Roncalli attended the assembly of Catholic writers. "The presentations at the Mutualité [conference center, 24 Rue Saint-Victor, Paris], of Speaight, Guardini, and Gilson, but especially Gilson, struck a strong papal note."

91 Étienne Gilson, "Souvenirs du Père," *La France Catholique*, June 7, 1963, 1–2.

92 Letter from Étienne Gilson to the editors of *Revue thomiste*, December 26, 1968; published in *Revue thomiste*, 1994, 528.

93 Étienne Gilson, "Wandering among the Ruins," in *The Tribulations of Sophia*, trans. James G. Colbert (South Bend, Ind.: St. Augustine's Press, 2021), 97.

94 Étienne Gilson, "Suis-je schismatique?," *La France catholique*, July 2, 1965, 1.

95 Jean-Luc Marion, "Le découvreur d'un continent," *Le Monde*, October 7, 1978: "Unquestionably, we must salute Étienne Gilson as one of those who renewed Thomism, an original and powerful thinker to whom the university in France owes much of its greatness. But for the generation that has entered philosophy only in the last ten years, that debt does not count—rather it is denied to us."

subject's medieval foundations against Heidegger and the supporters of Descartes, considered until then the inventor of the "modern discipline."[96] The year 2015 saw the publication of a volume to commemorate the hundredth year of Gilson's thesis defense, an unusual homage.[97] In a sense, perhaps the Mountain of Ste. Geneviève is more faithful to Gilson's memory.

But we must be careful not to gild the picture. As Léon Brunschvicg put it at the end of the nineteen thirties, the Middle Ages of Paul Vignaux are no longer those of Gilson.[98] Gilson the Catholic polemicist, like the Gilson of "the metaphysics of Exodus"—I AM WHO AM, was also sharply criticized, including by some who recognized themselves as indebted to him, since henceforth, with Jean-Luc Marion, one was supposed to think of a "God without being."[99]

IMPETUS VEHEMENS ET CONCASSANS

The varying reactions to Gilson's work should surely be connected to his plainspoken character, both "blunt" and "just,"[100] "aggressive in order to maintain good sense by paradox,"[101] as both friends and those close to him emphasized along with colleagues and opponents. Thus, in May 1935, Maritain wrote to Yves Simon, "Gilson is very kind! What a straightforward mind!" And Maritain underlined this *impetus vehemens et concassans*.[102] According

96 Alain de Libera, *Où va la philosophie médiévale? Leçons inaugurales* (Paris: Fayard-Collège de France, 2014); Alain de Libera, *L'invention du sujet moderne, Cours du Collège de France 2013–2014* (Paris: Vrin, 2015).

97 Dan Arbib and Francesco Marrone, eds., *Gilson et Descartes a l'occasion du centenaire de La liberté chez Descartes et la théologie*, Examina philosophica, "I Quaderni di Alvearium" 2 (Lecce: ClioEdu, 2015).

98 See Paul Vignaux, *Philosophie au Moyen Âge* (Paris: Vrin, 2004), 10.

99 Jean-Luc Marion, *Dieu sans l'être* (Paris: P.U.F., 1991), 109: "The principled denomination of ~~God~~ [sic] as being and by being cannot—let us immediately indicate our evidence—be justified by the pure and simple recourse to Exodus 3:14. Moreover, only its conceptual insufficiency allows us to attribute to the metaphysics of Exodus the dignity and merit of being a radical innovation." In the preface to the English edition (*God without Being* [Chicago: University of Chicago Press, 1991]) Marion acknowledges a number of teachers; Gilson is there, to be sure, but also Derrida, Althusser, Alquié, Levinas, Daniélou, and von Balthasar (xix).

100 Letter from Jacques Maritain to Charles Journet, June 24, 1932, *Correspondance Journet–Maritain*, vol. 2, *1930–1939* (Paris: Saint-Augustin, 1997), 246.

101 Jean Guitton, "Une sorte de lion de la pensée," *Le Figaro*, Thursday, September 21, 1978.

102 Letter from Jacques Maritain to Yves Simon, May 10, 1935, *Correspondance Jacques Maritain–Yves Simon*, 2:191.

to Henri Gouhier, Gilson was "the man without a mask," of "perfect frankness."[103] For Pierre Mesnard, Gilson was a "superb medieval baron," who had "carved out a significant fief in the domain of ideas" and who in springtime would go off to wage war "to the land of the Cartesians" or to demolish "some pseudo-constructions" on the frontiers of the Renaissance.[104] Lucien Febvre, who had expressed reservations about the history of ideas as practiced by Gilson, still enjoyed the "coherence of mind, security of experience, attentive vigilance, something powerful, solid, and firm that amounts to a signature."[105] For Pasteur Vallery-Radot, Gilson was a "cheerful man," even funny, for whom the eighth capital sin was sadness:

> You have kept the good laughter of a sixteen year old, that clear laughter, bursting with frankness that lights up your face. Happy those who arrive at the peak of their career without losing the freshness of sentiments of their early youth, who are still capable of giving themselves entirely to joy, enthusiasm, passion! Such persons know neither undercurrents nor the conventional attitudes that stunt the forces of personality.[106]

Fond of the good life, the wine of Burgundy, and tobacco, a tobacco that was always absent during the war where Pétain abounded,[107] Gilson thought of himself rather as an "enfant terrible"[108] and was aware of being "harsh" sometimes: "I always forget that there are human beings behind the ideas."[109] His letters were full of pugnacious vocabulary in spite of himself: "It will be necessary to polemicize, which I hate, with Léon Brunschvicg,

103 Letter from Henri Gouhier to Henri de Lubac, May 10, 1986, published in Henri de Lubac, *Lettres de M. Étienne Gilson adressées au P. de Lubac*, 258.

104 Pierre Mesnard, "Perspectives sur la Renaissance," in Maritain et al., *Étienne Gilson, Philosophe de la Chrétienté*, 159.

105 Lucien Febvre, review of *L'histoire de la Philosophie médiévale* (2nd ed., Payot, 1944). "Étienne Gilson et la philosophie du XIVe siècle," *Combats pour l'histoire* (Paris: Armand Colin, 1953, 1992), 184–88. In *Annales*, the review of the book has a different title: "Histoire des idées, histoire des sociétés: Une question de climat," *Annales* 1, no. 2 (1946): 158–61.

106 Pasteur Vallery-Radot, "Réponse au discours de réception d'Étienne Gilson"

107 This pun [translator: between "pétun" and "Pétain" and untranslatable] is found repeatedly in Gilson's correspondence with Fr. André Combes during World War II. Nouvelles acquisitions françaises [NAF] 28257, Bibliothèque nationale de France [BNF].

108 Letter from Étienne Gilson to Fr. Michel Labourdette, July 28, 1950, *Revue thomiste* (1944), 484.

109 Letter from Étienne Gilson to Fr. Marie-Dominique Chenu, October 17, 1946, APDF: "I hold my pen better than my tongue, and I usually end up distressing those who trust me enough to consult me. That has already happened twice in six months, and in both cases the word 'harsh' was used."

whom I love, so happy does he feel in his hermetic blindness."[110] In this fashion, he even wrote to Paul Valéry, whom he greatly esteemed, that he had cooked up two verses in "a variation thus far lost of the *Femmes Savantes*."[111] An old MRP senator dedicated two burlesque verses to the "rude old fighter" Gilson: "In the eternal fight, You're a puncher of might."[112] Maurice Halbwachs described Gilson as a "Parisian street brat."[113] Pierre Boutang mentioned Gilson's "bronze heart."[114]

Gilson's often pugnacious thinking wanted to shatter contradictions. "Who will deliver us from Thomism to give us Saint Thomas Aquinas?" he demanded during the Second Vatican Council.[115] Asked to comment on the Thomistic proofs of the existence of God, he answered that the question hardly interested him, that "the non-existence of God is what is questionable."[116] In the words of Jean Guitton, "Gilson appeared to me in the form of a lion, shaking his mane, affirmative and even dogmatic, truculent, generous, overflowing with life and certainty, and enjoying his paradoxes. . . . Gilson, in whom we admired a courteous ferocity, good sense like that of Diogenes, the joy of contradicting, the desire to be alone, even among us, to think what he thought."[117]

As an example of this rather singular way of thinking, of this style that gains adhesion by the strength of common sense, good reasoning, and eloquence of the evidence—and returning to the question of solder posed by Marc Bloc—we can cite the opening of an article published in the journal *Esprit* in 1946 about the "retrospective illusions" that one should not entertain about the agreement between Christianity and the modern world:

> To assert oneself about the crisis of the relations between Christianity and the modern world, it is necessary to first define the crisis. About what

110 Letter from Étienne Gilson to Gabriel Marcel, June 19, 1930, Fonds Gabriel Marcel, BNF.

111 Letter from Étienne Gilson to Paul Valéry, May 5, 1944, Bibliothèque Doucet—see the appendixes.

112 Verse by Barthélémy Ott, former MRP deputy and senator, no date; SMCA. [The French is: "Et dans l'éternelle bataille / Vous est un lutteur de taille."]

113 Halbwachs, "Ma campagne au Collège de France," 193.

114 Pierre Boutang, "Le cas du fuyard Gilson," *Aspects de la France*, February 9, 1951, 1.

115 Letter from Étienne Gilson to Jean de Fabrègues, November 27, 1964, CHSP.

116 Étienne Gilson, *L'athéisme difficile* (Paris: Vrin, 1979), 11–12.

117 Jean Guitton, *Réponse au discours de réception d'Henri Gouhier*, Académie française, November 22, 1979. Available on the website of the Académie française.

> "modern world" do we want to talk? Is it about what it is for us or what it is for Christianity? All disciples of Christ lived in a modern world, and the problem for them has always been to live in it, because whatever its form, it was there, but they were not of it. The first point to clarify is that. Nothing is less modern than the crisis of the relations between Christianity and the modern world.[118]

Once that is stated, the history lesson can begin. On the grounds defined in this way, Gilson was almost surely the only one able to go back in time from twentieth century philosophy to antiquity.[119] We believe that it is worthwhile to follow him in order to try to understand him.

Strictly speaking, the present work is only a biographical essay on Gilson the historian and intellectual in the *polis*. Let us state clearly that the objective is to resolve the kind of enigma that he poses and that perhaps leads us as much to his own internal evolution as to his many readings and readers. For Étienne Fouilloux, "Gilson refuses to abandon his role as university man and to play to his audience in order to intervene in the Church's intellectual life. . . . Étienne Gilson? A strong personality, an important output, which has drawn medieval philosophy out of undeserved oblivion, but with limited religious impact."[120] Without much nuance, this personality has been regarded as a professor without influence, either in the city of men or in the Church, "rather isolated at the Collège de France,"[121] but also as a brilliant historian who established the historicity of *philosophia perennis*,[122] as an ardent

118 Étienne Gilson, "Monde moderne, monde chrétien: Pas d'illusions rétrospectives," *Esprit* 14, no. 125 (1946): 192.

119 See the letter from Étienne Gilson to Jean de Fabrègues, January 27, 1968, CHSP, for the chronological mechanism: "I would assure Fr. Daniélou that atheism is not a sickness of modern man. Renan already stated, and rightly, that there is not a single negation from the eighteenth century that cannot be found already in the thirteenth century. I would add Cicero's remark, I believe in the *Topics*."

120 Fouilloux, *Une Église en quête de liberté*, 124.

121 According to René Rémond, Gilson was "rather isolated at the Collège de France" in the 1930s, in what concerned philosophy, whereas Maritain was marginalized: René Rémond, Jacques Julliard, Daniel Lindenberg, "L'histoire des intellectuels catholiques: Interview de René Rémond," *Mil neuf cent* 13 (1995): 17. See also Étienne Fouilloux, *Une Église en quête de liberté*, 124. —Étienne Gilson is not mentioned in René Rémond, *Les catholiques dans la France des années 1930* (Paris: Cana, 1979). Likewise, he is not mentioned in Hervé Serry, *Naissance de l'intellectuel catholique* (Paris: La Découverte, 2004).

122 Eco, *Écrits sur la pensée au Moyen Âge*, 1005.

defender of philosophical pluralism and a model of "ideological neutrality"[123] or, in the opposite direction, as a defender of a timeless and monolithic Thomism, whose entire output falls under the sign of apologetics.[124]

The biographical genre, despite its admirable successes, is today often shunned by the learned, who find little to recommend it.[125] We are warned that there can be a danger of excessive faith in the subject, "worn out narrative procedures," singling out the person and de-emphasizing society as a whole with its underlying forces and the anonymous masses. I do not accept the criticisms of that history uniformly—even if frequently I will try to give a hearing to voices critical of Gilson's work. Moreover, issues of pure medieval history as well as questions of metaphysics and of history of philosophy will essentially be set aside. There will be those who think with good reason that this is an extraordinary narrowing of perspective in order to grasp good old Gilson. I answer simply that I am completely aware of the intrinsic limitations of biography, on the one hand, and of the risk of reductionism connected with intellectual history, on the other. It is not possible, even in a thousand pages, to grasp everything. Also, a thousand times it has been suggested that I should clarify the philosophical questions posed by the authors considered. Ultimately, in my opinion, the subject of "political Gilson" has interest and importance for the century in which he was situated, and that before climbing a peak or simply prolonging a walk, it is helpful to know the terrain well.

123 Alain Boureau, "Des politiques tirées de l'Écriture: Byzance et l'Occident," *Annales.* Histoire, Sciences Sociales 55, no. 4 (July-August 2000): 883: "The first works on medieval subjects by the two great Thomist scholars, Fathers Chenu and Congar, date from this epoch. The two were themselves very much engaged in their century, but were able to give complete autonomy to their historical research. The case of Étienne Gilson must also be mentioned. He pushed scrupulous ideological neutrality to the paradoxical consequence of writing a very remarkable *Histoire de la philosophie médiévale* that excluded theology."

124 Catherine König-Pralong, "L'histoire de la philosophie médiévale depuis 1950: Méthodes, textes, débats," *Annales. Histoire, Sciences Sociales 64*, no. 1 (2009): 143–69. In contrast with Boureau's article, König-Pralong's piece is a violent criticism of Gilson's historical writings, which are accused of all the faults of the discipline—teleological, unhistorical, spiritualist, monolithic, timeless, a stream, something inherited from the nineteenth century, and so forth. For the author of this article, Father Chenu and Paul Vignaux (two of Gilson's closest friends, who continually declared what they owed to Gilson) would have opened up "ways that are alternatives to timeless Thomism" and "broken Étienne Gilson's monolithic solidity" (153).

125 On the issue of method, see the dossier edited by Antoine Compagnon and Philippe Roger, "Biographies, modes d'emploi," *Critique* 6-7, nos. 781–782 (June-July 2012): 483. See notably the elegant and demanding clarification by Michel Winock, "Histoire d'historiens," *Critique* 6-7, nos. 781–782 (June-July 2012): 511–23, on the subject of the biography of Pierre Nora by François Dosse and of Marc Ferro's autobiographical conversations.

1

A Catholic Academic and Intellectual

A visit to the cemetery of scientific doctrines that were irreconcilable with Revelation would take us by a great many tombs. In our own lifetime, in the names of how many doctrines, since abandoned by their very authors, have we been summoned to abandon the teaching of the Church?[1]

In October of 1924, Fr. Habert, a professor at the major seminary of Meaux and the author of many books on sociology and philosophy, tore into Gilson in the pages of *La Vie catholique* with no circumspection: "Let us not be fooled. The professor at the Sorbonne admires the architecture of the temple [i.e., of medieval philosophy]; occasionally, he lets himself be moved by sacred music, by a thought that modern philosophy takes up and transposes; but he always remains an outsider."[2] The *ad hominem* attack shows how badly informed its author was. It is important to understand how Gilson, far from being an outsider to the subject he examined, had

1 Étienne Gilson, "L'intelligence au service de Christ-Roi," in *Christianisme et philosophie* (Paris: Vrin, 1936), 167 ["The Intelligence in the Service of Christ the King," in *Christianity and Philosophy*, trans. Ralph McDonald, CSB (New York: Sheed & Ward, 1939), 124].

2 O. Habert, "Notes sur les études médiévales," *La Vie catholique*, October 25, 1924, 9–10.

become the Catholic intellectual who was simultaneously professor of the Sorbonne and professor of the Collège de France and, within the Church, an outstanding member of what Gilson called, with genuine humor and detachment, the "Thomist school."[3]

The defining characteristics of Catholic intellectuals have been set out by historiography. Chateaubriand and Louis Veuillot are the precursors. The great guardian figures on the literary side would be Paul Claudel, François Mauriac, or Francis Jammes. The ways in which Catholic intellectuals enter the secular world bring us back to the space created by publishing houses, collections, newspapers, and magazines, such as Cerf or Desclée De Brouwer and *La Croix*, *Sept*, the renowned *Roseau d'or*, or *Dieu vivant*. The social events are those of the Catholic Writers Week, of *Pax Romana*, or of the Catholic Center of French Intellectuals, according to the period. For Claude Langlois, the model of the Catholic intellectual was, "by successive elimination" of the other competing figures, Jacques Maritain, who was anchored in the renewal of Thomas Aquinas's philosophy recommended by the teaching Church and by Rome, acknowledged abroad for its scientific legitimacy and marked by a capacity for autonomy, critical distancing, and freedom in regard to the Church to which it belonged.[4]

Gilson is a paradigmatic case of the group thus defined. As a plain-clothed theologian, he admitted the primacy of theology in the degrees of knowledge. In this way, he hoped to contribute to "restore the theological values in their fullness,"[5] at the same time that he emphasized the necessity of studying theology on the historical level.[6] "My conclusion," Gilson wrote in 1951, "and I intend to go to Rome to state it, is 'Zurück zur Theologie!'

3 Étienne Gilson, *The Philosopher and Theology*, 202.

4 Claude Langlois, "La naissance de l'intellectuel catholique," in *Intellectuels chrétiens et Esprit des années 1920*, ed. Pierre Colin (Paris: Cerf, 1997), 213–33. Claire Toupin-Guyot, *Les intellectuels catholiques dans la société française: Le Centre catholique des intellectuels français, 1941–1976*, preface by René Rémond (Rennes: Presses universitaires de Rennes, 2002). See also Hervé Serry, *Naissance de l'intellectuel catholique* (Paris: La Découverte, 2004).

5 Étienne Gilson, *Christianity and Philosophy*, 124–25. Gilson continues (125): ". . . to do so in such a way that they descend into the thought of the savant who calculates or who experiments, into the reason of the philosopher who meditates, into the intelligence at the service of Christ the King, is to promote the coming of His reign, by aiding nature to be born again under the fruitful action of His grace and in the light of His truth."

6 Letter from Étienne Gilson to Fr. André Combes, August 29, 1942, NAF, 28257, BNF: "We can revalue theology by history only by its own history, whose sense so many theologians of our time have lost. It is doubly intelligent to call upon the great theologians, because they knew what they were talking about, and they have retained the authority that they had to talk about it."

[Return to theology]. Of course, I have just discovered the moon, but I am surely going to be accused of fideism," he adds in jest.[7] This phrase, "return to theology" is precisely what de Lubac inscribed in his *Mystère du surnaturel* in 1965.[8] On the peak of a ridge between intellectual circles and the historical, philosophical, and theological disciplines, Gilson acted on the two stages of university and Church. He counted on this dual recognition and expected to enjoy the absolute freedom that belonged to him not only in regard to state and Church. For example, he denounced the absence of neutrality in *laicité* in the nineteen thirties. Equally in regard to the Church's theologians, he pointed the finger at the "Thomism of some professors at the Angelicum, which was in an advanced state of decomposition,"[9] denouncing during the World War II the equivocal stance of the French bishops,[10] and took delight, for example, in "not being tied to any institution subject to ecclesiastical discipline," in the lamentable context of the placement of his friend Fr. Chenu on the Index in 1943.[11] Gilson scattered his activities throughout many Catholic meeting places, newspapers, and magazines (*Sept*, *Vigile*, *Pax Romana*, *Documentation catholique*, *L'Autre*, and so on) and published in non-confessional media (*La Revue de métaphysique et de morale*, *Les Nouvelles littéraires*, *L'Européen*, *Le Monde*, and others). As a kind of hybrid, Gilson frequently articulated his dual debt in education: to the Petit Séminaire de Notre-Dame-des-Champs and to the Sorbonne. "I never had the impression that they were two rival and much less enemy educations. I would be nothing without Notre-Dame-des-Champs and the Sorbonne; both are in me."[12]

Similarly, Gilson developed his own strategy within his academic environment thanks to the bookstore and publishing company owned by his

7 Letter from Étienne Gilson to Michel Labourdette, OP, August 12, 1950, printed in *Revue thomiste* 94 (1994): 502.

8 In *Le mystère du surnaturel* (Paris: Aubier, 1965), 9, Henri de Lubac cites Gilson, among others: "Buried under more than five centuries of debris, ignorance of itself is the most serious ill from which Scholasticism is suffering. To cure it, let us listen to the counsel of history. Return to theology!" Étienne Gilson, "Les historico-critiques et l'avenir de la scolastique," in *Scholastica ratione historico-critica instauranda* ed. Carol Balič (Rome: Pontificum Atheneum Antonianum, 1951), 40–48, at 42. [See also de Lubac, *Letters of Étienne Gilson to Henri de Lubac*, 77n1; and the letter from Gerard Smith, SJ, to Henri de Lubac, July 19, 1965, 201.]

9 Étienne Gilson, *Réalisme thomiste et critique de la connaissance* (Paris: Vrin, 1939), 7.

10 Letters from Étienne Gilson to André Combes, July 23, 1942; May 3, 1943; NAF, 28257, BNF.

11 Letter from Étienne Gilson to André Combes, July 18, 1943, NAF 28257, BNF.

12 Talk by Étienne Gilson reported by Vallery-Radot, "Réponse au discours de réception d'Étienne Gilson," May 19, 1947.

friend Joseph Vrin in Place de la Sorbonne. While the first edition of *Thomisme* was published in Strasbourg in 1919, Vrin brought out the second edition in 1921. Two years later Vrin took over the Collection Études de philosophie médiévale founded at the University of Strasbourg in 1921. Starting in 1926 Vrin also published the scholarly journal *Archives d'histoire doctrinale et littéraire du Moyen Âge*, directed by Gilson and Fr. Gabriel Théry.[13] Gilson was not comparable to Maritain and his collections Roseau d'or and Îles, nor to Mounier, who founded *Esprit* outside university circles. Gilson's reputation grew not only through the publication of his own scholarly work, but also through the editorial labor he undertook that allowed him to direct scholarly publications and promote authors like Henri Gouhier in 1924 with *La pensée religieuse de Descartes*, or Alexandre Koyré in 1929 with his tome on Jacob Boehme, *Étude sur les origines de la métaphysique allemande*. Gilson likewise deserves the credit for the appearance of Paul Vignaux's 1935 book *Luther, Commentateur des Sentences*, Louis Gardet's *Avicenne* in 1948, and Marie-Dominique Chenu's 1957 *La théologie au XIIe siècle*. Similarly, Gilson was reponsible for the appearance of works by André Combes, Raoul Carton, Émile Bréhier, Palémon Glorieux, Aimé Forest, Vladimir Lossky, and others.

GILSON: A MODERNIST TURNED ANTI-MODERN?

In his diary of the World War II period, Maurice Halbwachs (1877–1945) gave a rather unflattering portrait of young Gilson: "ambitious," "pushed on by priests and a bit of a Father Morality." Both were agrégés [held their teaching certificates], and were students of Henri Bergson and Lucien Lévy-Bruhl, but "poles apart," as Halbwachs put it, in philosophy and religion. Seven years younger, Gilson rapidly mastered the stages in his career. Halbwachs visited Gilson at the end of October 1942 in the context of the search for a successor to Marcel Mauss at the Collège de France. Halbwachs's depiction of Gilson is most interesting.

> My relation with Gilson goes back to Poitiers, where we used to meet for the baccalaureate examinations. He would come from Rochefort [Gilson taught at the Lyceum in Rochefort during the school years 1908–1910],

13 On Gabriel Théry, see Dominque Avon, "Une polémique catholique sur les origines d'Islam. Autour des travaux de Hanna Zacharias," in *Mélanges offerts à Gérard Cholvy*, ed. Michel Fourcade and Dominique Avon (Montpellier: Publications Université Paul-Valéry Montpellier 3, 2004), 203–37.

> and I from Tours. We visited the Roman churches together. A practicing Catholic, he was at that time in complete sympathy with the Modernist movement and very worked up against the pope [Pius X], who had blocked the road by eliminating the Modernists from all the seminaries. Gilson also indulged in slightly ridiculous tirades about the immorality that existed in the port district of Rochefort. Newly married, he was appointed to Tours to substitute for me while I was in Germany for the year 1910–1911, and he bought a house. My return greatly inconvenienced him. He was able to get himself appointed at Angers and gave his course there, but lived in Tours. We used to see each other a little. (I was not yet married.) He loved music, without playing it, but he read it very well.—Gilson came from a very modest family—a small tailor who produced ready-made clothes in a poor neighborhood—a family with many children. He was dominated by the priests: catechism of perseverance, singing in church choirs, and so forth. Along with that, he had a strong personality, a Parisian street brat, and a lot of ambition.—At Tours, he worked on his thesis on the will in Descartes, while I worked on mine, the working class and living standards. We were poles apart because what interested him in Descartes was the influence (as Gilson thought) of medieval philosophy. Gilson cared very little for Descartes the researcher oriented toward modern science, the scientific philosopher.[14] Gilson did not know even the basics of mathematics. We presented our theses at about the same time in 1912. He was named *maître de conférences* [tenured junior professor] on the eve of the war (in preference to me) [in July 1913].[15] I met him again at the University of Strasbourg [where Gilson taught 1919–1021], which he left rather quickly for the Sorbonne [in 1921]. Friendly relations at Strasbourg; perhaps *friendly* is excessive, because I perceived some coldness, if not hostility in him.... One of his brothers is a priest in Paris.[16]

Beyond verbal thrusts between young colleagues and rivals, in Halbwachs's image of Gilson, less sympathetic than what he would depict later in

14 The statement needs to be nuanced. In 1931, Gilson wrote in his *Exposé des titres* for the Collège de France: "A necessary link must be established between the history of philosophy and the history of the sciences. Here again, and still more if possible, unity is a fact of which the historian has an obligation to become aware."

15 There was a heated dispute between Gilson and Halbwachs on the subject of the Lille position. See Laurence Shook, *Étienne Gilson* (Toronto: PIMS, 1984), 58–59.

16 Halbwachs, "Ma compagne au Collège de France," 189–229. The original is found in Halbwachs, *Journal*, notebook IV, 195–98, Fonds Halbwachs, IMEC.

the nineteen thirties,[17] we detect the problems that preoccupy Gilson in his thirties: Church membership, stability in the university, Modernist inclination since his twenties,[18] which his involvement with the group surrounding Laberthonnière reinforced during his years of studies.[19] On the other hand, there is his "anti-modern" philosophical project, since Gilson's thesis maintained in Laberthonnière's presence (May–June 1913)[20] consisted of showing continuity between the medievals and Moderns against the widely accepted ideas of Victor Cousin and Octave Hamelin.[21] Must we read as a symbol the approximate coincidence of the presentation of Gilson's thesis and the placement of the journal *Annales de philosophie chrétienne* as well as some works of Laberthonnière on the Index of Forbidden Books (May–June 1913)? According to Gilson, Descartes, far from being a blank slate and liberator from prejudices, derived his vocabulary from medieval philosophy (whence Gilson's *Index scolastico-cartésienne* published in 1913). In a sense Descartes's work amounted to an impoverishment of medieval philosophy. Edmund Husserl elegantly describes the debt that contemporary Cartesianism thus owes to Gilson: "Descartes had a firm will to liberate himself radically from all prejudices. But thanks to recent research and notably thanks to the elegant and profound research of Gilson and Koyré, we know how many unclarified assumptions, inherited from Scholasticism, are still contained in the *Meditations*."[22]

17 Halbwachs and Gilson were good friends and took Atlantic voyages together in September and December, 1930. See the introduction to chapter 4, below.

18 On this point see the letter from Étienne Gilson to Fr. Lucien Laberthonnière, April 12, 1906, included in the appendixes, NAF 28025, no. 70, BNF.

19 Fr. Laberthonnière's correspondence in 1912–1914 (NAF 28025, BNF) shows how much this member of the Oratory was in contact with students, doctoral candidates, and junior professors (Gilson, Delbos, Xavier Léon, Boutroux, Baruzi, Le Roy, and so on.)

20 Undated letter from Gilson to Fr. Lucien Laberthonnière, NAF 28025, no. 36, BNF: "I thank you very much for the inconvenience you took on by coming to my thesis."

21 There are many references to this. See Paul Vignaux, "Sur la place du Moyen Âge en histoire de la philosophie," in *Bulletin de la Société française de philosophie. Séance de samedi 24 novembre 1973* (Paris: Armand Colin, 1974), 6: "It suffices to recall Victor Cousin's judgment: 'There are only two really distinct periods in the history of philosophy as in the history of the world: ancient and modern.' He adds; 'The second age begins with Descartes.' In the first years of the twentieth century, Octave Hamelin still taught, 'Descartes comes after the ancients, nearly as if there was nothing between them and him except the physicist.' That tells the importance of Gilson's thesis in 1913."

22 Edmund Husserl, *Méditations cartésiennes*, trans. Gabrielle Peiffer and Emmanuel Lévinas (Paris: Vrin, 1947; repr. 1992), 51.

Paradoxically, Gilson was a Modernist who became anti-Modern. On the eve of World War I, he indeed developed in an environment of Modernist Catholicism. In February 1913, in the same issue as an article by Louis Canet, Gilson published his "Notes on Campanella" in the journal *Annales de Philosophie chrétienne*, which was put on the Index in May 1913. He felt the shock of the sanctions (as did his wife) and asked Fr. Laberthonnière to give her a little spiritual peace, "something I do not want for myself but very much desire for her."[23] When Pius X died in 1914, Gilson wrote to his mother that he would surely get along better with the next pope. However, Gilson became "anti-Modern," if we define the term in the literary sense of Antoine Compagnon's book, *Les Antimodernes* (Paris: Gallimard, 2005, 2016). Simplifying, the anti-Modern is an "intellectual who goes forward looking at the rear view mirror," "the rear guard of the avantgarde," a Modern disillusioned about Modernity's Modernity, who has been vaccinated against the idea of progress. That said, quite unlike Bloy and Péguy, two of the models used by Compagnon in his typology, Gilson did not use the term anti-Modern and tried to show how Modern thought is rooted in medieval thought. "My conclusion, which has forced itself on me with increasing clarity starting from Roger Bacon, is that modern philosophy did not have to win the rights of reason against the Middle Ages. On the contrary, the Middle Ages conquered the rights of reason for modern thought."[24] "I wear myself out reconquering evidence that should have been at our disposal when we were eighteen years old."[25] In a similar vein but certainly with more finesse, Gilson quoted Goethe's *Faust* on the first page of the fifth edition of *Thomisme*, which appeared during World War II: "*Was du ererbt von deinen Vätern hast/ Erwirb es, um es zu besitzen.*" (Conquer what you have inherited from your parents, to make it yours, to possess it.) Gilson's words are situated in the dynamic of recapturing a philosophical heritage that Modernity and Modernism, through prejudice, negligence, forgetfulness, or willful ignorance, have not transmitted.

To clarify the question of the dialectic Modernity–anti-Modernity–ultra Modernity in Gilson's work, we can emphasize that after World War II Gilson adopted Maritain's term "ultramodern" without ever, to our knowledge, employing Maritain's related term "antimodern," with which Maritain

23 Letter from Étienne Gilson to Fr. Lucien Laberthonnière, April 13, 1914, NAF 28025, no. 40, BNF.

24 Letter from Étienne Gilson to Léon Brunschvicg, November 5, 1920, IMEC.

25 Letter from Étienne Gilson to Gabriel Marcel, June 19, 1930, Fonds Gabriel Marcel, BNF.

had toyed in a spirit of paradox since 1922.[26] "Medieval ideas come back to us today through German or Danish philosophies," Gilson confided to the journalist Paul Guth in 1946. "Accordingly, it is better to go back to the origins. One must be ultramodern to devote one's life to the Middle Ages."[27] Like Maritain, Gilson was convinced that Thomism, "the philosophy of the future," is, so to speak, ahead of the game and allows us to envisage a "consistent" existentialism without recurring to the output of a Heidegger or a Kierkegaard. Gilson loved his time, even if he sometimes made fun of it ironically: "Many of our contemporaries prefer to remain on the ground; they put their glory in seeing nothing at all unless they can see it by their own efforts, and console themselves for their petty stature alleging their advanced age. It is a sad old age that loses all its memories."[28] Again, in a pained tone, notably at the end of World War II, Yves Simon reported: "Stories from San Francisco: Gilson is very depressed by the frame of mind of French youth and says: 'There are now three philosophies in France, that of the absurd, that of nausea, and that of desperation.'"[29] Strictly speaking, Gilson did not refute the concept of Modernity, but he wanted to go beyond it and, above all, to restore it to its proper place in the *continuum* of the centuries. For example, he often said that he loved Bergson, Debussy, Rodin, and Monet. Paul Vignaux confirms, "The affirmation of 'philosophical constants' is not accompanied in the old professor by lack of attention to contemporary novelties."[30] Gilson appreciated contemporary literature from Paul Valéry to Pierre Seghers. He even appreciated popular entertainment. On transatlantic voyages, he "never missed the daily movie session."[31]

26 Jacques Maritain, "Antimoderne," in *Oeuvres complètes*, vol. 2 (Fribourg: Editions universitaires, and Paris: Editions Saint-Paul, 1987), 928 ("Antimoderne" was originally published in Paris: Editions de la Revue des Jeunes, 1922): "What I call *antimodern* could just as well have been called *ultramodern*. Indeed it is well known that Catholicism is as *antimodern* for its unshakable attachment to tradition as *ultramodern* for its boldness in adapting to new conditions that arise in the life of the world."

27 Étienne Gilson, "Le monde va-t-il vers un nouveau Moyen Âge? Entretien avec Paul Guth," *Le Littéraire*, December 28, 1946, 1, 3.

28 This is the conclusion of Étienne Gilson, *The Spirit of Mediaeval Philosophy* (New York: Charles Scribner's Sons, 1940), 426. [*L'esprit de la philosophie médiévale*, 2nd ed. (Paris: Vrin, 1944), 402].

29 Journal of Yves Simon, June 13, 1945, 25, University of Notre Dame Archives [UNDA]. Simon learned of Gilson's remark from his friends the Greenwoods, who met Gilson in San Francisco.

30 Paul Vignaux, "Étienne Gilson," *Revue de métaphysique et de morale*, no. 3 (1979): 290.

31 Maurice Halbwachs, "Missions à Chicago," folios 94, Fonds Halbwachs, IMEC.

> But I cannot forget that before modern man there is simply man, he whose aesthetic demands are as fulfilled by Paestum or the Parthenon, as were those of the architects who constructed these temples. For every look backwards to be an absurdity, we would need to be able to affirm that humanity constantly remains at the highest level of such and such particular person. Now, experience demonstrates, to the contrary, that humanity often forgets, as it occurs that an individual declines from himself, and that then his first duty is to collect himself in order to re-encounter himself.[32]

The example was quite fresh in the mind of Gilson, who had gone to Italy in 1924. At the time, he had written to his old teacher Lévy-Bruhl: "I have left [for Italy] without faith in the progress of man (I mean of human nature). I have returned from Paestum, Pompei, and the Museum of the Baths of Diocletian convinced that we have regressed. I would be a bad reporter for *Le Quotidien*. It is all too evident."[33]

In his examination of conscience, published in 1932 in the magazine *Vigile*, Gilson tried again to set out the terms of his personal journey. Was the man he had become "pre-awaited" in the young man he had been? He hesitated and ended by answering in the negative. In his terms, he did not want to "warp his inner truth," which he wanted to grasp in its entirety, "even if it wounds him." "The truth is that instead of attaching myself to Scholasticism because it served Catholicism, for years I have had to make the most painful efforts not to separate myself from Catholicism on account of what I believed Scholasticism was. I set out against Scholasticism not only as a philosopher but as a believer. It was a two-fold obstacle for me."[34] In a 1962 letter to Henri Gouhier, Gilson was more explicit: "Understanding none of what Fr. Laberthonnière wrote, I almost let myself be separated from the Church (but not for a second from the faith) by the scandal that the theologians belonging to Action Française gave at the time."[35]

Maurice Halbwachs's testimony and Gilson's expression indicate a strong political, philosophical and religious tension, born out of the jolts of the

32 Étienne Gilson, during a conversation with Frédéric Lefèvre, published as "Une heure avec Étienne Gilson," in *Nouvelles littéraires*, January 3, 1925, 1–2; republished in Frédéric Lefèvre, *"Une heure avec . . . ," Third Series* (Paris: Gallimard, 1925), 63–79.

33 Letter from Étienne Gilson to Lucien Lévy-Bruhl, July 8, 1924, IMEC.

34 Étienne Gilson, "Examen de conscience," *Vigile*, no. 2 (1932): 85–99.

35 Letter from Étienne Gilson to Henri Gouhier, January 30, 1962; published in *Revue thomiste* 94 (1994): 473.

Modernist crisis and of Gilson's closeness to Fr. Laberthonnière, his philosophical adviser and spiritual adviser to Gilson's wife Thérèse in 1914.[36] They involve a series of ruptures and turns that ought to be clarified. The break with Modernism and Fr. Laberthonnière is presaged by the progress of Gilson's thesis on the medieval sources of Descartes's philosophy but is not immediately evident, because Gilson's Descartes interested Fr. Laberthonnière.[37] There is the break on account of the confession of faith within university circles. Very reticent on this point, Gilson unceasingly denounced the anti-Catholicism of the Sorbonne in the first third of the twentieth century and lamented the silence of his Catholic colleague Victor Delbos. There was a break in philosophical orientation at the time of World War I. In the trenches and in the prisoner of war camps, Plato and Descartes gave way to St. Bonaventure and St. Bernard.

Gilson's Catholic activism, which dated from before World War I, became public in 1924–1925 because of an article he contributed to *Vie catholique* in November 1924 in answer to the same Fr. Habert who labeled him a "foreigner."[38] Then Gilson granted an interview to *Nouvelles littéraires* in January 1925: "I would like to think that a day will come when in the face of the rising tide of materialism and mechanization, Catholicism will fully commit itself in the struggle for the rights of the soul and of religious life in the completeness of its tradition."[39] We have a break here, not in Gilson but in the face that Gilson presented to the public thereafter. This is apparent, on the one hand,

36 On this point see the Papiers Laberthonnière, NAF, 28025 numbers 40 and 42, BNF. See also letter from Étienne Gilson to Henri Gouhier, October 31, 1932, *Revue thomiste* 94 (1994): 471.

37 Letter from Étienne Gilson to Fr. Lucien Laberthonnière, April 28, 1914: "I am very happy that my Descartes has interested you." Papiers Laberthonnière, NAF, 28025, no. 40, BNF. Laberthonnière attended what Xavier Léon called the Gilson Session in March 1914 at the Société Française de Philosophie. Laberthonnière wrote an account of the session for the *Revue de métaphysique et de morale* (NAF 28025, numbers 40, 42, and 43).

38 Étienne Gilson, letter to the editor, "Pour travailler tranquille [to work in peace]," *La Vie catholique*, November 1, 1924, 2. Regarding this letter, see the letter from Étienne Gilson to Henri Gouhier, October 26, 1924, Archives Gouhier: "The more this goes on, the surer I am that the planet has to choose between religion and savagery, and that God is in Catholicism. But if it is good to be a Catholic to avoid Guignebert, it is equally necessary to avoid Habert. By definition, Catholicism is the exclusion of sects." See the letter from Étienne Gilson to Francisque Gay, October 25, 1924, Institut Marc Sangnier: "Attached to this letter is my reply to Fr. O. Habert. You will see that it is a bit long; but in fact, I have set apart the lesser falsehoods to reformulate my statement and sum up my state of mind in a few lines. Misunderstandings like this inevitably occur."

39 Étienne Gilson, "Une heure avec . . ." *Les nouvelles littéraires*, January 3, 1925.

in Maritain's favorable letter to Frédéric Lefèvre about Gilson,[40] although he had not been friendly with Gilson up until then. On the other hand, the position of the Paris newspaper *Le Temps* is symptomatic. Paul Souday, who had always shown himself to be well disposed to Gilson, clearly distanced himself this time, writing tersely: "Gilson's interview with Frédéric Lefèvre raises serious objections."[41]

FAMILY SOURCES

The descendant of a family from Burgundy that settled near Paris after the Revolution, Gilson was born on June 13, 1884, in the clothing store on La Motte Picquet Avenue, Paris, owned by his parents Paul-Anthelme Gilson (Melun, 1838–1917) and Caroline Rainaud (Cravant, 1851–1937). The Gilsons had five boys, Émile, Paul, Étienne (1884), André (1886–1959), and Maurice. The family home was at the corner of Rue de la Santé and Boulevard de Port-Royal, at number 91. Their father was in poor health and became an invalid. The mother, always addressed as "my dear little Mum," in the hundred or so of Gilson's letters to her that are preserved, bore the weight of the family by herself.

Baptized at home on July 7, 1884, by the family friend Fr. Escaré, Gilson was officially received into the Christian community at the parish of Saint-Pierre-de-Gros-Caillou in the seventh arrondissement on August 17. His godmother was a cousin on his mother's side; his godfather a first cousin, a young graduate of the faculty of medicine and future benefactor of the Angoulême hospital.[42] In *Le Philosophe et la théologie* (1961), Gilson narrated his theological childhood. "Nobody is born a Christian, but a man born in a Christian family soon becomes one without being consulted. . . . I do know that, in the full awareness of what I am doing and with the inner certainty of making a free choice, I still formally renew the vows made in my name a few days after my birth."[43]

40 Letter from Jacques Maritain to Fréderic Lefèvre, January 3, 1925, FG, SMCA; also AM, BNUS.

41 Paul Souday, "Les Livres," *Le Temps*, January 21, 1926, 3, col. 6.

42 Étienne Gilson, preface to *À la mémoire du Dr. Henry Gilson, 1857–1932* (Liège: G. Thone, 1932), 7–15; reproduced as "Preface: À la mémoire du Dr Henri Gilson (1857–1932)," in Étienne Gilson, *Oeuvres complètes*, vol. 1, *Un philosophe dans la cité 1908–1943*, ed. Florian Michel (Paris: Vrin, 2019), 801–6.

43 Étienne Gilson, *The Philosopher and Theology*, 8–9.

For his primary education, Gilson was indebted to Catholic institutions. He was enrolled at the age of six in the school run by the Brothers of the Christian Schools in the Saint-Clotilde neighborhood. Notably, he tells us that he learned Latin there. In 1895, he enrolled in the seventh class at the minor seminary of Notre-Dame-des-Champs founded by Bishop Dupanloup at the end of the 1840s. Gilson was a pupil there from "seventh" to "rhetoric" in 1902. The minor seminary of Paris, Notre-Dame-des-Champs, had an excellent reputation and formed many ecclesiastics and part of the Catholic élite of the capital city and the nation.[44] Gilson frequently stressed what he owed to this institution. He defined himself as "a gift from private education to the University." The minor seminary of Notre-Dame-des-Champs

> . . . was a mixed institution open to future laymen as much as to future priests, where there were excellent professors and where, along with religious faith and strict morality, there reigned the most open humanism. Entertainment there consisted in representing *Antigone* or *Iphigenia at Aulis* in Greek; or in making the same actors play the parallel scenes from Molière or Plautus, or in representing Méhul's *Joseph* in its entirety with orchestra and chorus.[45]

The boys enrolled in the seminary could go on to the major seminary at Issy, as did André Gilson or, like Maurice and Étienne, enter the university. Gilson's teachers were priests and religious, the Christian Brothers or Fr. Lucien Paulet (1876–1915), who taught at Notre-Dame-des-Champs, and then was professor of philosophy at the seminary of Issy, where as a "Bergsonian priest," he constructed a "Bergsonizing Scholasticism,"[46] and because of this was banned from teaching after the condemnation of Modernism. Finally, there was Fr. Thorelle, who insisted that Gilson join the school choir,[47] and who instilled in him both musical taste and expertise. Gilson never ceased to repeat that he owed these "admirable priests" his love, not only for the Church but also for French literature, literary style, the fine arts, history, Latin, and music. Given to study and to piety, on February 6, 1894, at the age of fourteen,

44 See, notably, the bulletin of the Notre Dame-des-Champs Alumni Association published until 1950. In the 1950 issue, which still mentions the Gilson brothers who studied at Notre-Dame-des-Champs, there are large numbers of bishops, priests, religious, generals, physicians, lawyers, and so on.

45 Étienne Gilson, "Une heure avec . . ." *Les nouvelles littéraires*, January 3, 1925.

46 Étienne Gilson, *The Philosopher and Theology*, 43, 44, 45.

47 Shook, *Étienne Gilson*, 8.

Gilson joined the Congregation of the Holy Angels, whose motto was "Piety, Docility, Work."[48]

It was clear from the beginning of Gilson's adolescence that he did not have a vocation to the priesthood but wanted to marry and become a professor. He left the *champistes* after his rhetoric year in 1901–1902,[49] but always remained very devoted to his alma mater, which would serve as a model in his reflection on education, and he developed a strong *esprit de corps* with his fellow alumni.[50] Notre-Dame-des-Champs lived by Bishop Dupanloup's intuitions, which Gilson summed up in 1934 as: discipline, respect for the child's freedom and vocation, a sense of the Church, and a sense of France. The minor seminary had to close in 1908 after the separation of church and state for reasons of finances and of the physical plant.

> It was an extraordinary house of education.... We are a spiritual family in the process of extinction.... This spirit will always live on in the writings of Bishop Dupanloup, for those who want to to know it.... Like future priests, laymen have their vocations. Have no doubt, dear companions, you who will work in the world as I do, your teachers have treated you, you too, with all the respect that they felt for you, for your future vocation, that is to say, for God's will for you. I dare say that is why we have been royally treated, and better than kings; we have been treated as free men.[51]

48 Shook, *Étienne Gilson*, 9.

49 See Archives de l'Archevêché de Paris [AHAP], 1 H 12 17, for results of the rhetoric program in 1901–1902. The graded exercises are as follows: Latin translation, Greek translation, Latin verse, Latin speech, French speech, German translation, history, mathematics. Gilson was better in Latin, Greek, and French speech, where he is placed among the six highest, than in mathematics, where he appears in the middle of the roll. In July 1902 Gilson won first prize in French speech.

1 H 12 33, AHAP, Étienne Gilson's Honor Notebooks for second class 1900–1901.

1 H 12 35 AHAP, Étienne Gilson's Honor Notebooks for the rhetoric course. The Honor Notebooks indicate the following subjects of French essays: "Evaluate this thought of Pascal: The whole succession of human beings in so many centuries must be considered as a single person who always subsists and constantly learns." "Why do the Romantics place Corneille above Racine?" For the Latin theme we find an extract from Sully-Prudhomme titled "The Gallop," and in the Latin version it was a portrait of Pompei.

50 Étienne Gilson, "Discours," in *Association fraternelle des anciens élèves de Notre-Dame-des-Champs* (Paris: Louis de Soye, 1934), 16–21: "This is why, just as a cat that meets another cat always enjoys smelling, when a *champiste* meets another *champiste*, there is a kind of perceptible pleasure in their handshake, the purely instinctive mutual recognition of two members of the same species who meet, that immediate experience of a similarity of structure that creates the strongest bond between them."

51 Étienne Gilson, "Discours," *Association fraternelle*, 18–19.

At the beginning of the academic year 1902–1903, Gilson changed to the Lycée Henri IV in the philosophy program to prepare for the baccalaureate. There he encountered the painter André Dunoyer de Segonzac.[52] He just missed Jacques Maritain, who was two years older than he, and who had also taken Hector Dereux's philosophy courses. Dereux taught a mild form of spiritualism that Victor Cousin himself would not have disowned. The unifying function of reason was the good Mr. Dereux's ideal: "He probably taught me something more, but I have forgotten it."[53] Gilson received the baccalaureate with the indication *pass* in summer 1903.

With his bachelor's degree, Gilson immediately fulfilled his military obligation, that "school of loafing,"[54] during which he read Descartes and Léon Brunschvicg, whom he had met at the baccalaureate oral examinations. Gilson directed the local orchestra in the army.[55] His year of military service ended successfully in the summer of 1904. His captain liked his good humor and intelligence, and judged that he would make an excellent reserve officer later on.[56] "Cheerful character, full of energy, was a good influence on his companions, [Gilson] showed a great deal of energy during the practice marches," the captain noted.[57] Gilson recalled some observations that attest to his temperament: "This first contact with the men frightened me a little; that has passed now, but I have retained the unpleasant sensation that one experiences entering cold water. I am rather disillusioned."[58] On the eve of the Great War, Gilson repeated his training.

By comparison with Maritain, in the socio-political sphere of Gilson's youth there is no shadow of Jules Favre, the imposing maternal grandfather and one of the founders of the Third Republic. Neither are there the feminist struggles of Geneviève Favre, nor the friendship with Ernest Psichari and the Psichari family. Again, in Gilson's youth there was no contact with Charles

52 Shook, *Étienne Gilson*, 10. On this point, see Gilson's account at the time of Lucien Lévy-Bruhl's death. "Mon ami Lévy-Bruhl, philosophe, sociologue," *Les nouvelles littéraires*, March 18, 1939, 1: "A little wary of what I was taught in the Lycée Henri IV under the heading of philosophy and whereas for his part Dunoyer de Segonzac took his emergent genius out to play hooky, my curiosity led me to the Sorbonne."

53 Étienne Gilson, *The Philosopher and Theology*, 17.

54 Shook, *Étienne Gilson*, 13.

55 Shook, *Étienne Gilson*, 14.

56 Shook, *Étienne Gilson*, 14.

57 Letter from Étienne Gilson to his mother, August 1904, SMCA.

58 Letter from Étienne Gilson to his mother, August 1904, SMCA.

Péguy, whom Gilson appreciated and criticized on occasion.[59] There was no influence of Léon Bloy, whom Gilson, by contrast, did not admire at all.[60] Moreover, Étienne Gilson did not experience conversion to Catholicism, with all the uprooting that conversion supposes. Nor was there the presence of a charming Russian Jewish girl like Raïssa Oumançoff. Maritain was a pure product of public education at Lycée Carnot and Lycée Henri IV. His parents were complicated, to put it charitably. His father, Paul Maritain, died in 1904. His mother, Geneviève Favre, was literally shattered by her son's religious conversion. Gilson's social background was both less prestigious and less open, but also less troubled and more stable. Many of Gilson's remarks in different autobiographical reports and letters let us see the loving sweetness and the peaceful existence where religion, music, studies, brotherhood, and philosophy are harmoniously united. "My generation was fortunate enough to live those years of study with no other care than to bring them to a happy completion."[61] He explained:

> To understand the experience that brought several among us to metaphysics between 1900 and 1914, let us read "music" instead of painting, and let us not say Leonardo da Vinci but Bach, Beethoven, Schumann, Wagner, or Debussy. Disciples of Bergson, brothers of Romain Roland's Jean-Christophe, their life was spent as happy victims under a music spell, to which they passionately consented.[62]

Gilson was aware of being part of the Parisian Christian and republican petite bourgeoisie. "I did not belong to Le Sillon, nor for that matter to any political party, but there were many of us who felt very close to Marc Sangnier and at

59 Étienne Gilson, *The Philosopher and Theology*, 21–22: "Charles Péguy, whom we admired so much in those days, wrote an account that surprised me. . . . The sociological terror so vividly described by Péguy, of which Durkheim would have been the Robespierre, never existed except in Péguy's poetic imagination."

60 Letter from Étienne Gilson to Stanislas Fumet, December 5, 1967, NAF, 28171, BNF: "I emerge from your *Léon Bloy* shaken and confused. What a man! I hardly know him, because I must confess that I began with *Les derniéres colonnes de l'Église*, and I have never been able to recover from it. My friend Charles Blondel, Protestant, skeptic, and ironic by nature, is an enthusiastic admirer of Bloy's style and made me read *La Femme pauvre*, but the mixture of keys spoiled the author's music for me. So, I am a bad public for *Le Mendiant ingrat*, I would be skeptical even about his spirituality were it not for the unquestionable and irrefutable proof of his impact on many diverse souls. A power of this order and magnitude forbids the slightest doubt."

61 Étienne Gilson, *The Philosopher and Theology*, 30.

62 Étienne Gilson, "Compagnons de route," in *Étienne Gilson: Philosophe de la Chrétienté* (Paris: Cerf, 1949), 275–95, at 282–83.

one with him in his struggle.... Most of us were Christians and republicans belonging to the middle class. All we knew was that a Christian devoted to the Republic was somewhere fighting for us. The condemnation of his movement [by Pope Pius X in 1914] was for many of us a thunderbolt."[63]

Only a few things are known about Gilson's two older brothers. Émile Gilson seems to have taken over his parents' store. Paul Gilson appears to have remained on Avenue de la Motte Picquet. He was "a prototypical Gaul."[64] In any case, Paul Gilson was the father of one of the great figures of French radio, also Paul Gilson (1904–1963), who was at the same time poet, reporter, film director, producer, and announcer at the ORTF.[65] The fifth brother, Maurice, became a radiologist at the Necker Hospital. Andrew, the fourth brother was ordained a priest for the Archdiocese of Paris. Educated like Étienne and Maurice at Notre-Dame-des-Champs, he entered the major seminary of Issy-les-Moulineaux in 1906. After his ordination by Bishop Amette in July 1909, he taught for five years at the Fénélon School in the eighth arrondissement, before being mobilized like his brothers in 1914. He received the *Croix de Guerre*, and after the war he had different assignments as a curate at the parish of Saint-Mandé and then at the Basilica of Sainte-Clothilde.

After receiving his *agrégation* [certification as a junior professor], Étienne married Thérèse Ravisé on February 11, 1908, at Saint-Aspais in Melun. Thérèse is described as a second cousin.[66] Gilson presents the matter thus:

63 Étienne Gilson, *The Philosopher and Theology*, 56–57.

64 Germaine Decaris and Pierre Mac-Orlan, *Paul Gilson*, Poètes d'aujourd'hui (Paris: Pierre Seghers, 1959), 19.

65 See Philip Nord, *France's New Deal: From the Thirties to the Postwar Period* (Princeton, N.J.: Princeton University Press, 2010), 425n129. This work has been translated as *Le New Deal français* (Paris: Perrin, 2016). Nord refers to the dossier gathered by Hélène Eck, "Poète et directeur: Paul Gilson," *Cahiers de l'histoire de la radiodiffusion*, no. 36 (1993): 61–68. According to Philip Nord, Étienne's brother Paul Gilson was a general, which is untrue. —On Étienne's nephew Paul Gilson, see Decaris and Mac-Orlan, *Paul Gilson*. See also the collection of testimonies gathered by F.-J. Temple, *Paul Gilson: Hommage et contribution bio-bibliographique* (Lausanne: Éditions le Front Littéraire, 1983). There is a genealogical tree in Étienne Gilson's archive. Étienne's brother Paul married Louise Duvelleroy. They were the parents of Paul Gilson (1904–1963), who married Christiane Dourif. Paul and Christiane were the parents of Alain and François Gilson. —According to Eck, "Poète et directeur, Paul Gilson," 64, the nephew Paul Gilson "is to be counted among the agnostics and even anti-clericals." We have no indication of any considerable communication with his uncle, who loathed the radio. Letter from Étienne Gilson to Stanislas Fumet, June 1, 1973, NAF, 28171, BNF: "I never speak on the radio. I am allergic to ORTF, which I regard as a permanent disgrace to France.... If I could sing a little ditty of the Brassens type, it would be different." He signs the letter, "An old friend entered into senility." There was a clear cultural and familial fissure.

66 Shook, *Étienne Gilson*, 29.

"Her grandmother and my grandfather were brother and sister. She was probably the first woman I saw as a woman. I first met Thérèse at Cravant when I was about eighteen. . . . I decided on the spot I would marry her."[67] Gilson explains that Thérèse was the final cause of his success in the exams at the Sorbonne. Thérèse, sometimes called "Chouchette" or "Femmette" in their correspondence, and Étienne had three children: Jacqueline (1912), Cécile (1913), and Bernard (1928). "So, the only thing left to us is to thank God through a good life and, I have promised Him that, by raising the children he may give us, in fear and love of him, we will make them little saints," wrote Thérèse after her future husband's success in the teaching certificate process.[68] Often separated, first by World War I, then by the yearly trips to North America that Gilson made, the spouses maintained a magnificent and tender correspondence throughout four decades. There is a lovely depiction of Thérèse in a letter to Fr. Laberthonnière as "an independent soul," as a person "of total sincerity," and "devoted by nature to the religious life."—"And do not look for traces of me in it. I send her to you as I have received her," the husband specifies.[69] In December 1914, Thérèse composed a spiritual letter to Fr. Laberthonnière to "thank him for his kind letter" [which we have not found] and for "all the interest you devote to my husband." "I have to repeat to you, my Father, the good that your encouragement and your kind words have done for me. I have regained a great calm."[70] Thérèse Gilson was then reading "Sur le chemin du catholicisme," a booklet by Laberthonnière, put on the Index in 1913.[71]

Their oldest child, Jacqueline, was a talented artist formed by Maurice Denis, to whom Gilson was close.[72] Jacqueline's work is in the line of the Ateliers d'Art Sacré. Notably, she painted the magnificent Way of the Cross

67 Conversation with Fr. Shook in 1974, quoted in Shook, *Étienne Gilson*, 29–30.

68 Letter from Thérèse Ravisé to Étienne Gilson's mother, October 13, 1907, SMCA.

69 Letter from Étienne Gilson to Fr. Lucien Laberthonnière, April 13, 1914, NAF 28025, no. 40, BNF.

70 Letter from Thérèse Gilson to Fr. Lucien Laberthonnière, December 2, 1914, NAF 28025, no. 42, BNF.

71 Letter from Thérèse Gilson to Fr. Lucien Laberthonnière, no date, NAF 28025, no. 42, BNF.

72 Letter from Étienne Gilson to Maurice Denis, February 5, 1933; October 27, 1942; November 19, 1943, Musée Maurice Denis. In the November 1943 letter, Gilson writes a letter of condolence to Denis's widow shortly after his death: "Jacqueline, who owes everything to him, is inconsolable, and your grief is also our family's grief." Gilson possessed several paintings by Maurice Denis and greatly appreciated his drawings and his prints. "For myself, who owes you everything that my daughter owes you, I don't know how to thank you. This sketch will soon accompany those prints of yours that I already possess, and that are a source of endless joy to me."

of the Basilian Fathers Chapel at St. Michael's College. In her father's view, she was a "commercial failure."[73] Gilson complained that he was her principal buyer. He dedicated *Painting and Reality* (Washington, 1957) to her. Cécile, a nurse and social worker, also had an excellent mastery of English and translated some of her father's works into English, notably *The Philosopher and Theology* (New York: Random House, 1962). Bernard, whose relations with his father were stormy,[74] carried out important work in political science and in philosophy, with publications on presidential government, John Locke, and Henri Bergson. Thérèse died of leukemia in November 1949, leaving her husband who had been called back from Canada bereft and crushed for many years. The burial mass took place in the church of Saint-Léon in Paris in the presence of the Canadian Ambassador to France, Georges Vanier and his wife. "I am a wreck. I am devastated," wrote Gilson to a Canadian friend.[75] To another friend, he said, "I write to you from the new desert and the new land of desolation where I must dwell now."[76] "There are no words for this, but the affection of friendships like yours [Monsieur and Madame Francisque Gay] helps me bear a cross whose weight I never would have imagined.[77]

In the realm of personal spirituality a touching self-portrait of Gilson is found in a letter directed to Fr. André Combes, a former student, dear friend, and future specialist in the spirituality of St. Thérèse of Lisieux. Gilson presented himself as someone who, in the eyes of the world, is a good husband, good father, good citizen, and good Catholic, but who testifies at the

73 Letter from Étienne Gilson to Ralph Barton Perry, May 22, 1950, Harvard University Archives.

74 This was an upheaval in Gilson's inner life. He delicately opened up about it to Thomas Merton in the letter of June 17, 1968, Thomas Merton Center, Louisville: "Thank you for sending me your blessing. I need it, and your prayers for my son, who announced to me two years ago, that he had ceased to believe. I do not know why: I just go on with him as though I did not know that something has happened. And I am praying, of course, but I suppose I have loved him too much. It is my experience that every human love must be paid for. And what is the prayer of so many saints, if not a long complaining?" Rumor had it that Bernard Gilson fell into "loose behavior." See the letter from Fr. Gagnebet to Fr. Labourdette, February 27, 1951 (Archives of *Revue thomiste*): "As for Gilson, I find all the fuss made about his departure displeasing. I believe that the explanation is to be found rather in the drama of his son, who has become an alcoholic and fallen into loose behavior,they say, rather than in politics in which Étienne Gilson would have done better never to have gotten mixed up." Document provided by Michel Fourcade.

75 Letter from Étienne Gilson to Fr. Gerald Phelan, November 12, 1949, quoted by Shook, *Étienne Gilson*, 292.

76 Letter from Étienne Gilson to Anton Pegis, November 26, 1946, quoted by Shook, *Étienne Gilson*, 292.

77 Letter from Étienne Gilson to Francisque Gay, November 16, 1949, Institut Marc Sangnier.

same time to the poverty of his spiritual life. Fr. Combes then invited him to co-direct Vrin's series History of Spirituality. Initially, Gilson rejected the suggestion (which he ultimately accepted) and argued thus:

> We are dealing with an area in which my Christian life is intimately involved. Anatole de Monzie [France's first Minister of Education, 1876–1947] said one day jokingly in my presence: "How funny it would be to catch Gilson in a big scandal!" If the past indicates the future, that will never happen. God has averted occasions of my scandalizing my neighbor. Good husband, good father, good citizen, and so on. That said, I know myself a little from inside and, as Joseph de Maistre used to say about the conscience of an honest man, it is frightful. I'm also what is called "a good Catholic," but may it please Heaven that this is true in God's eyes as it is in men's. I mean, may it please Heaven that my spiritual life were less completely wretched than it is. I certainly can read, understand, and learn everything that the saints say about meditation and contemplation, but I am unable to sustain the smallest prolonged prayer. I can certainly say that the thought of God haunts me, day and night. But I have never lifted myself above the level of the Our Father, the Hail Mary, and the *De Profundis* [Psalm 130, not to be confused with the poem by Oscar Wilde]. Along with the penitential psalms, those are my constant prayers. As for the prayers of the mass, God knows my feeling of unworthiness as I associate myself with them. In short, the background of my religious life is the deep constant conviction of its complete impoverishment. It has often happened to me in my solitude that I berate myself and express the horrible revulsion that my weakness inspires in me. This is not the spiritual life of a man whose name could appear on a series of spiritual books. If I refuse, my answer is that of someone who could give his life for the faith, if God had judged so and made him worthy of such good fortune, but who knows himself all too well to be among the last of the last in God's eyes for me not to be horrified by the possibility that some people might take him for something he is not.[78]

THE SORBONNE: STUDIES, PROFESSORS, AND EXTENSIONS (1905–1913)

Étienne Gilson's academic trajectory was quite traditional. He received his baccalaureate in July 1903. After his year of military service, he received his *license* in philosophy at the Sorbonne in 1905. His professors were Victor

78 Letter from Étienne Gilson to Fr. André Combes, September 19, 1943, NAF 28257, BNF.

Brochard, Gabriel Séailles, André Lalande, Lucien Lévy-Bruhl (his thesis director), Émile Durkheim, Marcel Mauss ("the prophet of Durkheimian sociology"),[79] and Victor Delbos ("one of the teachers I loved most" and one to whom Gilson owes part of his historical method).[80] There were also Léon Brunschvicg, who rebelled against the Jewish fast by eating exactly one bean on a day of fast, and Fréderic Rauh and Léon Brunschvicg.[81] Gilson was also taught by Félix Alcan, Xavier Léon, and Élie Halévey. The last two were among the three founders of the *Revue de métaphysique et de morale*. From this incursion into the world of the Sorbonne, Gilson retained close bonds to good friends, marking his academic relationships.

As his thesis for the Diploma of Higher Studies of Philosophy, Gilson presented *Descartes et la scolastique* under the direction of Lévy-Bruhl in 1906. He was ranked sixth in the philosophy teaching certification or *agrégation* in 1907 in his first try, after David, Peltier, Ray, Leroux, and Sarrien.[82] He presented his doctoral thesis at the Sorbonne in 1913, again under the direction of Lévy-Bruhl, "the least medieval man" Gilson ever met, the one who suggested to him that he ferret out the medieval origins of Descartes's thought.[83] Gilson published both theses. The "little" thesis was published by Alcan in 1912 with the title *Index Scolastico-cartésien*. The major thesis, *La liberté chez Descartes et la théologie*, was also published by Alcan the following year [*Theology and the Cartesian Doctrine of Freedom*, 2018]. After five years of teaching as an instructor in different lycées from Bourg-en-Bresse

79 Étienne Gilson, *The Philosopher and Theology*, 27.

80 On Victor Delbos, see Étienne Gilson, "L'État sans philosophe," *Sept*, no. 5, March 31, 1934, 2. — Étienne Gilson, *The Philosopher and Theology*, 96: "There had been considerable naïveté in my early decision to apply to the theologians of the Middle Ages the same method of inquiry that Lucien Lévy-Bruhl and Victor Delbos had taught me to apply to the study of modern philosophers."

81 Étienne Gilson, *The Philosopher and Theology*, 34.

82 *Le Temps*, August 15, 1907, 2.

83 Étienne Gilson, *Discours de réception à l'Académie française* (Paris: Firmin-Didot, 1967), 6: "As a young student in search of a subject for a thesis on Descartes, I went to consult my teacher Lucien Lévy-Bruhl. . . . This heir to the pure rationalism of the Enlightenment, this great mind remains even now in my memory as the least medieval man I have ever met. Not only did he judge with Auguste Comte that metaphysical systems are not worth refuting and that it is enough to let them fall into disuse, but he thought that among so many dead philosophies, none is more irrevocably dead than medieval Scholasticism, of which it could be rightly said that it is dead by universal consent. Yet it is he who, by advising me to seek in medieval thought the possible origin of certain doctrines taken up by Descartes, made me open the *Summa Theologica* for the first time, about which both he and I suspected that, having opened it once, I would never decide to close it again. Thus, in the twentieth century, the author of *La Mentalité primitive* (1922) [*Primitive Mentality*, 1923] recruited a new disciple for St. Thomas."

to Rochefort, from Tours and Angers to Saint-Quentin, in summer 1913 his doctorate allowed him to be named almost immediately a lecturer (*maître de conférences*) at the faculty of letters of the University of Lille.

In his autobiography, Gilson clearly describes the "new Sorbonne" of his youth, dominated by neo-Kantian philosophy (*The Critique of Pure Reason* had become "the charter of a philosophical training")[84] and by "pure scientism": outside the sciences, there was no knowledge worthy of the name. "In the end, both criticism and scientific positivism agreed on this point, of paramount importance in their eyes, that the problems of the world, of the soul, and of God were out of date."[85]

Reading Gilson's letters, we can understand what a shock the Sorbonne was for him at the age of twenty. He wrote his mother in 1904: "I work, as I have often told you, for God, to carry out his work, for me, because I want to be someone, and for you so that my success will be part of your reward on earth."[86] In August 1907, when Gilson achieved his *agrégation* [philosophy teaching certification] "the only person from the Sorbonne" that year, he wrote again: "We will never thank the good Lord enough for the grace he has just given us. . . . When I attribute my success to Providence, it is not a phrase. The fact is that I am quite convinced. . . . I cannot explain my success except by the good Lord's will."[87] There were only seven certificates of *agrégation* granted that year, of which four went to normal school graduates.

A letter from Lucien Lévy-Bruhl testifies to the criticism and "bad humor" of François Picavet after the approval of the thesis in June 1912:

> Follow Picavet's advice when it seems good and forget the rest! What matters is that he approved you. He must be in a bad mood, and I am the one responsible. . . . I deprived him of the pleasure of directing you. I hope to act in a way that no problems for you stem from that. In any case, if he bothers you, do not show it, and scrupulously observe good form. My thinking is that ultimately the mockers will not be on his side. . . . Your thesis means something and offers something really new, in its method and results, about problems where the old methods could no longer offer anything. One doesn't see that every day.[88]

84 Étienne Gilson, *The Philosopher and Theology*, 36.

85 Étienne Gilson, *The Philosopher and Theology*, 37.

86 Letter from Étienne Gilson to his mother, August, 1904, SMCA.

87 Letter from Étienne Gilson to his mother, August 14, 1907, SMCA.

88 Letter from Lucien Lévy-Bruhl to Étienne Gilson, June 3, 1912, SMCA.

The tribunal consisted of Professors Picavet, Lalande, Delacroix, Lévy-Bruhl, Rébelliau, and Delbos. A report on the thesis defense and the published book appeared in the newspaper *Le Temps* on February 15, 1913.

> In his latest work, Gilson tries to show that the Cartesian doctrines of divine and human freedom are not explained if we fail to relate them to the three predominant theological tendencies in the Catholic Church that Descartes experienced: the theology of St. Thomas, that of the Oratory's Augustinianism, and that of nascent Jansenism. By carefully tracing Descartes's attempt to adapt Catholicism's traditional teaching to the requirements of the new physical science, we often discover the true meaning of this or that doctrine and the explanation of the apparent contradictions that its passages on freedom contain. This new thesis, which Gilson skillfully defends, will be read with profit by all those concerned with the history of philosophy and of religion.[89]

We can state unequivocally that indeed Gilson's thesis signaled a shift in the approach to the history of ideas, both in method and results. To hear Gilson, his method was not at all original and was completely laid out by the methodology of the Sorbonne, that of his professors Lucien Lévy-Bruhl and Victor Delbos. Accordingly, in his book *Héloise et Abélard* (Paris: Vrin, 1938, 184) Gilson writes: "My ambition to do for Abelard, St. Thomas, and Duns Scotus what Lucien Lévy-Bruhl has done for Descartes, Hume, Berkeley, and Comte, is one whose presumption I think I can gauge." In his autobiography he adds:

> There had been considerable naïveté in my early decision to apply to the theologians of the Middle Ages the same method of inquiry that Lucien Lévy-Bruhl and Victor Delbos had taught me to apply to the study of modern philosophers . . . Besides, history is not exactly the forte of Scholasticism. Deep within themselves, Scholastics rather despise and mistrust history. The University practiced it better and, as a result, the understanding of the theology of St. Thomas doctrine has greatly benefited from it.[90]

Gilson gladly acknowledged his debts and sometimes exaggerated them a little. Lévy-Bruhl was better known for his works on anthropology and sociology than on history of philosophy. The radical novelty of Gilson's

89 *Le Temps*, February 15, 1913, 4.

90 Étienne Gilson, *The Philosopher and Theology*, 96–97.

works, starting with his thesis, was, in any case, to apply that method of the Sorbonne to a set of philosophical objects that not only had evaded it until then, but were adverse to it. The simple consequence of the method taught and applied to a new area had to call into question the content of the lesson imparted by these same professors. Gilson underlined the sensation of initiating a break in 1913 after the thesis defense: "Looking back across forty-five years, I distinctly remember the feeling of fear I experienced on the day when, after holding back my pen for a long time, I finally wrote this simple sentence: 'On all these points, the thought of Descartes, in comparison with the sources from which it derives, marks much less a gain than a loss'" (*The Philosopher and Theology*, 88–89).

Gilson's idea has been so widely accepted that it is difficult to recognize the violation of a commandment, a broken idol, but Gilson had challenged a dogma of the new Sorbonne, denying the existence of an "intellectual night" between the Greeks and Descartes that Victor Cousin and so many others had described. This initial rupture, widely criticized by Gilson's professors after the thesis defense,[91] bore the profound imprint of continuity that, over the course of years, Gilson built into a method of the history of ideas. We find the method replicated in other passages in his books regarding the point of connection between the Middle Ages and the "Renaissance"; about Petrarch, whose inner life is nourished by St. Augustine; on Rabelais, a staunch reader of the medievals and of Duns Scotus in particular. But also between antiquity and the Middle Ages, there is Heloise reciting Lucan's *Pharsalia*, as she approached the altar where she was to take the veil. There is St. Bernard, who renounced everything but the art of writing well. There is Alcuin, who was full of nostalgia for antiquity in his reconstructed dialogues with Charlemagne; or Roger Bacon, commenting upon important passages from Seneca for the pope. In 1939 Gilson gave a course whose unpublished four-hundred-page manuscript, preserved in the St. Michael's College Archives in Toronto, is titled *The Continuity of Classical Culture from Cicero to Erasmus*. The spirit of Gilson's method is most noticeable in the series of lectures collected and published with the title *Les idées et les lettres* (Paris: Vrin, 1932).

> The arbitrary compartments that we invent to isolate the great periods of the history of our art and of our ideas in general are only the projec-

91 "Thèse de M. Étienne Gilson, agrégé de philosophie," *Revue de métaphysique et de morale* 21, no. 3 (May 1913): 24–32. The review of Gilson's thesis was published at the same time as the review of Maurice Halbwachs's thesis (19–23).

> tions upon the past of our secret hatred and our current preferences. We want those from whom we separate ourselves to have been separated in order to distance ourselves more securely from those who still relate to them. Instead of violently introducing our divisions into the past, perhaps it would be wiser to start from the unity of our common history so as to become aware of the illusory vanity of our divisions. The study conducted thus would be more beneficial only because it would be truer.... We don't have so much of the past that we cannot be ourselves. Let us accept our whole tradition; let us lovingly cut into the old tree, let us penetrate at length the sap that still rises from its roots in order that we may bear in our turn, as one of its branches, leaves, flowers, and fruits.[92]

Henri Bergson's singular magisterial role likewise emerges from these years of studies. Like many others, Gilson would go to the Collège de France to listen to him.[93] Gilson testified to this frequently. In a 1914 letter to Xavier Léon, Gilson, by then at the University of Lille, mentioned that he was soon to speak at a meeting of the *Revue de métaphysique* along with Maurice De Wulf of the Louvain: "I hope that Bergson will not be there. If he should be, don't introduce me. I have known friends who told me, 'I have written to Bergson, I am going to see Bergson,' with the same calm that they might have in telling me, 'I have written to Plato.' I don't know how they can do it."[94] Gilson wrote from the trenches in 1915 that Bergson is "the fourth great philosopher after Plato, Descartes, and Kant.[95] We emphasize that, at this date, Gilson did not designate any medieval author. It is only in 1922 that Gilson began to correspond with Bergson, who held Gilson's works "in high esteem."[96] The correspondence shows that they read each other. Bergson appreciated, variously, Gilson's Cartesian studies, his introduction to St. Augustine, the mystical theology of St. Bernard, and the studies on Heloise and Abelard. In 1967, Gilson still called Bergson "My dear Teacher." "Allow

92 Étienne Gilson, *Les idées et les lettres* (Paris: Vrin, 1932), 261.

93 François Azouvi, *La gloire de Bergson: Essai sur le magistère philosophique* (Paris: Gallimard, 2007).

94 Letter from Étienne Gilson to Xavier Léon, March 13, 1914, Fonds Xavier Léon, Bibliothèque interuniversitaire de la Sorbonne [BIS], MSVC 361.

95 Letter from Étienne Gilson to Xavier Léon, August 24, 1915, Fonds Xavier Léon, BIS, MSVC 361.

96 Letter from Henri Bergson to Étienne Gilson, June 18, 1922, SMCA. The Gilson-Bergson correspondence between 1922 and 1939 consists of nine letters from Bergson (SMCA) and two letters from Gilson (June 5, 1939 and October 20, 1939, Bibliothèque littéraire Jacques Doucet.

me to give you publicly the name that you have long had in my heart."[97] Like Maritain, Gilson felt the greatest appreciation for Bergson, but unlike Maritain, Gilson seems to have reached a point where he refused to read Bergson so as not to have to criticize him publicly and in this way avoided committing a sort of parricide. This is the meaning of a letter to Henri Gouhier in 1958:

> The truth, which seems improbable, is that I have never read *The Two Sources* [1932] ... Why? I think that in a way I am afraid. I have never dared to face what perhaps would put me in the obligation of saying this time an absolute no to this great mind who was philosophy in the flesh for me, like Socrates, the guide toward the source of philosophy beyond philosophy.... I have always been afraid of the deep pain of having to separate myself totally from him on a point that is so vital for me.[98]

Gilson concluded with a beautiful homage to his professors during those years studying at the Sorbonne: "When I recall those faraway years, I realize that our masters constituted a republic and thereby made it possible for us to enjoy the benefits of a republican regime.... In sum, and this is no light praise, our youth had no other burden to carry than freedom."[99]

PHILOSOPHIZING DURING WAR (1914–1919)

Mobilized in August 1914 as a sergeant and then as a machine gun officer, Gilson was involved in the battle of Verdun in February 1916. On the third day of the offensive, he survived a strike by a shell that left him buried in a blockhouse before being captured by the Germans on February 23, 1916.[100] As he was taken prisoner, one of the Germans had the flash of humor to shout: *Morgen, wir sind keine Barbaren.* [We are not barbarians.][101] "I am a prisoner of war and not wounded, which is something greater than a miracle, given all

97 Étienne Gilson, "Hommage à Henri Bergson: Allocution de M. Étienne Gilson," speech given at the Pantheon, May 11, 1967, printed in a booklet (Paris: Firmin-Didot, 1967), 6.

98 Letter from Étienne Gilson to Henri Gouhier, June 4, 1958, printed in *Revue thomiste* 94 (July–September 1994): 468.

99 Étienne Gilson, *The Philosopher and Theology*, 40–41.

100 Laurence Shook's biography is very precise factually about the combat and Gilson's imprisonment. See Shook, *Étienne Gilson*, 66–87.

101 Shook, *Étienne Gilson*, 82.

I have seen," he immediately wrote to Thérèse.[102] In the newspaper *Le Temps*, he then became an archetype of a civilized French soldier, a kind of Marcus Aurelius without rank, who despite the war, the bombs, and imprisonment stoically continued his philosophical work. In 1947 Vallery-Radot narrated Gilson's war to the Académie française:

> We are in 1914. We are at war. You are mobilized with the rank of sergeant. You are at the Courtine Camp, at a center for machine gun instruction. You take apart and put together every machine gun known at the time. These are surely the only mechanisms whose secrets you have had to penetrate! In 1915, you manage to be sent to the front. You join the forces at Verdun as a second lieutenant in a machine gun unit. One day you are given the task of choosing twenty-four mules for our company. You need to learn to distinguish mules from horses, a problem that initially seems unsolvable. It is not the same to be a philosopher as to be a mule driver. On the third day of the Battle of Verdun, you are buried in a blockhouse. When you are dug out, you have the *croix de guerre* but are a prisoner. Men of your era do not know what discouragement is. You make months of captivity into months of work and reflection. In every field, even the field of reprisals to which your irreverent mind, allied with your hatred of the enemy, ought to lead you, you organize courses on metaphysics as well as on psychology and sociology. In a camp near Magdeburg, you write an article for the *Revue philosophique* that you title "On the Foundation of Aesthetic Judgements." It is honored by a critique of Paul Souday. Your time is divided between conferences, articles, and lectures. But that is not enough. You learn Italian with an Italian prisoner. English with a Canadian prisoner, and Russian with thirteen Russian prisoners.[103]

This connection with the Russian language was to be important in Gilson's life.[104] Furthermore, Paul Souday's articles in *Le Temps* signaled the beginning of Gilson's fame and his good reception by the press. He appeared

102 Letter from Étienne Gilson to Thérèse, March 7, 1916, quoted in the letter from Thérèse Gilson to Lucien Lévy-Bruhl, April 4, 1916, IMEC.

103 Vallery-Radot, "Réponse au discours de réception d'Étienne Gilson."

104 Gilson went to Ukraine in 1922. He communicated with the Communist delegates in San Francisco in 1945. Again in 1969, he wrote to Jean Laloy, "Russia, from which I have distanced myself with age, still dwells within me always. . . . What I regret is having lost familiarity with the Great Russian language, so sweet to speak and pleasant to hear, even when it sounds in all its majesty. I remember the public recitation in Moscow of a scene from Boris Godunov: what music!" (Letter of December 21, 1969, Archives familiales de Jean Laloy, private archive letter communicated courtesy of the son of Jean Laloy.)

three times on page one of the daily. If Paul Souday argued with the artistic theses that Gilson developed, the essential point was evidently the moral argument that the writer draws from it: people still philosophize in the trenches.

> Another example is provided by a young Bergsonian philosopher, Étienne Gilson, who published an article titled "Art et métaphysique" in the last issue of the *Revue de métaphysique*, and dated it "in the campaign, November-December 1915." Marcus Aurelius composed his thoughts during a campaign against the Quadi or the Marcomanni [two Germanic tribes]. But the barbarians of that period had less artillery than those of today, and the higher rank of the imperial Stoic perhaps guaranteed him a bit more comfortable quarters in the camps. Étienne Gilson's article is very interesting. One might not accept his conclusion. Gilson denies any relation of art with science or philosophy. That is to go rather far. According to him, art is not a representation or contemplation of nature, but a complete creation that introduces a new object into the world.[105]

While Gilson was a prisoner in Germany, he was praised three times by the newspaper for continuing to philosophize in captivity. In June 1917, we find a long critique of Gilson's, and Paul Souday's comparison with Marcus Aurelius:

> Thinkers continue to believe that Marcus Aurelius moralized in his tent and would have done the same if misfortune had sent him into captivity. A philosopher and aesthetician in the prisoner of war camp at Magdeburg, Étienne Gilson, composes a study on the "foundation of esthetic judgements." Even in the heart of this historic crisis, French intelligence cannot be idle or abdicate. And behold a happy promise for the future.... Gilson, all of whose development we cannot accompany, as we see it, attributes too much to subjectivity and too little to serious criticism. But he perceives the truth when he considers that the standard to be sought is the judgment of the competent and of better minds.[106]

Gilson wrote many letters during the war: to his mother, his wife, his university colleagues, and to Fr. Laberthonnière. Gilson composed a notebook on the battle of Verdun, sent to Thérèse in installments from June 1915

105 Paul Souday, "Dans la tranchée," *Le Temps*, May 8, 1916, 1. See also Souday's article "Sur Flaubert," *Le Temps*, June 26, 1916, 1.

106 Paul Souday, "Un esthéticien en captivité," *Le Temps*, June 8, 1917, 1.

to February 1916. Large excerpts have been published in English.[107] He wrote to his mother in 1915, "Becoming a genuine *poilu* is not easy"[108] In 1915–1916 from Verdun, Gilson wrote, "I arrived this morning at the front line, in a very tranquil, peaceful place."[109] "My cheerful temperament came with me."[110] "I always bring a book and a candle when I have to take shelter during a bombardment, which has the virtue of insanely amusing my captain."[111] Gilson always wrote with incredible tenderness, reassuring his mother while assuring her that he read *The Imitation of Christ*: "Good evening, dear little Mum, your little boy hugs you tenderly, and he pats you as he always loved and will always love to do."[112]

Gilson continued to write articles for the *Revue de métaphysique et de morale* and for the *Revue philosophique de la France et de l'étranger* in 1916 and 1917.[113] He became more religious than ever, consoling and hearing the confession of one of his dying men.[114] He narrated a terrible bombardment on Christmas eve 1915, where only those at midnight mass were saved.[115] The letters exchanged between Gilson and Xavier Léon are priceless because of the way they reveal Gilson's mettle. They touch upon philosophical readings, thanksgiving for past years and for favors received, good humor, prayers for the unity of the French people, who will "no longer have the right to hate each other on the soil where we will rest." In Gilson's writing, the issue of the unity of France and of Europe seems to spring out of the heart of the conflict. Let us quote at length a letter of Gilson, also cited elsewhere:

> Your proofs return to you corrected after having heard a blast that seems to indicate that the restocking of munitions is carried out regularly in all countries. . . . With joyous confidence in the future, I have renewed my subscription for 1916. . . . The first issue has reached me in the trenches.

107 Shook, *Étienne Gilson*, 73–75.

108 Shook, *Étienne Gilson*, 76.

109 Letter from Étienne Gilson to his mother, June 19, 1915, SMCA.

110 Letter from Étienne Gilson to his mother, June 27, 1915, SMCA.

111 Letter from Étienne Gilson to his mother, February 5, 1916, SMCA.

112 Letter from Étienne Gilson to his mother, January 25, 1916, SMCA.

113 Étienne Gilson, "Art et métaphysique," *Revue de métaphysique et de morale* 23, no. 1 (January 1916): 243–67; "Du Fondement des jugements esthétiques," *Revue philosophique de la France et de l'étranger* 83 (January–June 1917): 525–46.

114 Shook, *Étienne Gilson*, 76.

115 Shook, *Étienne Gilson*, 79–80.

> At the time, philosophical speculation seemed a faraway mist, so that I was surprised to discover that I devoured the volume in two days at the front line. I was like a convalescent who does not think he is hungry and is surprised when he devours everything he is given. . . . It is unnecessary to say that I am well morally and physically. Besides, we lead a very harmonious existence, because it is simplified. When I look at my past life as something that can end this evening, I see it flowing with more riches than a hundred years of existence. I have found all the deepest joys of my heart in the lives of my mother, my wife, and my daughters. I have found the deepest joy of the mind in dwelling assiduously on the works of Bergson, and I am infinitely happy to have seen with my own eyes the fourth great philosopher known to humanity, after Plato, Descartes, and Kant. From the societal viewpoint, I have the pleasure of having belonged to French higher education. So I look at my past without worry. I view the present with a peaceful soul, because here duty is clear, simple, and need not be sought out in anguish. The future remains. Imagining it, I express only one wish: May the French understand that they will no longer have the right to hate each other on the soil where we rest.[116]

> I have mailed you an essay that three weeks of rest behind the lines allowed me to start. I finished it as best I could, even at the front line, because one should not hide the fact that a machine gun nest is a very appropriate place for meditation. Nothing is more like a Benedictine's cell than a machine gun officer's shack. There is just less light there, and from time to time the neighbors on the other side dump carts full of rubbish in one's vicinity. . . . It almost came to pass that someone other than myself sent these papers to you. We had a horrible Christmas Eve in muck and blood. My socks were red from it and my boots still oozed it two days later. The balance for the machine gunners: eight killed, two with amputations, six with lighter wounds. The calm returned, and the stubborn wait began again. Some good friends help put up with it: books.[117]

Gilson described his philosophical and religious readings to Fr. Laberthonnière in detail. Thus, in December 1914, while Gilson was far from the front in barracks where non-commissioned officers and companies were trained, he waited to be sent to the front. "When the time to leave comes, I will put my St. Bonaventure in my bag, and I will go to read his marvelous

116 Letter from Étienne Gilson to Xavier Léon, August 24, 1915, Fonds Xavier Léon, BIS.

117 Letter from Étienne Gilson to Xavier Léon, January 6, 1916, Fonds Xavier Léon, BIS.

Itinerarium elsewhere. Finishing my reading of the *Breviloquium* a few days ago, I found this phrase from St. Bernard: *Deus futurus est rationi plenitudo lucis, voluntati multitudo pacis, et memoriae continuatio aeternitatis.* Such are encounters that let one close the book and spend a few instants of leisure in the trenches."[118]

While Gilson in prison camp gave other prisoners lectures on Bergson and took notes on the works of St. Bonaventure, appropriately reviewed by the German censors, his wife Thérèse exchanged letters with Xavier Léon:

> I did indeed read the article by Souday that appeared in *Le Temps* but I simply confess that I do not share his interpretation of my husband's conclusion, and I wonder if he has grasped its precise meaning. I have mentioned the article to my husband, but I am not taking the chance of sending it to him. I believe that the Boches would not accept it. I am going to send him an extract, because he asked me for one, so that there is no difficulty in sending it. My husband continues to do well. He exercises every day, but I only receive postcards. Letters are still suppressed in his camp. This new sacrifice is really painful for me.[119]

> In the letter of May 18 that came yesterday, my husband asked me precisely to send him the issue of the journal [*Revue de métaphysique*] where his article will appear. That does not seem prudent to me, but I think I can send him the excerpt without creating problems for him. He will be happy. Very fortunately, it is possible to write to him at one's pleasure. It is a joy and consolation for him. He asks that people write to him, and indicates the letters he has received.[120]

Gilson's letters to Lévy-Bruhl let us see his work in prison. He organized courses for prisoners (letter of April 18, 1916). "After school" he had a commitment to compose reviews of German, English, and Italian works (letter of February 1917), and demonstrated his love for the fine arts. Gilson requested music, notably Fauré's Lieder (letter of April 25, 1916). The letters also show that Gilson had moments of deep despondency:

> My dear teacher: There is a serious question that I cannot settle without you. Won't the history of medieval philosophy be an unwanted luxury after

118 Letter from Étienne Gilson to Fr. Lucien Laberthonnière, December 21, 1914, NAF, no. 52, BNF.

119 Letter from Thérèse Gilson to Xavier Léon, June 2, 1916, Fonds Xavier Léon, BIS.

120 Letter from Thérèse Gilson to Xavier Léon, June 8, 1916, Fonds Xavier Léon, BIS.

> the war? I am still young enough to modify my activity, and I like action enough to want to cooperate in the great task that awaits us. I believe in applied experimental psychology, especially pedagogy. I believe that since 1914 something has changed in the problem. I have reread and burned my essays on the issue [probably on "the psychic organism," which was the theme of the letter of February 1, 1917]. This sub-Bergsonianism sickens me. In twenty years, after living the realities, I will return to abstractions.[121]

At Christmas 1918, after almost three years spent in German prisons (February 1916 to November 9, 1918) and after having observed the so-called "German revolution" of 1918 from rather close up, Gilson was back in his home at Melun. He gave a brief account of his painful experience as a prisoner.[122] "The lies and the theft cannot be described." "We were treated as means and not as ends." For Gilson, the experience in Germany was "humiliation and refined slavery." Repression and harassment of prisoners were constant: reduced rations, blocked mail, ten men per room, high cost of food. After leaving the camp, Gilson saw the red flag floating over it on the day the Kaiser abdicated. However, wrote Gilson, "Apart from that, nothing changed." "The flag is red. The commandant accepted it. The Kaiser's flag floats over many buildings." The officers keep their positions. "They have not yielded." "The main impression is that this is a revolution that considers itself genuine, but that is not profound.... The mindset that is both cause and effect of the regime remains. This [German] revolution does not stem from a movement with ideas.... A revolution like that of 1789 is a spiritual conversion. There is none of that here.... The spiritual elements likely to produce war are still going to continue with increased animosity."[123] It would be interesting to delve into the political culture of the prisoner of war camps in Germany. Of course, Gilson did not see what was happening in Berlin or Moscow. But he was in constant contact with Germans and Russians in the camps, and consequently could see how they viewed and interacted with each other.

Demobilized in January of 1919, Gilson was awarded the Croix de Guerre. "Here I am finally, back with my own people. What a price in fatigue but what a reception! Everything is so good and so beautiful that all the pain will vanish like a bad dream.... The only thing left is to rest in order

121 Letter from Étienne Gilson to Lucien Lévy-Bruhl, April 16, 1918, IMEC.

122 Étienne Gilson, "Impressions d'Allemagne," no date, three manuscript pages, SMCA. This document appears to be the draft of a lecture.

123 Étienne Gilson, "Impressions d'Allemagne," SMCA.

to go back to work in good form. That is what I am going to do."[124] In the spring, at Lévy-Bruhl's request, Gilson agreed to review books for the *Revue philosophique*.[125] In March 1919, Gilson applied for a position as professor of medieval philosophy at the University of Strasbourg, where he began to teach at the beginning of the following academic year.

FROM THE UNIVERSITY OF STRASBOURG TO THE UNIVERSITY OF PARIS (1919–1932)

Gilson's stay at the University of Strasbourg was short. It lasted only two years, from autumn 1919 to autumn 1921. In November 1919, Gilson attended the solemn opening of the university by Raymond Poincaré. "The opening was completely beautiful, aesthetically and morally. I believe that we have 'scored' as our English friends say."[126] Gilson presided ("brilliantly" in Lucien Febvre's report)[127] over the election of the dean of the faculty of letters, Christian Pfister. At Strasbourg Gilson encountered Gustave Cohen, Sylvain Lévi, Marc Bloch, and Lucien Febvre.[128] Re-working courses given at the University of Lille on the eve of the war, Gilson published the first edition of *Thomisme* in 1919–1920, as well as the first edition of *Études de philosophie médiévale*, at Strasbourg.

In November-December 1921, Étienne Gilson was appointed to the Sorbonne and to be director of studies at the Religious Studies Section of the École pratique des hautes études (EPHE), succeeding François Picavet (1851 to May 1921). At the EPHE, Gilson had received nine out of eleven votes, and

124 Letter from Étienne Gilson to Xavier Léon, January 14, 1919, Fonds Xavier Léon, BIS.

125 Étienne Gilson, review of two works by Alfred Loisy, *De la discipline intellectuelle* and *La paix des nations et la religion de l'avenir*, published in *Revue philosophique de la France et de l'étranger* 88 (1919): 129–31; review of *Le retour à la scolastique* by Gonzague Truc, *Revue philosophique de la France et de l'étranger* 88 (1919): 322–24.

126 Letter from Étienne Gilson to Xavier Léon, December 2, 1919, Fonds Xavier Léon, BIS.

127 Lucien Febvre, "Souvenirs d'une grande histoire: Marc Bloch et Strasbourg," in *Combats pour l'histoire* (Paris: Armand Colin, 1953; repr. 1992), 391 [the review is online: https://www.persee.fr/doc/ahess_0395-2649_1946_num_1_2_3203]: "A very young Étienne Gilson presided brilliantly over a meeting where we agreed upon the installation of a dean."

128 For the relations between Gilson, Bloch, and Febvre, see the published correspondence between Bloch and Febvre, as well as Lucien Febvre's review of *L'Histoire de la philosophie médiévale*, 2nd ed. (Paris: Payot, 1944), "Histoire d'idées, histoire des sociétés: Une question de climat," *Annales* 1, no. 2 (1946): 158–61. The review was reproduced in Febvre, *Combats pour l'histoire*. The text will be analyzed below.

notably joined Marcel Mauss, who held the chair of religions of primitive peoples, and who had been the first to suggest Gilson as François Picavet's successor,[129] as well as Sylvain Lévi, who taught the religions of India and of ancient Egypt.

Until 1932, Gilson taught the history of medieval philosophy in both institutions, fully aware of the significance of the mission he had been given. He wrote in this vein to Xavier Léon in September 1921:

> To speak of medieval thought in this University of Paris and especially in this faculty where it was born is, if my historical interpretation of the Middle Ages is correct, a beautiful responsibility to undertake. One does not have the right to be mediocre in this place. I would like to devote a whole life to teaching the French, *all* the French, the profound sources of their moral unity.[130]

At the Sorbonne, Gilson achieved notable success among the students, whereas some of the other professors seem to have been more reserved. Louis Bouyer (1913–2004) reports in this regard that he and his young colleagues at the Protestant seminary were "free to take the course on Thomistic philosophy that Gilson was giving at the Sorbonne during those years, a course that passionately interested us. . . . Gilson's first lecture had a great impact on me."[131] For his part, in *The Philosopher and Theology*, Gilson recalls an astonishing anecdote that shows the resistance met from within. He was reproached for "religious propaganda."[132] In articles that he published in *Sept* in 1934, the suspicion and preconceptions that he had to confront were perceptible. "The secret of the matter is known by all, but it is not good form

129 See the minutes of the Council of the Section of Religious Studies, June 26, 1921, Notebook 2, p. 685, Archives École pratique des hautes études: "Professor Mauss declared that if the section decides in favor of retention [of the description of the position of François Picavet] two very qualified candidacies will be presented: Émile Bréhier, professor at the faculty of letters in Paris, and Étienne Gilson, professor at the faculty of letters in Strasbourg. The council entrusted the study of the issue and preparation of a report to a committee composed of, along with Maurice Vernes and Toutain, members of the office, Sylvain Lévi, Mauss, Alphandéry, de Fay, and Hubert." On November 13, 1921, the report of the aforesaid commission was read by Monsieur Alphandéry at the section council meeting and it concluded: "The Council will propose Étienne Gilson to the Minister to be entrusted with the open position in the history of doctrines and dogmas." "Gilson received nine votes and Bréhier two votes. Gilson will be recommended to the Minister" (687–88).

130 Letter from Étienne Gilson to Xavier Léon, September 17, 1921, Fonds Xavier Léon, BIS.

131 Louis Bouyer, *Le métier de théologien: Entretiens avec Georges Daix* (Geneva: Ad Solem, 2005), 27.

132 Étienne Gilson, *The Philosopher and Theology*, 34.

to acknowledge it. It is that metaphysics is 'reactionary.' A metaphysician may be an impressive thinker but there is no need for him. Rather, there is a need that he not be there. Say everything good about him that you like, he will never be dependable as 'a man of the left.' That is the very nature of his profession."[133]

At the École pratique, Gilson attended the sessions of the council of the fifth section. The minutes of these sessions are very revealing, sketching a broad range of social contacts and readings. In numerous meetings we encounter the names of Mauss, Sylvain Lévi, Gouhier, Koyré, and Alfred Loisy, who was already at the Collège de France and the director of studies at EPHE from 1923 to 1927; the diplomat Jean Marx, for the study of mythology and Celtic folklore, session of November 23, 1923, named director of studies in 1927; Maurice de Gandillac, Gilson's substitute in 1930; Paul Vignaux, his substitute in 1932–1933; Alexandre Kojevnikoff [to be known as Alexandre Kojéve], about whom Gilson composed a report after the January 21, 1933, session on the subject of his study of "the religious ideas of Vladimir Solovyov."[134]

The École pratique's yearbook referred to some fifty regular students in Gilson's two weekly seminars. In 1922, Gilson began a seminar for the study of Augustinian texts relating to divine illumination. The second seminar was devoted to the influence of the Franciscan spirit upon medieval philosophy. From 1922 on (the yearbooks provide a good record) there are at least two of Gilson's students who will become longtime friends. They are Henri Gouhier (1898–1994) and Alexandre Koyré (1892–1964), both of whom initially worked along Gilsonian lines. At Gilson's recommendation, Gouhier was invited to give a series of courses at EPHE (council meeting of June 20, 1923). The Bibliothèque de l'École pratique des hautes études published Gouhier's first book, *La pensée religieuse chez Descartes*, in 1922. In 1923, Gouhier published *L'idée de Dieu dans la philosophie de saint Anselme.*[135]

133 Étienne Gilson, "L'État sans philosophie," *Sept*, no. 5, March 31, 1934, 2.

134 See the minutes of the Council of the Religious Sciences Section, January 21, 1933, Notebook 3, p. 839, Archives École pratique des hautes études.

135 Regarding Alexandre Koyré's participation in Gilson's seminars, see Koyré, *De la mystique à la science: Cours, conférences, et documents, 1922–1962* (Paris: EHESS, 2016), 43: "In the history of theology, the preferences of a student of Husserl and Picavet tended to Augustinianism and Scotism rather than Thomism, but they did not prevent [sic] Koyré from attending Gilson's lectures."

In 1929, Gilson was a member of the tribunal for Koyré's thesis on Jacob Boehme. The thesis was published that year and dedicated to Léon Brunschvicg and Étienne Gilson. "Where others have not even tried, you have succeeded fully," Gilson commented at the time.[136]

In 1923, Gilson devoted a seminar to Albertus Magnus and another to Duns Scotus. Paul Vignaux (1904–1987) was registered among the regular participants. In 1929, Gilson analyzed texts of St. Bonaventure and investigated the causes of the "Thomistic reformation." The seminar attained a cruising speed with more than thirty participants. In 1927, Gilson commented on St. Anselm and Scotus Eriugena. Among the participants were Paul Vignaux, Marie-Thérèse d'Alverny, Maurice de Gandillac, and Mohammed Abd-El-Jalil, who presented a study of Sufism that was commented on and approved by Gilson at the section council meeting. In 1929, Gilson presented Robert Grosseteste, Roger Bacon, and the medieval commentators on St. Augustine. Emmanuel Mounier told his sister that in January 1930 he would attend Gilson's lectures on "the medieval doctrines of intelligence" and "speculative mysticism from St. Bernard to Dante" as an auditor.[137] In 1931, Gilson analyzed the relations between Luther and medieval theology and continued the examination of Duns Scotus. That year we find among his auditors the future Dominican cardinal Yves Congar and Fr. André Combes. In 1932 Paul Vignaux took over teaching responsibilities for the chair of history of doctrines and dogmas, when Gilson was elected to the Collège de France. The Sorbonne courses were lectures and less directed toward research. We have a very precise description of them in the notes of André Gilson, Étienne's priest brother, who attended the lectures during the academic years 1929–1931.[138]

The seminars at EPHE and the Sorbonne courses in the 1920s were the preparation for Gilson's publications and re-editions. Also, in 1924 Gilson published *La philosophie de saint Bonaventure* (Vrin) [*The Philosophy of St. Bonaventure*, 1965], which reaped the fruits of the 1922 and 1924 seminars. In 1927, the third edition of *Thomisme* appeared [*The Philosophy of St. Thomas Aquinas*, 1929]. In 1927, *L'introduction à l'étude de saint Augustin* saw the light [*The Christian Philosophy of St. Augustine*, 1960]. In 1930 Gilson brought

136 Koyré, *De la mystique à la science*, 44.

137 Letter from Emmanuel Mounier to his sister Madeleine, November 5, 1929. Published in *Œuvres complètes*, vol. 4, *Recueils posthumes. Correspondance* (Paris: Seuil, 1963), 452.

138 Shook, *Étienne Gilson*, 195–97.

out *Études sur le rôle de la pensée médiévale dans la formation du système cartésien*. In the decade 1922–1932, the frequency of Gilson's publications was notable, as was the growing fame that led to his presence at international philosophical conferences: Oxford in 1921, Naples in 1924, Harvard in 1926. The very clear positions he took in regard to historical method and his religious commitment were also striking. In December 1926 and January 1927, Gilson spent time at Harvard, Toronto, and New York, to which he returned in September 1927. At the height of the Action Française crisis, whereas Maritain fought fiercely with *Primauté du spirituel* (1927), *Pourquoi Roma a parlé* (also 1927). amd *Clairvoyance de Rome* (1929), Gilson launched the project of the Institute of Mediaeval Studies at Toronto.

In regard to Gilson's teaching at the Sorbonne, Stanislas Fumet expressed a perceptive observation. "Gilson's powerful personality has a great deal to do with forcing the University to consider Scholasticism, which was so disparaged, with a little less disdain."[139] Fumet notes that the main thing was that a philosopher emerging from the University itself promoted this rediscovery:

> The Sorbonne continued to stroll through all the philosophical highways of the world, avoiding the path of St. Thomas, as if there were a risk of finding a new tree of knowledge of good and evil in it, . . . when one of the University's own, Étienne Gilson, placed the treasury of medieval philosophical thinking before the indifferent eyes of professors who were convinced that between Greek philosophy and the totally French philosophy of René Descartes, there were only gloomy shadows for the human mind, to use the common phrase.[140]

FROM THE COLLÈGE DE FRANCE TO THE ACADÉMIE FRANÇAISE (1932–1950)

Gilson's social network in the period between the world wars testifies to his roots in the state university system, in the palace of the republic of letters, and in Catholic intellectual circles. In this regard, his path was closer to that of Louis Massignon, professor at the Collège de France, where Gilson was a

139 Stanislas Fumet, *Histoire de Dieu dans ma vie* (Paris: Cerf, 2002), 234.

140 Fumet, *Histoire de Dieu*, 315.

member of the tribunal for his doctoral dissertation,[141] or of Paul Claudel, French ambassador and member of the Académie française, than to the trajectory of Jacques Maritain, Gabriel Marcel, or Emmanuel Mounier, all of them philosophy teachers but far from the Sorbonne and other state institutions. Gilson occupied a position that could be considered both eminent and middle of the road.

Gilson's election to the Collège de France in January 1932 reveals tension in the Paris intellectual life of the early thirties. Reading certain accounts by Gilson, it might seem that his election was settled in advance. "The designation of the chair of medieval philosophy at the Collège de France was a success," he wrote to a Canadian friend in 1931. "All that is left is to designate its titular, and that will be me. So, all goes well, and the only cloud on the horizon has dissolved."[142] Again, he wrote on January 17, 1932, "I have been appointed today to the Collège de France as professor of medieval philosophy, thirty votes against seven. It was difficult to hope for a better result."[143] Gilson's adversary overwhelmed in the vote was the "plagiarist" Louis Rougier.[144] Alexandre Koyré had presented his candidacy in "second place." "I am not a candidate against Professor Gilson," Koyré explains to the administrator of the Collège.[145] The minutes of the meeting of the Assembly of Professors confirms Gilson's remark. Out of thirty eight present, Gilson received thirty

141 See Marie-Thérèse d'Alverny, "Nécrologie. Étienne Gilson," *Cahiers de Civilization médiévale* 22, no. 88 (December 1979): 427.

142 Letter from Étienne Gilson to Mme Thibadeau, November 16, 1931, quoted by Shook, *Étienne Gilson*, 207.

143 Letter from Étienne Gilson to Fr. Henry Bellisle, January 17, 1932, quoted by Shook, *Étienne Gilson*, 207.

144 On this point, see the letter from Étienne Gilson to Henri Gouhier, November 21, 1931, Archive Gouhier: "I cannot believe that between the plagiarizer and the plagiarized person, the plagiarizer would be chosen." Louis Rougier (1889–1982) was professor of philosophy at the universities of Besançon and Caen. He was the author of a work titled *La Scolastique et le Thomisme*, where he copied Gilson word for word. This was demonstrated in the review of the work published in the *Bibliothèque de l'École de Chartres* 87 (1926): 411–13, whose author places the works of Gilson and Rougier in parallel columns. Gilson treats the matter in detail in his "Examen de Conscience," *Vigile*, no. 2 (1932): 98–99: "I am simply surprised that things that lack any value in my book could become, complete with its periods and commas, the expression of a free spirit and a critical spirit by passing into the text of someone who copies them. When I see the bards of independent thinking recommend my own prose to me as a model to follow, solely because one of their own has seized it without warning, I vehemently begin to doubt the purity of their intentions. In fact, do you really believe they are freer than I? Perhaps they will also write an apology."

145 Koyré, *De la mystique à la science*, 59–60.

votes.[146] However, when we read the confidences that Gilson made to Charles Du Bos, we perceive that the election was painful for Gilson,[147] with its set of uncertainties and "combinations of string pulling," to use Sylvain Lévi's expression.[148]

The election turned out to be the result of a compromise worked out by the two "parties" that existed at the Collège de France. In Halbwachs's description the compromise was made necessary by the victory "won with difficulty" by Marcel Mauss (1872–1950) in 1930 in the third round of voting.[149] "Mauss had ~~to present himself three times~~ [crossed out in the manuscript] to fight for nearly two years (three meetings at six-month intervals in which the Collège was split exactly in half) before succeeding by one vote. With Simiand, there were finally two Durkheimians at the Collège de France. Gilson also succeeded (at the end of November 1931)."[150] Like his uncle Émile Durkheim, Mauss had already failed against Alfred Loisy in 1909. In November 1929, at the moment when it was hoped that Mauss could succeed Jean Izoulet, the deceased occupant of the chair of social philosophy who had defeated Durkheim in 1897, two rival proposals were made. The first was for a chair of sociology for Mauss, and that was defended by Sylvain Lévi and Antoine Millet. The second was for a chair of the history of medieval philosophy, made by Édouard Le Roy, Bergson's successor, and by the historian of Africa Stéphane Gsell. The chair of sociology and the chair of medieval philosophy received exactly the same number of votes, twenty-two out of a total of forty-four. The faculty meeting of November 6, 1929, left the question undecided: "Given this result, the meeting is adjourned and the matter

146 Koyré, *De la mystique à la science*, 60.

147 See Charles Du Bos, *Journal*, vol. 9 (Paris: Éditions de la Colombe, 1991), 111–12: "I cannot forget a conversation with Gilson one evening when his wife and he came to dinner to talk with us about the matter [the possible election of Du Bos to the Collège de France]. Gilson, who knew me well, . . . told me how much he had suffered himself in this regard, and the picture he drew was as vile as that which represents a candidacy to the Académie française itself."

148 Christophe Charle and Christine Delangle, "La campagne électorale de Lucien Febvre au Collège de France (1929–1932). Lettres à Edmond Faral," *Histoire de l'éducation* 34 (1987): 56.

149 This fact is ignored by the "Maussians" other than Maurice Halbwachs. See Marcel Mauss, "Un inédit: la leçon inaugurale de Marcel Mauss au Collège de France," presented by J. F. Bert, *Terrain* 59 (September 2012): 138–51. "The election ended in the first round, November 29, 1931. Marcel Mauss was elected. Maurice Halbwachs was the reserve candidate (Laurent Mucchielli and Jacqueline Pluet-Despatin, 1999)."

150 Maurice Halbwachs, "Journal," Notebook 1, 124, IMEC.

postponed until the next assembly."[151] There was a tense negotiation. Gilson, who had attended Mauss's courses at the Sorbonne, withdrew his candidacy on December 30, 1929, not wanting to risk his success or failure at the Collège on an election. "I have just written to Professor Le Roy to request the unconditional withdrawal of my candidacy. Chance alone would have decided an election of this kind, and it does not seem reasonable to leave the decision to chance."[152] Gilson wrote to Lévy-Bruhl that his withdrawal was a gesture of conciliation, by yielding to his personal feelings for Mauss.[153] Afterwards, the two would be colleagues in the fifth section for a short decade. The January 4, 1930, meeting again adjourned without resolving the choice of a successor to Jean Izoulet.

In April–June 1930 Mauss continued with his candidacy while Lucien Febvre was forbidden to put his own forward in order not to hinder the operation of the left at the Collège de France.[154] But two changes had occurred. Édouard Le Roy now supported the candidacy of the philosopher Jacques Chevalier, while a group of friends led by Louis Massignon continued to support Gilson,[155] who after a period of hesitation, agreed to present himself

151 Minutes of the faculty meeting of November 6, 1929, AP IV 439, Archives du Collège de France. See especially Édouard Le Roy's letter of October 14, 1929: "I have the honor of proposing the assignment of the funds left available by the death of Professor Izoulet to the creation of a chair denominated 'History of Philosophy in the Middle Ages.'" —See also the letter from Professor Gsell, November 1, 1929: "Gilson has devoted his most recent book to the great African (St. Augustine). Having had to study St. Augustine at length for my work in African history, I have been able to appreciate Professor Gilson's enormous knowledge and his keen, critical mind. I strongly recommend Professor Le Roy's proposal." The minutes of the faculty meeting indicate Professor Monceaux's support of Gilson.

152 Letter from Étienne Gilson to Edmond Faral, December 30, 1929, Fonds Edmond Faral, 58 CDF 10–12, Archives du Collège de France.

153 Letter from Étienne Gilson to Lucien Lévy-Bruhl, February 10, 1930 IMEC. "My return [from Canada] has, moreover, been poisoned by the events at the Collège de France. I intended to make a gesture of conciliation by giving in to my personal feelings for Mauss, and you know what has come out of that. I do not think that Mauss can be accepted for now. Chevalier has taken my place, and since my old supporters seem satisfied with him, he is the one who will go forward. Several friends here urge me to come back, which I would happily do, but I am exploring the terrain."

154 Christophe Charle and Christine Delangle, "La campagne électorale de Lucien Febvre," letter from Febvre, end of April 1930: "The Mauss supporters met and considered two candidacies of 'reconciliation,' mine and Gilson's. Ultimately, it seemed to them that Gilson, who was better situated to bite into the 'right,' would have a better chance than myself to win a majority." Mauss belonged to the SFIO [Section française de l'Internationale ouvrière]. Febvre was a "moderate socialist" and "secularist."

155 Letter from Étienne Gilson to Edmond Faral, May 10, 1930, Fonds Edmond Faral, 58 CDF 10–12, Archives du Collège de France. In this letter Gilson presents his candidacy again and acknowledges, "The situation is confused through my fault." "Professor Le Roy judges that he now ought

again. Because of the division between the philosophers, Mauss's election was possible, as well as the rejection of Chevalier, sunk by Gilson.

At the assembly of June 15, 1930, Louis Massignon supported the project of the creation of a chair of the history of medieval philosophy. His skillful organization, mobilizing both the figure of Renan and Le Roy's speech, did not succeed in winning the votes for Gilson:

> This is essentially a return to the proposition that our colleague Édouard Le Roy presented at our November 16, 1929, session. Since nobody among us, I think, has forgotten this exposition of the reasons, so simple, so nuanced, and so persuasive, my role is made all the more simple. . . . In this very place, Renan indicated insightfully the characteristics of this medieval pre-renaissance, founded on texts re-translated two and three times, passed from Greek into Syriac, then into Arabic, and finally from Arabic into Latin. . . . As Professor Édouard Le Roy indicated to you seven months ago, Professor Gilson is eminently suited to be recommended for the chair envisaged: consider his editions of texts, indices of technical terms, and syntheses of philosophical systems like Thomism or Bonaventurian Augustinianism.[156]

Édouard Le Roy, probably shocked by Gilson's rather quick withdrawal in December 1929, was in a difficult position because, though cited by Massignon in favor of the creation of a chair of medieval philosophy, he argued nevertheless in favor of the creation of a chair of "French philosophy," that was in favor of Jacques Chevalier, markedly on the right. With wonderful persistence, Antoine Meillet, Pierre Janet, and Charles Andler proposed the creation of a chair of sociology for Mauss. When the vote took place, the philosophers divided and permitted the creation of that chair in the third round in place of a chair of social philosophy. "Sociology" received twenty-four votes, the slimmest majority. "French philosophy" got sixteen votes, and the "Philosophy of the Middle Ages" received six.[157] Therefore, this was a serious setback for Gilson, who measured the influence of Le Roy and the happy surprise of the sociologists: "You are quite right to say," Gilson wrote to Administrator Faral, "that we could not know what would happen

to support Jacques Chevalier, but adds that his chances are slight and he would be disposed to go back to my candidacy eventually, if the situation changes on that front." Gilson emphasizes Sylvain Lévi's support and concludes: "I am invited by both sides."

156 Louis Massignon, "Proposal for the creation of a chair of history of philosophy in the Middle Ages," Assembly of Professors, June 15, 1930, 16 CDF 156, Archives du Collège de France.

157 Minutes of the faculty meeting of June 15, 1930, AP IV 442, Archives du Collège de France.

in the first round [twenty-one votes for sociology, twenty-three votes for philosophy divided between medieval philosophy (seven) and French philosophy (sixteen)]. Mauss's friends found themselves faced with a success for which they no longer dared hope and which changed their plans. No hope remained then for me, and I am all the more moved by the support you have so generously given to a lost cause."[158] Marcel Mauss was elected as the first occupant of the new chair of sociology, November 23 of the same year, with Halbwachs in second place.[159]

All the same, Gilson presented his candidacy to the Collège again in October 1931.[160] He was unfailingly supported by Louis Massignon. This time Édouard Le Roy rejoined him,[161] abandoned Chevalier's candidacy, and suggested that the chair of Celtic languages and literature, held by Joseph Loth, be abolished. Gilson was likewise supported by Antoine Meillet, friend and supporter of Mauss the previous year. On November 15, the faculty assembly ratified the abolition of the chair of Celtic language and literature and adopted the proposal to create a chair of medieval philosophy by a sizable majority: twenty-four votes in favor, nine votes in favor of a chair of diplomatic history, and six blank ballots. On January 17, 1932, Gilson was elected "in the first place" for the new chair. Alexandre Koyré was elected "in second place" with a similar majority.

158 Letter from Étienne Gilson to Edmond Faral, June 18, 1930, AP IV 442, Fonds Faral, 58 CDF 10–12, Archives du Collège de France.

159 Marcel Fournier, "L'élection de Marcel Mauss au Collège de France," *Genèses* 22 (1996): 160–65.—See also Marcel Fournier, *Marcel Mauss* (Paris: Fayard, 1994), 586–88. Maurice Halbwachs comments: "A victory won with difficulty, but a decisive outcome for the Durkheimians, all the more in that the resistance was obstinate." On Maurice Halbwachs, read the article by Danièle Hervieu-Léger, *Dictionnaire des faits religieux* (Paris: P.U.F., 2010), 464–68.

160 Letter from Étienne Gilson to Edmond Faral, October 12, 1931, 16 CDF 156, Archives du Collège de France: "I have the honor of presenting my candidacy to the chair of history of philosophy in the Middle Ages, which the Collège de France has just voted to create."

161 Letter from Édouard Le Roy to Edmond Faral, October 14, 1931, 58 CDF 5c, Archives of the Collège de France. Letter from Édouard Le Roy to the administrator, October 12, 1931, AP IV 448, Archives of the Collège de France: "I propose the appropriation of funds left available by the retirement of our colleague Professor Loth to the establishment of a chair whose title would be History of Philosophy in the Middle Ages." Antoine Meillet supported this proposal (letter of October 2, 1931, AP IV 448, Archives of the Collège de France) and thereafter was one of the supporters of the chair of medieval philosophy. See also Gilson's inaugural lecture at the Collège de France, "Le Moyen Âge et le naturalisme antique" [The Middle Ages and Ancient Naturalism], *Archives d'Histoire doctrinal et littéraire* 7 (1933): 5–37; and *Héloïse et Abélard* (Paris: Vrin, 1938), 182: "Accordingly, this is the creation of a new area of teaching. However, no one would believe me if I pretended to create it from nothing."

Upon Mauss's election in November 1930 (whom Halbwachs succeeded in 1944), after Jacques Chevalier's failed candidacy sunk by Gilson, that of Gilson followed in January 1932. The first group consisted of the sociologists and Durkheimians with pronounced socialist inclinations (Charles Andler, Sylvain Lévi, Antoine Meillet, Paul Langevin, Henri Maspero, and so forth). The second included the "philosophers" and "historians" with a strong Christian bent (Louis Massignon, Édouard Le Roy, Alfred Loisy, the paleontologist priest Henri Breuil, and so forth), happy to be labeled conservatives, and anti-Durkheimians or anti-sociologists by Mauss.[162] Both succeeded in electing their candidates in a period of fourteen months. Perhaps in Gilson's memory a trace of this confrontation of method and goal remained when he wrote, in *The Philosopher and Theology*, that for Mauss the objective of sociology was not "to attack religion but to dissolve it."[163] But at bottom, the elections of Mauss and Gilson are a sign of compromise between the parties, testifying to Gilson's academic sociability.

On April 5, 1932, Gilson gave his inaugural lecture, "Le Moyen Âge et le naturalisme antique," which was first published that same year in the *Archives d'histoire doctrinale et littéraire du Moyen Âge* and then again as an appendix of *Héloise et Abélard* (1938). He taught at the Collège de France until his retirement in 1950. From 1932 on, a large part of Gilson's social relations in France were organized around the Collège: teaching, lectures, and meetings. After Gilson's election, Bergson wrote how "happy he was because of [Gilson's] admission to the Collège de France, which Ronsard, who was a professor there, would surely judge today 'flourished in its greenest newness.' Those who listen to you there will soon become disciples."[164] Gilson's correspondence is replete with his exchanges with Edmond Faral, the administrator of the Collège, with other faculty members, and with successful or failed candidates like André Siegfried, Paul Valéry, Marc Bloch, Lucien Febvre, Maurice Halbwachs, Gustave Cohen, and so on. The seminars of the Collège de France, like those of the École pratique or of the Institute of Mediaeval Studies in Toronto, sometimes sought to answer philosophical questions posed by our own time. Thus, for example, the 1943–1944 seminar

162 Mauss, "Un inédit: la leçon inaugurale de Marcel Mauss," 138–51.

163 Étienne Gilson, *The Philosopher and Theology*, 27.

164 Letter from Henri Bergson to Étienne Gilson, March 13, 1932, SMCA. Bergson thanks Gilson in passing for Gilson's tribute to him during the inaugural lesson.

was devoted to the "problem of being and existence from its Greek origins to the fourteenth century." Most often the seminars were sketches of works in progress. The seminars of 1947–1948 and 1948–1949 dealt with the "metamorphoses of the City of God," returning to a course given in Toronto in 1933 and announcing the book published in 1951 with the same title.

When Gilson resigned in December 1950 in the context of the Gilson Affair, his replacement became an issue in January-February 1951. Alexandre Koyré appeared to be his legitimate heir. Gilson's student, his quasi-successor at EPHE, elected "in second place" behind Gilson in 1932, Koyré was unsuccessfully supported by the physicist Francis Perrin and by Lucien Febvre for a chair of the "history of scientific thought."[165] By a small margin, the Collège opted for the historian of philosophy Martial Guéroult.

Gilson's second particularly prominent role in society was his membership in the Académie française, where he was elected to Chair 23 in October 1946 by eighteen votes out of twenty-four. The chair had been left vacant by the expulsion of Abel Hermant for his acts of collaboration during the war. Elected that year were Paul Claudel, Maurice Genevoix, René Grousset, Robert d'Harcourt, Jules Romains, Marcel Pagnol, Henri Mondor, and others. In June 1939, Gilson had been unsuccessful in second place after Albert Rivaud as a candidate to succeed Lévy-Bruhl at l'Académie des sciences morales et politiques. The episode won him very affectionate letters from Bergson: "I am sure that you are already *persona grata*, indeed *gratissima*, and that is why your academic future inspires no concern in me."[166]

In 1945, Mauriac, who had been elected in 1933, likewise gave clear indications about the possible election of Gilson to the Académie: "Your place is in the Académie, at least in the Académie as I picture it."[167] Gilson had written him repeatedly to seek advice:

> Our friend Fr. Maydieu told me last Thursday that you would not consider my candidacy to Bergson's chair to be unreasonable. I am very moved that you think that way, and I thank you. I permit myself to assure you that if this is really your opinion, I would trust you entirely, and would present or

165 All of the dossier's contents have been published in Koyré, *De la mystique à la science*, 181–95.

166 Letter from Henri Bergson to Étienne Gilson, July 12, 1939, SMCA.

167 Letter from François Mauriac to Étienne Gilson, March 16, 1945, SMCA.

> not my candidacy for this chair or another according to what you might be so kind as to advise me.[168]

Mauriac answered that Édouard Le Roy, Bergson's successor at the Collège de France, would be elected to the chair. "But there are many other chairs. That is not what is missing. It is necessary to talk to Duhamel with a clear head. He knows the chessboard best. Your place is with us."[169] Gilson would wait several months to return to Mauriac.

> In your absence, I have been trapped by an academic whirlpool, and I have failed to come to an agreement with Baron Sellière. How I regret not being able to consult you! In the end, I have abstained in order to avoid unnecessarily troubling several of his friends who are colleagues of mine. Nevertheless, it is possible that I may declare my candidacy before leaving for Canada around the twentieth of this month. First, I must revisit Georges Duhamel, but I would be equally happy to speak with you. Not that I have any illusions! If I had had any, I would have lost them already. First I was told that there were fifteen seats to fill. Then, they began to tell me that there are twelve practically filled already. . . . Nevertheless, I can't act as a candidate without consulting you.[170]

Gilson conducted his campaign in good and proper form, as his correspondence with Louis Madelin[171] and Jules Romains[172] attests. Pasteur Vallery-Radot, professor of medicine and grandson of Louis Pasteur, was "godfather" to Gilson, who was officially received under the cupola of the Académie in May of 1947. His portrait of Gilson is delightful:

168 Letter from Étienne Gilson to François Mauriac, March 4, 1945, Bibliothèque littéraire Jacques Doucet.

169 Letter from François Mauriac to Étienne Gilson, March 6, 1945, SMCA.

170 Letter from Étienne Gilson to François Mauriac, February 8, 1846, Bibliothèque littéraire Jacques Doucet.

171 Letter from Étienne Gilson to Louis Madelin, May 26, 1946, 355 AP 3, Archives nationales: "Sir, I have the honor of requesting you to kindly grant me a meeting in order that I may announce my candidacy to the Académie française in person."

172 Letter from Étienne Gilson to Jules Romains, October 14, 1946, NAF 28403, BNF: "Sir, I have presented my candidacy to the chair of Abel Hermant and I would like the pleasure of presenting myself to inform you of this personally, if it is possible to do so before the election on the twenty-fourth of this month. It is unnecessary to say that your choice of day and time will be suitable and I will be grateful furthermore for the opportunity to meet you after having spent so many days and so much time in the company of your books. Yours faithfully. Étienne Gilson SUF, 10.85." In pencil in the margin of the letter: "phone him."

> Sir, you are a philosopher and one of the finest of our time. I will confess to you that, the more I consider you, the more I am amazed. I used to imagine the philosopher with a serious, almost somber, demeanor, and here I have before me a playful, smiling person, beaming, with the joy of living, thinking, and expressing himself. You are, sir, the greatest expert in philosophy of the Middle Ages. You love Romanesque and Gothic churches, from those of Vézelay and Auxerre to those of Notre-Dame de Puy and Chartres. You know their smallest stones, from clocks to crypts. But near St. Thomas's *Summa*, I am certain that on your work table you keep one of those libertine fables who delighted our fathers; and I know that, along with churches, you love to frequent good inns. "I am sure," you said to me confidentially one day, "that there is not a single white wine of the countryside that goes from Étaules to Chablis, and from Tannay to Coulanges-la-Vineuse that I cannot name," and you added, "along with the name of the right cheese." You are right, Sir, and this is what makes France this extraordinary mixture of the most perfect spirituality and sensuality. You are one of the most perfect specimens of Frenchmen.[173]

In his chronicles, Mauriac described the Académie française's political-literary activity before the Liberation as a sounding board for Vichy. Even in the postwar period that voice managed to reinforce itself through Maurras, Farrère, Bainville, Chaumeix, the Tharaud brothers, Massis, and so forth. Gilson entered the Académie with a "batch of leftists," in Mauriac's phraseology. Later, in *Le Figaro littéraire* of May 14, 1955, he deplored Gilson's separation from the Académie: "After cruel vicissitudes, loathing makes me, me too, abandon the field of battle. Among those elected from the left, the only one with fighting spirit, the only one who could oppose the right, if not with a tactic at least with the violence of a great mind, Étienne Gilson in his turn departs, and we will not see him again."[174]

GILSON, CHRISTIAN INTELLECTUAL: ENCOUNTERS, FRIENDSHIPS, CONTROVERSIES

Gilson evolved perceptibly in his relations with religious intellectuals during the years between 1920 and 1930. His social circle increased—notably including those who surrounded Maritain: Charles Du Bos, Gabriel Marcel,

173 Vallery-Radot, "Réponse au discours de réception d'Étienne Gilson."

174 François Mauriac, *La paix des cimes: Chroniques 1948–1955* (Paris: Bartillat, 2009), 547.

Emmanuel Mounier, among others. Gilson's correspondence likewise reveals contacts with Russian émigrés as well as English and German Protestants. Gilson's writings began to reach more confessional readerships.

Gilson also participated in ecumenical meetings. His involvement in this area was both particular and discreet. It took the form of meetings with Lev Shestov, one of the fathers of existentialism, between 1923 and 1936; with Nikolai Berdyaev in January 1931;[175] with Karl Barth at Juvisy in 1934 after a conference organized by Fr. Congar.[176] His dialogue with the Russian Shestov (1866–1938) is rather significant. Upon his return from Russia in 1923, Gilson read in Russian and greatly appreciated Shestov's studies on Nietzsche, Tolstoy, and Raskolnikov.[177] In March 1936, when Shestov was writing his study on Athens and Jerusalem, Gilson sent him this short note:

> Dear M. Shestov,
> I have just devoured your two articles [marginal note in pencil by Nathalie Beranoff-Shestov: this probably refers to *Revue philosophique*, November-December 1935, and January-February 1936.] Of course, I have particular reasons for being interested in them, but I cannot help believing that they will awaken rather general interest because of the problem's importance and the subtle, living, penetrating way in which you discuss it. It seems quite remarkable to me that in a presentation on "The Humanism of St. Thomas" at the Naples Convention in 1924, I also quoted Tertullian's phrase,[178] "What does Athens have to do with Jerusalem?" but added an

175 See Gilson and Maritain, *Correspondance 1923–1971*, 42–43.

176 Étienne Fouilloux, *Les catholiques et l'unité chrétienne du XIXe au XXe siècle: Itinéraires européens d'expression française* (Paris: Le Centurion, 1982), 218–19.

177 Letter from Étienne Gilson to Lev Shestov, April 4, 1923, MS 2115/f. 264, BIS: "I have just taken advantage of my first days on vacation to read the extraordinarily interesting book that you had the kindness to send me. . . . The presentation of Tolstoy has been a total revelation for me of something I hardly perceived and only as a vague resistance instinctive in me." The two met again before this letter of 1923. "I understand why you told me Solovyov wrote badly. Evidently he was very far from having your marvelous ease, picturesque turn of a phrase, and as far as a foreigner can perceive, the precision of your expressions."

178 Étienne Gilson, "L'humanisme de saint Thomas," in *Atti del quinto Congresso Internazionale di Filosofia,* May 5–9, 1924, Società filosofica italiana (Naples: Società Anonima Editrice, 1925), 976–89; see 985–86 for the quote from Tertullian, taken from *De praescriptione haereticorum*: "Quid ergo Athenis et Hierosolymis? Quid academiae et ecclesiae?" Gilson answers: "Jerusalem cannot be separated from Athens without being separated from Rome. . . . What is common to Athens and Jerusalem is the human being. The human being, indivisible unity of body and soul, who cannot be saved without Christianity, but without whom Christianity would have nothing to

> answer: Rome. This is evidently the heart of the debate. You return, if not to Luther, at least to what there is of Luther in your dear Dostoevsky. I believe, on the contrary, that God speaks through the Church of Rome, that his revelation continues through her, and that, moreover, her purpose is to place the complete revelation before us. The Old Testament contains more than arbitrariness. But these are global questions that no individual text settles. Attitudes govern the texts. I regret that I do not possess a copy of my 1924 paper, but I will send you something that I hope you will find interesting.[179]

Shestov's book *Athènes et Jérusalem. Essai de philosophie religieuse* was published by Vrin in 1938. In the part devoted to medieval philosophy, Shestov deals at length with works by Gilson. The book opens with Tertullian's question *Quid ergo Athenis et Hierosolymis*?[180] With a thousand nuances, Shestov holds Gilson's position: "Can we today, in this case, speak of Judeo-Christian philosophy? I think we can."

As to the Protestant world, in 1932 Gilson gave the Gifford Lectures at the University of Aberdeen, where he became aware of the need to establish a dialogue with Protestant theologians.[181] Gilson began to study Luther at the École pratique, in the context of the debate about Christian philosophy, and to read Karl Barth, whose writings he knew well and to whom he often referred in his 1933 courses at Toronto and again at Science-Po in 1947, and whom he sometimes criticized.[182] Some twenty Protestant ministers participated in the seminar on Luther at the EPHE in 1932. In April 1936, Gilson gave a lecture at the Protestant theology faculty on Boulevard Arago, Paris, which was the origin of the little book *Christianity and Philosophy.*[183]

---

save, and who is saved by guaranteeing, through a perfect human life, the complete fulfillment of his divine destiny" (986).

179 Letter from Étienne Gilson to Lev Shestov, March 11, 1936, MS 2119/f. 143, BIS.

180 Lev Shestov, *Athènes et Jérusalem: Essai de philosophie religieuse* (Paris: Vrin, 1938), 251–380, at 378.

181 Shook, *Étienne Gilson*, 203.

182 Étienne Gilson, *Christianisme et philosophie* (Paris: Vrin, 1936), 64, 114, 151; idem, *Christianity and Philosophy*, trans. MacDonald, 44, 47–48, 82, 87, 110–11.

183 In this regard, see Gilson's letter to Fr. Marie-Dominique Chenu, April 29, 1936, APDF, published in its entirety by Francesca Murphy, editor, "Correspondance entre Étienne Gilson et Marie-Dominique Chenu. Un choix de lettres (1923–1969)," *Revue thomiste*, 105 (2005): 36–40: "It so happens that I have just had to give another lecture at the faculty of Protestant theology in Paris, on Christianity and philosophy. It has been given, and *the* Lutheran and the Calvinists have concurred in saying that I had correctly interpreted their positions. In reality, I did not prepare one lecture but four, because having written what I was able to say to them, I had to write many

> The greatness of Karl Barth's work, insofar as it holds for every Christian confession, is to have affirmed and maintained for our time unconditional respect for the word of God. It is inevitable that over the course of centuries the divine message would be burdened with human elements that at least offend it, unless, what is still worse, they manage to mistake themselves for it. Consequently, the truth of Scripture is mixed with philosophy, archeology, and finally literature. It is good, it is necessary to produce a restoration of pure theology, returned to its eminent dignity as science of the word of God. For those of us who are Catholics, that has been the most valuable part of Karl Barth's message. We have received it all the more joyfully in that, ready to receive it, we were formulating it ourselves in the secret recesses of our hearts. To restore theology to its place and to its own eminence is to work for all Christians, whoever they are, and for my part, I am deeply grateful to Karl Barth for having done it....
>
> Everything that brings us closer to Jesus Christ also brings us closer to each other. It is not Kant or Schleiermacher, or even Kierkegaard, who have the words of eternal life, and God was not incarnated in St. Thomas Aquinas to save us. On the contrary, what gives St. Thomas incomparable theological greatness, from the outset of his *Commentary on the Sentences*, is having identified wisdom with Christ.[184]

During the war, Gilson wrote in the same vein to a Benedictine friend to denounce the Church's "hardening" and "absurd suspiciousness" in regard to the Bible because of the Reformation: "One will always be a Christian through God's Word, by the converting power of his word, which is infinitely above that of St. Thomas."[185] In the context of Rome's generalized suspicion of ecumenism, Gilson's letter to Barth was little appreciated in certain spheres of the Eternal City. In his personal notebook, dated December 11, 1947, Maritain noted: "Monsignor Montini, whom I encountered in a reception hall, expressed certain unease about a study by Gilson published in a

things that I felt the need to say to myself. After reading Calvin and the Calvinists, I wanted to know whether we committed the crimes of which they accused us. That is a dangerous temptation, because it led me on a steep slope to the problem of Christian philosophy, of which I am literally horrified." Francesca Murphy quite rightly remarks that on p. 87 of *Christianisme et philosophie* [translator note: possibly p. 61 of *Christianity and Philosophy*], Gilson finds a Calvinist theologian right and Cardinal Mercier wrong.

184 Letter from Étienne Gilson to Karl Barth, January 15, 1946, published in *Hommage et reconnaissance: Recueil de travaux à l'occasion du soixantième anniversaire de Karl Barth, Cahiers théologiques de l'actualité protestante* (Paris: Delachaux et Niestlé, 1946).

185 Letter from Étienne Gilson to Fr. Irénée, April 26, 1942, APQV.

collection in honor of Karl Barth." We learn from a "well-placed source," according to the expression of Fr. Delos, the ecclesiastical advisor of the French embassy to the Holy See, that Gilson was denounced to the Holy Office.[186] "A remark made in passing by Monsignor Montini has made me anxious about an article Gilson has published in a Collection in honor of Karl Barth. The article seems to have been denounced as unorthodox. Dear Lord, they get alarmed easily!" Maritain commented to Charles Journet.[187] In December, Fr. Delos asked Fr. Congar to write a short note titled "On the Subject of Étienne Gilson's Contribution to a Festschrift for Karl Barth," in order to end the criticisms. Congar explained: "Gilson occupies such a place and has rendered such services that a public condemnation of him would have a disastrous effect.... He is quite famous in Canada, the United States, and England. Everywhere, he appears as a straightforward, unreserved defender of Catholicism."[188] The matter went no further, because Gilson's great strength, as he said years later, was "that I am not a priest": "Had Maritain and I been monks or priests, neither of us would have been able to write the hundredth part of what we've written. We would have been, as they say here, *crucified*."[189] His fame, his status as a layman, and his academic position protected him, unlike Chenu and de Lubac, from censure. Furthermore, Maritain was ambassador to the Holy See at the time. In that capacity, he had organized a meeting in April 1947 between Gilson and Pope Pius XII. Gilson

186 Letter from Fr. Delos to Fr. Yves Congar, December 19, 1947, Fonds Congar, V 832–121, 1946–1948: "I have learned from a well-placed source that after Professor Gilson published a contribution to the Festschrift for Karl Barth, his article was denounced to the Holy Office. I confess that I know nothing about this collection. . . . Could you do me the favor of providing reports on the matter, and if it is not asking too much, tell me your feelings about it?"

187 Letter from Jacques Maritain to Charles Journet, December 22, 1947, *Correspondance Journet-Maritain*, vol. 3, *1940–1949* (Paris: Saint-Augustin, 1998), 605.

188 Yves Congar, "Au suject de la contribution de M. Étienne Gilson à un hommage pour Karl Barth," December 23, 1947, Papiers Congar, APDF—documents reported by Étienne Fouilloux. See Fouilloux, *Les catholiques et l'unité chrétienne*, 884. See also Fouilloux's thesis for the state doctorate, *Catholicisme et oecumenisme en Europe francophone au XXe siècle* (University of Paris X [Nanterre], 1980), 1186, 1444. —See also the Papiers Congar, APDF: letter from Fr. Delos, canonical advisor to the French Embassy, to Fr. Congar, December 19, 1947; see Fr. Congar's note of explanation, December 23, 1947. Congar argued by pointing out that Gilson had criticized the Reformers and Karl Barth in his interpretation of St. Anselm and in his interpretation of human nature saved by grace. On this point see Étienne Gilson, *Christianisme et philosophie*, 151 [*Christianity and Philosophy*, trans. MacDonald, 28–30].

189 Letter from Étienne Gilson to Henri de Lubac, April 1, 1964, in de Lubac, *Letters of Étienne Gilson to Henri de Lubac*, 69.

filially esteemed the Pope,[190] who was aware of his own "insufficiency," something that Gilson appreciated. He thought, however, that the Pope "wrote too much and too close to the Gregorian," as he would recall.[191] In the spring of 1947, Gilson would also meet Monsignor Montini, then assigned to the Vatican Secretariat of State. Maritain started to work in January 1948 to ward off the accusation.[192]

Gilson's relations with Maritain testify to the increasing integration of Gilson into the circles of Christian intellectuals. The two began to correspond in 1923. Despite the closeness of their initial trajectory, they hardly knew each other in the 1920s, something that was gradually attenuated. Their first letters tried to pinpoint differences in their analyses. Maritain dedicated a copy of *Trois réformateurs* (Plon, 1925) [*Three Reformers*, New York: Scribners, 1929] to Gilson in measured terms of "sympathetic hommage."[193] Gilson answered with the greatest affability to better indicate that he did not share Maritain's reading of Descartes, "I am very inclined toward your Rousseau. I do not feel competent about Luther, although I have studied him a bit, and many aspects of his personality are disconcerting to me. I am less incompetent about Descartes, and I confess that I do not conceive him as you have made him out to be."[194] A letter from Jacques Maritain to Frédéric Lefèvre in January 1925, of which Gilson was aware, shows both real enthusiasm and some reservations on Maritain's side:

> Your last interview was magnificent. I have read it with keen interest, and I assure you that in spite of the reservations that I would make about certain theses of Gilson, it has been a great consolation. Having known the Sor-

190 Shook, *Étienne Gilson*, 277, cites Gilson's letter of April 25, 1947, reporting the meeting to Anton Pegis: "Had I found my own father alive, I don't believe he would have shown me more fatherly love."

191 See Gilson and Maritain, *Correspondance 1923–1971*, ed. Prouvost, 161; and the letter of April 9, 1947, in *Correspondance Journet-Maritain*, 3:545. For echoes of the meeting, see Gilson's letter to Jean de Fabrègues, January 27, 1968, CHSP: "The admirable Pope Pius XII (who wrote too much and too close to the Gregorian) told me literally one day: 'We are an inadequate pope. Do you see what is happening in Russia?'"

192 Letter from Fr. Delos to Fr. Yves Congar, January 12, 1948 (1947 appears erroneously in the letter), Papiers Congar, V 832 121, 1946–1948, APDF: "My sincere thanks for the care you have taken to send me this information; I have hastened to transmit them to the Ambassador, who, at this very moment while I am writing you, is using the information."

193 Gilson Library, SMCA.

194 Letter from Étienne Gilson to Jacques Maritain, June 27, 1925, in Gilson and Maritain, *Correspondance 1923–1971*, 32. The correspondence consists of 107 letters (1923–1971).

> bonne twenty years ago in its scientistic pride (which it has not completely lost), having seen Péguy's suffering and struggles, and having ourselves been almost suffocated by an abject philosophy against which only Bergson reacted, what joy now to have a university professor talk about St. Thomas, about Scholasticism, the Middle Ages, about Catholicism, the preserver of metaphysics—in the terms in which Gilson expresses himself. One might find that he acknowledges a few too many teachers, and one might ask what philosophical truth is for him. But I want to believe that the purely historicist position is still provisional and, in any case, what I take away in the first place from your interview are the declarations about which I have just spoken.[195]

Gilson was often forced to justify himself against this reproach of historicism. At the level of method, he was on a razor's edge: "I am not a philosopher who defines a priori, but a historian who asks history for the material from which he will take his concepts."[196] In the diary of Albert Camus, we find traces of a critical tribute to Gilson's position: "We read more than we reflect. We have no philosophies, only commentaries. This is what Gilson says when he judges that the age of philosophers who occupy themselves with philosophy has been replaced by the age of professors of philosophy who concern themselves with philosophers. There is both modesty and impotence in this attitude."[197]

In May 1937, Gilson wrote again to Gouhier about Maritain: "That is why, having become a Thomist without having studied St. Thomas [which is not accurate], and by a kind of act of faith, [Maritain] began believing that it was urgent to be an anti-Bergsonian in order to be a Thomist. As I showed my intention to try to discover in what St. Thomas's doctrine consisted, before taking a position about its intrinsic value, [Maritain] accuses me of being a historicist, as if the immediate and peculiar goal of the historian could be something other than history."[198] In January 1926, however, Gilson wrote more amiably to Gouhier about Maritain's article "Grandeur et misère de la métaphysique": "Have you read Maritain in the *Croniques*? He is excel-

195 Letter from Jacques Maritain to Frédéric Lefèvre, January 3, 1925, FG, SMCA; and AM, BNUS.

196 "Étienne Gilson—Thomas Deman. OP, Lettres inédites," ed. B. Hodel, OP, and F.-X. Putallaz, *Nova et Vetera* (Fribourg) 87 (2012): 458.

197 Albert Camus, *Carnets II. Janvier 1942–mars 1951* (Paris: Gallimard, 1964), 88.

198 Letter from Étienne Gilson to Henri Gouhier, March 3, 1973, published in *Revue thomiste* 94 (July –September 1994): 474–75.

lent, and for the first time, I believe I am totally in agreement with him."[199] Thereafter, Gilson and Maritain continued to draw closer, without Gilson ever being integrated into the "Maritain crowd" in the 1920s, sharing many intellectual concerns: "It will take one hundred years to realize what Maritain has done for us," Gilson proclaimed in 1939.[200] "Jacques Maritain has been admirable. The man is a genius and really great."[201] "We two have the good fortune to have found freedom in friendship and friendship in truth," wrote Gilson to Maritain in August 1939."[202] In the social and political controversies that surrounded Maritain's work, Gilson often took up his defense. Against Paul Claudel, who attacked Maritain in 1938–1939, Gilson wrote: "Is, therefore, the most authentic genius not free of stupidity?"[203] During the controversy about the common good in 1945–1947, Gilson criticized Charles De Koninck: "Old Quebec, Quebec does not love us much."[204] "You have never been attacked in my presence without being defended."[205]

Gilson's relations with Blondel are more complex and harder to define. Regarding Blondel, a perceptive commentator noted here that "between dialogue, which Gilson thought was impossible, and condemnation, which he refused to make, he chose silence, the first degree of that philosophical pluralism within the Church (whose *de facto* legitimacy Gilson would devote himself to proving)." Indeed, according to Henry Donneaud, the absence of debate between the two men was due to their having no common ground.[206]

199 Letter from Étienne Gilson to Henri Gouhier, January 10, 1926, AG.—Maritain's article "Grandeur et misère de la métaphysique" was published in the first issue of *Chroniques* of "Roseau d'or," December 1925. A revised version became the introduction to the *Degrés du savoir* (Paris: Desclée De Brouwer, 1932) [*Degrees of Knowledge*, trans. Bernard Wall and Margot Adamson (London: Geoffrey Bless, 1937).]

200 Remarks in Gilson and Maritain, *Correspondance 1923–1971*, 152.

201 Letter from Étienne Gilson to Monsignor André Combes, February 10, 1939, NAF 28 257, BNF.

202 Letter from Étienne Gilson to Jacques Maritain, August 19, 1939, in Gilson and Maritain, *Correspondance 1923–1971*, 136.

203 Letter from Étienne Gilson to Jacques Maritain, August 19, 1939, in Gilson and Maritain, *Correspondance 1923–1971*, 137.

204 Letter from Étienne Gilson to Jacques Maritain, November 26, 1945, in Gilson and Maritain, *Correspondance 1923–1971*, 144.

205 Letter from Étienne Gilson to Jacques Maritain, January 29, 1953, in Gilson and Maritain, *Correspondance 1923–1971*, 184.

206 Henry Donneaud, "Étienne Gilson et Maurice Blondel dans le débat pour la philosophie chrétienne (1931–1933)," *Revue thomiste* 99, no. 3 (1999): 497–516.

From 1912 on, Gilson and Blondel were not kindred spirits, as the letter from Gilson to Fr. Laberthonnière reveals on the subject of an article by Édouard Le Roy that Gilson judged admirable and that had been demolished by Blondel. "Note that I esteem and admire Blondel very much. But his letter really seems too much like an encyclical. One pope is enough for us."[207] The Blondel archives include only four letters from Gilson plus a rough draft of a letter from Blondel (1928–1932),[208] while Gilson did not keep any original document except a work by Blondel dedicated to him in the most respectful terms.[209] The exchange of letters began in April 1928, when Blondel sent the first edition of his conversations with Frédéric Lefèvre, published with the title *Itinéraire philosophique*. Gilson replied and clarified his underlying intentions, which Blondel seemed to have misunderstood: "I am deeply moved by your subtle allusion to St. Bonaventure. Allow me to tell you in this regard that, like you, I do not consider the antithesis Thomas-Bonaventure (or rather Thomas-Augustine) to be insurmountable. I speak as a historian and for the thirteenth century only."[210] Gilson emphasized the differences of method, formation, and intention. "I think that my generation of Catholics suffered from profound ignorance of its own tradition, and I consider its tradition to be that of the entirety of Catholic thought."[211] "I beg your pardon for having misunderstood certain of your intentions," Blondel immediately answered.[212] Having begun with a misunderstanding, the correspondence ended in 1931–1932 with amiable disagreement on the issue of Christian philosophy. On the subject of Blondel's theses, Gilson wrote to Blondel: "I find so many difficulties that I cannot help believing that I do not understand you, and I will say so at the end of my reply. In our two texts, a good continuation

207 Letter from Étienne Gilson to Fr. Lucien Laberthonnière, August 12, 1912, NAF 28025, no. 36, BNF.

208 Fonds Maurice Blondel, Catholic University of Louvain. The main documents are reproduced in the appendixes below.

209 Dedication of *Le problème de la philosophie catholique* (Paris: Bloud et Gay, 1932), Gilson Library, SMCA: "To my dear colleague Étienne Gilson, in expression of my highest esteem and cordial devotion, M. Blondel." Was the mention of devotion a bit of Blondelian humor?

210 Letter from Étienne Gilson to Maurice Blondel, April 29, 1928, Fonds Blondel, Catholic University of Louvain. See the appendixes below.

211 Letter from Étienne Gilson to Maurice Blondel, April 29, 1928, Fonds Blondel, Catholic University of Louvain. See the appendixes below.

212 Letter from Maurice Blondel to Étienne Gilson, May 8, 1928, Fonds Blondel, Catholic University of Louvain. See the appendixes below.

of the session may be found: little agreement but immense good will."[213] In 1932 Blondel published *Le problème de la philosophie catholique*, a whole chapter of which is a criticism of Gilson. "Is there in fact a philosophy that can be called Christian philosophy from the historical point of view?" "No, the solution, just like the problem, does not depend on history alone."[214] In his critique, Blondel rejected the "radicalism," "doctrinal historicism," and "error of interpretation" of Gilson, who "gets into difficulty in history, in intellectualism, and in an essential query of the Christian mind,"[215] who "mutilates Thomism in its historical balance and in its Christian soul."[216]—After reading these pages, Gilson avoided any subsequent exchange with Blondel.

The first encounter of Gilson with Berdyaev and Maritain's ecumenical group took place January 20, 1931. Berdyaev and Maritain jointly invited Gilson. "My friend Nikolai Berdyaev asks me to invite you on his behalf to the meeting that will take place in his home next Thursday, January 20," wrote Maritain. "Du Bos and I have spoken about you regarding these meetings where Russian Orthodox philosophers and French Catholic philosophers meet. If you wish to attend and help us, we would all be delighted."[217] The date is important because Jacques Maritain wrote in his notebook that it was the start of his friendship with Gilson. "To everyone's great surprise, Gilson declared that, if he had spoken thus [i.e. of St. Thomas as the forerunner of philosophy of pure reason], he was mistaken, and that he was in complete agreement with Raïssa and myself, and I was very moved by Gilson's attitude and by his authenticity in correcting himself. Our bonds of friendship with him date from that day."[218]

213 Letter from Étienne Gilson to Maurice Blondel, March 21, 1931, Fonds Blondel, Catholic University of Louvain. See appendixes below.

214 Maurice Blondel, *Le problème de la philosophie catholique* (Paris: Bloud et Gay, 1932), 135.

215 Blondel, *Le problème de la philosophie catholique*, 130.

216 Blondel, *Le problème de la philosophie catholique*, 132.

217 Letter from Jacques Maritain to Étienne Gilson, January 15, 1931, in Gilson and Maritain, *Correspondance 1923–1971*, 42–43. Berdyaev's letter to Gilson is published in a note on p. 43. Berdyaev indicates that Massignon, Jean De Menasce, Olivier Lacombe, Fr. Altermann, and others would be present.

218 Jacques Maritain, *Carnets de notes* (Paris: Desclée de Brouwer, 1965), 224.

Maritain read Gilson,[219] who accompanied him to Charles Du Bos's house in Versailles.[220] In February 1931, Gilson invited Maritain to the meeting of the Société Française de Philosophie at the Sorbonne to confer with Xavier Léon, Léon Brunschvicg, Édouard Le Roy, Jacques Chevalier, Maurice Blondel,[221] Émile Bréhier,[222] and others on the concept of Christian philosophy.[223] This was the point of departure for the well-known session of March 21, 1931, where Maritain and Gilson formed a common front against the rationalists Émile Bréhier and Léon Brunschvicg, on the one hand, and Maurice Blondel on the other. Gilson narrated the meeting in his memoires:

> But how could I forget the twenty-first of March 1936 [1931], the day when this the noble mind of Maritain honored with itspresence a meeting of the French Society of Philosophy? He spoke his own language. A philosopher who had come from Mars for the occasion would not have been less understood. The excellent Bouglé was the least fanatic among the representatives of secular philosophy. He was most anxious that his Catholic colleagues should feel they were trusted by him, and as a result he strove to prove it to them by courageous decisions. He came out of this meeting visibly preoccupied, even worried. "Say," he whispered in my ear, taking me by the arm in a friendly way, "what is the matter with him? I think he is crazy."[224]

219 Jacques Maritain, "Carnets de notes," *Cahiers Jacques Maritain*, no. 70, November 2015, April 26, 1930: "Read Gilson's St. Augustine." Tuesday, June 3: "Read Gilson." Monday, September 15, 1930: "Had breakfast at Versailles in Charles' house [Du Bos] with Gilson; the meeting was very cordial and may be important; he is pleased with my article on St. Augustine."

220 Letter from Étienne Gilson to Jacques Maritain, April 21, 1931, in Gilson and Maritain, *Correspondance 1923–1971*, 60.

221 Concerning the relations between Gilson and Blondel, see Donneaud, "Étienne Gilson et Maurice Blondel dans le débat sur la philosophie chrétienne," *Revue thomiste* 99, no. 3 (1999): 498–516.

222 Émile Bréhier, "Y-a-t-il une philosophie chrétienne?," *Revue de métaphysique et de morale* 38 (1931): 133–62.

223 On Christian philosophy we defer to the very lucid notes of Géry Prouvost, in Gilson and Maritain, *Correspondance 1923–1971*. See also Thierry-Dominique Humbrecht, "Étienne Gilson (1884–1978) et la philosophie chrétienne," in Étienne Gilson, *Introduction à la philosophie chrétienne*, 2nd ed. (Paris: Vrin, 2007), 7–26. See also Ruedi Imbach, "Paul Vignaux et la philosophie chrétienne," followed by Paul Vignaux, "La philosophie franciscaine et autres documents inédits," in *Paul Vignaux: Citoyen et philosophe (1904–1987)*, ed. Olivier Boulnois (Turnhout: Brepols, 2013), 129–40. See also the synthesis by Emilio Brito, "La 'philosophie chrétienne' a-t-elle un avenir?," *Revue théologique de Louvain* 36, no. 4 (2005): 508–38.

224 Étienne Gilson, *The Philosopher and Theology*, 203. Gilson situates in 1936 what took place in 1931. —See Gilson and Maritain, *Correspondance 1923–1971*, 45, and Jacques Maritain, "De la philosophie chrétienne," in *Oeuvres complètes*, vol. 5 (Paris: Desclée de Brouwer, 1932), 228.

Gilson developed the notion of Christian philosophy in *L'Esprit de la philosophie médiévale* (Paris: Vrin, 1932), and next in *Christianisme et philosophie* (Paris: Vrin, 1936), and *Introduction à la philosophie chrétienne* (Paris: Vrin, 1960).[225] For his part, Maritain published a short book in 1933, *De la philosophie chrétienne* (Paris: DDB) and dealt with the issue again in *Science et sagesse* (Paris: Labergerie, 1935). We will not return here to the documentation on Christian philosophy,[226] a "closed circle," or a "misunderstanding," according to Martin Heidegger, a concept that, according to its opponents, would ruin the autonomy of reason. However, it is important to underline that Gilson and Maritain agreed on Christian philosophy's existence in fact and on its possibility in principle. In Gilson's view, it is "an objectively observable reality" in history, in the sense in which the historian perceives Christian influence upon the progress of philosophy[227]: "If history shows that there have been Christian philosophers, it follows that the concept itself of Christian philosophy is possible."[228] The position was not widely shared and was greatly debated. Gilson lamented, "Dialogue became impossible!" In 1936, he acknowledged that he had "stopped setting foot in philosophical society."[229] The agreement between Gilson and Maritain was public knowledge. In *Esprit de la philosophie médiévale*, Gilson indicated (volume II, 289–90) that he is "entirely in agreement with Maritain." After 1931, Gilson turned not to the Sorbonne but to Maritain and Gabriel Marcel to carry on the discussion and focus the issue: "Xavier Léon has indicated that I should expect a letter from Gabriel Marcel for the *Bulletin de la Société française de philosophie*. I wanted to urge him to make his point of view known to us. On such an issue, even nuances are useful and some are necessary."[230] In May 1931, Maritain

—A disciple of Durkheim, Célestin Bouglé (1870–1940) was then assistant director of the École normale supérieure on Rue d'Ulm.

225 [English translations: *The Spirit of Medieval Philosophy* (New York: Charles Scribner's Sons, 1936); *Christianity and Philosophy* (New York: Sheed & Ward, 1939); and *Christian Philosophy: An Introduction* (New York: Doubleday, 1960).]

226 Regarding this data, see Thierry-Dominique Humbrecht's updating in the second edition of Étienne Gilson, *Introduction à la philosophie chrétienne*, 7–27.

227 See the letter from Étienne Gilson to Jacques Maritain, June 18, 1922, in Gilson and Maritain, *Correspondance 1923–1971*, 89.

228 Étienne Gilson, *Christianisme et philosophie*, 117.

229 Letter from Étienne Gilson to Henri Gouhier, October 30, 1936, Archives Gouhier.

230 Letter from Étienne Gilson to Charles Du Bos, April 25, 1931, Bibliothèque Doucet.

proposed that Gilson "drop the 'colleague' in order to keep the friendship pure and simple."[231]

The correspondence between Gabriel Marcel and Gilson has traces of meetings and debates around the 1920s.[232] They were simultaneously friends, close, and different on the philosophical level: "Continue to carve out the new thinking, as you are doing," Gilson wrote in 1930, "and be absolutely sure of the fact that you are doing something good, a good that proliferates and abounds of itself, passing from soul to soul."[233] In a letter of 1934, Gilson urged Marcel not to yield to the atmosphere of idealism in the name of philosophy of inwardness: "You also know that I have no essential reservations about your thought itself. You are on the side of 'according-to-Augustine.' Personally, I am less Augustinian. For me, *res sunt, ergo cogito*."[234]

Gilson's correspondence with Du Bos provides useful clarifications about the conversations at Versailles and Gilson's participation in the magazine *Vigile*. In May 1930, Du Bos extended the invitation: "In the difficult task of updating and even making the inner connections which an event like the one I have lived obliges, your works are the place where I have found the most solid support.... I would very much like to see you again, to speak to you about *Vigile*, whose first copy has already reached you, and I would like to ask for your cooperation and to talk with you."[235] Gilson suggested a meeting at Vrin,[236] and promised to participate: "I absolutely guarantee you that I will write first pages that are non-dogmatic and of general interest. Besides, if I send you something, you will always be free to return it to me, should you see any difficulty in publishing it in *Vigile*. I should like our friendship to be complete enough to make that freedom totally natural."[237] "Being able to

231 Letter from Jacques Maritain to Étienne Gilson, May 5, 1931, in Gilson and Maritain, *Correspondance 1923–1971*, 63.

232 See Fonds Gabriel Marcel, NAF 28349, BNF, where there are a dozen letters exchanged between 1928 and 1972. We notice a gap of twenty years between 1946 and 1967. See likewise Étienne Gilson, "Un example," preface to *Existentialisme chrétien: Gabriel Marcel* (Paris: Plon, 1947), 1–9. See also Étienne Gilson "Un philosophe singulier: À propos de Gabriel Marcel," *Nouvelles Littéraires*, June 19, 1958, 1, 7.

233 Letter from Étienne Gilson to Gabriel Marcel, June 19, 1930, NAF 28349, BNF.

234 Letter from Étienne Gilson to Gabriel Marcel, January 12, 1934, NAF 28349, BNF.

235 Letter from Charles Du Bos to Étienne Gilson, May 26, 1930, Bibliothèque Doucet.

236 Letter from Étienne Gilson to Charles Du Bos, May 28, 1930, Bibliothèque Doucet.

237 Letter from Étienne Gilson to Charles Du Bos, July 3, 1930, Bibliothèque Doucet.

count on your cooperation is one of the very scarce but completely luminous certainties that this endeavor brings me, whose complexity you know as well as I," Du Bos answered.[238] "Perhaps you recall that it had been understood that you would meet Maritain at my house before you left for Canada. I want to recall that good promise and ask Mrs. Gilson and yourself to give my wife and me the pleasure of lunching here next Monday, September 15 [1930] at one o'clock. Only Maritain and perhaps his wife, her health permitting, will be present. We will be able, you and I, to chat with Maritain in complete peace."[239] The invitations and encounters continued: "I send you this note to say that the next of the little gatherings about which I have corresponded with you and in which you have promised to participate, will take place here on Monday, January 19, at 3 P.M. The previous meetings have been interesting and useful. Only Jacques and Raïssa Maritain, Gabriel Marcel, François Mauriac, my wife and I will be present. As I have told you, the problems posed by Gabriel Marcel touching upon the connection he seeks to establish between his faith and his reason are what has given birth to the gatherings and what has guided the course of the questions examined."[240] "Thank you for your kind invitation," wrote Gilson in 1931. "I will be at Versailles Monday, January 19, unless something unexpected prevents me from going. But it will be rather to learn than to teach, because our friend Gabriel Marcel has posed a large question for you. Of course, the old Sorbonne is open to you. My course on St. Bernard takes place at eleven o'clock (instead of ten) in the English Room, second floor, left, at the end of the corridor. If you come, you will hear me *study* St. Bernard, because I am only an old student myself, and have never really decided to become a professor. The course is public."[241]

Gilson submitted two very valuable articles to Charles Du Bos for *Vigile*. In 1939, he published "La tradition française et la chrétienté," which was his first composition that dealt so directly with the theory of Christendom; its viewpoint was debated by Fr. Altermann and Maritain: "I think I have a great deal to say about the ideal of Christendom, because it is dear to my heart, and I am happy that my propositions have been submitted to good judges, because we have no right to be mistaken. I will not publish anything

238 Letter from Charles Du Bos to Étienne Gilson, July 4, 1930, Bibliothèque Doucet.

239 Letter from Charles Du Bos to Étienne Gilson, September 10, 1930, Bibliothèque Doucet.

240 Letter from Charles Du Bos to Étienne Gilson, January 7, 1931, Bibliothèque Doucet.

241 Letter from Étienne Gilson to Charles Du Bos, January 7, 1931, Bibliothèque Doucet.

without their approval."[242] "Since I saw Jacques Maritain yesterday, I have worked non-stop day and night to review and re-write in part and complete my article. It had to be done immediately, while my conversation with him was still fresh in my mind, and I could benefit from his very valuable observations."[243] In 1932, Gilson submitted an article for *Vigile* titled "Examen de conscience," an important introspective milestone in the development of Gilson as autobiographer, who seeks to resolve the question of apologetics within his work.[244]

After the crisis of February 6, 1934, there were Christian responses. The creation of the weekly magazine *Sept* and the publication of *Manifeste pour le bien commun* also marked a break for Gilson that indicated the beginning of his intellectual involvement in the affairs of the city. As he explained to Gouhier in 1934, he regretted that up to that point he seemed to have pursued "Platonic dialogues in Pompei on the eve of the eruption."[245] Henceforth, he desired less to leave Pompei than to maintain dialogues engaged with current events. In reply to the crisis stemming from February 6, 1934, the "Maritain set" published an authentic "essay on practical Christian politics"; as Maritain said to Journet,[246] with the clear title "For the Common Good: The Responsibilities of Christians and the Present Moment." Gilson was one of the fifty signatories, along with Étienne Borne, Charles Du Bos, Jean Lacroix, Emmanuel Mounier, Stanislas Fumet, Yves Simon, and others. Gilson was close to Mounier and Maritain at this point: "Saw Gilson yesterday," Maritain wrote to Mounier in May 1934: "He was deeply moved by your letter and spoke to me about it quite movingly."[247] If Mounier's letter to Gilson seems to be lost, and if it can be viewed as expressing reservations that Mounier might have about *Pour un ordre catholique* (DDB, November 1934), Gilson entered socio-political debates with a position that was neither partisan, nor conformist, in the vein of Maritain's *Lettre sur l'indépendance* (1935), and in agreement with the editorial aims of the Dominican weekly *Sept*:

242 Letter from Étienne Gilson to Charles Du Bos, February 8, 1931, Bibliothèque Doucet.

243 Letter from Étienne Gilson to Charles Du Bos, no date, shelf number MS 33845, Bibliothèque Doucet.

244 Étienne Gilson, "Examen de conscience," 98.

245 Letter from Étienne Gilson to Henri Gouhier, August 31, 1934, Archives Gouhier.

246 Letter from Jacques Maritain to Charles Journet, May 16, 1934, *Correspondance Journet-Maritain*, vol. 2, *1930–1939* (Paris: Saint-Augustin, 1997), 382.

247 Letter from Jacques Maritain to Emmanuel Mounier, May 1934, in Maritain and Mounier, *Correspondance. 1929–1949*, ed. Sylvain Guéna (Paris: Desclée de Brouwer, 2016).

"Neither left nor right, independent of politics, to better serve the City, praise good, denouncing evil, we are indebted only to truth."[248] A simple numerical argument could be enough to illustrate the new part of Gilson's output. Between March 1934 and August 1935, Gilson published sixty-one articles in *Sept*, twenty-six of which were selected to make up the book *Pour un ordre catholique*. Along with others, he appeared as one of the master thinkers of a magazine whose circulation, before its condemnation in summer 1937, was sizable, since it had at least twenty-five thousand subscribers and an average circulation of fifty-thousand copies. Its readership went far beyond professed Catholics.[249]

After the mid-1930s, Gilson fully assumed the status of Catholic intellectual, putting his "intelligence at the service of Christ the King," as he wrote in 1936.[250] He was simultaneously a professor at the Collège de France, a journalist and editorial writer, and a person with ecclesiastical and socio-political commitment. Furthermore, on the eve of World War II, he published some twenty articles in Francisque Gay's *L'Aube*, more than a hundred articles in Hubert Beuve-Méry's *Le Monde*, and many others in *La Vie intellectuelle*, the New York magazine *Commonweal*, *Esprit*, *Politique*, and so on. He offered the example of a hybrid model of committed intellectual, not comparable to Bergson, who, though very present in the City and purely speculative, distanced himself from any coterie and wanted to confine himself to a "pure philosophical magisterium."[251] Nor was Gilson comparable to Maritain, whose strategies were different and in whom the Sorbonne was not inter-

248 Editorial in *Sept*, March 10, 1934.

249 By order of Rome, the magazine had to stop publishing abruptly in August 1937. Regarding this event, which has been thoroughly studied by historians, see Coutrot, *Un courant de pensée catholique. L'hebdomadaire Sept (mars 1934–août 1937)*; Magali Della Sudda, "La suppression de l'hebdomadaire dominicain *Sept*: Immixtion du Vatican dans les affaires françaises (1936–1937)?," *Vingtième siècle. Revue d'histoire* 4, no. 104 (2009): 29–44. Della Sudda quotes testimony of Msgr. Saliège (Archives of the Congregation of the Doctrine of the Faith), titled "Notes on the Disappearance of the Weekly *Sept*": "It is a fact that the abrupt disappearance of the weekly *Sept* caused a considerable emotional reaction in the Catholic circles that were most docile to papal directives. In fact, beyond the environment of Catholic Action, *Sept* had succeeded in reaching university populations and intellectuals favorable to Catholicism and had even interested groups that were not specifically Catholic, including persons in the government. On the one hand, that is explained by an attitude that seemed new and courageous and, on the other, by the very remarkable team of laymen who contributed to it (Mauriac, Gilson, Maritain, and so on)."

250 Étienne Gilson, "Intelligence au service de Christ-Roi," in *Christianisme et philosophie*, 142–68. This material is reproduced in *La Vie intellectuelle*, 181–200.

251 Azouvi, *La gloire de Bergson*, 327–28.

ested, though as François Azouvi notes, "The modern history of French philosophy can be written without pronouncing the word Sorbonne."[252] Gilson was also not similar to young Emmanuel Mounier, who, separated from the university, tried to found a magazine and make the "event" into his "inner teacher,"[253] while Gilson thought of nothing apart from the long span of history. Again, Gilson's manner of existence and his role as a Catholic intellectual in French society, his network and widespread recognition, and his relationships were quite different, because of his position.

252 Azouvi, *La gloire de Bergson*, 329.

253 Letter from Emmanuel Mounier to Jean-Marie Domenach, September 1949, in Mounier, *Oeuvres complètes*, vol. 4 (Paris: Seuil, 1963), 817.

2

Against Secular Ideologies
To Build Christendom

Pope Pius XI builds as much of contemporary history as Mussolini or Lenin. If there is a difference, it is that he has created better and for the longer term.[1]

In France we are astonishingly provincial.[2]

Étienne Gilson wrote no systematic work denouncing twentieth-century ideologies. However, the critique of secular ideologies, of all those failed metamorphoses of the City of God, to put it in Gilson's language, nourishes the deep philosophical reflection of the methodical realist that Gilson intended to be.[3] It suffices to read him, including his most philosophical works,[4] with a bit of attention, to reconstruct clearly his interpretation of current political events, where his analysis made very few concessions. With

1 Étienne Gilson, "L'Église et la liberté," *Sept*, no. 43, December 21, 1934, 3.

2 Interview of Étienne Gilson by Paul Guth, "Le monde va-t-il vers à un nouveau Moyen Âge?," *Le Littéraire*, December 28, 1946, 3.

3 Étienne Gilson, *Le réalisme méthodique* (Paris: Téqui, 1935).

4 See for example, Étienne Gilson, *Les métamorphoses de la Cité de Dieu* (Paris: Vrin, 1952), 61, 151, 286–287 [trans. James G. Colbert as *The Metamorphoses of the City of God*, (Washington, DC: The Catholic University of America Press, 2020), e.g., 231–33].

the notable exception of Dante's country, (and infrequently Mussolini's),[5] Gilson was completely hostile to what he called "Germanism," situating Hitler in the long span of German history, to the Marxism in practice that was bolshevism and Stalinism, and to different kinds of French nationalisms like those represented by Maurras, Pétain, and even de Gaulle. Likewise, Gilson was critical of "industrial capitalism," which in 1930 he judged to be a "more dangerous plague than Marxism."[6] After 1945, he described it as the regime of "destitution for the many," as opposed to communism, which was "destitution for all."[7] Criticism of capitalism was not a mere stylistic pose for Gilson. "If bourgeois capitalism is a reactionary regime, Stalin's Leninism is not less so. Really, there is no essential difference between the two regimes, because neither is capable of picturing human beings as other than exploiting or exploited. Both cheerfully speak of democracy but neither thinks about it."[8] We find conscious rejection of all ideology in Gilson: "Not a single 'ism' agrees with all the facts. Irenicism is the only one we ought to care about, and have no doubt that I address that lesson to myself," he wrote to a Belgian colleague in 1949.[9] Gilson readily shared the frame of reference of the "non-conformist generation" that denounced the "established disorder," as Jean-Louis Loubet del Bayle understood it,[10] although Gilson was twenty years older than thinkers like Emmanuel Mounier, Alexandre Marc, or Jean de Fabrègues.

Befitting this being "neither right nor left," "neither conservative, nor revolutionary,"[11] Gilson missed no opportunity to break a lance in private or in public against these ideologies. "During the ideological war of the 1940s,

5 On this point see in the appendixes the observation of Fr. Pierre Boisselot in his "Notes sur l'histoire de Cerf," 1943, Fonds Boisselot, APDF. Thomists were divided on this point. Yves Simon published *La Campagne d'Éthiopie et la pensée politique française* (Lille: Société d'Impressions Littéraires, Industrielles et Commerciales, 1936; subsequently, Paris Desclée de Brouwer, 1937). In 1935, Étienne Gilson's nephew, Paul Gilson, published a condemnation of the Ethiopian regime; Paul Gilson, *Le roi des rois* (Paris: Denoël et Steele, 1935).

6 Étienne Gilson, "Giovanni Papini et saint Augustin," *L'Européen*, March 5, 1930, 5.

7 Lecture of Étienne Gilson, "Justice politique et justice sociale," at Hamilton, summary published in *La Survivance*, September 10, 1947; and also in *Relations* 7, no. 73, October 1947.

8 Étienne Gilson, "En lisant Staline," *L'Aube*, February 12, 1947, 1.

9 Letter of Étienne Gilson to Ferdinand Van Steenberghen, March 23, 1949, published in *Revue philosophique de Louvain* 87, no. 4 (1989): 616.

10 Jean-Louis Loubet del Bayle, *Les non-conformistes des années 30: Une tentative de renouvellement de la pensée politique française* (Paris: Seuil, 1969; repr. 2001).

11 Letter from Étienne Gilson to Jean-Augustin Maydieu, May 28, 1944, 2–3, Fonds Maydieu, APDF.

Gilson was not too much this or too much that," Msgr. Jean Rupp reported.[12] Was this a consequence of moderation acquired in his Parisian Catholic bourgeois education? The explanation seems insufficient. Gilson bluntly criticized the "frightened lump" who was a Parisian bourgeois in July 1935.[13] Gilson's class consciousness was rather detached: bourgeois certainly, but above all Burgundian. Besides, Gilson knew Germans and Germanic culture through his experience in the war. He also spoke Russian and had gone to Ukraine in 1922. Fourteen years before André Gide's *Retour de l'URSS* (1936), Gilson's testimony was a model of lucidity. A realist, he missed no occasion, as we will see, to say that he had seen what he criticized.

The first positive challenge in his reflection is Maritain's watchword: "That the order of bodies should be established under the primacy of the spiritual, that is authentic salvation, but spiritual persons will wait in vain for it to be offered to them. It is up to them to establish it."[14] For Gilson, this requires social democracy on the political level. *Ut fiat aequalitas*, he recalls with St. Paul. "Socialism" is another of the Christian truths, sprung from the Mosaic law, but cut off from its root and thus from its strength. Every human being must receive a basket of manna.[15] The primacy of the spiritual likewise requires politics based on the consideration of the person, body and soul, without losing sight of the Church's social doctrine or the ideal of a universal society as "Christendom" would propose it.

The second positive issue is an open question. Gilson was certainly a liberal. But the issue is to discover the nature of his liberalism, which is neither economic, nor moral, nor theological, nor in the English Darwinian

12 Jean Rupp, "Gilson tel que je l'ai connu," *L'Homme nouveau*, March 4, 1979.

13 Letter from Étienne Gilson to Henri Gouhier, July 4, 1935, Archives Gouhier. Gilson encountered a bourgeois attacked by a proletarian. "The bourgeois, pummeled with hooks and swings, howls pitifully: 'But defend me, defend me.' This frightened fathead, whimpering under the blows of the giant, gave me a pathetic idea of my 'class'."

14 Étienne Gilson, "Giovanni Papini et saint Augustin," *L'Européen*, March 5, 1930, 5. Gilson employs the expression "primacy of the spiritual" in at least two other articles, "Autour de Julien Benda: La mare aux clercs," *L'Européen*, May 29, 1929, 4; and "Les vrais problèmes," *Sept*, number 50, February 8, 1935, 3.

15 Étienne Gilson, "Un gomor de manne," *La Vie intellectuelle*, November 1946, 17: "Perhaps it is not too late to acknowledge within this truth of socialism an old Christian truth that goes back at least to St. Paul: *ut fiat aequalitas* (2 Corinthians 8:14). Unless it goes back to Moses: a basket of manna for everyone, and let no one ever have more or less. It is true that the basket has been lost, but as we said, it was the tenth part of an ephah. It ought to be possible to make another."

model, which Gilson denounced on occasion, and whose end he believed he could see in 1936: "This extravagant society, from which we have just begun to emerge, and which is charmingly called 'liberal society.'"[16] Gilson's liberalism, a theme that does not even appear on the horizon of *Pour un ordre catholique*, involved first of all freedom of conscience, freedom of the Church, and freedom of the act of faith. Gilson was very clear on this point in an article that he published in 1949, where he defined religious freedom as the "only practical condition" for progress of religion:

> Religious freedom is not religious life and still less the triumph of religion, but it is the practical condition for the only real progress and the only real triumph of the Christian religion in the world. There is not the slightest trace of a doctrinal liberalism here, which would be only a beginning of religious indifference. To the contrary, the unique truth of the Church of Christ is presupposed by the whole political attitude of Catholics in the debates that concern it. The fact is just that one can become Christian or remain Christian only by a series of free acts and that it is equally contradictory for the State to be able to prohibit anyone to be Christian or compel anyone to become Christian. States themselves are not mistaken here. They know the Church's tremendous strength when it is free, and that is why we see them continually hesitate between the only two methods known for subjecting the Church: to persecute it or "protect it."[17]

As a counterpoint, there was also a negative presentation written by Gilson, in the sense that he defined himself by what he was not and what he vehemently rejected. "I do not believe in either Hegel or Marx, and not even in Luther, who was at least Christian," he wrote to Fr. Chenu after the

16 Étienne Gilson, "La corporation médicale dans un ordre social-chrétien," *Cahiers Laënnec* 2, no. 1 (January 1936): 1–15: "This is why the individuals who remained afterwards were able to behave as if they were authentic ends, and this is what gave birth to this extravagant society from which we have just begun to emerge, and which is charmingly called 'liberal society.' The liberalism that flourished in England is a society of individuals, each one of whom behaves as if he or she had the rights of a person. Everyone for himself but God for everyone. Let them act, do not control. Who will succeed? The strongest. It is the struggle for life. All these persons in the name of liberalism grasped for themselves the right to be taken as ends, in so far as individuals and in their temporal, material interests; with that they entered into a struggle with each other, and Darwinism was right: the survival of the fittest by the elimination of the weakest."

17 Étienne Gilson, "Le catholique et la politique," *Culture catholique. Présence de la Pensée chrétienne*, no. 1, (June 1949): 119–28.

Second Vatican Council.[18] Gilson proposed a valuable, though rambling, contribution to the theologico-political history of the twentieth century. In autumn 1933, he argued that if the German ideal, adoration of the state, was pursued, it would mean war. If the Russian ideal was pursued it would mean slavery and certainly famine. Gilson concluded his lectures by putting communism and Nazism in biblical perspective: "I should say that as Lenin was Anti-Christ, so Hitler is anti-Moses. He is the prophet of his appointed people, which is contrariwise to what the Jews had done. God has elected the Jewish people, but the German people are electing their God."[19]

The connecting thread of our analysis in this chapter is the unpublished typescript of a fall 1933 course titled "Christian Social Philosophy," which Gilson gave in Toronto in English. This series of nine lectures is important for two reasons. We are dealing with the first attempt to write the *Métamorphoses de la Cité de Dieu*,[20] which Gilson published as a book only in 1952. In addition to long, carefully composed expositions on the issue of Russia,[21] and about the German question,[22] there are many elaborations upon Nazism, nationalism, Stalinism, and Maurrasism that would not be retained in the published *Metamorphoses*.[23] In the 1933 series, Gilson already proposes the *Letter to Diognetus* as the cornerstone of political reflection for Christians in the 1930s: "'They live in homelands that are not their own, but as pilgrims. They share the life of citizen and endure the lot of foreigners. It is like that

18 Letter from Étienne Gilson to Fr. Marie-Dominique Chenu, November 5, 1969, published in "Correspondance entre Étienne Gilson et Marie-Dominique Chenu: Un choix de lettres (1923–1969)," *Revue thomiste* 105 (2005): 82.

19 Étienne Gilson, "Christian Social Philosophy," a lecture on Germany, p. 7, 1933, SMCA; in Étienne Gilson, *Oeuvres complètes*, vol. 1, *Un philosophe dans la cité 1908–1943*, ed. Florian Michel (Paris: Vrin, 2019), 263.

20 Étienne Gilson, "Christian Social Philosophy," first lecture, p. 1, 1933, SMCA: "I am going to rewrite the history of the City of God." In *Oeuvres complètes*, 1:210.—Final lecture, p. 1: "We have followed the history of the City of God in the wanderings through different parts of the world in the different periods of human history." *Oeuvres complètes*, 1:279.

21 Étienne Gilson, "Christian Social Philosophy," lecture on Solovyov, 1933, SMCA. *Oeuvres complètes*, 1:245–53.

22 Étienne Gilson, "Christian Social Philosophy," lecture on Germany, 1933, SMCA. In *Oeuvres complètes*, 1:253–63.

23 Étienne Gilson, *The Metamorphoses of the City of God*, 231n10. Marxism is excluded from consideration there, because, as Gilson tells us, it is only an impoverishment of Auguste Comte's philosophy.

today. This tells the whole story."[24] Thirty years prior to the well-known expressions of Fr. Chenu,[25] Gilson was aware of the "end of the Constantinian era" and of the political and moral secularization of the world produced by Modernity, war, and nationalisms, and he sees the "distance between our ways of thinking about them and those of the world."[26]

GERMANISM, NAZISM, AND ANTI-SEMITISM

In line with Pius XI's papacy, and like Jacques Maritain on this point, Gilson exhibited evident philo-Semitism throughout the 1930s. Thus, in March 1933, he was among the signers of a declaration in favor of German Jewish intellectuals threatened by Nazism.[27] In May 1933, he told an American correspondent that one of his German friends, a Franciscan, had arrived in Paris with his old Jewish botany professor to bring him to safety, that the "admirable Cassirer" had been chased out of Hamburg, that "Heidegger is said to have become a full-fledged Nazi," and German Catholics have completely caved in to the anti-Catholic concept of race." "Madness prevails everywhere," he concluded."[28] In regard to Heidegger, the reference is important. From May 1933 on, Gilson was aware of rumors about the latter's involvement with Nazism. Thereafter, Gilson would be rather circumspect, to employ a euphemism, about the German philosopher.

Gilson was very clear about Germany. At Cologne in the summer of 1932, he observed the virulence of the crowd, and walking beside a priest he was treated ... as a communist: "There was no middle ground between a complete Communist revolution and that powerful and in some ways more dangerous reaction."[29] From 1933 on, Hitler's coming to power meant to Gilson that a

24 Étienne Gilson, "Christian Social Philosophy," first lecture, 2, 1933, SMCA. In *Oeuvres complètes*, 1:213.—The same quotation appears in *Metamorphoses*, 18.

25 Marie-Dominique Chenu, "La fin de l'ère constantinienne," in *Un concile pour notre temps* (Paris: Cerf, 1961), 59–87.

26 Étienne Gilson, "L'intelligence au service de Christ-Roi," in *Christianisme et philosophie* (Paris: Vrin, 1936), 150.

27 See *Paix et droit, organe de l'alliance israélite universelle*, March 1933, 7, for the manifesto. Over 250 signatures appeared in the March and April issues.

28 Letter from Étienne Gilson to Ralph Barton Perry, May 23, 1933, Harvard Archives. About Heidegger, the exact statement is: "By the way, Heidegger is said to have become a full-fledged Nazi. But this is only from hearsay."

29 Étienne Gilson, "Christian Social Philosophy," lecture on Germany, 1933, SMCA. *Oeuvres complètes*, 1:255.

war was approaching for which it was necessary to be prepared. "France is in an almost desperate situation," he wrote to a colleague. "Morally obliged to disarm, with the absolute certainty that Germany is rearming and another war in sight, in which we shall be left to ourselves by all those who are now urging us to destroy our guns.... It will be *finis Galliae*."[30] There we find a disparate summary, but one with foresight of what was to come. In autumn 1933, Gilson had read enough fragments of *Mein Kampf* to compare the German and English versions.[31] On his way to the September 1934 Prague Philosophy Congress, Henri Gouhier made a detour to Nuremburg to observe a Nazi rally. In a letter to him, Gilson showed that he grasped the danger to which the world was exposed as well as the anti-religious nature of Nazism:

> I regret not having seen Nuremberg. My consolation is that an *alter ego* was there. I believe that what happened there is of planetary importance. A pure essence was unveiled; after being sought for so long, it was finally acknowledged publicly. Since the birth of Jesus Christ, nothing more truly important can have happened than the rejection of Jesus Christ. That took place. What astounds me is that our French adversaries of Hitler do not see that they work for him while hoping to save man from enslavement by man. They are shamefaced Hitlerians. Above all, if they do not think that Hitler is great—in his horror—they are dangerous imbeciles.[32]

The phrase "to save man from enslavement by man" from Gilson's pen is probably a summons to emerge from secularized anthropocentrism, whether capitalist or Marxist, and to recover the meaning of God and the taste for Christian salvation. In a 1938 letter, Gilson was very firm about the means to be employed: it is necessary to be "dogmatic," he explained, in order to denounce the intrinsic evils of communism and fascism. It is necessary not to tolerate freedom of expression for those who hold these doctrines; otherwise, he writes, "one works for fascism."[33]

30 Letter from Étienne Gilson to Ralph Barton Perry, May 27, 1933, Harvard Archives.

31 Étienne Gilson, "Christian Social Philosophy," lecture on Germany, 1933, SMCA: "If you read the book of Hitler, you will find sentences which are in the original text but not in the English translation. That English edition has been carefully revised." *Oeuvres complètes*, 1:262.

32 Letter from Étienne Gilson to Henri Gouhier, Toronto, October 6, 1934, Archives Gouhier.

33 Letter from Étienne Gilson to Ralph Barton Perry, August 15, 1938, Harvard Archives: "Don't you see that to express an opinion is already to act? It is the very beginning of the corresponding action. Dear Perry, do you know what you are working for? Fascism."

Gilson attentively followed events and commented upon them in his correspondence. In a 1935 letter he remarked: "The German religious situation is abominable. More than one hundred priors or abbesses are in prison. I have a great deal to tell you about that, but these are matters about which one cannot be cautious enough."[34] In 1936, Gilson wrote again: "What one sees from here [Harvard] is clear as daylight and dominating everything is the hard and fast absolute will of Germany to unleash a new war. It is horrible, and there is no choice but to be prepared for what seems quite inevitable."[35] On the subject of the Munich agreement and Chamberlain's speech, Gilson wrote to Gouhier: "This makes one weep." In April 1939, Gilson again spoke of Chamberlain's "noble stupidity."[36] In the same letter, Gilson lamented the fate of one of his Italian students, a specialist in Petrarch who was about to leave Paris to be mobilized in the Italian army and fight against France. The poor lad was in tears, Gilson explained. This inevitable war, Gilson wrote in 1939, is the triumph of the worst demon, whose name is Stupidity."[37]

Gilson continually wondered about the correct line of conduct. Should he "be quiet and hope for a better future?" he asked in 1936.[38] In July 1939, Gilson reminded the French public of Heinrich Heine's lesson: "He clearly saw and rightly said that the history of Germany is essentially a progressive restoration of its old paganism against the Christian civilization that Rome had once imposed."[39] On the eve of the war he tried to send some of his students to Canada[40] and recommended his colleagues, notably Alexandre Koyré,[41] to American institutions, so that they could cross the Atlantic and find refuge. In February 1940, he tried to explain the meaning of the war and

34 Letter from Étienne Gilson to Gerald Phelan, postscript, May 5, 1935, in French, SMCA.

35 Letter from Étienne Gilson to Henri Gouhier, October 30, 1936, Archives Gouhier.

36 Letter from Étienne Gilson to Ralph Barton Perry, April 4, 1939, Harvard Archives.

37 Letter from Étienne Gilson to Ralph Barton Perry, April 4, 1939, Harvard Archives. The letter states: "The poor boy was actually crying. We had been working together on Petrarch for two solid years, little knowing whether Petrarch was an Italian or a Frenchman. How, I ask you, can that youngster fight us? How could I fight against Italy? Italy, Perry, think of it. What a triumph for the worst of all devils, whose name is Stupidity!"

38 Letter from Étienne Gilson to Ralph Barton Perry, May 27, 1933, Harvard Archives: "The wiser course is perhaps to keep quiet and hope for a better future."

39 Étienne Gilson, "Henri Heine a-t-il prévu Hitler?," *Les nouvelles littéraires*, July 1, 1939, 1.

40 Letter from Étienne Gilson to Ralph Barton Perry, April 4, 1939, Harvard Archives.

41 Letter from Étienne Gilson to Alexandre Koyré, 1940, sales catalogue of Librairie Vignes, 2007.

of Nazism to the American public, "a revival of pan-Germanism."[42] During the occupation, Gilson himself hoped for a time to take his whole family to Harvard in 1941–1942, where he was invited to give a new series of William James Lectures,[43] but the project failed because of administrative complications—"the road to the United States goes through Vichy."[44] In 1940, Gilson attempted to help Emmanuel Levinas, from whom, after the Liberation, he received a letter overflowing with thanks for the assistance given in 1940:

> It is not only the text of your article in *Le Monde* of October 28–29[45] and its lucid generosity for which you need no compliments. The two words of the signature are what provoke this letter. They remind me of the words that in autumn 1940 I found at the bottom of a sheet of paper that you directed to me, when I had written to you at the beginning of a captivity that was to last for five years. An Israelite and naturalized Frenchman, I already glimpsed what awaited us. Charles Blondel was dead. Maurice Halbwachs was under suspicion—and powerless—looking forward to martyrdom. Many turned away. Louis Lavelle, the philosopher of the eternal presence, then Secretary General of the Ministry of National Education, had the presence of mind not to answer a timid, respectful letter. A letter that came from you, where you told me, me whom you did not know, with a clarity that could compromise you, of your confidence in the return of a situation that seemed lost forever; and where, without hiding from me the dangers you perceived for me and my people, you proposed that I use your name as needed, brightened that loneliness in solitude to which my status as an Israelite prisoner condemned me. It was an act for which at that moment I could only make a vow to thank you some day, on some far off day for which your letter gave me the first hope. That day has come. Among the elderly, the empty spaces are still more gaping. From my own family, I have only my wife and my little boy. No joy at our return is unmixed. But what I feel in saying these words of gratitude to you has preserved the purity it had when there was only hope. And the excuse that your article in *Le Temps* [*Le Monde*] has attenuated a little my phobia against indiscretion.[46]

42 Étienne Gilson, "A French View of the War," *America*, no. 62, February 3, 1940, 452–56. "The rise of Nazism can be explained partly as a result of the World War, and partly as a revival of pan-Germanism, which was not an effect of the World War, but one of its causes."

43 Archives of the Collège de France, 16 CDF 156.

44 Letter from Étienne Gilson to Albert Béguin, March 11, 1951, "Journal à plusieurs voix," *Ésprit* 19, no. 78 (1951): 596–99.

45 Étienne Gilson, "L'éducation des Nations Unies," *Le Monde*, October 28–29, 1945, 1.

46 Letter from Emmanuel Levinas to Étienne Gilson, October 29, 1945, SMCA.

On the level of historical analysis, from 1933 on, Gilson's position consisted of connecting Nazism to what he calls "Germanism" and opposing French thinking, the idea of the universal, to German thought, the anti-Roman notion of the national.[47] He begged his audience to excuse his "over-simplification" of the question. But he recalled his long stay in prisoner-of-war camps: "As I spent several years in Germany, I feel authorized to say something about it."[48] Gilson enlisted Dostoevsky and Thomas Mann; he went back to the Roman defeats in the Germanic forests—"the start of the perennial protests against everything Roman." He recalled the long struggle between Germanic emperors and the popes: "Once again it is the same problem, an effort to protest against everything spiritually universal." He underlined the continuity between the Lutheran reform ... and those who opposed Napoleon—Napoleon being the "bearer of the universal ideals of the Revolution." Gilson reconsidered the recreation of a German empire in 1871 and then the war of 1914, during which "Germany had the whole world against it." He commented upon Spengler, Fichte, and Hegel—notably the well-known section on "Reason in History"—and on the Prussian state as the meaning of German history. He concluded that German history is essentially a state-controlled protest, in a larger sense than the Protestant Reformation, against the sense of the universal and the sense of the catholic. Gilson commented on "the German order," the sense of service, the "servant of the German state, the race question in Germany, to put forth an original comparison with the Catholic Church. "In the German order," "the individual is sacrificed on the altar of order itself," "it is submitted to the state," everything converges on "the good of the German state." By contrast, in the Church, the least among the laity, although certainly subject to the pope, "can be a better Catholic than the pope." In Catholicism, Gilson explained, there is a sense of hierarchical order, which not only does not abolish the sense of equality before grace in the members of that order, but even guarantees the possible excellence of the least of them. Gilson's position on German racism in 1933 is very classical and quite clear: "Every scientific attempt to demonstrate the

47 Étienne Gilson, "Christian Social Philosophy," 1933, lecture on Germany, SMCA; in *Oeuvres complètes*, 1:256.

48 Étienne Gilson, "Christian Social Philosophy," lecture on Germany, 2, SMCA; in *Oeuvres complètes*, 1:255.—On Gilson's captivity, see chapter 1, above.

existence of a German race has failed. There is no serious scientific work in favor of this idea to ground it rigorously."[49]

Concluding this autumn 1933 course, Gilson emphasized that "the persecution of the Jews is not accidental, not something that could or could not have happened. All that is not Aryan must be eliminated."[50] From Hitler's viewpoint, "the only solution is war and blood. He must eliminate all Christian influence, and the first stage is the elimination of the *Zentrum*. The second stage is the elimination of all Christian pacifists, whether Catholics or Protestants." Gilson recalled the Lutheran Church's collaboration with the Nazis. Some of its bishops had forbidden the reading of the old Testament as "too Jewish." "I read the solemn protest of Karl Barth against that question of German nationalism.[51] He says that this is contrary to the Lutheran spirit, and I suppose so, but when he says that Luther had nothing to do with that question, I think he is wrong. I call your attention to the fact that Luther had placed the Church entirely under the control of the temporal power.... The Lutheran Church [whose bishops are named by the Reich] must know its proper function, which is to be the faithful servant of the Third Reich."[52] Gilson's observations during fall 1933 were confirmed by the Barmen Declaration of Faith (May 1934) and the foundation of the "Confessing Church." Only a schism in the strict sense within the German churches could detach the Lutheran Church from the Third Reich.

COMMUNISM AND STALINISM

For all that he read Hitler, Gilson was not sure that he had ever read a single line of Karl Marx. By contrast, Gilson read Stalin[53] and was not always troubled by the subtleties in treating the subject: "Communism is a terrible trag-

49 Étienne Gilson, "Christian Social Philosophy," lecture on Germany, 6, SMCA; in *Oeuvres complètes*, 1:262.

50 Étienne Gilson, "Christian Social Philosophy," lecture on Germany, 6, SMCA; in *Oeuvres complètes*, 1:262.

51 Before the declaration of Barmen (May 1934), Barth allowed a pamphlet to appear (July 1933), which would give rise to the Confessing Church, and which Gilson mentions here. In summer 1933, in the ecclesiastical elections, the "German Christians" supported by the Nazis obtained 75 percent of the votes; see *Oeuvres complètes*, 1:263.

52 Étienne Gilson, "Christian Social Philosophy," lecture on Germany, 6, SMCA; in *Oeuvres complètes*, 1:263.

53 Étienne Gilson, "En lisant Staline," 1.

edy for the whole world," he explained to his 1933 students. "We may call it communism or bolshevism. It does not make much difference what term we use. Technically speaking, however, bolshevism in a sense completes communism.... Therefore bolshevism means pure and unadulterated communism. The situation in Russia can be described without exaggeration as the complete enslavement to matter. The present order in Russia is nothing but disorder."[54] Gilson always showed biting irony: "As Joseph Stalin says in his excellent treatise *On the Principles of Leninism*, 'The proletarian State is a machine to crush the bourgeoisie.' Nothing could be clearer. What is less clear is that after having crushed the bourgeoisie, the proletarian State still proposes to exploit it."[55]

Anti-communist instinctively and by culture, as much as a republican bourgeois can be, Gilson's experience with communism is still extremely interesting. In August-September 1922, Gilson, a Russian speaker since his stay in the prison camps in Germany, went to Russia and to Ukraine in the Volga region, to bring assistance to the starving. Gilson thereby witnessed the great famine of 1921–1922, whose victims are usually estimated at five million dead.[56] Gilson talked to professors in the Saratov region, met people's commissars, read the press, and brought back valuable souvenirs and photographs of starving children.[57] He explained the purpose of his mission to Henri Gouhier: "As a good disciple of Descartes, I am going to close my books for five or six weeks to read the book of the world and to cleanse myself in action. I almost certainly leave August 12 for the starving regions of Russia. I hope that, upon my return, my testimony will help to save some unfortunate people and, who knows, perhaps some thousands. I intend to concern myself particularly with children and intellectuals."[58]

This experience served Gilson throughout the absolute, irrefutable demonstration of communism's noxiousness and of the "merciless struggle"

54 Étienne Gilson, "Christian Social Philosophy," lecture on Germany, 1, SMCA; in *Oeuvres complètes*, 1:254.

55 Étienne Gilson, "En lisant Staline," 1.

56 See the review of *Guerre, guerres civiles et conflits nationaux dans l'Empire russe et in Russie soviétique 1914–1922*, by EHESS, in *Cahiers du Monde russe* 38, nos. 1–2 (January–June 1997): 223–41.

57 One of those photographs was published in *The Étienne Gilson Collection* (Toronto: PIMS, n.d.), 15.

58 Letter from Étienne Gilson to Henri Gouhier, July 28, 1922, Archives Gouhier.

that it conducted against Christianity.[59] In 1933 Gilson depicted his mission to Russia and Ukraine for his Toronto students: "I was there in 1922, and I will show you from photographs which I took myself the actual state of affairs in Russia at that time."[60] "I will never forget the day I met my colleagues at Saratov. . . . They were reduced to a state of complete slavery. I have never felt such humiliation as these men were living."[61] In the spring of 1934 the controversy returned in a polemic launched by Edmond Humeau in *Esprit* against Gilson and *Sept*. "I do not talk about Communist Russia to be a yes-man," Gilson wrote. "I went there. I saw it. And I did not go there like one of those bureaucratic sheep, who are shown only what someone wants them to see, or like someone unable to listen or communicate, who cannot speak the country's language," explained Gilson, who then recalled the dead child he picked up, the empty schools, the starving children, poverty, moral and intellectual degradation, disappearance of morality."[62] An anonymous note in the May 1934 issue of *Esprit* viewed this article by Gilson as an act of allegiance to big capital, bankers, and pro-fascist forces: "Why is it necessary that Gilson in *Sept* tries to howl with the wolves like some [Henri] Béraud? . . . Our Christ is not a worldly social order that the government of the tsars, Dollfuss, or Doumergue might defend against a mafia of bogeymen." With a touch of sorrow, Gilson answered sharply and explains his position in the May 19 issue of *Sept* in an article titled "Intermède soviétique," rejecting the "game of sham" in which *Esprit* was indulging: "Between bolshevism and us, any cooperation is impossible." "Bolshevik Marxism is an inhuman doctrine." "I am ready to go back to Russia with you, Mounier," protested Gilson, who described in detail the circumstances of his 1922 trip and concluded: "The remedy is not to replace capitalist exploitation with a still worse exploitation. . . . Are we going to flirt with Marxist materialism under the pretense of better achieving the ends that the gospel sets for us? Let whoever wants to do so lend himself to the sham. . . We are not here to stand guard over the chests of the wealthy or the coffers of the Soviets, but over

59 Étienne Gilson, "La croisée des chemins," *Sept*, April 14, 1934, 2: "Materialism and atheism are the very negation of Christianity against which, moreover, they carry on a merciless war. No Catholic will hesitate on this."

60 Étienne Gilson, "Christian Social Philosophy," lecture on Solovyov, 5, SMCA; in *Oeuvres complètes*, 1:253.

61 Étienne Gilson, "Christian Social Philosophy," lecture on Germany, 1, SMCA; in *Oeuvres complètes*, 1:254

62 Étienne Gilson, "La croisée des chemins," *Sept*, April 14, 1934, 2.

the treasure of our faith."[63] Edmond Humeau, the author of the anonymous note erroneously attributed to Mounier, presented his apologies (*Esprit*, June 1934, 512–13), still expressing the desire that the U.S.S.R., which alone had begun the anti-capitalist revolution, not be abused. . . . In 1947 Gilson again described a conversation that he had with an officer of the Red Army: "I remember once making the trip from Odessa to Saratov in the company of a young Red Army officer, recently graduated from his academy. It was a long magic spell for me. He knew absolutely everything, not only what, according to the system, he ought to think, but even what, according to the system, I myself was obliged to think. My feeble efforts to persuade him that I sometimes thought otherwise on this or that particular point left him so unmoved that I soon had to give up."[64] In 1949, Gilson still remembered: "It is enough for me to close my eyes for an instant to see again, in the villages of Ukraine and on the banks of the Volga, those dead children in 1922, whose little corpses lay abandoned in their deserted schools, or again, along the railway tracks, those bands of feral children that later had to be got rid of by machine guns."[65]

There were echoes of Gilson's Ukrainian mission in the contemporary press. The newspaper *Le Temps* narrated its start: "M. Gilson has left with the mission to inspect the French soup kitchens organized in the Volga region by the French committee to aid Ukrainian children, and to visit the regions currently affected by the famine, in particular Ukraine, in order to study the conditions in which new French soup kitchens could be opened. The Soviet government has given the necessary authorizations to enable this mission." [66] Likewise, the newspaper published a short announcement by Gilson: "Étienne Gilson, professor of philosophy at the Sorbonne, sent on a mission by the French Committee to Assist Children, whose headquarters is in Paris at 10 rue d'Elyssée, to the areas of Russia and Ukraine affected by famine, has just sent the president of the committee, Madame René Dubost, the following telegram from Odessa, dated September 1: 'From Odessa to Kherson over a hundred fifty kilometer swathe, the famine looms more terrible than that of last year. The harvest is non-existent. The situation of children is particularly

63 Étienne Gilson, "Intermède soviétique," *Sept*, May 19, 1934, 2

64 Étienne Gilson, "Le système et l'esprit," *Politique* 4, no. 27 (October 1947): 637–77.

65 Étienne Gilson, "Les terreurs de l'an deux mille," *Revue de l'Université d'Ottawa* 19 (1949): 67–81.

66 *Le Temps*, August 15, 1922, 3.

tragic. A redoubled effort is necessary. The French soup kitchens function splendidly at Odessa and Kherson. But it is absolutely necessary to provide each of them with bathrooms and showers and sleeping space, without which the children saved from famine will die of cold and epidemics. I will provide an exact picture of the situation. Gilson.'"[67]

Upon his return, Gilson published a long, detailed ten-page description in the *Revue de la Croix-Rouge*, where he recalled the conversations he had had and gave his impressions of the trip:

> From the moment of entry into Ukraine it is impossible not to be painfully struck by the pathetic situation of the little children. Despite considerable efforts by the Ukrainian government and an incredible increase of asylums created to take in orphans and abandoned children, there is no railroad station of any importance or railroad junction where one does not find unfortunates whose life is exactly similar to that of lost dogs in our country. The situation is explained by the tragic fate of Ukraine during the course of recent years. Not only was it pummeled during the war years, but it has also borne the greatest burden of the civil war. The devastation there has been still deeper and harsher than elsewhere.[68] The conclusion of Gilson's report was blunt: it was absolutely urgent to assist the children. With Painlevé and Paul-Boncour, he attempted to organize several meetings at the Sorbonne to alert the national media and raise funds for starving children. If we believe his declaration in 1934, there was no real success.[69]

On the level of politico-religious analysis, like Lutheranism in Germany, the Russian example showed Gilson the danger of placing the Church too close to the throne: "When the Russian empire was demolished after the war, the power of the czar was entirely destroyed and at the same time the Russian Church was destroyed as a necessary consequence. That Church, because of its very structure and organization, is now without a head."[70] As for communism, Gilson concluded his 1933 course emphasizing that:

67 *Le Temps*, September 11, 1922, 2.

68 Étienne Gilson, "Enquête sur la situation actuelle des enfants en Ukraine et dans les régions de la Volga: Enquête pour le Comité français de secours aux enfants, 15 août–15 septembre 1922," *Revue de la Croix-Rouge*, October 1922.

69 Étienne Gilson, "Intermède soviétique," *Sept*, May 19, 1934: "When I returned, I quickly realized that no one wanted to listen to me."

70 Étienne Gilson, "Christian Social Philosophy," lecture on Solovyov, 5, SMCA; in *Oeuvres complètes*, 1, 253.

> Communism is a kind of inverted universalism. Communism is really and truly anti-Christ. For Christ is truly spiritual life itself. Communism is the idealization of material life, but I say that it is an inverted universalism, because it is a universalism of matter instead of being a universality of spirit—it is a universal submission of all things to the universally material necessities—the slavery of all men to matter, which is the direct antithesis of universal and spiritual freedom.[71]

For that set of reasons, to Gilson the U.S.S.R. had become the "kingdom of the Antichrist." "Russia attempted to organize all of society on a purely materialistic basis."[72] His position was fixed. During his brief stay in the Palais du Luxembourg, Gilson dueled with the communist members on the issue of free schools in the nationalized coal mines in Aquitaine, the Loire, and the Cévennes. The communist group, headed by Alphonse Bouloux, presented a motion to abolish the private schools that the MPR group intended to defend.[73] We also find expressions of Gilson's anti-communism all during the Cold War, when he rigorously opposed any political blurring of Catholics and communists.

> What the Church forbids Catholics, and has the right to do, because they appeal to her, is not "sovietism," but "Marxism." That is to say, less a political regime than an ideology, one of whose principal foundations is atheism. Without betraying itself or simulating this betrayal to deceive others, every Marxist regime starts from atheism as a principle and tends to it as an end. Forbidding adhesion to Marxism is not a political act. Therefore, it could not in any way reduce the political freedom of the faithful, which remains in its totality insofar as it does not attempt to be used outside of its peculiar realm and legislate on the subject of religion. These principles are fairly simple, but the particular problems that their application entails are, by contrast, so complex that a general solution cannot be proposed. Leaving to the virtue of prudence the care of resolving the problems one by one,

71 Étienne Gilson, "Christian Social Philosophy," lecture on Germany, 3, SMCA; in *Oeuvres complètes*, 1:257.

72 Étienne Gilson, "Christian Social Philosophy," lecture on Solovyov, 5, SMCA; in *Oeuvres complètes*, 1:253.

73 Étienne Gilson, "Rapport fait au nom de la commisssion de l'Éducation nationale tendant à inviter le Governement à prendre d'urgence les mesures nécessaires pour conserver ou restituer à leur usage normal d'écoles publiques laïques les bâtiments scolaires acquis régulièrement," Conseil de la République, 1re législature, annexe no. 902, séance du 17 decembre [Report submitted on behalf of the National Education Committee to take necessary measures to preserve or restore duly acquired school buildings of secular public schools to their normal use", Council of the Republic, First Legislative Term, appendix, number 902, session on December 17, 1947], 692–93.

> according to the particular factors that define them, it remains possible to direct our reflection toward areas where it is foreseeable that the problems will be posed.[74]

In 1961, Gilson again denounced:

> . . . the immense undertaking of world domination carried out today by Moscow, [which] reveals its character, is not at all internationalist but profoundly nationalist. . . . On the largest scale, but in exactly the same spirit, the same undertaking begins again. Just as Napoleon once undertook to Frenchify Europe in the name of freedom, as Hitler lately undertook to Germanize Europe in the name of racial rights, so also the Muscovite state today tries to Russify Europe, and if possible the entire earth including its satellite, in the name of Its Majesty the Working Class. The phenomenon is not new. The same nationalism is its cause, except that the idealist pretext, with which the undertaking is adorned each time, has just changed its name once more.[75]

ON FRENCH NATIONALISMS

Gilson has no more liking for any of the sprouts of the various French right-wing movements than for German National Socialism or Russian National Communism. He was not a Bonapartist, a monarchist, a Barrésian,[76] a Maurrasian,[77] or a colonialist. "First of all it is necessary that we undergo amputation, or that we crumble. Between greatness and smallness, catastrophe is inevitable for us."[78] "I am haunted by the fear of a bloodbath in

74 Étienne Gilson, "Le catholique et la politique," *Culture catholique. Présence de la Pensée chrétienne* (Paris, La Colombe), no. 1, June 1949, 119–28.

75 Étienne Gilson, "L'unité spirituelle de l'Europe du Moyen Âge à l'heure actuelle," in *L'unification européene: Realité et problèmes; Atti del V Covegno di cultura europeana* (Bolzano, 1961), 23.

76 Gilson opposed the visit of Barrès to the University of Strasbourg in 1920. See the letter from Étienne Gilson to Léon Brunschvicg, November 5, 1920, IMEC: "It is troublesome that the year begins with the unfortunate Barrès, against whom I protested in vain." See also *Aspects de la France*, February 9, 1951, 1, which thirty years later made the reproach: "Gilson was the only person to oppose Barrès's course on the 'Genie of the Rhine.'"

77 Gilson opposed Maurras in the name of St. Thomas Aquinas. See *The Philosopher and Theology*, 59: "It is enough to open the *Summa Theologiae* at the right place to know that this [that Charles Maurras and St. Thomas Aquinas agreed on the notion of 'the best possible political regime' is not true." Gilson's positions were published in the magazine *Sept*.

78 On this point, which was hardly developed by Gilson, see his letter to Henri Gouhier, October 6, 1934: "Like you, I would like France to become a Spain. But, alas, we are an empire, the second

Algeria."[79] Gilson was no longer a de Gaulle partisan of strict observance. Pasteur Vallery-Radot reproached him for that in February 1951 in *Carrefour*. Gilson defined himself as a liberal republican, attached to social democracy and *libertas academica* (torn down by the "dictatorial and totalitarian character" of "Bonapartist Caesaropapism")[80] and to the inclusion of France in a transnational history, with a keen sense of the universal.

Gilson wrote many elegant public statements between 1934–1935 and 1949–1950 against Charles Maurras and Action Française.[81] His silence was noted in 1926–1927 at the moment of the formal condemnations of Action Française by Pope Pius XI, when Gilson was wending his way between two continents and did not yet possess the academic freedom he achieved upon his election to the Collège de France. Gilson's refutation of "politics first" was clear and distinct. For Gilson the national stage had no relevance to the solution of the great social, economic, and *a fortiori* religious questions. In 1933, Gilson stressed to his Canadian students the paradox of those "pagans" who intended to utilize the Church for political goals:

> Take for example the Action Française. These men will keep the Church even though they are at heart pagans. The State cannot live without the Church and the reason is precisely that they cannot overlook the fact that France as well as Germany and England were made by the Church. Consequently, they will stick to the Church as a political means of keeping their own country alive. It is a complete distortion of the proper historical truth, because the Catholic Church cannot help France unless the Church

---

largest in the world, and our body is too large." See likewise the report presented by Gilson to the Counseil de la République at the July 30, 1947, session: "aiming to encourage the government to create courses on overseas law at the metropolitan faculties of law." "The more methods of conquest are obliterated by the organization of peaceful cooperation for the common good, the more it becomes necessary to study objectively and sympathetically the social and juridical customs of the peoples who henceforth are part of the union. It is easy to anticipate that in the face of such diversity of customs and traditions with which the very survival of certain ethnic groups is directly involved, certain legal arrangements will be necessary."

79 Letter from Étienne Gilson to Jacques Maritain, July 4, 1991, *Correspondance Maritain-Gilson*, 211.

80 Étienne Gilson, "L'État, l'Université et les universités," *Politique*, no. 5 (September–October 1948): 674–77. For Gilson, the imperial university is only an enterprise in "university totalitarianism."

81 Étienne Gilson, "Christian Social Philosophy," fourth lecture, Autumn 1933, SMCA; in *Oeuvres complètes*, 1:241; "Par-delà le Sillon et l'Action Française," *Sept*, no. 69, June 21, 1935, 4; "Action politique et action catholique," *Sept*, no. 70, June 28, 1935, 4; "En marge de l'Action Française," *Sept*, no. 71, July 5, 1935, 4; "1940–1950," *Le Monde*, January 14, 1950, 1; "La plaie," *Le Monde*, January 21, 1950, 1–3; "La plainte," *Le Monde*, January 25, 1950, 6.

> is actually the Catholic Church and is an entity which in no way can be subordinated to the French State.[82]

Again, in an article that appeared in *Sept* in June 1935:

> If Charles Maurras does not manage to convince us, it is not for lack of skill on his part, nor for lack of compelling rigor in his reasoning. It is simply that he evades the problem from the beginning of his premises. The end, he says with St. Thomas and common sense, is prior in the order of intention but posterior in the order of execution. Therefore, precisely because politics is *for* religion, it goes before religion "as the means to reach an end is utilized before reaching that end. " Nothing is more correct than this principle, and we would be in agreement about the consequences drawn, if the means and the end that are proposed to us were of the same order. The whole problem is precisely to know whether, very far from being the means of the religious person, politics does not suppose the religious person in order to be itself what it ought to be. That is to say, in order that it, politics, may function as a means. Because it envisages a transcendent end, politics requires the help and direction of higher means which this end alone can put at its disposal. In a word, the issue is to discover whether we will make politics the means of the religious person, without religion itself preceding politics for us, not only in intention, but at each moment of execution.[83]

During World War II, Gilson kept as far away as possible from Henri Massis, who wanted to publish a text by Gilson in *Revue universelle*:

> You have certainly seen that I am horrified by compromises. I make an effort to keep myself completely away from anything that has the slightest relation to Action Française, above all at this moment. The movement's leaders are certainly interested or at least may be interested in giving the impression that certain people adhere to their movement. They are far from having my support and even farther than ever at the national level.[84]

The passage in *The Philosopher and Theology* where Gilson labels Maurrasism "doctrinal teratology" is equally well known: "Posterity will have more leisure than we have, and the future will see things from a distance that is lacking to us. Those who are curious about doctrinal teratology will enjoy unraveling

82 Étienne Gilson, "Christian Social Philosophy," fourth lecture, 3, SMCA; in *Oeuvres complètes*, 1:241.

83 Étienne Gilson, "Action politique et action catholique?," *Sept*, number 70, June 28, 1935, 4.

84 Letter from Étienne Gilson to Fr. Irénée, December 18, 1942, APQV.

the intricacies of such an alliance [between Maurras and St. Thomas]."[85] For Gilson, Maurrasism is nothing but a sheep with five legs, a monster in the biological sense. Maurras, "dripping sophisms and bad faith, running over with hatred and unscrupulously using violence through intermediaries,"[86] is a student who has not understood—or not wanted to understand, St. Thomas Aquinas's lessons on political philosophy. In 1967, Gilson again spoke to Jean de Fabrègues, who had been close to Maurras in his youth:

> I have greatly suffered from the hatred with which Maurras and his friends have sought and obtained the condemnation of Fr. Laberthonnière, Le Roy, and others. I all but left the Church when I saw Christians, priests, ready to die for their faith, if it were necessary, morally and religiously tortured at the urging of men, all of whose action was inspired by the pagan State's "politics first." That Rome seemed to let itself be directed by the leaders of a purely (or essentially) political maneuver was an unbearable scandal.[87]

The testimonies to Gilson's "intellectual resistance" during World War II came from different sectors. The mere fact of having worked with Jean Giraudoux and Jean Marx at the Commissariat Géneral d'Information in 1939 automatically placed him in the opposition. In a private letter in September 1943, Gilson commented with his usual humor about a box of Vichy candies a former student had sent him: "So something good can come from Vichy."[88] More seriously, Maurice Halbwachs recounted the conversation he had with Gilson in October 1942 and emphasized his "very resistant" commitment: "The general situation is discussed. He is very bitter. Catholics are persecuted in the countryside, the instigators continue. . . . And that happens under Pétain! I answered that, on the contrary, there seemed to be a rapprochement against the common enemy. He doesn't believe it. He makes fun of *Bonnardi* [Abel Bonnard (1883–1968), Minister of Education from April 1942 until August 1944]. Very resistant, he lets loose against the youth camps. He has great confidence in America."[89] In his private correspondence, Gilson was very critical of Pétainist bishops and theologians: "We

85 Étienne Gilson, *The Philosopher and Theology*, 58.

86 Letter from Étienne Gilson to Jean de Fabrègues, February 4, 1967, Archives Fabrègues, CHSP.

87 Letter from Étienne Gilson to Jean de Fabrègues, February 4, 1967, Archives Fabrègues, CHSP.

88 Letter from Étienne Gilson to Fr. André Combes, September 20, 1943, NAF 28257, BNF.

89 Maurice Halbwachs, "Ma campagne au Collège de France," *Revue d'histoire des sciences humaines* 1 (1999): 195.

expect of our priests that they give us and our children God, not philosophy or politics."[90] "I don't ask for our cardinals' heads, but I suggest that they be given a good scare, enough so that their successors remember once and for all not to meddle in politics, even to tell us who is the legitimate chief of state. If they get into trouble this time, I would not have a single word to excuse them, because my conscience does not suggest any."[91] In 1947, Gilson asked Maritain to draw the Holy See's attention to the delicate issue of bishops' involvement in temporal matters: "During the occupation, the bishops judged themselves qualified to tell us what was the legitimate government of France. Again, recently, in regard to the constitution, Bishop Saliège advised yes, while another bishop, equally respected by all, Bishop Théas, advised no. . . . A religious catastrophe is brewing in France that nothing can avoid."[92]

In spring 1947, Pasteur Vallery-Radot received Gilson under the cupola of the Académie française with these words: "We are convinced that a single concern guides you, the greatness of France. Your attitude during the occupation is a sure guarantee of that. In the course of dark years, you unceasingly, both in private conversation and in public, even in your courses, expressed your faith in the victory and refused any compromise with the enemy.[93]" The affirmation is significant and confirms Halbwachs's expression referring to Gilson, "very resistant." Indeed, in Gilson's courses at the Collège de France, he continually quoted and commented upon the English-speaking authors he knew, Whitehead, James, Perry, and Hocking. Gilson reported: "The mere sound of the English words was enough to make them mad. One could not do much, but what we could, we did.[94]

After Liberation, Gilson was awarded a certificate from the OCM [The Civil and Military Organization], the network of Resistance members of the CNR [National Resistance Council]. OCM president Maxime Blocq-Mascart (1864–1965) signed the certificate, recognizing that Gilson, "soldier without

90 Letter from Étienne Gilson to Fr. Irénée, June 29, 1942, APQV.

91 Letter from Étienne Gilson to Fr. André Combes, October 28, 1944, NAF 28257, BNF: "Beware of the pro-rector of the Catholic Institute of Paris who is irremediably Pétainist. And has Fr. Sertillanges lost a drop of blood, he who used to 'stamp' his foot when he was told that we were not beaten?"

92 Letter from Étienne Gilson to Jacques Maritain, January 12, 1947, in Gilson and Maritain, *Correspondance 1923–1971*, 157.

93 Pasteur Vallery-Radot, :Réponse au discours de réception d'Étienne Gilson," May 19, 1947, https://www.academie-francaise.fr/reponse-au-discours-de-reception-detienne-gilson.

94 Letter from Étienne Gilson to Ralph Barton Perry, May 5, 1945, Harvard Archives.

uniform" had "fought in the ranks of the OCM for the Liberation of the Homeland."[95] The OCM recruited in intellectual circles and Catholic networks, as is shown, for example, by the clandestine magazine published in October 1943.[96] Does that mean that Gilson served and fought actively in the Resistance network? Gilson said nothing of that. It is not the "medal of the Resistance." No documents from Blocq-Mascart's archives or writings clarify Gilson's degree of involvement with the Civil and Military Organization. However that may be, Gilson's spirit of resistance is confirmed by the facts. Immediately after the conflict, Gilson was not gentle with "traitors."

> Going to give his course, a professor at the Collège de France first passed in front of the Lycée Saint-Louis, where the Field Marshal's guards, submachine guns under their arms, forbid French youths from upsetting the German order. Fifty meters further on, at the bookstore of the Left Bank, he would see Brasillach in person signing his last book with prestige and profit for the enjoyment of German officers and their collaborators. Ten minutes later entering his lecture hall, the same professor looked for the faces of resistance that he knew, who had disappeared, this time to be deported, tortured, and shot by those whose hands Brasillach was clasping at the same time. There are regrets that justice itself forbids judges to feel.[97]

The controversy was bitter, as three articles from January 1950 show, in which Gilson had to reply to the "pile of insults" "before his eyes, which go from the most refined to the crudest."[98] The most developed document on Pétain was the draft of an article addressed to Canadian readers and written at an unknown date, probably the end of 1944. The title was unequivocal: "France against Pétain," and described the direct opposition (a bit simplistic in truth) between the people of France, who had not lost hope for victory (Gilson mentioned the inhabitants of Vermonton, his village in Burgundy,

95 Document published in *The Étienne Gilson Collection* (Toronto: PIMS, n.d.), 14. On the Civil and Military Organization, see the article by Guillaume Piketty, "Bouquins," in *Dictionnaire de la France Libre* (Paris: Robert Laffont, 2010), 1096–98. The author indicates 65,000 members of the Resistance network in summer 1943. See also the classic work by Arthur Calmette, *L'OCM. Organisation civile et militaire: Histoire d'un mouvement de résistance de 1940 à 1946* (Paris: PUF, 1961).

96 OCM, "Chronique de la Résistance," section 2, "Les catholiques et la Résistance," *Les Cahiers: Études pour une révolution française* 4, October 1943, xix–xxx. Available online at gallica.bnf.fr.

97 Étienne Gilson, "1940–1950," *Le Monde*, January 14, 1950: "Notre conscience de 1950 nos presse de grâcier, celle de 1941 nous interdit d'absoudre. [Our sense of duty in 1950 pushes us to pardon; our sense of duty in 1941 forbids it.]"

98 Étienne Gilson, "La plaie," "La plainte," "L'amnistie." *Le Monde*, January 21 and 25, 1950.

who suggested to the members of the SS that they should learn to swim to reach England) and Marshal Pétain, the paradigmatic traitor, who had yielded to the "mortal temptation of despair."

> Pétain only knew the language of despair. . . . That a French field marshal could hand over to the enemy an army that was beaten but of which great portions could have been saved, could immobilize an intact fleet and break his sworn oath, all that seemed so extraordinary that for a long time some Machiavellian plan was sought behind what was apparently incomprehensible, one subtly disguised but whose meaning would appear some day. Pétain is shrewd, say those who still want to defend him. He seems to cooperate with Hitler, but that is to win time and re-form the army of Africa, which will enter into action when the moment comes. . . . After Montoire, after Pétain's public and solemn endorsement of Laval's policy, no one can be deceived any longer. No ambiguity is possible this time. According to Pétain, France was so completely and definitively defeated that nothing remained for her but to work for her conqueror, to prepare the advent of that new Europe whose master would be Hitler, to subscribe to the expressions of national socialist orthodoxy and, repudiating ten centuries of Christian civilization, to fight for an ideal that horrified her. Pétain simply accepted, as the only good we could hope for, our incorporation into a Europe directed by the old Prussian ideal. That was to despair of France. When it became clear that such was Pétain's goal, the last hesitation disappeared. From that point, there was a complete break between him and the people he still expected to lead.
>
> A simple error on his part, it might be said. Not a simple error but a crime, and all the more irreparable, since it is despair, the sin of Judas. Courage is needed to say so, and we certainly do not say it with a light heart, but we also ask that an effort be made to understand it, if at least we want to understand the attitude of the immense majority of the French toward the person who calls himself their leader. If we have forgotten the definition of despair, let our old theologians remind us of it. To despair, Thomas Aquinas said, is not only to lack hope, it is to distance oneself from what ought to be one's hope, because it is deemed impossible to achieve. This is exactly what Pétain has done, and we do not reproach him for any other crime, but that is enough to condemn him. In the past four years, he has done everything, in word and deed to persuade the French of the impossibility of a liberation of France, when they obstinately believed it still possible. These were four years of cooperation with the looting of the country, the deportation of its workers, the expropriation of its peasants and the enlistment of its soldiers to the benefit of an enemy whose ultimate victory, by a kind of

> incredible madness, he wishes to ensure. This is what Pétain has done. He has wallowed in the defeat of France so much that after having proclaimed it to the world as a fact, since he began to fear that the defeat was not total, he has worked with all his might to accomplish it. Sometimes it is asked whether Pétain has betrayed France. Yes, like all who despair, he is a traitor to hope.... That is his crime, and the crime against one's country is nothing but treason. If a French court is to be convened some day to judge him, may God not will it, no other verdict will be possible.[99]

Gilson's attitude toward General de Gaulle and Gaullism was both friendly, developing, and nuanced. Gilson esteemed the man of 1940 and that of 1958, the hero of the Resistance and the founder of the Fifth Republic, but decidedly less the party leader after the Liberation. On Christmas day, 1940, Gilson wrote cryptically: "The problem of cold is frightful. Thank God *nescio quid luminis* is perceptible, which permits hope through the pain that still awaits us."[100] In November 1944, he wrote to a Canadian friend: "I have always been openly for de Gaulle and against the shameful armistice and against the not less shameful Pétain."[101] In 1970, Gilson told General de Gaulle of his feelings in June 1940: "Reception of the first volume of your collected speeches has touched me more deeply than I can say, and I thank you with all my heart. The book's design is impeccable in every way. I immediately opened the volume to June 18. I re-read what I distinctly remembered having heard and that corresponded exactly to my own expectation and that of millions of Frenchmen. Re-reading your words I re-encountered the thrill that I had felt in listening to them. Your confidence then, as you took charge of France, still seems to me admirable and authentically great, in the sense in which greatness was once Roman."[102]

However, in 1946, Gilson supported the constitution that de Gaulle did not want: "I think that we should vote 'yes' for the Constitution against General de Gaulle's advice, and I have organized meetings in the country in favor

99 Étienne Gilson, "La France contre Pétain," 5 pages, late 1944, Archives Vrin. In the first lines of the document, Gilson writes: "Finally, the first letters from Canada after these five years of separation and mortal anguish. They arrive, and the question I knew was inevitable comes up: What do you think about Pétain?" Those first letters arrived in October–November 1944.

100 Letter from Étienne Gilson to Monsignor André Combes, December 25, 1940, BNF 28 257.

101 Letter from Étienne Gilson to Madeleine Thibaudeau, November 3; Shook, *Étienne Gilson*, 251.

102 Letter from Étienne Gilson to General de Gaulle, May 5, 1970, AG 5(1)/1177, AN.

of the MRP."[103] In 1947, the philosopher bluntly criticized "the mystique of the leader" in MRP Christian-Democratic circles in time of peace, and Gaullist mystification, an illusion "between prestige and virtue" and a "confusion" between what is required in time of war and what the future makes desirable in times of peace:

> The most noble, the greatest leader, whose personal stature is blended for us with the greatness of France, poses a very different problem for our choice. In times of serious national crisis, the "appeal to the soldier" naturally presents itself as the quickest and only efficacious remedy. To unite every Frenchman behind a guide who embodies the will of France itself, above all if this leader has many claims to our trust and our gratitude—what could be more wise?
>
> Nothing, certainly, provided that the leader himself knows clearly how directing an army differs from directing a people. Those to whom he attends have the duty to listen to his voice, but also to weigh his purposes before committing themselves to follow him. They also have the right to tell him their doubts and to ask him for clarification. Because for him, it is a question of adapting a way of preparing and directing war, or a people in time of war, to the organization of a country in the period between wars that nowadays adorns itself with the name of peace. There is only one way for a people to say no to the enemy. There are several possible ways to say yes to the future....
>
> That is why the methods and the spirit that inspire the leader should not be the same when the issue is to guarantee the unity of the people in national resistance during wartime or its union in the activities of peace. "It is not a question of virtue," General de Gaulle answers us, "and evangelical perfection does not lead to an empire. The man of action is not conceivable without a strong dose of egoism, pride, hardness, and guile." To be sure, but the point is first to discover whether the people are for the leader's empire or the leader's empire is only there for the people. In the first case, all the Machiavellieanism in the world will not be too much. In the second case, let us not hesitate to affirm that the evangelical perfection of a good servant of the country retains some merit. There are reasons why this exaltation of the leader insists so much on the necessity of "prestige." In other times people knew exactly what this word meant. It simply means "delusion."[104]

103 Letter from Étienne Gilson to Anton Pegis, October 9, 1946; Shook, *Étienne Gilson*, 272.
104 Étienne Gilson, *Notre démocratie*.

In 1951, in the middle of the Gilson Affair, the avid Gaullist Pasteur Valery-Radot, without specifying further, reproached the philosopher for having "spoken badly" of the General: "A party made the mistake of pushing Gilson into politics. He was created to concern himself with St. Thomas and St. Augustine. Three years ago, in my presence, he spoke badly of de Gaulle. An evil sign that bodes no good."[105]

After the inception of the Fifth Republic, a rapprochement between the two men was observable. De Gaulle sent volume III of his memoirs to Gilson, who replied assuring de Gaulle of his "admiration" and "unqualified approval of the courage and admirable lucidity thanks to which [the President] is in the process of saving our country."[106] De Gaulle visited Toronto in April 1960 and met Gilson, who had been invited to the official dinner. Shortly thereafter, he wrote Gilson a touching note. "My dear teacher, your book *Le Philosophe et la théologie* is a very beautiful work. You reach the peaks of thought.... Allow me to say that I was happy to meet you the other day in that Toronto where you shine."[107] Somewhat later, Gilson wrote to de Gaulle: "There are millions of Frenchmen in whose thoughts you are always present and who are grateful to you for having reconstructed for them a self-confident France that is respected abroad. This had not happened for a long time."[108]

In a 1964 letter to François Mauriac, Gilson was very explicit about the odd nature of his Gaullism:

> Thanks to you, I have just come to grips with the extraordinary man about whom I had stopped wondering. Like you I have lived with the myth of the man in London, suddenly, totally, without nuance or reservation. Then, involved in a political movement, the MRP, for the only time in my life, I watched him separate from his best troops. I voted for the constitution he did not want. I was completely mistaken about that, because he was right, as I saw only too clearly afterwards. I found in him then, and I still find, the defects that I detest most in any person, which he praised in his incredible *Homme de caractère*, the perfect portrait of a leader after the heart of St.

105 Pasteur Vallery-Radot, "L'Académie française devrait exclure M. Gilson!," interview by Pierre-Louis Berthaud, *Carrefour*, February 20, 1951, 1.

106 Letter from Étienne Gilson to Charles de Gaulle, November 18, 1959, AG 5(1)/1177, AN.

107 Letter from Charles de Gaulle to Étienne Gilson, May 23, 1960, SMCA, and replica at AG 5(1)/1177, AN.

108 Letter from Étienne Gilson to Charles de Gaulle, April 21, 1963, AG 5 (1)/1177, AN.

> Ignatius Loyola, the leader maker of leaders. His pride, scorn of others with this great *salegenoso* [partly illegible word] drips—that horrifies me as much as ever. However, I surrendered and acknowledged, I was overcome by his greatness. Nothing he does surprises me any longer. I accepted him as I accept Mont-Blanc, without argument. In any case he is a leader. He has never pardoned a desertion, nor forgotten a fidelity. May God preserve him for us, with his great projects for which men are always waiting—yesterday Algeria and Africa, today Germany and tomorrow France herself—but never ceasing to climb his old peak![109]

Gilson probably voted for General de Gaulle in 1965. In June 1968, amid the student riots, Gilson voted with conviction for the Gaullist candidate of his district.[110] "You very soon formed 'a certain idea of France.' The only thing you lacked was Frenchmen who were worthy of it," Gilson wrote to de Gaulle in May 1970.[111] After the death of Georges Pompidou in 1974, Gilson showed his admiration for the "unusual man" who was General de Gaulle's successor.[112]

The problem that haunted Gilson was not the nation but universal society. On what intellectual foundation can universal society be thought out, built, and made the most rational and just? A universal society founded on

109 Letter from Étienne Gilson to François Mauriac, November 2, 1964, Archives littéraires Jacques Doucet. —On the constitution of the Fourth Republic, see the letter from Étienne Gilson to Francisque Gay, January 4, 1956, Institut Marc Sangnier: "The moment I voted for the Constitution, I realized I was mistaken. De Gaulle was the one who was right. I know very well what a combination of fear of the person and juridico-political reasons influenced our decision then. Nevertheless, it was bad. We are a country without an executive, and therefore adrift."

110 Letter from Étienne Gilson to Madeleine Thibaudeau, June 17, 1968, SMCA: "The Gaullist candidate will be elected in the Vermenton district. But de Gaulle would like a massive (!!) vote in his favor and in this case all votes count. I will also be able to vote for Cécile, who delegated to me: two voices for the great Charles! The Americans hate him and are afraid of only one thing: to see him lose the election.

111 Letter from Étienne Gilson to Charles de Gaulle, May 5, 1970, AG 5(1)/1177, AN: "I have found once more the same style in the speeches I have begun to re-read, the same security, the same power, the same *imperatoria brevitas*. I have also admired a certain art of abstract insult and scorn that you know how to do without lowering yourself, one that seems to me all your own. Alas, the speech makes one recall all the innumerable occasions where the country you saved failed you. You formed 'a certain idea of France' very early. The only thing you lacked was Frenchmen worthy of it."

112 Letter of Étienne Gilson to Madeleine Thibaudeau, April 3, 1974, SMCA: "Why spare an old fellow like me and take away an unusual man whom the country needs so much? *Fiat voluntas tua*."

the nation, on historical materialism, the concept of class, or full fledged secularism was a contradiction in terms for him. The Bolshevik revolution was only the beginning of a long civil war, and communism itself was only a by-product of secularization.

> After all, are not socialism and communism products of the decomposition of the de-Christianized society in which we are now living? That is, if we accept the possibility of a purely temporal society, of a society that has no relation whatever to any spiritual order, and still less submitted to a spiritual order—accepting that ideal as a possible means of providing men with the necessities of life in the temporal order and nothing else, then I say I do not see how such a society can live for any length of time without developing necessarily such historical effects such as socialism and communism, or if we choose to adopt the abstract name, Marxism.[113]

For Gilson, to grant primacy to reason and the spiritual order was the surest foundation for universal society, which alone would be able to bring peace. In the language of the period, for Gilson, that meant to "build Christendom."

RE-THINKING UNITY AFTER THE WAR: UNIVERSAL CHRISTENDOM

In Gilson's winter 1933 course at Toronto, on Christian Social Philosophy, he wrote that, in his view, "The Prussian State is the normal conclusion of every kind of German dialectic. It is just as native to the German mind as the idea of a universal Christendom is to my mind."[114] What exactly did Gilson mean by a universal Christendom that is native to his mind? It is easy to conceive that he referred to a long French insistence from the Enlightenment up to Auguste Comte on "thinking universally," and held that this insistence is the heir of an older Catholic pattern of things that Gilson interpreted as the "invincible Catholicity of our tradition."[115] By contrast, it is not so simple to establish that a concept of "universal Christendom" was common or peculiar to contemporary French Catholics. From Gallicanism to the description of

113 Étienne Gilson, "Christian Social Philosophy," final lecture, 46, SMCA; in *Oeuvres complètes*, 1:279.

114 Étienne Gilson, "Christian Social Philosophy," lecture on Germany, 31, SMCA; in *Oeuvres complètes*, 1:258.

115 Étienne Gilson, "La tradition française et la chrétienté," *Vigile*, no. 1 (1931): 86.

France as the "older daughter of the Church," French Catholicism in general was not free from a form of spiritual provincialism. According to the period, it appeared as the defense of the prerogatives of the French church within the universal Church, or as the emphasis on the French language in missions because Catholicism was considered an element of national history, or else by a certain exceptionalist view of French Catholic society. Gilson denounced this last characteristic when he criticized the "nationalization of the religious."[116] Gilson was rather original in his line of interpretation of "universal Christendom," reinforcing medieval studies with a graft of universality, doubtless characteristic of Roman Catholicism, but also typical of French philosophical ideals.

The concept of Christendom, a sensitive issue, certainly requires that one begin by eliminating certain misunderstandings. To interpret Gilson's position, we must detach ourselves from a post-Vatican II reading of "Christendom." Up to the 1950s, even in Mounier, who appealed to a "new Christendom" against the moribund "feudal and bourgeois Christendom," the term had connotations of openness.[117] A commonplace since Péguy—"May Christendom continue!"—Christendom was called upon by authors like Paul Vignaux, for whom the Jeunesse Étudiante Chrétienne had the mission of Christendom.[118] Likewise, we find that Monsignor Bruno de Solages intended "to rebuild Christendom." Jacques Maritain in *Humanisme intégrale* (1936) [*Integral Humanism* (1968)], and Fr. Marie-Dominique Chenu developed the theme of "profane Christendom" that is no longer "sacral." Alphonse Dupront has pertinently shown that democracy has ended up becoming "the

116 Étienne Gilson, "L'esprit de chrétienté," *La Vie intellectuelle*, February 1945, 25.

117 Emmanuel Mounier, *Feu de la Chrétienté* (Paris: Seuil, 1951), 25–26: "An error or a heresy can be refuted, condemned. A drama cannot be refuted, and Christendom in its superficial peace is confronted today by the most formidable drama in which it has been yet involved. Christendom is not menaced by heresy. It no longer creates sufficient passion for that. It is threatened by a kind of silent apostasy, produced by the surrounding indifference and by its own distraction. The signs are unmistakable: death is near. Not the death of Christianity but the death of western feudal and bourgeois Christendom. A new Christendom will be born tomorrow or the day after, from new social strata and new non-European buds. Still, it is necessary that we not suffocate it with the cadaver of the other Christendom."

118 See Jean Lecuir, "*De philosophia franciscana*, L'esprit franciscain de Paul Vignaux (1920–1930)," in Boulnois, *Paul Vignaux: Citoyen et philosophe*. Vignaux is the symbol of an intellectual generation. He adopts Christendom as the spirit of the JEC—Jeunesse Étudiante Chrétienne [Catholic Student Youth]—in 1929: "Faith impels us to find it natural to win all society for Christ, to remake civilization into Christendom."

secular name for the ideal of Christendom" in the twentieth century.[119] In these authors, the theme of Christendom certainly implies historical continuity, but even more the reconstruction of a Christian cultural substratum in the recent sense that the term "reconstruction" might assume after World War I, without reference to a single, neo-medieval model: "There is only one Church. There can be Christian civilizations, different Christendoms," noted Maritain in 1933.[120]

In Gilson's writings, the definition of Christendom is rather elusive. "What is Christendom? If we do not ask, we know it, because none of us fail to talk about it. But if we wonder about it, we are quite unable to define it."[121] Gilson pointed out the gaps in theory: "We still lack a theology of Christendom."[122] For Gilson, Christendom was the "Republic of the faithful" in the sense of Roger Bacon, the "doctor of Christendom."[123] It "is the temporal replica of the mystical body of the Church."[124] Christendom is situated at the meeting point and also the point of "subordination between the temporal and the spiritual." "In its essence, it is temporal, because it is essentially composed of a certain number of peoples. But at the same time, it is a temporal order that is subordinated to spiritual ends; it is aware of this subordination and accepts it."[125] Gilson was completely conscious of secularization and of the great impact of secular ideologies upon the masses, as well as of "the decadence of the spirit of Christendom."[126] In 1923, he published a "religious

119 Alphonse Dupront, *Le mythe de croisade* (Paris: Gallimard, NRF, 1997), 1218.

120 Jacques Maritain, *Du régime temporal et la liberté*, in *Oeuvres complètes*, 5:407. In this passage Maritain refers to reflections that Gilson developed in the 1931 *Vigile* article.

121 Étienne Gilson, "Les intellectuels dans la Chrétienté," lecture given April 12, 1947, at Palazetto Venezia, Rome; published in *Travaux et documents*, May-June 1947, 3–15; republished in *Les Intellectuels dans la Chrétienté* (Geneva: Pax Romana / Mouvement International des Intellectuels Catholiques, 1948), 159–78, at 161.

122 See, for example, Étienne Gilson, *The Metamorphoses of the City of God*, 66–67. Gilson often returns to the absence of a definition of Christendom. For instance, in "L'esprit de chrétienté," *La Vie intellectuelle*, February 1945, 18: "For centuries the term 'Christendom' has been used to designate something other than Christianity, but there does not seem to have been an effort to define a precise concept corresponding to 'Christendom.'" Or again in Étienne Gilson, *La Philosophie au Moyen Âge*, 2nd ed. (Paris: Payot, 1944), 257: "There is no known written work particularly devoted to grounding the concept of Christendom doctrinally."

123 Étienne Gilson, *La Philosophie au Moyen Âge*, 253; *Metamorphoses of the City of God*, 67.

124 Étienne Gilson, "La tradition française et la chrétienté," *Vigile*, no. 1 (1931): 57.

125 Étienne Gilson, "La tradition française et la chrétienté," 62.

126 Étienne Gilson, "L'esprit de chrétienté," *La Vie intellectuelle*, February 1945, 24.

balance sheet of the nineteenth century in France," and drew up an almost irrefutable report:

> To limit ourselves to France, it seems clear that the de-Christianization of the general population and of the bourgeoisie has taken place very rapidly. In certain areas of the countryside, the labor of evangelization would have to begin again as in a completely pagan country. There are no more priests; the churches are in ruins; and the name of God is only a linguistic inheritance, conserved in set phrases, values, or momentarily forgotten feelings.[127]

In his presentation of diplomas at the Collège de France, in 1931, Gilson defended history as an endeavor of "restoration" and of "restitution of spiritual riches that are ours and from whose definitive loss only history can spare us."[128] Again in 1945, Gilson denounced "the inorganic status" of Christendom following five years of war.[129] A papalist and a Guelph certainly, the person whom his friends labeled philosopher of Christendom in 1949,[130] he was lucid about it and had no nostalgic vision of reconstructing Christendom in a geographical-spatial, continental, inclusive, slightly totalitarian form, under the temporal *and* spiritual authority of the Supreme Pontiff.

The present study has attempted several times to clarify this theme of Christendom from the standpoint of intellectual history, from Chateaubriand to Alphonse Dupront,[131] and from Gilson's own viewpoint, notably through the analogy so often raised by Gilson himself with the monk Alcuin.[132] In retrospect, our sense is that these attempts failed because of an overly

127 Étienne Gilson, "Le bilan religieux du XIXe siècle français," *Foi et vie: Revue de quinzaine*, no. 21, December 16, 1923, 1198.

128 Étienne Gilson, "Présentation de titres au Collège de France," 1931, 2. [This comes from Gilson's talk, "Un enseignement des philosophies médiévales," reproduced in *Oeuvres complètes*, 1:165–68, see especially 166–67.]

129 Étienne Gilson, "L'esprit de chrétienté," *La Vie intellectuelle*, February 1945, 27, 34.

130 See the volume in his honor, *Étienne Gilson, Philosophe de la Chrétienté*, with contributions by Jacques Maritain, Bruno de Solages, Aimé Forest, Henri Gouhier, Henri-Irénée Marrou, Maurice de Gandillac, Paul Vignaux, Pierre Mesnard, M. Chastaing, Roger Verneaux, Louis-Bertrand Geiger (Paris: Cerf, 1949).

131 Florian Michel, "La chrétienté, nom commun à l'époque contemporaine," in *La chrétienté dans l'histoire: Une notion mouvante*, ed. Nicole Lemaitre (Paris: Parole et silence, 2014), 47–67.

132 Florian Michel, "Étienne Gilson, nouvel Alcuin d'une nouvelle Chrétienté?," *L'Amitié Charles Péguy* 143–44 (July–December 2013): 419–40. See also "Gilson fondateur," in *La pensée*

literary and insufficiently political approach. The curative dimension of the concept of Christendom was central for Gilson. Christendom is both a temporal goal—which Christians live in the "Republic"—but also an *ideological remedy* for the evils of the moment. Gilson's notion of Christendom was less dependent on Pius XI and Jacques Maritain, with whom, however he ended by agreeing in this area. Rather, it began in the trenches. Then it developed in Gilson's writings, starting in 1922 with the publication of *Philosophie au Môyen Âge* (Paris: Payot), and it was elaborated in the course of the years between the world wars, as a de-nationalizing and de-secularizing political counter-ideology in order to offer a "program" to Christians and to "men of good will": "The formula is simple, the program immense. Let us neglect the vast area of past Christendom, whose grandeur history obstinately works to reveal to us. Let us think only of present Christendom, whose reality shrouds us in every direction."[133]

Gilson's Christendom is at the same time a recharging of religious energy against anti-Christian ideologies, a transnational remedy for the period's nationalist evils, and a cultural project oriented toward peace—the Pax Romana that Gilson defends but that he extends to the Americans and Russians during the Cold War, without confounding Christendom with Europe.[134] As ecumenical,[135] Gilson's Christendom protests against the barriers of race and class,[136] against imperialisms, since Christendom cannot

catholique en Amérique du Nord: Réseaux intellectuels et échanges culturels entre l'Europe, le Canada et les États-Unis (années 1929–1960) (Paris: Desclée de Brouwer, 2010), 97–115.

133 Étienne Gilson, "L'esprit de chrétienté," *La Vie intellectuelle*, February 1945, 33.

134 Étienne Gilson, "L'unité spirituelle de l'Europe de Moyen Âge à l'heure actuelle," in *L'unification européenne: réalité et problèmes, Atti del V Convegno europeana* (Bolzano, 1961), 21–24.

135 Étienne Gilson, "L'esprit de chrétienté," *La Vie intellectuelle*, February 1945, 34–35: "How could we forget all our separated brethren? . . . Orthodox, Protestants, and Catholics are nevertheless united among themselves and distinguished from all other human beings by this remarkable singularity: all of them appeal to Christ, believe in his word, and profess to live by it. How could it be that they have nothing to say to each other, and that human beings who, gathered in different churches, are still inspired by the same gospel, would have no occasion to cooperate? The more the world that surrounds them becomes different from them, the more they resemble each other. Accordingly, it is foreseeable that in the future the areas will be continually multiplied from which the shared principles by which they live will not allow them to escape."

136 Étienne Gilson, "L'esprit de chrétienté," *La Vie intellectuelle*, February 1945, 20: "Let us enter a church in Charlottesville at mass time. I will not say that whites and people of color do not tend to sit in groups, but that is surely by habit, because the groups are mixed, and it is obvious that no benches are specially reserved for whites. Above all, there is a moment during mass in which even the memory of the social prohibition that separates them seems to be erased: it is the moment of communion. United in the same faith, all go together to kneel side by side at the table of the same Father, whose children they all are alike. Will I confess that I expected my Church be enclosed within the "framework of an empire,"[137] and against nationalisms, the soil of totalitarianisms.[138] For Gilson, the "transnational" dimension was a Christian sign. At the level of principle, *Unam Sanctam* is at once pre-national in the sense in which the Church is prior to national structures. meta-national, and "de-national" (as our Academician explains somewhat optimistically with a neologism created for the occasion). According to him, "one of the most notable effects produced by Christianity has been denationalization."[139] Gilson regards culture as the paradigmatic "transnational" place, in the sense in which the goal of all culture "passes beyond the national order," "transcends this nation's common good."[140]

The correspondence of Gilson and Xavier Léon, editor of the *Revue de métaphysique et de morale*, is a good reference point to situate the origin of the theme of Christendom. The letter Gilson sent Léon in April 1921 is a road map for a whole section of his work in the thirty years ahead and in particular seems to serve as the plan for the article that appeared in *Vigile* in 1931. Gilson wrote:

> I have gone away for a bit during vacation, because I needed a little rest. I came back in perfect form and ready to start work again. You know that if I work up a philosophical article, it will be for you. I am thinking about an essay in the history of ideas, which will present in broad strokes the French transformations of the idea of humanity. There are three stages. Middle Ages: humanity equals Christendom. Union of all human beings in a body whose solidarity is guaranteed by the adoption of a common

there? It was certainly she. I recognized her in this sign, that *everywhere the love of God breaks the barriers of races and classes, there also is Christendom*."

137 Étienne Gilson, "La tradition française et la chrétienté," *Vigile*, no. 1 (1931): 60.

138 Étienne Gilson, "L'esprit de chrétienté," *La Vie intellectuelle*, February 1945, 24: "Insofar as European nations have recognized the existence of this wider spiritual society above them, which is the Church, and the legitimacy of its peculiar goals, they avoided the mortal danger that has always threatened them afterward, of national totalitarianism, to which all of them are exposed and which finally has just ruined several of them."

139 Étienne Gilson, *The Metamorphoses of the City of God*, 18.

140 Étienne Gilson, "L'esprit de chrétienté," *La Vie intellectuelle*, February 1945, 18–36: "Indeed the point is to find out whether all human ends are included in those of the nation, or whether to the contrary, there exist ends of human beings that transcend the nation's common good as such. It cannot be doubted that there are such ends, and the fact that they are pursued in and by the nation does not diminish their transcendence in any way. That a nation experiences the need to promote the development of the arts and sciences does not keep art and science from essentially belonging to an order that transcends that of the nation."

> doctrine. Foundation equals faith. Second stage: Italian Renaissance. The idea of the Church is retained, but in place of dogma, which has shown itself to be incapable of guaranteeing universal unity, there is an attempt to substitute philosophies. It is a Catholicism of reason that replaces a Catholicism of faith. Campanella, Leibniz. Why does this compromise fail to have a representative in France? Third stage: establishment of humanity, always by the acceptance of a common doctrine, but without a Church. Encyclopedists, French Revolution, showing the origins of the movement in Montaigne and Descartes. Conclusion: the meaning of Comte's reform; the significance of the idea of humanity as the ideal connection of human beings in the acceptance of the same truth. I believe more and more in the continuity of our development since the Middle Ages and in the successive transformations, but also in the persistence of our medieval religious ideal. If I can suitably put the study together, I will submit it to you.[141]

Besides the 1931 article, the course already mentioned in 1933 and *Métamorphoses de la Cité de Dieu* were in gestation. Subsequent letters revealed Gilson's hesitation and his ambitions. "I believe I could successfully complete during vacation the study I spoke to you about. I would like to call it *De l'unité de la pensée française*. The hard thing is not to turn it into a book, but I wonder if it is not always possible to say in thirty pages what might be said in three hundred."[142] After his appointment to the Sorbonne, Gilson again wrote that he would like "to devote his whole life to teach the French, *all* the French, the deep source of their moral unity."[143] In 1922, Gilson published *Philosophie au Moyen Âge*, where considerable space, notably the volume's closing pages, was devoted to the question of Christendom. The work was reviewed on the first page of *Le Temps*... in order to support France's political positions after World War I:

> At the end of the excellent book that Étienne Gilson has devoted to the philosophy in the Middle ages, which is to say to an intellectual movement whose epicenter was the University of Paris, he wrote: "It was in the thirteenth century at Paris and in the mother of European universities, that France, by imparting to the whole world the common truth that grounds and defines Christendom, was penetrated forever by the messianic dream of humanity, organized and bound by the purely intelligible bonds of one

141 Letter from Étienne Gilson to Xavier Léon, April 3, 1921, BIS.

142 Letter from Étienne Gilson to Xavier Léon, May 12, 1921, BIS.

143 Letter from Étienne Gilson to Xavier Léon, September 17, 1921, BIS.

> same truth. The University of Paris's old dream, which was first the Church's dream, still today inhabits every French brain: to think the truth for all humanity which is established under the same constraint that the acceptance of truth imposes on it." That is certainly our national tradition. It does not date from yesterday. The French have enough glory in their past so that one more victory does not go to their head. They remain enamored of an idea that reason will impose on humanity.[144]

Gilson, however, did not think he had treated the question as he wished. In a letter of November 30 to Xavier Léon, he proposed a presentation on "Christendom and Humanity" to the International Philosophy Congress, to be held at Harvard in autumn 1926, instead of a required topic that he initially rejected: "I do not know how such an absurd subject came to ensnare me. Believe me, I want nothing to do with it. Very probably it will be something like: "Christendom and Humanity: Historical solutions of the Problem." Since it is understood that I am speaking in the history section, "Christendom and Humanity" will be satisfactory."[145] However, the topic Gilson proposed did not satisfy the organizers of the International Congress, and Gilson rather quickly gave up the presentation he had just proposed: "I agreed to surrender and deal with the subject they designed especially for me. Since they chose the person and the issue, I felt I should not slip away from the topic. I value following the rules of the game. . . . This is not at all the question about which I had dreamed but instead, *The role of philosophy in the history of civilization*."[146]

In the second half of the 1920s, Gilson did not deal with the theme of Christendom. We must wait, on the one hand, for the invitation of Charles Du Bos on behalf of the magazine *Vigile* in the spring of 1930, which led to the publication of the article already indicated, "The French Tradition and Christendom," of 1931,[147] and on the other hand, for the autumn 1933 course in Toronto where Gilson greatly expanded on the theme defined in the April 1921 letter to Xavier Léon. Between 1921 and 1931–1933, the environment evolved perceptibly. The beginning of the papacy of Pius XI and notably the

144 "Le discours de M. Poincaré," editorial, *Le Temps*, Saturday, June 3, 1922, 1. Gilson's work is used to emphasize the truth of the position set out by Poincaré in Parliament.

145 Letter from Étienne Gilson to Xavier Léon, November 30, 1925, BIS.

146 Letter from Étienne Gilson to Xavier Léon, December 5, 1925, BIS.

147 See chapter 1, above. See also Étienne Gilson, "La tradition française et la chrétienté, *Vigile*, no. 1 (1931).

publication of the encyclical *Quas Primas* on Christ the King (1925) was a significant moment. Gilson greatly respected Pope Pius XI, and in 1936 he explained that he intended to "put his intelligence at the service of Christ the King." However, he never commented on or quoted *Quas Primas*. Gilson's Christendom did not seem to be connected to Pius XI's socio-political project based on the "royalty of Christ." Maritain, who, as we have seen, played the role of second reader of Gilson's articles in *Vigile*,[148] was present in Toronto in January-March 1933. At the time, he was preparing the composition of *Du régime temporel et de la liberté* (DDB, 1933), the first sketch of *Humanisme intégral*. Gilson's 1933 course is valuable in that it shows us a professor speaking very freely to his Toronto students about current events: "A united Christendom failed in the Middle Ages, that is, it was the ideal of the Middle Ages, but it was never carried into execution. Do you despair of seeing that ideal carried into execution in the twentieth century? It is my feeling that even at the present time this ideal is being carried into execution." Gilson took the example of the Lateran Agreements, an "ideal," he said, "which seemed to the people of that age as almost impossible. So that, what was impossible in the thirteenth century has become a reality in the twentieth."[149]

Gilson's publication and correspondence give evidence that he thought of himself as living in Christendom. In 1929, he wrote to Gouhier in that vein. "I returned this morning to Chicago after having preached the gospel of Robert Grosseteste in the cornfields of the Midwest, where they have never heard of him and will never hear about him again."[150] In 1945, he continued:

> Therefore, where have I known Christendom? First of all, the name conjures up in my memory a multitude of churches, great and small, that have received me and revived me, sometimes for an hour, sometimes for weeks or even months, when I was going from town to town like a wandering scholar of times past. It is impossible to name them all. . . . What is the name of that church in Chicago not far from the station on the right in the direction of Michigan Avenue? I no longer know. . . . Where were we? Not in America, nor in France, nor in any geographical point in the world. But we were all right there, because we were at home. We were in Christendom.[151]

148 See chapter 1, above

149 Étienne Gilson, "Christian Social Philosophy," final lecture, 53, SMCA; in *Oeuvres complètes*, 1:290.

150 Letter of Étienne Gilson to Henri Gouhier, November 24, 1929, Archives Gouhier.

151 Étienne Gilson, "L'esprit de chrétienté," *La Vie intellectuelle*, February 1945, 18–19.

After Chicago, Gilson evoked St. Agnes in New York, St. Basil in Toronto, St. Paul, near Harvard, Our Lady of Rio de Janeiro, and a chapel in Moscow where he went to collect his thoughts in 1922. The conclusion is that there exists "everywhere an immense spiritual society that knows no geographical barriers or political frontiers, and where the Christian always feels at home." A new public expression of this is found again in a letter from Gilson to Albert Béguin in 1951, composed in the context of the Gilson Affair, where he compares himself to Alcuin:

> The secret of my public life, if there is one, is found in the dedication of my book, *La Philosophie au Moyen Âge* [1944]. In the middle of the German occupation, I dedicated it to an Englishman, Alcuin, tutor of France. He is a hero on my scale, not a genius or even highly talented, but one who abandoned England at Charlemagne's invitation, because he saw at a glance the importance of the civilizing work he was asked to take on. In 1927, when two priests I did not know sought me out at Harvard University to offer me, in the name of the Church, an incomparably more modest task, but an analogous one, I thought that a French Catholic had no right to refuse. I accepted. I worked for more than twenty years to bring to America a part of that Christian civilization of the Middle Ages that France once inherited from Rome through Alcuin.[152]

In 1947, the Quebec Dominican Benoît Lacroix had already noted the analogy between Alcuin and Gilson.

> Gilson compares his vocation as intellectual missionary throughout the western and American world with that of the "itinerant teachers of the Middle Ages." I am ready to push the indiscretion to the point of identifying the itinerant with the monk Alcuin, who came to France from York in times of Charlemagne. This time York is Paris, and France is Canada. Thanks to the new Alcuin, the trees of Paradise continue to grow here with their fruit.[153]

The foundation of the Pontifical Institute of Mediaeval Studies of Toronto in 1929 gives meaning to the comparison between Alcuin and Gilson and allows an expansion of the concept of Christendom. In 1949, Maritain's preface to his *Étienne Gilson, Philosophe de la Chrétienté* explained its

152 Letter from Étienne Gilson to Albert Béguin, March 11, 1952, published in "Journal à plusieurs voix," *Ésprit*, 19, no. 178 (April 1951): 596.

153 Benoît Lacroix, "Un centre de savoir et culture," *Relations*, 1947, 317.

title. He wrote: "By employing the term *Christendom*, I think I have treated Étienne Gilson's great concern and nostalgia, in both the speculative and practical orders, for the great dream that stirs up his heart and for the great task of achieving the rich clarity that he brings to our time."[154] Upon reading those lines, Gilson immediately sent a letter telling Maritain how touched he was by the kindness and appropriateness of his evaluation: "Praise apart, you have infallibly discerned the virtues that I esteem and the great ideas that I would have liked to serve better than I have."[155] The preface moved Gilson most deeply, as he would reveal to Fr. Maydieu, the architect of a volume of tributes to Gilson.[156]

In 1931, as we have indicated, Gilson offered an article for *Vigile* entitled "La tradition française et la chrétienté."[157] In 1945, he wrote "L'esprit de chrétienté" for the Dominican magazine *La Vie intellectuelle*.[158] In 1947, in Rome during the Congress of Pax Romana, he gave a lecture on "Les intellectuels dans la chrétienté."[159] Not to be overlooked are the 1936 Harvard lecture *Medieval Universalism and its Present Value*,[160] *La Philosophie au Moyen Âge* (1922 and 1944),[161] and *Les Métamorphoses de la Cité de Dieu* (1952),[162] where the concept of Christendom, absent from the three titles, is nonetheless at the center of the reflection. Accordingly, a first glance at Gilson's work suggests that the title "philosopher of Christendom," conferred on him by his friends in 1949, is legitimate. Without reviewing Gilson's whole treatment of

154 Jacques Maritain, preface to *Étienne Gilson, Philosophe de la Chrétienté*, 11.

155 Letter from Étienne Gilson to Jacques Maritain, July 28, 1948, in Gilson and Maritain, *Correspondance 1923–1971*, 170.

156 Letter from Étienne Gilson to Fr. Jean-Augustin Maydieu, July 28, 1948, Municipal Library of Bordeaux: "Jacques Maritain performs miracles. He has just made living water flow from the most arid rocks. May God forgive me, but reading Maritain, I have begun to find myself interesting for the first time in my life. What frightening lucidity our friend has! For me, these pages are the honor of my life. Thinking of the portrait, I tell myself what Degas used to say to one of his models: 'And now, sir, you have nothing left but to look like it.' With the help of his friendship and yours, I have to diminish the gap between what I would like to be and what my friends think of me."

157 Étienne Gilson, "La tradition française et la chrétienté," *Vigile*, no. 1 (1931): 33.

158 Étienne Gilson, "L'esprit de chrétienté, *La Vie intellectuelle*, February 1945, 18.

159 Étienne Gilson, "Les intellectuels dans la chrétienté," published in *Les Intellectuels dans la Chrétienté* (Geneva: Pax Romana, 1948), 161–78.

160 Étienne Gilson, *Medieval Universalism and Its Present Value* (Cambridge, MA: Harvard University Press, 1937), 22.

161 Étienne Gilson. *La Philosophie au Moyen Âge*. See particularly "Chrétienté et Societé," 252–58.

162 Étienne Gilson, *The Metamorphoses of the City of God*, 235.

Christendom, let us agree that an essential point flows from it: for Gilson, the collective institutions, in the first place the university, are what manifest the organic unity of Christendom. The whole conclusion of the chapter of *La Philosophie au Moyen Âge* devoted to Christendom is so significant that it should be quoted in its entirety:

> Nothing shows us the reality of the Christian people better than the collective endeavors they have undertaken, a number of which they brought to a successful conclusion. Among these enterprises, let us especially mention the medieval schools and universities, for example the universities of Paris and Oxford, whose nature is incomprehensible from any other standpoint than that of Christendom. It is precisely in these schools that *doctrina sacra* is established and taught and, taken in its totality, will be the expression and bond of the very unity of Christendom.[163]

The university played a major role in Gilson's argument. In its very name and its reality it succeeded at the same time in illustrating, proving, and concluding that Christendom really exists. The university manifests Western Christendom's intellectual unity. Gilson explained this upon his reception into the Académie française in 1947:

> Committed to the intellect, the Middle Ages were also committed to universality. What time has seen that intellectual cooperation among the peoples of the world flourish more than the Middle Ages? . . . What were the great names at the University of Paris? William of Auvergne was French; but Albertus Magnus was German; St. Bonaventure and St. Thomas were Italians; Roger Bacon was English; Henry of Ghent was Belgian; so many illustrious masters of whom no other passport was ever required than their genius.[164]

Intelligence and Christendom are inseparably linked, as Gilson again explained to his colleagues of *Pax Romana*: "There is Christendom where there is Christian civilization, and there is Christian civilization where there is Christian thought. In a word, Christian thought and civilization are the soul from which Christendom is born and lives."[165] This theme has an immediate,

163 Étienne Gilson, *La Philosophie au Moyen Âge*, 258.

164 Étienne Gilson, *Discours de réception à l'Académie française*, 12.

165 Étienne Gilson, "Les intellectuels dans la Chrétienté," Pax Romana, April 12, 1947, in *Les Intellectuels dans la Chrétienté*, 164.

political aim in Gilson. In 1931, he wrote: "At any rate, Christendom could only be identical in spirit, but entirely different in practical modalities, from medieval Christendom."[166] In 1945, he declared even more energetically: "Let us neglect the vast panorama of past Christendom, whose grandeur history works tenaciously to reveal. Let us think only of present Christendom, whose reality surrounds us on all sides, and which we still know so badly."[167] There was no trace of nostalgia in Gilson, as his words at the 1947 Rome congress again revealed: "Let us remember, as the profound theologian Fr. Journet loves to repeat, that Christendoms pass, but Christianity remains. We have to make one worthy of our time in order that, after us, others may make a still more beautiful one."[168] As long as there is a Christian people, as long as there exist institutions and projects common to the Christians of all countries, a spirit of Christendom will subsist, according to Gilson. As the modern world's Alcuin, Gilson drew up a report: "A Christendom wider than the ancient one has been born, and I have seen it already."[169]

Gilson's Christendom included the new world. He refused to equate the term with Europe. Europe "will be scholarly, but it will not be Science. It will give birth in beauty but it will not be Art. It will be just, but it will not be the Law. We hope it will be Christian, but it will not be Christendom."[170]

> Since the end of the Middle Ages up to our time, there have always been philosophers and historians who have bound together tightly the concepts of Europe and of Christendom. We can say without exaggeration that this has become an authentic commonplace. "Europe and the Faith," that is to say, the unity of Christian faith has created the spiritual unity of Europe, and the latter will not survive without the former. Perhaps the arms of the cross open so widely to better embrace all human beings without excepting Russians and Americans.[171]

Gilson was a *philosopher of Christendom*. The expression means two things. He became its historian in order to become its philosopher, in the

166 Étienne Gilson, "La tradition française et la Chrétienté," *Vigile*, no. 1 (1931): 64.

167 Étienne Gilson, "L'esprit de Chrétienté," *La Vie intellectuelle*, February 1945, 33.

168 Étienne Gilson, "Les intellectuels dans la Chrétienté," *Pax Romana*, April 12, 1947, in *Les Intellectuels dans la Chrétienté*, 164, 178.

169 Étienne Gilson, "Les intellectuels dans la Chrétienté," Pax Romana, April 12, 1947, in *Les Intellectuels dans la Chrétienté*, 164, 177.

170 Étienne Gilson, *The Metamorphoses of the City of God*, 184.

171 Lecture of Gilson, manuscript, no date, in French, from the 1950s, SMCA.

sense that he philosophized *about* and *in* Christendom, but also in the sense that as a philosopher he belonged on the ground floor of this new Christendom that he loved, taught about, and augmented. For him, the university was the most resounding proof of yesteryear's Christendom, of the universality of intellect, and of the unity of western culture.

In 1948–1949, in the preface to the collective work *Étienne Gilson. Philosophe de la Chrétienté*, Maritain tried to characterize the solder (to use Marc Bloch's term) mentioned in our introduction and found some felicitous expressions to define Gilson's comings and goings: "the scholar *savant*," "the great missionary that France sends to Christendom," caught between the demands of medieval philosophy and action. "Gilson is not satisfied with describing the work of the masters," Maritain wrote, "he has allowed himself to be caught by them. If the historian is a fowler, he has let himself be captured by the birds' song." Furthermore, Maritain added: "Gilson lives the lesson of his teachers. He has been led by them into the country where they dwell."[172] Gilson had certainly been led by his teachers into the country where they dwelled, but as a realist he knew how to *return* from it too.

Beyond Gilson, it is difficult to gauge the reception of Gilsonian Christendom as he describes it. The theme is certainly transnational, trans-imperial, ecumenical, republican—about the *Respublica omnium fidelium*. But the project remains elitist in its very definition, and therefore without impact on the masses in the short run, and in the long term awaiting a "re-Christianization from above." Did Gilson assume that perspective? "If I compare the mediocre character of the Christianity lost by the masses with the excellent quality of the Christianity of the elite, I believe I can hope for a re-Christianization of the West from above, and for a duration whose limit we cannot foresee," he optimistically wrote in 1923 to indicate a line of hope after having emphasized the profound de-Christianization of French rural areas in the nineteenth century.[173]

The subtitle of the appendix of *Humanisme intégrale* (1936), "Temporal and Spiritual Problems of a New Christendom," seemed to echo

172 Jacques Maritain, preface to *Étienne Gilson: Philosophe de la Chrétienté*, 10–11.

173 Étienne Gilson, "Le bilan religieux du XIXe siècle français," *Foi et vie*, no. 21, December 16, 1923, 1199.

(unconsciously, it appears) a phrase of Gilson from 1924–1925.[174] In the appendix, Maritain used several of Gilson's arguments. He introduced his reflection on the "structure of action" by recalling that in a *Sept* article Gilson "showed perfectly how the activities of the Christian are distributed over three levels," the spiritual, the temporal, and the one where the spiritual meets the temporal.[175] The section is important, because, in it, Maritain developed his well known distinction between acting "as a Christian" and acting "insofar as a Christian."

Ten years later, Gilson was quoted in Cardinal Suhard's Lenten Pastoral Letter of 1947, titled *Development or Decline of the Church*. Gilson's work was associated here with the Church's magisterium precisely in the theme of Christendom. The future Msgr. Jean Rupp, a former student of Gilson and the author of a historical study on Christendom,[176] had contributed to the composition of Cardinal Suhard's pastoral letter.[177] To reject the nostalgia that might be engendered by the theme of Christendom, Cardinal Suhard quoted Gilson's article that appeared in *Esprit* the previous year,[178] "The error is always to confuse the Church with passing forms. 'Now, the Church's task,' as Professor Gilson says very well, 'is not to preserve the world as it is, even if it has become Christian, but to preserve the Christian as he never ceases to become different. In a word, the Church does not have the task of preventing

174 Echoing the lecture he gave at Naples in May 1924 on the "Humanism of St. Thomas," Gilson indeed employs the expression "integral humanism" in 1925 in the introduction to his *Saint Thomas d'Aquin*: see the new edition, entitled *Saint Thomas: Textes sur la morale* (Paris: Vrin, 1998), 10.

175 Jacques Maritain, *Humanisme intégral*, in *Oeuvres complètes*, vol. 6, *1935–1938* (Fribourg, Switzerland: Éditions Universitaires, and Paris: Editions Saint-Paul, 1984), 617.

176 Monsignor Jean Rupp, *L'idée de Chrétienté dans la pensée pontificale des origines à Innocent III* (Paris: Les Presses modernes, 1939).

177 On this point, see Fonds Cardinal Suhard, 1 D 14–13 and 1 D 14–15, Archives de l'Archevêché de Paris [AHAP].

178 Étienne Gilson, "Monde moderne, monde chrétien: Pas d'illusions rétrospectives," *Esprit* 14, no. 125 (1946): 192–96: "The main difficulty, at least in the West, is that Christianity, which is a permanent revolution at the heart of the world, is taken to have been a successful revolution in the past. Many Christians pine for the good old days, when Christ's message was finally accepted by the world and would have penetrated and completely informed, as it were, temporal society including the State itself. From that comes nostalgia for the past triumph, sadness for the present decadence, and hope for a future that will resurrect the past. There would be much to say, certainly not against the faith of ancient times, but against the so-called perfections of former Christian societies. . . . Thus the present is lost in salvaging a past that really never existed. It is high time to renounce that illusion."

this world from passing but of sanctifying a world that passes.'"[179] Gilson wrote to the archbishop of Paris:

> As soon as I returned from Rome, I found the *Pastoral Letter for Lent 1949*. I read it at once from beginning to end with ever increasing emotion and admiration. It is not appropriate for me to congratulate you, but I am as happy to be able to express with all simplicity the complete adherence of one of your flock and the certainty that feels at finding himself before a pastoral letter that is probably unprecedented in a French diocese or perhaps in the world. For me it is an act of liberation at the same time as the surest guide and the perfect example of the attitude it recommends. I hold it to be a very great honor to be associated with it.[180]

The cardinal archbishop of Paris answered Gilson with a personal letter to emphasize the "philosopher's authority" in the first rank of Catholic elites: "The complete adherence to the spirit and directives for action that I have tried to draw up for the contemporary faithful of my diocese provides me with a new proof of the development of the Catholic elites in which you have a leading place."[181]"I am confident of your power," wrote Mauriac to Gilson at the time. "Thanks to you, the Church, in spite of everything that could be said, once again becomes a light for unbelievers, the Light."[182]

179 Cardinal Suhard, *Essor ou déclin de l'Église, Lettre pastorale, Carême de l'an de grâce 1947* (Paris: Éditions Lahure, 1962), 63.

180 Letter from Étienne Gilson to Cardinal Suhard, April 22, 1947, AHAP.

181 Letter from Cardinal Suhard to Étienne Gilson, April 30, 1947, SMCA.

182 Letter from François Mauriac to Étienne Gilson, April 1947, SMCA.

3

An Atlantic Intellectual

God alone creates. We ourselves make, and the Americans make a lot: they have built a civilized continent quickly, where San Francisco is as far from New York as New York from Le Havre. I prefer to contribute my stone rather than toss out a sarcastic remark. We ought to assist this gigantic work because, in great measure, western civilization will be what it becomes in the United States.[1]

In the literary republic, since Chateaubriand and Tocqueville, there has existed an informal circle made up of authors, lecturers, and professors within France who have the experience of and a taste for North America. From Henri Bergson to Paul Ricoeur, from Saint-John Perse to the *French Theory* philosophers; from Alexander Koyré to Jean-Luc Marion, from Julien Green to Claude Lévi-Strauss, a considerable portion of French culture has been written, thought out, translated, and introduced on the American continent. We know how much the phobia toward America has shaped opinion and discourse.[2] There seems to be less awareness that North America, certainly more than other cultural areas, has

1 Letter from Étienne Gilson to Henri Gouhier, December 30, 1926, Archives Madame Gouhier (private archive, Paris).

2 Philippe Roger, *L'ennemi américain: Généalogie de l'antiaméricanisme français* (Paris: Seuil, 2002).

offered a favorable environment for the maturation, reception, and influence of French authors.

These Atlantic intellectuals created their own jargon. First of all, for them the "CGT" meant the Compagnie Générale Transatlantique, otherwise known as the "French Line." They had their modes and places of socialization. They loved the transatlantic voyage and conversed on the ships between the two continents before the airlines provided transportation for the most privileged of them starting at the end of the 1940s. They spoke English or learned it very quickly. They were introduced into publishing and university circles. They met again on the campuses of Columbia or Yale, which long fascinated the French, who perceived their elite character. In the "diary of his election to the Collège de France," Maurice Halbwachs testified to this: "I decided to go to see Edmond Faral, administrator of the Collège. In September 1930, I had made the crossing from Le Havre to New York on the Compagnie Transatlantique's ship *De Grasse* with him, Gilson, Strowski, and Father Chenu. During those eight or ten days we were bound together. On my return, I saw him [Faral] in New York. He had invited me to breakfast at his club and to go for a walk in Columbia University."[3] Painting a portrait of "The Transatlantic Paul Hazard," Antoine Compagnon indicated the basic characteristics of this passage across the Atlantic as it appeared in French literary history in reference to Gustave Lanson (in 1911), Bernard Faÿ (starting in 1923), and Paul Hazard, professor at the Collège de France, author of *Crise de la conscience européene* (1935) [(*Crisis of the European Mind* (1961)]. He was a colleague and friend of Gilson, and he went to the United States regularly between 1923 and 1940.[4]

Gilson in particular, who served as guide to Fr. Chenu and Maurice Halbwachs in 1930,[5] was an example of a French intellectual open to the

3 Maurice Halbwachs, "Ma campagne au Collège de France," *Revue d'Histoire des Sciences Humaines* 1 (1991): 189.

4 Antoine Compagnon, "Paul Hazard transatlantique," lecture at the Collège de France, May 19, 2016, presented during the colloquium, "Histoire et historiens des idées: Figures, méthodes. problèmes," May 18–20, 2016. —See Paul Hazard, "Six professeurs français à l'Université Columbia," *Revue des deux mondes*, October 1923, 622–33. See likewise the letter from Paul Hazard to Étienne Gilson, November 26, 1941, SMCA: "Thank you, my dear friend, for your beautiful missives. . . . My gratitude for this spiritual nourishment along with my friendship."

5 See the letter from Maurice to Yvonne Halbwachs, September-December 1930, Fonds Halbwachs, assignment at the University of Chicago, folios 93–103, IMEC: "Gilson is very kind and always the same. Gilson was accompanied by a Dominican, Fr. Chenu, who was going to teach in Canada. . . . Gilson has been exquisite. He took charge of me and has been my father and mother.

North American world, exercising real influence upon it, and integrating an American touch in his works and a noticeable trace of cosmopolitanism. In the nineteen thirties Gilson's lectures and books were commented upon with obvious sympathy.[6] *The Choir of Muses*, published in 1953, was dedicated to his wife and to the women who inspire men—"Daughters, God bless them!," title of an article in the *Boston Pilot*—was reviewed more than fifty times in the local and national American press from the *Los Angeles Times* to the *New York Times*, in the majority of big city daily papers like Sacramento, Nashville, and Brooklyn, and even on the radio.[7] Gilson's philosophical work turned the lives of some readers upside down, as Thomas Merton recounted in his spiritual autobiography, *The Seven Storey Mountain*, published in 1941. Similarly, the thinking of John Wright, bishop of Pittsburgh and subsequently prefect of the Congregation of the Clergy, was greatly influenced by Maritain, de Lubac, and Gilson.[8] The famous literary critic Richard Gilman of Jewish ancestry, in search of the Ineffable, upon reading Gilson's *The Spirit of Medieval Philosophy*, ended against his will, requesting baptism one fine summer day in 1952, before leaving the Church eight years later.[9]

He was pleased by my enthusiasm, which was not an act. . . . Gilson put me in my Pullman car to Chicago and gave his final instructions. . . . He has extraordinary pluck. He continually sprouts amazing remarks. He sees a great deal and enjoys himself like a king."

6 William L. Laurence, "'Non-Racial Truth' Called Liberator," *The New York Times*, September 3, 1936, 15. The article comments upon and quotes long sections of Gilson's lecture on medieval universalism given at the celebration of Harvard's third centenary. —Padraic Colum, "The Light of Medieval Thought," *The New York Times*, January 29, 1939. The article is a combined review of Maritain's *True Humanism* and Gilson's *Reason and Revelation in the Middle Ages* (New York: Scribners, 1938). —On this point see the file of fifteen articles in the University of Notre Dame Archives [UNDA] on "Medieval Universalism and Its Present Value," CSAW, 313–36.—See also George Weigel, "Ways of Thinking and Believing, *The Philosopher and Theology* by Étienne Gilson," *The New York Times*, July 22, 1962: "It is an unmitigated pleasure to read almost any page of it."

7 In this connection, see the impressive collection of newspaper articles included in the file *Choir of Muses*, CSAW, 33–15, UNDA.

8 George Vecsey, "John Cardinal Wright Dies at 70: Top-Ranking American in Vatican," *The New York Times*, August 12, 1979, 32.

9 Richard Gilman, *Faith, Sex, Mystery: A Memoir* (New York: Simon & Shuster, 1986): "I was trembling and scraping my shoes on the floor in an effort to turn round and get away. I put [the book] back on the shelf. I turned around, found myself without any power to move, turned back again, took the Gilson book from the shelf once more, put it back, repeated the whole mad cycle three or four more times and then, besieged, light-headed as though I had a fever, nearly sick to my stomach, put the book with my others. . . . [After reading] I saw the world in a new way, saw explanations where there had been frustrating mysteries and alluring mysteries where there had been unsatisfying explanations. . . . I saw the supernatural as real, not a myth, not a human construction out of longing. . . . The idea of God as the Word, Logos, was especially seductive, since I'd lived by words, craving them, struggling with them and trying to bend them to my poor aspiring

From 1926 to 1973, counting a round trip each year except during the war, Gilson crossed the Atlantic some forty-eight times. In the magazine *Esprit*, to answer the critics who accused him of fleeing from France during the Gilson Affair, he humorously tabulated each of his trans-Atlantic flights, suggesting the reasons for his missions in America.

> I am an old recidivist in escaping to America. I fled there for the first time in Easter 1926 on the *Montcalm*. The second escape took place the same year on the *Savoie* in July to teach for six months. Harvard University offered me a chair of the history of philosophy.... I escaped to America again in September 1927 on the *Paris* and in September 1928 on the *De Grasse*.... In September 1929, I fled to America for the fifth time on the *Empress of Scotland* for a four-month stay. From that point on, my escapes multiplied. In 1930 on the *De Grasse*, in 1931 on the *La Fayette*, in 1932 on the *Ascania*. ... Since then I have taught each year in Toronto without missing a course at the Collège de France.... From that point, there were new annual flights each autumn for a three-month stay in America: on the *Ascania* in 1932, on the *Alaunia* in 1933, in 1934 on the *Ascania* again (the return each time was on the *Champlain*). In 1935 a variation took me to Brazil in July on the *Eubée*. I went from there to Canada to teach until January. The return was on the *Île de France*. The twelfth flight was on the *La Fayette* in 1936. The thirteenth escape was on the *Duchess of Richmond*, and the return in January on the *Normandy*. In 1939 after the declaration of war, the fifteenth flight was from Liverpool on September 15 aboard the *Duchess of York*. I came back from New York on April 6, 1940. My stay in France lasted uninterrupted until the beginning of April 1945.
>
> After the Liberation, the sixteenth flight was on the *Nea-Hellas* in April 1945, and the return on the *Ville-de-Strasbourg* departing on August 12. The seventeenth escape from March to May in 1946 was on an American Liberty Ship. From 1947 on I replaced ships with airplanes to flee more quickly, and I relapsed each year: 1948, 1949 (twice in the same year) and lastly in 1950. In short, and barring some mistake on my part, there were twenty-two escapes in twenty-six years. During those twenty-six years, I added sixty-eight months of teaching abroad, which is to say, nearly six years, to my uninterrupted teaching in France.[10]

uses for so long." —See the review by Christopher Lehman-Haupt in the *New York Times*, January 5, 1987, p. C 18. Richard Gilman's obituary appeared in the *New York Times* on October 31, 2006.

10 Letter from Étienne Gilson to Albert Béguin, March 11, 1951, published in "Journal à plusieurs voix," *Ésprit*, April 1951, 593–94.

In addition to these teaching missions, chiefly at Harvard and Toronto, along with other incursions into the academic network at the University of Virginia and Notre Dame, which Gilson visited regularly from 1931 on, he assumed the burden of administrative and diplomatic tasks. He was appointed to the French national committee for the observance of the fourth centenary of Jacques Cartier.[11] Beginning in 1937, Gilson presided over the Institute Scientifique Franco-Canadien, which coordinated university exchanges between France and Quebec. Likewise, he was commissioned by the French Ministry of Foreign Affairs and the Commissariat Général à l'Information to explain France's position in 1939–1940 to American neutralist public opinion. The Ministry asked him to join the French delegation at the London and San Francisco conferences in 1945. In 1946, Gilson privately complained about the American occupation of France.[12] Under the cupola of the Collège de France, he advocated for the literature of Quebec until the explosion of the Gilson Affair, which showed that an eminent Atlantic intellectual and shrewd admirer of North America could be other than an "Atlanticist" (which is to say, a supporter of the NATO project).

EXCHANGE SCHOLAR, HARVARD

Shook's biography of Gilson devotes a whole chapter to the year 1926.[13] In many respects it was an admirable year, since for the first time Gilson embarked for Quebec in April and a second time in the summer for the United States. It was his first exploration of Francophone America and the first plunge into the North American university world. The great event was Gilson's lecturing at Harvard from September 19, 1926, to January 1927.

First of all, Gilson participated in a philosophy conference at Montreal, where he replaced the Rector of the University of Paris, who had been invited but was forced to cancel his trip.[14] Gilson gave two lectures, one on Scholastic

11 See the newspaper *Le Temps*, March 3, 1934, 4.

12 Letter from Étienne Gilson to Jacques Maritain, September 3, 1946, in Gilson and Maritain, *Correspondance 1923–1971*, 140: "As for me, I often re-read a page or two [of *Les grandes amitiés*] to create the illusion of being with you again. What is to be made of the more pleasant of the two occupations of French territory? And to say that when I wrote 'Le baromètre américain' in *Le Monde* last March I was labeled a pessimist!"

13 Shook, *Étienne Gilson*, 132–68. —See also Florian Michel, *La Pensée catholique en Amérique du Nord*, chap. 1.

14 Shook, *Étienne Gilson*, 133.

philosophy at the congress, the second, under the auspices of the University of Montreal, "St. Thomas and Franciscan Thought." Gilson discovered the cities of Quebec and Montreal. He was enchanted by his first contact with the Quebecois, "more ourselves than ourselves."[15]

A second trip immediately followed the first. In July 1926, Gilson embarked for the United States. Richard McKeon, one of his students at L'École des Hautes Études, met him as he disembarked.[16] The first objective was the International Congress of Philosophy, where Gilson was a regular participant. It was held at Harvard in mid-September. Along with Léon Robin, Célestin Bouglé, and Lucien Lévy-Bruhl, Gilson represented French universities at the Congress,[17] where he met John Dewey. After the Congress, from mid-August to the beginning of September, invited by Professor Albert Balz, Gilson gave a summer course at the University of Virginia in Charlottesville, where he discovered the South and the racial problem. Also after the Congress, helped by Professor Xavier Léon's American network[18] and international university agreements set up with a view to promoting peace,[19] Gilson remained at Harvard, again for a semester, under the auspices of a program of faculty exchange with the Sorbonne.

Gilson left Harvard in mid-January 1927, not to return to Paris, but to go to the University of Chicago and then to Montreal, where, as the first to be invited by the newly created Institut Scientifique Franco-Canadien, he gave five lectures at the end of January. On January 30, Gilson was invited to St. Michael's College in Toronto for the first time. He left New York in February 1927 and arrived in Paris after a seven-month absence.

This long stay was a premier in many senses. A semester's teaching at a United States university was doubled by a series of lectures throughout Canada and the American Northeast, the inauguration of the Institut

15 Shook, *Étienne Gilson*, 135.

16 Letter from Étienne Gilson to Richard McKeon, September 5, 1926, McKeon Papers, University of Chicago Archives [UCA].

17 See *Proceedings of the Sixth International Congress of Philosophy*, Harvard University, Cambridge, Mass., September 13–17, 1926, ed. Edgar Sheffield Brightman (New York: Longman's, Green, & Co., 1927).

18 See letters from Alfred North Whitehead to Xavier Léon, 1914, MSCV 367-1, folios 162–63; letters from Ralph Barton Perry to Xavier Léon, 1921–1929, MSCV 365, folios 72–90, Fonds Xavier Léon, Archives of BIS.

19 See the thesis of Guillaume Tronchet, "Savoirs en diplomatie: Une histoire sociale et transnationale de la politique universitaire internationale de la France (années 1870–années 1930)" (PhD diss., Université Paris 1 Panthéon-Sorbonne, 2014).

Scientifique Franco-Canadien by a French Thomist and finally, Gilson's meeting with the Basilian community at Toronto.

Beside the itineraries and chronologies, it is important to clarify Gilson's connections at Harvard. Harvard was the beginning of his American adventure, which is somewhat surprising since neither metaphysics, nor Thomism, nor history of philosophy were part of local academic activity.[20] Medievalism was certainly in fashion on campus, since Harvard housed the Medieval Academy of America, recently founded (December 1925) by Edward Rand, Charles Haskins, and Ralph Cram. *Speculum*, one of the first American journals devoted to the Middle Ages, first appeared in January 1926.[21] It was one of the sources of the future Mediaeval Institute of Toronto.[22] But the philosophical Middle Ages were hardly examined in the United States, and Harvard's great philosophical figure was the pragmatist William James (1842–1910), brother of the novelist Henry James. William James was dominant enough so that the important series devoted to philosophy and psychology became the Williams James Lectures in 1930. Speakers included John Dewey, Arthur O. Lovejoy, Étienne Gilson, Bertrand Russell, Karl Popper, and many others.

Indications of disagreement between Harvard's philosophical luminaries and Gilson are easy to find, all within an atmosphere of friendship and academic courtesy. Gilson wrote in 1926:

> As for the history of philosophy, they don't see any use for it. [Ralph Barton] Perry is quite upset. He thinks that too much studying of the systems of others prevents young people from finding one of their own. It's like saying that visiting museums and studying masters prevents one from becoming a painter.... Such, you see, is the milieu I am working in. It is a desert waiting to be cultivated.[23]

In 1936, Gilson wrote: "It is the same everywhere. Today one of the Harvard logic professors whom I greatly esteem [Alfred Whitehead] explained to me that two rabbits plus two rabbits ordinarily make four rabbits, but that

20 See Bruce Kuklick, *A History of Philosophy in America, 1720–2000* (Oxford: Clarendon Press, 2001), especially chap. 9, which is devoted to pragmatism at Harvard.

21 On this point see Florian Michel, "Le Moyen Âge au Nouveau Monde: L'enjeu culturel des 'Mediaeval Studies,'" *Archives des Sciences sociales des religions* 149 (January–March 2010): 9–32.

22 Étienne Gilson, "Mediaevalism in Toronto," *Commonweal* 9, no. 26, May 1, 1929, 739.

23 Letter from Étienne Gilson to his wife, Thérèse, October 6, 1926, quoted by Shook, *Étienne Gilson*, 150.

logically speaking, there could be sixteen of them. This type of logic is very much in fashion."[24] Despite the disagreements, there were powerful reasons for Gilson's presence at Harvard. They included the 1926 Philosophy Congress and the agreement between the Sorbonne and Harvard. Furthermore, Gilson was also a friend of Ralph Barton Perry, the disciple of William James. Perry was a member of the Harvard philosophy department, who spoke French, and whom Gilson had met in Paris. In October 1925, Gilson wrote to him:

> I plan to attend the Philosophy Congress. Circumstances would have to make the trip completely impossible for me not to do so. . . . Also, I have been informed about the offer made for me to go to Harvard as an exchange professor, and I would very much like to go. The prospect of leaving my wife and two daughters for six months makes me very hesitant, to say the least. I rather think that I will wait for ten years until my two daughters are married. It is true that in ten years perhaps it will not be worth the trouble to make me cross the ocean.[25]

However, Gilson accepted both the Congress and the exchange. He provided the French public with a review of the Congress that gave him the opportunity to relate unusual and amusing variations on scenes of life in America.[26] After the Congress, Gilson began to teach in the Harvard philosophy department. He did so for three years. During the first year, autumn 1926, Gilson was an exchange professor. In January 1927 the philosophy department offered him a chair in the history of philosophy. The following years in autumn of 1927 and 1928, Gilson returned, no longer as an exchange professor but with the status of visiting professor. If Gilson had some doubts about the situation at Harvard, Harvard did not show any about him. Gilson's approach seems to have been seductive.

William Ernest Hocking wrote to President A. Lawrence Lowell that Gilson was a great professor. His impact had been immediate and profound. He had astonishing mastery of English. It is evident that he felt at home at

24 Letter from Étienne Gilson to Henri Gouhier, October 30, 1936, Archives Madame Gouhier, Paris.

25 Letter from Étienne Gilson to Ralph Barton Perry, October 15, 1925 (in French), Harvard University Archives.

26 Étienne Gilson, "Le VIe Congrès international de Philosophie: Harvard University, Cambridge (USA), 13–17 septembre 1926," *Revue de Métaphysique et de Morale* 33, no. 4 (1926): 509–44.

Harvard. He would strengthen the philosophy department in what was then its weakest link, namely history.[27]

Another testimony is found in a letter from Alfred North Whitehead, also directed to the President of Harvard University. Whitehead reported that after an informal discussion about the philosophy department's activity, Woods, Hocking, Perry, and he had agreed that they needed to convey to the President something evident to them: naming Professor Gilson to a chair would be an immense service to the department's strength and reputation .... Professor Gilson was the intellectual authority on Scholasticism and its relation with sixteenth [sic] century French thought. His lectures had been a remarkable success. They profoundly clarified the historical method and the exact analysis of the development of thought between the periods for his Harvard students.... This period was fundamental for the comprehension of philosophical problems stemming from the natural sciences of the twentieth century and also for the philosophy of religion.... Gilson's presence in the department would strengthen it and complete it in dealing with questions that interested young people of the time ... Professor Gilson was singularly at ease in the American way of life, and his sincere admiration and affection for the environment at Harvard. He was a charming colleague and popular among students.[28]

In January 1927, President Lowell agreed to appoint Gilson, and Gilson accepted the offer, as did the administration of the Sorbonne. Gilson reported to Perry that, truly, everyone in Paris realized the importance of close relations between Harvard and the Sorbonne.[29] Letters from Gilson to friends and to his wife show that, despite philosophical disagreements, he was happy with his American students and his discovery of the New World. Regarding his August 1926 summer courses at the University of Virginia, Gilson wrote to Richard McKeon that his teaching was not the total failure that he dreaded, since his courses were followed by acceptable examinations, and four or five good students seemed to have discovered the history of philosophy. After a laborious reflection following an explanation of Malebranche, one of them

27 Letter from William Hocking to President A. Lawrence Lowell, December 21, 1926, Harvard University Archives.

28 Letter from William Hocking to President A. Lawrence Lowell, December 21, 1926, Harvard University Archives

29 Letter from Étienne Gilson to Ralph Barton Perry, April 10, 1927, Harvard University Archives. [Letter is in English.]

confided to Gilson: "I wonder if they make us read the philosophers themselves often enough in our universities." Gilson was perfectly delighted with having led them to this conclusion without directly suggesting it, by simply taking them for an hour more each day in order to make them translate some Descartes, some Malebranche, and some Comte into English and by conversing with them about the meaning of the texts.[30]

Regarding his course at Harvard in fall 1926, Gilson commented:

> My courses unfold easily here. I have twenty students who work on Descartes and Malebranche. There are forty working on medieval philosophy. I give tests, and my English does not seem to be completely unintelligible, because I find what I have told my students in their notes. Since I have nine hours of classes per week, there is hardly any time left to work. That is too bad, because Widener Library is the finest instrument I have ever had at my disposal. Its organization is astonishing.[31]

We should observe in regard to the phrase "my English does not seem to be completely unintelligible," that, unlike Maritain, Gilson possessed obvious linguistic ability. He even seemed bilingual. He wrote humorously to his wife Thérèse:

> Since I was congratulated on my English, I did what I always do now. I confessed that I had lived in England for a long time. On the first occasions, I limited myself to telling the truth, namely that I spent almost ten days there. You remember that. People remain skeptical and clearly are convinced that I was posing as one who came into the world knowing English or who has a genius for language. With the new system, that happens by itself, so I no longer have to argue further: "You must have lived in England for a long time." "Oh yes, for a very long time." People are satisfied and that is the end of it. How odd it is to be reduced to lying to seem to tell the truth.[32]

Accordingly, Gilson was content with his American experience. The echo of his success crossed the Atlantic. Bergson congratulated him.[33] Despite that, and even if "Harvard is Harvard," as Gilson said in spring 1928, he submitted his resignation and decided to attempt the adventure of the Institute

30 Letter from Étienne Gilson to Richard McKeon, September 5, 1926, "McKeon Papers," UCA.

31 Letter from Étienne Gilson to Henri Gouhier, October 9, 1926, Archives Madame Gouhier, Paris.

32 Letter from Étienne Gilson to his wife, Thérèse, October 19, 1926, SMCA.

33 Letter from Henri Bergson to Étienne Gilson, March 1, 1928, SMCA.

of Mediaeval Studies in Toronto. It was a real adventure. On the one hand, there was the prestige and age of a three-century-old university. On the other there was an unknown or nearly unknown college, less than a hundred years old, a project that was still badly defined at this point, and the promise of the Basilian Congregation, with which Gilson was probably unfamiliar before coming to America. Gilson's decision had a certain flair. He sent his Harvard colleagues letters explaining the reasons for his departure to Toronto.

To C. I. Lewis, Gilson confessed that it seemed to him that the work he would have to carry out in Toronto would be more to his taste. He had an unexpected opportunity to do something there of which he had never dared to dream: to see his own concept of medieval studies embodied in an institution that would survive him and that he hoped would be of genuine value for the advancement of this branch of knowledge.[34]

Gilson wrote to James Haughton Woods that he knew that only Harvard was Harvard, but that he had a unique opportunity to achieve his ideal in medieval studies.[35] He sent a long letter to his friend Ralph Barton Perry, apologizing and declaring that his the letter was hardly what it should be and failed to do justice to his personal feelings, Gilson expressed his genuine sorrow at having to leave Harvard and seeming to show ingratitude for the warmest and most touching reception he had ever received in his life.[36]

A bit later again, Gilson conceded to Perry that the University of Toronto did not have the same rank of Harvard. In his judgment, the decisive factor was the unique opportunity given him to organize the teaching of medieval philosophy at Toronto that had no possible comparison.[37] Gilson lectured at Harvard again in fall 1928, when he gave three courses: on the great intellectual systems of the Middle Ages; on Descartes's philosophy; and on Thomas Aquinas's philosophy. He returned in November 1933 to give a lecture on "Duns Scotus and Heidegger's Phenomenology" (*The Crimson*, October 2, 1933) and then in autumn 1936 at the university's third centenary to give a lecture on "Medieval Universalism and Its Present Value," dedicated to

34 Letter from Étienne Gilson to Clarence Irving Lewis, January 26, 1928, Harvard University Archives.

35 Letter from Étienne Gilson to James Haughton Woods, January 28, 1928, Harvard University Archives.

36 Letter from Étienne Gilson to Ralph Barton Perry, January 26, 1928, Harvard University Archives.

37 Letter from Étienne Gilson to Ralph Barton Perry, March 3, 1928, Harvard University Archives.

Ralph Barton Perry. This lecture was particularly well received in the press. *The Nation* echoed that praise.[38] *The New York Times* reproduced a great deal of the lecture and made Gilson's thesis its own: medieval universalism is the best remedy to overcome totalitarian states, deification of the state, and racism. "A powerful revival of the medieval feeling for the universal, non-national, and non-racial character of truth is the only protection of humanity against the encroachment of the totalitarian state."[39] In October 1936, Gilson again gave a series of lectures, the William James Lectures, out of which *The Unity of Philosophical Experience* was born (New York: Scribner, 1937). In spring 1940, Gilson gave a series of lectures at Harvard on "God and Philosophy." Until the eve of World War II, his Cambridge friends always hoped to get him to return.

> On my side, there is nothing but desire to go back to the Institute [PIMS]. My Harvard friends have tried and are still trying to get me back with them. Perhaps I might accept to give them a second series of the same [William James] lectures, which I have been kindly invited to do, but since you still wish to have me, I will stay with you as long as God will keep me strong enough to do honest work."[40]

Harvard was not a parenthesis. It was the *incipit* of Gilson's American biography. In Gilson's correspondence and his journey, Harvard was the road taken but not continued. Harvard was the place of genuine friendship with philosophy professors like Perry and Whitehead. As Gilson wrote to Perry in May 1933, when he was to return to Cambridge in November, his only problem at that point was where to live at Harvard. He had already promised and re-promised Mrs. Whitehead that it would be with them. But he reminded Perry that his heart was powerfully drawn by the white house behind the white fence.[41] Gilson's stays were the occasion for long exchanges, whose echoes Gilson sometimes offered us in his correspondence[42] or his memoirs:

38 See the report of Harvard's third centenary observance, "The Truth Shall Set You Free," *The Nation* 143 (1936): 294: "The keynote of the meeting was the speech of the medievalist Professor Étienne Gilson of Paris."

39 William L. Laurence, "'Non-Racial Truth' Called Liberator," *New York Times*, September 3, 1936, 15.

40 Letter from Étienne Gilson to Fr. Gerald Phelan, November 3, 1944, SMCA.

41 Letter from Étienne Gilson to Ralph Barton Perry, May 27, 1933. Harvard University Archives.

42 Letter from Étienne Gilson to Joseph Vrin [?], no date, Archives de la Librairie Vrin, Paris: "This book [by Fr. Rostand] has, however, made me remember an incident. During one of my stays at

> The mathematician and philosopher A. N. Whitehead, coauthor with Bertrand Russell of the *Principia Mathematica*, was a sparkling conversationalist. . . . Wanting to please a Catholic colleague, during the course of one of their long Harvard evenings, Whitehead told him point-blank, "Those judges of Galileo, you know, they were not far wrong! Had they told Galileo only that he had not demonstrated the motion of the earth, they would have been three centuries ahead of the science of their time."[43]

It is easy to recognize Gilson in the reference to Whitehead's Catholic colleague at Harvard. One imagines them chatting about epistemology and philosophy of mathematics. But it was also the place where Gilson measured the impossibility of shared understandings and became aware of what he did not want to do:

> I am remembering the fatherly and brotherly goodness of Fr. Muckle, when we arrived in Toronto. I remember our first meeting at Harvard, when he came with Fr. Phelan to convince me to try Toronto. I am glad that I allowed myself to be persuaded. Besides, I suppose that God wanted me somewhere else than in the country of the last puritans.[44]

THE PONTIFICAL INSTITUTE OF MEDIAEVAL STUDIES, TORONTO

The principal cause of Gilson's coming to Toronto was that there was a teaching order there resolutely decided to uphold the cause of the Middle Ages, and to whom the University of Toronto allowed great freedom of action. In 1929, Gilson founded the Institute of Mediaeval Studies, which, after some hesitancy, won pontifical approval in 1939, and whose *de facto* head was Gilson for more than forty years.[45] The Institute has played a major role in

Harvard, I asked my friend, the philosopher-mathematician Alfred North Whitehead, 'How do we know that a mathematical conclusion is true?' Whitehead was very patient and put up with my most naïve questions."

43 Étienne Gilson, *The Philosopher and Theology*, 223.

44 Letter from Étienne Gilson to Fr. Laurence Shook, May 27, 1967, SMCA.

45 For the history of the Pontifical Institute of Mediaeval Studies [PIMS], see the brochure by Ruth Ellen St. Onge, "The Étienne Gilson Collection" (Toronto: PIMS, 2012). See likewise Michel, *La pensée catholique en Amérique du Nord*, chap. 1. The history of this institute and of its background is well established. After our first publications on the subject, the only novelty has been the development of medieval studies in North America[46] and is evidence of the importance of higher education during the reign of Pope Pius XI.[47]

If we believe what Gilson said about Toronto, there is no use in describing the place or its environment. He wrote in 1932 that he would spend three months there in perfect calm, leading the little, provincial life of the good people of Toronto. He described Toronto as a horrible place, where there was practically no social life around the university. The university itself was nothing. Nevertheless, it was true that, though it was pure *nihil* in comparison to Harvard, for that very reason, for Gilson, there was no better place for his noble experiment. His students were very good, and St. Michael's did everything possible to make the Institute a success.[48]

Did Gilson darken the picture because of nostalgia for Boston and the East Coast? At the time, Toronto had more than six hundred thousand inhabitants. It was the principal city of English-speaking Canada. The population of Toronto was more than eighty percent of British origin. Consequently, the proportion of Catholics in the city was low, less than fifteen percent.[49] In a sense, the Pontifical Institute of Mediaeval Studies seemed out of place, situated in a culturally Protestant, modern city. Toronto's Britishness was very marked. "It is enough to have breathed the air at Hart House at the University of Toronto to feel nearer to Oxford and Cambridge in England than to that other Cambridge so close in distance, where Harvard University flourishes in the state of Massachusetts."[50] The University of Toronto was founded in 1850 and initially included three colleges, Victoria College (United Church of Canada), Trinity College (Episcopal Church), and University College (without religious affiliation). St. Michael's College was the last to join the

---

the opening in 2006 of the Archives of the Congregation for Catholic Education (Rome) for the pontificate of Pius XI.

46 Florian Michel, "Le Moyen Âge au Nouveau Monde: l'enjeu culturel des 'Mediaeval Studies,'" *Archives des Sciences sociales des religions* 149 (January–March 2010): 9–32.

47 Florian Michel, "Les universités pontificales, un lieu de gouvernance pour le Saint-Siège? Perspectives comparatistes entre la France, les États Unis et le Canada dans l'entre-deux-guerres," *Le gouvernement pontifical sous Pie XI. Pratiques romaines et gestion de l'université*, ed. Laura Pettinaroli (Rome: École Française de Rome, 2013), 757–73.

48 Letter from Étienne Gilson to Ralph Barton Perry, August 19, 1932, Harvard University Archives.

49 James Lemon, *Toronto Since 1918: An Illustrated History* (Toronto: Lorimer Publishers, 1985), 2002.

50 Étienne Gilson, "L'équilibre canadien," *Chronique de France* 9 (1945): 17–20.

federation. Founded in 1852 by the Congregation of St. Basil, St. Michael's was admitted into the University of Toronto in 1881, which took on its present form: four colleges joined under the name of University of Toronto, divided by religious denomination, autonomous in undergraduate studies, federated for graduate studies.

St. Michael's was privileged to have the only philosophy department at the University of Toronto. Wanting to follow the teaching of *Aeterni Patris*, the Basilians were aware of the Scholastic renewal in Europe at the beginning of the 1920s. In April 1919, Maurice De Wulf, a professor at the University of Louvain, came to lecture on medieval history and philosophy for the first time. One of the professors of St. Michael's College, Fr. Gerald Phelan, had studied at Louvain, whose influence showed up again with the arrival of Msgr. Léon Noël in 1926. Accordingly, Gilson found a favorable but also Catholic place in a country that is not very Catholic and a place that was also interested in not falling behind in the Scholastic renewal that was sprouting in America.

An essential point in the Institute's history, and consequently in the history of Thomistic renewal in America and in Gilson's North American sojourn, was the role of the Congregation of St. Basil.[51] Founded in France after the Revolution by Archbishop d'Aviau of Vienne and Fr. Joseph Lapierre, it was established in l'Ardèche between Annonay and Viviers. It was given canonical approval in 1822 as an association of priests. In 1850, the bishop of Toronto called upon the association, which had only around twenty members, to found a minor seminary. The Congregation of St. Basil was expelled from France in 1905 and almost disappeared in Europe, though it flourished in the United States and Canada. Distance and difference in size hindered good relations between the French and North American branches, which decided to separate in 1922. After that date, the French branch was designated as the Congregation of Priests of Saint Basil of Viviers, while the North American branch was officially the Congregation of Priests of St. Basil of Toronto. In 1954 the two branches re-united. In France, the Basilians have never recovered from the expulsion. In America, the Congregation had a real success story, whose source was Toronto. The place of formation of Basilian novices and the residence of the superior general were there. St. Michael's was for a long time the only college run by Basilians. From Toronto, the Basilians

51 Charles Roume, CSB, *Origines et formation de la communauté des prêtres de Saint Basile, Contribution à l'histoire religieuse de Vivarais* (Privas, France: Volle, 1965).

moved into English-speaking Canada and the United States, with a presence in Rochester, Detroit, Houston, and Phoenix.

When Gilson passed through Montreal in April 1926, he met Fr. Edmund McCorkell, superior of St. Michael's College, along with Fr. Henry Carr, the congregation's superior general. In the first letter from Gilson to Fr. McCorkell, we learn that in April 1926 the latter had invited the French scholar to give some lectures in Toronto. Gilson replied that he had kept in mind McCorkell's very kind invitation. He remarked that he had never forgotten the interesting conversation they had in Montreal, and expressed his strong desire to continue it.[52] Gilson had precisely that invitation in mind when, at the International Philosophical Congress at Harvard in September 1926, Fathers Muckle and Phelan, who were attending, made an effort to recruit Gilson. Gilson wrote to his wife: "At 11:30 one of those strangers wanted, or so it seemed to me, to march me right back to Toronto with him."[53] The university there was set on getting him. Gilson proposed to Fr. McCorkell that he would come to Toronto at the end of January 1927 to give lectures on St. Bonaventure, St. Thomas, and Duns Scotus.[54]

On Gilson's first trip to Toronto, the idea germinated of building a center for medieval studies, which for the time being remained a very hazy project. When he departed from Toronto that year, Gilson left behind him only a question mark. In the University's yearbook, he published an article titled "Why Not?" He asked why St. Michael's College and the University of Toronto should not inscribe their names among the pioneers of the great task of medieval studies. What was required for this undertaking, he explained, was an authentic laboratory with the necessary instruments (books, scholarly journals, photocopies of manuscripts) under the direction of several professors.[55]

The question "why not?" provoked at least one other. Why did Gilson consider working with the Basilians? The answer is to be sought in the "pure *nihil*" that he used to describe the situation in Toronto. Whereas the older congregations, Dominicans, Franciscans, or Carmelites, had their intellectual traditions, the Basilians had none. Starting in 1929, they were and always

52 Letter from Étienne Gilson to Fr. Edmund McCorkell, October 9, 1926, General Archives of the Basilian Fathers [GABF], Toronto.

53 Letter from Étienne Gilson to Thérèse Gilson; quoted in Shook, *Étienne Gilson*, 145.

54 Letter from Étienne Gilson to Fr. Edmund McCorkell, October 27, 1926, GABF, Toronto.

55 Étienne Gilson, "Why Not?," *St. Michael's College Year Book*, October 27, 1926, 32–33.

would be Gilsonians. Edmund McCorkell explained that Gilson left Harvard to come to Toronto, because he saw a young religious congregation, not shackled by religious traditions and open to new ideas.[56] That *nihil* was a cause, even if it was at the very least a negative one. Why Toronto? Because there is nothing there for philosophy. Fr. McCorkell contemplated other reasons:

> Why did [Gilson] come to Toronto? What advantages did he find here that Harvard did not have? There were several. He found the philosophy of Thomism in a state of considerable advance. He found a good medieval library here. He found the creative impulse of a new movement in a small campus of a great modern university. He could count on having students who knew Latin, so indispensable to research in the medieval field.[57]

In Toronto, Gilson found a religious community ready to work, as well as a structure that met his needs. That is to say, he discovered a structure at St. Michael's College, but an empty structure. He would later observe that long before the Institute came to be, there was the idea of such a center for medieval studies, which awaited its realization in any place in the world. At the same moment there was a body prepared to receive that idea. But it was several years before the two encountered each other in Toronto.[58]

Neither the French university system nor Harvard offered the body that Gilson sought and that he found in Toronto. A kind of alliance was formed between Gilson and the Basilians starting in 1927, based on mutual trust. "A small group of Basilians, now old or dead, gave me their word. I trusted them, and my whole life has been completely transformed by the fact that they trusted me as I trusted them."[59]

On the spiritual level, the foundation in Toronto was the occasion for Gilson to bear witness to his Christian commitment. He wrote in this vein in 1927:

> Once more in my life, I feel that I am not acting but acted [upon] by God. To be the occasion of such a foundation in Canada is not more surprising

56 Edmund McCorkell, "The Spirit of the Pontifical Institute, *The Basilian Teacher* 5, no. 3 (1958): 37–40.

57 Edmund McCorkell, "Institute of Mediaeval Studies." *Varsity Graduate* 4, no. 3 (July 18, 1956): 116.

58 Minutes of the Institute Council, November 21, 1939, SMCA.

59 Letter from Étienne Gilson to Anton Pegis, May 28, 1933, SMCA.

> for me than to be teaching about Thomas Aquinas and St. Augustine at the University of Paris in the year of Our Lord 1927, *Poincaré regnante* or at Harvard University.... I am always doing things I am perfectly unconscious of and thankful for afterwards. Now I think that this is precisely what we foolish Christian people call Providence.... Let us pray to God, and hope.[60]

In 1929, Gilson wrote in the American Catholic press: "We are planting; we are confident that God will give us the increase.... The spirit of the Institute will be one of humility, of honesty, and useful work. Above everything else, it will be one of love for truth, which is but another name for God."[61] To confine ourselves to the foundation's beginning, in 1930 Gilson employed a series of very revealing metaphors:

> All goes well here. A healthy unease spreads throughout the university about what we are doing, particularly since it has become known that we are studying the medieval sources of the poet Spencer. Can we really teach them something? Yesterday I was invited to the English professors' club to give a lecture on the sources of medieval English literature. The ferment is at work in the dough. You will see how many "ladybugs" are going to take flight from Ottawa and Toronto.[62]

Pontifical recognition of the Institute required five years of negotiations with the Congregation for Seminaries and Universities. In March 1934, Gilson sent a letter to submit the request for the erection of the Institute as a Pontifical Institute, with authorization to grant canonical degrees:

> At a time when medieval studies are developing in America, where public universities establish chairs of medieval philosophy, where the Mediaeval Academy of America [at Harvard] has just been established, it is absolutely necessary that Catholics not fall behind in an area that ought to belong to them. It corresponds to them to teach the Middle Ages, in order not to allow Protestant scholars to spread a false image of it, dangerous for the situation of the Catholic Church itself in the United States and Canada. Therefore, this scholarly work is also, and even first of all, an apostolic work through historical science.... This very year, two American universities (Harvard and Los Angeles) have asked me to leave Toronto to organize

60 Letter from Étienne Gilson to Fr. McCorkell, November 21, 1927, SMCA.

61 Étienne Gilson, "Mediaevalism in Toronto," *Commonweal* 9, no. 26, May 1, 1929, 740.

62 Letter from Étienne Gilson to Marie-Dominique Chenu, November 29, 1930, Fonds Chenu, APDF.

teaching about the Middle Ages on the same model. I refused, judging that it is necessary to establish a Catholic center thoroughly before building on Protestant ground, where the dangers are only too evident.[63]

Gilson's request, supported by a letter from Fr. Chenu that was added to the dossier,[64] was examined twice in plenary sessions of the Congregation for Seminaries and Universities, in June 1934 and March 1936. Gilson's proposition was not accepted definitively, but nevertheless was rewarded with words of encouragement to make the labor undertaken deeper and stronger.[65] Gilson's initiative was esteemed for its boldness in creating a serious Catholic endeavor in Protestant territory. But in the background, there was a barrier of obstacles: for instance, from Msgr. Cassulo, the apostolic delegate stationed in Ottawa;[66] also from Msgr. Corrigan, rector of the Catholic University of America in Washington, who had been consulted in this regard.[67] The Congregation received many reports, some of them anonymous;[68] there were

63 Report from Étienne Gilson to Cardinal Bisleti, March 24, 1934, Allegato 1, Università di Toronto, Busta 1929–1934, Archives of the Congregation for Catholic Education (Rome) [ACCE].

64 Letter from Fr. Chenu, December 10, 1932, Università di Toronto, Busta 1929–1934, ACCE: argument for the historical method applied in the area of medieval thought; resurrection of dead and withered texts; destruction of the "stupid prejudice about ignorant Middle Ages."

65 See the minutes of the plenary session of the Congregation, March 24, 1936, two pages: "The initiative undertaken at Toronto ought to be encouraged and supported." But it was still not mature enough: "We have decided to defer canonical recognition." The decision was confirmed in an audience by Pius XI, March 25, Università di Toronto, Busta 1929–1934, ACCE.

66 See Msgr. Cassulo's letter to the Congregation of Seminaries and Universities, July 20, 1934, Università di Toronto, Busta 1929–1934, ACCE. Cassulo expressed reservations because the Institute was too new. Furthermore, there was a change of archbishop in Toronto. What would the new archbishop do?

67 Letter from Msgr. Corrigan to the Congregation, July 18, 1939, Università di Toronto, Busta 1929–1934, ACCE: "The scope and influence of this institute did not seem to me to merit the condition of pontifical erection.... An institute of medieval studies of first-class character would be a very desirable addition to Catholic education, since in the United States, particularly, a number of the great secular universities are showing an awakened interest in the culture of the Middle Ages."

68 Letter of December 26, 1934, Allegato IV, "Informazioni circa l'istituto di studi mediaevali in Toronto." An anonymous source transmitted the information to Fr. Pietro Boetto, SJ: "It is not clear what advantages the Medieval Institute will gain by being raised to the rank of Pontifical Institute. For the Basilians, the laymen, and others who take courses there, what matters is to have degrees from the University of Toronto. Those degrees alone will allow them to teach in other universities or in colleges affiliated with the University of Toronto. Consequently, the pontifical degrees would seem to be completely subordinated and secondary and something purely accidental. It is difficult to see what benefit the English-speaking population would derive from them. In education, they are still in a pioneering stage here. There is neither tradition nor general culture. Consequently, it is too soon to engage in this sort of work. However, one can understand that men like Gilson

those like Fr. Gemelli who valued the initiative and its apostolic worth but in the last analysis emitted a negative judgment.[69] A reviewer denounced the University of Toronto as "Protestant in name and atheist in fact." The same source declared that the Basilians did not require enough of those enrolled in medieval studies and gave them too much freedom, "in the fashion of the Protestants, which is not without serious danger." The institute "has not borne much fruit," and shows "a pretentious character."[70]

Gilson strongly resented these setbacks. He opened up to Cardinal Bisleti on June 23, 1934:

> I have abandoned an important post at Harvard University to undertake a labor that I believed had to be very useful for the future of Catholicism in America. Harvard University has asked me several times to return and let the Institute develop without me, since it had been founded. The Ministry of Foreign Affairs in Paris would much prefer that I work at Harvard, for French influence in North America, than at St. Michael's College for propagation of our faith. I have resisted all these entreaties. But I permit myself to ask in all simplicity what I should do.[71]

It was not until 1939 that the new apostolic delegate supported Gilson's request in order to "neutralize the influence of anti-Catholic schools that flourish in the Province of Toronto."[72] Cardinal Achille Liénart likewise gave his support to the Institute:

> Your excellency will permit me to explain my thinking about the Institute of Mediaeval Studies of Toronto. The work seems remarkable and even

---

and Maritain have produced a favorable impression in non-Catholic circles and exerted a positive influence on behalf of Scholastic philosophy at the University."

69 See Gemelli's first *voto*, addressed to Msgr. Ruffini, July 5, 1937. Gemelli had examined the Institute's statutes. "It is evident that under the garb of medieval studies, it is possible to present the substance of the Catholic Church's doctrine to the North American World." But the statutes did not correspond to the university reform fomented by Pius XI. See Gemelli's second *voto*, February 6, 1939. He acknowledged that it would be good for Toronto. But there were too few professors, too scarce means, too few books, too few journals for a field as broad as medieval studies. Università di Toronto, Busta 1929–1934, ACCE.

70 See the document "Osservazioni intorno alla Sezione di Studi Medievali nell Collegio San Michele dei PP. Basiliani, Toronto, affiliato all'Università di Toronto in Canada," no name, no date, two pages, Università di Toronto, Busta 1929–1934, ACCE.

71 Letter from Étienne Gilson to Cardinal Bisleti, June 23, 1934, Università di Toronto, Busta 1929–1934, ACCE.

72 Report of the Apostolic Delegate to Msgr. Ruffini, January 16, 1939, Università di Toronto, Busta 1929–1934, ACCE.

> unique to me, in the sense that this institute is the only center exclusively devoted to the study of the Christian civilization of the Middle Ages in all its forms. The foundation has all the more importance in that it is situated in the city of Toronto, rightly called the capital of English Puritanism. It is remarkable that more than a third of the very carefully selected students are converts from Protestantism, entranced by Catholic intellectual high culture and resolved to become themselves propagators of Catholic thought in Protestant environments. What a power of diffusion this Canadian university will have in twenty years when it has formed hundreds of expert professors.... Through its reputation as a Pontifical institute, it could attain considerable authority at the same time as encouragement and an apostolic stimulus that cannot help but augment its prestige.[73]

To finish the portrait of Toronto, the great institutional labor of Gilson's life, its ecclesial objectives must be emphasized. "The work has been undertaken for the Church," he wrote to Cardinal Bisleti in 1934.[74] The freedom given Gilson by the Basilian Congregation played a preponderant role. His *carte blanche* was one of the material causes of the foundation of the Institute at Toronto at the same time as the point of departure of a somewhat risky cultural adventure that was going to unite the Old and New Worlds in a far-reaching intellectual project: introducing Latin culture, the Middle Ages, and medieval philosophy to North America.

The Toronto Institute is just one of the links in the network of institutes for medieval studies that Gilson wove beyond the Atlantic. Starting in 1931, he went regularly to Notre Dame University, "a most powerful center of Catholic influence."[75] "I spent a few days at Notre Dame, where I helped them to arrange an Institute of Medieval Studies. Is it going to be a new fad?"[76] Gilson joked in 1934. By then Gilson had already contributed to building, besides Toronto, another institute of medieval studies for the Dominicans in Ottawa.[77] Gilson explained to Fr. Congar that he refused to give a lecture in England and asked him to encourage the English Dominicans in Oxford

73 Letter from Cardinal Liénart to Msgr. Ruffini, January 5, 1939, Università di Toronto, Busta 1929–1934, ACEC. Cardinal Liénart was a member of the Congregation of Seminaries and Universities.

74 Letter from Étienne Gilson to Cardinal Bisleti, June 23, 1934, Università di Toronto, Busta 1929–1934, ACCE.

75 Letter from Étienne Gilson to Fr. O'Donnell, October 26, 1931, UPCO 3/98, UNDA.

76 Letter from Étienne Gilson to Ralph Barton Perry, November 25, 1934, Harvard University Archives.

77 On this point, see Michel, *La pensée catholique en Amérique du Nord*, chap. 2.

and Cambridge to do the same and create a center of studies: "Everything else is chatter. They will happily multiply lectures and impose lecturers. Nothing serious or lasting will be accomplished.[78]

In 1949, Gilson invited Robert Schuman to visit PIMS, the Pontifical Institute of Mediaeval Studies, which he described in these terms: "An institute that teaches in English, almost all of whose professors were educated in France or are my students, and who work for the Church. In twenty years it has become an active center of French intellectual activity in the most British part of Canada."[79]

Gilson's reception in North America outside of Catholic circles ought to be measured more precisely. His Harvard friendships illustrate how Gilson maintained a network in secular universities. His readers went beyond pious parishioners. For instance, the prominent writer of the *New York Herald*, Dorothy Thompson, sent an interesting letter to Gilson in February 1952:[80]

> I have just received a reprint of your lecture "The Breakdown of Morals and Christian Education," and I want to express my gratification in finding a reference in it to me. I am not a Catholic and come from a family of the most ancient protestant lineage, but I am sick at heart over the way protestant communities, in their attacks on Catholic education... are more concerned to fight Catholicism than to uphold their Lord and Savior against the atheists and agnostics. Paul Blanchard's books, with their almost unbelievable ignorance of Catholicism, have sold hundreds of thousands of copies in this country's "Bible Belt." When recently asked (by a prominent protestant minister in Alabama) for my opinion of them, I remarked that there is no indication in them that Blanchard is a Christian at all, and that the logical end of his thesis was not anti-Catholic but anti-Christian and pro-totalitarian. I regret to say that the ancient preacher did not know what I was talking about.

78 Letter from Étienne Gilson to Fr. Yves Congar, May 14, 1927, APDF.

79 Letter from Étienne Gilson to Robert Schuman, August 29, 1949, Maison de Robert Schuman.

80 Letter from Dorothy Thompson to Étienne Gilson [in English], February 15, 1952, FG, SMCA.

INSTITUT SCIENTIFIQUE FRANCO-CANADIEN, MONTREAL

In December 1937, Gilson was unanimously named[81] president of the Institut Scientifique Franco-Canadien (ISFC) in Montreal, an institution thoroughly analyzed by historians. Its archives are located on the University of Montreal campus.[82] It was founded in May 1926 by the biologist Louis-Janvier Dalbis (1881–1937) and the jurist Édouard Montpetit (1881–1954) at the suggestion of Paul-Émile Naggiar,[83] who headed the consulate general of France at Montreal from 1921 to 1923 and was transferred afterwards to the "Service des Oeuvres" of the Quai d'Orsay, the Foreign Ministry's cultural affairs bureau. The Institute's goal, as set out in the first article of its statutes, was to "tighten the intellectual bonds between France and Canada" through the exchange of professors and the organization of scientific missions.

The Institute was both a very ambitious undertaking and a modest one in the sense that it did not possess classrooms, libraries, or laboratories. Housed, starting in 1931, at the University of Montreal, under the auspices of the Montreal Polytechnic School, it was subsidized by the Province of Quebec, the newly founded University of Montreal, and the Quai D'Orsay. Notably, its board of directors included the rector and deans of the University of Montreal, the various directors of other institutions of higher education in Montreal (the Polytechnic School, the Montreal School of Commerce), as well as provincial and diplomatic representatives. There was a parallel committee in Paris, including the rector of the Académie de Paris, the rector of the Institut Catholique, professors of the Sorbonne, and various other representatives of higher education.

In the four decades from 1926 to 1967, the Institute sponsored exchanges, chose lecturers, financed trips, organized lecture series, and thereby shaped

81 Letter from Édouard Montpetit to Étienne Gilson, December 3, 1937, P 12 E 14, Archives of the University of Montreal [AUM], quoted by Gérard Fabre, "L'Institut Scientifique Franco-Canadien pendant et au sortie de la Seconde Guerre mondiale, sur la présidence de Gilson et Montpetit," in "50 ans d'échanges France-Québec 1910–1960," special issue of *Bulletin d'histoire politique* 20, no. 1 (Autumn 2011): 84–97.

82 See the inventory of Fonds P 12 in the AUM. Read especially the remarkable article by Gérard Fabre mentioned in the previous note. See also Catherine Pomeyrols, "La formation des intellectuels québécois dans l'entre deux guerres" (PhD diss., Université Bordeaux Montaigne, January 1994), vol. 3, document 13, 75–84.

83 Hermas Bastien, "L'Institut Scientifique Franco-Canadien," *L'Action universitaire* 6, no. 5 (April 1940): 5.

intellectual cooperation between France and Quebec. As Henri-Irénée Marrou (Gilson's successor in 1951 as head of the ISFC and its last president) declared with concern, seen from France, the Institute was a "victim of the [Gaullist] policy of destruction of intermediate bodies."[84] On the Quebec side, the Institute was rather the victim of university reforms and upheavals in the second half of the 1960s. The ISFC became "lethargic"[85] after 1967, the year of the last meeting of its general assembly. It was finally dissolved in 1972.[86] At that point, the ISFC was "included in the machinery of cooperation," as Marrou put it with concern,[87] and its functions were placed within the "state services" that were set up in France and in the Quebec of the peaceful revolution.

The role of Étienne Gilson in the ISFC was most important. In January 1927, Gilson gave the ISFC's memorable inaugural lecture on St. Bernard's mysticism. An account of it was written by Hermas Bastien:

> The inaugural meeting took place on January 22, 1927 at Saint-Sulpice Hall. The felicitous idea of inviting Étienne Gilson. who was teaching at Harvard at the moment, had occurred to the Institute. Gilson spoke of St. Bernard, founder of medieval mysticism, to a captivated audience that included Msgr. Gauthier,as well as the consul of France, Senator Dandurand, Sir Lomer Gouin, Msgr. Piette, the representative of the provincial government C.-J. Simard, and many other intellectual figures. Never was a speaker listened to more attentively and more religiously. A short speech by the Institute President Monsieur Dalbis preceded the lecture. It was followed by thanks given by Fr. Ceslas Forest, O.P., dean of the faculty of philosophy.[88]

All during the 1930s and almost every year, Gilson, helped by the Institute's generous resources, was invited to give public lectures at the University

84 Letter from Henri-Irénée Marrou to Léon Lortie, April 13, 1970, P 12 E 47, AUM: "Our Institute has been the victim of what Gaullism's adversaries call its policy of destruction of intermediate bodies. Our little organization was doing very well, and I am not sure that the new arrangement, which requires that our proposals pass through ministerial channels, represents genuine progress for University exchanges between France and Quebec."

85 Letter from Henri-Irénée Marrou to Léon Lortie, March 31, 1970, P 12 E 47, AUM. In this archive there is a collection of letters from Marrou expressing the impossibility of reforming the ISFC in the new Quebec university environment of 1967–1970.

86 Letter from Roger Gaudry, rector of Laval University, December 7, 1972, P, 12 E 48, AUM.

87 Letter from Henri-Irénée Marrou to Léon Lortie, March 31, 1970, P 12 E 47, AUM.

88 Hermas Bastien, "L'Institute Scientifique Franco-Canadien," *L'Action universitaire* 6, no. 5 (April 1940): 5–9.

of Montreal and McGill University. The Institute had an important role in bringing French medieval studies to North America. It was responsible for the presence of Fr. Marie-Dominique Chenu in 1930, 1931, and 1935, contributing in this way to the foundation of the Dominican Institute of Medieval Studies in Ottawa. Likewise, the ISFC invited Jacques Maritain in 1934 and Yves Simon in 1946.

The ISFC named Gilson president in December 1937. For almost fifteen years, except during World War II,[89] Gilson played a major role in it. The ISFC required interaction with French diplomatic authorities, so Gilson communicated frequently with Quai d'Orsay's cultural services, which viewed his appointment to head ISFC most favorably.[90] Gilson met frequently with the French representative in Ottawa as well as with his cultural advisor. "Count on total support,"[91] wrote Madame Leïla de Dampierre to Gilson. She dedicated to Gilson in the friendliest terms a little volume entitled *Ballade des diplomates errants* (SMCA) that she published in 1949. De Dampierre affirmed her strong interest in ISFC and negotiated directly with the Quebec government for the continuation of the Institute's subsidy.

As the Institute's president, Gilson decided who should or should not participate in the exchange program. Gérard Fabre has shown the tension between Étienne Gilson, Édouard Montpetit, and Jean Bruchési, the Duplessis government's secretary of state for cultural affairs, on the subject of the invitation to the Pétainist adherent Louis Rougier and the Maurraissian Pierre Gaxotte. In 1946, Gilson explicitly opposed these invitations. He managed to block the way to his old opponent Louis Rougier, the eternal plagiarist, and vetoed him: Jean Bruchési wrote: "It is much too much, as a question of principle, that the invitation already extended to Rougier by the Institut Scientifique Franco-Canadien should not be maintained. Tell me simply whether the case has been decided negatively because he needs a visa to enter Canada and the French Embassy denies the visa, or because the Institut

89 See Fabre, "L'Institut Scientifique Franco-Canadien pendant et au sortir de la Seconde Guerre mondiale."

90 Letter from Jean Marx to Étienne Gilson, December 29, 1937, Archives Vrin: "My dear friend: I have learned of your appointment to be Director of the Institut Scientifique Franco-Canadien. We immediately congratulated the Committee in Montreal for the choice. I would like to see you as soon as possible in order to arrange for the Institute's functioning during the coming years. The death of poor Dalbis has left a void and produced a gap that ought to be filled."

91 Letter from Madame de Dampierre to Étienne Gilson, March 7, 1938, Archives Vrin.

accepts Gilson's veto."[92] But some months later Gilson did not succeed in his opposition to the invitation to Gaxotte, despite the clear expression of his position. In 1948, Gilson planned to resign as president of ISFC, because he found it unacceptable that his decisions were disputed in Quebec.[93] The official transition took place in 1951. Henri-Irénée Marrou succeeded Gilson as president of ISFC until 1967–1970.

PHONY WAR PROPAGANDA (1939–1940)

Gilson left Paris on September 12, 1939, to go to Toronto by way of Liverpool and Quebec. He did not return to France, via Lisbon, until April 15, 1940.[94] Gilson was excused from teaching at the Collège de France and informally granted leave from the Collège to the Ministry of Foreign Affairs.[95] Gilson remained in America during all of the phony war. Autumn 1939 was occupied in the usual pattern of different courses and lectures at the Institute of Mediaeval Studies in Toronto.[96] He was in Paris after the collapse of France in June 1940. A point that his biographer Lawrence Shook makes, without elaborating upon it,[97] justified Gilson's presence in America until April 1940. Like Jacques Maritain,[98] Gilson in effect was dispatched by the Ministry of

92 Letter from Jean Bruchési to Édouard Montpetit, Quebec, February 19, 1946, P 12 A1, AUM, quoted by Fabre, "L'Institut Scientifique Franco-Canadien pendant et au sortir de la Second Guerre mondiale."

93 Letter from Étienne Gilson to Édouard Montpetit, Paris, April 28, 1948, P 12 A1, AUM, quoted by Fabre, "L'Institut Scientifique Franco-Canadien pendant et au sortir de la Second Guerre mondiale."

94 Letter from Étienne Gilson to Gerald Phelan, April 20, 1940, sent from Paris, SMCA: "I reached Lisbon in complete calm, after a crossing without problems."

95 Letter from Édmond Faral to Étienne Gilson, April 20, 1940, Archives Vrin: "You have just carried out an important mission in the United States and Canada, which we know will produce positive results. In the present circumstances it is clear that the kind of services you can provide abroad must call for very generous accommodations in what concerns your teaching obligations at the Collège de France itself. I see only benefits from leaving you at the entire disposition of the Minister of Foreign Affairs and the Minister of National Education for new missions that they will entrust to you."

96 Shook, *Étienne Gilson*, 238–41.

97 Shook, *Étienne Gilson*, 237; "As an officer retired to the reserves, Gilson's services now became the property of la Republique." Again, 238: "On September 12, Gilson probably visited one or more of the French ministries."

98 Florian Michel, "Jacques Maritain pendant la drôle de guerre: Notes et documents," *Cahiers Jacques Maritain* 59 (December 2009): 4–57.

Foreign Affairs to explain the issues in the current war to the North American public, both French and English speaking.

There are very precise reports addressed to Édmond Faral, the administrator of the Collège de France, and to the Ministry of Foreign Affairs.[99] Gilson's private correspondence of the period testifies to an involvement against a background of grief. Gilson summed up *his* war in the New World for his old friend Henri Gouhier in December 1939: "I have to fight only against opinions and, furthermore, rather in the United States than in Canada, infinitely more among American Catholics, who are fiercely neutralist, than among Protestants, who mostly are pro-Allies. It is a little war without glory and without interest, except for the spectacle of human stupidity that it offers and of which it allows us to observe new varieties."[100]

Gilson wrote to Ralph Barton Perry in January 1940: "The French government will probably appoint me as a war propagandist at Harvard, at least for one or two weeks. In case you were still in favor of taking such a chance with me, I would suggest from four to six lectures on the explosive subject: 'Petrarch and the Problem of Fourteenth-Century Humanism.' This series of lectures would be entirely paid for by the French Government."[101] Unenthusiastically involved in the service of intellectual propaganda, Gilson nonetheless spared no effort to explain the rectitude of the Allied cause.

In February 1940, the Ministry of Foreign Affairs indeed granted Gilson a subvention of fifty thousand francs,[102] or $1125,[103] a considerable amount at the time. Gilson accounted for the use of this subvention in a letter to the minister, dated April 26, 1940. He had gone to Toronto, Ottawa, and Montreal. He had undertaken a "thirty-five day tour" in the United States: Buffalo, Cleveland, Indianapolis, Bloomington, Rochester, Boston, and New York. He had also toured Franco-American groups in New England: New Bedford, Worcester, Manchester, and Woonsocket. He hosted dinners at Harvard and Montreal. He distributed off-prints of his "propaganda articles," "more than

99 See the draft of these reports in the archives of Librairie Vrin.

100 Letter from Étienne Gilson to Henri Gouhier, December 4, 1939, Archives Mme. Gouhier.

101 Letter from Étienne Gilson to Ralph Barton Perry, January 2, 1940, Harvard University Archives.

102 Letter from H. de Lageneste of the French embassy in Canada to Étienne Gilson, February 26, 1940, Archives Vrin: "Dear Sir: We have just received instructions to pay you the sum of 50,000 francs as compensation for your travel expenses in Canada and the United States. This amount will be disbursed by the Consulate General of France in Montreal."

103 Draft of the letter from Étienne Gilson to the Minister of Foreign Affairs of France, April 26, 1940, Archives Vrin.

two thousand copies." Gilson compiled a detailed list of all his activities for Edmond Faral in a report of April 18, 1940. He listed thirty-nine lectures in seven months, sixty-four classes given in Toronto, and four propaganda articles published in magazines or newspapers.[104] The French diplomatic archives also contain evidence of Gilson's lectures: the French consul in Boston, François Brière, sent a detailed report dated May 1, 1940, to Ambassador de Saint-Quintin in Washington.[105]

From the four articles published, we must conclude that Gilson did not soften his words. He spoke frankly and directly. On December 9, 1939, Gilson gave a lecture titled "Europe and Peace," at the Cercle Universitaire de Montreal. It was published in March in the Montreal academic journal *Revue Trimestrielle Canadienne*.[106] On February 3, 1940, Gilson published an article in the United States, in the Jesuit Magazine *America*,[107] where he developed the same ideas as in Montreal, aimed this time at English speakers. In fact, the article was a letter that Gilson had sent to the magazine on December 23, 1939, in order to challenge the neutralist editorial stance of American Jesuits.[108] On March 19, 1940, Gilson gave a talk at Woonsocket in Rhode Island in French, titled "La France dans le conflit actuel," published in the magazine of the Union Saint-Jean-Baptiste, which *L'Indépendant de Woonsocket* reviewed and praised the next day.[109] Gilson gave a vivid description of France occupied by Nazi Germany, "dismembered," "torn to pieces" by "jackals who wait only for the opportunity to take a bite of the corpse. . . .

104 Draft of the letter from Étienne Gilson to Edmond Faral, April 18, 1940, Archives Vrin. The document is reproduced in the appendixes at the end of the present book.

105 Report of the French Consul in Boston to his Excellency de Saint-Quintin, French Ambassador in Washington, SOFE, 425, Archives du Ministère des Affaires étrangères (La Courneuve) [AMAE]. The document is reproduced in the appendixes at the end of this book.

106 Étienne Gilson, "L'Europe et la paix," *Revue Trimestrielle Canadienne* 26, no. 101 (March 1949): 27–43.

107 Étienne Gilson, "A French View of the War," *America*, no. 62, February 3, 1940, 452–55.

108 See the letter of the editor of *America* to Étienne Gilson, December 26, 1939, Archives Vrin: "I am indeed appreciative of your letter of December 23, stating your reactions to the editorial comment in *America*, December 23. It gives me the greatest pleasure to assure you that your letter is being published without any change whatsoever in our issue of January 6. I am sure that your exposition will be found most enlightening to our readers. . . . Certainly, our sympathy turns toward the allied cause. We have, however, insisted that though the present European conflict has a relationship with the United States and its future, we have not concluded that there is a just cause for American military participation."

109 Étienne Gilson, "Étienne Gilson à Woonsocket," *L'Indépendant de Woonsocket*, March 20, 1940, 1.

France entered the war coldly, calmly, but also with an unshakable determination for its existence, . . . keeping in its heart that beautiful French virtue that is called hope."[110] Similarly, Gilson published an article titled "Maginot Line and Domitian line," in *L'Indépendant de Woonsocket* on May 28, 1940: "The Domitian Line is called the Maginot Line, and the soldiers who fight or keep watch there are not only soldiers of France but the defenders of every country in the world that renounces violence for order, force for justice, barbarism for civilization."[111] In the Montreal conference, Gilson slashed at the American Catholic neutralists and posed the issue in these terms:

> The controversy about neutrality is a purely American issue. Nothing is more natural than that public opinion in the United States be divided on such a serious issue. What is less natural is that in this division of opinions, the mass of Catholic opinion in the United States seems to form a block on one side and that this should be the side of neutrality.[112]

Gilson rejected both the position of American journalists and that of Catholic readers hostile to the French and British empires. He retorted: "The happy people of the United States have so completely forgotten its predecessors in the territory it occupies that it does not even remember having eliminated them."[113] Against the angelism of the Los Angeles diocesan newspaper, Gilson used every rhetorical weapon on the point of combatting American non-involvement:

> Our capital vice as eventual allies is that we are not angels! That, I fear, has no remedy. Have the Poles and Czechs been wiped out? It is their own fault, since they are not angels. As its name requires, the Archdiocese of Los Angeles only agrees to ally itself with angels and only fights for angels. Let us be consoled, because, even if we were angels, the Archdiocese would look twice before helping us. After all, in the only war known among angels, there were good and bad angels. This time there would only be bad angels,

110 Étienne Gilson, "La France dans le conflit actuel: Causerie de M. Étienne Gilson, philosophe français, à l'occasion d'une visite officielle au Bureau général," *L'Union: Organe officiel de l'Union Saint-Jean-Baptiste* 40, no. 4 (April 15, 1940): 1–2.

111 Étienne Gilson, "Ligne Maginot et Ligne Domitien," *L'indépendant de Woonsocket*, March 28, 1940, 1.

112 Étienne Gilson, "L'Europe et la paix," *Revue Trimestrielle Canadienne* 26, no. 101 (March 1940): 27.

113 Étienne Gilson, "L'Europe et la paix," 29.

> and just as the first time, troops from California would not be seen on either side. Opportunities to laugh are rare in time of war.[114]

The deliberately ironical tone is sometimes aggressive: "'Americans must keep their heads,' *America* proclaims. Agreed. That is in everyone's interests. Let Americans not lose their heads, but let them not make us lose ours, and let them begin by putting something in their own."[115] With this, Gilson attempts to "clear away a false liberalism no longer capable of distinguishing between the just and the unjust." He reminded Americans that war is licit in certain cases, and concluded with St. Augustine in his letter to Boniface that it is necessary "to have the courage to proclaim this simple truth, that the war in which our English, Canadian, and French soldiers fight is a just war, undertaken without hatred for a just cause with a view to the just end that St. Augustine so perfectly formulated: 'Be peace loving even in making war, in order to attain the benefit of peace for those whom you conquer, by conquering them.'"[116] Gilson commented on certain passages from *Mein Kampf* and showed the insertion of "Germanism" throughout history. Arnold Lunn presented arguments from the English viewpoint. The magazine also opened its pages to a German author, Friedrich Baerwald, who published an essay titled "Hitlerism is not Germanism," so that the belligerents were represented. In *America*'s February 17 issue, the letters showed how divided opinions were. For one reader, Gilson's "is by far the best article of the three." For another reader, "Gilson's article merits great respect." For a third it is "a pure propaganda piece"—bad faith, bad information.[117] All the same, after his return to France, Gilson felt that the situation had improved: "Furthermore, I think that the Americans begin to understand, even Catholics, who along with the communists have been the worst opponents of the allies at the beginning of this war. We see them now returning to their true generosity, their eyes opened, and with the courage to speak."[118]

It is helpful to compare Gilson's articles with those of Maritain on the same issues, since the latter, dispatched in the same circumstances for the same task, also attempted to fight against American neutralism. Gilson

114 Étienne Gilson, "L'Europe et la paix," 34.

115 Étienne Gilson, "L'Europe et la paix," 40.

116 Étienne Gilson, "L'Europe et la paix," 43.

117 Letters, *America*, February 17, 1940, 521–22.

118 Letter from Étienne Gilson to Msgr. André Combes, June 7, 1940, NAF 28 257, BNF.

published in *America*, Maritain in *Commonweal*. Their positions in the argument are similar. The difference between the two is chronological. Maritain arrived in North America in January 1940. Gilson returned to Paris in April. His propaganda activity was truncated by the defeat of France, and he was reduced to silence in political affairs by the machinery of the Vichy State. By contrast, Maritain, in New York in June 1940, continued his activity until the end of the war, with all the good results that we know.[119]

Naturally, the Institute of Mediaeval Studies asked itself what role it could play in the war. In the 1940 annual report, the Superior of Saint Michael's College wrote that cooperation in wartime, which cannot wisely be avoided, must take the form of assistance to refugee professors.[120] The destruction of Louvain during World War I and the closure of the Catholic Institute of Paris are cited in this regard. Without drawing any conclusion referring to Gilson, who was by now in France, Maritain presented the Basilian Fathers with the opportunity to put their intention into practice in January 1941 by supporting the case of Paul Vignaux.[121]

119 Michel Fourcade, "Jacques Maritain, inspirateur de la Résistance," *Cahiers Jacques Maritain*, no. 32 (1996): 14–57. See also Fourcade, "Maritain et l'Europe en exil. 1940–1945," in *Jacques Maritain en Europe: La reception de sa pensée*, ed. Bernard Hubert (Paris, Beauchesne, 1996), 281–320.

120 *Annual Report of the Superior of Saint Michael's College, 1939–1940*, General Archives of the Basilian Fathers, Toronto.

121 Letter from Jacques Maritain to Gerald Phelan, January 30, 1941, SMCA: "My very dear friend, this is a postscript to my letter. I have forgotten to speak to you about Paul Vignaux, who, as you know, is the friend and best French student of Gilson. (He occupies Gilson's chair at l'École des hautes études.) He has written and cabled us here several times that he wishes to come to America. The Ministry of National Education is disposed to let him go. I have done all I could for him with the authorities at the New School and the Rockefeller Foundation, who have been authorized by the State Department to invite a hundred or one hundred fifty professors. All that I have achieved is that they are disposed to invite Vignaux, that is to say, to make him get an American visa, if another American university decides to give him an appointment for at least two years. If you think that a teaching post at the Institute can be considered, the best thing would be for you to write directly to Dr. Alvin Johnson, President of the New School for Social Research. . . . Vignaux has sent us a real SOS."

TOWARD UNESCO: THE SAN FRANCISCO AND LONDON CONFERENCES (1945–1946)

We shall try to be better in peace than we have been in war.[122]

At the end of March 1945, when Germany had not yet surrendered, Étienne Gilson was appointed to the French delegation to the San Francisco Conference (April 26 to June 26, 1945).[123] He next was sent to the London Conference (November 1 to November 16, 1945), where UNESCO's founding document was signed. In 1946, he participated in UNESCO's first activities in Paris and in debates that surrounded the birth of UNESCO and its first president, Julian Huxley. As a man of peace and supporter of international cooperation and a polyglot who spoke English and Russian, a university professor with abundant connections in the world of press and diplomacy, Gilson's mission from the Provisional Government of France allowed him to check the functioning of the "Gilsonian system," which included both involvement in action and press coverage, with equal doses of realism and medieval utopia.

On the diplomatic level, the San Francisco Conference was a major milestone in the postwar readjustment of international relations.[124] The Dumbarton Oaks agreements had to be re-examined. The groundwork of the operation of the United Nations had to be laid out. Many delicate technical issues had to be solved. The right of veto, the composition of the Security Council, economic and financial issues, the Court of Justice, cultural, economic, and financial issues, all had to be determined. After two months of negotiation, the final documents were signed on June 26 by one hundred fifty diplomats from fifty countries.

The Provisional Government intended that France should be heard again in international diplomacy. France became a permanent member of the Security Council at San Francisco. Along with English, French was

122 Letter from Étienne Gilson to Ralph Barton Perry, February 1, 1945, Harvard University Archives.

123 Letter from an official in the Ministry of Foreign Affairs personnel office (whose signature has not survived the ravages of time), to Étienne Gilson, March 27, 1945, SMCA: "I have the honor of communicating to you that you have been designated to be part of the French Delegation to the San Francisco Conference. . . . The date of departure from Paris is set for Tuesday April 3, by railway, at 8:30 A.M., North Station."

124 "Fonds Nations Unies—organisations internationales," 372 QO, dossiers 1–7, AMAE. See also Fonds Naggiar, 199PAAP/47, AMAE.

recognized as an official language in the future functioning of the United Nations. At San Francisco, by General de Gaulle's explicit order, Georges Bidault demanded the translation of speeches by American diplomats into French.

During the negotiations, the French delegation included ministers, ambassadors, and high officials, as well as many translators and stenographers. The Council of Ministers decided on its composition on March 2, 1945. The appointed delegates were Georges Bidault (Minister of Foreign Affairs), René Pleven (Minister of Finance), François Billoux (Minister of Public Health), Joseph Paul-Boncour (head of the delegation in Bidault's absence and permanent delegate of France to the League of Nations), and Henri Bonnet (French ambassador to the U.S.). The assistant delegates were Jean Monnet, Paul-Émile Naggiar, Jules Basdevant (the legal advisor of the Ministry of Foreign Affairs), General Alphonse Juin (Chief of the General Staff), and Admiral d'Argenlieu (Vice President of the Naval Council).

The French delegation also included a number of "technical advisers," jurists, economists, university professors, as well as members of the cabinet, personnel from the French embassy in Washington, and a team of ambassadors, mostly from Gaullist circles. Accordingly and at random, we can name Jacques Fouques-Duparc (Secretary General of the French delegation), Raoul Aglion, Hervé Alphand, Étienne Burin des Roziers, Émile Servan-Schreiber, François Charles-Roux, Geoffroy Chodron de Courcel, René Hofherr, Jean Laloy, Christian de Margerie, Bernard de Menthon, Élisabeth de Miribel, Roger Seydoux, André Siegfried, Étienne Gilson, and others.

The work of the national delegations was carried out in particular within three large commissions, each subdivided into numerous committees. Along with André Siegfried and Roger Seydoux, Étienne Gilson was assigned to Committee III of Commission II. The committee was in charge of "economic and social cooperation" and "eventually intellectual cooperation" (the last being an addition suggested by the French delegates). UNESCO, which was in the process of gestation, was on this committee's horizon. The work was done under the direction of Ramaswahni Mudaliar, president of the Indian delegation. Marshall Jan Smuts, delegate from South Africa, and Peter Fraser from New Zealand had notable interventions. This committee met twenty-one times in plenary session. The sub-committee in charge of drafting its report met nineteen times. The reports show clearly that France proposed four amendments on the subject of "economic and social problems contained in the project for international organization" as it had been adopted at

Dumbarton Oaks.[125] France would have liked to see the powers of the Economic and Social Council strengthened, to guarantee a just representation of the world's economic powers within the Economic and Social committee, to explicitly anticipate the creation of regional economic organisms, and to develop "intellectual cooperation." The addition of the term "intellectual," a French demand, had been ratified by Committee III, which now intended to develop "international cooperation in education and the intellectual realm." It became part of the current text of the United Nations Charter, where we find that intention to promote "international cooperation in the areas of intellectual culture and education" (articles 55, 57, and 62 of the Charter), a small French semantic victory.

However, it is impossible to measure Gilson's exact contribution to the Committee's work through archival files. Obviously, the term "intellectual" must have seemed prudent to him. If the opportunity presented itself for him to defend the French motion, he did so eloquently. The reports are always anonymous. No public speech by Gilson is recorded. Beyond Gilson's presence and modest participation in the elaboration of the United Nations Charter, what matters is the account he gave of the event and the conclusions he drew from it in his correspondence. In a letter to Fr. Phelan, he wrote:

> I am here, where I am supposed to act in the capacity of a technical adviser on all problems related to intellectual co-operation. There will be some problems, and we are already confronted with the curious reluctance of a great Eurasian state, a well-known champion of democracy in the world, to accept the principle of unrestricted freedom of information. Strange, is it not?[126]

Gilson indicated, as well, that he played an important role in the translation of official Conference documents from English to French: "I am now sitting on a committee of six (including Canada, Belgium, and Haiti) for the drafting of the French text of the charter. Since the English (or American) text is continually altered, it is a heartbreaking job. Moreover, to respect the intentional vagueness of the English formulas is also very distressing, both literally and morally."[127]

125 "Fonds Nations Unies—organisations internationales," 372 QO, dossier 3, folder: "Travaux des commissions et comités"; sub-folder: "Commission II, comité 3," AMAE.

126 Letter from Étienne Gilson to Gerald Phelan, April 30, 1945, in Shook, *Étienne Gilson*, 255–56.

127 Letter from Étienne Gilson to Gerald Phelan, June 11, 1945, in Shook, *Étienne Gilson*, 256.

In Gilson's work, there were numerous references to, as well as deeper analyses of, the San Francisco Conference. In a later article, titled "Neutrality for France?" (1950), Gilson recalled "the good old days of the San Francisco Conference,"[128] the last fair weather before the Cold War. In an homage to Paul Claudel, Gilson explained that he understood *Le soulier de satin* after having "attended a show at the great Chinese theater in San Francisco, with everyone speaking and eating freely, children who played in the aisles between the chairs in the pit, the continual din of the percussion orchestra underlining the lyrics by rumbling, rattling, grating, sudden explosions of gongs and cymbals, not to mention the comings and goings of the props staff."[129] In a 1946 *Esprit* article, Gilson implied that he argued about the existence of God with a "drunken sailor" in a San Francisco bar.[130] Also, Gilson was invited by the American government to watch an overabundance of Hollywood films that he found disagreeable and that prompted him to criticize the Blum-Byrne agreement and to support the position of the Communist Party organ *L'Humanité* on the subject.[131] In his inaugural speech at the Académie française in May 1947, Gilson returned to the French

128 Étienne Gilson, "Neutrality for France?," *Bulletin of the Atomic Scientists* 6, no. 7 (July 1950): 203–5.

129 Étienne Gilson, "Paul Claudel poète catholique," in *La pensée religieuse de Claudel*, ed. Centre catholique des intellectuels français, Recherches et débats (Paris: Desclée de Brouwer, 1969), 31–44.

130 Étienne Gilson, "Une aristocratie de l'homme moyen," *Esprit* 14, no. 127 (1946): 672–82: "However little someone has lived in the United States, that name alone conjures up so many contradictory images that it seems useless to sort them, classify them, and compare them. Where does one begin and by what right does one choose? Everything that one has seen and lived is America: from the scholar and humanist who lives in Widener Library to the drunken sailor who argues about the existence of God in a San Francisco bar."

131 Étienne Gilson, "Une erreur franco-américaine," *Le Monde*, June 12, 1946, 3: "Make no mistake, the current average French movie is incomparably better than the corresponding American film, whose complete decadence everyone in the United States knows. We owe real masterpieces, like *Green Pastures*, to that powerful industry, of which the French public cannot get enough. It would be easy to mention others, but the American film industry no longer produces them, and the United States government itself has proved this by presenting each night during two months the première of a brand new movie at the San Francisco Conference. Sadly, this was decisive. . . . A friend of the United States speaks here and someone who likes cinema. Countless Americans and even, I know well, people in Hollywood itself think this way." — Étienne Gilson, "La poutre et la paille," *Le Monde*, January 6, 1948: "On January 3, *L'Humanité* lamented the plight of French film-making, sold out to Harry Truman by Léon Blum. We have been the first to sharply criticize the Blum-Byrnes Agreement, and the experience of eighteen months that has followed has not changed our mind. *Humanité* is right to observe that apart from some courageous or excellent films that would have delighted us, the American studios have dumped on France a mound of fodder that we could do well without."

translation of the United Nations Charter, "that curious document," which lets American puritanism be glimpsed between the lines.[132] The most complete commentaries can be found in *Le Monde*. On October 29, 1945, on page one, Gilson presented the debates in which he had participated at San Francisco and enthusiastically argued for the new organization:

> An international conference for intellectual cooperation will convene soon in London. It originated from a recommendation by the French delegation to San Francisco that was unanimously and enthusiastically adopted by the conference on May 25, 1945. The decision will surprise no one, least of all the French. It is true that since the place for the reunion was not decided, a number of people thought it would take place in Paris. And rightly so, since Paris is the seat of the Institut de Coopération Intellectuelle, created by France in 1920 as one of the permanent organs of the League of Nations.... Here one must weigh one's words, because the consequences of the tower of Babel press heavily upon international undertakings. Where we write *intellectual*, the English write *cultural*, and the Americans prefer *educational*. Doubtless, our intellectuality implies culture and education, as American education implies intellectuality and culture, but with different emphases about which those who follow future debates ought to be forewarned. In particular, France should never lose sight for an instant of the fact that what will dominate the impending conference at London, or at least what will exercise a very deep influence, will be concern about organizing a new international education, without which the international spirit, which is precisely the spirit of San Francisco, will never rule.

132 Étienne Gilson, "Discours de réception à l'Académie française," 1947: "If future commentators scrutinize the curious document that is the French version of the United Nations Charter, they will have many surprises, but it will be too late, because those who composed it will no longer be there to clear them up. For example, when they read that the United Nations will guarantee 'the rights of man and the fundamental freedoms for everyone without distinction for race, sex, language, or religion,' there is no one in France who would not seize his or her pencil and restore the necessary logical order: 'without distinction of sex, race, language, or religion.' How, it will be asked, did our delegates fail to rectify this clumsy order? They did so, and I am a witness, three times, and nobody disputed that the distinction of genders is more general than that of races, so that it ought logically to go first. But when the same English phrase came back for the third time, before the same commission, imperturbably following the same order, a light began to dawn in French brains. Only one possible explanation remained, about which, using the necessary prudence, one could ultimately be sure that it was right. If race obstinately kept passing into first place, it was to hide what it is certainly sometimes good to name but sometimes cannot be seen! In this unequal struggle between logic and propriety, who will blame logic for having given up the fight? Of all the sacrifices that France has made for world peace, few will be cited that are less costly or more instructive."

> We will enter a new world and a new era, which are the world and the era of the United Nations. Under the risk of being separated from our own time, we must first learn to pronounce this name that is new to us, comprehend it fully, and love it. Six months ago, many of the French present at San Francisco were put off by this neologism. People have begun to get used to it, and soon it will be as familiar as the name of the United States, from which it derives. Henceforth, the United Nations exists, and we are part of it, to such a degree that the destiny of France, even as a nation, is inextricably linked to it. The time of isolationism has ended for all the countries of the world.

Almost immediately upon his return to France, in September 1945, Gilson was named to the French delegation to the London Conference led by Léon Blum. He was a member of the committee charged with writing the constitution of UNESCO, along with Archibald MacLeish, head of the American delegation. Gilson crossed paths with Léon Blum in a hallway, and reported that Blum wanted to talk with him about St. Thomas.[133] Gilson wrote immediately to André Combes:

> The Conference has begun well for us, but if I believe that it continues well also, it also seems to me that taken as a whole, it is out of kilter, for other countries as it is for France. Russia is absent. I think I know why, and I regret to say that I think Russia is right in the issue. The Conference was not called by the only organ that had the authority to do so.... Léon Blum is excellent from every point of view. He has the appropriate tone and attitude, which is not the case for all heads of delegations.... I have just been named to the committee in charge of drawing up the Conference's report. I know what that means. If it is like San Francisco, we will all spend our days and nights there.[134]

Twenty years later, Frank Cowell, a member of the British delegation, reported an important aspect of Gilson's participation at the London Conference.[135] It was taken up again by Gilson's biographer in 1966,[136] and since then

133 Shook, *Étienne Gilson*, 261.

134 Letter from Étienne Gilson to Msgr. André Combes, November 6, 1945, NAF, 28 257, BNF.

135 Frank R. Cowell, "Planning the Organisation of UNESCO, 1942–1946: A Personal Record," *Cahiers d'histoire mondiale, Journal of World History, Cuadernos de Historia Mundial* 10, no. 1 (1966): 210–34, at 225.

136 Shook, *Étienne Gilson*, 262.

it has been re-told in UNESCO's official channels.[137] The English diplomat recalled the figure of Gilson with obvious sympathy:

> Where so much has been forgotten, it is pleasant for the author of this brief account to remember a cold November morning in a small unheated room, where the Drafting Committee was preparing the final version of the Constitution and endeavouring to ensure equivalent English and French texts. The energetic leadership of Archibald MacLeish, leader of the United States delegation, the deeply thoughtful contributions of Dr. Jaime Torres Bodet, and the fecund inspiration of Étienne Gilson from France aroused an admiration that the passage of years has not dimmed. It was then that Mr. MacLeish picked up Primer Minister Atlee's remark . . . "It is in the minds of men that the defenses of peace must be constructed." It was also at that time that M. Gilson minted the happy phrase "the fruitful diversity of cultures," and that, on a more pedestrian level, this writer persuaded the Committee to include the promotion of "the rule of law" among the primary purposes of the Organisation. The text of the Article I (Purposes and Functions) had been agreed, everyone was cold and already late for lunch, but Mr. MacLeish . . . said that he thought that real progress had been made in the morning. Turning to M. Gilson, who never had any illusions about the strenuous difficulty of the committee's task, and who did not share some of its apparent psychological assumptions, he added, "Well, M. Gilson, I think that you will agree that it is better now!" "No," replied Gilson, amid general laughter: "it is no better; but I am getting used to it."[138]

The London Conference was something of a failure for Gilson. It was a renunciation of the "intellectual" and a defeat of "intellectuals" as an "intermediary body." The term "intellectual" was left out of the organization's name in favor of Education, Science, and Culture, which for Gilson was a failure in regard to what was accomplished in San Francisco. Intellectuals were not represented as such, but by their governments. Gilson wrote detailed accounts for *Le Monde* of the London debates and what was at stake there. The first article was titled "L'équivoque de Londres," and appeared on page one of the newspaper on November 21, 1945. The ambiguity in the article's

137 Frank R. Cowell's article was republished in *What UNESCO for the Future? Forum of Reflection* (Paris: UNESCO, 2006), appendix, i–xxxi. The anecdote is repeated in Daniel Janicot, *Rapport au Ministre des Affaires Étrangères: La France et l'UNESCO*, October 21, 2013, 143, available online: https://www.coalitionfrancaise.org/wp-content/uploads/2013/10/Rapport-Synthese-UNESCO1.pdf

138 Cowell, "Planning the Organisation of UNESCO, 1942–1946," 225.

title is connected to a serious question of principle, in which Gilson defended Russia. The San Francisco Conference called for another conference in order to continue the debates on social, economic, and intellectual questions. The invitation to the London Conference was made jointly by Great Britain and France. Russia was absent and did not accept the legitimacy of the meeting.

> The charter of the United Nations Education, Science, and Culture Organization was signed last Saturday at London. Overall, the charter is satisfactory because it stems from a sincere effort for cooperation among forty nations and is the surest guarantee, by the spirit that inspires them, that this cooperation will be continued in the future. It is a fact, and it is better that this be known, that the conference that has just established this agreement met in circumstances that allow some doubt about the practical value of the work. Article 62 of the United Nations Charter confers the power to take initiatives in culture and education upon the economic and social council. Furthermore, in the terms of a French proposal that was unanimously approved last May 25 at San Francisco, the United Nations must "convoke within the space of a few months, a general conference charged with establishing the statutes of an international organization for intellectual cooperation." The conference that has just ended, therefore, ought to have been convoked by the United Nations, which is to say, in the current state of affairs, by its provisional commission established in London.
>
> This is not what happened. An entirely different organization, the conference of allied ministers of education, which had met regularly in London since 1942, took the initiative of convening the general conference in the meeting that France had requested at San Francisco. In fact, we find an essentially British initiative that deliberately replaced what the United Nations ought to have done, and at the right moment certainly would have done. . . .
>
> We cannot say that it was legally improper to convene the London conference, and the fact that forty nations, among them the United States, agreed to go there, confers unquestionable authority on the results of its deliberations. However, let us observe that even among the states that took part in its activities, several would have preferred that it had been convoked by the United Nations itself under the San Francisco charter. At least one state demonstrated this preference in the most striking manner by refraining from sending a delegation to the London conference, namely Russia. No invitation could have persuaded Russia to join a meeting that, according to her, had to be conducted under the auspices of the United Nations and not under the auspices of the two governments that convoked it. This misunderstanding is regrettable.

The second article, titled "L'UNESCO et ses membres," was published in *Le Monde*, December 5, 1945, also on page one. Again, Gilson shows himself to be both disgruntled and confident in the future.

> What is this monster? It is the first child of the UN, that is to say the United Nations Education, Science, and Culture Organization. Do not protest! Everything that you could say against it has already been said unsuccessfully. In the land of Descartes and Pascal, it is hard to conceive of intellectual culture that dispenses with science. And without either one, what would become of education? Unhappily UNESCO has no sire, it has only accomplices. American educators wanted education to be mentioned in the name in order to interest Congress. The British delegates wanted science to be mentioned so as to console the scholars for its not appearing anywhere else. As a word to designate arts and letters was certainly necessary, they fell back on "culture." Accordingly, from compromise to compromise, Germanic *Kultur* has come to be displayed in the very title of an organization from which Germany is excluded....
>
> Let us dream about it without becoming discouraged. We are offered an organization that is not at all what France desired, but the French position was right, and in practice it will ultimately prevail. Is it not the case that as "observers," the intellectuals already have a foot in the door, and if we think that governments are bent on letting them get out of sight, it is difficult to imagine that those governments could dispense with their advice in the era of atomic energy. Moreover, there are philosophical and religious explosives as powerful as those of nuclear physics, and not all bombs are invented in laboratories. Accordingly, let us be confident and accept the United Nations intellectual organizations that we are offered. in order to guarantee the free cooperation of spiritual forces for the good of the whole world. UNESCO is a beautiful promise. France would have liked one still more beautiful.

Gilson attended the UNESCO general conference that was held in Paris from November 20 to December 10, as an assistant delegate of the French government.[139] The French delegation was led by Léon Blum. On December 1. 1946, Gilson participated in a debate broadcast by NBC radio the following day. The debate took place in Paris with J. B. Priestley of the British delegation and two members of the American delegation, Richard McKeon

139 See *Conférence générale: Première session, tenue en la Maison de l'Unesco, Paris, 20 novembre–10 decembre 1946*, available online at the UNESCO Digital Library, unesdoc.unesco.org.

(a former student of Gilson at the École pratique) and George Stoddard. In the broadcast, Gilson mixed UNESCO projects, the reality of medieval Christendom, the international character of the thirteenth-century university, and the "nationalization" of universities planned by the reforms of the Liberation. George Stoddard, president of the University of Illinois, did not fail to ask Gilson the fundamental question: "You would not want to return to the Middle Ages, would you?" Gilson answered that the question was very embarrassing for him. He would very much like to, but he knew, he said, that this was hardly possible.[140]

In two further *Le Monde* articles during December 1946, Gilson again returned to the subject UNESCO, specifically, the place of philosophy within the organization. He was concerned in particular with UNESCO's first president, Julian Huxley, the "evolutionist philosopher," who intended to make his own philosophy that of the organization.

> "UNESCO delegates belong to the intellectual pioneers of the world. If they follow their path with courage and faith, UNESCO can become the symbol of humanity's moral side." These noble words of the prime minister of India were still present in my memory, when I entered the ballroom at the Majestic, where these intellectual pioneers of the world were discussing the place of philosophy within the totality of education, science, and culture. It was at the same time comforting and baffling, because I heard first that the report of the corresponding commission had included philosophy in the social sciences, and then in the human sciences. [Gilson argued for its inclusion in the Humanities] ...
>
> As Mr. Hoffmeister, head of the Czechoslovakian delegation, correctly observed, this conference of men of science and artists is under the dictatorship of the administration and of diplomacy and, if we are allowed to add something, of international politics. It was only too easy to foresee this menace. Since the preparatory conference in London, the French delegation tried in vain to rule it out. Today, the facts are there, and the very future of UNESCO is at stake, because its peculiar mission is to put all the resources of intelligence in education, science, and culture at the service of all human beings without exception. I believe that one cannot conceive a more beautiful mission humanly speaking, but UNESCO cannot fulfill it by being inspired by contempt for intelligence.[141]

140 "Can UNESCO Educate for World Understanding?," *The University of Chicago Round Table*, December 1, 1946, 5–7.

141 Étienne Gilson, "Les pionniers intellectuels," *Le Monde*, December 4, 1946, 1.

> That the philosophers meet to define the fundamental concepts that inspire UNESCO is excellent. Especially if they reach an agreement some day. But let us not wait for them to agree before we go to work, and let us not speak as if they had been able to agree before consulting each other. At the beginning of the conference that just ended , Sir John Maud said wittily: "There are a hundred projects about which we could agree immediately, although perhaps we ought never agree on the reasons for which we agree." Those were golden words. Julian Huxley believes in UNESCO. Everyone knows he is completely devoted to it. No one doubts that he is equal to his task, and if his evolutionist humanism is to help him personally to accomplish it, we will grant it to him most gladly. But if he renounced burdening the organization with that dead weight, the organization would become much more effective and the philosophy would lose nothing by it.[142]

That was the apple of discord in the agency's early years. The issue found only a provisional solution in Mexico, in November 1947, with Maritain's lecture on the "way of peace." Julian Huxley renounced the imposition of his philosophy upon the agency he directed at that time.[143] In the 1950s, Huxley's successor faced similar criticism: promoting a single positive culture, disinterested in local realities, in order to build "the best of all worlds."[144]

Outside of the fact that the phrase about "the fertile diversity of cultures," inscribed in UNESCO's foundational document and destined to an abundant afterlife, was a suggestion of the Thomist Gilson, the results of Gilson's involvement are ultimately modest. He certainly supported the U.N. and the creation of UNESCO. But, as we have seen, he criticized the way that the London Conference was convened, the abandonment of the term "intellectual," which had been accepted in San Francisco, and the modes of UNESCO's foundation and governance. In this instance we see clearly the combination of three roles—university medievalist philosopher, public figure, and journalist.

As already mentioned, Gilson was concerned about the definition of "intellectual." He was faithful to the Latin and Augustinian sense of *intellectus*,

142 Étienne Gilson, "L'UNESCO et sa philosophie," *Le Monde*, December 20, 1946, 1

143 Michel Fourcade, "L'apport de Maritain à la philosophie de l'UNESCO," in *60 ans d'histoire de l'UNESCO: Actes du colloque international, Paris, 16–18 novembre 2005* (Paris: UNESCO, 2007), 143–47; available online: https://unesdoc.unesco.org/ark:/48223/pf0000154122.locale=en. —Chloé Maurel, "L'UNESCO de 1945 à 1974" (PhD diss., University of Paris 1, Pantheon-Sorbonne, 2005), 63–65.

144 Maurel, "L'Unesco de 1945 à 1974," 47–57, and 76 ff.

a word that he had engraved on his Academician's sword along with *fides* with the sense for Gilson of St. Anselm's phrase *fides quaerens intellectum*. At the time, the English envisaged the figure of the intellectual as it was popularized immediately after the war, notably in certain famous Parisian cafés. Reminiscing about the London Conference, Gilson recalled in 1948:

> When we asked, moreover, if, rather than the word "education," the phrase "intellectual culture" would not suffice to designate science, general consternation transformed Anglo-Saxon faces. We had perceptibly committed an indiscretion. Not "culture" but "intellectual" annoyed them. A mind nourished by St. Augustine's teaching—*intellectum valde ama* [love intellect intensely]—is surprised when he troubles friends by using such a noble and rich term. To be clear in my own mind, the next day I asked one of the British delegates, whose perspicacity had greatly impressed me, what the word "intellectual" suggested to her. "I see," she answered, "a man who is still young, pale, with a thin face, hair a little too long, unfortunately lacking practical intelligence, and who excitedly makes statements whose meaning is not immediately evident." "I think I see him," I told her, "but what will we say about 'culture'"? To which, I received the charming answer: "Culture is the same thing with a little embroidery."[145]

THE GILSON AFFAIR (1949–1951): FROM DEBATE WITH RAYMOND ARON TO INTERNATIONAL CONTROVERSY

Supported by Emmanuel Mounier and Hubert Beuve-Méry, Gilson was one of the first and staunchest critics in 1948–1949 of the North Atlantic Treaty Organization, as it was debated and then signed in 1949. That made him neither an ally of the communists nor an anti-American intellectual, but a precursor of those who considered that the Atlantic alliance was far from perfect at the military level, both in its wording and in its intention, and consequently one who believed that Europe ought to re-arm.[146] During the first years of the Cold War and especially during the Korean War, Gilson

145 Étienne Gilson, "Culture et civilisation," in *Les cents ans de l'Institut canadien de Québec: Compte rendu des fêtes du centenaire en septembre 1948*, ed. Alphonse Desilets (Québec: L'Institut Canadien de Québec, 1948), 76–84, Québec, Fonds Alphonse Désilets.

146 The bibliography on the Gilson Affair is scant. See Philippe Roger, *L'ennemi américain*, 423–29. See, likewise, Raymond Aron, *Mémoires: Édition intégrale inédite* (Paris: Robert Laffont, 2010; 1st ed., 1983).

took exception to its terms. He suggested a strong, neutral and non-aligned Europe, a Europe of the "third way," on the Swiss or Swedish model. In his view this was neither "a sign of cowardice" nor a diplomatic impossibility. Nor was it a question of "biting the hand that feeds us," but of asking that the feeding hand "not keep a tight grip on us."[147]

Raymond Aron, who had taken Gilson's courses at the Sorbonne, narrated in his 1983 memoirs what became known as the "Gilson Affair," "a quarrel among Catholics, in which Aron had no part,"[148] although he was the principal though anonymous object. Aron's written account was rather personal. He cast himself in favorable light and happily assumed the gift of foreknowledge,[149] in the realm of unverifiable counterfactual history, since in the end the U.S.S.R. did not invade Western Europe. This "first great postwar debate," as Aron summed it up, concerned "the North Atlantic Treaty and the neutrality of Europe in the nascent Cold War."[150] "The rejection of the North Atlantic Treaty did not imply neutrality. The debate about neutrality or neutralism developed with some confusion between Gilson and *Le Figaro* (myself included), and between Hubert Beuve-Méry and Pierre Brisson."[151] Aron rightly emphasized that the exchanges with Gilson and Beuve-Méry remained courteous although a bit sharp, in "the tone of honest controversy, without polemical excess."[152] *Polemics*, however, is precisely the title used by Aron in 1955 for the second publication of the article prepared against the neutrality supported by Gilson.[153] Aron, whose pro-Atlantic positions were ultimately victorious, wrote that he succeeded in convincing General de Gaulle that those positions were right. Initially, de Gaulle seems to have been a "Gilsonian"—"Gilson is right," the General wrote,—but he ended by becoming an Aronian who supported the North Atlantic Treaty even if its formulation was equivocal. "Aron," de Gaulle affirmed in a conversation

147 Étienne Gilson, "Neutrality for France?," *Bulletin of the Atomic Scientists* 6, no. 7 (July 1950): 205.

148 Aron, *Mémoires*, 355: "I neither had nor have anything to do with this quarrel among Catholics."

149 Aron, *Mémoires*, 353.

150 Aron, *Mémoires*, 342–57.

151 Aron, *Mémoires*, 342.

152 Aron, *Mémoires*, 347, 354.

153 Raymond Aron, "Neutralité ou engagement?" report presented to the Congress for Freedom of Culture at Berlin in July 1950, published under the title of "Impostures de la neutralité," in *Liberté de l'Esprit* 13 (1950), and in *Polémiques* (Paris: Gallimard, 1955), 199–217.

reported by Aron, "is right in denouncing the weakness of Gilson's argument."[154] Better an ambiguous treaty, according to Aron, than no treaty at all. Aron cast doubt on the importance of the precise expression of the obligations of the signatories.[155] To that Gilson, a philosopher who knew the United States well, could hardly agree. "The Atlantic Treaty does not bring us any real guarantee. It does not commit America to anything in case of aggression that its interest would not have automatically dictated," Mounier commented, supporting Gilson's analyses.[156]

In public, the controversy between Aron and Gilson culminated on French Radio, on December 28, 1949. Aron recalled in passing his distant memories of Gilson's classes at the Sorbonne. The two men opposed each other in company with Jules Romains (1885–1972), Georges Bourgin (1879–1958), and Joseph Paul-Boncour (1873–1972) on the program "The Paris Tribune" in a session devoted to "a half century of world history."[157] The conversation transpired on a very high level. It pitted different contemporary political tendencies against each other: Christian democracy, liberalism, and the different strands of French socialism. Paul-Boncour was a veteran of SFIO, a socialist republican. Romains was close to the radical socialists. Bourgin was a historian of the 1848 revolution, the Commune, and more generally of French socialism. Aron's nuanced pessimism on the subject of France and Western Europe clashed with Gilson's also nuanced optimism, since Gilson declared during the broadcast that he was horribly pessimistic about human nature but an optimistic voluntarist in politics. France and Europe would be what their peoples made of them, what they want them to be, Gilson insisted. Aron emphasized the decline of Europe, its disintegration, its decomposition, its exhaustion, joined together with the rise of the peripheral powers, the United States and the U.S.S.R., and the risks of the Cold War, comparing Europe to Greece at the time of the Peloponnesian War. Gilson recalled the cultural, aesthetic, and spiritual greatness of the previous half century and the efforts to build Europe that were in progress.

154 Raymond Aron, *Mémoires*, 348–49.

155 Raymond Aron, *Mémoires*, 350.

156 Emmanuel Mounier, "Le pact atlantique," in *Carnets de route*, vol. 2, *Les certitudes difficiles* (Paris: Seuil, 1951), 341.

157 Broadcast of December 28, 1949, "The Paris Tribune," "A Half Century of World History," with Étienne Gilson, Raymond Aron, Jules Romains, the former President of the Council of Ministers Joseph Paul-Boncour, and Georges Bougin; from the national archives, Inathèque. The program lasted a little more than twenty-eight minutes.

"I will speak only of what I have lived," he declared. The memories flowed. [Gilson evoked Bonnard, Bergson, Debussy, and the première of *Pelléas and Mélisand.*] "I find that those fifty years that I have lived were really worth the trouble to have lived," he explained, even though his life had been shattered twice by wars. In reply, the socialist Georges Bourgin foresaw, without much nuance, a future socialist world and the abolition of private property. Gilson retorted that the term *socialist* changed meaning continually and that, for his part, he believed in "the progressive destruction of leftist extremes"—"a radical is someone genuinely and extremely inoffensive nowadays." In answer to Aron, Gilson counted on "the reserves of energy, lucidity, and willpower that still remain in Western Europe and in the rest of the world that is still free." Taking Jules Romains's title and the liturgical invitation to "persons of good will who are not concerned with any political label," Gilson appealed for tolerance—knowing how to accept each other for laboring together, to serve "the same work." Without yielding in the political sphere, Aron agreed with Gilson in what concerned the intellectual and artistic richness of the epoch, while rejecting his opponent's invasive optimism. "One would think that we are still in the period of Juarès. [People speak of] "working together, accepting each other," [but the] "catastrophic situation" awaited a different language. The program host gave Gilson the last word. He concluded: "We are entangled in the words optimist and pessimist that have nothing to do with the question." It is necessary to work "as if there must not be universal catastrophes."

Gilson used a variety of ways of communicating his positions in France and in the United States,[158] newspaper and magazine articles, prefaces, and radio broadcasts. From April to September 1950, Gilson tried to define the terms of the debate—neutrality toward the East, neutralism toward the West—before proposing an epilogue in *Le Monde*: "Let us not always think that playing the role of a satellite is a healthy policy for Western Europe, not even (and we have repeated this constantly) if it is in the military interest of the United States!"[159] In the conclusion of the article, he also suggested again that the model of Swedish neutrality was the path for peace. Accordingly,

158 Étienne Gilson, preface to Jacques Nantet, *Soyons neutres* (Lyon: Éditions LAC, 1950). See also "Neutrality for France," *Bulletin of the Atomic Scientists* 6, no. 7 (July 1950): 203–5, answering an article by Raymond Aron in April 1950 in the *Bulletin*. Consult the bibliography, below, for a listing of many of Gilson's periodical articles. [Translator: The bibliographical lists do not claim to be comprehensive.]

159 Étienne Gilson, "Épilogue," *Le Monde*, September 29, 1950, 1–2.

Gilson published "Neutralité vers l'Est" in *Le Monde* on April 29. Aron replied May 4 in *Le Figaro* with an article titled "Neutralité vers l'Est?"

The controversy turned venomous in December 1950. On the one hand, Gilson's request to the Collège de France[160] was immediately interpreted as a desire for voluntary exile far away from an impotent Europe, soon to be occupied by Russian tanks. Also, Waldemar Gurian had informed Raymond Aron of ambiguous remarks made by Gilson in private on the campus of Notre Dame University in Indiana.[161] Gurian was a Catholic intellectual, close to Jacques Maritain and Yves Simon. He taught political science at Notre Dame and was the founder of the *Review of Politics*. Although Aron apparently did not believe the letter, Gilson was alleged to have said that Aron was a paid agent of the United States "and that there were witnesses who supported this accusation."[162] On December 15, 1950, Gurian published an open letter to Gilson in the Catholic magazine *Commonweal*, which was immediately translated and published by *Le Figaro littéraire* on January 27, 1951. Gurion, who had not heard the remarks directly, wrote publicly to Gilson:

160 It is important to quote Gilson's letter to Edmond Faral, the Collège de France administrator, in its entirety. It shows the reasons for which Gilson asked to retire. He indicated, in passing, his intent to return to France in July 1951: "39 Queen's Park, Toronto, 5, Canada, 5/12/1950. My dear friend, it is time to return, and for the first time in my life, I find myself without courses prepared that are worthy of the Collège de France; and without the energy for the task. I need complete rest, and it is available here. At bottom, I do not really believe that I will ever return to what I was. That is why, in the concern not to leave empty a chair that someone else could occupy usefully, I address you the attached request to be allowed to retire because of age and length of service. I have in mind only the good of the Collège in so doing. Among everything that I owe to the Collège de France, our friendship will always remain particularly dear to me. I hope to repeat it to you in person next June or July. My dear friend, I am most affectionately yours, Étienne Gilson." Archives du Collège de France.

161 Waldemar Gurian (1902–1954) was a German writer and political scientist, an anti-Bolshevik and anti-Nazi . He emigrated to the United States in 1937. On the eve of World War II, he founded and was editor of *The Review of Politics*. See the issue *In Memoriam* of 1954, with an article by Jacques Maritain. See also his biography by Heinz Hürten, *Waldemar Gurian, Ein Zeuge der Krise unserer Welt in der ersten Hälfte des 20. Jahhunderts* (Mainz: Matthias-Grünwald-Verlag, 1972). Likewise see Illen Thümmler, *Katholischer Publizist und amerikanischer Politikwisssenschaftler. Ein Intellektuelle Biographie Waldermar Gurians* (Baden-Baden: Nomos-Verlag, 2011).

162 Aron, *Mémoires*, 354. Aron dates the letter December 5, 1950. The manuscript is dated December 2. "Gilson, who is presently at Notre Dame has reported that *you are an agent in the pay of the United States*. Witnesses will confirm that Gilson made this accusation. But I think that it has only increased interest in you." For the whole letter see the Archives of Raymond Aron, NAF 28060 (209), BNF. No other letter from Gurian to Gilson is preserved in the Aron Archives of the Bibliothèque Nationale.

> You have spent the last few days here at Notre Dame, where you not only gave splendid lectures on Duns Scotus, but also spread the somber gospel of defeatism. You have most categorically accused a well-known and highly respected writer and scholar [Raymond Aron] of being on the American payroll, a person who has insisted that France should stand firmly alongside the United States and that in consequence has stood against the idea of French neutrality in the current world conflict. You have astonished those to whom you predicted that the Red Army would occupy France without resistance and without any significant involvement of the United States. You have told us that you do not intend to return to France, because you are not willing to live under a new occupation.... It would have been possible for you to be a mediator between Europe and the United States, more particularly between France and the United States. Indeed, you have made many trips to the New World. Americans have always been very proud to have you as their guest. But what have you done? They have always been and still are ready to benefit by your teaching. You have talked about the United States in the same way as narrow-minded observers who, not knowing about American life, apply the stereotypical label "materialistic" to it. You contribute to the growth of mutual suspicion. You have made yourself the spokesman of capitulation, because in practice, in the current state of tension in Europe, which has two sides, the debate upon neutrality centers upon that point. You affirm in advance that France and Europe are lost! I cannot believe that this is your last word. Nor do I believe that you are on the side of those who are overwhelmed, blinded by the difficulties and threats of the present moment. In conclusion, therefore, I beg you to give up your campaign of despair and accusation and that in the future you find words of encouragement and understanding."[163]

It is impossible to know the exact terms of Gilson's remarks. However, there is a measured description written by Yves Simon, which he obtained from his wife, Paule Simon:

> You know that the account published so indiscreetly by Gurian was completely exact with the two following exceptions. First Gurian, without saying so, allows us to think that Gilson made public declarations. Second, it turns out to be impossible to establish the terms used by Gilson about Aron. It seems as though things took place as follows. When somebody

163 Waldemar Gurian, "Europe and the United States: An Open Letter to Étienne Gilson," *Commonweal*, December 15, 1950, 250–51; "Lettre ouverte à Étienne Gilson. Champion de neutralisme," *Le Figaro littéraire*, January 27, 1951.

> said to Gilson, "Not all the French think like you, look at Aron," he pounced impatiently and replied that Aron's articles were paid at twenty-five cents per line, and his at five cents. (You be the judge of the level.) Then somebody said, "Do you want to tell us that Aron is an agent for hire, a traitor?"—According to Paule (I wasn't there), Gilson simply answered: "Call it what you want." Perhaps he had drunk a glass too many.[164]

To our knowledge, there is no testimony more definite or closer to the cause of the Gilson Affair. The expression "Call it what you want," without being an affirmative answer to the question, is not a firm negative either, and already entertains the allegation that Aron was an American agent. Aron had difficulty believing that Gilson had raised the alleged accusation against him.[165] He decided to remain above the Affair, even if he was the unnamed object of it in Gurian's open letter. The suggestion that Aron was an American agent was much too delicate to be raised casually. The authenticated CIA financial support for certain periodicals, for certain groups of journalists, and for certain political positions would be something to study at greater length.[166]

Without Aron and because of Gurian's letter, the polemic took on a less courteous tone thereafter. Public opinion was at white heat. In a textbook case of journalistic lynching, the Gilson Affair mixed politics, trans-Atlantic relations, internal Catholic tensions, and very French passions. It grew into continuous sparring in the columns of *Le Monde* between Pierre Emmanuel, denouncing "Imperial America," and Paul Claudel, contradicting him.[167] Gilson found himself enrolled in the Stalinist press for having criticized American movies and the Blum-Byrnes agreement,[168] and for denouncing

164 Letter from Yves Simon to Jacques Maritain, April 2, 1951, published in *Correspondance Jacques Maritain—Yves Simon*, vol. 2, *Les années américaines* (Paris: CLD, 2012), 384–85.

165 Aron, *Mémoires*, 356.

166 See Pierre Grémion, "Preuves dans le Paris de guerre froide," *Vingtième siècle* 13, no. 1 (1987): 63–82. —See likewise Frances Stonor Saunders, *Qui mène la danse? La CIA et la guerre froide culturelle* (Paris: Denoël, 2003).

167 On this matter, see the Fonds Beuve-Méry, BM 73, CHSP.

168 Unsigned article, "Thèmes et buts du film américain," *La Nouvelle Critique*, no. 12, January 1950, 114, quoted by Philippe Roger, in the chapter titled "Biographies, modes d'emploi," in *L'ennemi américain*, 425. Roger, however, goes too far when he refers (425–26) to "the cultural anti-Americanism that the philosopher does not hide. Gilson is not satisfied with resurrecting Uncle Shylock. He valiantly undertakes a whole labor of excusing the French. . . . Gilson's new reading of the period between the World Wars is, accordingly, in step with the Stalinist

the "blood tax" that the Pact "required." Pierre Debray defended Gilson in the magazine *Action*, which *Aspects de France* utilized in its March 2 issue (4) to show the philosopher's alignment with Moscow. "Certain short-sighted persons mistakenly take me for an anti-American," Gilson wrote to his friend Perry at Harvard that his real feelings in regard to the United States were admiration, gratitude, and affection. He had said again and again that the future of western civilization depends on the United States. But he saw both sides of the situation. The USA *could not* and *must not* be on the ground in Europe to prevent Russian aggression.... Europe's only military chance was to be re-armed and proclaim its neutrality.[169] Certain commentaries from moderate, competent persons did not score a bull's eye. Gilson was buried under a tidal wave of letters. "Do you really think that Soviet propaganda for peace is pacifist," Jean Laloy asked, "or that the Communal Partisans for Peace has as its only goal to wipe the love of fishing out of the hearts of the citizens? . . . I think that on this subject everyone ought to tremble about being mistaken. It is not easy to see clearly here."[170] Other readers approved the "great courage" of Gilson's powerful voice of wisdom in taking a position in the debates that "irritates our allies and replies to our adversaries' propaganda," and denounced "the insane French *furia*."[171] Gilson refused to join those who held the "war against Russia to be a sacred duty in the strictly religious sense of the word."[172]

For Albert Béguin it was a "campaign of insults resting on old Maurrasian methods."[173] According to Étienne Borne it was "a furious press campaign,"[174]

re-writing that emphasized the great culprits: the criminal French bourgeoisie and the American arch-enemy."

169 Letter from Étienne Gilson to Ralph Barton Perry, May 22, 1950, Harvard University Archives. The emphasis is Gilson's.

170 Letter from Jean Laloy (assigned to the General Secretariat of the Quai d'Orsay) to Étienne Gilson, April 28, 1950. Laloy commented on Gilson's article in *Le Monde* that day titled "En marge de négociations atlantiques: 1. Défaitisme et neutralité," 1–2. —For background, see Georges-Henri Soutou, *La paix de 50 ans* (Paris: Fayard, 2001). —About Jean Laloy, see Claude Dulong, *Notice sur la vie et les travaux de Jean Laloy (1912–1994)* (Paris: Palais de l'Institute, Gauthier-Villars, 1996).

171 See the letter from T. Sekutowicz to Hubert Beuve-Méry, May 4, 1950, Fonds Hubert Beuve-Méry [BM] 133, CHSP. The author presents himself as the second secretary of the French embassy in China and as a former member of the French Foreign Legion.

172 See the letter from Étienne Gilson, *Le Figaro littéraire*, February 17. 1951.

173 Letter from Albert Béguin to Étienne Gilson, February 17, 1951, SMCA.

174 Étienne Borne, "Feu l'affaire Gilson," *L'Aube*, Sunday Supplement, March 17–18, 1951, 1, 5.

and rather sordid political vengeance against a free man." Starting in January 1951, the Affair entangled many intellectuals and media personalities. In *Aspects de la France*, Pierre Boutang concentrated on the "cowardly neutralism" of Claude Bourdet and as well as Robert Schuman, who was the "bridge" between Stalin and Truman (January 19). Boutang also blamed René Pleven, who "fled to Washington," (January 26) and then aimed his bludgeon against the "fugitive Gilson" (February 2 and 9). As it went on, the Affair fed upon all the opposition resentment provoked by the MRP. At its height, the Collège de France, by majority vote, refused to grant Gilson honorary status (February 1951).

The controversy had spread and was commented upon by the entirety of the press from the *Journal de Genève* to *Le Monde*, from *Aspects de la France* to *Le Figaro*, press bosses, magazine editors, Hubert Beuve-Méry, Pierre Brisson, Albert Béguin, Pierre Boutang, and intellectuals like François Mauriac (who waxed poetical in *Le Figaro* about broken bonds, February 20–21, 1951), Daniel Halévy, Jean Paulhan, or Gabriel Marcel (in *Aspects de la France*), Étienne Borne (in *L'Aube*, March 18, 1950), Pasteur Vallery-Radot, Gerald Phelan (then director of the Notre Dame Institute of Medieval Studies), all took up their pens for and against Gilson. Yves Simon tried to smooth the rough edges by inviting his friend and neighbor Gurian to offer an apology, which Gilson accepted in October 1951.

The Affair was exploited by Maurrasians and MRP Gaullists, otherwise adversaries between themselves. Gabriel Marcel's brother-in-law Pierre Bernus in the *Journal de Genève* on January 27, like Pierre Boutang in *Aspects de la France* (February 2) denounced the "fugitive Gilson" in chorus. The case occupied the Maurrasian newspaper until the end of March. A broad "survey" conducted by Boutang, collected commentaries of Daniel Halévy, Gabriel Marcel, Jean Paulhan, Henri Boegner (son of the Reverend Alfred Boegner and another of Marcel's brothers-in-law), Colonel Rémy, as well as the Belgian Marcel De Corte. The campaign took on the appearance of settling scores against Gilson, who had dared to label Maurras as a "collaborator" with Germany and who had opposed Barrès' coming to Strasbourg in 1920. Thus, Gabriel Marcel, who until 1946 had corresponded with Gilson as a friend, now wrote:[175]

175 Fonds Gabriel Marcel, NAF 28349, BNF. The correspondence between Gilson and Gabriel Marcel consists of twelve letters exchanged between 1928 and 1972, with a gap of more than twenty years between 1946 and 1967. The last letter from Gilson to Marcel before the Affair is

> Étienne Gilson's secession seems grave to me, and seeing the conditions in which it has occurred, quite close to treason. That a person who has been harshly tested and perhaps worn down feels incapable of facing certain trials is a fact that may be deplorable but that by itself calls for no condemnation. But the incredible publicity that Gilson has given to his decision in America completely transforms his act. In fact, he has provided formidable weapons to all those on the other side of the Atlantic, who claim that France is lost, that she knows it, and that there is no reason to furnish her with the military assistance that she requests. One must say sorrowfully: here is a first-rate man, a universally respected scholar, who turns into an accomplice of our enemies. That is not all. Here is a Catholic who abandons himself to absolute fatalism, who does everything in his power to shut us up in despair. Finally, isn't it inconceivable that the man who has become the champion of an entirely chimerical neutrality, instead of holding his ground to defend to the end an idea in which he at least purports to believe, should go far away to prophesy at his ease? What makes the situation even more terrible in my view is that in a circumstance that I know well and perhaps in some others, Étienne Gilson has taken the position of an inflexible purist. But it must be said very loudly that, from the French point of view, the conduct of the Marshall's [Pétain] supporters was infinitely more defensible than what Gilson has just advocated. Recently, I had the occasion to observe the hideous scandal that this abdication has caused everywhere. We would like to think that Étienne Gilson now measures the consequences of his action. But unfortunately, it is irreparable. This problem of flight has obsessed me for some time. It provided the theme of the work [*Rome n'est plus dans Rome*] that I finished a few days ago.[176]

This statement by Marcel is a key to his character Pascal Laumière in *Rome n'est plus dans Rome*. Laumière is a member of the Académie Sainte-Beuve, a wretched resistant, a bad patriot, frightened, only concerned with publication of his articles, an expatriate by cowardice in a Catholic university in Brazil in order to "take cover." Laumière certainly conjures up the figure of Gilson. In the work's final scene, Laumière collapses on the ground after having declared on French emigrant radio: "We were wrong to leave. We should have stayed. We should have fought on the spot. The delusion that

very friendly (December 8, 1946): "I need you personally. I re-read two or three pages by you at random, when I feel that I have fallen into an inner crevice, and I need a friend to pull me out." The next letter was dated April 15, 1967.

176 Gabriel Marcel, "La réponse de M. Gabriel Marcel," *Aspects de la France*, February 9, 1951, 6.

one can take his country with him can only come from pride and the most insane presumption.[177]

The Affair provoked reactions from many readers as well, famous and unknown. Traces are found in the archives of Gilson and of Hubert Beuve-Méry.[178] Some faithful readers wrote indignantly to cancel their subscriptions or to strongly agree. Marshall Pétain's admirers took vengeance on Gilson, "the inflexible purger" of 1945. Gilson the fugitive in Canada was anti-national; he was a traitor to the homeland, and the best proof was that Pasteur Valléry-Radot and Gabriel Marcel had said so. But Field Marshall Pétain, the shield of France, was still in prison in France.[179] Others, like Jean-Baptiste Duroselle defended Waldemar Gurian's intellectual valor, without condemning Étienne Gilson.[180] Some judged that Gilson had a "badly constructed mind," "full of medieval nonsense," "a character without rectitude," with "interminable quibbling and convoluted arguments"; "the lengthy practice of medieval Scholasticism is no doubt tied up with his turn of mind."[181] An academic specialist in the Middle Ages was a target of facile humor: "May he finish his work on Duns Scotus in peace," Jean Paulhan proclaimed, "rather than meddle in public affairs." "Is it true that Duns Scotus and the Canadian students couldn't wait?" Henri Boegner asked.[182] Pamphlets were still written in 1952 against neutralism: "Gilson has not succeeded in hiding his deep hostility toward America by paradoxically expressing a verbal sympathy that fools nobody, nor is he able to conceal his basic belief that France and Europe must inevitably be conquered by the totalitarian empire."[183]

It is impossible to review exhaustively the published documentation or the content of archives. Perhaps what is best is to begin at the end, when the passions diminished, and the witness cited by Gurian, notably James Corbett in a letter in *Le Monde* in April 1951, declined to testify; when the accusers gave a cringing apology, and when institutions made amends for the harm

177 Gabriel Marcel, *Rome n'est plus dans Rome* (Paris: La Table Ronde, 1951), 148.

178 See some sixty letters contained in the file "Neutralisme," Fonds Hubert Beuve-Méry, BM 133, CHSP.

179 Letter from Yves Wallant to Hubert Beuve-Méry, February 23, 1951, BM 133, CHSP.

180 Letter from Jean-Baptiste Duroselle to Hubert Beuve-Méry, March 7, 1951, BM 133, CHSP.

181 Letter from Henri Bocqué to Hubert Beuve-Méry, March 7, 1951, BM 133, CHSP.

182 Hervé Boegner, "L'Affaire Gilson n'est pas close," *Aspects de la France*, March 16, 1951, 4.

183 Association des intellectuels antitotalitaires (Jean Le Dantec, secretary), *Le neutralisme* (Paris, 1953), Fonds Hubert Beuve-Méry, CHSP. This is a 46 page pamphlet, devoted to condemning neutralism and in particular Étienne Gilson and Henri Beuve-Méry.

Gilson as both rabbit and new example of Buridan's ass, hesitating between the U.S.A. and U.S.S.R.
Aspects de la France,
February 9 and March 2, 1951.

Gilson as frightened hare,
fleeing across the ocean at a gallop
Aspects de la France, February 9 and 16, 1951.

done. In a tone very different from that of his article "Les amarres rompues" [The Broken Moorings] (February 21–22, 1951), François Mauriac wrote on March 14, 1951: "We are delighted to learn today that we have been misled and that Étienne Gilson has not left us with no intent to return." Étienne Gilson was no longer a fugitive. As occurred with Bernanos before World War II, where Gilson went, French culture accompanied him. In May 1951 *Commonweal* published an honorable correction. "We regret our failure."[184] At the end of September and beginning of October, Waldemar Gurian offered humble regrets: "In quoting private conversations I made an error for which I would very much beg your pardon. I especially regret the personal attacks against you."[185] "I did not personally hear the remarks reported in my open letter [published in *Commonweal* and then in *Le Figaro*]. I also admit that to guarantee more certainly the exact meaning of your thinking, it would have been preferable to consult you."[186] "Good faith does not guarantee truth,"

184 "The Gilson Controversy," *Commonweal*, May 18, 1951, 134: "For those failures on our part, we sincerely apologize to Professor Gilson."

185 Letter from Waldemar Gurian to Étienne Gilson, September 29, 1951, SMCA and UNDA. This letter was written in French with the help of Yves Simon, who tried to correct Gurian's draft.

186 Letter from Waldemar Gurian to Étienne Gilson, October 4, 1951, SMCA and UNDA.

Gilson serenely reminded him and lamented that "the sincerity of political passions should have been taken to be a proof of truth."[187]

In 1956, five years after the Affair, the Collège de France finally undid the injustice to Gilson by voting almost unanimously to confer the honorary status that a small majority had denied him in February 1951. The Collège administrator Marcel Bataillon wrote tactfully to Gilson: "When an institution in the public eye commits a serious error, one that creates a scandal, it is difficult to repair it without recalling the earlier scandal. We have not escaped this recollection. *Le Monde* [in the December 27, 1956 issue] has inflicted it upon us with the style that characterizes it, as did the newspaper *Combat* with the stupidity of the writer in charge of the operation."[188] "Justice has been done to Étienne Gilson," was *Combat's* headline on December 28, 1956." The editorial added: "We would like those who criticize the Atlantic alliance to acknowledge now that somebody else was right before them." "How can it happen," *Le Monde* commented for its part, in defense of itself, "that Étienne Gilson and *Le Monde* made the mistake of having been right too early? The polemicists who used to accuse them of treason because they dared to criticize this or that feature of American policy, now attack it with the greatest sharpness and violence."[189]

A letter from Jean Paulhan to Étienne Gilson on January 8, 1963 (SMCA and IMEC) is revealing: "I am very deeply ashamed of a document directed to you that I signed [*Aspects de la France*, February 16, 1951] some years ago, and I beg you to pardon me. The strong desire to see you remain with us in France, in what was certainly a critical period, pushed me to absurd and excessive lengths." Gilson replied magnanimously: "Your letter is unnecessary, but it touches me most deeply, and I thank you. Please do me the favor, I beg you, of forgetting this misunderstanding and consider, as I do, that it never happened."[190] In his *Memoires*, published in 1983, Aron recalls a meeting with Gilson that took place after the Affair: "Some years later, after the crisis about neutrality, Gilson told me spontaneously that he only subscribed

187 Letter of Étienne Gilson to Waldemar Gurian, September 29, 1951, SMCA and UNDA.

188 Letter from Marcel Bataillon to Étienne Gilson, February 11, 1957, SMCA.

189 "Les professeurs du Collège de France confèrent l'honoriat à M. Étienne Gilson" [The Faculty of the Collège de France confer honorary status on Étienne Gilson], *Le Monde*, December 27, 1956.

190 Letter of Étienne Gilson to Jean Pulhan, January 10, 1963, Fonds Pulhan, IMEC.

to *Le Figaro* to read my articles. Waldemar Gurian had irresponsibly reported comments he had not heard and that Gilson always denied."[191]

In 1978, at the time of Gilson's death, André Fontaine published a fine article in *Le Monde* to put the issues and details of the Affair into larger perspective:[192]

> Étienne Gilson contributed regularly to *Le Monde* from June 1945 to September 29, 1950. For the most part, his articles were based on American and Canadian experiences. In 1948–1949 that experience moved him to pose questions about the North Atlantic Treaty Organization, which was in the process of negotiating certain issues that touched off very strong reactions. Without denying the determination of President Truman and of the State Department to support the countries of Europe with whom, for the first time in the history, the United States was preparing to conclude an alliance in time of peace, Gilson very much doubted the likelihood that the United States Senate would make a commitment to armed intervention. He was right. As it was concluded, the pact left it to the United States to determine in what manner it would come to the aid of its allies in case of aggression. It is precisely because doubt remained about that situation that France subsequently acquired nuclear armament. In Gilson's view, the countries of Europe thereby risked being threatened by the U.S.S.R. because of their declared ties to the United States without, however, being absolutely guaranteed U.S. assistance. Gilson, therefore, dared wonder whether in those conditions, the solution of European armed neutrality did not merit consideration. Despite all the foreign pressure on Sweden and Switzerland, there was something, perhaps in part their military preparedness, which had succeeded in preserving neutrality during two World Wars and that they were resolved to preserve in case the Cold War became hot. Gilson even judged that after November 1949, it would be necessary to make room for a re-armed Germany in Europe. Some days later, the National Assembly voted for a resolution excluding both rearmament of the Federal Republic and its admission to the North Atlantic Treaty Organization. We know what came of that resolution. When we re-read Gilson's articles today and the commentaries they provoked, the bad faith of his critics must be obvious. He had asked whether Europe's armed neutrality had to be excluded from that list of possible outcomes. In the articles of his critics, he had become

191 Aron, *Mémoires*, 356.

192 André Fontaine, "L'Affaire Gilson," *Le Monde*, September 22, 1978.

> "the champion of neutralism."[193] To put it differently, he became the champion of defeatism, of the refusal to fight. His hostility to communism was complete. He became its accomplice.
>
> On September 7, 1950, after the new treaty was signed and ratified, Étienne Gilson observed somewhat bitterly in an article in Le *Monde* that he had failed. "Evidently, the idea of a strong enough Europe to remain free in its politics and to keep its freedom by its own weapons has not penetrated into the French brain." It would be correct to classify this language as rather Gaullist. . . . Deeply affected by the attacks against him, coinciding with a painful death in his family [Thérèse in November 1949], he stopped writing to return to the courses in Canada again, as he had each year since 1926.

After the Gilson Affair, the philosopher became an outsider on the Paris intellectual stage, established himself in Toronto, fleeing from the bipolar polemic in Paris, the media controversies, the ghost of Thérèse, and more positively, seeking to re-encounter the Institute of Mediaeval Studies and to teach. As an Atlantic (but not "Atlanticist") intellectual, confronted with American neutralism during the phony war, but a philo-Atlantic neutralist on the eve of the Cold War, his position was difficult for the editorial writers in the national press to decipher, although not lacking internal coherence. Gilson was aware of continuing to be the political target of a fanaticism that could always rise up again. He took refuge in silence, his only protection,[194] and in his Canadian retreat, interrupted during the first half of the 1950s by a few brief stays in Paris and in his dear Burgundy.

193 See the article by Waldemar Gurian, "Lettre ouverte à Étienne Gilson, champion du neutralisme ," *Le Figaro littéraire*, January 27, 1951.

194 Letter from Étienne Gilson to Gerald Phelan, November 4, 1951, SMCA. [Letter is written in English]

4

Convulsions of the City of Men

The Church has no system. It has only principles.[1]

As a university man and an intellectual, Étienne Gilson chose his strategies and defined their places and moments of expression, sometimes by default. Often abroad, always occupied by research or by committees entrusted to him, he said nothing about momentary emergencies. He often lamented leading an insane life, going from committee to committee,[2] and sometimes described himself as having no intellectual freedom, an "unfortunate person who rushes from government ministries to shipping companies."[3] Trapped by the demands of his time, he pondered, "The situation within is horribly unhealthy. Only Mauriac fights, magnificently. Every time I sit down to prepare a lecture on St. Augustine, I have the impression of betrayal. What is it necessary to betray? What betrayal is our duty today?"[4] Paul Vignaux wrote: "Gilson intervened in the public life of his country only episodically. He kept in mind

1 Letter from Étienne Gilson to Fr. Jean-Augustin Maydieu, May 28, 1944, 2, Fonds Maydieu, APDF.

2 Letter from Étienne Gilson to Fr. Gabriel Astrik, May 13, 1947, UNDA.

3 Letter from Étienne Gilson to Fr. Irénée, February 14, 1946, APQV.

4 Letter from Étienne Gilson to Jacques Maritain, January 1, 1946, in Gilson and Maritain, *Correspondance 1923–1971*, 147.

the ideal social dimensions of Émile Durkheim's Sorbonne."[5] There may well be a discrete reproach in what Vignaux wrote. By contrast with Gilson, his political and union activity was more continual, sometimes overriding his scholarly work. But what is an intellectual by episodes? Is he an incomplete, overwhelmed, opportunistic intellectual taking offense with the press magnates, refusing work, choosing his moments and his causes? Is it a an intellectual who "commits treason" by omission? Is it necessary to "betray" in the sense of abandoning good authors or our own society? Gilson's periods of silence and absences give more meaning to his involvement in the *city*, which was ordered around two great moments, the years 1934–1935 in answer to the crisis of February 6, and the years 1945–1950, when Gilson became one of the figureheads of French Christian Democracy and, as we have seen, of neutralism.

OCCASIONAL INVOLVEMENT: AN INTELLECTUAL WHO DID NOT COMMIT TREASON

Julien Benda's 1927 book started a long polemic about the "the betrayal of the *clercs* [intellectuals]." Benda denounced the role of intellectuals in nationalist propaganda and "brainwashing" after World War I. Gilson had taken a clear position with the publication of two articles *in L'Européen* in May and July 1929. In the ideological chaos between the world wars, unlike Maritain whom Benda attacked explicitly,[6] Gilson escaped the wrath of the pamphleteer, whose underlying intentions Gilson approved, though he lamented the *ad hominem* attacks:

> So far, Julien Benda has not met with the gratitude his last two books deserve. *La trahison des clercs* and *La fin de l'Éternel*, even if we dispute this or that affirmation of detail, are two works that will remain in French intellectual history as the signs of a re-birth we all hope for wholeheartedly. However, everywhere and as they say in military jargon, from right to left indistinctly, there are only recriminations and vituperative complaints. No intellectual has betrayed, except perhaps his neighbor and adversary, although at the end Julien Benda will remain the only real traitor in this story. So what has happened and what has he done?

5 Paul Vignaux, "Étienne Gilson," *Revue de métaphysique et de morale* 84, no. 3 (1979): 291.

6 Julien Benda, *La trahison des clercs* (Paris: Grasset, 1927), 206: "Maritain declares that not everyone can philosophize and that the essential thing for human beings is to choose a teacher for oneself." [*The Treason of the Intellectuals*, translated by Richard Aldrington, New York, William Morrow and Co., 1928.]

> Simply this: he has betrayed all the parties consciously and deliberately, because they did not remain faithful to the only Truth. This is not a small thing. That the partisans of every stripe reproach him harshly is all too natural. Human beings do not like to confess, but they have still more horror of someone who confesses for them. It is more alarming that no one has desired to consider the central theses of Benda's books, to make their examination of conscience and to beat their breasts saying, I have betrayed, we have all betrayed. Intellectuals, we ought to thank the person who denounces us in the name of our own ideal. It has to be said: Benda is right. For our part we will add this: These two books are not an episode or an accident. They begin the necessary recovery that ought to lead the French general public to rediscover the authentic meaning of the word *philosophy*...
>
> Julien Benda himself is a little to blame. What he wants is to give us the feeling or rather the clear idea of what truth is in itself, because this point decides all the rest. Instead of dealing with this metaphysical difficulty as a metaphysician, he wants to proceed as a historian. He continually judges particular cases in the name of universal principles. That is wrong. The particular is the inexhaustible and therefore the ungraspable. It is not just what is never recognized in the universal. It is what does not let itself be reduced to the universal. That is why the particular turns bitterly against Benda today. Our fathers knew better how to do better, and there are profound reasons why proper names are as rare in St. Thomas's *Summa Theologiae* as in Spinoza's *Ethics*. One need only throw impersonal paving stones into the pond of intellectuals to allow each of them the joy of believing that the [stones] fall only on his neighbors.[7]

Some months later, Gilson returned to the subject: "People dispute with each other. One can only refute ideas. To want to refute human beings is to undertake a task whose very essence implies contradiction. It seems to me that Benda has undertaken it, and that he will not escape it."[8] In 1931, Benda wrote to Gilson to invite him to a round table organized by the *Union pour la Verité*, expressing "his high intellectual consideration" for Gilson."[9]

Was Gilson an intellectual who *betrayed*? Had he betrayed the ideas of the universal and of truth in the name of ideology? He was aware of his

7 Étienne Gilson, "Autour de Julien Benda: La mare aux clercs," *L'Européen*, May 29, 1929, 4

8 Étienne Gilson, "Métaphysique de la réfutation: Autour de Benda," *L'Européen*, July 10, 1929, 4.

9 Letter from Julien Benda to Étienne Gilson, March 15, 1931, FG, SMCA.

weaknesses and what was impossible for him. In 1926–1927, Gilson did not write a line in the midst of the crisis of Action Française, since, as we have said, he was in North America for seven months. We would search in vain for a minimally elaborated statement about separation of church and state in France (he was twenty years old and passing his competitive examinations), or about the Popular Front before World War II (he was at Harvard for a semester), or on the Spanish Civil War, the Munich Accords, the collapse of France in June 1940, colonial issues, and so forth. His statements are sometimes expeditious and irrevocable. In 1935, he wrote to Gouhier, "I regret leaving right in the middle of the controversy about Action Française. They are childish impudent types, who treat their public as idiots, moreover, as it deserves to be treated."[10]

Two calendars, that of current events and that of academic obligations, were at loggerheads here. Erudition sometimes served as a refuge. Academic writing was also a flight from politics. At the end of July 1940, after the vote granting full powers to Marshall Pétain, Gilson wrote in private: "Our duty and salvation will be to continue to serve God and our country as we were doing. How do we accomplish that? It is too soon to know. Let us continue our work. God will take care of us."[11] Unlike Maritain, who was in the United States after the defeat of France and remained "an exile" during World War II, Gilson had no freedom to speak. As an internal emigrant, he therefore continued his work and fell back into silence and a form of dejection inhabited by hope. "The sadness that overwhelms us is so bleak that it would hide God, if we let it. Still a little light glimmers at the end of the tunnel." [12]His public attitude had great moral clarity. Gilson rejected "any compromise with the enemy,"[13] and with "Marshalism" [i.e., Pétainism]. However, he did not publish a line in any clandestine magazine between 1940 and 1945 or in the Éditions de Minuit, where Maritain's *À travers le désastre* was published, or in *Cahiers du témoignage chrétien.*

Gilson cared for his Burgundian garden in the literal sense: "Everything is calm here. I garden. I work," he wrote in 1942.[14] In 1943 he declared, "I

10 Letter from Étienne Gilson to Henri Gouhier, July 4, 1935, Archives Gouhier.

11 Letter from Étienne Gilson to Fr. André Combes, July 29, 1940, NAF 28257, BNF.

12 Letter from Étienne Gilson to Fr. Irénée, December 4, 1942, APQV.

13 Pasteur Vallery-Radot, "Réponse au discours de réception d'Étienne Gilson," May 29, 1947. Complete text available on the Académie française website.

14 Letter from Étienne Gilson to Fr. André Combes, April 9, 1942, NAF 28257, BNF.

dream a little when I think about the Benedictine Rule with its alternation of work and contemplation. After having handled the spade and the rake for two hours, I am hardly in condition to think."[15] In November 1944, Gilson wrote to a Canadian friend: "We have lived supported by our daily work. I continue to teach and to write, with no other concern than to go unnoticed. Being totally against Vichy and Pétain from the first day of the disaster that was the armistice, I could expect nothing from that quarter. The Germans made two attempts to enroll me in their propaganda apparatus, and I must say that, despite their complete failure, they did nothing afterward to bother me."[16] Gilson kept his distance in an obvious withdrawal. That is somewhat surprising given the number of articles he published on current events before June 1940. There are rare exceptions. In the middle of the war, Gilson dedicated the second edition of his book on St. Augustine (Vrin, 1943), emphasizing his fidelity to the "allied camp": "To the professors and students of the Harvard Philosophy Department from E.G., who remains one of their own." In 1942, Gilson published his only wartime article of both scholarly and general interest, some of which should be read between the lines. Titled "Sagesse et société," the article appeared in the journal *Témoignages*, published by the Benedictine Abbey of La Pierre-qui-Vire in Burgundy. "If the censors of *Témoignages* knew their trade, they would have rejected my article."[17] "God having blinded the censors, he obviously wanted *Témoignages* to appear."[18] Gilson began his study quoting the poet Prudentius: "God wills the unity of mankind." "Christ's religion must be founded upon social peace and friendship among peoples."[19] He denounced the "outdated pagans" who "even today" build altars to victory just as do "all the social reformers and messiahs without mandate," to conclude with St. Augustine that only God is above man. It was easy to decipher the essay's political meaning under the erudite ornamentation. If the blind censors saw nothing, the public was not deceived. "I am happy that certain readers of my article were more clear-sighted than its appointed censors. We can depend upon this phenomenon in general."[20]

15 Letter from Étienne Gilson to Fr. André Combes, May 3, 1943, NAF 28257, BNF.

16 Letter from Étienne Gilson to Madame Thibaudeau, November 6, 1944, SMCA.

17 Letter from Étienne Gilson to Fr. Irénée, June 29, 1942, APQV.

18 Letter from Étienne Gilson to Fr. Irénée, July 29, 1942, APQV.

19 Étienne Gilson, "Sagesse et société," *Témoignages*, no. 1 (1942): 39–54.

20 Letter from Étienne Gilson to Fr. Irénée, December 4, 1942, APQV.

Gilson was a spiritual resistant and acknowledged as such at the time of the Liberation, but his message was encrypted under the banner of "Prudence."

It is difficult to evaluate the success of an intellectual position. Gilson did not hesitate to refuse requests and to withdraw, despite his own recommendations, to his ivory tower or, by contrast, to take a position and commit himself body and soul to a cause. In 1934–1935, his invitation to "First, be Catholics," sometimes seemed to lack specificity. Certainly committed and in the fray, but for what positive goals? In 1941, he wrote:

> Our first positive duty as Catholics is to work with all our might for the establishment of a Catholic order in our country. It must be said that the point is not to create a Catholic party, a kind of Centre français. Even if we were capable of doing so, the solution would be completely wrongheaded . . . and would only increase political compromises. . . . It is no longer a matter of returning to an ivory tower and reflecting at leisure there, while others fight. The Catholic, less than anyone else, is not above the fray.[21]

The historian can find Gilson's signature at the end of some (few) manifestos, as we pointed out in the introduction. In March 1933, he signed a manifesto against anti-Semitism.[22] Gilson was evidently concerned with the problem, although he did not elaborate greatly. "Anti-Semitism is stupid for a Frenchman. In a Catholic it is a monstrosity," he wrote in 1934.[23] In 1946–1947, he taught his students in the School of Sciences-Po, "Christianity is inseparable from Judaism. The Catholic is an heir to Judaism. It is either a Jewish heresy or the fulfillment of Judaism. They cannot be separated."[24] Likewise, as has been indicated, in March 1934, Gilson participated in the Manifesto for the Common Good, which arose under the leadership of Maritain and Mounier, after the extreme rightist disturbances of February 6, 1934.

The historian should also note the real impact on public opinion of certain articles that Gilson published in the magazine *Sept* in 1934–1935 or in *Le Monde* between 1945 and 1950. Some of his successes in public esteem

21 Étienne Gilson, "Entre la tour d'ivoire et la tour de Babel," editorial, *Sept*, no. 14, June 2, 1934, 1.

22 See the issue of *Paix et droit, organe de l'alliance israélite universelle*, March 1933, 7. The list of around 250 signatures was published in the March and April issues.

23 Étienne Gilson, *Pour un ordre catholique*, 184.

24 Étienne Gilson, "Les données chrétiennes de la politique nationale," lesson one, Sciences Po 1946–1947, 1, SMCA. The course devoted a whole lecture to the Jewish origins of transcending nationalism, 1–3.

were institutional failures—like the short-lived magazine *Vigile*, "the Catholic *NRF*" (*Nouvelle Revue Française*) that Gilson decided to support in 1930–1031, even though in 1966 he lamented the "unauthorized theological inquisitors" of the "*Vigile* incident."[25] At the same time, he refused to work with Emmanuel Mounier in the foundation of the magazine *Esprit*. Why did Gilson support *Vigile* and not *Esprit*? The guiding conceptions of the two magazines are not similar. *Esprit* is more involved in the socio-political realm, younger and less literary. Gilson was also closer to the writer Charles Du Bos, two years older than he, than he was to Mounier, a former student, twenty years younger. In a letter to Jacques Chevalier in April 1931, Mounier indicated that he was counting on Gilson's cooperation: "I thus intend to represent all branches and all opinions, yourself, Gilson, and Maritain."[26] Gilson answered him in May 1931:

> Thank you for your kind letter, which I found upon my return from Oxford. Presently, I am so overwhelmed with work and responsibilities that I have made a rule not to add any more. What you want to do seems very important to me, and I devoutly wish you success. It may even be that I can give you some effective help later, and I will do so gladly. But it is better that I limit myself entirely to the projects underway, at least as long as I do not see their conclusion clearly. I ask you to please not use my name and to leave me out of the foundation, which in no way excludes future collaboration, if you suggest it, and when it is possible.[27]

In the 1930s, Gilson published nothing in *Esprit*. Between 1946 and 1951, he submitted four articles to *Esprit*, one of them a defense of the United States with dissertations upon the "aristocracy of the average man." "Let us abandon the endeavor's waste products for the idea itself. It is beautiful in itself and worth pondering." There is also a plea on his own behalf in the context of the Gilson Affair.[28] In February 1947, Mounier obtained little support from the Academician:

25 Letter from Étienne Gilson to François Mauriac, January 19, 1966, Bibliothèque littéraire Jacques Doucet—see the appendixes.

26 Letter from Emmanuel Mounier to Jacques Chevalier, April 29, 1931, IMEC. The document was communicated to the author by Jean-Victor Elie.

27 Letter from Étienne Gilson to Emmanuel Mounier, May 11, 1931, IMEC.

28 Étienne Gilson, "Monde moderne, monde chrétien: Pas d'illusions rétrospectives," *Esprit* 14, no. 125 (1946): 192–96. —"Un aristocratie de l'homme moyen," *Esprit* 14, no. 127 (1946): 672–82.

> Your project seems very interesting to me, but if you will excuse me for answering selfishly, I am in a moment when I avoid with horror all involvement in any undertaking at all. I find sadly that I am absolutely unable to work in Paris. There are nothing but telephone calls, visits, letters, and meetings. So I am torn between the desire to encourage a project that I judge very useful, and being afraid that I cannot participate in it myself. To encourage you in these conditions does not seem to me very elegant.[29]

Mounier is not the only one to suffer Gilson's polite refusals, which abound in the archives. Other instances concern Fr. Laberthonnière's *Annales de philosophie chrétienne* in 1912;[30] or the *Revue thomiste* of the Dominican Province of Toulouse in February 1937;[31] or the publishing project, in 1938, of the rector of the Académie de Paris, Sébastien Charléty;[32] or students, like Maurice Denis's daughter Noële, to whom Gilson wrote in 1922 that "in conscience" he felt "obliged to dissuade [her] from a doctoral project at least for the present."[33] Alexandre Koyré hardly succeeded in getting a line from Gilson: "It would be better for you not to count on me at all."[34] Gilson's correspondence with Fr. Maydieu in the years 1937 and 1938, regarding possible collaboration by Gilson in *La vie intellectuelle*, lets us see a person both ready to enter a kind of "inner solitude," according to Vignaux's expression,[35] and sufficiently humble to write that he had nothing to say on important subjects at a moment when it was necessary to act, not to speak:

> Not for a minute do I lose contact with you in heart, in spirit, even if I am not in agreement with what you are doing. On the contrary, I think it nec-

—"Une drame d'amitié, Charles Du Bos et André Gide," *Esprit* 18, no. 171 (September 1950): 415–19. —"Letter to Albert Béguin," *Esprit* 19, no. 178 (April 1951): 593–96.

29 Letter from Étienne Gilson to Emmanuel Mounier, February 7, 1947, Fonds Mounier, IMEC.

30 Letter from Étienne Gilson to Fr. Lucien Laberthonnière, no date, 1912, NAF, 28025, 34, BNF: "I would not dream of denying you my cooperation, but I would want it to be compatible with my regular work."

31 See *Revue thomiste* 94, no. 3 (1994): 479.

32 See the letter from Étienne Gilson, February 18, 1938, Fonds Larousse, IMEC. "Gentlemen, I greatly regret that my many work commitments do not permit me to participate in the project you are planning about the great figures of humanity. I would be delighted to work under Charléty, but it is really impossible for me, and I beg you to excuse me."

33 Letter from Étienne Gilson to Noële Denis-Boulet, March 26, 1922, Fonds Boulet, IMEC.

34 See the letters from Gilson to Koyré, October 26, 1931; June 8, 1932; May 15, 1933, Archives du Centre Alexandre Koyré.

35 Paul Vignaux, "Étienne Gilson," *Revue de métaphysique et de morale*, 290.

essary for that to be done, and that you do it as well as possible. It is simply that I cannot honestly stay on that level, and moreover, it may be that I am condemned to be alone.[36]

In the spring of 1938, Gilson, rather lucid and quite depressed about France's situation, gave a lecture that "discouraged" his audience. Fr. Bernadot gives us some sense of it: "Lecture of Professor Gilson—Intellectual Center. Professor Gilson is very pessimistic about the state of France. More teaching of ethics in the university. The only case in history where a people does without ethics. All the same, there are Christian activities and the Christian press that reach many Frenchmen. This lecture seemed discouraging to me."[37] The philosopher avoided the question again in autumn 1938: "I will be abroad until the end of December [1938], and I have lost contact with my country too much to be able to talk about it. Besides, I do not think that the best opinions can help much nowadays. Acts are what is necessary, and philosophers cannot act. They have none of the levers of power in their hands."[38]

After the Gilson Affair, our philosopher took refuge in an "overly long silence deplored by friends and admirers."[39] In the first half of the 1950s, Gilson was sick. To his friends, he commented once in a great while on news that was seldom encouraging: "I am finishing my last days finishing my last books."[40]

SEPT AND *POUR UN ORDRE CATHOLIQUE* (1934–1935)

Therefore, the series of almost sixty articles that Gilson produced in fifteen months during 1934–1935 is extremely significant. The Dominican weekly *Sept*, which has been thoroughly studied by historians,[41] published some

36 Letter from Étienne Gilson to Fr. Jean-Augustin Maydieu, March 24, 1937, Bibliothèque municipale de Bordeaux.

37 Diary of Fr. Bernadot, entry for March 28, 1938, Fonds Bernadot, APDF.

38 Letter from Étienne Gilson to Fr. Jean-Augustin Maydieu, October 28, 1938, Bibliothèque municipal de Bordeaux.

39 Letter from Étienne Gilson to Francisque Gay, July 3, 1953, Institut Marc Sangnier.

40 Letter from Étienne Gilson to Francisque Gay, July 7, 1953, Institut Marc Sangnier.

41 Aline Coutrot, *Un courant de la pensée catholique. L'hebdomadaire Sept (mars 1934–août 1937)* (Paris: Cerf, 1961). —Magali Della Sudda, "La suppression de l'hebdomadaire dominicain *Sept*, 29–44. —See also Jacques Prévotat, "Étienne Gilson est-il un chrétien modéré?," in Prévotat and Vavasseur-Desperriers, *Les "chrétiens modérés" en France et en Europe (1870–1960)*, 433–53.

sixty articles by Gilson, twenty-five of which were republished in *Pour un ordre catholique* (DDB, 1934).[42] Let us make it clear that not all the documentation of these articles has been preserved or found. In the weekly's first number (March 1934), Gilson participated with an article titled "En marge de Chamfort," where he makes the case for theology, "the only intellectual activity absolutely free of temporality." He depicts the "modern Chamforts," that is to say all the "lay intellectuals" who have come down in the world, who want to live the life of the mind and occupy the first places by virtue of their intellectual activities: "The communism of many intellectuals hardly expresses more than the rancor of those who have come down in the world."[43] How was Gilson involved with the Dominicans? Did he attend meetings of the editorial board? We guess that he did, but we do not know. Nevertheless, it can be affirmed that Gilson did not spare either effort or his name for the magazine. He even became a pillar of the publication, contributing to three quarters of the issues between March 1934 and August 1935, and made a public relations argument for *Sept*: "I suggest that *Sept* should become the center where French Catholics, by helping each other to define their duties, may become conscious of their unity.[44]

After Gilson's involvement, we find a valuable commentary in the unpublished account that Fr. Pierre Boisselot wrote in 1942. Fr. Boisselot was the assistant to the publication's editor, Fr. Marie-Vincent Bernadot. For Bernadot, Gilson's articles were what "really got *Sept* off the ground."

For him, the abrupt interruption of Gilson's collaboration in August-September 1935 ought to be linked to the matter of Italy and Ethiopia, whereas Gilson's biographer is inclined rather to consider the material cause to be the Gilson family's stay for six months in Brazil and North America, from July 4, 1935, until their return in January 1936.[45] Fr. Boisselot's opinion on this point, presented in its entirety in the appendixes, is questionable. Gilson's remarks about "Mussolini's Thomism" were reported by Fr. Boisselot, who would have gotten them from Fr. Maydieu. Gilson, however, never wrote anything of

42 Étienne Gilson, *Pour un ordre catholique* (Paris: DDB, 1934; republished by Parole et Silence, 2013). The latter edition includes an appendix containing reactions that appeared in *Sept* about the "cult of incompetence."

43 Étienne Gilson, "En marge de Chamfort," *Sept*, no. 1, March 3, 1934, 8.

44 Publicity handbill, Fonds *Sept*, APDF.

45 Letter from Étienne Gilson to Henri Gouhier, July 4, 1935, Archives Gouhier: "I am in a frightful rush of a departure from the Cook Agency. . . . We leave today for Le Havre. We will be happy to be back in Paris in six months."

the kind, either in private or in public, so that Fr. Boisselot's testimony—he hardly knew Fr. Maydieu—stands absolutely alone and might represent either a simplification of Gilson's thinking (the famous *reductio ad Hitlerum*) or Gilson thinking in anger (*ira brevis furor*), which in no way excuses the remark's tenor. In both hypotheses (the first of which seems more likely to us), the rupture indicates precisely Gilson's heated temperament as well as his sporadic involvement, without thereby being his last word. When the weekly, suspected in Rome and in the upper levels of the hierarchy of being "reddish Christian," was struck with an interdiction in August 1937, Gilson sent a very friendly letter to Fr. Bernadot.[46] When *Sept* disappeared, Boisselot commented, "There are more letters. The ones from Gilson and Mauriac are stunning and consoling about many things. Nothing new here."[47] On the eve of World War II, Gilson published many articles in *La vie intellectuelle* at Fr. Maydieu's request.

One of the interesting features of Gilson's involvement in the Dominican network is to emphasize that the book *Pour un ordre catholique* (criticized, as we have seen, by Emmanuel Mounier, Marc Bloch, and Maurice Halbwachs as the expression of Catholicism of the inner self) was offensive to certain bishops and initially taken to be the expression of a self-critical Catholic position. Let us yield the floor to Fr. Boisselot:

> Another much larger and further-reaching polemic was provoked by a series of articles by Gilson on education. These articles really set *Sept* on its feet. Until then, success was unclear. The newspaper was attractive, but it was not clear where it was going, what were its guiding concepts. There were good features, courage, youth, authenticity, a desire to separate the Church from its recognized protectors. But that was still vague. There was still no teacher who asserted himself. Gilson became that teacher, and his involvement had an immense reverberation among French Catholics. . . .
>
> He offered sound doctrine, supported by a remarkable talent as a writer. Not that he was brilliant or brisk as one would expect from a journalist. Not at all. He was an improvised journalist. He had a philosopher's style, but such a powerful and clear philosopher that his style had a clarity and force that carried conviction. . . .
>
> Gilson confronted the problem of schooling in France. . . . He called things by their names. What a scandal! As long as he limited himself to

46 The whole document is reproduced in the appendixes.

47 Letter from Fr. Pierre Boisselot to a Dominican brother, August 30, 1937, Fonds *Sept*, APDF.

> demonstrating the need for Catholic schooling and to denouncing the secularist metaphysics that public education hid, he had only admirers. But when he began to criticize (very objectively) private education, to denounce its flaws, and to call for structural reform, there was a hue and cry. The bishops seized upon it. Bishop Richaud dumped his concerns and advice on Fr. Bernadot's doorstep. Bishop Beaussart, the champion of private education, echoed him. I recall meeting Fr. Bernadot at Faubourg Saint-Honoré, on the feast of Saint Dominic, August 11, 1934. He attacked Gilson violently, as well as Fr. Chenu, who was there. The latter, however, was not impressed, and answered point by point. Having published a particularly accurate article about the technical mediocrity of our private education and having unfortunately titled it with the aggressive heading "The Cult of Incompetence," we received so many protests that there was no choice but to answer. Gilson did so masterfully. He posed the problem on its real ground: "Is it necessary to say" . . . Must Catholics draw a modest veil over their blemishes and with their usual Pharisaism pretend that everything is well with them and that their failures are the fault of their enemies? Rather, is it not better to acknowledge what is wrong with us, uncover it, and together loyally seek to remedy it? The second solution was always our choice. It was already Gilson's. He showed the need for a master's hand.[48]

Aline Coutrot notes that "the agreement [among *Sept*'s collaborators] on the subject of Italy was not perfect" and that "a little earlier Étienne Gilson had ceased to contribute because he was reproached for seeming to justify the Italian attack."[49] The language seems excessive. Gilson's rare public reference to the Ethiopian issue invites us to nuance it.

> All European politics is bathed in lies nowadays, and that runs the risk of damning Europe. England protects Abyssinia in the name of justice, but an Italian Abyssinia in its colonial empire is the only thing that bothers England. Italy claims Abyssinia in the interest of civilization, but it is because Italy needs Abyssinia that it wants to take it. France opposes the Anschluss in order to safeguard Austria's independence. . . . But the result of general elections in Austria might embarrass France. . . . The duty of Catholics toward nations as toward parties is to recall that nothing solid is ever built on a lie.[50]

48 Pierre Boisselot, "Notes sur l'histoire du Cerf," 1943, Cahier II, 83–87, Fonds Boisselot, APDF.

49 Coutrot, *Un courant de la pensée catholique*, 175.

50 Étienne Gilson, "Action catholique et action politique" *Sept*, no. 77, August 16, 1935, 4, column 4.

Since Gilson never considered that having a need gives a right, we must conclude that he is not justifying the Italian attack, any more than he is defending the English or French position. On September 6, 1935, the weekly *Sept* had a first-page article on the Ethiopian question in a very optimistic editorial: "The pope has spoken. Conscience is rescued." The battle of manifestos during the following October would show that consciences were not at all rescued. Gilson's break with *Sept* took place in the second half of August. Fr. Boisselot's testimony, upon which Aline Coutrot bases herself, is rather crushing for Gilson. It must be taken—as we have said—with prudence, in the measure that Boisselot recounted in 1943 a discussion that he did not hear in 1935. No document discovered so far has proven the remarks attributed to Gilson by Boisselot.

> The year 1935 was marked by *Sept* and *La vie spirituelle* taking a position on the war in Ethiopia that would be the first public grievance to be held against us subsequently. It is certain that we sided resolutely against Italy and for Ethiopia, or rather in favor of international law and morality. . . .
>
> However, our team itself was not unanimous. On this occasion, Étienne Gilson left us and did not conceal his motive, with that brutal frankness that is one of his charms. He stopped contributing and, despite our insistence, did not yield. One day, Fr. Maydieu went to see him, accompanied, if I remember correctly, by one of our friends who was also President of our Board, M. Coyne, and Gilson demolished our position. For him, Mussolini acted as a perfect Thomist! He was in charge of Italy's common good. This common good required that a large population should have new outlets. Mussolini found them in the uncivilized parts of Abyssinia, which was the only part of Africa not yet conquered. He took possession of it all to feed his own people and civilize the other one. Nothing is more in conformity to theology and Thomism. This argument did not convince us, and we left Gilson to his beloved studies without thereby loosening the friendship and gratitude that tied us to him.[51]

Jacques Prévotat, for his part, specifies that if events in Italy did end Gilson's involvement in *Sept*, Gilson was not thereby in favor of either the Italian invasion of Ethiopia or the rejection of international sanctions that were contemplated against the Fascist state.[52] In fact, Gilson did not sign the

51 Pierre Boisselot, "Notes sur l'histoire du Cerf," 1943, Cahier III, 27–35, Fonds Boisselot, APDF. See the appendixes.

52 Jacques Prévotat, "Étienne Gilson est-il un chrétien modéré?"

Manifesto of French Intellectuals for the defense of the West and the Peace of Europe," which praised Mussolini's action in Ethiopia and the civilizing conquest of one of the most backward countries in the world. This manifesto, published October 4, 1935, in *Le Temps*, obtained several hundred signatures of "right-wing pacifists," among them Henri Massis, Msgr. Baudrillart, Henry Bordeaux, Léon Daudet, Pierre Drieu La Rochelle, Abel Hermant, Abel Bonnard, Maurice Denis, Jean de Fabrègues, Gabriel Marcel, Henri Boegner, Charles Maurras, Thierry Maulnier, and others in support of Italy and to denounce the sanctions contemplated by the League of Nations. Gilson did not add his name to the counter-manifesto either, signed by the majority of his own students and friends: Jacques Maritain, François Mauriac, Fr. Bernadot, Charles Du Bos, Georges Bidault, Étienne Borne, Maurice de Gandillac. Marc Sangnier, Emmanuel Mounier, Paul Claudel, Henri-Irénée Marrou, Yves Simon, Pierre-Henri Simon, and others. The position was very clear and had an elevated moral and geopolitical vision. It was titled "For Justice and Peace." "Neither the need for expansion nor the work of civilization to be carried out has ever given the right to seize the territories of others and inflict death." The signers rejected the sophism of inequality of races, lamented both Italian and Abyssinian deaths, and recalled their commitment to peace through justice. It was published in *Sept* (October 18, 1935, 5) and in *La vie catholique*, and later in *L'Aube*, *Le Figaro* (October 20, 1935, 4) and in *Esprit* in November 1935.

Consequently, in the controversy about Ethiopia, Gilson was neutral in the strict sense. He supported neither Mussolini nor the defenders of the Ethiopian state. Outside of the passage quoted he did not declare himself in public. His private correspondence was rather reticent on it. To our knowledge, only a brief section of a letter to Henri Gouhier gives any indication: "The idea that one could supply arms to a band of savages against the country of Dante and Michelangelo, and do so in the name of civilization, morality, and justice, seems to me to be a disarming stupidity," he wrote on November 10, 1935. Gilson believed he had first-hand information about "the band of savages." His nephew Paul Gilson, then a freelance reporter and future executive of the French Radio and Television Organization (ORTF),[53] had just published an interesting assigned study of Haile Selassie, the Negus, the king of kings, the heir to Solomon's throne, the strength of the Trinity, whom

53 On this point, mentioned in chapter 1, see Philip Nord, *France's New Deal*.

he had had the opportunity to meet.[54] Paul Gilson had also interviewed the Ethiopian critics of the Negus. According to him, Ethiopia was still only a feudal regime. The King of Kings had weak moral and dynastic legitimacy. Starting as regent in 1924, he had seized his position after the death of the daughter of Emperor Menelik by executing the emperor's heirs, notably his grandson Lij Iyasu. Paul Gilson reported His Majesty's plans, which were to live in peace with his neighbors, modernize the country, abolish slavery, educate the people, and make sure that the Geneva pact and the country's territorial integrity were respected. But the result was a vitriolic picture of the existing regime: spies as numerous as fleas, police surveillance, state violence, propaganda, frequent hangings in the streets, a parliament worthy of Hollywood whose only purpose was to be the setting when the King wanted to give a speech, an impoverished and muzzled opposition. . . . The book's illustrations are significant: a debtor chained to his creditor, a slave merchant, and so forth. Not without reason, Yves Simon criticized these terrible and generally pro-fascist descriptions of the internal situation of Ethiopia: "The situation within Ethiopia offers a very dark picture to the most benevolent observers."[55] Was it, however, the case that the nephew had influenced his uncle's views? This is a likely hypothesis, to which we add a certainty. Despite Mussolini, Italy remained the country of Dante and Michelangelo for Étienne Gilson.

This Ethiopian affair is important here precisely insofar as it reveals Gilson's intellectual position: neutralism and balance. The five dozen articles published by Gilson in *Sept* do not for the most part concern international relations, but issues of French politics—democracy, monarchy, the involvement of French Catholics in debates, Catholic principles, and notably Catholic Action (one of whose founders was Gilson), as well as questions linked to education. Despite the vague disagreement on the Ethiopian question, *Sept*'s positions in large part were defined by Gilson's doctrinal articles. The book *Pour un ordre catholique* was regarded as "a masterpiece that should be the map of our action" (*Sept*, January 11, 1935, 15). It can also be seen in the self-description of an article that appeared February 14, 1936:

54 Paul Gilson, *Le roi des rois* (Paris: Denoël et Steele, 1935), 42 pp.

55 Yves Simon, *La campagne d'Éthiopie et la pensée politique française* 2nd ed. (Paris: Desclée de Brouwer, 1937), 63.

> *Sept* is Christian first of all, not red, white, or any electoral shade. As Étienne Gilson wrote here, answering certain accusations, "*Sept* is not a democratic newspaper by the simple fact that democracy is a political doctrine, and if we take the greatest interest in political doctrines in order to judge them from the Christian viewpoint, *qua* Catholics, we profess none of them." We are neither monarchists nor supporters of dictatorship. But we call all Catholics to us, whether of left or right. . . . "To clarify the situation in a way that never ties the truth of Catholicism, which is eternal, to this or that form of political organization, which is temporal and transitory by nature, that is what *Sept* works for above all." These statements of principle that we take from Gilson are essential to understand the authentic meaning of our action.[56]

The newspaper then returned to a June 1935 article by Gilson, where he explained that keeping to the level of principle, for the same reasons, he refused to condemn democracy or monarchy.[57] As was his custom, Gilson did not hesitate to break lances with newspapers and magazines of other sectors, who responded to him as well: for example, with *Esprit* in May and June 1934 on communism;[58] with *Action Française* in summer 1935 on the subject of "politics first," which Maurras logically intended to maintain;[59] with the *Nouvelle Lanterne* in June of the same year. At the conceptual level, Gilson rejected the idols of homeland, capital, and working classes. He trounced laicism (November 23, 1934) and "free thought," the paganism of moral license and of pornography (May 3, 1935), as well as communism, nationalism and the cult of youth.

The twenty-five articles republished in *Pour un ordre catholique* can be analyzed in two ways, by their intrinsic content and by the reactions and debates they provoked. The proud, martial title, *Pour un ordre catholique*, indicates one direction, that of Catholic Action, for which Gilson was both the advocate and one of its theoreticians.[60] The expression came from the title of an article by Gilson that appeared in *Sept* on June 9, 1934:

56 "Notre position," *Sept*, February 14, 1936.

57 Étienne Gilson, "Pour éclairer *La nouvelle lanterne*," *Sept*, no. 68, June 14, 1935, 4.

58 See the exchanges with Edmond Humeau analyzed in chapter 2.

59 Accordingly, see P. Tuc, "Politique d'abord," *L'Action Francaise*, January 26, 1935, 5. Between June 19 and August 6, 1935, *l'Action Française* devoted no fewer than nine articles to answer pieces written by Gilson in *Sept*.

60 On this point, see Coutrot, *Un courant de la pensée catholique*, particularly the section "Catholic Order and Catholic Action," 81ff: "Therefore, the articles in *Sept*, taking into account their

> What must be understood by *Catholic order*? I mean to indicate that between Catholics' private religious life and the political groups in which they participate as citizens, there is an order of institutions created by Catholics to guarantee the realization of the Catholic objectives for which the state does not take responsibility. As long as you did not create that order, there is only one answer to the question you pose about what Catholics can do for their country: Pray as individuals and make yourselves better. Socially there is nothing, because socially you do not exist. The first step to take at the bottom of a long, hard climb that awaits us, is to understand that, if Catholicism is not to submit to a party or to become a supplementary political party, it can still do a great deal for France. But it can do it, only if it is given the means. Here too, I will say with the politicians that we are dealing with a specific order, with its end and particular means. Its end is to wholly satisfy the requirements of a fully Catholic life in a state that is not Catholic. Its means are the institutions to be created or coordinated in order for these requirements to be wholly met. When this order exists, although it is not at all political, we will not have to wait long to see that, even without seeking it, the presence of this order weighs heavily upon the life of the parties. As long as it does not exist, we will have nothing to say and we will be able to do nothing. We will not even have set foot on the path that leads to the end, as long as it has not been understood.[61]

The expression "Catholic order" was itself open to criticism. Gilson was aware of that and wanted to respond in his article of January 1935 "Catholic Order and National Unity":

> The most serious objection that can be made against the concept of a Catholic order is that carrying it out would risk producing a kind of inward migration and making French Catholics into a state within the state, separating them from the other French people. . . . Can we wish for a French Catholic order, which is to say, our schools, our charitable institutions, our hospitals, our youth and worker activities, without going it alone and separating ourselves from the rest of the nation? Let us first acknowledge that such a result would be abominable, and the system would be absurd, as much for the Church as for the country. However, the point is in no way this sort of secession. . .

early date and the stature of their authors [Maritain and Gilson], are fundamental contributions to the doctrine of Catholic Action."

61 Étienne Gilson, "Pour un ordre catholique," *Sept*, no. 15, June 9, 1934, 2. Reproduced with the title, "L'ordre catholique et la France," in *Pour un ordre catholique*, 100–107.

> What must be done for France to remain or return to being livable for us? Should we demand and wait for justice to be done to us? Nothing is wrong with doing that, but above all it is necessary to act. To act with the firm certainty that the surest way to see our Catholic order recognized and respected by the state some day is to do what French Catholics have always done: to organize outside the state. Let us make this order exist. Once it exists, the danger will no longer be for it to remain on the sidelines, but to keep the order from being absorbed by a state impatient to glory in it and benefit itself by it.[62]

The existence of this Catholic order was certainly the first difficulty. Gilson intended to pose real problems in his February 8, 1935 article, which "are the problems of Catholic Action" and the "practical modes of their solution in the country."[63] Gilson did not envisage all of the features of Catholic Action, but chiefly the ones that concerned education. "Private education is an endeavor that is always threatened by its adversaries and persecuted with the most tenacious hatred" (1934, 126). For Gilson the first remedy was the repeal of the Combes Laws. "So where do we find the remedy? I have stated it: in the return of our teaching congregations and by granting the complete freedom that their schools ought to enjoy, by the mere establishment of a democratic state, which the French State again professes to be" (192). Gilson's second target was the mediocrity of French Catholic education. "Does private education have competent teaching personnel? To that question, I regret having to say that this is not my impression.... If I had to formulate a general rule, it would be that devotion dispenses [the teacher] from competence" (153). In the book's conclusion, we again find mention of a problem that haunted Gilson all his life: "The principal problem is simple: those responsible for selecting teachers must keep in mind that if a Catholic school is, religiously, a Catholic activity, it is, technically, a school" (227). In a resounding article on "the cult of incompetence" that appeared on July 21, 1934, Gilson emphasized the necessity of good Catholic teaching at the level of elementary and secondary schools just as in higher education: "To have Catholic teachers, it is necessary to prepare them, and state institutions can be of no help here. Catholic education is not state education received by Catholics. It is not a ready-to-wear garment, still less something admirably tailored, perhaps for somebody else, with which we might make do ourselves.

62 Étienne Gilson, "Ordre catholique et unité nationale," *Sept*, no. 47, January 18, 1935, 3.

63 Étienne Gilson, "Les vrais problèmes," *Sept*, no. 50, February 8, 1935.

It ought to be education made to order, which is to say, by Catholics for Catholics. Now, there is only one intellectual and religious authority that is capable of saying what such an education ought to be and of organizing it. It is the authority of the Catholic Institutes" (171-72).

Further on, after showing that private education was more attractive and more successful in Belgium, England, the United States, and Canada, than in France, Gilson added:

> Our French people are rather different. Just as they count on Clovis's new baptism to ensure the future of Christianity in their country, they hope for a new Charlemagne to provide them with the schools they need. But don't talk to them about organizing the schools. It is not that they feel unable to do so. They do not even want to, because, if you will permit me the expression, "They don't see what that is good for." . . . The reason for that is simple. It is the lack of Catholic spirit. They understand schools being opened to teach science and letters, law or medicine, because in their view, all that is useful for something. But to pay out of their pockets for someone to teach Holy Scripture, theology, canon law, or Christian philosophy—they are so uneager to do so, that one is forced to believe that in their view all that is useless. . . . All Catholicism rests on these two pillars, the sacramental order by which Christians participate in the life of grace, and the Church's doctrine by which they participate in the faith. Suppress the study and teaching of that doctrine, and Catholicism breaks down. Let these activities vegetate, and Catholicism's very life slows down. (174–76)

The reception of Gilson's book and *Sept* articles is not difficult to measure. It largely depended on the readers' position in the French ecclesiastical spectrum. "Your articles are admirably clear and relevant. You can't imagine how much the directives you draw up are discussed. Quantities of letters testify to that, and *Sept* certainly owes you real gratitude and, through *Sept*, all of Catholicism," Fr. Boisselot wrote to Gilson in May 1934.[64]

Marc Bloch and Lucien Febvre could not criticize Gilson sharply enough. Bloch went so far as to refer to "voluntary ignorance" in Gilson, though adding that some passages in the criticized book "ought to be pondered by the most secularist among us."[65] For his part, Febvre commented in a lively, gripping manner: "The Gilson of *Pour un ordre catholique*, which

64 Letter from Fr. Pierre Boisselot to Étienne Gilson, May 5, 1934, SMCA.

65 Letter from Marc Bloch to Lucien Febvre, February 11, 1935, *Correspondance Marc Bloch—Lucien Febvre*, 2:209.

I have just gone through —The man is crazy. This is not about Gilson. He ought to have gone away six years ago. He gave us his last good moments at Strasbourg."[66] *L'Action Francaise* was equally critical, without ever discussing Gilson's arguments. The nationalist newspaper fulminated and labeled the philosopher "illogical" (May 26, 1935). By contrast, the pro-rector of the Catholic Institute of Paris praised Gilson's "soundness" and "robust clarity."[67] The editorial writer for *La Croix*, Jean Guiraud, deemed Gilson "one of the most respected witnesses to religious truth" and devoted a long first-page column to comment upon the work, whose clarity and frankness he praised, though he expressed "reservations on certain points." Guiraud was enamored of the "Christian state," quite distinct from the Gilsonian "Catholic order."[68] As for Mounier, he certainly recognized an agreement on principles that permitted a "first liberation from liberal anarchy" and "a first protection against the totalitarian threat," but (his criticism is biting) he acknowledged an authentic "disappointment" and "fear" regarding the steps suggested by Gilson. To Mounier, the Catholic order seemed to be dictated by a "class position," a very "center-right" political position, that would tend to enclose Catholicism in "resentment."[69] Mounier specified, "There is a risk of an instinctive tendency to the right, because the mass of Catholics tends that way, and to re-constitute the two Frances." Claudel valued at least one of Gilson's suggestions: "Dear Sir, I have read your article in *Sept* with great interest, where you correctly blame the stinginess of the Catholic faithful."[70] Maritain, who expressed minor reservations, overall was delighted: "The vigor and clarity with which you remind our French Catholic brothers of so many truths that they have forgotten wins my admiration. Your book is full of the most accurate comments.... It is a Socratic book, a spur to energize Athenians and bishops."[71]

66 Letter from Lucien Febvre to Marc Bloch, June 24, 1935, *Correspondance Marc Bloch—Lucien Febvre*, 2:261.

67 René Barbier de la Serre, pro-rector of the Catholic Institute of Paris, "Pour un ordre catholique," *Sept*, January 25, 1935, 3.

68 Jean Guiraud, "La croisée des chemins," *La Croix*, January 23, 1935, 1–2. See also Guiraud, "La collaboration des catholiques à l'enseignement laïque," *La Croix*, January 29, 1935, ; and Guiraud, "L'humanisme, terrain d'entente?," *La Croix*, February 1, 1935, 1.

69 Emmanuel Mounier, "Étienne Gilson, *Pour un ordre catholique*," *Esprit* 3, no. 30 (March 1935): 959–64.

70 Letter from Paul Claudel to Étienne Gilson, July 24, 1934, SMCA.

71 Letter from Jacques Maritain to Étienne Gilson, January 4, 1935, in Gilson and Maritain, *Correspondance 1923–1971*, 122–23.

The French bishops were indeed stung. According to Cardinal Baudrillart, "All in all, the book is very good and courageous, full of truths, with the single defect of reproaching us for doing nothing about the teaching of things that we have done or attempted . . ."[72] Gilson wrote to Fr. Phelan: "My book *Pour un ordre catholique* has been very well received in Rome, including by Bishop Pizzardo and the Holy Father. It has been translated into Spanish [by José Bergamín with a study by Alfredo Mendizábal] and into English."[73]

On the subject of the "cult of incompetence" that Gilson had denounced, he was criticized by some bishops, in particular the auxiliary bishop of Versailles, Paul Richaud, President of the National Committee for Private Education, and Bishop Beaussart, President of the Alliance des Maisons d'Éducation Chrétienne. On August 7, 1937, Gilson replied to Fr. Bernadot on the recommendations urging prudence: "I am unable to speak if I do not feel free, and if we published the continuation, there would again be a general outcry. I am horrified by any conflict with religious authorities. Since those who are in charge judge that I serve badly, it is a formal invitation to me to cease my services, because I am incapable of serving otherwise."[74]

A week later, still on the subject of the "cult of incompetence," Fr. Bernadot received a diplomatic letter from Emmanuel Suhard, then archbishop of Reims:

> Let us acknowledge that the author has written articles on private education with an excellent touch that can only be admired. On the particular issue considered in this article, while his intent is above all reproach, certain things he has written, and particularly the way of presenting them, cannot help offending some Catholics. That is what happened. . . . All this, dear Father, leads to the conclusion that Professor Gilson will do a very great service if he also accepts friendly supervision. It could be given to him by any of your priests able to know what should be said and what (even if true) should not be said, what should be said in private and what should be shouted in public.[75]

72 *Les Carnets du cardinal Alfred Baudrillart, 1932–1935* (Paris: Cerf, 2003), 1079–80.

73 Letter from Étienne Gilson to Fr. Gerald Phelan, March 8, 1935, SMCA.

74 Letter from Étienne Gilson to Fr. Bernadot, August 7, 1934, 1934, quoted by Coutrot, *Un courant de la pensée catholique*, 158.

75 Letter from Archbishop Suhard to Fr. Marie-Vincent Bernadot, August 14, 1934, quoted by Coutrot, *Un courant de la pensée catholique*, 158.

Gilson had already answered Archbishop Suhard's suggestion, saying that he needed to feel free. The polemic died down. The article about the "cult of incompetence" was forgotten. It reappeared in a volume with a dulcified title, "Competence and Goodwill." Gilson continued to write in *Sept.* "Accordingly, the incident had limited reverberation," Aline Coutrot concludes. But it is worth studying the events further because, for example, Bishop Richaud, as we noted President of the National Committee for Private Education, included Gilson's recommendations in a report of July 1936, prepared for the meeting of French cardinals and archbishops.[76]

The analysis of Gilson's involvement with educational issues ought to be pursued in depth. In France, at the end of World War II, Gilson continued to defend the freedom of "private education," which he always deemed to be threatened. His ideal was simple to sum up and difficult to put into practice: "Absolute freedom in absolute equality of obligations, compensated with absolute equality of support."[77] After the Liberation, as he had in the 1920s, Gilson often attempted to act as a mediator. In 1925, he wrote about those pseudo-rivalries that the two parties carefully exploited, since they really needed to foment the hatreds by which they lived, which did not exist in reality. "The law is that there is a constant exchange of students and teachers between the two forms of education and that they complement each other mutually."[78] In 1945, Gilson wrote again:

> This is the situation. There are two educations, that of the Church and that of the Republic, neither of which properly speaking is national education. Both of them sin by excess and by defect. What we lack is another school that would be the French school properly speaking, from which a national education could be expected, since it would be education of the nation, by the nation, and for the nation.... To formulate the issue differently, let us say that the point is to achieve Henri Marrou's perfect formula, to which I subscribe unreservedly: "The imperative that ought to silence every partisan, secularist or Christian, is *to restore the common will of the French to form a*

76 "Une déclaration de Mgr. Richaud," *Sept*, July 17, 1936: "I have reproduced in a recent report the suggestions made in books by Pierre-Henri Simon and Étienne Gilson."

77 Letter from Étienne Gilson to Jean-Augustin Maydieu, May 28, 1944, 9, Fonds Maydieu, APDF. See appendixes in the present volume.

78 Étienne Gilson, "Une heure avec...," *Les Nouvelles littéraires*, January 3, 1925, 1–2.

> *nation*. Schools ought to be at the service of the common climate." Indeed, the national education we hope for will be just that, or it will not be.[79]

Gilson proposed a "liberal solution" (in a rather vague sense, it must be said), which sought a just middle ground. "What matters in this realm, as in so many others, is that our country should be able to find the path that goes between individual choice and state choice by giving national social structures a freedom of action that is their very life, and that our country should find in time without waiting to be forced to it ultimately by the fatal decadence of its institutions."[80] Going beyond the perspective *of Pour un ordre catholique*, Gilson specified his analysis of the French educational system in the magazine *Politique*,[81] *La documentation catholique*,[82] *La Vie intellectuelle*,[83] *L'Aube*,[84] *Le Monde*,[85] and even in his participation in the Conseil de la République in 1947, where, as a member of the National Education Committee, he advocated an increase in university budgets: "Consequently, it is necessary that we remedy the chronic ill that threatens to become a mortal ill if this country does not finally understand that, in a modern state, science is not a luxury, but a necessary condition of its economic and national independence."[86]

79 Étienne Gilson, "Pour une éducation nationale," *La vie intellectuelle*, April 1945, 116–32.

80 Étienne Gilson, "L'État, l'Université, et les universités, *Politique*, no. 5 (September–October 1948): 690.

81 Étienne Gilson, "L'État, l'Université, et les universités, *Politique*, no. 5 (September–October 1948): 673–90.

82 Étienne Gilson, "La question de l'enseignement libre en France," *La Documentation catholique* 45, September 12, 1948, 1163–69.

83 Étienne Gilson, "Pour une éducation nationale," *La vie intellectuelle*, April 1945, 116–32.

84 Étienne Gilson, "Le droit d'enseigner," *L'Aube*, August 14, 1948, 2.

85 Étienne Gilson, "Instruire ou éduquer?," *Le Monde*, January 9, 1945, 1–2.

86 See Gilson's remarks at the Conseil de la République's August session the research budget, "Rapport fait au nom de la commission de l'Éducation national tendant à inviter le Governement à créer des cours de droit d'outre-mer dans les facultés de la métropole, qui n'en possèdent encore" [Report made on behalf of the national education budget encouraging the government to create courses in the faculties of law of the metropolis that do not yet have them on the law of overseas French territories], Conseil de la République, first legislative session, session of July 30, 1947, appendix number 485, 507.

See also "Rapport fait au nom de la commission de l'Éduation nationale tendant à inviter le gouvernement à prendre d'urgence les mesures nécessaires pour conserver ou restituer à leur usage normal d'écoles publiques laïques les bâtimments scolaires acquis régulièrement," [Report submitted on behalf of the National Education Committee recommending that the government urgently take the necessary steps to preserve or restore to normal use as secular public

MRP (MOUVEMENT RÉPUBLICAIN POPULAIRE) AND CONSEIL DE LA RÉPUBLIQUE (1945–1950)

After Gilson's exile within France during World War II, he undertook a new period of political activism alongside Francisque Gay, Georges Bidault, and Robert Schuman, within the Mouvement Républicain Populaire.[87] It is not certain that French Christian Democrats have a precise memory of Gilson's intellectual role within their network immediately after the War. Jean Marie Mayeur has recalled the seminal role and "considerable influence" of Jacques Maritain and *Integral Humanism* on the Christian Democratic activists, whereas Mounier acted as a "stern judge" against the democratic parties with Christian inspiration.[88] Jean-Dominique Durand points to Gilson, among many others like Maritain, Mounier, Borne, Blondel, Bergson, Berdyaev. as one of the creative intellectuals of Christian Democracy.[89]

Gilson was not a judge or founding father, neither was he a simple fellow traveler. However, he did not spare his effort on behalf of the MRP, whose European, Christian, pacifist, social, and republican program corresponded to his own deep aspirations. After the Liberation, he gave lectures, organized meetings, published pamphlets and articles in *Le Monde*, *Temps présent*, and *L'Aube* to defend the MRP's political position and attack socialists, communists, radicals, and Gaullists. Hubert Beuve-Méry wrote to him in 1946: "Your prose does not pass unnoticed."[90] The following year, Gilson became "Senator in spite of himself,"[91] representing the MRP in the Conseil de la République. His university teaching is nuanced by his political commitments of the period: "Christian doctrine is often presented as defending safe deposit boxes. Perhaps it has been used to play that role. It is not its own,"

schools the school buildings that were legally acquired], Conseil de la République, first legislative session, session of December 17, 1947, appendix number 902, 692–93.

87 Letter from Étienne Gilson to Robert Schuman, August 29, 1949, Maison Robert Schuman: "When I think of the admirable role you are playing and the service you perform for France (Perhaps much more still in Germany than the country imagines), I am a humbled by the little that a person of good will can do by teaching. Your friends console themselves with the thought that their affection for you gives them a kind of participation in your merits."

88 Jean-Marie Mayeur, *Des partis catholiques à la Démocratie chrétienne XIXe–XXe siècles* (Paris: Armand Colin, 1980), 152–53.

89 Jean-Dominique Durand, *L'Europe de la Démocratie chrétienne* (Brussels: Éditions complexes, 1995), 111.

90 Letter from Hubert Beuve-Méry to Étienne Gilson, August 27, 1947, Archives Vrin.

91 Shook, *Étienne Gilson*, 272.

he explained to the students at Science-Po, quoting St. Paul and Fénelon's *Telemachus*, while suggesting that Marx's communism is a Christian heresy born of Scholasticism and showing that capitalism only developed against Christianity.[92] This political activism was a novelty in Gilson's personal history in comparison to the 1930s; still there was a background of continuity represented by the network of magazines and the figures of Marc Sangnier and Francisque Gay, with whom Gilson corresponded after 1919. A sympathizer of Le Sillon during his youth, but totally ignorant of its theory,[93] Gilson re-encountered its founder in the MRP. In 1924, Gilson subscribed to *La vie catholique* that Gay had just founded.[94] In the 1934–1935 *Sept* articles, Gilson still intended to stay on the level of principles exclusively, and was afraid of the creation of a political party like the German *Zentrum* and never mentioned the Italian Christian-Democratic Party, eliminated by fascism and the Lateran Treaty. It would be necessary to trace the steps precisely from the group around *Sept* to the construction of the MRP. The Gilson Affair and his departure from the Collège de France marked an end to this period of engagement.

At the time of the debates about the adoption of the constitution of the Fourth Republic, Gilson was very close to Francisque Gay. "The Minister of State, Francisque Gay, President of the MRP, is coming next Saturday to hold a council-of-war in my country house [Vermenton]. I have converted my priest [Abbé Breuil] to the MRP despite the decided opposition of my archbishop. But I have not yet agreed to run for deputy."[95] In October 1946, Gilson supported the draft of the constitution of the Fourth Republic against

92 Étienne Gilson, "Les données chrétiennes de la politique nationale," third lecture, Sciences-Po, 1946–1947, 6, SMCA.

93 Étienne Gilson, *The Philosopher and Theology*, 56–57: "I did not belong to Le Sillon, nor for that matter to any political party. . . . Quite apart from any political doctrine, our hearts leaned toward Marc Sangnier."

94 Francisque Gay began publishing the weekly on September 20, 1924. In a letter of October 9, 1924, Gilson commented on the event to Henri Gouhier: "I have subscribed to *La Vie catholique* because the paper seems to me to meet a real need, and until now I would criticize it for only one somewhat excessively firm editorial, especially for a first issue." The editorial was by Francisque Gay. See the letter from Étienne Gilson to Francisque Gay, February 18, 1925, Institut Marc Sangnier: "I at least want to take advantage of this occasion to tell you with what interest I read your newspaper and to send you my best wishes for complete success."

95 Letter from Étienne Gilson to Anton Pegis, September 25, 1946, quoted by Shook, *Étienne Gilson*, 272.

de Gaulle and delighted in fighting the communists.[96] In December 1946, Gilson took himself out of the Yonne senatorial elections. He was designated by the MRP committee director for the next local elections. He accepted, then hesitated, and sought in vain to join Francisque Gay and Georges Bidault. He ended by declining in favor of another candidate, because an express message to him suggested that he stand for election "thinking about a later election." "What made me accept was precisely the perspective of being able to act in the Conseil upon a plan of general interest, by raising the level of the debates each time it was possible, in other words, by showing that the MRP embodied the idea and the will of a certain France. I think that it was the best way to serve the party . . . without worrying about preparing for my 'later election' as the famous express mail said."[97] All the same, Gilson was elected, not by the expedient of a local election, but by an unusual procedure foreseen by the new constitution.

Gilson was not elected to the Conseil de la République (Herriot called the assembly "as inefficient as possible") by the usual path.[98] Once the constitution of the Fourth Republic was adopted (October 27, 1946), elections for the two houses of the assembly were organized. Article 3, line 6, established that "the National Assembly can name members of the Conseil de la République not to exceed one sixth of the total number of members." In November-December 1946, fifty out of three hundred fifteen counselors were elected by the Assembly. New perspectives from civil society appeared in the Conseil and profoundly modified its membership: the Senegalese writer Alioune Diop, the communist intellectual Jean-Richard Bloch, the socialist Gilberte Brossolette, wife of Pierre Brossolette, and Maurice Blondel's son-in-law Charles Flory, for example. In 1946 Gilson appeared as the substitute on the list presented by the MRP for the Conseil de la République after Auguste Champetier de Ribes, chosen as first President of the Conseil de la République in December 1946, by virtue of age. He died on March 6, 1947. Gilson was declared elected and entered Luxembourg Palace at the end of

96 Letter from Étienne Gilson to Anton Pegis, October 9, 1946, quoted by Shook, *Étienne Gilson*, 272: "We should vote 'yes' for the constitution against de Gaulle's advice, and I have organized meetings in the country in favor of the MRP. Fighting with communists is really fun."

97 Letter from Étienne Gilson to Francisque Gay, December 25, 1946, Institut Marc Sangnier. Gilson ended the letter with the words: "This in no way lessens my deep gratitude for the honor paid to me, nor the regret I feel for having responded so badly to it, but I hope to find other ways of serving, and I will not fail to involve myself in them."

98 Marc Baroli and Dominique Robert, *Du Conseil de la République au Sénat, 1946–1958* (Paris: PUF, 2015).

March 1947. He joined the MRP group (the most numerous of the Conseil with a quarter of the seats and seventy-six elected members). He became a member of the National Education Committee and the Pension Committee. Six months after Robert Schuman's appointment to Luxembourg Palace, the "father of Europe" and an MRP senator wrote to Gilson: "My friend, do not thank me for a gesture that has only been the unanimous ratification of disinterested services that you have continually performed within and beyond our boundaries."[99]

Basically Gilson's work within the Conseil de la République centered on the after-effects of World War II: social problems, the research budget, education, reclassification and improvement of the legal status of victims of war, also the situation of deportees and confined members of the Resistance, aid to private schools, reform of old age insurance, revisions of excessive pensions, and higher education budget. Gilson was involved in senate debates at least five times, whether in the context of resolutions or reports from the National Education Committee, or questions put to the government.[100] The

99 Letter from Robert Schuman to Étienne Gilson, September 1, 1947, SMCA.

100 Proposition de Résolution tendant à demander aux houillères des bassins d'Aquitaine, des Cévennes et de la Loire à donner à bail aux associations des parents d'élèves les locaux des anciennes écoles privées des mines" [Resolved; to request the coal mines of the Aquitaine, Cévennes, and Loire basins to lease to the association of parents of school children, the sites of the old private schools of the mines], Conseil de la République, first legislative session, 1946–1947, appendix number 482, meeting of July 30, 1947, 505.

"Proposition de Résolution tendant à inviter le Gouvernement à régulariser dans les plus brefs délais la situation des fonctionnaires détachés de leur adminsitration d'origine dans d'autres adminsitrations" [Resolved: to request that the Government normalize in the shortest possible time the situation of functionaries detached from their original position in the administration], Conseil de la République, first legislative session, 1946–1947, appendix number 974, meeting of December 30, 1947, 767.

"Rappport fait au nom de la commission de l'Éducation nationale tendant à inviter le Gouvernement à creer des cours de droit d'outre mer dans les facultés de la métropole qui n'en possèdent pas encore" [Report on behalf of the National Education Committee requesting that the Government create, in those faculties of law of the Metropolis that do not yet possess them, courses of the law of French overseas territories], Conseil de la République, first legislative session, appendix 485, meeting of July 30, 1947, 507.

"Rappport fait au nom de la commission de l'Éducation nationale tendant à inviter le Gouvernement à prendre d'urgence les mesures nécessaires pour converser ou restituer à leur usage normal d'écoles publiques laïques les bâtiments scolaires acquis régulièrement" [Report on behalf of the National Education Commission requesting the government to take urgent measures to preserve or restore legally acquired school buildings to their normal use as secular public schools], Conseil de la République, first legislative session, appendix 902, meeting of December 17, 1947, 692–93.

most interesting was the one where Gilson argued for a significant increase in the research budget at the August 5, 1947, session:

> Minister, ladies, my dear colleagues, since I cannot speak about the entirety of the National Education budget, which would be a huge subject, I will limit my remarks to the higher education budget, and on this point I will not try to tell you as quickly as possible as many things as possible in the least possible time....
>
> What I would like to tell you is not that our 1947 budget is insufficient, but that the budget is always insufficient. The constancy of this phenomenon precludes easy explanation, because the easy explanation is always the same. What do you want France to do, when it is as poor as it is? Yes, it is true that France is poor. It regrets not having spent its money better when it was rich. But as it becomes rich again, it continues not to know how to spend.
>
> Consequently, it is necessary that we should remedy the chronic evil that threatens to become a fatal evil if the country does not finally understand that in a modern state, science is not a luxury but a necessary condition of its economic and national independence. It would be interesting to seek the cause of this evil. But stating it would be another thing. And to seek the remedy with you would be a third thing. Let us leave the issue for later. But some day in this chamber (something of which there is no sign yet), if we agree on time to reflect [*smiles*], your Assembly perhaps will want to remember these two problems whose importance is urgent, which the discussion of the 1947 budget did not let us resolve but that it will have at least permitted us to pose [*unanimous loud applause*].[101]

Gilson, likewise, helped to define the general orientation of the MRP. In the magazine *Politique*, he presented a resounding plea in favor of the Christian democratic party:

> Those who complain that the Movement Républicain Populaire has no manifesto to which it may always refer as the party's bible are simply people who do not know their good luck. But that does not mean that we have no need to think and nothing to say. It does not even mean that we believe we are dispensed from reasoning in an orderly methodical way, because, if the MRP has no system, it has principles. In that sense, one can even say that it has a doctrine, but that doctrine is very simple, because it always consists of applying the same principles to the study of the different political,

101 Minutes of the Conseil de la République, August 5, 1947 session, 1482–83.

economic, and social problems, which must urgently be resolved for the common good of our country.

The particular objective of the *Société d'Éditions Républicaines Populaires*, which has just been founded and whose first books appeared a few days ago, is precisely to set out the principles and show the different practical applications to which the principles lead by the publication of pamphlets, brochures, and books. The first duty of a movement is to retain its freedom of movement, which simply means that practical reason must move comfortably and with agility amid the complex facts it needs to structure. There is no party rigidity to be found here, but everywhere we find the unity of a mind that remains faithful to its principles in the diversity of its investigations, its problems and its solutions.

This is why firmness will always be united to freedom. Moral problems are practical problems. So are political problems, and all practical problems are particular problems. The things that Mouvement Républicain Populaire advocates, insofar as they relate to the political level, are all related to this particular political problem: how can France, ruined by the two most terrible wars of its history, be reconstructed so as to make justice reign in a spirit of common friendship? The idea is simple but we must not fail to understand that it is irresistible in its very simplicity, and those who see only a safe formula will be very much out of touch, because it is inspired by the most effectively revolutionary forces that the world has ever known: charity and reason.[102]

On February 11, 1948, Gilson gave a long lecture "by invitation of several of our friends, to define democracy as the Mouvement Républicain Populaire understood it." Gilson did not plan to "dogmatize," as he says himself, "just to "clarify my own thoughts for myself."[103] The original manuscript is in the Senate Archives. It was then published separately and in articles in *L'Aube*, with the title "Notre Démocratie."[104] The opening indicates its tone:

To define democracy as the Mouvement Républicain Populaire understands it, is not to desire to establish dogmas in the name of our movement.

102 Étienne Gilson, "Le système et l'esprit," *Politique* 4, no. 27 (1947): 673–77.

103 Étienne Gilson, "Notre Démocratie," February 11, Senate Archives, 16 pp.: "This talk prepared for our parliamentary group, whose informal tone we have retained, took place February 11, 1948, in the Conseil de la République. By allowing it to be reproduced as it stood, we hoped to broaden the conversation without changing the tone of the conversation."

104 Étienne Gilson, *Notre démocratie* (Paris: SERP, 1948), 30 pp. The talk was subsequently re-published in *L'Aube*, April–May, 1948.

> None of us has received the charge of doing that, and we have no intention of binding ourselves once and for all to any political system. Nonetheless, we all are interested in clarifying our own thoughts on the subject and communicating our reflections to others in the hope of benefitting their thinking. Perhaps this examination of political conscience will have some usefulness.[105]

The lecture was remarkable. Gilson established a rather convincing analogy between Renan and Maurras on the issue of hostility toward democracy. He denounced the "mystique of the leader," radical democracy," "Marxist democracy" in all its variants, in order finally to characterize "republican democracy," that of the MRP. At the core of that democracy is the "human person" and not individuals or masses: "The human person is an end. The state is there only to permit the human person to attain the full development of which it is capable," namely democracy of freedom in all its senses, including liberty "in its soul," equality before the law, and fraternity:

> Finally fraternity, because the republic that we want will not be Marxism's hive, where production is sufficiently guaranteed by the discipline that the state imposes, but the free cooperation of persons obeying the orders of reason and of love that reason elucidates. It is not our intention to perpetuate the race of Caliban in order to save the culture of some élite or so-called élite, not even to improve it, as Renan began in his old age to think was possible. It would be better to suppress it. There is politics that consists in taking advantage of humankind. That is not ours. There is politics that consists in serving humankind. That is ours. But to serve it, one must begin by loving it.

Gilson concluded

> We have an end: the democracy of human persons. We have a method to attain the end: it makes the state the protector and guide of natural social groups whose totality constitutes the people. We have a precise rule of political action, which does not consist in wanting to act differently from others, but rather to do exactly that in which the others take no interest and which we want to do: eliminate evil by eliminating its cause. It is not a political program to direct violent action against communism, because a program worthy of the name is never *against* but *for*. The only effective way of being against communism is to create a social order that removes

105 Étienne Gilson, *Notre démocratie*, 1.

> all of communism's reason for being. It is to resolve communism's particular issues more intelligently than it does. It is always to favor, whatever the problem, the state intervention that will help citizens themselves more effectively to achieve their own proper ends.

On January 18, 1950, Gilson gave another public speech under the MRP banner in the presence of Pierre-Henri Teitgen in the fifteenth arrondissement of Paris. There was a large crowd. The speech had not been delivered previously and was titled "Political Freedom and the Parties."[106] At the end of the speech, Gilson was booed by the Maurrasians, notably by the monarchist lawyer Georges Calzant, one of the founders of *l'Aspects de la France.* Calzant intended to defend the honor of Maurras against Gilson's attack on the subject of the limitation of the collaboration ordered by Maurras. In the course of the speech, Gilson related his experience in the area: meetings of MRP federations; encounters with voters who questioned him about the price of milk or wine; the mail he received; the relations among parliamentarians, and among parliamentarians and ministers. Gilson developed Bidault's theme of "revolution by law" and, in a moment of eloquence, described the party he desired (38–48):

> To describe the party of my dreams I will sum up its program in four points:
>
> First, in France, it accepts the family as a natural fact. . . . It cannot be killed without killing the whole social body. . . . Second, the party will accept this other social fact, namely, the socialization of certain natural resources or of certain means of production and distribution. . . . Third, my party will accept the third fundamental fact of social democracy as it is actually organized before our eyes in trade-unionism. . . . The fourth and final point is that this party will have to accept that each French citizen is not a number but a human, that is to say a moral person with intelligence and will. . . . The party will remember that formerly *minister* in Latin meant *servant*. . . . There will be no state religion; I say *none*, especially in the interest of the churches. There will be no official philosophy or official science, in the interest of philosophy and science. There will be freedom of education, and I say not only freedom of education in private schools, but I call for this freedom even more in state schools , where it is infinitely more threatened than

106 Étienne Gilson, "La liberté politique et les partis," January 18, 1950; 75 typewritten pages, introduction by Monsieur Cayeux and a report on the debates (50–75), SMCA. The speech was disrupted by militants of Action Française, who reproached Gilson for articles in *Le Monde* about Maurras.

> elsewhere. In short, the state will understand that it cannot think because it has no brain, and even if it had one, it would not be more intelligent all by itself than forty million French men and women. . . . If I try to define this party of which I dream, I will say that it takes as its primary goal the creation of the conditions of all their liberties of those French men and women within the framework of France. . . . The most extraordinary thing is that this party exists and that one of the most beautiful things in my life is to have found it. . . . Perhaps there may be parties where one cannot enter without leaving one's freedom at the front door. But I know one and only one whose very doctrine compels it to protect your political freedom at the same time as everyone else's. It is the MRP.

Gilson's experience as counselor of the Republic and political activist was short. It was full of lessons, dissatisfaction, and "perplexity," for him.[107] Fundamental problems were not considered; documents were overburdened with secondary questions; the counselors lacked time to reflect; they faced governmental song and dance, along with inconsistency and irresponsibility of the parliamentary system as it actually functions.[108] The parliamentarians were impotent because of their mediocrity.[109] It was urgent to reform the constitution.[110] The Third Force was irrelevant, a "worm eaten plank" because of lack of civic spirit.[111] There was electoral manipulation, and so on. To all

107 Étienne Gilson, "Perplexités parlementaires," *Le Monde*, September 11, 1948, 1–2.

108 Étienne Gilson, "Gouvernement et parlement," *Le Monde*, July 28, 1948, p. 3: "The government must always be responsible to the Parliament that approves it, but the Parliament must be responsible before the country for the choice of leaders in whom it deposits its confidence. One can conceive of making a mistake once, twice, three times perhaps. If [the Parliament] is mistaken a fourth time, its duty is to dismiss the leader like the others, but also to acknowledge that it is incapable of giving its trust wisely or of keeping it for those who deserve it. Governments will have unheard of stability in France if the fall of one of them will quickly bring the moment when, if a minister departs, the Parliament that dismisses him must depart with him." See also Étienne Gilson, "Soigner la chute," *Le Monde*, September 6, 1948: "When Parliament is unable to demonstrate yet again its impotence, it will have no other choice than to ally itself with wisdom or, if that is impossible, in a healthy distaste for itself, to find the courage to commit suicide."

109 Étienne Gilson, "L'assemblée des Trente," *Le Monde*, August 21, 1948 : "Parliament members are not happy persons, at least in these times of crisis, when everything pushes them to use their mandate to abdicate the rights that it confers on them. It is not that they fail to see the necessity, but in the moment of taking the plunge, what scruples they have!"

110 Étienne Gilson, "Le plus pressé," *Le Monde*, August 31, 1948.

111 Étienne Gilson, "La planche vermoule," *Le Monde*, September 18, 1948: "Whatever regime France prepares for itself, let us advise it to follow Switzerland's example where no children get their certificates unless they have at least a four over a possible ten in a subject, but must receive at least a six in civic education. The road is long, but there is no other. Unless we are to perish, we must go that way."

this, a series of articles in *Le Monde* during 1948, written with caustic humor, bear witness. For example, on February 23, 1948, Gilson writes on "Parliament and the Rabbits":[112]

> I have just gone to look for the package of laws upon which I must reflect today as the people's representative. It is extremely interesting. For instance, the main sewer of the great city of Orleans seems to require Parliament's attention. It will be necessary to take care of it, because the matter is urgent. However, perhaps we ought to fix the problems of the "usage of the secondary lines of general interest from Châteaumeillant to La Guerche and from Sancoins to Lapeyrouse." This, item number 3258 of the National Assembly, also deserves to be examined carefully. I would certainly place it first in my reflections if I did not also have in front of me the number 3276 of the same Assembly, which poses the otherwise serious problem of rabbits. The wild rabbits are not happy. Let us specify that we are dealing with rabbits in Sologne and more particularly in Loir-et-Cher. It seems that they can be hunted at any time with the authorization of the prefect or sub-prefect on properties of more than ten hectares, but not smaller ones. This discrimination wounds their democratic sentiments. . . . One of the most urgent problems is that of administrative reform. As long as it is not done and well done, Parliament inevitably will have to continue to distinguish the bootmaker from the cobbler, to preside over the sewers of our cities, and to deliberate about rabbits.[113]

Again, in an article about "parliamentary vacation," Gilson wrote:

> The approach of vacations, which the members of Parliament speak about without daring to believe in them, slows down a little the rain of proposals for laws, resolutions, and reports of all kinds on which deputies and counselors of the Republic must, as they somewhat condescendingly say, look into. It is still pouring, and in any case, it has poured a great deal. . . . What are the great issues that urgently demand an answer? Stabilization of the executive and revision of the Constitution, administrative reform, fiscal reform, rational organization of a modern French army, standardization of industrial production, organization of a national education worthy of the name, and still other things, not one of which has been the object of a debate in the whole chamber during an eighteen-month session. These huge problems have sometimes been touched upon indirectly in the con-

112 Étienne Gilson, "1=3," *Le Monde*, September 16, 1948.

113 Étienne Gilson, "Le Parlement et les lapins," *Le Monde*, February 23, 1948, 3.

text of the hasty discussion of some budget or some particular law. And they are always touched upon in the same way, less to deal with them than to say that the day will have to come when Parliament will be free to carry out the functions that really belong to it and will give an answer to those questions. That day has never come, and this is why Parliament sees itself driven, however unwillingly, to give itself a vacation not only from its work but from its function.[114]

How were Gilson's biting articles received? We have no idea. However that may be, the form of election to the Conseil de la République was changed for the renovation of November 7, 1948. The MRP no longer needed the services of Gilson, who considered himself dismissed. Gaston Monnervile, who followed Champetier de Ribes as president of the Conseil, inquired of Gilson in November 1948:

> My dear colleague, I don't know whether you left us deliberately or whether [your colleagues'] "stupidity in the face of the bull" is what has separated you from us, through an ostracism to which intelligent people are too often exposed. In any case, I have to tell you that I am deeply sorry. Thought and disinterested culture are not so frequent in parliamentary bodies that they can be flouted. I very deeply lament your absence from our body, where you had marked your place deeply and lastingly.[115]

Gilson answered immediately:

> My dear President, your charming letter has given me the greatest pleasure because, between us, I will confess that you are the only one who has noticed that I am no longer in the Conseil de la République. It would have been impossible for your words to have been more friendly or delicate, but what touched me much more is that you thought of writing to me. I am very grateful and cannot thank you enough. What happened is very simple, and there was no bad faith on anyone's part. After the elimination of appointed members, I informed the office of the MRP movement that I was at their disposition for any candidacy for any post on any party list. It seems that they could not find a way to use me and, indeed, given the results [the MRP lost more than fifty seats in the Conseil de la République between 1946 and November 1948], it appears that there were probably no possible arrangements. In any case, I did not turn my back on the Conseil.

114 Étienne Gilson, "Vacances parlementaires," *Le Monde*, August 16, 1948, 3.

115 Letter from Gaston Monnerville to Étienne Gilson, November 19, 1948, Archives Vrin.

> I offered my services. It was found that there was no need for them. Should I lament that? I have three times more work than I ought to have, if I am to do it well, even without counting the Conseil de la République. If I had been reelected, I would have requested a leave of absence from the Collège de France in order to devote myself entirely to my assignment in Parliament. I'm sorry about the battle in which the remaining republicans must close ranks. I particularly regret not being there to give you my vote in the election for the presidency of the Conseil. But there is still enough to do in France and abroad for me to have no fear of being idle.[116]

Gilson, however, continued to comment closely on current politics in *Le Monde* and put together a sad picture of the partisan fragmentation of the Republic in the period of the Third Force:

> The Mouvement Républicain Populaire asks only to cooperate with the socialists, the left wing of the first party, getting along rather well with the right wing of the second. But this lateral communication is also broken by a vertical split caused by the secularist issue. We can do everything to dismiss it or forget it, but the split is still there. Since it reappeared, the socialists are closer to certain radicals, whom they detest in social policy, than to their neighbors in the MRP, whose Roman religious obedience, at least overall, troubles them only slightly less than the political obedience of the Muscovites. There again it would be desirable to work together, but it is often necessary to split.
>
> Further right is General de Gaulle, who moreover does not at all want to be on the right, but you always end up where other people put you, and he has certainly been put there. His idea is great and simple, as all his ideas that we have known were. It seems to be that France is dying of impotence in every area, because of this fragmentation that the parties impose on it. He is completely right, but to diagnose the illness is not to find the remedy. Despite his intentions, he has only succeeded in founding another party that contributes greatly to parliamentary disorder and aggravates the malady of which its leader wants to cure the nation.[117]

The echoes of this political and parliamentary experience in Gilson's writings and correspondence are rather bitter. In a 1953 interview with an American newspaper publisher, who asked him about his political beliefs,

116 Letter from Étienne Gilson to Gaston Monnerville, November 19, 1948, Fonds Gaston Monnerville, GM 69, CHSP.

117 Étienne Gilson, "Le cloisonnement cellulaire," *Le Monde*, February 14, 1950.

Gilson answered: "I used to have some political beliefs (MRP), but since the only political party in which I believe does not believe too much in me, I am afraid I have no right to any political beliefs."[118] In June 1954, Gilson went to the Florence Conference organized by Giorgio La Pira,[119] where he blasted "nationalistic thinking" and a Europe too narrowly conceived. His correspondence with Francisque Gay is full or remorse: "I am no longer capable of anything but to wallow in the memory of the great opportunities that we were unable to grasp," Gay wrote.[120] Gilson shared Gay's regrets: "The leaders of the movement have preferred to be crafty."[121] "To tell the truth, I believe that our leaders have used the movement for purposes of their own personal prestige, convinced, and making us aware of their conviction, that they alone were more intelligent than their whole band."[122] In 1956, Francisque Gay still expressed himself sharply to describe his own "immense helplessness" and that of the Christian Democratic activists:

> I don't know if you grasp how dismayed some of the best activists of prewar *L'Aube* are. Events seem to surpass us and crush us. No group, no publication offers solutions that we could confidently accept. It seems that no one dares to try anything that has the possibility of getting positive results. People drift with the current. General de Gaulle and the last block of his adherents do not try now any more than in the past to specify to us the regime they would like to substitute for the "system." As for our friends in the MRP, it is easy to see that their apparent agreement rather badly hides deep differences. Sadly, they even seem to be as troubled as the rest by personal rivalries or ambition. . . . Excuse all this chatter. I am somewhat hopeful that you will take up your pen again on behalf of your French friends.[123]

118 Interview of Étienne Gilson, June 3, 1953, CSAW 25–73, UNDA.

119 Philippe Chenaux, *Une Europe vaticane? Entre le Plan Marshall et les Traités de Rome* (Brussels: Éditions Ciaco, 1990), 221–22.

120 Letter from Francisque Gay to Étienne Gilson, July 3, 1953, Institut Marc Sangnier. See the appendixes, below.

121 Letter from Étienne Gilson to Francisque Gay, July 7, 1953, Institut Marc Sangnier. See appendixes, below.

122 Letter from Étienne Gilson to Francisque Gay, August 5, 1953, Institut Marc Sangnier. See appendixes, below.

123 Letter from Francisque Gay to Étienne Gilson, December 26, 1956, FG, SMCA.

In 1968, Gilson lamented:

> Once I hoped that the French MRP would establish itself as a Christian Party in the likeness of the *Democristiani*. Bidault and Gay were always opposed. I am such a bad politician that I wonder whether they were not right. In any case, the Mouvement Républicain Populaire has ceased to exist. It dissolved by itself and nothing is left of it.[124]

In 1973, a former Christian Democratic Senator wrote to Gilson again, "The MRP has not even known how to die. Politically, I feel completely orphaned."[125]

In conclusion, it is necessary to take stock of the cultural and political failure of Gilson's endeavors. *Vigile*, a magnificent magazine, did not reach its third anniversary. The weekly newspaper *Sept* was condemned by Church authorities in 1937. There were Nazi anti-Semitism, Soviet Communism, Sartre's existentialism, and unbridled liberalism triumphing in turn. The Fourth Republic was not reformed by the MRP in 1948–1950, but by de Gaulle in 1958. Gilson acknowledged the correctness of de Gaulle's vision but did not greatly esteem him as a leader. The MRP sank in the quicksand. Western Europe, unarmed, attached itself to the United States. Colonial wars again exhausted France, though Gilson advocated in 1947 that we should "proceed with enlightened prudence" toward the peoples who "henceforth form part of the Union."[126] The unpleasantness of the Gilson Affair, combined with his bereavement, chased the philosopher from Paris. We see many events where Gilson placed himself against the tide of history or of public opinion. Gilson, whose optimism Aron missed, as we have seen, offered tragic narratives of the twentieth century and did not bypass any of its dramas in silence: world wars, revolutions, mass graves, or ruins.

> The dead pile up while they are still in our hearts, so that we may mourn them, a whole race intended for destruction, savagely annihilated, pursued with learned and ferocious hatred, of which only human beings are capable toward human beings. Germany opened mass graves for the Jews and put in them numbers we do not yet know. Certainly, everything had to

124 Letter from Étienne Gilson to Augusto Del Noce, May 8, 1968, *Cher collègue et ami*, 168. .

125 Letter from Georges Aguesse to Étienne Gilson, May 16, 1973, SMCA.

126 Report presented by Étienne Gilson proposing the creation of courses in the metropolitan faculties of law on law in France's overseas territories, *Documents parlementaires, Conseil de la République*, session of July 30, 1947, appendix number 485, p. 507.

> end with a liberation, but we know what it had to cost in other deaths and other ruins, including that bomb at Hiroshima, whose solemn detonation announced to a horrified world, along with the alleged end of a war that has not yet been followed by peace, the advent of a new epoch, where science, formerly our hope and our joy, will be the source of the era's greatest horror.[127]

We might conclude that Gilson the historian, in proposing another route situated at an already faraway bifurcation, was not a visionary, and that it is simpler to write works of metaphysics than to be a political activist and anticipate the turning points of history. Or we might see Gilson as a sign of contradiction for the tragic twentieth century. Was he politically vanquished by history? Certainly, but let us add that this happened without any detriment to the philosopher—except the sadness of never or almost never being understood, and that the arguments put forward and the moderate positions, defended by Gilson and his family in the broad sense, perhaps would have helped pacify the past century.

127 Étienne Gilson, "Les terreurs de l'an deux mille," *Revue de l'université d'Ottawa* 19, January–March, 1949, 67–68.

5

The Conciliar Moment (1960–1978)

And let us pray to God that he pleases to forgive us for everything![1]

In his memoirs, Gilson compared the Church to "a noble ship, which for so many centuries has carried her load without ever straying from her course." How can we believe now, he asked, without seeing the upheaval and the coming crisis, after John XXIII announced the opening of the Second Vatican Council, that [the Church] is "today about to alter [its course] or to reach its term?"[2] "The Church's history is slow history," Gilson taught in 1933.[3] In 1942, he wrote again, "For Christians, history's wave length is immensely long."[4] Before the application of the first decrees of the Council, Gilson, aware of the long duration of history, could not imagine the coming Council in terms of a turning or a dramatic event. From 1960, even before the liturgical reform, he already complained of

1 Letter from Étienne Gilson to Jean de Fabrègues, February 4, 1967, CHSP; letter from Étienne Gilson to Jacques Maritain, July 3, 1967, in Gilson and Maritain, *Correspondance 1923–1971*, 242.

2 Étienne Gilson, *The Philosopher and Theology*, 236.

3 Étienne Gilson, "Christian Social Philosophy," 1933, final lecture, p. 8, FG, SMCA.

4 Étienne Gilson, "Sagesse et société," *Témoignages*, no. 1 (1942): 40.

the "degradation of the liturgical texts by their translation into gradually deteriorating vernacular."[5]

Fifteen years later, in April 1975, Pope Paul VI, who had read Gilson as a young man,[6] wrote an unusual and very personal letter to the "venerated professor Étienne Gilson," by then in his nineties, to indicate the Church's gratitude and to thank him for his contribution to the development of Christian thought. The two men had known each other since Easter 1947 and had, it seems, maintained a brief correspondence.[7] The 1975 letter, a real consolation for Gilson, began as follows:

> Notwithstanding your modesty, the passage of time has not eclipsed the merits you have earned by your intellectual activity over such a long period and of such vast extent, as well as by your exemplary fidelity to the Church. Giving thanks to the Lord for the years you have filled with such an efficacious contribution to the spread of Christian thought, We have to express personally to you today an esteem We have long held for you, along with the gratitude you deserve from the Church.[8]

Gilson died in September 1978, less than a month before the election of the Polish Pope John Paul II, who was formed during his student years in the existentialist Thomism of Gilson and Maritain. After being elected, he proposed ten thinkers, among them Gilson, as models of Catholic intellectuals, at the time of the publication of his encyclical on faith and reason.[9]

Between the initial gesture of John XXIII in January 1959 and the end of Paul VI's papacy and beginning of Wojtyła's "takeover," there were twenty years of *aggiornamento* marked by a protean collection of crises, transformations, and renewals. Gilson had a part in the post-Council debates that was

5 Étienne Gilson, *The Philosopher and Theology*, 13.

6 Gian Battista Montini, *Scritti Fucini (1925–1933)* (Brescia: Istituto Paolo VI, 2004); see p. 274 (on St. Thomas the ethicist) and p. 430 (on St. Augustine).

7 Letter from Étienne Gilson to Fr. Michel Labourdette, OP, August 12, 1950, printed in *Revue thomiste* 94 (1994): 499.

8 Paul VI, "Letter to Professor Gilson," first published in *L'Osservatore Romano*, September 11, 1975; reproduced here from *Letters of Étienne Gilson to Henri de Lubac*, 203; also available on the Vatican website.

9 Bernard Lecomte, *Jean-Paul II* (Paris: Gallimard, 2006), 158; Philippe Portier, *La pensée de Jean Paul II: La critique du monde moderne* (Paris: Les Éditions de l'Atelier, 2006), 30–31. John Paul II, *Fides et Ratio* (Boston: Pauline Books and Media, 1998), 93, §74.

both modest and definite.[10] Was he one of the "game leaders,"[11] as he depicts it to defend himself in a 1967 letter? The term is exaggerated. In any case, for some, he was a "grumbling old man," good for "the inauguration of the status quo,"[12] or an "old dribbler,"[13] that the "modern and ignorant" young clerical new guard unceasingly denounced. In 1968, Gilson found himself labeled a "Mandarin" by the Action Committee for Revolution in the Church, as the "prosecutor for the bourgeoisie" and the "papal gendarme."[14] For others, he was the wrinkled witness to Tradition, with the "holy arrogance" of a kind of twentieth-century St. Jerome, whom the bishops of Rome (more than the archbishops of Paris) in turn have honored. In the "dialogue of the deaf between integrists and progressives,"[15] and lamenting the excesses on all sides, Gilson, according to his habitual practice, tried to occupy a position that he defined as centrist. In 1967, he had this expression of his own to describe the area of tension: " I think that following the norms of the Council badly does not authorize other people to refuse to submit themselves to them."[16]

10 We have tried to clarify certain aspects of this matter in *Traduire la liturgie: Essai d'histoire* (Paris: CLD, 2013), notably in chapter 2, on the controversy about *consubstantialem*. See likewise Florian Michel, "Étienne Gilson et *Les Tribulations de Sophie*: Une théologie sans philosophe?," in *Un nouvel âge de la théologie? 1965–1980: Colloque de Montpellier, juin 2007*, ed. Dominique Avon and Michel Fourcade (Paris: Karthala, 2009), 45–67.

11 Letter from Étienne Gilson to Jean de Fabrègues, February 4, 1967, CHSP: "That allows some people to regard me as an integrist (*consubstantial* is rightist, *nature* is leftist), while others place me among the "play-makers."

12 Jean-Marie Paupert, *Vieillards de chrétienté et Chrétiens de l'an 2000* (Paris: Grasset, 1967), 75, 82–83.

13 Letter from Étienne Gilson to Fr. Marie-Dominique Chenu, August 5, 1965, APDF: "I have no illusions about what your young men [in Le Saulchoir] must have thought about the old dribbler. Their irremediable ignorance facilitates their being *modern*."

14 "MM Edmond Michelet, François Mauriac, Étienne Gilson, et treize autres personnalités expriment leur reconnaisance au pape," *Le Monde*, December 18, 1968, p. 13. The initiative to compose the letter came from Henri Rollet and Fr. Jean Daniélou. —See the letter from the Comité d'Action pour la Révolution dans l'Église, December 22, 1968, 4 EM 967, Archives Michelet.

15 Letter of Jean de Fabrègues to Étienne Gilson, December 20, 1966, FG, SMCA.

16 Letter from Étienne Gilson to Jean de Fabrègues, February 4, CHSP.

TOWARD THE COUNCIL: NEITHER LA NOUVELLE THÉOLOGIE NOR DOCTRINAL CONDEMNATIONS

In Cardinal Suhard's 1947 pastoral letter, Jacques Maritain and Étienne Gilson were used to define a middle way between "modernism" and "integrism."[17] During the "nouvelle théologie" period (1940–1950),[18]and then of a "new age of theology,"[19] Gilson felt no particular need either to subscribe to any of these "novelties" or to see them condemned by Church authorities. This 'neither-nor" was not indifference. Gilson knew that novelty is rarely "new" and sometimes uncertain. He had witnessed firsthand the condemnation of Fr. Laberthonnière in 1906–1913, that of *Sept* in 1937, and of Fr. Chenu in 1943. Gilson was involved with the objects of those sanctions, since he published articles in Laberthonnière's *Annales* and *Sept* and was quoted in Chenu's book that was put on the Index.

In the same context, Gilson defined himself as a "historian of philosophy scrubbed with theology,"[20] in the sense that he knew the rudiments of theology and he scrubbed himself in it often, urging a constant return to it in the desire to safeguard the distinction and also the sacred union of the historic philosophical and theological disciplines. Gilson had a doubly ancillary conception of the subalternation of the disciplines: History is the servant of philosophy, and the latter is the servant of theology. "Let not the handmaid quarrel with the mistress, and let not the mistress carp at the handmaid. A stranger might come who would rapidly settle the question."[21] During the period from 1940 to 1960, Gilson's position remained the same as in the 1931 debate about Christian philosophy in the sense that, according to him, the Christian who philosophizes is called to do philosophy in faith. More

17 Cardinal Emmanuel Suhard, *Essor ou déclin de l'Église: Lettre pastorale, Carême de l'an de grâce 1947* (Paris: Éditions A. Lahure, 1962), 64 ff. and 89 ff.

18 See the clarification by Fouilloux, *Un Église en quête de liberté*, 193—244, "Nouvelle théologie?"

19 See Avon and Fourcade, eds., *Un nouvel âge de la théologie? 1964–1980*.

20 Letter from Étienne Gilson to Marie-Dominique Chenu, April 29, 1936, APDF.

21 On this point, see Jean-François Courtine's introduction to Étienne Gilson, *Le philosophe et la théologie* (Paris: Vrin, 2006), i–iv, where two formulas of Gilson's are quoted: "True Scholastic philosophers will always be theologians" (1951). "A theologian is not improvised. Theology is learned only under a teacher, and fifty years of metaphysics are not enough to introduce the apprentice to the doctrine's rudiments" (1960). *The Philosopher and Theology* opens with a passage from Péguy: "Philosophy is the handmaid of theology. Of course. (After all, Mary is the handmaid of the Lord.) But let not the handmaid quarrel with the mistress, and let not the mistress carp at the handmaid. A stranger might come who would rapidly settle the question."

precisely, Gilson wrote: "I call Christian every philosophy which, although keeping the two orders formally distinct, nevertheless considers Christian revelation as an indispensable auxiliary to reason."[22] On this point, Gilson coincided with Mounier in *Feu la chrétienté*: "This supernatural help is necessary to wounded reason for it to function as right reason. But then it is not less reasonable, it is more reasonable, more whole in its order than 'independent' reason, which is to say than reason that remains sick and refuses a physician. Furthermore, the help reason receives carries perspectives that make reason not only healthier but richer in gifts and openness."[23] In 1960, Gilson published his *Introduction à la philosophie chrétienne*, where he enlarged and clarified his position. Delving into the question of the "metaphysics of Exodus" (chapters 1 and 3), he again made the summons, "And because in the final analysis it is not in our power to make the act effective, all God asks of us is that we make his word heard. What Christian would dare refuse him this request?"[24] Gilson explained that after 1950 he had stopped frequenting the Société Française de Philosophie, where, he said, he had "the effect of a dinosaur."[25] In his 1960 remarks, like a tired boxer, he explained: "From where I now stand, I can see looming in the distance some new philosophies still groping for their forms, and I know that I shall have neither the time nor the strength to follow them to their point of perfection."[26]

For institutional and generational reasons, we cannot attribute to a layman like Étienne Gilson the preparation of the great theological minds of the postwar period. Gilson, however, was close to the architects of the renewal. For instance, Gilson maintained an intense dialogue with the Jesuit Henri de Lubac, twelve years younger than he. However, Gilson's works were not easily available in the Jesuit scholasticate in Jersey, where de Lubac studied. They were kept in a locked cabinet that was opened only during

22 Étienne Gilson, *The Spirit of Medieval Philosophy*, 37.

23 Emmanuel Mounier, *Feu de la Chrétienté* (Paris: Seuil, 1951), 87–88.

24 Étienne Gilson, *Christian Philosophy: An Introduction*, trans. Armand Maurer (Toronto: PIMS, 1993), 134. In the French original, *Introduction à la philosophie chrétienne* (Paris: Vrin, 1960, 2007), 204.

25 Letter from Étienne Gilson to Fr. Michel Labourdette, September 26, 1950, published in *Revue thomiste* 94 (1994): 515.

26 Étienne Gilson, *The Philosopher and Theology*, 235.

vacations.[27] The correspondence between the two men,[28] some thirty letters between 1956 and 1975, was very friendly. Its late start in 1956, when Gilson was over seventy, should not hide the initial differences. "Besides, how easily Fr. de Lubac would save the whole truth that he holds dear, if he finally understood St. Thomas," Gilson wrote to a Dominican correspondent in 1950.[29] Their correspondence shows important agreement on Fr. de Lubac's main theological principles, as well as major differences on Blondel and Teilhard, whom Fr. de Lubac defended tenaciously, "suffering from acute Teilharditis," and completely devoid of lucidity,[30] according to Gilson, when de Lubac spoke about his fellow Jesuit.

The absence of friendship between Pierre Teilhard de Chardin (1881–1955) and Gilson was of long standing. The two men, who were roughly the same age, met, although there is no exact documentation. In 1954 they met at the symposium organized for the bi-centenary of Columbia University. At the time, Teilhard wrote: "I have to meet my friend Julian Huxley and my non-friend Étienne Gilson (whom I like very much, but with whom I am at odds intellectually)".[31] The expression and the meeting are important. Gilson often alluded to their private exchanges during the 1960s. Teilhard has described the circumstances in New York: "We were nicely split (between scientists and so-called humanists) on the question of 'ultra-evolving.'" You will suspect on which side I was (in good company moreover). But I was interested and sad to observe that, other than myself, all of the participant with a Catholic education (Gilson, the Lebanese Charles Malik of the United Nations, Rector Battaglia of the University of Bologna, Van Düsen, who is the

27 Henri de Lubac, *Mémoire sur l'occasion de mes écrits* (Paris: Cerf, 2006), 15n6, 67.

28 See the new revised and enlarged edition of their correspondence, prepared under the direction of Jacques Prévot, in Cardinal Henri de Lubac, *Oeuvres complètes*, vol. 47 (Paris: Cerf, 2013). [The correspondence is also available in English as *Letters of Étienne Gilson to Henri de Lubac*, trans. Mary Emily Hamilton (San Francisco: Ignatius Press, 1988).]

29 Letter from Étienne Gilson to Fr. Michel Labourdette, OP, September 26, 1950, published in *Revue thomiste* 94 (1994): 512.

30 Letter from Étienne Gilson to Augusto Del Noce, August 14, 1967, *Cher collègue et ami: Lettres d'Étienne Gilson à Augusto Del Noce, 1964–1969* (Paris: Parole et Silence, 2011), 156–57.

31 Letter from Teilhard de Chardin to Fr. André Ravier, New York, October 24, 1954, in *Lettres intimes de Teilhard de Chardin à Auguste Valensin, Bruno de Solages, Henri de Lubac, André Ravier, 1919–1955, introduction and notes by* Henri de Lubac (Paris: Aubier-Montaigne, 1974), 444–45.

leader of neo-Protestantism in America along with Niebuhr, and so forth) were against me."[32]

For his part, the Dominican Yves Congar participated in several of Gilson's seminars in the 1930s: "I am not the only one to notice that your teaching has spiritual value," Congar wrote to Gilson in 1932."[33] The two men exchanged some letters thereafter until after the Second Vatican Council. Gilson was very friendly with Marie-Dominique Chenu (1895–1990) during the 1930s and 1940s, but the correspondence became infrequent in the 1950s. Louis Bouyer, an Oratorian and former Lutheran student at Boulevard Arago, recalled Gilson's classes in his autobiography as "passionately" taken in: "I can say that this lesson had a great impact on me, because without my having ever been a Thomist properly speaking, I have always been receptive to what was at the heart of the thinking of St. Thomas, who renewed the biblical and especially Pauline vision of the unity of man and of the cosmos, certainly better than the Augustinian tradition."[34]

Twice, in 1947 on the subject of Chenu's "school of Saulchoir" and in 1948 of Henri de Lubac's "school of Fourvière," Gilson sought either to convince Roman authorities that condemnation was useless, or to prevent a condemnation that he knew would be inopportune. For all that, Gilson did not subscribe to the theses of the "new theology." Accordingly, he wrote euphemistically that Fr. Henri Bouillard, the author of a thesis on grace and conversion in St. Thomas, would do well to "keep an eye on his style."[35] At Easter 1947, Gilson went to Rome and met with Msgr. Montini. He vigorously defended his friend Fr. Chenu, whose *Une École de théologie: Le Saulchoir* had been placed on the Index in 1942.[36] Gilson's position in the matter was known—all the more in that Chenu explicitly placed himself in the line of Gilson's studies, quoting the professor of the Collège de France several times to criticize the transformation of St Thomas's philosophy into a closed and ahistorical

32 Letter from Teilhard de Chardin to André Ravier, New York, November 6, 1954, *Lettres intimes de Teilhard*, 447.

33 Letter from Yves Congar to Étienne Gilson, March 3, 1932, FG, SMCA.

34 Bouyer, *Le métier du théologien*, 27.

35 Letter from Étienne Gilson to Jacques Maritain, in Gilson and Maritain, *Correspondance 1923–1971*, 162.

36 Marie-Dominique Chenu, OP, *Un École de théologie: Le Saulchoir* (Kain-Lez-Tournai, Belgium: Le Saulchoir, 1937; re-published Paris: Cerf, 1985 [page numbers refer to the 1985 reprint]).

system.[37] In this brief work, Chenu, like Gilson and with him, defended a historical-critical approach to "make the reading of St. Thomas improve by the technique and light that modern exegetical procedures have provided for the explanation of texts in contemporary university training" (*Une École de Théologie: Le Saulchoir*). It was at this meeting that Montini told Gilson, "It pertains to authority not to justify itself"—a rather illiberal expression that Gilson long remembered and quoted many times after the election of Paul VI.[38] We have a second-hand account of the meeting between Montini and Gilson from Fr. Congar:

> Sunday, January 11, 1948. Breakfast at Vrin. Sat beside Gilson. He told me he had gone to Rome at Easter, 1947. He saw Monsignor Montini. Gilson told him that neither he nor anyone who knew Fr. Chenu could accept his condemnation. That the accused book was in no way modernist. That Rome discredited itself by such condemnations. Msgr. Montini answered that 1) he, Msgr. Montini, knew nothing, had not known anything, could not do anything about these things; 2) that things happened this way: a commission read a book, extracted propositions from it, which another commission reduced to five, three, or one. . . . Gilson answered that he absolutely did not believe that, occupying the post that Msgr. Montini did, he was not aware and could do nothing in this matter. After Msgr. Montini told him that the Church condemns very seldom, Gilson answered him that Maritain complained about being continually obliged to become involved in order to prevent unfortunate incidents.[39]

In the summer of 1950, in the context of Fr. de Lubac's suspension and of the preparation and publication of the encyclical *Humani Generis*, Gilson did not defend the persons condemned. Nor did he defend the Roman condemnations. As he wrote to his Dominican friends at Le Saulchoir and the *Revue thomiste*, in 1950, he refused to sign a petition in favor of the "new theology." He considered that this theology is indefensible and added that

37 See Marie-Dominique Chenu, OP, *Une École de théologie: Le Saulchoir*, p. 123: "The system had taken on value in itself, as if it were the object of philosophy, with the result that centuries went by 'philosophizing about philosophies, instead of philosophizing about problems' (Étienne Gilson). People refuse to pose problems."

38 Shook, *Étienne Gilson*, 248, 365.

39 Manuscript notes of Fr. Yves Congar, January 11, 1948, "Papiers Congar," V 832 121, 1946–1948, APDF.

the proposition "every syllabus is bad" is not "an evident proposition."[40] "Fr. Bouillard and even Fr. Daniélou fight for a cause that is not mine."[41] "My paper [at the Rome Thomistic Congress]," Gilson wrote to Fr. Chenu on August 21, 1950, "is going to put me in the middle of historicism, which the radio has just informed me an instant ago was condemned today along with existentialism and I do not know what else. I am horrified by historicism, independently of any condemnation, but those who confuse dogmatism with ignorance of history are going to believe themselves encouraged in their path."[42] Questioned by the Secretariat of State, Gilson wrote to Msgr. Montini in 1948 that a condemnation of the Jesuit fathers of Fourvière would do no good "at the price of the harm that its exploitation by people for whom Christian faith is of minimal interest."[43]

To clarify the background of the petition that Gilson did not sign in 1950, since he did not preserve any of the exchanges, we must retrace the issue in the correspondence of André Latreille (1901–1984) and Joseph Vialatoux (1880–1970). André Latreille had the idea of the petition because of the sanction against Henri de Lubac in June 1950.[44] Wanting to mobilize the CCIF

40 Letter from Étienne Gilson to Fr. Michel Labourdette, August 12, 1950, *Revue thomiste* 94 (1994): 500.

41 Letter from Étienne Gilson to Fr. Marie-Dominique Chenu, August 28, 1950, APDF.

42 Letter from Étienne Gilson to Fr. Marie-Dominique Chenu, August 21, 1950, APDF. Pope Pius XII's 1950 encyclical *Humani generis* states explicitly (https://www.papalencyclicals.net/pius12/p12human.htm): "6. Such fictitious tenets of evolution which repudiate all that is absolute, firm and immutable, have paved the way for the new erroneous philosophy which, rivaling idealism, immanentism and pragmatism, has assumed the name of existentialism, since it concerns itself only with existence of individual things and neglects all consideration of their immutable essences. 7. There is also a certain historicism, which attributing value only to the events of man's life, overthrows the foundation of all truth and absolute law both on the level of philosophical speculations and especially to Christian dogmas."

43 Letter from Étienne Gilson to Fr. Michel Labourdette, August 12, 1950, published in *Revue thomiste* 50 (1950): 499: "Two years ago . . . I wrote to Msgr. Montini to insist how little good a condemnation would do, and the harm that would surely be done through its exploitation by people for whom the Christian faith has the slightest importance." Gilson described the content of a letter to Madiran, published in Jean Madiran, *Chroniques philosophiques* (Paris: Difralivre, 1992), 31–32. He recalled it again in a letter to Maritain, June 9, 1967, in Gilson and Maritain, *Correspondance 1923–1971*, 237: "I do not understand what my friend Fr. Henri de Lubac is doing. And let me say that when you made me meet Msgr. Montini in the Vatican, I tried to defend the good intentions of the Fourvière Fathers, about whom he spoke to me."

44 See Henri de Lubac, *Mémoire sur l'occasion de mes écrits*, Collection Œuvres complètes du Cardinal Henri de Lubac 33 (Paris: Cerf, 2006), 68ff. See likewise, in relation to Latreille, the article of Fr. François Bédarida, "Les intellectuels catholiques et le Vatican en 1952–1953: Un épisode inédit," in *Mélanges offerts à M. le doyen André Latreille* (Lyon: Audin, 1972), 242–52; see also Toupin-Guyot, *Les intellectuels catholiques dans la société française*.

[Centre Catholique des Intellectuels Français] and Catholic intellectuals, he approached Gilson with the request to compose a letter in de Lubac's defense, which Gilson declined to do on August 9 in fairly clear terms at the doctrinal and prudential levels:

> I am surprised that Fr. de Lubac was affected because I had not noted anything out of the ordinary in what I read of his. But some others are hard to defend. What happened was inevitable, to my mind, for the simple reason that these theologians, who ought to have been prudent, have, on the contrary, gone on the offensive against Thomism and proposed such personal interpretations of it that overt hostility would have been more honest. [No doubt the reference is to Bouillard and Daniélou.] I am the last to say anything against them, but I must confess that what has happened does not surprise me. As for a new Syllabus of Errors, about which I know nothing, we will certainly see. In any case, it seems to me impossible to intervene about any question, even of principle, without knowing what the issue is. If this document appears, we will have to examine it closely, all the more in that, as always, the theologians will be at odds in the manner of interpreting its meaning and scope. As for me, who has never pretended to speak in the name of the Church, I intend still less to get into a debate with her. If the way in which I believe I can serve the Church in my soul and conscience were disapproved by the Church, I would immediately become silent without posing any question or raising the slightest protest. One can only serve the Church as it is and according to the ways that she approves or permits. This is to tell you how little I am inclined to recommend the presentation of a memorandum to the French bishops in the expectation of a document whose content we do not know and and in the wake of an incident whose victims were only too vulnerable. I am not speaking here of an excess of boldness on their part, but of their frightening ignorance of the meaning of the approved doctrines that they attack. If we recalled that we have been invited to be firm, it would be easy to answer that excessive firmness, alas, was the least of their defects. Do not take me for an integrist. I only think that the word *orthodoxy* does not just have a negative value, and that whoever we are, the Church is not wrong to keep us from playing with the truth at the risk of shattering it as children do with their toys.[45]

Latrielle was stung and immediately answered Gilson on August 20, 1950:

45 Letter from Étienne Gilson to André Latreille, August 9, 1950; mimeographed partial copies in the Carlhian papers, Diocesan Archive of Lyon, and in the Vialatoux papers (Archives of the Philosophy Faculty of the Catholic University of Lyon). Étienne Fouilloux provided this document.

> Allow me to tell you that [your letter] amazes me, not on account of its refusal, but because of the manner in which it is expressed. When I directed myself to a colleague with fraternal confidence in order to consult him about a point that other friends judge important for a Christian conscience, I did not expect to receive such a sharp lesson about loyalism toward ecclesiastical authority. Those for whom I speak have so far demonstrated their devotion to the Church. Some of them have demonstrated that they know how to maintain the most noble silence in the face of unpleasant measures. But they believe that it is incumbent upon Christians to bring to the hierarchy what each observes in their environment and that it is a duty to *warn* their shepherds before certain decisions are taken, which it would be impossible to reverse. I believe this like them and also believe that frank speech on the threshold of the Church is a proof of that: the deep distress caused in the best Catholic sectors in Quebec by the resignation of Msgr. Charbonneau; ... the lesser unease caused by measures taken against Fourvière in ecclesiastical circles, and afterward the cardinal of Lyon, even seminarians and our students. You do not think that these facts should be noted in the name of higher doctrinal concerns. So be it. It is not a question of taking you for an integrist. The cultivation of history has steered me away from these rough classifications. I only regret not having learned the serenity that allows all Thomists to brand as having "frightening ignorance" and almost as being dishonest those who make the mistake of serving Christ and his Church under other banners than those of Scholasticism.[46]

Gilson responded to this letter from Latreille with a second letter on August 23, 1950. Between Gilson's two letters, the situation had changed considerably, since on August 12, the encyclical *Humani Generis* was published, and it condemned in bulk a set of "modern opinions and errors threatening to undermine the foundations of Catholic doctrine." Gilson became aware of the encyclical's content on August 21, as the letter to Fr. Chenu cited above showed. Gilson specified to André Latreille:

> I believed that you were consulting me on the appropriateness of a certain action. It is evident that I could not recommend it without committing myself to join in, nor could I without carrying out myself an examination of the questions.... I know that there are "unpleasant measures," even some that in my soul and conscience I cannot justify, as in the case of my dear friend Fr. Chenu, which makes no sense to me. I have said so to Rome as

46 Reply from André Latreille to Étienne Gilson, same day, August 20, mimeographed copy, Carlhian Papers and Vialatoux Papers. Étienne Fouilloux informed us about this document.

loudly as possible. Generally speaking, I have always thought that particular condemnations do more harm than good. This is what I permitted myself to write to Msgr. Montini two years ago in regard to Fr. de Lubac and those who are called the Fourvière Fathers, at the moment when I was questioned about them. I wrote as clearly as I just wrote to you, to beg that they be left in peace. I did not succeed, but I tell you this so that my true feelings may be known to you.

That said, I have never pretended to give you a "lesson on loyalty" or any lesson. Questioned by you, I answered that *I* do not believe myself responsible for warning or informing my shepherds. If they question me, as they have done, I will answer, as I have answered. If they pay no attention to my answer, I can do nothing more. My personal rule (good or bad) is that *I respond before, I do not protest after*. I have warned Msgr. Montini about the trouble such a measure would cause. Indeed, there is trouble, and I regret it, but I think it is irreparable and that it would only be increased by intervening after the fact.... As for the end of your letter, I am too old for it to wound me. I am only afraid that your "all the Thomists" does not put the finger on the wound. Your "almost with dishonesty" is gratuitous. "The irremediable ignorance" is mine, and I recognize that it is not very apt. I ought to have written "irremediable incomprehension." And I maintain that. They do not understand St. Thomas at all, which is comprehensible, but why do they attack him? I do not understand Maurice Blondel at all. You will not find a *line* of mine against him. I know that I do not understand. Therefore I am silent. When he attacked certain positions of mine, and completely distorted them, I did not answer a single word. . . . I am horrified by "banners" and by all "schools" without exception. As for the "School," I have spent my life demonstrating that it does not exist.[47]

In September 1950, in the heavy atmosphere of the new "Syllabus," Gilson attended two meetings in Rome, Scotist and Thomist. Notably, he delivered a paper on "Historical Research and the Future of Scholasticism" and disputed publicly with Fr. Garrigou-Lagrange on the subject of an open and inviting expression in *L'être et l'essence* (1948) that Fr. Garrigou-Lagrange thought was off-hand and dangerous; "The history of philosophy is not closed," Gilson wrote. "On the contrary, the narrative of so many adventures faced by thought, invites us to new ones, and perhaps the moment has come

47 Letter from Étienne Gilson to André Latreille, August 23, 1950; mimeographed copy, Vialatoux papers. Étienne Fouilloux provided the document.

to attempt the most beautiful."[48] "Therefore, for you," Fr. Garrigou-Lagrange said to Gilson, "metaphysics is an adventure, which is to say, an arbitrary story and made up as one wishes." The professor of the Angelicum warned Gilson that he was going to state the opposite publicly at the next session of the congress, namely that "metaphysics is not a great adventure" whose "history is not closed." Gilson answered him: "Father, if you do that, I will leave Rome immediately." Fr. Bouyer, who had invited Gilson, said to him at that point, "Garrigou-Lagrange will be pleasant with you, *as long as you are there*."[49]

On the eve of the Ecumenical Council, Gilson belonged to a third party, a rather large one in fact. He was critical of Rome to the point of being denounced to the Holy Office himself, as we have seen, for his letter sent to Karl Barth in 1946. He absolutely lamented the condemnations and supported Chenu's position, which, in fact, was his own at the methodological level. He sought to prevent the blows that were to fall upon Fouvière, without sharing the Jesuits' position. In 1950, for André Latreille, Gilson represented "the School." For Garrigou-Lagrange, who had been the first to denounce the "new theology,"[50] he was a liberal.

GILSON THE AUTOBIOGRAPHER (1960)

Gilson published his intellectual autobiography just before Vatican Council II. It is not that he had ever rejected autobiography or even certain staging of himself. Gilson's itinerary reflected meanderings through the history of ideas and institutions that he, often with biting humor, labeled: "the moves and countermoves of a historian lost in the past who looked at the flow of events from the wrong end."[51] The totality of articles and books of an autobiographical nature is one of the touchstones of Gilson's polemical realism. Did he criticize Marcel Mauss, Émile Durkheim, Alfred North Whitehead,

48 Étienne Gilson, *L'être et l'essence* (Paris: Vrin, 1948), 328.

49 An account of the congress and of this dispute is found in a letter from Étienne Gilson to Fr. Marie-Dominique Chenu, September 25, 1950, APDF. For complementary references, see the critical apparatus of the Gilson-Chenu correspondence, "Correspondance entre Étienne Gilson et Marie-Dominique Chenu: Un choix de lettres (1923–1969)," ed. Francesca Murphy, *Revue thomiste* 105 (2005): 64.

50 Reginald Garrigou-Lagrange, "La nouvelle théologie, où va-t-elle?," *Angelicum* 23, no. 3-4 (1946): 126–45.

51 Étienne Gilson, *The Philosopher and Theology*, 5.

Fr. Laberthonnière, or Fr. Teilhard de Chardin? He had read them, met them, and rubbed shoulders with them. He had debated with each of them at the Sorbonne, the École pratique, Harvard or Columbia. Did he denounce the U.S.S.R. or Fourth Republic parliamentary practices? He went to the Ukraine in 1922, where he saw Marxism's starving people in real life. He frequented the Palais du Luxembourg during several semesters. Gilson's life was a repertoire of arguments for him.

In November 1924, the article "Pour travailler tranquille" was thus an answer in method and existence to the reproaches of an ignorant cleric.[52] In January 1925, there was a long interview with Frédéric Lefèvre that Gilson published in *Les nouvelles littéraires*. In 1932, his "*Examen de conscience*" appeared in *Vigile*. "I thought I was studying Descartes for himself, but I was studying him for St. Thomas Aquinas, St. Thomas Aquinas for St. Bonaventure, St. Bonaventure for St. Augustine, and St. Augustine for St Justin—and all of them for the Gospel."[53] In 1934–1935, once again, articles appeared in *Sept* in which Gilson narrated his conversations with Lévy-Bruhl and Victor Delbos. In 1947, his speech after he was inducted into the Académie française included many autobiographical details. A January 17, 1953, French radio broadcast, *Permanence de l'Académie*, gave a very clear, colorful picture: "Gilson is bursting with life and good humor. He reminded one of a successful wine grower, glass in hand, after a magnificent harvest." "For me," Gilson repeated, "France is a country whose capital is Auxerre." "Music set him on fire. Nineteen times he listened to Pelléas at the Opéra Comique. One Sunday in 1906, he made such a racket at Châtelet to prevent the Cologne Orchestra from playing a Mendelssohn concerto that he was taken to the police station."[54]

The appearance of *Le Philosophe et la théologie* (*The Philosopher and Theology)* in spring 1960 fit into a traditional vein in Gilson, who in a way recapitulated in the book his past publications and took them further. Moreover, the practice of writing memoirs was customary among academics and philosophers of his age. Maritain published *Le philosophe dans la cité* (Paris:

52 Étienne Gilson, Letter to the Editor, "Pour travailler tranquille," *La vie catholique*, November 1, 1924, 2.

53 Étienne Gilson, "Examen de conscience," *Vigile*, no. 2 (1932): 98.

54 Script of the radio broadcast devoted to Étienne Gilson, prepared by Paul Guth and Francine Leullier, "Permanence de l'Académie," May–June 1952, Radio France, 20000392/11, AN. The broadcast is available at Inathèque.

Éditions Saint Paul, 1960) and was preparing to publish *Le Journal de Raïssa* (*The Journal of Raïssa*) (Paris, 1962). However, publication of Gilson's memoir was due to external circumstances. He had to be begged to reply favorably to a 1959 request from Henri Daniel-Rops. He explained to Anton Pegis in Toronto:

> The forty fellows of the Académie française . . . are all invited (in turn!) to contribute one volume to the series. They like memoirs, which I feel unable to write. So I answered in the negative, saying that a life spent in rediscovering the true meaning of the word "theology" was not a fit subject for such a collection. But Daniel-Rops replied: "Oh, but yes! You sit down and write a book entitled *Le philosophe et la théologie*. Do it without opening a single book."[55]

Gilson finished the rough draft of the book in twenty-three days and then spent six months revising it. "The title of the book is a gift of our colleague and friend," Gilson explained in the foreword.[56] Daniel-Rops wrote a two-page presentation for the media: "A vigilant irony retains the right to smile. At the age of sixty-five, Étienne Gilson is young, as full of hope as in his brilliant beginnings. . . . This is a book of reflections wrapped in memories, a book of memories interspersed with reflections. Everything is closely linked in this autobiography of Gilsonian thought."[57] According to Shook, the book "was too hastily written to be great Gilson" and "was not received well by the new pre-conciliar theologians."[58]

Fr. Chenu does not seem to have become acquainted with *Le Philosophe et la théologie* at the time of its appearance. The correspondence between Gilson and Chenu does not mention it, but the fact is that the two were not close at the time.[59] Despite their proximity, Henri de Lubac only sent a simple acknowledgment that he had received the autobiography in May 1960[60] and

55 Shook, *Étienne Gilson*, 345.

56 Étienne Gilson, *Le philosophe et le théologien*, 9. [Translator: The acknowledgment does not appear in my English version.]

57 Henri Daniel-Rops, "Étienne Gilson, *Le philosophe et la théologie*," 2 pages, FG, SMCA.

58 Shook, *Étienne Gilson*, 347.

59 There is a gap of three and a half years in their correspondence between September 1959 and January 1963, APDF.

60 See the letter from Henri de Lubac to Étienne Gilson, May 18, 1960, in *Lettres de Monsieur Étienne de Gilson adressées au P. de Lubac*: "Your book [*Introduction à la philosophie chrétienne* (Paris: Vrin, 1960)] arrived just at the right time, when I am alone and can read it at my leisure.

seems to have considered that it was "not a lucky book,"[61] as Fr. Shook recalls. Francisque Gay was very touched by Gilson's testimony, but like de Lubac,[62] regretted that Gilson had not said more about Maurice Blondel in this philosophical journey: "Your silence about Blondel will seem harsh to his disciples, just as the references that you make here and there to Édouard Le Roy's *Dogme et critique*."[63] "Blondel played no role in my life. I have never been able to read a single book of his to the end. When one does not understand, one should be silent. Why didn't he do the same in my regard? But he was looking for a fight," Gilson bluntly responded to Gay, remembering a certain chapter of Blondel's *Problème de la Philosophie catholique* published in 1932.[64] Maritain wrote a lovely letter expressing fundamental agreement, all the more in that the book contained very warm praise of him:[65]

> I have read your defense and philosophical illumination of theology with an interest that is all the more lively in that, since I am fundamentally in agreement with you, I have the impression that we often approach the same problems and the same events from opposite directions, which creates for me delightful contrasts against a background of agreement.
>
> There is one particular point on which I think completely differently from you. I am convinced that, at the end of his life, Bergson really had faith. Conversations with Jeanne Bergson and Fr. Journet leave no doubt about that, and in having herself baptized she knew she fulfilled a wish of her father.

It is as delightful as the other [*Le philosophe et la théologie*], but it is wine that runs the risk of seeming bitter to throats that are too tender." [Translator: I have not found de Lubac's letter in the English version, but in *Letters of Étienne Gilson to Henri de Lubac*, 40n1, there is a reference to the reception of the two books.]

61 Shook, *Étienne Gilson*, 345. Shook does not give a reference for his source here.

62 *Letters de Monsieur Étienne Gilson adressées au P. de Lubac*, 253: "When I questioned Fr. de Lubac about this lacuna in Gilson, he [de Lubac] answered that his [Gilson's] great failure was not to have shown more sympathy to Blondel. He insisted and elaborated upon this point."

63 Letter from Francisque Gay to Étienne Gilson, October 21, 1960, Institut Marc Sangnier.

64 Letter from Étienne Gilson to Francisque Gay, October 30, 1960, Institut Marc Sangnier. See also Maurice Blondel, *Le problème de la philosophie catholique* (Paris: Bloud et Gay, 1932), 127–35.

65 Étienne Gilson, *The Philosopher and Theology*, 201–2: "The only Thomist in contemporary France whose thought was lofty, bold, and creative, capable of meeting the most urgent problems and, so to speak, stand ever ready before all emergencies, was rewarded for his zeal by the incessant, active and venomous hostility of unhappy creatures who have little else to put in the service of God than the hatred of their neighbors. True enough, greatness as such is unbearable in their eyes."

But what I want to tell you most of all is my gratitude for what you have written about me in such affectionate terms, ones that honor me so much. This testimony of a philosopher truly within the faith and of a comrade in arms who is so well equipped is absolutely precious to me. I am deeply grateful to you as a friend.

I was moved to see that we took our philosophy class at Henri IV, with the same very good and very inconclusive Monsieur Dereux. Do you recall the funny way in which he pronounced certain words by adding an f at the end? It is strange that a few years apart, we sat on the same benches, to meet later in so many adventures.[66]

Stanislas Fumet likewise wrote a long letter to indicate his "very great admiration":

Dear Sir and Friend: How can I express the joy and, something else, the emotion that comes from a certain contact with the True that the reading of your book, *The Philosopher and Theology*, has given me? It is not only your personal case that has excited me in this confession; it is also and still more the light that your experience sheds. Lastly, the concept of theology that excludes all those gloomy or pretentious theologians, capable or guilty of sterilizing everything; that denunciation in such a courteous tone of the mediocrity of our catechetical "reforms" and of the poverty of the new translation of the holy texts, worthy of Fr. Gelineau's music. There are so many reasons for me to be delighted. [Passage crossed out: But more than anything else, what I believe is most important in your book is the way in which you situate theology insofar as it participates in uncreated Wisdom; in regard to the freedom of human philosophies.] Unfortunately, ignorance of St. Thomas's thinking is such that I am afraid that, for many, you are preaching in the desert. May God will that your book is not hushed up, for despite its Christian . . . affability, there is something implacable about it. Your way of viewing Bergsonian philosophy in regard to faith and your critique of the two sources definitively clarify the question you deal with. The example is striking to the point of knocking down a wall, the wall of the most lamentable confusion. Allow me to congratulate you with all my heart. The passage about Maritain is superb, but why are we so old and not thirty, the age when one has a taste for battle? Doubtless we always see clearly a little bit late, when the sun itself rises over the rubble after the

66 Letter from Jacques Maritain to Étienne Gilson, June 22, 1960, in Gilson and Maritain, *Correspondance 1923–1971*, 207–8.

> battle. I anxiously look around me for new faces to replace us. Dear Étienne Gilson, I thank you and assure you of my greatest admiration.[67]

Newspapers and magazines published book reviews, which allow us to understand Gilson's reception in ecclesiastical debates on the eve of the Second Vatican Council. The dividing line was not where one might imagine. In *Le Figaro littéraire*, the critic André Rousseaux devoted a half page to a sympathetic presentation of the book. "No one less resembles a forbidding scholar than Étienne Gilson. An evening spent with him is time in the company of a decent man." There is only praise in six columns of commentary: "a desire for soundness," "search for balance," "delicious and nourishing reading," "strong human health," "wisdom smiling" on the "troubled stream of fanaticism." The critic emphasizes Gilson's middle of the road position on the chessboard: "Modernism was a bundle of errors for which those who maintained them were responsible. But we too often forget what responsibility of a different order weighs upon those who permitted that the truth was so often unknown or not understood by their own fault."[68] In the same spirit, Fr. Pie Duployé, the Dominican admirer of Péguy, devoted a full page of *Témoignage chrétien* in November 1960 to the work by Gilson, whom he regarded as the last humanist."[69]

> The Catholic Church has waited a century to take its revenge on Renan, and this revenge is Gilson. They are both men of the Church. Regarding Renan, Péguy said in an unforgettable passage that he had never ceased to be Catholic and that the Church had never ceased treating him as such. Regarding the second, the beautiful book that has come out this year and that is the object of this article, *The Philosopher and Theology*, by its very title reveals that its author's existence has been strictly and technically clerical in the sense in which the Middle Ages understood the word and the thing. The

67 Letter from Stanislas Fumet to Étienne Gilson, June 14, 1960, NAF 28171, boîte 27, BNF. See also the letter from Étienne Gilson to Stanislas Fumet, June 25, 1960, NAF 28171, boîte 27, BNF: "Allow me to thank you [for your letter], however inadequately, because it was very touching. We are people who have offered their testimony. Perhaps we have been understood more often than we can know. Our replacements are doubtless there also, without our knowing how to recognize them, but I also dread a sort of new eighteenth century, as limited in its vision and as pleased with itself as its predecessor. A France of Albert Bayet. . . . God help us!"

68 André Rousseaux, "L'aventure de Étienne Gilson," *Le Figaro littéraire*, July 16, 1960. See likewise the very favorable review in the student newspaper *Paraboles* of the Richelieu Center in the Sorbonne (May 1960, 1, 12).

69 Pie Duployé, "Le dernier des humanistes," *Témoignage chrétien*, November 18, 1960, 11.

> paradox is that this "intellectual" has had a career in the university, the French University, which presents itself as totally secularist and that it is an understatement to say that Gilson is loyal to the university that gave him his living. I do not know a more complete and more pertinent praise of that University than what is given in the first chapter of *The Philosopher and Theology*.

In *Nova et Vetera*, Charles Journet devoted a long review to Gilson's autobiographical work.[70] Like Maritain, he fundamentally agreed on the issue of Christian philosophy. Journet valued the "humor," the "witticisms," the "paradoxes," the "correct and fair views." But there was also a clear reservation regarding Bergson's religious views. Journet wrote:

> Let me confess that one phrase startled us in this lovely and substantial exposition: namely, when the author—starting from the fact that in Bergsonian philosophy there are only two types of knowledge, *intelligence*, reduced to the reasoning of scholars, and *intuition*, related to instinct—abruptly concluded: "It is not enough to say that Bergson had no faith. He did not even know what it was. I mean by this that he never suspected the sense of this word in Christian philosophy" (p. 177). Let us not talk about Bergson's philosophy. Let us talk about Bergson. Would he consequently have been unaware, would he have "never suspected" Pascal's third order, the order of the heart? Would he not have placed metaphysical intuition, which he had as a philosopher, on a different level from mystical intuition, which he attributed only to the saints and which he desired?. . . We have the moral certainty that this was not the case.

The review occasioned an exchange of correspondence between Gilson and Journet. The debate was both blurred and technical.[71] It refers to the interpretation of Bergson after the publication of *The Two Sources of Morality and Religion*, to the way it was received in Catholic circles, to the "desire for baptism" expressed by the philosopher, and to Jeanne Bergson's spiritual closeness to the future Cardinal Journet, who baptized her. Gilson replied to Journet that he simply did not want to enter into debate.

70 Charles Journet, "Chronique de philosophie," *Nova et vetera* 36, no. 2 (1961): 141–57. See the appendixes below for a longer quote on this issue from Journet's review.

71 On this point see the notes of *Correspondance Journet–Maritain*, vol. 3, *1940–1949* (Paris: Saint-Augustin, 1998), 175ff; as well as Catherine Chalier, *Le désir de conversion* (Paris: Seuil, 2011).

> The expression that shocks you was not an inadvertence on my part. I simply thought that there would be no interest or benefit for anyone or for any truth to provoke a controversy that would be both late and premature. Time will clarify all that, and we should look forward. Above all, we should not divide our forces. At least I have forbidden myself to do so, and I hope to continue that in the future.[72]

Jean Lacroix, a partner in *Esprit* and philosophy professor in the normal school arts preparation course, emphasized for his part in *Le Monde*, June 28, 1960, "Gilson's tranquil power" and pointed out at the same time some questions about Christian philosophy. The very long review allows us to take the measure of the tributes and of pending questions:

> A Catholic philosopher, rigorous, and solid unwavering thinker, expresses his gratitude to the University that taught him and the Church that formed him. He achieves a kind of genius of balance and good sense. A Catholic of the sort we no longer see, he insults no one, not even other Catholics. He passes by in silence those who do not share his views, limiting himself to saying that they do not understand him. In the face of so much peaceful strength, perhaps we would feel a respectful and distant admiration, if there were not also in him a deeply human sense of humor, an always penetrating and always contained sensitivity.... It is doubtless in his opinions of human beings that Gilson gives the full measure of his fairness....
>
> But ultimately, it is certainly good to come to the author's thesis. Because there is a thesis. This autobiography narrates "the adventure of a young Frenchman, raised in the Catholic religion, owing all his education to the Church and all his philosophical formation to the University, sent by Clio to grapple with the problem of finding an exact sense for the concept of theology, spending part of his life in the discussion of this problem and finding the answer too late for him to be able to use it." The answer is that there is only Christian philosophy inside, so to speak, of theology. Even in philosophy, there exists a primacy of the word of God. The first sources of all Christian philosophy are Scripture and Tradition. Here I would like to express some reticence. Gilson has great skill in presenting as evident propositions that perhaps become evident only with great difficulty. Accordingly, when he says that he always judged that it is necessary to think about something and not about thought, he puts laughter on his side and seems to enunciate a truism. It is not evident. Moreover, he acknowledges that:

72 Letter from Étienne Gilson to Charles Journet, June 22, 1961, Archives of the Cardinal Charles Journet Foundation. See the appendixes below.

> "If Kantianism is madness, it is a craziness that is very widespread among philosophers, and when we see so many crazy people around us it is prudent to have oneself examined." Without being a Kantian, it is possible to believe that the mind would know nothing if it did not recognize itself in every act of knowledge and to wonder whether this recognition of oneself by oneself does not imply a foundational, strictly spiritual affirmation.
>
> But the essential point is to find out whether, to be a Christian philosopher, it is necessary to be a theologian at the same time. It is indisputable that St. Thomas is a true philosopher and that one can build a great philosophy by being directly inspired by him. The magnificent and so deserved homage that Gilson pays to Jacques Maritain offers a decisive proof.... What troubles us are not the affirmations of these books, but sometimes their exclusivism. We are afraid the author turns his particular itinerary into a general thesis. Perhaps first of all it is better not to be a theologian at all than to be one by half—and from the practical point of view it looks bad, for example, for future professors obliged to such a long preliminary state!

Jean Lacroix's reservations about Thomist "exclusivism" and Gilson's anti-Kantian realism do not have the same scope. St. Thomas (and we will return to the issue) was one of the themes of the Council. Regarding Thomist exclusivity, which is a habitual objection formulated against the Thomists, Gilson (who wrote books about St. Augustine, St. Bernard, St. Bonaventure, Duns Scotus, and others) would surely have reminded Lacroix of some of the positions clearly affirmed in his autobiography and in several earlier writings. In 1925, Gilson wrote in this sense: "In the service of the true, the good, and the beautiful, a Christian only knows co-workers. This is not a more or less adroit modernization of some old attitude, and here I do not constitute myself as the spokesman of any 'new spirit.' It is the very charter of Christian thought, defined by St. Justin in the second century. All that is true is ours."[73] In a letter made public in 1946, Gilson likewise had written to Karl Barth in a form that is clear cut, to say the least: "God was not incarnated in St. Thomas."[74] In *The Philosopher and Theology*, we read again: "The perfect expression of this liberty of the Christian man is that of Saint Augustine: *Dilige et quod vis fac: Love and do what you will.* In exactly the same spirit and the same

73 Étienne Gilson, "Une heure avec . . . ," Les nouvelles littéraires, January 3, 1925, 1.

74 Letter of Étienne Gilson to Karl Barth, January 15, 1946, in *Hommage et reconnaissance: Recueil de travaux publiés à l'occasion du soixantième anniversaire de Karl Barth*, Cahiers théologiques de l'actualité protestante (Paris and Neuchâtel: Delachaux et Niestlé, 1946), 41–42.

deep sense, but in no other, the disciple of Saint Thomas can likewise say: *Believe, and think what you will.* Like charity, faith is a liberator."[75] Later, after the Council, Gilson would write again: "We hope to be able to be excused from recalling that St. Thomas 'is not the only valid source of true philosophical knowledge.' Who ever was so simple as to think so and so indifferent to ridicule as to say so?"[76] In Gilson's writings, his position is non-exclusive, but at the same time he affirms his own preference for St. Thomas.

The philosophers and theologians at Louvain and Brussels took notice of Gilson's memoirs and published long reviews in the *Revue philosophique de Louvain*,[77] and the *Nouvelle revue théologique*.[78] The first one was initially positive. "Gilson has given us a perfect harmonization of faith and reason and has revealed it to us." "This testimony of the harmony between faith and reason seems profoundly impressive." But in the last part, the reviewer wanted to nuance and discuss "Gilson's very sharp affirmations" as to the unconditional maintenance of the primacy of God's word *even in philosophy*." At bottom, the whole controversy about Christian philosophy was the backdrop of the review:

> Faith does not positively imply any determined philosophy. Its role is not that of a philosophy professor. For the philosopher, revealed truths are hypotheses that certainly can guide his research, at least in certain areas, but that he will accept in philosophy only if he succeeds in establishing and grounding them by philosophy's own methods. In this perspective, there will no longer be the serene harmony between faith and reason that we admire in Gilson. As in any dialogue there will be a certain tension, always an unstable equilibrium between two interlocutors who seek to make everything agree, while respecting each other's perspectives. Must we regret this situation? Isn't such tension rather the very condition of progress in theology? Is not the theology that Gilson describes (cf. French p. 136, English p. 147) too static, too inert to attract the philosopher?
>
> If we must thank Gilson for having forcefully and proudly emphasized the importance of faith in the life of the Christian, we can not share

75 Étienne Gilson, *The Philosopher and Theology*, 204.

76 Étienne Gilson, *The Tribulations of Sophia*, trans. James G. Colbert (South Bend, Ind.: St. Augustine's Press, 2021), 113.

77 Georges Van Riet, "Le philosophe et la théologie," *Revue philosophique de Louvain* 58 (1960): 308–13.

78 André Thiry, SJ, "Le philosophe et la théologie," *Nouvelle revue théologique* 84, no. 4 (1962): 337–64.

> his opinion about the exact role that he would make faith play in rational activity. Meditating about his moving testimony, we feel less decided than ever to commit ourselves to the path that he traces for us. But certainly in the great family of Thomists, as in the Father's house, there are many mansions.[79]

The second, nuanced, review was written by Fr. André Thiry for *Nouvelle revue théologique* published by the Jesuits in Brussels. Almost thirty pages long, it was an extended, precise critique of Gilson's book. Thiry began: "It is not too late to speak of it. A book by Étienne Gilson is never a matter of indifference. Whether he deals with Descartes, St. Augustine, or St. Bernard, or narrates the misfortunes of Abelard or Heloise, or leads us to the discovery of pictorial reality,[80] he always sways the reader's mind and conquers his audience."[81] The reviewer shows the volume's timeliness: "The importance of the issue cannot escape our readers. The relations of philosophy and theology are on the agenda of contemporary thought." He mentions Kierkegaard, Jaspers, Heidegger, Marcel, Ricœur, and Blondel, and thanks Gilson. The first twenty pages delineate Gilson's exact itinerary as it is traced in the book. In the second part, the reviewer asks whether "the testimony will be accepted." "Nevertheless, it is permissible to wonder about the reception he expects and perhaps about the opposition he provokes, legitimate or not, in and around himself." For the reviewer, a series of issues in Gilson's account remain problematic: the subalternation of philosophy to theology; "philosophizing in theology"; "'the primacy of the word of God, *even in philosophy*,' has a jarring sound,"[82] the reviewer esteems. Given the plurality of theologies and Christian philosophies, "we have all the less difficulty in affirming that for the medieval period, we owe our full awareness of them to the works of Gilson."[83] What is characteristic of theology as a science—*ut palea*, as a winnowing device—is its "character of questioning, investigation, and method." The last page of the review seeks a point of balance and agreement: Gilson is too much a "man of the tradition" to "turn himself toward the past." The Gilsonian invitation, that theologians become more attached to science, must

79 Van Riet, "Le philosophe et la théologie," 313.

80 Thiry, "Le philosophe et la théologie," 337.

81 Thiry, "Le philosophe et la théologie," 354.

82 Thiry, "Le philosophe et la théologie," 359.

83 Thiry, "Le philosophe et la théologie," 360.

be understood in order to avoid repetition of the Modernist crisis. We can see that "such a program has demands. It is a call to unceasing effort, and that is not the least sign of its authenticity."[84]

The last review that we would like to recall is by far the most complex in the underground currents that it signifies. It appeared in June 1960, in the journal *Itinéraires*, whose editor was Jean Madiran (1920–2013). He was a neo-Thomist Maurrassian, who had received the Vichy decoration "La Francisque." He was close to the brothers André and Henri Charlier, and had been a spokesman of traditionalism and the French Catholic extreme right since the mid-1950s. Madiran was a fervent reader of Gilson. *Itinéraires* was founded in 1956. It was condemned by the French bishops in 1966. According to Étienne Fouilloux's phrase, the magazine was "the rallying point for those who rejected any evolution of the Catholic Church and dreamed of re-establishing a Christian social order."[85]

Recalling Madiran's attack on Gilson in *Revue universelle* in 1943,[86] and in *Aspects de la France* in 1950 under the pen name Pierre Boutang, it is rather surprising that we should now find in *Itinéraires* a twenty-page review under Madiran's own name, favorable to Gilson's autobiography.[87] "What a beautiful book. What a tranquil, profound, and great book, the conclusion of a whole life of research. Very personal testimony and balanced in tone, but it concerns everything essential in Christian thought today. And it is like a last word. Has Gilson finished his work in this way? One might say so."[88] With that, we have the first sign that testifies to Gilson's good standing in French traditionalist circles, where Maritain was methodically detested.[89] That would not fail to surprise Gilson himself, who in his memoir, once again expressed his affinity to Le Sillon, and did not spare criticism against

84 Thiry, "Le philosophe et la théologie," 364.

85 Étienne Fouilloux, "Madiran, Jean," in Julliard and Winock, *Dictionnaire des intellectuels français*.

86 On this point see *Revue universelle* and *Action Française* of December 1941, where Jean Arfel, the future Jean Madiran, sharply criticized Gilson's political position (*Revue universelle*, nos. 70 and 71, November and December, 1943; *Action Française*, December 18, 1943, 6.)

87 Jean Madiran, "Un témoignage chrétien: Le philosophe Gilson et la théologie," *Itinéraires: Chroniques et documents*, no. 44, June 1960, 46–67.

88 Madiran, "Un témoignage chrétien," 47.

89 Florian Michel, "Intégrisme catholique et politique," *Études*, September 2009, 211–22. See likewise Madiran, *Gilson:* Chroniques philosophiques, 16–17, 51–76.

the "monstrous " and "positivist Thomism" of the Master of Martigues, "so interested in Rome, but not at all in Jerusalem."[90]

To try to understand Madiran's acceptance of Gilson's work, one must note three points: rejection of the friendship between Maritain and Gilson, and distinction between the two philosophers; deemphasis of the political disagreements between Gilson and traditionalist circles on the subjects of Maurras, Le Sillon, and Christian democracy; and finally as much as possible, the effort to "conservativize" not Gilson but his work, by making him understand who his authentic readers were.

Gilson wrote a flattering portrait of Maritain, and Madiran reversed the portrait. "We had a philosopher among us. We did not recognize him. A philosopher who was also a writer. We reproduce the tribute Gilson paid to Maritain," Madiran explained, "but directed it to Gilson himself. The paragraph can be read replacing Maritain's name with Gilson's. . . . What Gilson wrote about Maritain, as a matter of fact, he also wrote about himself." Madiran's intent initially was to shift Gilson's favorable judgments about Maritain to Gilson himself, without considering the substance of those judgments. Madiran next claimed to offer an "attentive welcome" to the work of Gilson and Maritain. This welcome, he said, had the dual problem of being both critical and "not being situated, as necessary, in the areas or the shores toward which their hearts tended." Madiran went on to say that *Pour un ordre catholique*, which originated on the left within the publication *Sept*, was "forgotten, unknown, scorned" by Gilson's friends and companions, while traditionalist circles continually studied it and recommended reflection upon it.[91]Here, Madiran seemed unaware of the *Sept* articles against Maurras that were not reprinted in *Pour un ordre catholique*. (Madiran was only fourteen or fifteen years old at the moment when they appeared in *Sept*.)

In the 1960 article, Madiran did not mention the involvement of Gilson with Francisque Gay and the MRP. Madiran likewise rejected Gilson's positions on Fr. Laberthonnière and Le Sillon. Gilson would have been a victim of blindness about the "Sangnier myth." And naturally, Gilson did not know Maurras, as he did not know Sangnier. "Gilson seems not to have been much more familiar with the thinking and writing of Maurras than those of

90 Étienne Gilson, *Le philosophe et la théologie*, 68. [Translator: I have not found this reference in the English version, but the title "Master of Martigues" is a reference to Charles Maurras, founder of Action Française.]

91 Madiran, "Un témoignage chrétien," 50.

Sangnier." In relation to faith, Madiran established an audacious comparison between Maurras and Bergson, both of whom were in the antechamber of the Church. . . . "Doubtless, Gilson would be less scandalized, or more advisedly so, if he possessed a less unilateral view of these things [Action Française, Maurras]" (p. 64). The review's conclusion again set Gilson and Maritain at odds:

> Maritain's *christiana philosophia socialis* was very ambitious. It had a reason for being in so far as it was *christiana philosophia socialis*. His work did not reach the altitude of that legitimate ambition. Maritain's overall vision and his judgment about the meaning of history are false. . . . His general view on the temporal sphere is mistaken. . . . By contrast, and we will finish with this because it is a tribute to Étienne Gilson, his work *Pour un ordre catholique* had a modest, humble vision. It simply concerned freedom of education in 1934 France. . . . *Pour un ordre catholique* is an example and a masterpiece of *christiana philosophia socialis*. Naturally, nobody ever talks about that.[92]

Consequently, for Jean Madiran, Étienne Gilson became a temporary ally in 1960. Gilson was aware of the maneuver and accepted the risks of a reconciliation. In 1992, Madiran wrote again, "Gilson was not one of our people, but we are his. We admired him, we loved him, we owe him a great deal, we have said so. . . . He was on the left because of his friendships with Chenu and de Lubac. In that, he was not one of us. We have not tried to take him over during his life. We will not take him over after his death . . . . I have never met him. Our relations have been purely intellectual, purely epistolary.[93]

In the course of the 1960s, a series of realignments occurred in Thomist networks. Little by little, Gilson distanced himself from some of his best friends of the 1930s and 1940s, like Chenu, whom he no longer understood: "I have never questioned Maritain's Thomism. I will question still less your evangelism, which I do not understand at all. You seem to me to be the victim of a conventual perspective whose importance is very limited."[94] In 1967, Gilson learned that Chenu did not share his critique of the new *Credo*: "I

92 Madiran, "Un témoignage chrétien," 66–67.

93 Madiran, *Gilson: Chroniques philosophiques*, 15.

94 Letter from Étienne Gilson to Fr. Marie-Dominique Chenu, November 5, 1969, published in *Revue thomiste* 105 (January-March 2005): 82.

have been told that you disapprove of my opposition to 'of the same nature.' If that is true, it is more comic than anything I could have imagined."[95]

By contrast, Gilson began to correspond with integrist circles whom he had previously opposed and whom Maritain, in *Le Paysan de la Garonne,* considered (and the expression has not been pondered) "the worst offense to divine truth and human intelligence."[96] On March 11, 1967, Madiran addressed Gilson: "I would like to publish your work *Christianisme et philosophie* in *Itinéraires* in five installments."[97] Gilson replied three days later: "I feel profoundly in agreement with you on essentials. . . . I know *Itinéraires* very well. Its remaining Maurrasian character remains alien to me in tone and spirit."[98] As always, Gilson was politically lucid,[99] obviously well intentioned, but not a good strategist in regard to a magazine that had received an admonition from the French bishops:

> It is inevitable that Catholics should be divided on political problems relating to the temporal order, but these divisions are superficial and not really important compared to the profound, intimate agreement that unites members of the same Church. . . . We can do nothing useful to the Church without first situating ourselves in a climate of common faith, grace, and fellowship.[100]

The reaction against Gilson came quickly, and as it were, suspended the acceptance of his positions in postconciliar debates: "To say that I am now classified among the fundamentalists! We have seen everything," he lamented to Fr. Chenu in June 1967.[101] "I am now classified among the integrists, which

95 Letter from Étienne Gilson to Fr. Marie-Dominique Chenu, April 16, 1967, APDF.

96 Jacques Maritain, *Le Paysan de la Garonne* (Paris: Desclée de Brouwer, 1966), 17. There is a new edition prepared by Michel Fourcade, *Le Feu nouveau: Le Paysan de la Garonne* (Geneva: Ad Solem, 2007).

97 Letter from Jean Madiran to Étienne Gilson, March 11, 1967, SMCA.

98 Letter from Étienne Gilson to Jean Madiran, March 14, 1967, published (in part) in Madiran, *Gilson: Chroniques philosophiques*, 16.

99 On this point, read the letter from Étienne Gilson to Jean de Fabrègues, February 4, 1967, Archives Fabrègues, CHSP: "Maurras has left a family of fortunately impotent politicians, but masters in the art of sophistry, lying, and slander, that they use above all against Christians in the name of Christianity."

100 Letter from Étienne Gilson to Jean Madiran, April 28, 1967, "Christianisme et philosophie," *Itinéraires*, April 1967, 39–65; republished in Madiran, *Gilson: Chroniques philosophiques*, 173–74.

101 Letter from Étienne Gilson to Fr. Marie-Dominique Chenu, June 7, 1967, APDF.

is funny, along with Maritain, which is more funny if possible," he commented to a Canadian friend a few months later.[102]

WAR BREAKS OUT: THE NEW LITURGICAL TRANSLATIONS (1965–1966)

In 1965, the approval of new liturgical translations stemming from the reform decided by the Council Fathers provoked Gilson's emergence from retirement and helped create several deeply felt controversies. For Gilson, more like St. Jerome than ever, the major issue was the translation of *consubstantialem* in the Nicene-Constantinopolitan Creed. The other, of less importance, dealt with the translation of *Sicut et nos* in the Our Father.

In June 1965, Gilson wrote parallel letters to Fr. de Lubac and Fr. Shook:

> I have just done something really dumb. I sent an article to *France catholique* protesting the new French translation which obliges us to recite in the *Credo*, that the Son is of the *same nature* as the Father. I maintain that they have been consubstantial from eternity, and that this is not exactly the same thing. I hope that Jean de Fabrègues will throw the article in the wastebasket.[103]

> I am going to create a scandal with a paper to be published by *La France catholique* under the title "Suis-je schismatique?" And why would I be such a monster? Because I refuse to say in the new French version of the mass, that the Son is "de la même nature que le Père." I am creating a new schism, that of the Nicaean paleo-Catholics who believe that the Son is of the same "substance" as the Father and that both are of the same nature only because they are "consubstantial."[104]

The article appeared on the first page of *La France catholique* on July 2, 1965. Jean de Fabrègues, an old student of Gilson, had a basically moderate conservative position, center-right one might say. Having come out of the Maurrasian matrix, he was Roman and papal, neither progressive nor

102 Letter from Étienne Gilson to Fr. Laurence Shook, November 14, 1967, SMCA.

103 Letter from Étienne Gilson to Fr. Henri de Lubac, June 20, 1965, in *Letters of Étienne Gilson to Henri de Lubac*, 83.

104 Letter from Étienne Gilson to Fr. Laurence Shook, June 29, 1965, SMCA. See Shook, *Étienne Gilson*, 370–71.

integrist, in the line of "Notre Démocratie" of Gilson's MRP.[105] "Am I Schismatic?" asks Gilson's provocative title. In a more peaceful time, anyone would have viewed the question that Gilson was posing, clumsy in itself, as rhetorical. Would Gilson in his eighties seriously want to break with the Church of Rome? He gave the embryo of a reply to a Canadian friend, explaining that his "interrogation about the schism was a purely rhetorical question."[106] But in 1965 the question was a detonator.

Elsewhere,[107] we tried to examine Gilson's arguments in depth and the reception of his articles, not only in the press (*La Croix, Le Monde, La France catholique, Le Figaro*), but also using the correspondence that readers sent directly to Gilson and the letters exchanged with the majority of the intellectuals and theologians of the period (such as the Maritains, Congar, de Lubac, Journet, Chenu, Mauriac, and so forth). It should not be necessary to go back to the whole demonstration. In July 1965, Gilson was the first to raise the prickly subject of *consubstantialem* publicly. On this issue he rediscovered private remarks made by Fr. de Lubac to some bishops in secret.[108] Supported by de Lubac, Maritain, and Congar, approved with reservations by Journet, who saw a blunder rather than a heresy, the argument on *consubstantialem* was taken up many times. Congar wrote to Gilson:

> I will permit myself to tell you of my agreement with you. In January, I myself supported the protest or interrogation of a priest in the same sense. He accurately observed that the semi-Arians had adhered to the formula "of the same nature," and that St. Hilary got himself exiled in order to not admit it.... The people at the Liturgy Center who translated the Symbol responded in January that nowadays there is no longer danger of Arianism.

105 On Jean de Fabrègues (1906–1983), see Véronique Auzépy-Chavagnac, *Jean de Fabrègues et la Jeune Droite Catholique: Aux sources de la Révolution national* (Villeneuve d'Ascq: Presses Universitaires du Septentrion, 2003).—Letter from Jean de Fabrègues to Étienne Gilson, March 22, 1967, SMCA: "A little brochure by you from the same period, published by the MRP: 'Notre Démocratie,' continues to be at the heart of the efforts of the team at *La France catholique*."

106 Letter from Étienne Gilson to Fr. Laurence Shook, July 11, 1965. Shook, *Étienne Gilson*, 371.

107 Florian Michel, "Entre tradition et traduction: Philosophes, philologues et théologiens dans un débat conciliaire," *Revue de l'histoire de l'Église de France*, no. 229, July-December 2006, 435–75. The article is developed in *Traduire la liturgie: Esssai d'histoire* (Paris: CLD, 2013). See also Vincent Petit, Christian Sorrel, Bruno Dumons, eds., "La gestion de conflits et la gouvernance ecclésiale au temps de la réforme liturgique (1963–1975)," *Liturgie et société XIXe–XXe siècles* (Rennes: Presses Universitaires de Rennes, 2016), 205–23.

108 Document published in Cardinal Henri de Lubac and Jacques Maritain, *Correspondance et rencontre* (Paris: Cerf, 2012), 120–24.

> ... This is true. But as you say, it is also always necessary to express the faith correctly, and, in an article of such importance, this must be considered sacred. I would not want you to think that those who cooperated in the great opening up of the Church took dogmatic exactitude cheaply. What astonishes me is that the Holy Office, which reserved to itself approval of the translations, precisely in order to avoid whims, has allowed to slip past it what you raise.[109]

Alone among theologians and historians, the Dominicans Dubarle and Chenu,[110] along with Henri-Irénée Marrou,[111] supported the translation chosen by the liturgical bishops against the translators. The controversy was heated. A polemical publication banished Gilson to the "swamp of grumpy old men," where the names of Maritain, Mauriac, Guitton and so forth were also found. The author exploded in literary anger against Gilson because of his article in *La France catholique*. "Why the devil does the Burgundian Academician engage in an absurd war against the French translation of the Latin *consubstantialem* in the Creed by 'of the same nature'? To blow the epic trumpet in *La France catholique* and evoke councils and cry heresy, and that people die for that! Good heavens. How blood-thirsty and romantic these chapel members are. . . . Monsieur Gilson, in looking with your big eyes at the bishops and other big personalities, you have uttered a big stupidity with your big voice."[112] Louis Salleron denounced the "scandal of the translation of *consubstantialem*" in *La Nouvelle Messe*.[113] In 1970, integrist circles, Louis Salleron, Jean Madiran, and primarily the magazine *Itinéraires* organized a petition that gathered seven thousand signatures between 1967 and 1970, the figure provided by Salleron in the newspaper *Carrefour* on December 30, 1970. The signatures went beyond the usual integrist or traditionalist

109 Letter from Fr. Yves Congar to Étienne Gilson, July 6, 1965, SMCA.

110 On this point, see the letter from Fr. Marie-Dominique Chenu to Étienne Gilson, July 2 1965, published in *Revue thomiste* 105 (2005): 69–70: "Your philological and theological scruple is too great." Chenu cites two passages from St. Thomas where "substance" and "nature" are considered synonyms in Trinitarian theology.

111 See on this point *Cahiers Marrou*, no. 1, 2008, 24–28, where there is an exchange of letters between Louis Salleron and Henri-Irénée Marrou (May–June, 1966). Marrou reproduced an extract from the publication *Catéchèse*, no. 24, July 1966, and concluded: "For the great number of our contemporaries, *consubstantial* is a word with no meaning and that seems as bizarre to them as *anticonstitutionally*."

112 Paupert, *Vieillards de chrétienté et Chrétiens de l'an 2000*, 75.

113 Louis Salleron, *La Nouvelle Messe* (Paris: Nouvelles Éditions Latines, 1970), 23.

territory—Jacques de Bourbon-Busset, Henri Massis, Roland Mousnier, Gustave Thibon, Gabriel Marcel, Étienne Gilson, Stanislas Fumet, François Mauriac and so on. The petition, demanding the re-establishment of *consubstantial* in the name of St. Athanasius, was rejected by Cardinal Lefebvre, who claimed that it constituted "an act of defiance against the bishops." In the exchanges between Jean Fourastié, father of the "Glorious Thirty," and Fr. René Laurentin, the question was again posed in the briefest terms. Criticizing the deficient translation, Jean Fourastié tried to defend his position: "If war has been waged [against the translation of the Creed], I have not waged it"; Fr. Laurentin responded learnedly: "No, it is not you. It is Étienne Gilson." He added that in fact the translation "of the same nature as the Father" was more faithful to the Greek and the Syriac than was the Latin formula.[114] In 1974, one of the leaders of the integrist movement again employed the argument to denounce the cardinal of Paris as a heretic.[115] The controversy has not lessened since 1965.

The second point of the debate provoked by Gilson in *La France catholique* in February 1966 did not have the same theological importance. Gilson was more gentle—and also more ironic—in his remarks about the new ecumenical Our Father.

> A kind correspondent informed me about the new text of the Our Father, henceforth "common to all Christians." By that we obviously understand "all French-speaking Christians." My correspondent's parish and diocese are not the same as mine, and since so far no document of this kind has been sent to me, I can continue to say the old Our Father of my childhood without worrying about how others say it, but I have no illusions, and if I must undergo a shock, I prefer to be prepared for it.
>
> I hasten to add that I have no objection against the substance itself of the text that is beginning to circulate. It is true that in it we use the informal pronoun to address God, to which we are not accustomed. . . . A French speaker does not spontaneously use the familiar pronoun to address the King of kings. . . but if we are called upon to do so, we will. What would we not do to please our good Lutheran or Calvinist brethren? In any case, to the contrary of what my amiable correspondent thinks, it is the case that this new use of the familiar French pronoun is not "slavishly inspired by

114 Jean Fourastié, René Laurentin, *L'Église a-t-elle trahi?* (Paris: Beauchesne, 1974), 35–42.

115 Letter from Msgr. Ducaud-Bourget to Cardinal Marty, published as an offprint of a supplement of *Fort dans la Foi*, October 1974, 100.

> the German," *Vater Unser, der bist*. It correctly and precisely translates the liturgical Latin: *Pater Noster qui es in caelis*. The only thing that we can regret, in saying *Notre Père, qui est aux cieux*, is therefore a change of habit. But that is unimportant, because God understands many other versions, and we ourselves are not judges of the liturgy. In its texts as in its rites, the Church is in complete charge of deciding, without even having to consult us.
>
> Therefore, I will not follow my correspondent on this point.... However, I share his surprise when I read something a bit further on: "Pardon us our offenses as we also pardon those who have offended us." What is unusual in this expression? In the Our Father that I once learned from my mother and recited at catechism, we simply said "as we pardon those who have offended us." The adverb *as* means *just as, in the way that*. The word *also* does not figure in our version of the Lord's Prayer. But its equivalent figures in the Latin text: *Sicut et nos dimittimus debitoribus nostris*. Therefore it is natural to want to add it to the French prayer. One may be allowed to wonder, however, if the proposed translation is satisfactory. No dogmatic truth is at issue here. It is simply a question of a detail of style or rather of French grammar, and still more precisely of the place that properly corresponds to the adverb *also*... Do we want to say that we pardon, not only those who have not offended us, but also those who have offended us? .. . The Protestant Our Father traditionally and correctly said it: 'As we also pardon...." That has a beautiful power, and I certainly hope that the esteem in which the reformed Christians are held in the Church today will permit them to prevent a formula from being snatched away that is in such perfect agreement with the Latin Bible's *sicut et nos*. Not desiring to offer services that nobody has invited me to give, I will limit myself to observe timidly that to spoil what is good in the Protestant Our Father in order to obtain a prayer common to all Christians is not the best form of ecumenism that we could practice.[116]

By All Saints Day 2017, that is to say, half a century after the reform, new translations had been proposed by the French Episcopal Conference and approved by the Congregation for Divine Worship and the Discipline of the Sacraments, in agreement with the instruction *Liturgiam Authenticam* of 2001. The thoroughly debated term "consubstantial" has returned to the official translation of the Nicene Creed.[117] Gilson certainly would have been

116 Étienne Gilson, "*Sicut et nos*," *La France catholique*, February 18, 1966.

117 Read the interview of Nicolas Senèze with Archbishop Aubertin, *La Croix*, November 8, 2015. See also Nicolas Senèze, "Missel romain, bisbilles autour d'une traduction," *La Croix*, May 27, 2016, 14.

delighted, under the condition that certain groups should not gloat over their victory. It certainly was not a victory of integrist pressure groups, or the distant outcome of petitions initiated by Salleron and Madiran, or a sign of success of a confrontational strategy. In a sense, Gilson foresaw the return of *consubstantialem*, which, as he wrote in 1965, "will surely win back its place, because it is unacceptable that the local synod should abolish the Council of Nicaea. France cannot become Arian again."[118] Instead, there was a return to an understanding of the faith required by the Latin terminology. But it provoked a symmetrical controversy in its turn: the new translations were soon being criticized as unintelligible, conservative, and anti-pastoral at the very moment when the Holy See insisted on inculturation.

TRIBULATIONS OF SOPHIA (1967)

On June 9, 1967, Étienne Gilson presented his last work, *Les Tribulations de Sophie*, then at the printer's, to Jacques Maritain:

> The "Lectures on Thomism," whose spirit you approve, will appear as a pamphlet with a response from the Reverend Father Roger Garaudy, who marvelously imitates clerical unction. I have added a short chapter called "Wandering among the Ruins," written in the pressure of the moment about the Church's current situation in France and the United States. After the publication of Fr. Congar's "Response," I would like to draw his attention to his error of perspective."[119]

Here we have a quick summary of the contents of *Les Tribulations de Sophie*, which Vrin brought out in autumn 1967. In the *Tribulations*, there is a very traditionally crafted plea for the philosophy of St. Thomas Aquinas, "always current," according to Gilson.[120] He explained humorously, "The real revolutionary, on the contrary, is the person who holds a truth firmly, however old it may be, and though the whole world abandons it."[121] This gives

118 Letter from Étienne Gilson to Jean de Fabrègues, December 5, 1965, CHSP.

119 Letter from Étienne Gilson to Jacques Maritain, June 9, 1967, in Gilson and Maritain, *Correspondance 1923–1971*, 235–37.

120 Étienne Gilson, *Les Tribulations de Sophie* (Paris: Vrin, 1967). [English translation by James G. Colbert, *The Tribulations of Sophia* (South Bend, IN.: St. Augustine's Press, 2021), 35. Quotations and page numbers will be taken from the English translation.]

121 Étienne Gilson, *The Tribulations of Sophia*, 48.

a sense of the work's general tone: humorous, polemical, and generously untimely.

The work was important for the fault lines it revealed, the controversies it started, and for its agreement with Maritain's *Le Paysan de la Garonne* and with Pope Paul VI and other members of the clergy for whom the Church and humanity were in a state of "philosophical crisis."[122] Gilson's title recalled *Les Malheurs de Sophie* by the Countess of Ségur. But, Gilson added, it also alluded to Paul Claudel's *Les Aventures de Sophie*. "The new Sophia, whose misfortunes I lament, is not a little girl or an allegory, but none other than wisdom, *sophia*, *sapientia*. She is the doctrine that St. Thomas called supreme wisdom among all human wisdoms."[123] Accordingly, *Les Tribulations de Sophie* designates the torments and questions that Christian philosophy and Catholic theology are undergoing.

The *Tribulations* gathered a disparate group of pieces composed between spring 1965 and spring 1967. Three topics were treated at different lengths. The first, "Thomism and Its Current Situation," was given in Italy as a lecture series in spring 1965. With the addition of an appendix against Teilhard de Chardin, these lectures were published at the end of 1965 in the Roman journal *Seminarium*, the organ of the Congregation of Seminaries and Universities. The second part of *Tribulations* consisted of a critical discussion of Roger Garaudy, who tried to engage Catholics in his *Un Marxiste s'adresse au Concile*, Paris: Plon, 1965. *Seminarium* published Gilson's reply, "A Difficult Dialogue," in spring 1966. Besides the pieces on Teilhard and Garaudy, the last component was "Wandering Among the Ruins." Written in spring 1967, it responded to debates in France during the winter of 1966, although largely autobiographical in tone and containing Gilson's reflections on the post-Council Church.

Some background discussions form the horizon of the work's composition. The first took place in November 1964. During the third session of the Council, the Council Fathers discussed the place of St. Thomas in the

122 See, for example, Jerzy Kalinowski and Stefan Swieżawski, *La philosophie à l'heure du Concile* (Paris: Société d'Éditions internationales, 1965), 15: "Humanity [and] the Church are, alas, in a state of crisis, also philosophical crisis." Likewise in the letter from Henri de Lubac to Émile Mireaux, November 11, 1968, published in *Bulletin de l'Association Internationale Cardinal Henri de Lubac* 9 (2007): 4–5: "The crisis whose depth the events of May and June have shown, goes beyond the framework of economic, political, and social problems. Especially among the young, it indicates deep moral unease. I would even say spiritual and metaphysical unease."

123 Étienne Gilson, *The Tribulations of Sophia*, 4.

program of religious studies. Some argued for more attention to St. Thomas, notably Cardinal Ernesto Ruffini and the Congregation for Seminaries and Universities The others, led by Cardinal Paul-Émile Leger, archbishop of Montreal, backed by Fr. Chenu, no longer wanted this.[124] The battle was harsh and left scars. Gilson involved himself directly in this debate. The second controversy was both prior to and a corollary to the first. It shook Catholic seminaries and universities for ten years and concerned the place to be given in the curriculum to the thought of Fr. Teilhard de Chardin, who gained new influence through the proliferation of works published after his death. Was Teilhardism the precursor and foundation of the *nouvelle théologie*... or a great joke? The lines were drawn. The third debate swirled around *Le Paysan de la Garonne*, which appeared in autumn 1966.[125] The publication of *Les Tribulations de Sophie* in several installments explains how Maritain based himself extensively on the first part of it in *Le Paysan de la Garonne*, while Gilson quoted *Le Paysan de la Garonne* in the third part of the *Tribulations*, which was written in 1967. The two authors quoted and supported each other. The fourth debate was protean. It involved the feeling of Catholicism's decay, its decimation, according to Fr. Boyer, and of its ruins in the aftermath of the Council. It included Christian understanding, the place of religion in a secularized society, liturgical reform, moral change, the sexual revolution as well as an upheaval of the priesthood.

Les Tribulations de Sophie had various themes; it was circumstantial and responded to requests. Gilson willingly let himself be maneuvered by a

124 Read André Naud, "Le cardinal Léger au concile et la conduite de l'intelligence chrétienne," in *L'Église canadienne et Vatican II* (Quebec: Fides, 1997), 237–63: "Cardinal Léger suggests that we cease to require that what the *schema* calls *philosophia perennis* be taught" (247). The article clearly shows the opposition between Cardinal Léger and Cardinal Ruffini. "It is necessary to avoid exaggerated exclusivism," Cardinal Léger has said. "Unhappy the man of a single book! Unhappy the Church of single doctor." André Naud quotes a letter from Fr. Marie-Dominique Chenu to Cardinal Léger (248–50): "I permit myself to direct my respectful, solid, and fervent adherence without any precaution. Your Eminence and not Cardinal Ruffini (still less Msgr. Staffa) is the one who is faithful to St. Thomas." Read likewise Kalinowski and Swieżawski, *La Philosophie à l'heure du concile*, 137–40: "It happens that the conservatives are the ones who claim St. Thomas for themselves. . . . In that context the advocates of progress, even among the best intentioned and most cautious, spontaneously adopt the opposing attitude. . . . We are present at a combat. Meanwhile, St. Thomas runs the risk of a new failure, his failure at the Council. I hope that things will not go that far and that truth and wisdom will triumph. . . . If God permitted it, as he permitted the condemnation of the theses of St. Thomas in 1277 and 1284, it will only be a misadventure in the more than seven-century-old history of Thomism."

125 On this debate, see Jacques Maritain, *Le Feu nouveau: Le Paysan de la Garonne* (Geneva: Ad Solem, 2007), new edition prepared by Michel Fourcade.

faction of the Vatican Curia—more precisely, by the Secretary and the Prefect of the Congregation of Seminaries and Universities, Archbishop Dino Staffa and Cardinal Pizzardo. Gilson mentions the fact in the preface of *Tribulations*:

> Word, however muted, reached the Roman Curia and Archbishop Dino Staffa, Secretary of the Sacred Congregation of Seminaries and Universities at the time, expressed the desire to publish the lectures in the Vatican journal *Seminarium*. I gratefully accepted the honor. . . . Nowadays it is hard to speak of any theological subject without encountering Teilhard de Chardin. If you seek to avoid him, people trip you with him. Accordingly, I said a few words about him in the third lecture. Archbishop Staffa asked me to take up the question in greater detail, which I did unenthusiastically in what constitutes chapter four of the present work, "The Teilhard de Chardin Case." . . . This fourth chapter is not a lecture delivered in Italy. It is an essay written to respond to a request by Archbishop Dino Staffa to have my opinion on Fr. Teilhard's thought, taken in itself and not obliquely, as a possible substitute for that of St. Thomas Aquinas.

In his correspondence, Gilson indicated several times that it was Cardinal Pizzardo himself who asked him to publish the material. In a letter to Fr. Chenu in August 1965, Gilson explained:

> Furthermore, I had rambled through three lectures about St. Thomas (What can be done? I love him.) His Eminence Cardinal Pizzardo got wind of it and wanted to see them, then he wanted to publish them in *Seminarium*. (Am I an integrist?) Since, in the third lecture, I briefly mentioned Teilhard de Chardin, S.J., the cardinal asked me to devote a special article to him. I wrote it, and his Eminence is going to publish it at the same time as the other three.[126]

In Rome in the spring of 1965, Gilson had met Pizzardo and Staffa, who, to put it mildly, did not embody the progressive sector of the Fathers of the Council. As a Polish observer of the Council wrote with exquisite understatement: "Those who defended Thomism in the course of the debate were not taken from the Council's leaders or the most active promoters of necessary reforms, the real authors of *aggiornamento*."[127] Thomism and conservativism

126 Letter from Étienne Gilson to Fr. Marie-Dominique Chenu, August 5, 1965, APDF.

127 Kalinowski and Swieżawski, *La philosophie à l'heure du Concile*, 135.

in fact were associated. Gilson was under orders when, without naming him, he attacked Cardinal Léger, who argued for "de-Thomistification" of studies in his archdiocese: "I do not think I am mistaken," Gilson wrote, "in thinking that a sort of anti-Thomist offensive is being prepared in quarters where nothing would have invited us to foresee it."[128] He based himself on a November 1964 article published in the Montreal *Devoir*: "The Church should not give exclusive status to St. Thomas," summing up Cardinal Léger's intervention in the Council. This time, in his private correspondence, Gilson did not refrain from naming the cardinal:

> Alas, the general revolt against Thomism is justified, but it is perfectly useless to talk about it. On last November 26, a Monday, I gave a lecture at the University on "St. Thomas and Us." The morning of the lecture, the Montreal *Devoir* published an announcement of the warning of his Eminence Cardinal Léger, archbishop of Montreal, alerting the public to the excessive attachment to Thomism that some people demonstrate. It was only a coincidence, but it was unfortunate. Who am I to defend St. Thomas against our cardinals? It is true that in secondary schools here, students must learn the definitions in their manuals by heart. . . . Who will deliver us from Thomism to give us St. Thomas Aquinas?[129]
>
> I did not know that the Council had to concern itself with St. Thomas Aquinas. An inconceivable remark by Cardinal Léger had astonished me. (I am naive.) He complained that Thomas is taught too much. Now, for fifty years, I have shouted myself hoarse saying at the University of Montreal, for which the cardinal is personally responsible, that the Thomism taught there does not have much to do with St. Thomas Aquinas. So, he does not even know what he is talking about. After having taught their Thomisms instead of St. Thomas Aquinas, they now want to exclude the teaching of genuine Thomism to free themselves from the false ones they have instilled by force in its stead. I rightly say "by force," because in the diocese of Montreal there are secondary schools where the students must recite from memory answers from their manuals.[130]

Similarly, Gilson took a stand against certain undercurrents of society: the cultural relativism of the mass media that impose their own view of

128 Étienne Gilson, *The Tribulations of Sophia*, 14.

129 Letter from Étienne Gilson to Jean de Fabrègues, November 27, 1964, CHSP.

130 Letter from Étienne Gilson to Stefan Swieżawski, 1965, published partially in Kalinowski and Swieżawski, *La philosophie à l'heure du concile*, 247–48.

truth, namely western naturalism and secularism, and the attempt to secularize religion itself. He entered into a close discussion of three authors: Fr Teilhard de Chardin, Roger Garaudy, and Fr. Yves Congar. Gilson's critique of Teilhard (the two had met at length in New York)[131] is definitive. He dissected the Jesuit's "gnostic" work for itself as well as for the desire to replace St. Thomas with Teilhard.

> There still remain Blondelians, but the school no longer gains recruits. Young Christians in search of a philosophy turn rather toward the work of Fr. Pierre Teilhard de Chardin than toward this convoluted dialectic, difficult to follow, whose word choice and sentence structure reflect its indecision in thought. . . . I simply ask whether, after wanting to replace Thomism by Blondelism in teaching Christian theology, masters and students today will have to enlist in Teilhard de Chardin's school. I would like to explain my reasons to doubt it.[132]

For Gilson, Teilhard's theology was not a Christian theology. We are dealing with the cosmic theology of "Christ the evolver," which denies original sin and dwells in the noosphere and the "flowery meadows of the imagination."[133] Gilson wrote: "Teilhardian theology is one more Christian gnosis, and like every gnosis from Marcion to our day, it is *theology fiction*."[134] In the split over the acceptance of Teilhard's work, there was a watershed in the theology of the decade from 1960 to 1970.

Gilson's attack on Roger Garaudy was no less sharp. The two also knew each other, since Garaudy had traveled to Toronto to teach "Marxist ecumenism."[135] Gilson took advantage of the opportunity to re-visit the Teilhard material upon which Garaudy had based himself. Thus, in relation to

131 Thus, in his correspondence, Gilson recalled his encounter with Teilhard; see the letter from Étienne Gilson to Fr. Marie-Dominique Chenu, August 5, 1965, APDF: "He was an exquisite person, a great gentleman, about whom I sometimes wondered whether he did not like to scandalize a little the bourgeoisie. Finally, I must confess that he scandalized me the day he asked whether we would finally get the meta-Christianity that it seems we all await." See also the letter from Étienne Gilson to Msgr. Bruno de Solages, March 2, 1967, SMCA: "Teilhard does not teach evolution. He preaches it. It is his God. I was seated fairly close to him for three days while Julian Huxley presided."

132 Étienne Gilson, *The Tribulations of Sophia*, 42–43.

133 Étienne Gilson, *The Tribulations of Sophia*, 66.

134 Étienne Gilson, *The Tribulations of Sophia*, 45.

135 Letter from Étienne Gilson to Jacques Maritain, January 15, 1967, *Cahiers Jacques Maritain*, no. 37 (1998): 72: "Garaudy came to Toronto to stage one of his exhibitions of Marxist ecumenism. He left very good memories. I wonder whether there are possible limits to Catholic gullibility or not."

Garaudy's work, he mused: "There is a Marxist scholasticism (as convoluted as the other one) in which we may be excused from participating, since it does not concern us."[136] Gilson pointed out an unsolvable controversy between communists and Catholics. For him, there was an "abuse of confidence, and an endeavor to falsify history" in Garaudy's narrative.[137] Gilson asked in conclusion:

> Can we usefully dialogue with atheists? I doubt it if they are communists, and I even dread this dialogue if it is between Marxists as well informed about their doctrine as Roger Garaudy and theologians as badly informed about theirs as Fr. Teilhard de Chardin. In cases of this kind, the communists absorb the theologians with the greatest ease and feed on them with advantage. Only the ridiculousness of the adventure remains to us.[138]

Lastly, Gilson devoted a few pages to defending Maritain against Fr. Congar, whose critical view of *Le Paysan de la Garonne* in *Le Monde*, December 1966, titled "A Sort of Pain," had influenced a large sector of the clergy.[139] "What mosquito has bitten Fr. Congar?"[140] "What has brought Fr. Congar to attack Maritain,"[141] Gilson wondered in private. In the *Tribulations* he tried, not to dissipate Congar's "kind of pain," but rather to drive in Maritain's nail. "Our theologians, some of them among the best, are close to crying sacrilege if one allows himself to say that Hegel's philosophy is purely and simply false."[142]

> But our theologian [Congar], completely absorbed by what the Council has done, does not seem clearly aware of what the Council has not done.... It is true that pastoral, liturgical, ecclesiological and biblical theology were well represented there, but the theology of which Jacques Maritain does not speak but that he embodies throughout a whole life's work, never really got a hearing there. Scholastic theology, neglected today when it is not scorned, rather shone by its absence. The consequences were felt during the

136 Étienne Gilson, *The Tribulations of Sophia*, 75.

137 Étienne Gilson, *The Tribulations of Sophia*, 82–83.

138 Étienne Gilson, *The Tribulations of Sophia*, 96.

139 Maritain, *Le Feu nouveau: Le Paysan de la Garonne*, 417–20.

140 Letter from Étienne Gilson to Jacques Maritain, January 15, 1967, *Cahiers Jacques Maritain*, no. 37 (1998): 71.

141 Letter from Étienne Gilson to Fr. Marie-Dominique Chenu, June 7, 1967, APDF.

142 Étienne Gilson, *The Tribulations of Sophia*, 111.

> Council. Extravagant positions were held by certain pastors about whom one wondered where they led their flocks.[143]

The point of Gilson's response to Congar was a reflection on language and on philosophical vocabulary, the foundation of theological vocabulary: "The teaching of dogmatic theology is linked, in fact and by necessity, to the categories and language of certain philosophers."[144] Gilson blamed both that temptation to separate philosophy and theology and the idea that it is necessary to make an *aggiornamento* of our discourse about God, since a new language would certainly be necessary for a new theology. He remarked: "We do not ask that philosophical and theological Thomism be imposed, without which one can certainly be saved, but we would like the creeds, which express salvific truths, not to be destroyed."[145]

Les Tribulations had a very mixed reception. The work was not translated until 2021. The size of its circulation was not at all comparable to that of *Le Paysan de la Garonne*, which sold more than 60,000 copies in a few months. But the reception of *Les Tribulations* was not as bad as Gilson sometimes reported. For example, he told a Canadian priest friend:

> Of *The Tribulations* itself, nothing is said. Non-Catholic publications don't care for Catholic problems. Catholic publications either are leftist or cowish [sic] for fear of the leftists, so they say nothing, not even against. . . . Of all the French bishops, *not a single one* has deigned to write me one line of approval. The French hierarchy could as well not exist at all, nothing would be changed. Now of course, it is not for laymen to upbraid their clergy and to wake them up to an awareness of impending perils. So we do nothing.[146]

Gilson wrote to his former student Henri Gouhier in the same vein: "I am not in orbit, and the critics do not consider me as someone that it is necessary to mention in order to be up-to-date. I have even come to wonder whether it would be necessary to pay some critics to get an article from them."[147] Some months later, Gilson wrote to another Canadian friend in a

143 Étienne Gilson, *The Tribulations of Sophia*, 112–13

144 Étienne Gilson, *The Tribulations of Sophia*, 113.

145 Étienne Gilson, *The Tribulations of Sophia*, 113.

146 Letter from Étienne Gilson to Fr. Francis Lescoe, December 27, 1967, FG, SMCA.

147 Letter from Étienne Gilson to Henri Gouhier, July 28, 1967, Archives Gouhier.

more nuanced way: "The reactions of the Curia are excellent. Cardinal Staffa is delighted, and Cardinal Garrone is pleased. I never send my books to the present Pope; he has no time to read them. The French newspapers do not even mention the existence of the book."[148]

There were not many reviews, but Gilson exaggerated. Cardinal Journet's *Nova et Vetera* indicated Gilson's articles and books.[149] There was also a full page article in *France catholique*, January 1968, written by Jean de Fabrègues with the title "Étienne Gilson, défenseur de l'intelligence."[150] Likewise, in February 1968, there was a half-page article in *Le Monde* written by the Academician Pierre-Henri Simon. His evaluation was rather positive, even though the review ends with a musical metaphor and a demand for polyphony:

> Therefore, *The Tribulations of Sophia* refers to the disorder that invades Christendom today, because the Church's theology vacillates, since it is cut off from Thomism, the philosophy best suited to support it. Summed up in this way, Étienne Gilson's thesis seems bold and almost insolent. How come? Would Scholasticism be the remedy to restore the modern mind's health? Indeed, it is an endeavor that is not obviously up to date. But let us not assume that a great historian of philosophy, someone who has gotten to the bottom of all systems, is naive, and let us understand what he means. . . . It is not surprising that a Church guided by belief in a transcendent God and creator should have chosen this philosophy as the privileged foundation of its theology. Scholastic vocabulary, to be sure, better supports the absolute character of dogmas, but it engages with greater difficulty the dialectical and tragic vision that modern science tends to give us of our universe. Theology, like the organ, needs several keyboards.[151]

148 Letter from Étienne Gilson to Fr. Laurence Shook, November 14, 1967, FG, SMCA.

149 For *Nova et Vetera*, see number 4, 1965, 319–20, where there is a long quotation from "À propos de Teilhard de Chardin," *Seminarium*, summer 1965, 714–17. See also, number 2, 1968, p. 158, where there is a review of *The Tribulations of Sophia*: "The last part is a bit like the cry of anguish in Holy Week."

150 Jean de Fabrègues, "Étienne Gilson, défenseur de l'intelligence ou *Les Tribulations de Sophie*," *France catholique*, January 19, 1968. Jean de Fabrègues saw a ray of light in the midst of the "primeval chaos of the theologies of death of god and secular religion."

151 Pierre-Henri Simon, "*Les Tribulations de Sophie, Interrogations autour de l'essentiel*," *Le Monde*, February 28, 1968. Combined review of Gilson's work and that of *Interrogations autour de l'essentiel* by Jean Onimus.

Examining Gilson's correspondence, we find a collection of factors with which to evaluate the reaction of Gilson's readers. Cardinal Garrone was the least critical of his correspondents.

> I thank you very much for having decided to send me your reflections on *The Tribulations of Sophia*. I knew most of its components, but I have re-read them with the same pleasure and the same benefit. . . . I hope that the "nothingness" of Philosophy to which we have arrived will give people the courage to pull themselves together. It is difficult to be an optimist in the present state of things, but I think we can and must keep our hope, because in the Church's direction there is a guarantee that simply must make us take stock of our responsibilities. I permit myself to repeat how happy I was to be able to express in person my gratitude for so many things that I have received from you through your work.[152]

Maritain, in his turn, had no reservations about the part of the book published in *Seminarium*. In a 1965 letter he declared:

> These "Three Lectures" are truly authoritative, setting everything in the correct perspective, admirably reminding people (those few who have ears to hear something other than the radio) of love for Truth. If I may say so, they themselves are overflowing with truths. We ought to be very grateful to you for the freedom, courage and lucidity of such testimony. . . . What you have written about Teilhard is magnificent. I would like it to be printed separately and distributed everywhere. After that, it remains that the worst about Teilhard is not Teilhard himself. It is the need to which he responds: the need for a counterfeit intellectual coin.[153]

However, the appearance of *Les Tribulations*, and notably of "Wandering among the Ruins," brought some sour notes.

> As for the spectacle before us, I don't need to tell you how much I agree with your judgment about it. . . . I have read your "Wandering among the ruins" with passionate interest. (Thank you for what you say about the old peasant). . . . I have a regret, however, that you are too dear for me not to confess. You seem to have "put in the same bag" absolutely essential questions that touch upon truth, faith and theology along with other questions that are subordinate, like priestly celibacy. . . and the issue of modern ver-

152 Letter from Cardinal Gabriel Garrone to Étienne Gilson, November 6, 1967, FG, SMCA.

153 Letter from Jacques Maritain to Étienne Gilson, November 23, 1965, *Correspondance*, 224–25.

> nacular language.... Is this a sign that I have become extraordinarily liberal in telling you this... ? No, there is simply a certain hierarchy of problems for me.[154]

As much as Maritain loved what Gilson wrote against Teilhard, the same passages were disliked by Fr. de Lubac and Msgr. de Solages.[155] Thus, Fr. de Lubac wrote a letter in regard to the *Seminarium* articles:

> Dear Monsieur Gilson, I read you at Geneva. I would not wish to take on another dialogue about this "difficult dialogue," which would perhaps be less difficult.... Indeed, for at least three quarters of the way, I am with you and very glad of it; and your dialectic seems invincible to me. Everything essential is there, and the rest is marginal. Even on this small remainder, my problem is not with you. It concerns Roger Garaudy. I don't know why you should follow him faithfully after having accused him of breach of trust. It is very easy for the communist to absorb the theologian when the theologian is dead.... I would tell Roger Garaudy, I hold it against you. I even blame Fr. Teilhard a little, because the way in which, in spite of himself, he dominates you keeps me from praising your articles in *Seminarium* to the highest degree. But I do encourage people to read them, because if I defend Teilhard where I think he is defensible, I do not make him my idol.[156]

Gilson did not yield an inch and replied to de Lubac: "Teilhard will always have the upper hand, because he is remarkably inconsistent. He's like quicksilver."[157] Teilhard became the apple of discord between Gilson and de Lubac. The Jesuit answered:

> I am only convinced that if you had read Teilhard, entering more into his viewpoint and forgetting about everything that has been said about

154 Letter from Jacques Maritain to Étienne Gilson, November 15, 1967, *Correspondance*, 244–45.

155 See the letter from Étienne Gilson to Msgr. Bruno de Solages, March 2, 1967 FG, SMCA: "How do you want someone who talks about theology without being a theologian, to be able to do it without spoiling everything? Now, the exact truth is that Fr. Teilhard does not know what he is talking about.... In a time when as simple laymen we are showered with insults by priests against whom we struggle to save our faith, do not give us Teilhard as an example. I have read Teilhard enough to know that his religion is not that of the Church or mine."

156 Letter from Henri de Lubac to Étienne Gilson, April 2, 1967. *Lettres de Monsieur Étienne Gilson au Père de Lubac*, 152–53 [Translator: The English version of Gilson's letters to de Lubac contains Gilson's letter of April 2, to which de Lubac presumably refers here, but I cannot find de Lubac's letter in the English version]

157 Letter from Étienne Gilson to Henri de Lubac, April 7, 1967, Henri de Lubac, *Letters of Étienne Gilson to Henri de Lubac*, 134–35.

> him, your impression would be better. He would seem less incoherent to you. . . . I perfectly understand you when you say you would prefer to be Lutheran than Teilhardian. That brings you close to Teilhard, whose first and last principle was fidelity to the Catholic Church, which alone keeps Christ for us.[158]

The exchange continued after publication of *Tribulations* in the fall of 1967:

> Dear Monsieur Gilson: Upon my return from a long stay in Rome, I found *The Tribulations of Sophia*. Even amid tribulations, you do not lose your sense of humor. The tribulations are still real, and I confess that I share them with you in great measure. Perhaps even more troubling is that, as a member of the clergy, it is more difficult for me than for you to withdraw from combat. Yet I am less free (much less free) to publish what I think. Besides, you certainly know that there are other points on which I cannot entirely side with your opinions. I believe that, in addition to the insuperable differences of formation and orientation, your suffering takes you to some excess. You will please excuse me for saying that, because I do not say it to you as a reproach. It indeed only increases the affection I have had for you for a long time, as you know.[159]

Likewise, Fr. Congar responded to Gilson in the same sense as in the *Le Monde* article he had published on *Le Paysan de la Garonne*:

> My thanks for having sent *Les Malheurs de Sophie* [sic]. I read it immediately. Once more, it poses problems whose bite I feel. First of all, there is the place of St. Thomas among us. Young people do not neglect St. Thomas, but they think that very real problems, valid approaches to the truth, above all in anthropological topics, come to them from other philosophies and cannot be conceptualized in St. Thomas's philosophy. I am of the old school myself. It is an effort for me to enter into a vocabulary in which young people express themselves and find themselves as spontaneously as they breathe. . . . Secondly, there is the postconciliar Church. I do not deny and am not unaware of any of the wrongdoing that you deplore. But I would wish that you—or Maritain—could take more account of what is positive in the postconciliar Church. . . . I suffer seeing you so poorly connected to the postconciliar Church, which does what it can in the midst of a world

158 Letter from Henri de Lubac to Étienne Gilson, April 9, 1967, *Lettres de Monsieur Étienne Gilson au Père de Lubac*, 162–63.

159 Letter from Henri de Lubac to Étienne Gilson, November 7, 1967, *Lettres de Monsieur Étienne Gilson au Père de Lubac*, 172.

that is frightfully difficult for faith. There may be ruins in it, but there is something else too.[160]

Les Tribulations was a composite, polemical, postconciliar booklet and rarely received the reader's complete approval. Apart from such differing reactions, the questions Gilson posed about the new theological age are still important and deserve to be examined. The first concerned this new theology's direction, which Gilson continued to denounce even as the conciliar Church affirmed its desire to leave more room to the laity. Fr. Chenu, moreover, made the same observation in 1966: "Your letter reached me in Rome on the last day of the congress of philosophy—from which you were absent.... To tell the truth, the congress and the theology were very clerical, to the detriment of *theo-logy*, at the very moment when it is claimed that theology must be the work of the people of God as such."[161] Gilson's position on this issue was twofold. He complained both about the tacit denial of the sacrament of holy orders—thus in *Les Tribulations* he insisted on "the signs of a general tendency to erase the distinction between cleric and layman, which was a minor symptom of a growing desire to desacralize religion."[162] At the same time, he lamented that theologians did not give more attention to what the laity said. "The simple layman that I am, submitted to unprecedented clerical bossism, really has nothing to do but to yield to the American rule for the life of lay people: *Pay, pray, obey*."[163] In another letter to Chenu, Gilson again protests against "rampant clericalism that wants to impose on us theological attitudes that are contrary to tradition."[164]

The second issue is the Americanization of the new theology and, beyond it, of religious life itself. Gilson raised this point in the foreword of *Les Tribulations*:

> Over many years I have developed the routine of a three-month stay in the United States and Canada. Recently, the stay confronted me with a new situation. Returning from the U.S., Georges Duhamel once summed up his impressions in a book entitled *Scenes from Future Life* [*Scènes de la vie future*]. He attempted to make us aware that America's today could well

160 Letter from Fr. Yves Congar to Étienne Gilson, October 24, 1967, SMCA.

161 Letter from Fr. Marie-Dominique Chenu to Étienne Gilson, October 3, 1966, SMCA.

162 Étienne Gilson, *The Tribulations of Sophia*, 100.

163 Letter from Étienne Gilson to Fr. Marie-Dominique Chenu, April 7, 1967 APDF.

164 Letter from Étienne Gilson to Fr. Marie-Dominique Chenu, June 7, 1967 APDF.

> become our own tomorrow. The book's naive provincialism and haste to disapprove of all foreigners who change its [France's] customs annoyed me, but some of its predictions have come to pass. We are being Americanized before our very eyes."[165]

On this point, Gilson recalled the crisis of the priesthood, the marriage of priests, the naturalization of religion, the liturgical and creedal "revolutions" that he had first perceived in North America. He also cited, as we have seen, the position of Cardinal Léger, a leading figure both in the North American episcopacy and in the demand for intellectual renewal of the Church. The news that Gilson gave Maritain about North America in 1966 was explicit:

> Not everything is about the pill and of the marriage of priests... that women should read the gospel in a chapel in Toronto and, as regards doctrine, one would say that hundreds of priests have become aware that they never believed in anything. Fundamentally, this is the old, eternal naturalism that is coming to life. People do not want to *believe* anything any more but to know it or, in any case, to have opinions. Moreover, the opinions that one hears being offered are naive or frankly absurd, especially in a country like America, where we are only at the stage of discovering old modernism, with its god who is change, its cult of evolution, and other worn out twaddle.[166]

A colloquium on "Theology of Renewal," introduced by Cardinal Léger,[167] took place at Gilson's Institute of Mediaeval Studies in 1967.[168] Given

165 Étienne Gilson, *The Tribulations of Sophia*, 4.

166 Letter from Étienne Gilson to Jacques Maritain, December 29, 1966, *Correspondance*, 230–32.

167 Cardinal Paul-Émile Léger, "La théologie de renouveau de l'Église," in *La théologie du renouveau*, Laurence Shook, Guy Bertrand, editors, Montreal: Fides-Cerf, 1968, volume I, 7–20: "The Church has changed its ways of expressing the Christian mystery with our mental categories.... Nowadays, we too easily forget the scandal provoked by that genius among his contemporaries. Thomas Aquinas innovated, but his audacity merited the name of renovation, because, without losing a speck of revealed truth, Thomas's renovation crystalized a whole effort of theological renovation and corresponded to the demands of his century. This is the sort of audacity that we need nowadays again. Is this to say that simple translation or even transposition of Aquinas into the registers of contemporary thought can be considered the substance of the renovation that the Church must implement quickly to respond to the questions of the contemporary world? I do not think so. Much more will be necessary.... Sooner or later, the theologians must work as a team and organize research laboratories just as chemists and biologists do" (11–12).

168 Fr. Marie-Dominique Chenu, in a letter of June 6, 1967 to Gilson, APDF, emphasizes that the conference should take place at Gilson's home. "After a long resistance, I yielded to the invitation, because of the appeal to your friendship. In fact, my memory is going to recapitulate the title, the place, and the participants in the colloquium, a page in Catholic thinking was in the process of being turned.

The third question that Gilson posed regarded Pope Paul VI's place in the new age of theology. Gilson concurred with some of Paul VI's speeches. Notably we can recall the address in 1965, when the pope diagnosed an "abdication of intelligence, which tends to destroy the traditional doctrine of the preambles of faith" and in which he attempted to dispel the mistrust of some believers in regard to the "certainties belonging to philosophical wisdom."[169] Throughout *Les Tribulations* there are many references to Paul VI:

> But, if what the priest says is not believable for the layman, he becomes troubled. Is he the victim of prejudices that the Church herself asks him to reject? Or is the priest in the vanguard of that cry for novelty that blinds him to the true meaning of the message he has the mission of transmitting? If there is an arbiter, where is he? . . . . I see only one answer to that. The only effective remedy to the malaise is to assign again a place of honor to the traditional theology that Pope Paul VI has urged us to respect, follow, and advocate.[170]

Gilson's last word in *Les Tribulations* is an "Amen" to the words of the Supreme Pontiff at the opening of the Year of Faith in 1967. It must be emphasized how much this new age of Catholic philosophy is structured in depth around the acceptance or rejection of Paul VI's thinking. Louis Bouyer explained in what sense, after having been the progressives' great hope when he was still only Cardinal Montini and after having for some time been given the benefit of the doubt, Paul VI was re-classified as a conservative.[171] Hans Kung labeled Paul VI a kind of Vatican Hamlet in his *Memoirs*, though acknowledging in him some intellectual merits.[172] Fr. Chenu was also very critical of Paul VI, confiding to Fr. Congar:

> Despite the stupidity, clumsiness, and childishness, I am not a pessimist, and I regret that every other Wednesday Paul VI subjects us to clouds of

a whole slice of your friendship—among several—with joyful acknowledgment. . . . We will meet there, at your house!

169 Pope Paul VI, Address to the Sixth Thomist Congress, September 10, 1965, *La Documentation catholique*, October 1965, columns 1747–50,

170 Étienne Gilson, *The Tribulations of Sophia*, 118–19.

171 Louis Boyer, *La décomposition du catholicisme* (Paris: Aubier Montaigne, 1968), 19.

172 Hans Küng, *Mémoires. Mon Combat pour la Liberté* (Paris: Novalis-Cerf, 2006), 399–401.

> anxiety, partly justified, but partly the effect of fear and of authoritarian faith. By contrast, his intrepidness in the ecumenical terrain continues.[173]

> Very dear friend, here is the passage from Paul VI on "chronolatry" that I mentioned to you. It strikes me as painful, not just because of its abruptly unilateral character, but because of its misshapen form and platitudinous vocabulary. I am afraid that in this way and henceforth, one of Paul VI's intellectual characteristics will be tainted. This includes his position in *Humanae Vitae*.[174]

Les Tribulations criticized the weakening of the basis of theology. By rejection of metaphysics; by denying philosophical pluralism and yet demanding it; by ideological rejection of Thomism: "It is their time that refuses to dialogue with Thomists. It is not Thomists who refuse to dialogue with their time."[175] And by anti-intellectualism: "Whereas a Thomist agrees to let each person go toward God in the best way he or she can, the others do not want to let us go toward God according to the way that Thomas recommends and that the Church prefers. Their anti-Thomist intolerance is rooted in a radical anti-intellectualism. It conforms perfectly to personal salvation but not to the Peace of Wisdom."[176] The question posed by Gilson is again and always that of the place of philosophy in regard to theology. He was in agreement on this point with Maritain, who wrote:

> It seems to me that at the origin of the spiritual weakness shown by so many good fathers, there is the idea that, since philosophy is only an *ancilla* or instrument, theology can and even ought to employ any old concocter of concepts, according to the moment and one's convenience. An epistemology of theology is what is missing.[177]

173 Letter from Fr. Marie-Dominique Chenu to Fr. Yves Congar, December 15, 1967, "Papiers Congar," APDF.

174 Letter from Fr. Marie-Dominique Chenu to Fr. Yves Congar, August 27, 1968, "Papiers Congar," APDF.

175 Étienne Gilson, *The Tribulations of Sophia*, 18.

176 Étienne Gilson, "Plaidoyer pour la servante," paper presented at the International Theology Conference in Toronto, summer 1967, published as "Pour la servante" in the collection *La théologie de renouveau*, vol. I, 61–72; re-published in Étienne Gilson, *L'athéisme difficile*, (Paris: Vrin, 1979), 75–95; see 91.

177 Letter from Jacques Maritain to Étienne Gilson, June 16, 1967, *Correspondance*, 239.

In the summer 1967 colloquium, Gilson devoted his contribution, titled "Plea for the handmaiden" to this issue: "Perhaps we expect more services from the handmaiden than she can perform, particularly given the circumstances in which we force her to work."[178] Relations between philosophers and theologians were reconstructed according to the issues. In spring 1967, de Lubac indicated to Gilson his agreement about "mass liturgies."

> Your little book about *Mass Society and Its Culture* arrived at the same time as your letter. I immediately devoured the last chapter. Do I have to tell you how much it satisfied me? May you be heard this time on the translation of the *Credo*. What makes my hope fragile is not the obstinacy of a small group of translators who admit practically no criticism. It is that I observe the same thing as you: the indifference of those who could and ought to react.[179]

In 1968, Henri de Lubac confided his perplexity to Congar: "Yes, it is an effort for me to understand certain new requests and sympathize with them, all the more in that it is necessary to sort things within a torrential movement, to avoid letting oneself be swept away. In times of crisis, everything is mixed up first. Despite everything, the Apostle tells us, 'Do not extinguish the spirit.' But it is hard to discern."[180] *Les Tribulations de Sophie* wanted to contribute to this difficult discernment through negation and not without bitterness, but with a clear grasp of the task's difficulty. What theology should be constructed if we renounce the contribution of medieval philosophy?

DE SENECTUTE

After the publication of *Les Tribulations de Sophie*, the philosopher began to withdraw from the ecclesiastical battle. In his old age, he had a strong feeling of representing a lonely rear guard, someone apprehended in the act of being out of date. After his eightieth birthday, he had the impression that the effort of his whole intellectual life had been consumed by this postconciliar spirit that he labeled "neo-Modernism," with its portion of defrocked priests and apostates, and annihilated by the rupture between theology and philosophy.

178 Étienne Gilson, "Plaidoyer pour la servante," in *L'athéisme difficile*, 77.

179 Letter from Fr. Henri de Lubac to Étienne Gilson, May 18, 1967, *Lettres de Monsieur Étienne Gilson au Père de Lubac*, 168–69.

180 Letter from Fr. Henri de Lubac to Fr. Yves Congar, April 20, 1968, "Papiers Congar," APDF.

Within the French Church, Gilson, like de Lubac but better off, complained of lacking any influence within the episcopate. His correspondence had a tone of lamentation: "Since the majority of the hierarchy is against the ideas we defend, there is no reason for our books to sell. Furthermore, as for me, I am finished. I do not consider myself obliged to fight for a Church that does not want me as a soldier."[181] Gilson's friends provide background. In a letter from Jean Laloy about *Les Tribulations* we read: "What can be done? I have tried to speak to certain bishops. They say that you are right and do nothing. It is a very strange situation. Thank you in any case for sounding the alarm."[182] Let us add that on occasion Gilson criticized certain bishops by name and in particular the cardinal archbishop of Paris, Maurice Feltin (1883-1975). In the last chapter of *La société de masse et sa culture*, the archbishop was attacked by Gilson for having defined the new means of communication as "sacraments of public opinion:" "Only priests can dedicate as fervent a cult to the profane and withdraw so far from the limits of naivete."[183] Again, "The Hierarchy and the Orders had already broken down at the time of the Reformation.... But that had no relation to the rotting of a great tree on the spot, which we witness today. What frightens me is that, in private, eminent dignitaries will lament to me what they lack the will to oppose in public."[184] "The episcopacy seems to be in complete disintegration," he wrote in 1971.[185]

In 1971, in a document presented to a plenary session of the French bishops, Bishop Robert Coffy took note of the exhaustion of classical metaphysics. The bishop of Gap and future cardinal archbishop of Marseilles underlined the change of paradigm:

> A large number of fundamental concepts of the classical philosophy that Christian doctrine has utilized to formulate itself seems to have lost the power for our contemporaries that they used to have to structure a coherent vision of the world that would be common to all minds. This is the case for the concepts of substance, form and matter, character, infused virtue. The same goes for the theory of causes that expressed the efficacy of the sacraments. We are not dealing with a question about the appearance of

181 Letter from Étienne Gilson to Augusto Del Noce, May 8, 1968, *Caro collega et amico*, 162.

182 Letter from Jean Laloy to Étienne Gilson, October 12, 1967, SMCA.

183 Étienne Gilson, *La société de masse et sa culture* (Paris: Vrin, 1967), 145.

184 Letter from Étienne Gilson to Jean de Fabrègues, November 10, 1967, CHSP.

185 Letter from Étienne Gilson to Jean de Fabrègues, February 28, 1971, CHSP.

> revealed truth but of re-interpretation. . . . Christianity finds itself constrained to make a critical reflection and a re-interpretation under the risk of appearing to be, not a false system, but, what is worse, a system devoid of falsehood or truth, an unreal system.[186]

This is a serious point. But be that as it may, given the lack of support for Gilson in France, he, who was already Roman in many senses, became still more so, In August 1968, after the appearance of the encyclical *Humanae Vitae*, which Gilson explained, was a "legitimate prolongation" of the great encyclicals of Leo XIII, he published in the *Osservatore Romano* and in *La France catholique* a statement of support for Pope Paul VI.[187] "One of the great foundations of Leo's thinking is that one cannot sin against God without violating nature. . . . We can expect everything from the Church, especially pardon for our sins, but never approval of sin." A letter to Fr. de Lubac makes it clear how much Gilson revered the pope:

> The thought of paying Paul VI a visit would never enter my head, and maybe that's wrong, because this man of God, endowed with a prophet's soul, as you have said of him with perfect justice, could well be, at the same time, in great need of both comfort and simple human affection; and wouldn't comfort and affection help to make up for the indignities with which he is deluged—indignities that even some of his sons shower on him.[188]

He repeated his expression of support for the pope with Edmond Michelet, François Mauriac, Olivier Lacombe, Stanislas Fumet, Gabriel Marcel, and André Latreille in a letter published in *Le Monde* on December 18, 1968, reproduced in an article of P. Wenger in *La Croix* on the same day:

> Most Holy Father, at the close of this year of 1968, we wish to express our gratitude to you for the profession of faith as well as for all of the teachings in which you have affirmed the principles of faith and of Catholic discipline. We declare to you our sadness and scandal in the face of attacks against your person and your teaching. . . . We state the anguish of

186 Bishop Robert Coffy, *Église signe de salut au milieu des hommes* (Paris: Le Centurion, 1972), 22–23.

187 Étienne Gilson, *Osservatore Romano*, August 24, 1968, 4; *France catholique*, August 30, 1968.

188 Letter from Étienne Gilson to Henri de Lubac, September 3, 1938, *Letters of Étienne Gilson to Henri de Lubac*, 156.

> the Christian people in seeing the admirable effort for renovation of the Church, inaugurated by the Council and courageously continued subsequently, compromised by a small minority of agitators, clergy and laity, who aspire to dictate to the Church and everywhere sow trouble and doubt.

La France catholique reproduced the document on the front page on December 27, 1968, and January 3, 1969, and noted the thousands of signatures as "a burst from the Christian people." The initiative gave "great satisfaction to the Holy Father"[189] and provoked a curse from the Comité d'Action pour la Révolution dans l'Église: "When the hierarchical structures of the Church creak, it is not Christ who moans, it is the Grand Inquisitor. For the latter, Christ is only a nuisance, good to take to the police station with a dozen rabid people."[190]

Paul VI was familiar with Gilson's work. He had received Gilson in 1965 in the Vatican,[191] and quoted him in January 1966 in an address to diplomats.[192] In Paul VI's letter *Lumen Ecclesia* addressed to the Master General of the Dominican Order about the contemporary importance of St. Thomas, he also recalled Gilson's works, notably the sixth edition of *Le Thomisme* and the 1932 Gifford lectures [*The Spirit of Medieval Philosophy*].[193] A letter to the philosopher in 1975 would soothe 'old Gilson's' bitterness, as he insistently recalled that we must not forget the lessons of history.

The philosopher despaired about social developments. Society, university, morality—everything was decaying. When the survivor of Verdun commented upon the events of May 1968, he lamented the violent demonstrations.[194] In the context of the debates of the Veil Law, legalizing abortion, Gilson commented to a Canadian friend in 1974: "French society is falling apart more and more. Legalization of abortion, which is nothing less than legalization of murder, is something inconceivable that, however, is about

189 Letter from Henri Rollet to Edmond Michelet, March 10, 1969, Archives Michelet.

190 Open Letter to the Pope with sixteen signatures, composed by the Comité d'Action pour la Révolution dans Église, December 22, 1968, Archives Michelet.

191 There is a photograph of Pope Paul VI and Gilson dated only 1965, testifying to the meeting, Archives Vrin.

192 Address of Pope Paul VI to members of the diplomatic corps, Saturday, January 8, 1966, *La Documentation catholique*, number 1464, columns 279–284.

193 See Georges Cottier, "*Le Paysan de la Garonne* et la lettre *Lumen Ecclesiae* de Paul VI," in *Montini, Journet, Maritain: Une famille d'esprit* (Brescia: Pubblicazioni dell'Istituto Paolo VI, 2000), 172–95.

194 Letter from Étienne Gilson to Fr. Marie-Dominique Chenu, September 11, 1968, APDF.

to happen shortly. The murder of old people could just as well be legalized. Perhaps we will see it."[195]

According to Étienne Borne,[196] Gilson, "the last Christian philosopher" because of his exceptional longevity, became a solitary butte on the landscape of philosophy after Maritain's death in April 1973. "So to speak," Gilson explained, "there are no more philosophers but rather rhetoricians who want philosophy to be such that they can talk about it. Their ignorance of its history is perhaps connected to their fear that if they knew what others have said, it would keep them from inventing."[197] Until the end of his life, Gilson held to the dialectic of old and new. "To grow old is to accustom oneself to be dead. I have nothing more to say," Gilson wrote again to Gouhier in July 1973. "All in all, I no longer think.... Besides, my silence in no way deprives of anything those for whom I could still speak. I know now that I have nothing new to say, except that what is old, when it is true, should not be forgotten under the pretext that it is no longer new."[198]

On the ecclesial level, Gilson took refuge in caustic humor and flashes of wit. He wrote to Fr. McCorkell that he did not recognize the Church in which he was born and where he was baptized. It was impossible for him to follow the mass that priests said. The only thing to do with people of his age was to let them die and make room for another generation that perhaps will not be as bad as it seems to his generation.[199] "I am content to end my life in the Church of my childhood, while someone celebrates in front of me a semi-Lutheran Meal without even the dignity of a Reformation liturgy."[200]

Gilson died on September 19, 1978 at the Auxerre hospital complex. The Vicar general of the Auxerre diocese, Denis Poinsot, presided at his funeral in the Cathedral of Saint-Étienne. Fr. Chenu, members of the Académie française, and many religious attended. Gilson was buried beside Thérèse in the Melun North Cemetery in a very simple ceremony. Fr. Chenu said the

195 Letter from Étienne Gilson to Madelaine Thibaudeau, April 3, 1974, SMCA.

196 Étienne Borne, "Stature d'Étienne Gilson," *La Croix*, September 22, 1978, 10.

197 Letter from Étienne Gilson to Henri Gouhier, July 28, 1967, Archives Gouhier.

198 Letter from Étienne Gilson to Henri Gouhier, July 29, 1973, Archives Gouhier.

199 Letter from Étienne Gilson to Fr. Edmund McCorkell, December 1, 1968, SMCA.

200 Letter from Étienne Gilson to Jean de Fabrègues, February 28, 1971, Archives Fabrègues, CHSP.

final prayer.[201] The pastor and parishioners of Vermenton, Gilson's village in Burgundy, declared: "He was a Christian with roots in the Church's long tradition, someone who was humble and courageous in faith, with great spiritual discernment.... He was a modest person, one among others, faithful to common prayer and the Eucharist in the little Sunday gatherings. He was also a man for whom prayer to the Virgin Mary counted a great deal."[202]

ASYMMETRIC IMPACT

Acceptance of Gilson since his death seems to vary in two ways: some appreciate that he was very Catholic and very Roman, to the neglect of Gilson's personal trajectory. He certainly was Catholic and Roman, but he was also something else. But what works by Gilson are still read in faculties of history, philosophy, and theology? What is read in France and abroad? How are his works used and critiqued? Who *recovers* him? For the Christian world, it would be necessary to undertake a careful inquiry to examine Gilson's reception in the universities, the monasteries, and the works of Christian intellectuals to this point. The same should be undertaken in regard to secular universities. Without archives and an established corpus of work, answers are difficult. But the question ought to be asked in order to measure the low point between the crests of waves, to trace intellectual genealogies and penetrate varying cultural strategies.[203]

It would appear that the postconciliar moment in France has seen a weak influence of Gilson upon the generation of clergy and students in the process of being educated. In 1978, Jean-Luc Marion lamented that his generation had "arrived late," that it had not had more access to the master's work.[204] The "1968 generation" proudly ignored the old Gilson. The few normal school philosophers who read Gilson, such as Jean-Luc Marion himself, had seri-

201 Laurence Shook wrote a description of the Mass, "Etienne Henry Gilson (1884–1978)," *Mediaeval Studies* (Toronto) 41 (1979): vii–viii.

202 *Église dans l'Yonne*, no. 18, October 7, 1978, 330.

203 The 2013 publication of the translation by a "monk of Fontgombault" of Gilson's *Dieu et la philosophie* by Éditions Petrus et Stella, with a preface by Rémi Brague, is triply interesting: for the translation, the place of publication, and the author of the preface.

204 Jean-Luc Marion, "Le découvreur d'un continent," *Le Monde*, October 7, 1978: "There is no question that we must hail Étienne Gilson as one of the renovators of Thomism, a powerful and original thinker, someone to whom the French university owes much of its greatness. But for the generation that has entered philosophy only in the last ten years, that did not count—rather it was denied us."

ous reservations.[205] Jean-Robert Armogathe told how, "as a young student working for his *license*, he "often encountered the old teacher in his office in the basement of Librairie Vrin. At the age of eighty he had lost nothing of his freshness, critical sense, and above all intellectual curiosity."[206]

Gilson's friends tried to show the "topicality" of his thought in May 1979 during a two-day meeting at the Collège de France.[207] Despite the success of the event attended by an audience of two hundred, according to a witness (including in no special order Henri de Lubac, Yves Congar, Marie-Dominique Chenu, Jean-Robert Armogathe, and Henri Gouhier, to name only a few), Gilson studies did not pick up speed, despite hopes expressed a the time. We have to wait until 2009 to witness the birth of the International Étienne Gilson Society in Poland and the United States under the direction of Peter Redpath, in the perceptible absence of any philosophers from the French university system. In France, in the 1970s and 1980s, Michel Foucault began to publish his *Histoire de la Sexualité* [*History of Sexuality*]. Sartre and Raymond Aron went to Vietnam to observe and "save" the boat people. The magazine *Commentaire* was founded the year of Gilson's death. In the same period, Michel de Certeau published his book on the possessed of Loudun. The sample is brief, but it was obviously not a propitious moment for reading or re-reading Étienne Gilson. There was a slow erosion of his influence within the University system and at the Collège de France. "Yes, Tircis, it is time to retire." Gilson wrote in 1969.[208] In his classic work *Memory, History, Forgetting* (first French edition, Paris: Seuil, 2000), Paul Ricoeur cited dozens of authors and omitted Gilson. In France, Gilson is one of the forgotten figures of his generation's intellectual history. There is a Maurice Halbwachs

205 Jean-Luc Marion, "Le découvreur d'un continent," had great praise: "Gilson discovered a continent: medieval philosophy." "He definitely changed the practice of the history of philosophy." "To begin to speak after death belongs only to authentic philosophers." But there is underlying criticism that concerns notably the reading of Heidegger, "so oddly discussed by Gilson."

206 Jean-Robert Armogathe, introduction to *Gilson et Descartes à l'occasion du centenaire de La Liberté chez Descartes et la théologie*, ed. Daniel Arbib and Francesco Marrone, Examina philosophica, "Quaderni di Alvearium" (Lecce: ClioEdu, 2015), 6.

207 *Étienne Gilson et nous, la philosophie et son histoire, actualités de la pensée d'Étienne Gilson, 28–29 mai, 1979* (Paris: Vrin, 1980), contributors: Henri Gouhier, Jean-Luc Marion, Marie-Thérèse d'Alverny, Jean-François Courtine, Maurice de Gandillac, Pierre Hadot, Pierre Aubenque, Paul Vignaux, Marie-Dominique Chenu, Geneviève Rodis-Lewis, and others. There is an account of the event in the report by Charles Wenin, "Actualité de la pensée d'Étienne Gilson (Paris: 28–29 mai, 1979)," *Revue philosophique de Louvain* 78, no. 40 (1980): 590–594.

208 Letter from Étienne Gilson to Fr. Marie-Dominique Chenu, September 1, 1969, APDF. The allusion is to Racan's *Pastorale*.

Auditorium at the Collège de France and a Marc Bloch Room at the Sorbonne. Marc Bloch University is in Strasbourg. There are CNRS research centers named after Koyré, Mauss, and Durkheim, and there are Raymond Aron and Lucien Febvre Rooms at the EHESS [School for Advanced Studies in the Social Sciences] in Paris. Quai François Mauriac is in Paris. To our knowledge, one would look in vain for a Gilson space in the French university world.

By contrast, Gilson's acceptance by the successors of Pope Paul VI is quite remarkable. To be sure, for the historian, it testifies to an extraordinary reduction in potential readership of a professor at the Sorbonne and Collège de France, who hoped precisely to occupy a middle ground. Yet, John Paul II mentioned Gilson's work several times. In the general audience of September 12, 1979, he took up the Gilsonian theme of the metaphysics of Exodus, "I am who am." In 1992, by means of a telegram from Cardinal Sodano, John Paul conveyed "with all his heart his apostolic blessing" to the organizers, speakers, and participants in the colloquium on Gilson at the Collège de France, organized by Géry Prouvost:

> Informed about the colloquium to be held in Paris, October 9 and 10, on the reception of the thought of Étienne Gilson, the Holy Father expresses his warmest wishes for the success of its work. He desires that the thought of this man of culture and faith be ever better known, a person who was able notably to reveal medieval thought to many students as a rich source of philosophy. Today, his spiritual heirs have the mission of continuing to open up their contemporaries' understandings to metaphysics, as he himself did for generations of readers and listeners.[209]

In the encyclical *Fides et Ratio*, John Paul II indicated John Henry Newman, Antonio Rosmini, Jacques Maritain, Edith Stein, and Étienne Gilson as "significant examples of a process of philosophical enquiry which was enriched by engaging the data of faith." The pope continued: "One thing is certain: attention to the spiritual journey of these masters can only give greater momentum to both the search for truth and the effort to apply the results of that search to the service of humanity. It is to be hoped that now and in the future there will be those who continue to cultivate this great

209 Telegram from Cardinal Sodano to Géry Prouvost, September 5, 1992, Bibliothèque et archives du Collège de France.

philosophical and theological tradition for the good of both the Church and humanity" (*Fides et Ratio,* paragraph 74, Boston, Pauline Media, 1998, 93-94).

Étienne Gilson and Joseph Ratzinger met in Germany at the end of the 1950s. In 1959, Ratzinger, who completed a thesis on St. Bonaventure, wrote to Gilson to convey his thanks and "great respect." "As a student I already read your works with the greatest enthusiasm. They were a source of knowledge and joy."[210] It would be necessary to scrutinize Ratzinger's thesis on St. Bonaventure's theory of history on this point and acknowledge in what sense he testifies to his debt to Gilson, while showing at the same time his reserve in regard to certain positions defended by him.[211] In an interview on September 12, 2008, Benedict XVI again indicated: "I had very good personal relations with Étienne Gilson and Henri-Irénée Marrou. Accordingly, I really had a very deep, personal, enriching contact with the great theological and philosophical culture of France." The contrast between the relative flourishing of Maritain studies and the paucity of Gilson studies in France is another indication of a truncated acceptance of Gilson.

210 Letter from Joseph Ratzinger to Étienne Gilson, September 13, 1959, FG, SMCA: "Hoffentlich ist darin trotz einiger Verschiedenheiten in der Aufassung deutlich geblieben wieviel ich Ihren Werken verdanke, die ich schon als Student mit grösser Begeisterung gelesen habe, und die für mich eine Quelle der Belehrung und Freude geblieben sind. In aufrichtiger Verehrung und Hochachtung bin ich, Ihr ergebener, Joseph Ratzinger."

211 Joseph Raztinger, *La théologie de l'histoire de saint Bonaventure*, trans. Robert Givord (Paris: PUF, 1988), 42 (for Ratzinger's debt to Gilson) and 20, 26, 38, 179 (for the disputed points). The thesis was published in German with the title *Die Geschictstheologie des Heiligen Bonaventura* (Münich: Verlag Schnell und Steiner, 1959). [Translator: Available in English as *The Theology of History in St. Bonaventure*, trans. Zachary Hayes (Chicago: Franciscan Herald Press, 1971 and 1989). See, for example, on the one hand, p. 85: "This conviction of the sign-character of the entire creation is the root of the Bonaventurian symbolism of creation which Gilson has beautifully described in his book on Bonaventure." On the other hand, p. 133: "We must realize (more than Gilson has done) that the elaboration of this ideal of wisdom in Bonaventure is not at all self-evident."]

Conclusion
Gilson the Historian

So far as I am concerned, I am thoroughly disgusted with my Gifford Lectures. There is a very great difference between intellectual and biological procreation. Both are painful, but mothers are very fond of their children as soon as they are born, whereas we are usually perfectly dissatisfied with our books as soon as they are written.[1]

To conclude this essay without returning again to numerous questions raised and left unanswered, we would like to analyze, not Gilson the philosopher polished with theology (that is a prey to hunt elsewhere), but Gilson the historian. The fundamental intuitions of historical method, as he conceived it, seem to us to be a foundation for Gilson the philosopher, to guarantee, more than Thomistic philosophy does, "the unity of his being,"[2] and "the tranquil strength"[3] as well as the intellectual loyalty of his political and

1 Letter from Étienne Gilson to Ralph Barton Perry, August 19, 1932, Harvard University Archives.

2 We take Jean Lacroix's term to change his perspective. Jean Lacroix, "Un grand existant," *Le Monde*, September 22, 1978, 23: "It is in Thomistic thought that Gilson discovered this unity of his being. To take note of existence is the beginning as well as the foundation of all philosophical wisdom."

3 Jacques Maritain, preface to *Étienne Gilson, Philosophe de la Chrétienté*, 10.

ecclesiastical commitments. What is the secret of this Gilsonian "tranquil strength"?[4] As a good reader of Augustine, he seems to whisper "be a loving historian and do what you will." "We did not study history to free ourselves from the past, but to save from nothingness the whole past that would drown in it without history. We did it so that what without history would no longer even be past should be reborn to existence in this unique present outside of which nothing exists. In order that this human should exist again in his individual, concrete complexity, it is enough to know him. To enrich ourselves with his substance, it is enough to love him," Gilson writes in the conclusion of *Heloise and Abelard*.[5] According to Gilson, only love, faithfulness to oneself, and the sense of continuity permit one to create and carry out the work of a historian. Gilson proposes a kind of chart for the historian with "a religious soul":

> In modern society, a religious soul is assigned a place at the front, not the back; firstly to prevent human beings from forgetting themselves. In this regard, curiously, it is still not understood why Catholicism became the champion of Hellenic and Roman civilization, to then carry it further, as once did the poet of the *Divine Comedy*, the architects of Notre Dame in Paris, and the philosopher of the *Summa Theologiae*. Authentic Catholic tradition is there, in the continuity and unshakeable fidelity to itself, which alone allows us to create. Accordingly, the historian must be the memory of this tradition and the awareness of this continuity. More than anywhere else, his role is limited to setting out the inventory of wealth that he would not have been able to define *a priori* without limiting it to his own horizon or reducing it to his own measure. The noblest prerogative of history—and this certainly is why the humanists of all times have cherished it—suffices for it to remain modestly itself so as to help great things to endure.[6]

In Gilson's work, the muse of history seemed to be simultaneously the source, the question to be resolved, and, so to speak, the plumb line. In his intellectual and religious journey, Gilson plunged into history. He "found himself confronted by Clio with the task of discovering the precise nature of theology."[7] He considered that "Clio alone made it possible for us to bring

4 Jean Lacroix, "Un grand existant," 23.

5 Étienne Gilson, *Héloïse et Abélard* (Paris: Vrin, 1938), 180.

6 Étienne Gilson, "Une heure avec . . .," *Les Nouvelles littéraires*, January 3, 1925, 1–2.

7 Étienne Gilson, *The Philosopher and Theology*, 5.

some order to this confusion by unraveling its origins. But she could not do it without calling into question several accepted historical attitudes."[8] "Once more, I am indebted to Clio for having rediscovered, at a much later date, this notion [of Christian philosophy] by then fallen into disuse among philosophers."[9] The homage thus rendered to history's virtues, *ordonnantes* and *revivificantes*, to "Clio alone," gallant Clio, was not a small thing from the pen of the historian of philosophy whose historical appetite was opened by "the bad gruel" served him as a student in the Sorbonne. "It was the time of the great philosophical famine. . . . We almost died. Anything at all was eaten to cheat hunger, at the risk of poisoning oneself."[10] There was the same shortage on the religious level, in Gilson's opinion, the same ignorance, the same poverty grounded in the "cult of incompetence." "Fr. Laberthonnière," he recalled, "did me much good with his charity and much harm with the disorder of his charity, which deep ignorance of Christian tradition always cut off from its object."[11]

This Gilsonian recourse to history in view of philosophy, appreciated in the highest degree by Umberto Eco,[12] does not fail to provoke reservations on the part of some very well-established guilds. Gilson is criticized both by historians, who find him too philosophical, elitist, and not historian and social enough, and by philosophers, who look in an inverted mirror and find him too much of a historian. Certain practitioners of these two disciplines, of very varied orientations, come together to consider that Gilson is too exclusively Thomist, or too much of an apologist, and that these vices corrupt the better part of his work. The history of philosophy, by the very nature of the object it attempts to examine, is certainly hybrid. In the criticisms formulated against Gilson, this hybrid character of principles is not at issue, but rather

8 Étienne Gilson, *The Philosopher and Theology*, 87.

9 Étienne Gilson, *The Philosopher and Theology*, 177.

10 Étienne Gilson, "Examen de conscience," *Vigile*, no. 2 (1932): 85–99.

11 Letter from Étienne Gilson to Henri Gouhier, October 31, 1932, published in *Revue thomiste* 94 (1994): 471.

12 Eco, *Écrits sur la pensée au Moyen Âge*, 1005. Eco establishes a typology of the Middle Ages. He has distinguished "ten manners of picturing the Middle Ages," "ten types" that are distinct, among which is "the Middle Ages of the *philosophia perennis*." In passing, he notes that these philosophical Middle Ages have been able "to progress in greatness through Étienne Gilson," before capturing Maritain, Pius XII, and Wojtyła, and concluding that "these Middle Ages present aspects of philological exactness and others of anti-historical dogmatism." For Eco, Gilson is clearly on the first side.

the passionate, committed manner of writing history that Gilson claims as such: "History is a weapon," he explains in *Nouvelles littéraires*, 1925, "a much more effective one and a discipline more committed to the present than is imagined when someone turns it into serene a but sterile contemplation of the past." "That is the bankruptcy of objective, disinterested history," answers the journalist.[13] And Gilson agrees and offers the well-known formula:

> There are no disinterested historians any more than there are impassive scholars. What matters is to know whether the passion that moves a historian is of a kind that impels him to the study of facts or rather that prevents him from perceiving them. Let us set aside the shoals of hatred and concern ourselves only with the most noble intellectual zeal.

Certain criticisms of Gilson's works dissolve with time, whereas others gain force, become sharper, or are neutralized. For example, the difference increases in the way Gilson is received by philosophers of the Sorbonne, of the Institute Catholique of Paris, and by historians within the sphere of influence of *Annales*.

In 1925, Jacques Maritain expressed his deep appreciation for the "magnificent" interview that Gilson gave to Frédéric Lefèvre in *Les nouvelles littéraires*. But Maritain also expressed critical observations on the subject of Gilson's "purely historicist position."[14] Blondel likewise reproached Gilson for historicism in the debate on Christian philosophy. "Gilson considers more or less Christianized systems or systems juxtaposed in history as closed concepts, each one in its precarious historical arrangement. Oh historicism! I moan at having to answer."[15] The issue was debated by Gilson and Blondel from the time of their first exchange in 1928: "Consequently, I am not enclosed in a historical empiricism that would lead to the conclusion that what has been will be. I believe that it is necessary to know what has been, in order to make that which-ought-to-be take place," Gilson tried to explain.[16] In the faculty of philosophy of Laval University in Quebec, Gilson was not

13 Étienne Gilson, "Une heure avec . . .," *Les Nouvelles littéraires*, January 3, 1925, 1–2.

14 Letter from Maritain to Frédéric Lefèvre, January 3, 1925, AM and FG, published at length in Gilson and Maritain, *Correspondance 1923–1971*, 22–23.

15 See Maurice Blondel's letter of March 17, 1931, to Auguste Valensin, quoted in the Gilson–de Lubac correspondence, *Letters of Étienne Gilson to Henri de Lubac*, 120. See likewise René Virgoulay, *Philosophie et théologie chez Maurice Blondel* (Paris: Cerf, 2002), 51, 61, 63, and so on. Blondel never stopped denouncing the inadequacy of Gilson's historical approach.

16 Letter from Étienne Gilson to Maurice Blondel, April 29, 1928, Fonds Maurice Blondel.

esteemed much more. Like Fr. Chenu, he was reproached for quickly fitting St. Thomas into a system of historical index cards that freed one from having to read the *Summa*.[17] "A little clan sees a dangerous germ of relativism and therefore of latent Modernism in the historical study of the Middle Ages and of St. Thomas."[18] Historicism is an ambiguous concept, and the concern for historicity easily turns into the sin of relativism according to certain censors. They think that the true has no history; only errors would be historical. Historicist historians of philosophy would consider history as a kind of visit to a fine museum, or rather to a beautiful ossuary; or as the critical examination of a *panta rhei* [all things change] where, by definition, nothing lasts. Gilson does not share such a conception of the history of philosophy. In 1925 he responded to Frédéric Lefèvre, "I refuse to write the history of ideas in function of their content alone. Therefore, I do not introduce historicism in metaphysics; I make an effort to avoid metaphysicism in history. That is completely different."[19] Metaphysicism, an even more ambiguous concept than historicism, as Gilson explained it in the interview cited, would be "to reduce thinkers to an interplay of philosophically incompatible abstract theses," to essentialize de-historified authors in the library of history.

Gilson himself readily denounced his colleagues at the Sorbonne as historicists. In his terminology, historicism denotes an exclusive concern with mental archeology, with the ambition no longer to philosophize but to secularize and bury metaphysics and thus to become peaceful cemetery guardians. In 1934 Gilson wrote in this sense in regard to several university reforms:

> The point is to completely secularize French thought. Therefore, the faculties of theology have been suppressed. Then, they have worked to gradually eliminate metaphysics, whose theological stench made the atmosphere unbreathable for well-formed minds. Nothing is easier than to get there. Replacing philosophy with history of philosophy is enough, the sure means, provided that this history is understood as a kind of mental archeology or catalogue of human errors. For it was not enough for this history to be "objective," that is to say, to be uninterested in what it narrated; it was also

17 See Michel, *La pensée catholique en Amérique du Nord*, chapter 3.

18 Letter from Fr. Marie-Dominique Chenu to Étienne Gilson, March 13, 1947, Archives Vrin.

19 Étienne Gilson, "Une heure avec . . .," *Les Nouvelles littéraires*, January 3, 1925, 1–2.

necessary to be critical, that is to say, to legitimize all the "affirmations of modern consciousness."[20]

In his memoirs in 1960, after emphasizing that there was no method of teaching either metaphysics or general philosophy, Gilson wrote in the same sense that it was necessary to find a way out:

> It was found in the history of philosophy. Why not learn from Plato, or Descartes, or any other great thinker of the past, the way to ask and answer metaphysical questions? . . . [Formerly], the historian of philosophy . . . found himself acting as the caretaker of the cemetery of dead metaphysicians.[21]

Gilson did not intend to confine himself to this archeological approach of the historian of philosophy, which consisted in examining fossil philosophies. This refusal brought some clashes with his Sorbonne colleagues. Gilson gave neither name nor exact date on this point—was it Léon Brunschvicg? André Lalande? Someone else? In any case, Jean Wahl, who did not deal with Gilson in his *Traité de la métaphysique*, only arrived at the Sorbonne in the second half of the 1930s, after Gilson's departure for the Collège de France. Whoever it may be, the charge, even anonymous, is cutting:

> When I had become a professor at the Sorbonne, one of them [my colleagues] requested my presence at an important conversation. He had been told that I took advantage of my teaching of the history of medieval philosophies to carry on religious propaganda. . . . The question left me flabbergasted. . . . But I have always thought that in order to teach any doctrine, a historian should present in the fullness of its intelligibility and how can he show that a philosophy is intelligible, without somehow justifying it? . . . Not knowing what to answer, I immediately offered to exchange at the first occasion my chair of the history of medieval philosophy for a chair of the history of modern philosophy. . . . The offer was neither accepted nor ever renewed, and the matter was dropped.[22]

20 Étienne Gilson, *Pour un ordre catholique*, 47–48.

21 Étienne Gilson, *The Philosopher and Theology*, 38: "My friend Professor Bush of Columbia University had a charming phrase to describe this avocation: mental archeology."

22 Étienne Gilson, *The Philosopher and Theology*, 34

In 1948, Maritain wrote the introduction to the volume *Étienne Gilson. Philosophe de la chrétienté*. The time was past when he suspected Gilson of historicism.

> Nothing is more full of meaning than the intellectual adventure in which, beginning as a historian, Gilson has journeyed as a philosopher and affirmed with ever greater vigor and clarity his capacity as a metaphysician. With that very thing he has turned the history of ideas toward its real nature, while showing in it an infinitely valuable instrument of detection and verification, and one completely indispensable to philosophy. The whole drama and the whole problem of history have been lived and overcome in Gilson's personal experience. [23]

Maritain then acknowledged the strictly historical virtues of Gilson, who worked without "antiseptic procedure . . . without phenolated acid, rubber gloves, gauze over his nose . . . as a realist historian," in some way a Péguyist, who touched the real with both hands, and whose realism provided philosophy the touchstone it needs.[24] "It is not only the unity and authority of your work that appears to me with singular intensity, it is also the inner light by which this great philosophical monument is itself illuminated, and that is a better light than that of pure reason, a sweet and penetrating light that shines before the altar of the living God."[25]

The diagnosis is not shared among historians. If we leave aside Henri-Irénée Marrou and Paul Vignaux, two filial figures already mentioned, the circle of *Annales* offers a fine observatory to examine Gilson's reception outside of the coterie of the French school of the history of Christianity, which gladly recognized Gilson as one of its own and one of its outstanding minds.

Marc Bloch and Lucien Febvre are notable examples of the complexity of Gilson's reception among the body of *lay* historians of the university. It has been said that Bloch and Febvre did not understand *Pour un ordre catholique* (1934), a work too philosophically and too religiously committed, even if Bloch did conclude his commentary on the tome by remarking how, with Gilson, he sat in biblical fashion in his tower, "inclined to treat our

23 Jacques Maritain, preface to *Étienne Gilson, Philosophe de la Chrétienté*, 7

24 Jacques Maritain, preface to *Étienne Gilson, Philosophe de la Chrétienté*, 10.

25 Letter of Jacques Maritain to Étienne Gilson, October 22, 1949, in Gilson and Maritain, *Correspondance 1923–1971*, 173.

pedagogical methods as whitened sepulchers."[26] These founders of *Annales*, who happily read the Dominicans Chenu and Congar,[27] nevertheless appreciated not only Gilson's historical works, but also the man himself for the objective services he rendered and the good will shown to their group. Gilson and Febvre were both war veterans and old colleagues at Strasbourg during the time of the University's re-opening. They met again at the Collège de France, elected less than a year apart. In Gilson's "sparkling" presence, Febvre narrated his meeting with Bloch, after one of the University of Strasbourg's inaugural sessions, and that moment of happy spontaneity, in which "we were joined together, moreover with coherent, selected elements in a beautiful bond of friendship and devotion."[28] In the collection of documents related to Febvre's election (February 1933), even though the two men were likely competitors, one feels that, for Febvre, Gilson was less a rival than a respected ally and an honorable alternative to Jacques Chevalier. "I do not wish, I cannot be a candidate against Gilson," sighed Febvre in 1930.[29] In March 1934, as a friendly "mahout,"[30] Gilson defended the case of Marc Bloch in the assembly of the faculty of the Collège de France and submitted to the administrator of the Collège de France Bloch's study entitled "Project for Teaching the Comparative History of European Societies."[31] It was to

26 Letter of Marc Bloch to Lucien Febvre, February 11, 1935, in Marc Bloch and Lucien Febvre, *Correspondance*, vol. 2, *1934–1937* (Paris: Fayard, 2003), 209.

27 Fouilloux, *Les catholiques et l'unité chrétienne*, 212.

28 Lucien Febvre, "Souvenirs d'une grande histoire: Marc Bloch et Strasbourg," in *Combats pour l'histoire*, 391.

29 Christophe Charle and Christine Delangle, "La campagne électorale de Lucien Febvre au Collège de France (1929–1932): Lettres à Edmond Faral," *Histoire de l'éducation* 34 (1987): 55: "I do not wish to be, I cannot be, a candidate against Gilson;" 58. "The Mauss supporters met and considered two candidacies of 'reconciliation,' mine and Gilson's. Ultimately, it seemed to them that Gilson, who was better situated to bite into the 'right,' would have a better chance than myself to win a majority. I did not contradict that. I did not know anything. . . . It only remained for me to congratulate Gilson. I sent my good wishes to him by this messenger."

30 Marc Bloch and Lucien Febvre, *Correspondance*, vol. 1, *1928–1933* (Paris: Fayard, 1994), 463.

31 Letter from Étienne Gilson to the administrator of the Collège de France on the creation of a chair of comparative history of European societies, February 18, 1934, 4 AP 461, Archives du College de France: "Sir, I have the honor of informing you that at the next session on March 18, I intend to request that the credits freed by the death of Camille Jullian should be devoted to the creation of a chair of comparative history of European society. I take the liberty of adding that, to my mind, Marc Bloch should be designated as the holder of this chair, if it is created. Please accept, Monsieur Administrator, the assurance of my respectful devotion." In the file 4 AP 461, along with Gilson's letter, we find Marc Bloch's "Project of Teaching of Comparative History of European Societies" as well as the minutes of the March 18 session (four pages): "The meeting was occupied by two motions. The order in which they were considered was decided by drawing

no avail, because the Assembly had to be adjourned without a decision, and in April 1934 the chair to which Bloch aspired was not endowed after the higher education budget reduction by the Doumergue government. Bloch and Febvre, however, showed Gilson deep gratitude for the public defense of Marc Bloch's credentials.

In depth, Gilson's support shows how much the three men were united on the level of their historiographic intuitions: international awareness, sense for the long view, care about comparison, deconstruction of chronological limits, transcendence of national frontiers, passionate study, appreciation for the Middle Ages. In Bloch's splendid expression, on the politico-religious plane, the Middle Ages could no longer be regarded as "an empire within an empire" and ought to be extended well beyond their physical limits, in analysis of the past with a view to better understand the present. "One must run the movie backwards here, precisely in order to grasp the changes themselves," wrote Bloch.[32] In *Rabelais* (1942), Lucien Febvre retained (which is no small matter) Gilson's teaching on the Franciscan origins of the author of *Gargantua*, against the theses of Abel Lefranc, one of their predecessors at the Collège de France, who saw Rabelais as an anti-clerical writer situated at the foundation of secularism.[33]— That earned Febvre supercilious reproaches from Marcel Bataillon, who esteemed that Febvre had "indulged too much in the direction of Gilson's erudite investigations."[34]

However, *Annales*' criticisms of Gilson developed immediately after the Second World War in a tone of mutual esteem. They centered on two volumes

lots. Étienne Gilson proposed to devote the available funds to the creation of a chair of comparative history of European societies. Antoine Meillet supported this proposal." The session was dramatic: next came the turn of the second proposal, for the support of a chair devoted to ancient national history, proposed by Fr. Henri Breuil, then Eugène Albertini, then Camille Matignon, who began to speak and dropped dead "a few seconds later in the midst of his colleagues." The faculty assembly was adjourned at that time.

32 Marc Bloch, "Projet d'un enseignement d'histoire comparée des sociétés européennes," February 1934, five pages plus bibliography, 4 AP 461, Archives du Collège de France.

33 Lucien Febvre, *Le problème de l'incroyance au XVIe siècle: La religion de Rabelais* (Paris: Albin Michel, 2003; 1st ed., 1942), see especially 145, 165–66, 168, 258–59.

34 Marcel Bataillon, "Le problème de l'incroyance au XVI siècle d'après Lucien Febvre," *Mélanges d'histoire sociale*, no. 5 (1944): 5–26: "Posterity can have good reasons to consider Rabelais an ancestor of modern secularist thinking. Certainly, some will reproach Lucien Febvre for having indulged too much in the direction of Gilson's erudite investigations on Rabelais the Franciscan and re-inserted Rabelais in the religious environment of his century, by having explained him too much by what preceded, by what surrounded him, and by not having listened to certain accents of triumphant novelty that perhaps transfigured the old expressions of irreverence."

in particular and were connected to a background argument about the definition of what history of ideas ought to be. In 1946 in an essay titled "Histoire des idées, histoire des sociétés, Une question de climat," a piece included in the famous work *Combats pour l'histoire* (1953),[35] Lucien Febvre reviewed Gilson's *La philosophie au Moyen Âge* (Paris: Payot, 1944). Febvre stressed that it was "a book of daily importance." He repeatedly claimed the title of "historian" in the course of the review. He also objected to Gilson's challenges to disruptions of continuity. "For Gilson . . . the history of medieval philosophy has no gap between the thirteenth and fourteenth centuries. . . . I understand some of his reasons of a philosophical nature. But as a historian I feel troubled."[36] Yet Febvre's "historical self," perhaps intimidated by the philosopher, disagreed with Gilson, not for building bridges between centuries and disciplines, but for not having built enough of them. Febvre wanted to establish a definite relationship, between history of ideas and history of societies, more integrated in some way:

> I am not speaking of primacy [of social history over history of ideas]. I speak of interaction. Or if one prefers, of climate. . . . Étienne Gilson has made an effort to erect some bridges, situated at good places, between the evolution of literature and that of philosophy in the Middle Ages. He was quite right. I believe that it would have been easy for him to throw up some other bridges between general political and economic evolution and the evolution of philosophy in the Middle Ages, which would have given all those who use his treatise an incomparable breadth of vision. . . . I certainly do not ask the historian of doctrines to reinvent himself as a historian of political and economic ideas. I ask him always to leave open a door for communication, through which the world of ideas may again grasp in our minds the contact that it quite naturally posed with the world of realities when it was alive.[37]

In 1954, in a review of Gilson's *Métamorphoses de la Cité de Dieu*, Febvre returned to the same line of thought, deepening and hardening it.[38] He began

35 Lucien Febvre, "Étienne Gilson et la philosophie du XIVe siècle," in *Combats pour l'histoire*, 284–88.

36 Lucien Febvre, "Histoire des idées, histoire des sociétés: Une question de climat," *Annales* 1, no. 2 (1946): 158–61.

37 Febvre, "Histoire des idées, histoire des sociétés," 161.

38 Lucien Febvre, review of *Les métamorphoses de la Cité de Dieu*, by Étienne Gilson, *Annales* 9, no. 3 (1954): 371–74.

sarcastically to complain about not having received the volume. "This work of Étienne Gilson is a powerful book. There is no need to say that the *Annales* did not receive it. The publishers are admirably sagacious: they send their products only to buyers known in advance as such." After having dealt with Gilson's publisher, d'Harpagon, Febvre assessed the breadth of the book's subject, its free tone, the infinite talent with which Gilson dealt with these metamorphoses. Febvre liked the volume's "manly conclusion." Once that was stated, Febvre could formulate the core of his thinking and pronounce reservations in the name of the old antagonism, according to him, between "historians' history and philosophers' history." He harshly criticized Gilson for not respecting "his historian neighbors," and even for being contemptuous in giving a schoolboy definition of history. Febvre over-analyzed the phrase "clearly, by its own nature, it [history] can only report the past"—which Gilson used in the preface of *The Métamorphoses*. [Translator: I cannot find this statement. Gilson does say, for instance, 'Here, history is only the raw material for philosophical reflection.'] Febvre read a "lack of respect" into that, an "odd point of view," a paradox, since this "executed history" is, he said, the very food of "the intellectual history" that Gilson wrote.[39]

Febvre then commented upon the quotation from Fustel de Coulanges that Gilson appropriated in the same criticized foreword: "History does not study only material facts and institutions. The real object of study is the human soul. History ought to aspire to know what this soul believed, thought, and felt in the different ages of the life of humankind." Febvre specified that he, like Gilson, subscribed to this proposition, "on the condition of not restricting the remark to the ancient world. It holds for all ages, and in our age for the very human beings who profess themselves to be free of the grip of a religion." Febvre's recommendation was extremely interesting, since precisely on this point, he connected with Gilson: it is not necessary to secularize history even if one is secularized and "free from the grip of a religion." Febvre then described the development of this historical labor through the centuries, from Saint Augustine to Auguste Comte, pointed out its strength and its gaps, and concluded that the "long voyage becomes a little short":

> I believe that our analysis has brought out sufficiently what is, for us, the inevitable defect of any book of this sort. The author flies from peak to peak from great minds to great minds. It is a classic history of ideas, an aristo-

39 Febvre, "*Les métamorphoses*," 373.

> cratic history of ideas. Yes, it is a powerful book, but with a strength that is obtained at the price of a rather crude simplification. The fact is that human history is not all in the interplay of thought.... That interplay has a strength that is owed to the completely exclusive, if not arbitrary, concentration of a powerful and lucid brain upon a single and unique category of mental activities, and that gladly lets everything drop that ordinary humans call "Life." Here, quite specially, "social Life."[40]

Was Gilson familiar with these passages? Did he reply to them anywhere? What would he have answered? Ready to admit his mistakes and to acknowledge what was right in someone else's position, would Gilson admit certain criticisms and certain suggestions? We seek the social in his works in vain. Keep doors open, build bridges, Febvre suggested? Certainly. All that would remain unspecific for Gilson, and doubtless he would have asked that there be an understanding about the sense of the exercise he undertakes: not history for history, but to think through as philosophers what is still *actual* in past philosophies and serves the present time. Absent the "social," is the history of ideas consequently aristocratic (according to Lucien Febvre's expression, with the haughtiness and disdain that the expression carries)? Is the term excessive as Febvre's interpretation of what history would be for Gilson? Elitist, textual, and even airy, since, according to Febvre, Gilson's tome "flies from peak to peak," even masculine and rather clerical are perhaps some adjectives that might suffice to describe this history of ideas. That said, at the Pontifical Institute of Mediaeval Studies in Toronto, Gilson fully intended to study medieval civilization in its entirety, in a setting where there could be a kind of division of tasks among the investigators.

On the other hand, in his scientific works, Febvre never attacked Gilson publicly on the question of apologetics. There was not a shadow of a quarrel

40 Febvre, "*Les métamorphoses*," 374. Let us note that in this evaluation, which is simultaneously favorable to Gilson and critical of an elevated history of ideas cut off from its social basis, the *Annales* review is fairly consistent. In this sense see Lucien Febvre, "Synthèses," *Annales* 9, no. 2 (1954): 248–57; Georges Duby, "Encore un histoire de philosophie," *Annales* 12, no. 4 (1957): 674–75, where the issue is to review a work of Jacques Chevalier, "which does not, however, dispense one from reading Étienne Gilson"; Jacques Le Goff, "Au Moyen Âge: Temps de l'Église et temps du marchand," *Annales* 15, no. 3 (1960): 417–33. Le Goff bases himself on Gilson's authority for the history of medieval philosophy. Last, see the two articles quoted in the introduction: Alain Boureau, "Des politiques tirées de l'Écriture: Byzance et l'Occident," *Annales* 55, no. 4 (July-August 2000): 879–87, sees a great "punctiliousness about ideological neutrality" in Gilson, but Catherine Köning-Pralong, "L'histoire de la philosophie médiévale depuis 1950: Méthodes, textes, débats," *Annales 64*, no. 1 (2009): 143–69, reverses the interpretation, considering Gilson as having constructed a work of apologetics.

on this point. Febvre, quoting Gilson's own words, emphasized how the latter tried to be a docile son of the Church. "Gilson's is a manly conclusion," Febvre noted again. "Evidently, coming from the pen of a Catholic like Étienne Gilson, it is subtle. But it is also courageous. Doesn't the intellectual development in Europe of 1953 seem to justify what the author of the defeat says about the 'lay' endeavors and 'temporal' thinking even by great minds?"[41] One would like to have more precision about what Febvre indicated here too vaguely.

Since the question of apologetics was posed to him, Gilson naturally displayed it in his fashion and enjoyed doing so. Thus, in his "Examination of Conscience" published in 1932 and fashioned as a dialogue between Gilson and a quasi-omniscient spiritual adviser, we read the challenge:

> —My dear friend, except for the style, this is a philosophical appendix to the *Genius of Christianity*, which you are in the process of writing. If that is what you want to do, why do you claim that you are not an apologist? You would do better to say so frankly.
>
> —If I say so, it will be objected that I am not a historian and that I falsify facts to draw a defense from them.
>
> —But why in heaven's name are you so obstinate in passing for a historian?
>
> —Because, if I am not a historian, I will never be an apologist.

Two decades later, in 1950, Gilson wrote rather lucidly to Fr. Marie-Michel Labourdette:

> "From the point of view of simple apologetics, neo-Scholastic philosophy . . . seems to me a failure. It has convinced no one. . . . In a few words, what I am saying is the experience of a whole life, and I am persuaded, perhaps wrongly, that it [neo-Scholasticism] is the wrong path. Faith has converted more philosophers to Thomism than Thomist philosophy has converted philosophers to the faith. Nothing suggests that this state of affairs has to change.[42]

41 Febvre, "*Les métamorphoses*," 371.

42 Letter from Étienne Gilson to Fr. Labourdette, September 26, 1950, published in *Revue thomiste* 94 (1994): 515.

Gilson's personal position is thus summed up: To be a historian with no view of deriving the tiniest apologetic either from history or philosophy would lack meaning and effectiveness. But Gilson admitted that he had great need of being a historian, establishing historical facts scrupulously, and letting the readers extract an apologetic from them if they need to and if they are able.

> —I could have studied medieval philosophy to draw an apologetics from it, and I will never prove that I did not do that. I could also have studied medieval philosophy as history and have found an apologetic at the end of my history, which I was not seeking but that I was glad to have found.
>
> —It has been observed that Christianity has no need of it.
>
> —I would like to hope so, but mine was so mediocre that this apologetic did it a great deal of good. The wealthy do not think enough about the poor. Besides, if my studies were for me and certainly will always be only an apologetics, nothing obliges those who do not need one to consider it as such. The apologetic here, in any case, would only be worth what the history is.[43]

Working on an intellectual biography is sometimes like climbing a mountain in the Alps. In the course of the outing, a new landscape appears; upon arrival at the summit or just at a pass, one gets a sense of the panorama, with its peaks, its rocky ridges, its alpine prairies, glaciers, and the neighboring ridges, and one guesses everything that might be seen after another ridge or another peak. In his volumes, articles, and correspondence, Gilson gave his views on many cultural, religious, Atlantic, and political questions during almost seven decades of national and international life, from the trenches of 1914 to May 1968, from famine in the Ukraine to the Cold War, from noisy Paris performances of a Mendelssohn concerto to the poetry of Pierre Seghers.... Gilson proposed a different path, one that was certainly complex and demanding, that led from the Modernist crisis to the emergence from the postconciliar crisis, from Fr. Laberthonnière to Benedict XVI.

Gilson was a university man intermittently involved in the City of Men, which for St. Bonaventure and for Gilson after him is only the "suburb of the City of God." Gilson spun out the Bonaventurian metaphor—*quoddam*

43 Étienne Gilson, "Examen de conscience," *Vigile*, no. 2 (1932): 85–99.

suburbium—from 1924 to the 1950s.[44] Without respite he committed himself to the City of God, whose sad metamorphoses he denounced unceasingly. The *Civitas Dei* is intimately tied to and yet distinct from the *Eccclesia Dei*, according to Gilson,[45] who, with the greatest respect for the ecclesiastical institution, sometimes judged that the City of God had been "confiscated," as it were, and "institutionalized" by the Church. Gilson's position on this sensitive and debated point of Augustinian ecclesiology is complex. Gilson responded by messenger to Fr. Congar, who essentially maintained *Civitas Dei sive Ecclesia* in a 1957 article:[46]

> In what concerns me personally, I cannot free myself from a sensation of discomfort in the face of this progressive confiscation of the concept of City of God, or perhaps better, in the face of its 'institutionalization' in a process over many centuries that seems to have reached its end. At bottom, what bothers me no longer seems to bother anyone else. We have lost the heavenly Jerusalem like the other one, with the difference that we do not even conserve its memory. I am certainly mistaken in worrying about it, because the Church is sufficient in everything, but it seems to me that we have lost something."[47]

Étienne Borne, in *La Croix*, elaborated: "An undaunted layman, Gilson was horrified by clericalism, about which he wrote ferociously during the *Sept* period. And it is necessary to be very ignorant and a little silly to turn Gilson, as will inevitably happen, into an out-of-touch witness of a period labeled triumphalist."[48]

44 On this point, see Étienne Gilson, *La philosophie de saint Bonaventure* (Paris: Vrin, 1924), 385. Gilson quotes chapter 4 of Bonaventure's *Soliloquium*: "De hoc exilio quoddam suburbium caelestis regni." This is likewise the concluding expression of Gilson's *Metamorphoses of the City of God*, trans. James Colbert (Washington, DC: The Catholic University of America Press, 2020), 235: "The end is what commands. The City of Man can only be built, in the shadow of the cross, as a suburb of the City of God."

45 There we find a larger question at the level of understanding St. Augustine. See Étienne Gilson, *Metamorphoses*, 46–47, 193.

46 Yves Congar, "*Civitas Dei* et *Ecclesia* in St. Augustine," *Revue des études augustiniennes* 3 (1957): 3–14. The article is extraordinary. Read especially pp. 9–11, where Congar acutely discusses the theses of Gilson, who, in his judgment, "is both right and wrong."

47 Letter from Étienne Gilson to Fr. Yves Congar, September 22, 1959, in "Papiers Congar," APDF.

48 Étienne Borne, "Stature d'Étienne Gilson," *La Croix*, September 22, 1978, 10.

Gilson was certainly remarkable, taken in the logic of the temporal, academic, ecclesial, and ecclesiological realms. It is also necessary to say that Gilson was a remarkably incomplete intellectual. He was not like Henri Bergson, the man of pure thought, nor like Jacques Maritain, the bridgehead of a network, not the man of a magazine like Emmanuel Mounier, neither an "intellectual committed" on all fronts nor a "committed spectator" according to Raymond Aron's odd expression. Gilson who, in a radio round table with Aron, claimed not to be the "spectator of any event" but on the contrary to be "unfortunately for me an actor in all events so much so that I have not had time to watch them,"[49] hardly referred to anti-Semitism in the 1930s, segregation in the United States, the Spanish Civil War, decolonization, the nuclear threat, and so on. More substantially, in his view of French tradition, Gilson left an astonishingly small place for the French Revolution, whose legacy he certainly claimed, though he greatly nuanced its perspective. He declared to his fellow members of the MRP, "Accordingly, we certainly have the right to take up as our own the three great watchwords of the French Revolution. We should restore to them the meaning that they had for a very long time before the Revolution, the meaning whose memory, to our misfortune and its own, seems to have been partially lost."[50] On French Radio, in January 1948, Gilson lamented that the Revolution was not accompanied by "its completely indispensable complement, a social and economic democracy."[51] In his writings, Gilson evoked the occurrence of the Revolution in the context of educational issues and of Canada, which precisely did not live the Revolution. Gilson cited several revolutionary authors—Robespierre, Condorcet—without placing them in the totality of events and quotations, and therefore in the continuity of centuries of French history. A contemporary of Diognetus and Stalin, Alcuin and Maritain, Roger Bacon and Comte, the Abbé of Saint-Pierre and Robert Schuman, of Thomas Aquinas, Dante, and Joseph McCarthy, Gilson navigated through the centuries, certain centuries, thinkers, certain thinkers, and questions yet to be resolved.

The vocabulary that Gilson employed and whose meaning he reloaded—Christendom, the Catholic order, and even the MRP—carried traces of the

49 Broadcast of December 29, 1949, "Un demi-siècle d'histoire du monde," Étienne Gilson, Raymond Aron, Jules Romains, Joseph Paul-Boncour, G. Bourgin, available through Inathèque.

50 Étienne Gilson, *Notre démocratie*.

51 Broadcast of January 5, 1948, "Perspectives intellectuelles," with Étienne Gilson, Salvador de Madariaga, D. Rousset, C. Levi, M. Prichette, and others, available through Inathèque.

golden age of "Catholic renewal," but had slight resonance with such contemporary political issues of our own time as communitarianism, cultural pluralism, secularist neo-intransigence, religious neo-fundamentalism. François Daguet concluded his reflection on Thomas Aquinas's vision of politics with a well-founded observation of the expiration of Thomist political philosophy. But he, at the very least, acknowledged its merit of discernment and diagnosis: "Perhaps St. Thomas does not allow us to think through a political order for today, but he certainly helps understand pathologies within the political order."[52] *Mutatis mutandis*, we could say the same about Étienne Gilson, outdated, anchored in his time, responding to concerns of his epoch that sometimes are no longer ours, or even ours at all. At the same time, Gilson's work, based in its best part on the consideration of the long view, provides a good measuring stick to offer a diagnostic for the present.

What can we retain from Gilson, if we must retain something? Perhaps precisely the sense of the Christian long view, of human humility, and fertile liberty. Regarding the sense of the long view and of continuity, Gilson developed the thesis that religious facts are always contemporary, so much so that spiritual texts have an active value. When Pascal quotes Moses, and when Gilson quotes Pascal, Gilson can conclude that there is a "permanent presence of the religious past."[53] Similarly, we can recall the last paragraphs of the *Metamorphoses of the City of God*, which Lucien Febvre found so strong and so courageous:

52 François Daguet, *Du politique chez Thomas d'Aquin* (Paris: Vrin, 2015), 351.

53 Étienne Gilson, course given at the Paris School of Sciences-Po, Paris, 1947: "When I read in the book of Exodus: 'Thou shalt tell the sons of Israel that the God of their fathers, Abraham, Isaac, and Jacob, has sent thee to them, and this is the name he will be known by forever; it shall stand recorded age after age' [Exodus, chapter 3:15], and then I observe that a man like Pascal, in the seventeenth century, writes in his *Memorial*, 'God of Abraham, of Isaac, and of Jacob, not of philosophers and scholars,' I wonder what the date of the passage is. At what moment, if this text has meaning for human beings, at what date is it current, living, contemporary? Is it at the moment when God spoke to Moses? Is it at the moment when Pascal remembered this passage in his *Memorial*? Such facts—and perhaps it is characteristic of religious facts as long as religious forces are exerted—have no date. They are contemporary forever. Therefore, to want to look at them from the standpoint of 1947 is perhaps to condemn oneself to misunderstand them, unless we remember at the same time that in 1947 we are witnessing the unfolding of permanent spiritual forces in which what history considers as a sometimes-distant past is exactly today's present. I am going to try to direct myself to history without directing myself to the past. I don't know whether I will succeed in conveying the impression of this permanent present, but it is what I want to do. I will quote ancient texts to you, but to my mind, we will always be in the present."

> This Christian people, by whatever name it is designated, is the same as what the *Letter to Diognetus* and *The City of God* already described as spread throughout the world in the manner in which the soul is everywhere co-present to the body it animates. This Christian people has no other being than that of the Church, no other end than that of the Church, and it can only expect that end under the Church's guidance. Being outside time itself, the Church's truth can be expressed in a multitude of tongues and animate various temporal institutions that succeed each other in time and are spread about in space. That is why, even if this Christian people changes its appearance in the course of the centuries, because it inhabits different temporalities successively, it remains one in time, as it is one in space, because it lives off the one and unchanging life of the Church.... The City of Man can only be built in the shadow of the Cross, as a suburb of the City of God.[54]

Reading Gilson is a lesson in both humility and freedom. As someone who published six corrected and evolving editions of his own *Thomisme* (1919–1964), Gilson knew well that the historian's job is untenured. "I have no illusions about what we know of the Middle Ages today. In twenty years our nephews will know another, much truer one," he wrote to a young colleague in May, 1947.[55] Historians of ideas are "explorers in an unknown country," and merely write the diary of their trip.[56] Despite all efforts, not all the archives of Gilson have been located. No doubt in the future, some of Gilson's correspondence will be recovered that will re-orient the perspectives of our analyses.

However, as our journey nears its end, it is necessary to try to conclude and answer the question posed by Marc Bloch in 1935. Where is the "solder" in Gilson's work connecting the medieval historian, the Catholic philosopher, the professor of the Collège de France, and the committed intellectual? If the solder exists, it might be in Gilson's presence in the present time, both loving and without illusion. It is a characteristic that is doubly an inheritance of his Catholic background: on the one hand there is the law of the Christian *carpe diem*, since holiness consists in sanctifying the present instant, in being in the innermost part of the world without being of the world; and on the other hand Gilson belongs to his generation, that of fire, survivor of

54 Étienne Gilson, *Metamorphoses of the City of God*, 233–35, and all of chapter 10, "The Church and Universal Society."

55 Letter from Étienne Gilson to Fr. Gabriel Astrik, May 10, 1947, UNDA.

56 Étienne Gilson, *Héloïse et Abélard*, 180.

the battle of Verdun, an imprudent, hardboiled generation, certainly sharp-tongued but peace-loving in the depths of its heart. In Gilson's opus we feel a fighting concern for the unity of humankind and for humanity's global experience, as well as an authentic universal society. That requires the will to think through false divisions at the political, chronological, or ideological levels. Within the MRP, Gilson is the opposite of a partisan. In international relations, he rejects a feudal subjection of Europe to any side, whatever its ideology: Europe is not only not a vassal of the United States, but it is no longer a territorial Christendom. The U.S.S.R. is not Stalinism, even in 1950. A man of peace, Gilson finds that the bipolar organization of the Cold War is a dangerous absurdity, and that it is necessary to try to avoid it. For Gilson, Catholicism is the opposite of a sect.[57] In his judgment, France in 1956 "drifts aimlessly," because "her future is no longer in her own hands." She will find meaning only by serving an ideal that goes beyond herself.[58]

In the *Metamorphoses of the City of God*, Gilson recalls: "There is no longer local history. There is no longer exclusively national history whose events concern a particular people and it alone, in the sense that this people alone is the cause or will alone undergo the effects of those events."[59] He constantly invites us to keep in mind the cosmopolitan nature of thought as much as the "denationalization" produced by Christian identity and by the "Commonwealth of the faithful" scattered over the planet.[60] With Lucien Febvre, we can certainly always lament that other bridges toward social history have not been built, but certain Gilsonian intuitions, launched between the two World Wars, for the history of ideas—for an integrated, humanist, humble, realist history, which, in the absence of the social and of many modes, has a sense of human beings, of human singularity, and of the continuity of human beings on this earth—might very well still possess current relevance in the writing of history strictly speaking.

57 Letter from Étienne Gilson to Henri Gouhier, October 26, 1924, Archives Gouhier: "The more that goes on, the surer I am that the world has to choose between religion and savagery, and that God is in Catholicism. . . . Catholicism by definition excludes being a sect."

58 Letter from Étienne Gilson to Francisque Gay, January 4, 1956, Institut Marc Sangnier: "France has been able to live only by serving something above her, and in this moment there is nothing that France desires to serve. Thus she drifts aimlessly. Her future is no longer in her own hands. This is not pessimism but fact."

59 Étienne Gilson, *The Metamorphoses of the City of God*, 3.

60 On this point see Florian Michel, "L'Affirmation transnationale de la culture catholique française (années 1920–années 1960)," *Revue historique* 3, no. 679 (July 2016): 605–27.

Appendix A: Correspondence

LETTER OF ÉTIENNE GILSON TO FR. LUCIEN LABERTHONNIÈRE, APRIL 12, 1906

The "Fonds Laberthonnière" of the Bibliothèque nationale of France [BNF] (NAF 28025) contains at least twelve letters sent by Gilson between April 1906 and December 1914. Here, we include the first letter of the series. Gilson was not yet twenty-two years old and was preparing for the examination for the university teaching certificate, *agrégation*, in philosophy at the Sorbonne. This is the first document written by Gilson directed to someone outside of his family or educational institutions. On April 5, 1906, the Congregation of the Index had condemned Fr. Lucien Laberthonnière's *Essais de philosophie religieuse* and his *Le réalisme chrétien et l'idéalisme grec*, which Gilson will often recall in his memoirs or his correspondence with Gouhier, Fabrègues, and others.

NAF 28025, number 70, BNF.

> April 12, 1906
>
> My Father,
> I do not know whether my modest expression of sympathy will bring you any consolation, but I owe too much consolation and too much comfort in certain difficult moments to the books that have just been put on the Index for me to fail to take advantage of this sad occasion to express all my gratitude. I beg you not to abandon your labor for a single

instant, because the benefits I have obtained from it are not mine alone, and I know many others who have profited by it as I have. You have offered us the fullness of the interior life at a time when perhaps we were about to abandon everything, disgusted by a terminology both pedantic and sterile. By immersing ourselves along with you in the true tradition of Christian thought (not just the one that dates from the thirteenth century) we have re-encountered the peace and the strength to continue. The measure taken against you does not impress us, and I would add, does not surprise me personally. It saddens me. But let us return to the quest, in the tranquility of our consciences, taking as our guide the magnificent epigraph of the *Annales*.[1]

With deepest sympathy
"Blessed are those who are persecuted for the sake of justice."
Devotedly yours in the love of Christ,
Étienne Gilson—Licencié en Philosophie—Étudiant d'Agrégation

EXCHANGE OF LETTERS BETWEEN ÉTIENNE GILSON AND MAURICE BLONDEL (1928–1932)

Archives Maurice Blondel—Université catholique de Louvain.

We reproduce here the five pieces of correspondence preserved in the Blondel Archives. The Gilson Archives do not contain anything from this exchange. Gilson's last message is a simple acknowledgment of the reception of *Problème de la philosophie catholique* published by Blondel, in 1932. Unable to understand, Gilson chose to remain silent.

1 "Therefore, let us seek as they seek who must find, and let us find as they find who must seek again, for it is said: 'Reach thou the end of thy reckoning, thou must needs begin again' (Ecclesiasticus 18:6)." Saint Augustine.

April 29, 1928

My dear colleague,

My deep thanks for having sent me. your *Itinéraire philosophique.*[2] Fréderic Lefèvre has never better employed his commitment and his talent than by putting them at your service, and we are all in his debt for having made us hear your voice. I am quite touched by the discerning allusion you make to St. Bonaventure.[3] Allow me to tell you in this context that I do not consider the antithesis Thomas-Bonaventure (or rather Thomas-Augustine) to be insurmountable. I speak as a historian and only for the thirteenth century. All I ask is that we do not, under the guise of agreement, imagine a non-existent agreement, obtained by the tacit suppression of one of the two, which would make any real agreement impossible. To unite them, it is necessary first to contrast them, and to become deeply aware of their differences. Only by this effort will we find out what each tradition finds unacceptable, and will we see how each of them must go beyond itself. I think that my generation of Catholics has suffered from a deep ignorance of its own tradition, and I consider its tradition to be *all* Catholic thought. That is why, in my ignorance, I labor to inform myself about it, in order to give a better point of departure to those who will come after me. Consequently, I am not shut up in a historical empiricism that would lead to the conclusion that what has been will be. I believe that we must know what has been to make that which should be actually happen. We have wanted to invent what was there only to be learned. This is why we fail to invent where indeed it would be necessary to invent.

Excuse this fragment of an hour with Maurice Blondel. You will complete it with an hour with Xavier Léon, if he is still loyal to Aix-en-Provence!

With profound respect and gratitude,
Étienne Gilson

2 *Les nouvelles littéraires*, March 31, 1928, p. 1, announced the publication the following week of *L'Itinéraire philosophique de Maurice Blondel: Propos recueillis par Frédéric Lefèvre* (Paris: Spes, 1928), a long interview with the philosopher by Frédéric Lefèvre, in the series "Une heure avec . . ."

3 Maurice Blondel, *L'Itinéraire philosophique* (Paris: Spes, 1928), 246–47.

May 8, 1928

My dear colleague,

None of the letters that I have received about *L'Itinéraire* is more valuable to me than yours, and I want to thank you emphatically for your kindness, your judgments, and your corrections. I ask your pardon for having been ignorant about some of your intentions. If there is to be a new edition of Lefèvre's . . . book, I would like to delineate your position better, all the more in that it completely delights me and that I am happy to learn everything that we can still expect from you and to benefit by your teaching. Please excuse the brevity of this scribbling traced amid the shadows that invade my eyes, and please be assured, my dear colleague, of my great esteem and cordial devotion.

M. Blondel

August 28, 1929

Dear sir and colleague,

I am touched by the trouble you have taken to send me your evaluation on the occasion of my *St. Augustine*. [Florian Michel: The evaluation has not been found, which makes it difficult to understand Gilson's reply.] I do not think we are in disagreement, but we do not give the same names to the same things. First it is true that I consider Thomism and Augustinianism two heterogenous Christian systems from the philosophical standpoint. I would not say the same from the theological standpoint and, moreover, I believe that in the future they may shown to be compatible, but they are incompatible in the past. A doctrine where God is known by analogy to what is sensible (Thomism) and a doctrine where God is known by analogy to thought (Augustinianism) are philosophically antithetical. As they have been established, taken in their historical, temporal, finished, fixed reality, they will be so eternally. That they might be reunited later, in a new synthesis that envelops and goes beyond them, is something I hope for. The observation of historical irreducibility as they lie, *prout jacent*, in the past, far from making a future synthesis impossible, is its condition to my mind, in the sense that it makes impossible eclecticism and verbal reconciliations that, by papering over obstacles, make it impossible to overcome them. The same goes for the second point. Augustinianism's unfinished character perhaps is not connatural to it in itself, but it was connatural to St. Augustine's

Augustinianism. A finished technical elaboration remains possible, but we can never make it to have been done by St. Augustine.

In a word, you judge from the point of view of the philosopher who creates and moves in a dynamic reality. I judge from the point of view of the historian who observes and stands in a static realm. The future and even the present are therefore with you. I believe that their perspectives would be more brilliant than they are, if better knowledge of the past presided over their point of departure.

Be assured of my great esteem, most cordial yours,
Étienne Gilson

March 21, 1931

Sir and dear colleague,
We wanted to read your second version during the Saturday session, but the meeting had lasted beyond any reasonable length, so that we had to give up the plan. Several presentations that were scheduled had to be eliminated, and like yours will appear as letters included in the *Bulletin*. I have taken your second version home and will use it exclusively, dispensing completely with the first. I will send it shortly to Xavier Léon with a detailed reply to your objections, as well as my objections to the way you pose the problem. I find so many difficulties there that I cannot keep from believing that I do not understand you and will say so at the end of my reply. Our two texts will be a good continuation of the session: scant agreement but huge good will.

Respectfully yours.
Étienne Gilson

A calling card, no date (1932):

Étienne Gilson—Professor at the Collège de France. With my sincere thanks for sending your book and my congratulations on the happy completion of such a heavy task.

LETTERS OF ÉTIENNE GILSON TO CHARLES DU BOS (1930–1938)

Paris: fifteen handwritten letters—MS 33845 to MS 33859, Bibliothèque littéraire Jacques Doucet

Letter 1

May 23, 1930

Dear Sir,

Thanks to you I enjoyed a splendid Easter vacations, and I was firmly resolved to thank you for having sent me your *Itinerarium*, when your fourth series of *Approximations* arrived to make that an urgent duty. I have not yet read that book, but I have continually thought about the first, asking myself whether it will be possible to follow the subtle curve that it traces out of so many apparently disconnected [in English] observations. In fact, your intense and profound expressionism—because that is what interests you, in yourself and in others—predestined you to the Word, that which is the expression in itself, the absence of distinction between the expresser and the expressed. Consequently, your conclusion, about which all your friends, which I think is to say all your readers, are so happy, is absolutely necessary.

One small detail, but one that has filled me with delight, is our common admiration for [Pierre Loti's] *Fantóme d'Orient* [*Phantom from the East*]; its breathless and tragic pace of march toward nothingness has always affected me most intensely.

I hope that you will get used to loving souls who do not love themselves. You told me that you suffered because of this. For me, who does nothing else after twenty long years, I am convinced that we end by bringing them closer to each other by bringing each soul closer to itself, and I insist on it. We adhere less to the truth than to the way by which we attain it. It is not necessary to want it for human beings, if, incapable of completely detaching themselves from themselves to save themselves, they prefer their truth to the Truth. The Truth will know well, indeed unknown to them, it already knows, how to reconcile them.

Be assured of my deep acknowledgment of all the good your books have done me and of my firm friendship
Étienne Gilson

Letter 2

May 28, 1930

Dear Sir and friend,
I would be very happy to see you, but in Paris I have practically no free time except Tuesday afternoon. If that is feasible for you, I could meet next Tuesday at Librairie J. Vrin, 5 place de la Sorbonne, at a time that is convenient for you, from 3 P.M. on. We could find a peaceful corner in the Sorbonne to chat. If that does not work for you, I could come to see you some Saturday convenient for both.

I have received and read *Vigile*. It is a very beautiful idea, but how difficult to work out.

Furthermore, I am stealing time to read your *Approximations*. You have succeeded at least once in this fourth series with the feat of an absolutely expressive phrase. It is on p. 41. "They have acted with all their being . . ." There is one surprise, on p. 35, where Marius [illegible] thinks the role assigned by Epicureanism to memory is insufficient. Did Pater commit that error? When you can, look up Victor Brochard, *Études de philosophie ancienne et de philosophie moderne*, p. 296. But we agree on the amazing worth of Tolstoy and Chekhov.

May we see each other soon,
Cordially,
Étienne Gilson

Jacques Maritain's *Bergson* breaks my heart: *infidelia non amantis vulnera*.

Letter 3

May 28, 1930

Dear sir,
I have to come to Paris next Saturday for a meeting at 5 P.M. If you can come on that day to the address I indicated on my card, after 2:15, I will expect you at the time you like.

With very best wishes,
Étienne Gilson

Letter 4

July 3, 1930

Dear Sir,
I have just received the second issue of *Vigile*, which, from the little I have read, seems excellent. My heartfelt thanks. I tried to write something about Guigues, but was checkmated. The man does not allow comments on himself. One can only translate. I do not see how I could give you something for All Saints Day, and you would be wise not to count on me, but I absolutely promise you the first non-dogmatic pages of general interest that I do write. Moreover, if I send you something, you are always free to return it should you see any difficulty in printing it in *Vigile*. I would like our friendship to be complete enough to make that freedom totally natural.

Be assured of my best wishes,
Étienne Gilson

Letter 5

Friday, September 12, 1930

Dear friend,
I have found your letter at Vrin, and it will be a pleasure to accept your kind invitation next Monday at one. We are in the middle of moving in and my wife very regretfully sends her apologies for not coming with me, but workers continually come to do odds and ends, and she has to be there.

Until Monday with my best wishes,
Étienne Gilson
2 avenue Émile Acollas—VIIe

Letter 6

October 22, 1930

My dear friend,
I am at Ottawa for three days, where I am working to set up a center of medieval studies. The soil is rich, and later on the harvest will be of Canadian abundance. I have just received the charming visit of your secretary's father. I was able to tell him that I had simply intended to lunch with one of your nieces or cousins, at any rate, with one of the "children," which may give an idea of the place you have made for him among you. Inversely, you can assure your secretary that her father enjoys excellent health and is happy to know

she is with you. The time seems long to him too, but he hopes that the previous plans, whose fulfillment is delayed by the change of government in Canada, will eventually be carried out, which would permit his daughter to stay in Paris without being separated from all of her family. I join you in your wish that this happy combination of events occurs.

I hope that you and yours enjoy good health in your chosen refuge at Versailles. I have an unforgettable memory of the hours spent with Jacques Maritain and yourself. It is more than a memory; it is a lasting effect whose presence makes itself felt still.

Please give my regards to Madame Du Bos, and be assured of my warmest friendship,

Étienne Gilson
Dominican Convent
95 Empress Avenue
Ottawa

Letter 7

January 7, 1931

My dear friend,
Thank you for your kind invitation. I will be at Versailles Monday, January 19, barring something unforeseen that unexpectedly prevents me from going there. But it will be rather to be instructed than to instruct, because our friend Gabriel Marcel has posed no small question to you.

Of course the old Sorbonne is open to you. My course on St. Bernard takes place at eleven o'clock (instead of ten), in the English room, on the second floor, at the end of the corridor, left. If you come you will hear me *study* St. Bernard, because I too am only an old student and have never really decided to become a professor. The course is public.

In staunch friendship,
Étienne Gilson

Letter 8

January 14, 1931

My dear friend,
The unlikely event that I vaguely feared has occurred. I have been summoned to the École des Hautes études on Monday the nineteenth at 5 p.m. Since there is a quarterly meeting, and since I have

not been seen since the start of the year, I absolutely must attend—and must be absent from the meeting of our friends. Please give them my excuses, and say how sorry I am.

Your good friend,
Étienne Gilson

Letter 9

February 8, 1931

Dear friend,
Thank you for your telegram on Monday, for your letter, and for your greeting that is so encouraging. I think I have a great deal to say about the ideal of Christendom, so dear to my heart, and I am happy that my propositions have been submitted to good judges, because we have no right to be mistaken. I will publish nothing without their approval. I am terribly disappointed to be unable to go to Versailles on Monday. I have just restarted a candidacy to the Collège de France. It is not fun, but I must do it, and make visit after visit. On Friday I leave for Aberdeen, and I have to work twice as hard before I leave, so that being tied up with my courses Tuesday and Wednesday, I am an errand boy the whole day. It will be easy for you to believe that I would prefer to see our friends and you. I hope that you are completely over your attack of the flu. Take good care of yourself, because we need you.

Your good friend,
Étienne Gilson

Letter 10

[no date]
Friday evening

Dear friend,
After I saw Jacques Maritain yesterday. I have not stopped working night and day to revise, rewrite in part, and complete my article. It had to be done right away, while my conversation was still fresh in my memory, and I could take advantage of his most valuable observations.

Apart from that, I am overwhelmed with work, but I am doing well, and I only beg pardon for not seeing you and our friends, as I would like.

Yours very truly,
Étienne Gilson

Letter 11

Sunday, April 25, 1931

My dear friend,

This is certainly a kind of fate. I was suddenly convoked for an urgent meeting tomorrow, Monday. Once again this robs me of the pleasure of being with you and especially the intellectual benefit I would have gained from it. I am more grieved than I can say, and I ask you to give my excuses to our friends. Would you tell Gabriel Marcel in particular how sorry I am, and also that Xavier Léon has led me to anticipate a letter on Christian philosophy from him for the Society's Bulletin. I would like to insist to him that he should make his viewpoint known; on such a matter, even nuances are useful, and some of them are necessary.

Your good friend,
Étienne Gilson

P.S. Would you tell Jacques Maritain that Ventura di Raulica[4] is the Traditionalist, and that his interpretation of St. Thomas (he presents himself as a Thomist) is very tendentious. He hardens and falsifies Thomas. I have not seen Del Prado yet, but I find a huge literature on the question.

Letter 12

February 5, 1937

My dear friend,

I am happy about the good news you send regarding your health. I hope with all my heart that news will become better and better. As for the Collège, I agree about the interest that a chair of the history of autobiography would have. But I am very unsure as to the practical likelihood of getting it created. However, one must not despair. If Valéry takes charge of this after his election, there will be friends to support the project, and nothing allows us to say that it will fail. For the moment, we must wait until your health allows you to make at least the indispensable visits, without which any attempts to convince those who do not know you would be useless. I know well what the word *wait* means for you, but that is certainly what troubles your

4 Gioacchino Ventura de Raulica (1792–1861) was a Theatine (Superior General from 1830 to 1833). A theologian, philosopher, and preacher, he was exiled to France from 1849 on, following his participation in the Risorgimento in Sicily and then in Rome [indication of the BNF].

friends so much. They know it, and they feel incapable of moving the social obstacles with which you yourself collide so painfully.

Affectionately,
Étienne Gilson
2 Avenue Émile Acollas—VIIe

Letter 13

May 27, 1937

My dear friend,
I have just written out the essence of what I propose to say to you next Sunday. After having thought it over a great deal, I have come to the conclusion that it would be best to be very brief, since, to cut to the chase, this is a formality. The Collège must present two names for the minister's selection. That is the law. On occasion, the minister has even chosen the candidate presented in second place. He has the right to do so. He will not do that this time, but ultimately, the election is technically impossible without a second candidate and nothing would prevent other candidates from presenting themselves against Paul Valéry for the first place. Your candidacy makes Valéry's nomination possible, by assuring the presence of a second candidate who agrees that in no case will he present himself against the first. You do him a real service. The problem that presents itself to me is to act in such a way that you are not hurt by it and, if possible, that it helps you.

After careful thought, it seems to me that you ought to get all the benefit possible from this situation. I must confess that I think you do not have the slightest chance of holding a chair of English. There are always professionals to intrigue for that sort of chair, and against their weighty *quarto* sized volumes, your studies will seem lightweight. There is no point in complaining. It seems to me that must happen, and our protests will change nothing. To the contrary, Valéry is going to be elected. After a valiant attempt on his part, it may be that the task seems heavier to him than it had appeared and that he arranges for a substitute. Why not you? After the substitution, succession is not impossible. Accordingly, I am going to present your poetics of poetry as a particular case of your own more general poetics, which you are fully qualified to teach, when you will be able to present yourself at the level that belongs to you, rather than the place to which friendship leads you. This precise point is what I am eager to clarify as forcefully as possible. Here is my statement: "I find myself led simply by the dynamic of the circumstances to present for the second rank a writer, a critic, and an aesthetician who, to my mind, cannot belong anywhere but in the first." Above all, I am eager to save your dignity in this adventure, because it is certain that your rights in the future will rest upon it. That is why, after specifying the particular conditions in which your candidacy is proposed, I add: "It would, however, be unfair that the perfect courtesy of his gesture should give rise to a misunderstanding about his personal worth and about the importance of his work. I simply find . . ." In that way, far from losing something or other, I can subsequently take advantage of the circumstance to prepare for the future.

Therefore, finish getting back on your feet, and don't worry about anything. What is happening may some day have for us the value of a felicitous start of a journey.

Faithfully yours,
Étienne Gilson

Letter 14

December 5, 1937

My dear friend,

I am most happy to receive the seventh series of the *Approximations*. It has been my companion and my intellectual stimulus since I received it. It is an oxygen bottle in an atmosphere that is a little too thin. To be sure, Charles Du Bos in South Bend entails an almost catastrophic break in equilibrium, and in any case as surprising, but in a different way from the arrival of *Approximations* VII in Toronto! What I want to see there first of all is a sign of your physiological stability and the announcement of a few months without urgent material worries. I cannot tell you enough how happy I am for you. There is a hard law that intellectual freedom must be paid for by selling part of it. I have always consoled myself with the thought that what was left had only all the more vigor and was only all the more precious.

We get back to France on December 26. Unfortunately, South Bend is not on the route from Toronto to New York: far from it. I would have been happy, or rather both of us would have been happy, to see you again. It will be a short postponement. I do not know what is going on right now in the Collège de France, nor what problems are going to present themselves there. You know that your friends will do everything possible to support your wishes, but we must not hide the fact that the chances of entering into the Collège, for anyone, are roughly equal to those of winning first place in the National Lottery. I have stopped believing that these events are intelligible, and it would be imprudent to base one's future on this probability. South Bend is less pleasant but more secure.

My wife joins me in expressing our closest friendship,
Étienne Gilson

Letter 15

December 6, 1938

My dear friend,
I know that you have been invited to Toronto to give a lecture in French. St. Michael's College would like to take advantage of the opportunity to meet you. Accordingly, I have been instructed to invite you to give another lecture, this time *in English*, on *The Mysticism of Wordsworth*. St. Michael's can offer you fifty dollars for this lecture and, furthermore, would be pleased to have you as its guest during your whole stay in Toronto. There could be some benefit in your becoming personally known. I am convinced of it.

At your *French* lecture, you will have almost all the liberal arts professors in the audience. Why not give them your splendid lecture on Benjamin Constant.

Yours faithfully and cordially,
Étienne Gilson

ÉTIENNE GILSON AND THE MAGAZINE *SEPT* (1934–1935)

Extracts from *Notes sur l'histoire du Cerf* by P. Pierre Boisselot, 1943
Fonds Boisselot, Archives de la Province dominicaine de France, Le Saulchoir, Paris [APDF]
Notebook II, 83–87

Another polemic, on a much grander scale, was triggered by a series of Gilson's articles on education. These articles really launched *Sept*. Until then, success had eluded it. The magazine was attractive, but it was difficult to see where it was going, what ideas guided it. It had good elements, courage, youth, sincere openness, and a desire to separate the Church from its recognized protectors. But that was still unclear. As yet, there was no leader who stood out. Gilson was that leader, and his involvement had immense repercussion among French Catholics.

Étienne Gilson was a professor at the Collège de France and at the École des hautes études. He was a philosopher and a historian of philosophy. Knowing St. Thomas perfectly, he offered sure doctrine aided by admirable talent as a writer. Not that he was brilliant or sharp, as one expects from a generalist. Not at all. He was a self-made journalist. His style was that of a philosopher, but such a powerful and clear philosopher that it had clarity and power that carried conviction. His pace of thought was slow, a bit heavy, but grasping reality without letting anything get away, turning it over again and again in every direction, giving a sensation of irresistible good faith and gentle strength. With that came a dialectical power that could not be escaped and that did not let you go when it had bitten you with sometimes terrible teeth. His articles were a monument to intelligence, good sense, and frankness.

Gilson confronted the problem of education in France. This is one of the most important problems for the future of French Catholicism, a problem for which we have sacrificed enormously and which therefore deeply affects the average Catholic. The usefulness of private Christian education is so evident that the subject becomes taboo and all criticism is considered profanation.

Gilson advanced across this burning minefield at his heavy, clear pace, and called things by their name. That caused a fine scandal!

As long as he limited himself to demonstrate the necessity of Catholic education and to denounce the secularist metaphysics hidden in public education, he had only admirers. But when he came to criticize private education—quite objectively—to point out its flaws and demand structural reform, there was an outcry. The bishops latched onto it, and the ever present Msgr. Richaud went to Fr. Bernadot's home to bring his objections and advice. Msgr. Beaussart, the champion of free education, echoed him. I recall that on the feast of St. Dominic, August 11, 1934, having met Fr. Bernadot at Faubourg Saint-André, he subjected him—and Fr. Chenu, who was there—to a violent tirade against Gilson. Gilson, however, did not budge and returned blow for blow. Having published a particularly accurate article about the technical mediocrity of our free education and having had the misfortune of titling it "The Cult of Incompetence" we received so many protests that it was necessary to make a good response. Gilson did it masterfully. He posed the problem in its real setting: "Is it necessary to say this?" Is it good to tell the truth, or rather is it necessary to take refuge in a lie as is done at present? This took the debate to the most sensitive point for the first time. All the polemics that we had to maintain subsequently on the most varied topics were to bring this initial point. Is it necessary to say this? Must Catholics throw a modest veil over our weeds and with our customary Pharisaism pretend that everything is well with us, and that our defeats are motivated by the wicked, or rather is it better to acknowledge what is wrong in us, unveil it, and together loyally seek a remedy. We always chose this second solution. It was already Gilson's. He showed its necessity masterfully.

Notebook III, 27–35

The year 1935 saw *Sept* and *Vie spirituelle* take a position on the war in Ethiopia that would be the first political grievance subsequently raised against us. That is why it is important to dwell upon it. Certainly, we had firmly taken the side of Ethiopia against Italy, or rather the side of law and international morality. For it would be absolutely mistaken to imagine that we were led by political reasons. Let us never forget that *Sept* was a Catholic magazine that had taken as its motto *Catholics first of all*. So, in the event, if we involved ourselves against Italy, it could only be for non-political motives, which must be found in our very Catholicism. . . .

However, our team itself was not unanimous. On this occasion, Gilson broke with us and revealed his motives with the brutal frankness that is one of his charms. He stopped cooperating and, despite our appeals, did not yield. One day, Fr. Maydieu went to see him, accompanied, if I remember rightly, by one of our friends who was also president of our board of directors, M. Coyne, and it seems that Gilson made a formal critique of our position. For him, Mussolini was acting as a perfect Thomist! He was in charge of the common good of Italy. This common good required new outlets for an overpopulated country. He found them in the uncivilized lands of Abyssinia, which were the only part of Africa not yet colonized. He undertook all this to feed his own people and to civilize the other. Nothing could follow more clearly from theology and Thomism! This argumentation did not convince us, and we left Gilson to his beloved studies, without thereby loosening the friendship and gratitude that bound us to him.

LETTER FROM ÉTIENNE GILSON TO FR. BERNADOT, OP, AUGUST 26, 1937

Letters sent to Fr. Bernadot after the magazine's cessation, *Sept* Collection, Archives of Éditions du Cerf, APDF.

August 26, 1937

My Reverend Father,

My heart sank when I saw the headline: "Adieux à nos lecteurs" [Goodbye to our readers]. Thousands of them want to tell you that. I want you to know that their sentiments are my own. I have never stopped following, admiring, and supporting your effort, in the fashion in which I believed I could still do, and I intended to offer to resume my collaboration soon, since *Sept* recently had moved in the direction of a balance that did not exclude boldness. I would have done so, if I had known that this issue was to be the last. I at least want to assure you of my recognition of the courage and perfect fidelity with which you have supported me at a time when I certainly had not brought you only friends. There, as always, you have been admirable in you peaceful vigor, and I thank you for it from the bottom of my heart.

Many people want to ask you to begin again. But they will not give you the means to do so. Catholics know neither how to use their money nor how to give moral support to each other. I know that only too well. I have sometimes wondered if I committed the same fault in your regard. All considered, I do not think so. But I am not sure, and if I have done so, I beg your forgiveness.

My only consolation is to know that this crushing burden has just fallen from your shoulders. But *Sept* is no longer there, and the void it leaves will let everyone measure the place it occupied.

My most respectful and faithful affection,
Étienne Gilson
6 rue Collet
Vermenton (Yonne)

LETTERS OF ÉTIENNE GILSON TO LÉON BRUNSCHVICG (1928–1939)

Fonds Léon Brunschvicg, Institut Mémoires de l'édition contemporaine [IMEC]. The correspondence contains eleven letters from Gilson (1916–1939, IMEC). In the letter of July 4, 1927, Gilson laments a "certain lack of effort to accompany me, at least to the limit where we really must diverge" and lists the "points of disagreement." We publish the last three letters from

Gilson which give a fairly clear, although incomplete, idea of the Gilson-Brunschvicg debate.

Letter of Étienne Gilson to Léon Brunschvicg, May 18, 1928

Dear Sir and friend,
It is impossible for me to go to the joust tomorrow to which you so cordially invite me. My wife has to go to Paris to see a physician at four P.M., and I am on duty at home. Besides, I don't know what I would be able to do. I am not completely convinced that it is constructive to debate works like yours orally, at least among people who do not have the same concept of philosophy. You teach us what consciousness is, and I learn that. You are very far ahead, in a region of certainties that give you an absolute judicatory power, and we are full of naive questions that you have already overcome. How can we talk and converse? I think that if I found the time, I would like to ponder what is philosophy in general, *überhaupt*. That is where I am. I am also one wholeheartedly with all who will seek the truth tomorrow. Even to seek the truth is always beneficial.

Most cordially yours,
Étienne Gilson

Letter of Étienne Gilson to Léon Brunschvicg, March 13, 1936

My dear Teacher,
I thank you with all my heart for having taken up my little book so kindly. I knew that it would not please you. I also know that the realism that you call primitive is inconsistent in your view. You have explained this to me thoroughly in the past and again later, and I have done my best to believe it. I had to get past my fiftieth birthday to dare to say that I have never succeeded. I have always been a realist. That is also why I have never written as a philosopher, because, seeing myself as the sole exemplar of my species, at least in France, I always considered myself as touched by a kind of unspeakable philosophical disease. Consequently, I silenced myself, and I think I would have continued to do so, because I am far from having pushed my reflections to the point where I honestly should have pushed myself. Accordingly, I had to resign myself to think like a six year old child . . . at most.

As for the epigraph I borrowed from you, I do not think that anyone could be misled by it and attribute my own conclusions to you, any more than, when you cited my interpretation of Aristotle by Descartes to prove Aristotle's "childishness," anyone could believe that you attributed your own interpretation to me. I hope I have not done any injustice to your thinking by using one of your texts against you as you have used one of my texts against a doctrine I hold, or elsewhere quoting my own St. Thomas Aquinas to prove that Thomist realism is condemned to infallibility. You have the right to do so, because it is legitimate to take premises from an adversary, provided that one reports them exactly, as you have always done. It is evident that, since one draws different conclusions from the premises, one must understand them differently, but I hope I have no more misrepresented your genuine thinking than you have ever misrepresented mine. If I have done so, it would be without wanting to, and I would sincerely regret it.

Please be sure of my most grateful feelings,
Étienne Gilson

Letter from Étienne Gilson to Léon Brunschvicg, March 30, 1939

Dear teacher and friend,
I thank you for having sent your most recent book, which I have just read with constant pleasure and great admiration. I will not say that you write and compose better than in the past, because I do not think that is possible. *L'introduction* and its contemporary *L'idéalisme* are genuine models of philosophical style, and you yourself can not do anything to surpass them, but you have just equaled them. As for the content, you know what I think of your work. I think I am able to appreciate its importance as it will appear one hundred years from now, and this importance is very considerable, because it marks a *nec plus ultra* in its own line. In this sense, even this latest book represents an advance, if not in your thinking (because you were already there) at least in its expression. Your integral anti-realism eliminates, after the thing, the person still known as a thing, and this elimination is pursued even with God. My only objection is that when the operation has been carried out, nothing remains but nihilism, or rather a nihilizing activity whose efficacy seems to me to me most formidable. Evidently, what forces me to reject your attitude is what gives it its value in your eyes. It is a moment to recall the saying *mens non omnibus una* . . .

Be assured of my respectful friendship,
Étienne Gilson

LETTERS BETWEEN HENRI BERGSON AND ÉTIENNE GILSON (1939)

Bibliothèque littéraire Jacques Doucet and Saint Michael's College Archives (University of Toronto) [SMCA]

Dedication of *Héloïse et Abélard: Études sur le Moyen Âge et l'humanisme*

Bibliothèque littéraire Jacques Doucet

To Monsieur Henri Bergson
In homage of affection, admiration, and constant gratitude
I finally get up courage to send a book,
because it is not about philosophy

Étienne Gilson

Letter of Étienne Gilson to Henri Bergson, June 5, 1939

BGN 2733 3, Bibliothèque littéraire Jacques Doucet

My dear Teacher,

I do not want to have declared my candidacy to the Institute, a completely theoretical candidacy this time moreover, without telling you what pleasure it would have been to visit you in this circumstance, if you were still in Paris. I would not have gone to ask you for your voice or vote, but to tell you that the years have only increased my admiration for your work as well as my gratitude for the immense pleasure, truly and literally incomparable, which I owe to your teaching. Nothing has ever replaced, even remotely, the airy pleasure of being led by your intelligence from comprehension to comprehension. Dear God! How intelligent we were as we listened to you! Afterwards, what conversations I had with my friend Fr. Paulet,[5] professor of philosophy at Saint-Sulpice! He loved you so much that on Boulevard Saint-Michel I have seen him literally and physically

5 Lucien Paulet was born Paris, October 7, 1876; ordained June 29, 1901; became a teacher at Notre-Dame-des-Champs, July 1, 1905; director of the major seminary of Issy, October 12, 1905; chaplain at the Sacré Coeur de Monmartre, October 25, 1907; curate at St. Honoré, Eylau, March 9, 1908; volunteer chaplain-stretcher bearer, August 28, 1914; assigned to the 29th, 26th, and 19th battalions of alpine riflemen; assigned to Argonne, then Champagne; wounded September 28, 2015, at Suipes; died the next day; military medal awarded posthumously, *JO*, September 17, 1920: "A man of unusually elevated sentiments, exceptional devotion, carrying the spirit of sacrifice to its furthest limits. Gained the admiration of all the riflemen with the zeal and care displayed in the relief of the wounded, September 27, 1915. Mortally wounded in fulfillment of his duties, September 28. Cross with palm leaf."

stagger back from the shock of simply having crossed paths with you. This friend is dead, a volunteer enlisted as chaplain to infantry riflemen, killed in the charge with them, cross in hand, in order to be with the dying as they died. I know that you are surrounded on all sides with similar affection, but I do not think there has been one purer, or more complete than that one.

As for me, the more I go on, the more I feel that my thought, under the surface differences of expression, is in communion with yours. Whatever you may think of it yourself, and I don't know what you think of it, your whole endeavor seems to me a philosophy whose only conceivable theology is Christian theology. I beg your pardon for speaking so clumsily of these things, but I mean this, that every prayer addressed to the God of your metaphysics, and every inner ascent toward the God of your metaphysics, goes directly and infallibly to the God that I worship as a Christian. That can be seen better or more generally, if we understand that your theology is explicitly free of any revealed theology and that its greatness is to be the homage of pure thought to a God that it encounters as God himself has created it to do. Our theologians, and we Christians ourselves, are too inclined to confuse what our thought knows and what revelation teaches us. You have gone out to meet God with your whole soul, but with it alone. And I certainly think that he must have alerted you in some personal, secret manner, because it is truly He that you have encountered. The more certain I am of it, the closer I feel to you, and the happier I am.

Rest assured, my dear teacher, of my faithful and grateful affection,
Étienne Gilson

Letter from Henri Bergson to Étienne Gilson, July 12, 1939
SMCA

My dear Colleague,
My illness and above all the need to struggle against it unceasingly with the appropriate exercises leaves very little time in my day to write. But I do not want to delay further in thanking you for your letter last month and for your book on Heloise and Abelard (on two other subjects also). Let us talk about the book first. It is exciting from beginning to end. To elucidate so many and such delicate problems, even more than your great learning and your very acute critical sense, a sympathy—in the etymological sense of the word—is necessary that makes you penetrate into the soul of the Middle Ages. To

recreate sentiments sometimes quite alien to ours, one must also be a psychologist. Finally, to express these things, one must be a writer. All these qualities, all these gifts are present together in your work. As for the two essays that you have added to *Héloïse et Abélard*,[6] they present features of the Middle Ages that are little known and very interesting—very important as well. (Thank you for the kind reference, infinitely too kind, that you make to my lectures at the Collège de France in the first essay.)

I now come to your affectionate letter, written on the occasion of an academic candidacy that you had reason to present, yet that could not succeed immediately, because you present yourself for the first time and at the eleventh hour, but that will surely lead to the day when the way will be open. When you are on the inside, you will see how much the semi-commitments that were acquired in this or that prior election weigh upon an election. One would really think that Leibniz was thinking about academic elections or others of the same kind when he wrote, "The present is heavy with the past." But I am sure that you are already *persona grata*, indeed *gratissima*, and that is why your academic future does not give me any concern.

The last paragraph of your letter has deeply moved me. Here again you have seen clearly. The religion that was immanent, so to speak, in my first reflections, in my first conclusions, has ended by emerging. I ask myself how I did not perceive immediately, distinctly what now appears to me as clear as day.

My compliments for your beautiful book and my most cordial greetings,.
Henri Bergson

P.S. How I regret not having known Fr. Paulet of whom you speak so movingly. The War cut down so many of those who would be the moral and intellectual elite of our country.

6 This refers to the opening lecture of Gilson's teaching at the Collège de France, on April 5, 1932, titled "Le Moyen Âge et le naturalisme antique," [The Middle Ages and Ancient Naturalism] included in *Héloïse et Abélard* (Paris: Vrin, 1938), 183–224; and the presentation titled "Philosophie médiévale et humanisme [Medieval Philosophy and Humanism]," given April 24, 1935, at the Guillaume Budé Congress, held at Nice, included in *Héloïse et Abélard*, 225–45.

Letter from Henri Bergson to Étienne Gilson, September 5, 1939
SMCA

Dear colleague and friend,
How can I tell you what deep satisfaction I have just felt in reading you? Your article is infinitely too kind toward me.[7] You have looked at what is good in my books through a kind of magnifying glass, with a sympathy that, as you know, is reciprocal. With that reservation, I feel comfortable telling you that you have admirably understood and made understandable my work's intention, the method I employ, the results I would like to have reached. Above all, you have shown, and so penetratingly, how I tried to continue a great French tradition. Nothing could be more moving for me. When you wrote this article, the possibility of peace still seemed credible, devoting oneself to pure philosophy seemed possible. Today we must think only of war, of the need to save civilization, of the great, sublime France that once again is going to achieve its mission. But your article will remain in my memory as the last flash to shine in my eyes before the world enters the infernal night, a night from which we will emerge gloriously thanks to France.

Thanks to you with all my heart.
Henri Bergson

Letter from Étienne Gilson to Henri Bergson, October 20, 1939
BGN 867 4, Bibliothèque littéraire Jacques Doucet
The Institute of Mediaeval Studies-Toronto

My dear Teacher,
I have just received your letter of September 5, which must have been delayed and made some detours before arriving. I am happy to think that I did not misrepresent your intentions in an article that, in spite of everything, could not break out of the framework of a newspaper. But what also pleases me is to have received several letters from your admirers and friends who are much more happy than if I had been praising them. That, it seems to me, is the sincerest and most disinterested praise.

May Touraine welcome you. You are very near Marmoutiers, where Gaunilo insisted upon resolving metaphysical problems as

7 Étienne Gilson, "Ce que nous devons à Henri Bergson," *Les nouvelles littéraires*, September 2, 1939, 1–3.

a logician. Above all, you are very close to Saint-Martin, where the Englishman Alcuin set up residence in the eighth century to bring us Roman and Athenian classical culture. I am delighted to know you are there in this time of trial. No one has done more for France than you. It is right that you should be there when its new victory will once more have assured our civilization's survival.

My faithful and respectful affection to my dear teacher,
Étienne Gilson

PHONY WAR PROPAGANDA (1939–1940)

Rough draft of Étienne Gilson's letter to Edmond Faral, director of the Collège de France, April 18, 1940, Vrin Archives.

To the Director,
I gratefully accept the honor of representing the Collège de France at the University of Pennsylvania ceremonies next September.

Following the wish that Jean Marx has expressed, and with your consent, I likewise am going to prepare to resume my activities of propaganda in Canada and the United States on behalf of France during 1940–41.

For the academic year 1939–40, the Collège de France can be considered to have carried out the following activities through me:

1. Length of the mission: seven months (September 12, 1939 to April 15, 1940)
2. Main activity: five months of teaching at the Institute of Mediaeval Studies, Toronto, two months of which of which were unsalaried.
   a. Principal course: The Conflict of Eloquence and Philosophy during the Middle Ages (thirty-two lectures).
   b. Seminar: Dialectics and Theology in Saint Anselm (twenty-four lectures)
   c. Public Lectures: God and Philosophy (four lectures)
3. Secondary Activities
   a. Management of the Institut Scientifique Franco-Canadien, of which I am the honorary president.
   b. Six public lectures at Montreal on Cicero's *Eloquentia* and its influence in the Middle Ages
   c. Propaganda Lectures

      1939
      October 27, Alliance Française, Toronto

November 15, Wellesley College, Massachusetts, USA
November 17, Winooski College, Vermont, USA
November 19, Société des écrivains canadiens, Montreal
November 26, League of Social Action, Toronto
December 8, Alliance Française, Montreal
December 9, Cercle universitaire, Montreal
December 29 University of Ottawa

1940

10, Kiwanis Club, Toronto
January 17, Students Club, Toronto
January 26, Collège du Saint-Esprit, Ironside, Canada
January 27, Alliance Française, Ottawa
February 19, Catholic Action, Toronto
March 1–8, University of Indiana, Bloomington, Indiana

1. Philosophical Club
4. Mahlon Powell Lectures: "God and Philosophy"
1. Saint Charles' School
1. Newman Club
1. French Club
1. Faculty Club
1. Indiana Union

Total of ten lectures

March 11–24

4. Harvard University: four public lectures, "God and Philosophy"
1. French Club
1. New Bedford, Mass.
2. Worcester, Mass.
1. Augustinian Society, Boston, Mass.
1. Woonsocket, Rhode Island
1. Manchester, New Hampshire

Total of eleven lectures

For the record, I should mention that I had the honor of representing the Collège de France at the fiftieth anniversary of the founding of the University of Washington in November, 1939, and that we were the only French institution represented by a special delegate. Perhaps I should add my articles published on the war:

"L'Europe et la paix" (*Revue trimestrielle canadienne*)

"La France sous les armes" (reproduced by more than twenty newspapers and used as a French dictation text in a number of schools)

"Ligne Domitien et Ligne Maginot" (five or six newspapers)

"A French View of the War" (in *America*, issue sold out, a new edition in progress)

[Passage crossed out on the draft]
~~A final point about which it might be good for you to have exact information concerns the finances of this mission. As usual, I was paid at Toronto for my teaching from October to December. I have also been paid for my four lectures at the University of Indiana. All my other activities have been uncompensated and offered as such in the name of the Collège de France. The total time of my public speaking is 98 hours, fourteen in French and eighty-four in English. This seven-month mission has cost France: (1) my ongoing wages at the Collège de France; (2) a subsidy of 50,000 francs for travel expenses. Roughly two hundred dollars of this subsidy is left. That money will be used starting next September, when I resume my activity in the United States~~
[End of passage crossed out]

In closing, I would like to emphasize my gratitude for your ongoing support as Director, which has greatly encouraged me during this endeavor.

Respectfully yours,
Étienne Gilson

Report of the French Consul in Boston, François Brière, to French Ambassador de Saint-Quintin, May 1, 1940

SOFE, 425, Archives du Ministère des Affaires étrangères (La Courneuve) [AMAE].

Professor Étienne Gilson, whom I had met a few months ago at Wellesley College where he gave a remarkable lecture on Racine, agreed to give talks at associations of Franco-Americans of French Canadian origin in New England. Taking advantage of a stay at Harvard, where he gave a very successful series of lectures on Scholastic philosophy last March, our eminent compatriot greatly desired, with an enthusiasm and good humor I admire, to fulfill his commitment.

At the Alliance Française in New Bedford, to students of the bilingual Assumption College in Worcester, following the meeting of the directors of the Union Saint-Jean Baptiste at Woonsocket, and at the Société des Conférences in Manchester to an audience of some 350, setting aside his role as philosopher, Gilson presented himself to our Franco-American friends "as a simple son of France," speaking to them with great sincerity. Supporting his point with particular examples, he explained to them the reasons for which our country, which has been invaded so many times, wants to oppose the attempts at domination by Germany once and for all. Moreover, he showed great moderation in sketching the conditions of the firm but generous peace that we desire. Furthermore, by publishing an article in the Franco-American press titled "Ligne Maginot et Ligne Domitien" he gave particular expression to his fundamental theme, which is the defense of the civilization that is heir to that of the Roman Empire

Accurate accounts of his lectures have been published by serious Franco-American periodicals like the bulletin of the Union Saint Jean-Baptiste and the Manchester *Canado-Américain*. In the latter magazine, Fr. Adrien Verrette, director of the local Société des Conférences, who had given warm words of welcome to Gilson in the meeting, summed up his impressions in this way: "What a comforting message delivered to Franco-Americans by one of the most authoritative voices in France. . . . It is because France struggles for its existence that it must undertake this stupid war and it is right to hope for victory. . . . Monsieur Gilson's testimony gives food for thought. His lecture leaves more vigorous and better reasoned sympathy in every heart. May France triumph in order to preserve for humanity, in the words of Cardinal Verdier, 'the sacred principles of a wise liberty, authentic fraternity, and Christian equality.' This is the prayer of all Franco-Americans."

I had to quote these lines from the *Canado-Américain*, because they are in striking contrast with the attitude of Josaphat Benoit, advocate for Fr. Coughlin's thesis at the *Avenir National*. President Robert of the l'Association Canado-Américaine and Fr. Verette [sic], who are genuine friends of France, deeply lament their compatriot's attitude, and are rightly afraid that his intemperate language may bring discredit to their group in French circles that take an interest in Franco-Americans. Nevertheless, my impression is that Benoit is an isolated individual among Franco-Americans.

I would add that I have taken advantage of Professor Gilson's visit to Boston to offer a lunch in his honor, where I gathered some of his French and American colleagues at Harvard, particularly in the philosophy department, the chair of the French department of Wellesley College, and an important Irish-American figure at Boston College.

The expenses of Professor Gilson were covered by our consulate general at Montreal, and our eminent compatriot has generously refused any fee for his lectures.

LETTERS FROM ÉTIENNE GILSON TO PAUL VALÉRY (1942–1944)

Bibliothèque Littéraire Jacques Doucet, Paris

Letter 1

Library number: VRY 1570

December 19, 1942

My dear colleague,

You are pleasantly rid of flatterers, and I would not want to insult you by speaking well of your book, but I ought at least to be able to thank you for the immense pleasure you have given me. I would certainly try to take you with a bit of vinegar, if I was only sure that to have a thought, even a "bad thought" implies that one can put it in practice. I prefer to go on selfishly reading you, as if the good moments I spend with you, whether approving, or disconcerted, or repulsed, were still the best homage I could offer you. I wonder whether disconcerting your readers of good will might not be what amuses you most. You are a past master in this kind of sport, and you do it so kindly that one recovers and gets back on track awaiting the next shove. When one approves, one would like to be with you to continue the conversation: "Thinkers, granted that thinkers serve some purpose . . ." and so on. A hundred times I have taught this as an exact description of metaphysics. A metaphysician asks himself what happens if we admit that. . . . What stops me is the following difficulty: if the metaphysician cheats, it is not worth the trouble to read him, if he plays fair, his greatness condemns him to the system. Every impure position is harmful for the intellect; every pure position is absurd. It is necessary to think like Descartes, Spinoza, or Hegel, or not at all, which is to say to be condemned to the absurd, or to be content with a jumble of ideas unworthy of a "thinker."

Perhaps there would be an outcome, which would be to reestablish the communications of thought with the mystery of existence, two of your pet peeves (let us call them the Pascals), to which your whole labor pays homage, since they are your limit, and since your greatness has always been affirmed on its own limit. For my part, I do not believe that the intellect abdicates the least of its rights by acknowledging the existence of what happens to it. That is where I would have vinegar to offer you. Don't think that "existence" pleases philosophers. They are horrified by it. I would like to write a history of philosophy to show that "horror of existence is the beginning of wisdom." Being, yes, because it is a kind of concept, but existence is not. What a pity that you, who have unceasingly got inside the mystery of the existential act and whose incomparable art is so powerful in being able to give its shock as if with a presence, would turn against it in that way and speak of it only to exorcise it. It is true that written words surely can do nothing else.

I have not finished the book (p. 184). Nor will I have "finished" it when I have read it once. I do not want either to delay in thanking you or to hurry my pace at the risk of spoiling my pleasure. But be assured that you give me marvelous intellectual joy, and also of my perfect gratitude.

Étienne Gilson
2 Avenue Émile Acollas, VIIe

Letter 2

Library number: VRY 139 (4) In 12, and VRY 137 (15) In 12

May, 5 1944

Dear colleague,

What a delightful surprise when your two volumes arrived![8] I wanted to read *Arbre* first, with which I was not acquainted, but I could not refrain from starting with my favorite *Eupalinos* once again, and naturally, I continued on to the end. It is the art of perfect French prose enriched by three centuries of experience, handled by

8 Gilson first comments on one of the two books, which contains three works: Paul Valéry, *Eupalinos, L'âme et la danse, Dialogue de l'arbre* (Paris: Gallimard, 1944); then he comments on *Mémoires d'un poème* [*Fragments des mémoires d'un poème* (Paris: Grasset, 1938)].

an incomparable artist. I don't know how you do it, and despite M. Teste, I dare say that you don't know either.

Then I took up *Arbre*, and everything was going well. I reached Valéry, when an accident happened on p. 192:

> Tandis qu'à tes chansons, mon oreille se fie,
> Je crains d'être sans goût pour ta philosophie.
> [As long as my ear trusts your songs, / I fear I've no taste for your philosophy.]

I heard: "se fi-e" and "philosophi-e," as in French, in short, a hitherto lost variant of the *Femmes savantes*. From that point I was lost. These two rhymes no longer allowed me to fail to feel all the alexandrines with which the work's continuation is filled and that horribly annoyed me. Emerging from *Eupalinos*, they made me miss the exquisite sense of rhythm, of breaks, and of cadences that you have in the highest degree. The strangest thing is that, as I observed next, Tityre had already begun some time earlier without my having perceived the device, so much so that I do not even know whether these two verses are not what spoiled my enjoyment. I give you my impressions, because you surely know that nobody enjoys you more than I do. Yes, in spite of the Pascal problem!

I am in *Variété V*, but I want to take my time and read or re-read everything slowly. In regard to *Coquille*, don't you have anything to tell us about existence? I know well what you are going to answer, but you are precisely the one who still knows how to speak on the farthest frontier of the ineffable, the unspeakable. I have begun *Mémoires d'un poème*, but it is too important to be read without complete intellectual leisure. By contrast, as I was leaving an enactment of *Bérénice* yesterday, I threw myself upon *Phèdre femme*, which entirely satisfied me, and be sure that you were completely right in recounting your personal experience of the ending. Everyone will understand, and the ending is indeed decisive. I add that today only Bérénice herself remains for me today and that, like Phèdre, she alone survives. She has secreted the piece around herself as a pearl that would secrete its shell.

So, if you are reading me, I would say something else, which is that if the end does not justify the means for you, it is not *because there is no end*. I would say rather that it is because there are no means, because the means are already ends. Everything that exists is an end, and when you have written a page, it is an end. There is in Valéry's world something eternal that did not exist before, that could only exist through you, that enriches the sum total of the authentically beautiful and what is authentically being. You have increased the value of the world by prolonging its creation. I know well that you cannot feel it, precisely because you are the creator. I have just read Degas's letters, and I have been confounded to see that he, Degas, was not happy. He was not sure that he was really good. However, who comes to the world as a more absolute end than a Degas? More can be done but not anything more than something like *Phèdre* or *Bérénice*. And you, who create a work whose breadth equals its beauty, you have to envy no "line" in anyone. Do not doubt for an instant that you are a creator of absolute ends. I have come to recite some Valéry, all alone on a hill, as I have come to repeat a verse of Racine or a phrase of Pelleas, in order that this beauty should sound out in that place at least once in the history of the world, and for the first time since its creation. That also is an end in itself, quite modest, alas, but it is one.

Yours very truly,
Étienne Gilson
2 avenue Émile Acollas, VII

REPORT BY ÉTIENNE GILSON DIRECTED TO FR. AUGUSTIN-JEAN MAYDIEU, MAY 28, 1944

This report titled "Conversation with an Absent Friend," eleven pages long, is found in the Maydieu Collection at the Archives de la Province dominicaine de France, Le Saulchoir, Paris [Archives of the French Dominican Province; APDF] and contains the seeds of articles published by Gilson in *La Vie intellectuelle* between 1945 and 1946: Christendom, Catholic Action, educational issues, Catholic principles, social system, and so on. Answering a query from Fr. Maydieu about the eventual re-opening of *La Vie intellectuelle*, Gilson indicates his fundamental principles on the eve of the landing in Normandy and the basic lines of a program that the proximate and longed-for liberation required in his view. The Atlantic and transnational framework is clearly delineated, at the same time as criticism of the French bishops during the war. Gilson rejects both conservativism and revolutionary spirit in the Church, both clericalism and insubordination of laity. This is a *via media*, if ever there was one.

Articles by Étienne Gilson in *La Vie intellectuelle*:

- "L'esprit de chrétienté," *La Vie intellectuelle*, February 1945, 18–36.
- "Jacques Maritain au Vatican," *La Vie intellectuelle*, March 1945, 36–38.
- "Pour une éducation nationale," *La Vie intellectuelle*, April 1945, 116–32.
- "Le thomisme et les philosophies existentielles," *La Vie intellectuelle*, June 1945, 144–55.
- "Un gomor de manne," *La Vie intellectuelle*, November 1946, 6–19.
- "Révélation et unité des hommes," *La Vie intellectuelle*, February 1955, 6–24.

Discussion with an Absent Friend

[p. 1 - Gilson's pagination]

I would simply like to write a few marginal notes about the project conceived by Fr. Maydieu. This is not an opposing project or a criticism, but a conversation, where I think agreements ought to be noted as clearly as the divergences that might eventually arise. A project of this scope, furthermore, surpasses any individual competence, and I would limit these remarks to parts of the project upon which my personal experience allows me to reflect usefully.

My impression is that the point is not to break with *La Vie intellectuelle*, but to make a new start. I am so convinced of it that I do not even see that it is necessary to choose a new title. The magazine's present name has its good qualities and its defects, the chief of the latter being that the title is not directly Christian, at least for those who do not know the religious element that a Dominican puts in the meaning of the term intellect. If we want to emphasize the endeavor's real continuity, let us keep the name. On the other hand if we want to draw attention to the new element in the stage into which it has to enter, we might think of *Chrétienté [Christendom]*.

In any case, content matters more than name, and however hugely varied this content is, it will be efficacious only if it is a unity taken as a whole. Accordingly, this magazine must say one thing, and only one, for its message to be understood and ultimately accepted. If I myself **[p. 2]** were to define it, I would propose this simple formula: the Church has no system, it has only principles. By *system* here I understand every particular organization of reality that appeals to its principles and, whether in the political, economic, or intellectual order, expresses the manner in which, at some given moment of history, these principles are embodied in the particular, concrete situation. The permanent task that Christian life in the world presents is precisely to distinguish the principles of the different situations in which we find ourselves already entangled, to avoid confusing what Christianity has done from what it is, but also to detach the former from the latter if necessary, in order to assure its insertion into new systems, which, in any case, will arise. Truly Christian thought must equally steer clear of two dangers, either of which can give scandal, and both of which always threaten. The first is what could be called conservative Christianity. It consists of a kind of incapacity to distinguish Christianity itself from its temporal accomplishments. Let us acknowledge that it is not completely avoidable. Christianity's constant labor through the centuries consists in sanctifying the temporal as it develops, according to its specific demands, with its greatness and its weakness, throughout time. There has never been and there will never be a human reality, whatever its form, whose sanctification Christianity does not undertake. In the measure in which it succeeds, this reality becomes Christian. Consequently, it presents itself to us as the particular reality of Christianity, and all Christians, especially if history has not made them familiar with other realities, will naturally confuse it **[p. 3]** with Christianity itself. Consequently, their fate seems linked. To touch one is to touch the other. Christians are scandalized when it is revealed to them that this is not so. To give a particular example of the same idea, let us say that the relation of Christianity to the temporal in fact always resembles a concordat. Whether this concordat is explicit or not, it exists, but it is not always the same. Conservative Christians are those who believe that this concordat is always the same and that there can only be one.

The opposite to that danger is the one that the revolutionary Christian incurs. Revolutionary Christians are those who believe that Christianity perishes if it does not get aboard the last train, as if behind the last outbound train there were not always another that is being assembled. These Christians are rightly troubled at the sight of Christianity bound to particular forms that are obsolete in the whole temporal component. In the interest of Christianity, they want to create a revolutionary force capable of participating actively in the establishment of systems that are in the process of formation. Christianity ought to sanctify what is temporal, but it does not have to do directly with creating it. Human beings of the future will design their several dwelling places with the sweat of their brow, without the Church having to do anything but judge this effort and direct it from above in the light of these principles. For all systems that respect these principles, however diverse and unequal their temporal merits may otherwise be, are legitimate from the Christian standpoint. Every human construction that does not exclude Christ in principle, can be sanctified by Christian principles.

[p. 4] A Catholic magazine would perform a very beneficial role by helping Christians to situate themselves within the authentic maze presented by the problem of the place of Christians in the temporal order. This is why one of the most urgent tasks would be to expand the horizon of Catholics to the dimensions of the horizon of the Church. Whence comes the emphasis that it would perhaps be appropriate to place upon the concept of Christendom. The Church contains all the churches, among others the French church. Now, we are not acquainted with the others. French Catholics are always parishioners of the parish of France. That is excellent, but they should not be completely ignorant of the other parishes, if only in the interest of their own parish. To progressively initiate French Catholics in all the great social, aesthetic, and intellectual expressions of Catholicism would be a labor of vast scope. At its end, if the very nature of such a labor involves an end, a restoration of this sense of Christendom, which we so painfully lack, would be perceived. Moving forward with the labor, an expansion of perspective would certainly be gained that would help French Catholics to discern better what is permanent and what is temporary or local in their own Christianity. We would have all the less to lose doing in that, because French Christianity has never been truly great except at the moments when it is most completely identified with the essence of absolute Christianity. For Bossuet to be a doctor of the Church, the only thing missing was not to be a Gallican.

Not binding the Church to any particular temporal form does not mean that Christians need not involve themselves in temporal action and do so as Christians. Here we tackle the problem of Catholic action, and this is still an area **[p. 5]** where French lay people, if they are Catholics, need to be directed and continually advised. I do not mean that they themselves should not intervene in the debate, but their position in the Church is such that it is very difficult for them to express themselves. Indeed, this problem involves the relation of Catholics with the hierarchy to which they are subordinated, and that very relation is a notable example of the delay that systems suffer at certain times in regard to principles. However, their hierarchy continually involves itself for its part, without having consulted them, and involves them in its wake. It is as if we lived in the period when the hierarchy, creator and manager of the temporal order, still had to organize it. This time has ended. At least, let us say that the time in which we currently live in France is a completely different time. The initiative in temporal things, which the

Church never claimed in principle, except where the pope himself was a temporal sovereign, is not in fact acknowledged for the Church by any presently existing state. In France, it would be identified with what the man in the street most hates and most despises, clericalism. It is not often enough noted that, in its noble forms, this exasperation involves a very great tribute to the Church's spirituality. In this regard, the hierarchy's slightest error can have the most serious consequences. I am thinking here much less of the justification that it gives anti-Christian political actions than about the repercussions upon Catholic Action itself, because it makes it impossible. I cannot commit myself to any particular Catholic activity if the hierarchy to which I am subordinated as a Catholic takes initiatives in temporal things, **[p. 6]** where I am not subject to it and my conscience prevents me from approving. We are not dealing with some particular case, but with a problem that is now permanent and created by Catholic Action itself. If Catholic Action has to culminate in the laity being drafted and subjected to social or political directives from the hierarchy, the effect in each country would be the establishment of a priestly party that would be the very incarnation of clericalism. The consequences would be all too easily foreseeable. It is not that a clerical [sic] is bad or impossible in essence. I would not have to be pressed too much to confess that it is my most cherished utopia. I only observe that no state is Christian enough to want it, nor is any clergy so superlatively wise as to accomplish it. Therefore, taken as it is posed in the particular case, the problem of Catholic Action calls for the creation of new institutions or the transformation of old ones. In any case, it demands the creation of new habits that make possible the consultation of the laity by their leaders and consequently permit coordination of their action. It seems to me that it is up to our priests to demand and direct this reform. The magazine that we contemplate would helpfully offer them the chance to express themselves.

Only if the presently non-existent contact between the laity and their hierarchy comes to be established, will the still immense Christian forces of our country be able to place themselves at the disposition of the Church. The French hierarchy is that of a Christian France that is no longer today's France. If one may say so, it remains as the administrative body imagined by Napoleon I in a period when the pope himself **[p. 7]** was his prisoner in order to utilize most effectively the Christian forces of France for the political interests of the Empire. The bishop was then the prefect's delegate for ecclesiastical affairs, and the custom has taken hold so strongly. that the bishop sometimes still behaves in the same way, although by law he is no longer that.

One prefect, one bishop, is good enough for administrators but not good enough for shepherds of souls. We must insistently demand more bishops, assign at least one to the majority of our ancient cathedrals, and create new bishoprics if necessary. Spiritually, immense benefits would result from such a reform, and to keep to the specific problem of Catholic Action, it would allow the direct contract of bishop and faithful, which would avoid many disagreements, whose multiplication risks being the death of this action. Absent authentic collaboration, the Catholics will certainly not declare war on their own hierarchy, but they will be disarmed against those to whom the hierarchy itself will have furnished weapons to fight against it, and the faithful will abstain.

Similar problems are posed if we move from the structure of ecclesiastical institutions to Christian culture. Here again these problems are immediately posed regarding institutions, which though no longer belonging directly to the Church, are still its works. The school system, from Catholic secondary schools to elementary schools, without which Christian culture would be able to exist only with difficulty, immediately appears to be at stake. Huge obstacles oppose the public discussion of these schools, and anyone who dares to pose the simplest questions is certain to attract suspicions that soon turn into hatred. Let us take an example that is both simple and possible **[p. 8]** What Catholics, after having contributed all their lives to the expenses and maintenance of a Catholic school, have ever seen its budget? What means do Catholics have of knowing where the money they give goes? We know that the teachers are ridiculously badly paid. Is that because we do not give enough, or because what we give is steered toward things that are deemed more urgent, but for which we did not contribute on the day when we gave for the Catholic school? There is more. Have Catholics been consulted about what they expect from their Catholic schools or universities? How many of the thousands of Catholics who represent culture under all its modern forms and who are entrusted by the state itself to represent it, have been invited to express an opinion on this subject? I certainly understand that once more the hierarchy intends to reserve to itself the initiative and authority that, moreover, no one challenges, but what use does it make of them? Some Catholic has been able to teach the history of Christian philosophy in the Middle Ages, but is a layman. The Catholic Institute of Paris does not teach it. The state teaches it. Christian literature of North Africa has been taught at the Collège de France. There is a program for studies of the history of theology—at the École des Hautes Études. Many examples could be added.

They are not important. What is important is that Catholics have been able to present their own culture only in non-Catholic institutions, and that they would not have been able to do so, certainly not materially and doubtless not spiritually, in Catholic institutions where that culture rightfully ought to be presented. This odd situation calls for a deeper examination.

[p. 9] Questions related to secondary or primary schools, whose status and perhaps even existence are at stake today, are not posed with any more prudence. The users of these schools, who keep them alive, have never been asked for their opinion on what they would like the schools to be. It is hardly permissible, without attracting tenacious enmity, to speak, however discretely, about what they are. Above all, so far as I know, no opinion has been formulated on what it is desired that they should be, nor have the only conditions in which they could survive within a modern state been honestly formulated: absolute liberty in absolute quality of obligations, compensated by absolute equality of support. The problem is not peculiar to France, and here again the study of what goes on abroad would be of the greatest use. Nothing in France can be even remotely compared to the University of Louvain nor with the various Catholic schools systems recognized by the state in the United States or elsewhere. Experiments that are unlikely in France and that our hierarchy would be the first to condemn, no less than the state itself, have been carried out abroad. I know Catholic colleges, federated with Protestant universities, whose president is a Protestant minister, who congratulate each other on their association. If we looked a little outside, how many possible "systems" would appear before our eyes, whose existence we would never have thought conceivable. Certainly, what is possible here is not possible there, but knowing these things perhaps would awaken a desire to make proposals, take initiatives, invent, and create.

[p. 10] There are also problems posed by intellectual and artistic culture in all its forms. Here, *La Vie intellectuelle* has given such an excellent example that I see nothing better than to continue it. If there still exists a complete collection of the magazine, it must be preserved avidly. Readers of the future will be surprised at everything it contains. The only difficulty to be overcome is gathering around a magazine of this kind the big names, all the big names, of Christian letters and art. Our Catholic magazines have a second-class appearance. Major figures take their prose and their verse elsewhere. Doubtless, they are culpable in that, but perhaps the whole fault is not on their side. From this viewpoint, I don't know whether the format of *La Vie intellectuelle*, although it has its advantages, might not be blamed.

A format like that of the major magazines, *NRF*, *Mercure*, *Revue de Paris*, or *Revue des deux mondes*, seems to be indispensable. I may be mistaken in this, but the issue ought to be studied.

Do we have directions in this vast undertaking? Yes, the very ones you have stated and that come to us from the popes, especially from Leo XIII to Pius XII. Let us confess that we laymen are unfamiliar with them, perhaps because the way in which they are transmitted, not to mention the way in which they are expressed, does not help their dissemination. A publisher that committed itself to making them known gradually and to reminding us of them continually would be excellent. I know perfectly well that some of them would provoke an outcry. In this they are like the Gospel, and this is another reason to recall them.

[p. 11] In finishing, it seems to me that I have commented upon only some points of the text that I was sent. I think that there is too much about agreements in what I have said and very little or nothing about differences. Possibly, long friendship is sufficient explanation of that. In what circumstances could it achieve the form of a more complete and closer unity?

Pentecost Sunday, May 28, 1944
Étienne Gilson

LETTERS FROM ÉTIENNE GILSON TO FRANÇOIS MAURIAC (1945–1969)

MS 39435–MS 39442, Bibliothèque littéraire Jacques Doucet, Paris

There are eight letters sent by Étienne Gilson to François Mauriac between 1945 and 1969. It shows a friendship that was late, discrete, and deep between the two. The letters combine worldly subjects—Gilson's candidacy to the Académie française—as well as university or ecclesial issues. It casts a glance upon Gilson's daily readings and lets us capture his meetings with Pius XII or with other members of the Académie française. After Gilson's involvement with the Mouvement Républicain Populaire, the correspondence includes political considerations about General de Gaulle's France.

Letter 1

March 4, 1945

Sir:

Our friend Fr. Maydieu told me that you would not consider my candidacy to Bergson's chair to be an absurdity. I am deeply touched that you think so and thank you. If I may, I would like to assure you, that if this is really your opinion, I would leave it entirely to you, and I would submit my candidacy to this chair or to another according to your kind advice.

Most gratefully yours,
Étienne Gilson
2 avenue Émile Acollas, VIIe

Letter 2

February 8, 1946

Sir,

In your absence, I find myself buffeted by the academic whirlwind, and I had to enter into competition with Baron Seillière. How I regretted being unable to consult you. Finally I abstained in order not to trouble several of my friends unnecessarily, who also happen to be my colleagues.

Nevertheless, it is possible that I will present my candidacy before leaving for Canada around the twentieth of this month. First, I must meet Georges Duhamel again, but I would be happy to speak to you about it as well. Not that I have any illusions. If I had had any, I would have lost them already. I was told first: consider that there are fifteen seats to fill! Then they began to tell me that twelve of them were practically filled . . .

However, I cannot act as a candidate without consulting you. I am free every day except Monday and Tuesday mornings, and I would be grateful if you could kindly grant me a meeting as soon as you have recovered from the fatigues of your voyage.

Please accept my heartfelt gratitude,
Étienne Gilson
2 avenue Émile Acollas, VIIe

Letter 3

Conseil de la République

République Française
Liberté - Égalité - Fraternité
[handwritten note]

April 22, 1947

Sir and dear Colleague,
This morning I came back to Paris from Rome, where I had the honor of being received on Sunday, April 13, by the Holy Father. Since his Holiness asked me for news about the Académie française, I naturally related the session where Paul Claudel was admitted, at which point, he immediately spoke about François Mauriac, and indeed only about him. Pius XII had read the two discourses, but he spoke to me of yours in moving terms, and regarding the comment I made about the magnificent example of courage that you give us all, the pope literally answered: "Yes, a magnificent example. I read all François Mauriac's articles in *Le Figaro*. At least I can say almost all, because unhappily there are days when my work becomes too overwhelming to leave me the time. But we should not speak only of his courage. We must not forget the admirable perfection of the form in which he expresses his thought. He is a great Christian and a great writer." I asked the Holy Father if he authorized me to convey his words to you, and he immediately answered, with perceptible tenderness in his voice, "Yes, do that, tell him. Tell him for us."

So, there it is, and it is the first thing I promised myself to do since my return. What nothing can make you hear is the sound of that voice speaking of you in that way and the deeply moving reality of your living presence on Vatican Hill. Be assured that you are tenderly admired and loved there. For me, who love and admire you likewise—from a lesser altitude but not from close by—to have had the honor to bring you this message will remain one of the most intimate and dearest joys of my life. Once more, something I owe you.

In grateful friendship,
Étienne Gilson
2 avenue Émile Acollas, VIIe

Letter 4

July 20, 1950

Dear Sir and friend,

So now we have *Journal IV* published by Flammarion, placed after *Journal III* published by Grasset. How strange it is to re-read all those articles! We were reading them in the present so little time ago, and all that is irrecoverably past. Your art, poured out of your great heart, will have frozen forever the hopes and all kind of sentiments that were ours very little time ago, and for which we would have so little use today that, without you, we would no longer even remember them. You have never turned away anything but lying and hatred, but unfortunately that is the only food desired by those who know what they want. As for our friends, they swim in complete unreality and drown in a flood of words none of which cover reality.

It is frightful. Reading your articles, of which I have missed none, I often wonder what your mail must be. I wonder how your extraordinary sensitivity can put up with the assaults before which you continually place yourself. Stupidity is the worst curse of the human species. When one ponders the fact that the French are one of the most intelligent and cultivated peoples—at least so they say—whatever can the rest be like? We will know it before long perhaps, and then the problem of writing articles will not present itself. It will be the moment of the great peace. But why would Vermenton overshadow Malagar? You are there, I think, and I like to imagine that you set aside some hours for pure art. If I did not have to do some work myself that turns me away from so many anguishing subjects, I would no longer have the courage to live. Everything has failed. But while one writes, one no longer thinks [sic]. I have been away from Paris since Easter and I came back to the Academy only for the "prix de roman." That was enough for me. Once upon a time, I used to imagine that people there talked about literature, but I find only bickering about boots. So here I am in my solitude, which is the only place I can work a little. I have just read the last diary of Charlie and his correspondence with Gide. It is strange. It will give you a sorry notion of my literary taste, that I have no admiration for Gide's style. For me he is a kind of Anatole France and the height of artificiality. But I am very curious about the man himself. He must have been deeply unhappy. Why was he was not satisfied with being liked but not approved?

Don't waste time answering me. You have something else to do that will be more important for everybody. I reply to the reception of your book and take advantage of the happy occasion to repeat to you, still more than my admiration, my deep and faithful affection.

Please remember me to Madame Mauriac.
Yours very truly,
Étienne Gilson
6 rue Collet - Vermenton - Yonne

Letter 5

December 5, 1962

Distinguished colleague and friend,
Your last book [perhaps *Ce que je crois* (Paris: Grasset, 1962)], has suffered the fate of all those that you generously send me. I have read it at a sitting. Moreover I did not have to descend from some height to join you in your "little swamp," because it is mine too. I live there like you and so many others, and life is bearable there for me, in the frightful moral humiliation of old age, only because like you, I hope that God loves me as I am. Otherwise he would change me, as I have begged him a thousand times to do, without being heard. I have never expressed this feeling better than one day in Spokane in the United States, when I hardly expected it, at the end of the question time that customarily follows a lecture in American universities, some question or other had been put to me. I remember only the last part of my improvised reply: "In any case, one idea reassures me, which is that my sovereign judge will not be a *man*." With that the chair of the session immediately declared it closed.

Your book will do a great deal of good, and I do not see anything that could offend anyone, even at Rome. I allow myself to make that observation, because even your repentances at the end seem unnecessary to me.

Gratefully yours, with my very best wishes,
Étienne Gilson
9 rue Saint-Romain - Paris - VI

Letter 6

November 2, 1964

Dear and distinguished colleague,
How can I thank you for the book [*De Gaulle* (Paris: Grasset, 1964)] and its dedication. Thanks to you I have just sat down face to face with the extraordinary man about whom I have never stopped asking myself questions. Like you, I lived with the myth of the man in London—suddenly, totally, without nuances or reticence. Then involved in a political movement (the MRP) for the only time in my life, I saw him separate himself from his best troops. I voted for the constitution he did not want. I was completely mistaken in that, because he was right, as we have seen only too well since. I found in him then, and I still find, in him the defects that I most detest in any person, and whose praises he furthermore sings in his incredible "Man of Character," a perfect portrait of a leader according to the mind of St. Ignatius Loyola, that maker of leaders. The pride, the contempt for others of which this great *salegnoso* [illegible word] streams, all that horrifies me as much as ever. Yet, I have surrendered. I acknowledge that I am conquered by his greatness. Nothing he does surprises me any more. I accept it like Mont Blanc, without arguing.

In any case, he is a leader. He has never pardoned a defection or forgotten loyalty. God preserve him, with his great projects for which men are always lacking—yesterday Algeria and Africa, today Germany, and tomorrow France herself—but never ceasing to climb his old cliff!

With admiration and gratitude,
Étienne Gilson
9 rue Saint-Romain - Paris - VIe

Letter 7

January 19, 1966

My dear colleague and friend,
Aided by a temperature that invites one to stay home, I have just spent two days with you, fascinated, as always, by the style and the language, but this time equally by the author himself. I more or less knew all this, but a portrait of you done by you [Gilson probably refers to *Nouveaux mémoires intérieures* (Paris: Flammarion, 1965)]

confirms the picture already made and completes it. I think that you do yourself, as they say, true to life.

The *Vigile* incident had inspired me to write an article for the *Cahiers Charles Du Bos* against the self-appointed theological inquisitors, but Madame Du Bos opposed its publication. As I wrote to her then, what a triumph for Gide! The devil had foreseen everything. Our friend fell from Keats to Bérulle and from great critic to unauthorized spiritual author. Voltaire (or the medieval tumbler of Notre Dame) was a better theologian: let us cultivate our garden; even A.M.D.G. [*ad majorem Dei gloriam*], one can do no better. Spirituality is not a literary subject, alas, except for spiritual persons themselves, who are rare.

Thank you with all my heart and be assured of my faithful friendship
Étienne Gilson

Letter 8

No date [but after April 1969]

Dear and distinguished colleague,
A mishap never comes alone. Your stupid accident would have been a sign among the ancients, but at least as for you, we will see you again. I hope it will be soon and that your back will not cause too much pain from now until then.

Why doesn't the Academy welcome General de Gaulle rather than General Béthouart? It is true that he must have enough of all the disasters. The thought that he is going to have some rest consoles me a little for his failures, and also the thought that he alone could reverse himself.

May you have a good convalescence and quick recovery, my dear colleague.
Yours very truly
Étienne Gilson
6 rue Collet - Vermenton - Yonne

P.S. In two months I will send you a little book about language.[9] It will be unreadable for you, but I send it only for the pleasure of offering it to you.

9 Étienne Gilson, *Linguistique et philosophie: Essai sur les constantes philosophiques du langage* (Paris: Vrin, 1969).

LETTERS BETWEEN ÉTIENNE GILSON AND THOMAS MERTON (1951)

The Thomas Merton Center, Bellarmine University, Louisville, Kentucky

November 4, 1951 [Original in French]

My Reverend Father,

My thanks for your beautiful book [*The Ascent of Truth*], where I re-encounter so many doctrines lived and alive in you, about which a poor Christian like myself—a small scale pedestrian—has never been able to speak except in the language of their author. You do so as well, but with the free familiarity of someone who speaks from experience. In this admirable and moving American people there is a crowd of elite souls who will understand you and whom you will draw after you toward the heights. God has chosen you to speak for him about these secret things. I am sure you will be understood about him.

I live in extreme spiritual poverty, which is not that of afterwards, but, alas, that of before everything you speak of. But I believe in the Kingdom of God, and I live awaiting it on earth as in heaven. I am convinced that the United States is to play a huge role in this story, and that the coming will be prepared by the United States. The substitution for Europe, which is too far from the Orient, is necessary. It seems to me that yor work and your person are a sign. I find it moving that it should come from that Gethsemane about whose existence I learned many years ago in Michael Williams's moving passages, which I have never forgotten.

I know how much I owe to your prayers that have sustained me during tragic months of my life, and I thank you with all my heart. God has heard you, but think of me still sometimes in the mass for ordinary sinners, the mediocre, who are not even bad enough for someone to learn something from them.

Be assured, Father, of my respectful gratitude and my filial devotion,
Étienne Gilson Toronto
8 Elmsley Place, Ontario, Canada

Nov. 12, 1951
Our Lady of Gethsemani
Trappist-Cisotercian Abbey
Trappist, Kentucky

Dear Professor Gilson,
Deeply moved by your beautiful letter, I want to do what I should have done long ago—write you a line to assure you of my recognition of a spiritual debt to you which I too sketchily indicated in the pages of *The Seven Storey Mountain*, and in a rather badly constructed section of the book at that. To you and to Jacques Maritain, among others, I owe the Catholic faith. That is to say I owe my life. This is no small debt. Can you feel as abandoned as you do when you are handing out to other people as great a gift as is the Kingdom of Heaven? But indeed, it is the privilege of those who bear such spiritual fruit to feel abandoned and miserable and alone, for poverty of spirit is the patrimony of the children of God in this world, and their pledge of glory in the world to come: "for theirs is the Kingdom of Heaven."

What greater thing can we have than to be empty, to be despoiled, to be orphans and exiles in this world? Your exile is not merely metaphorical. It is something you suffer and offer to God for the France He loves and which nevertheless tends to reject Him and those whom He sends.

Thank you for the kind words you say about *The Ascent to Truth*. In none of the books that I have written do I feel that I have said what I wanted. I do not know whether or not in this one I have said what needs to be said to any except a few. I have the consciousness of having disappointed many who wanted me to say something to *them*. Also I have an even greater consciousness that I have nothing to say to anyone except the oaks of our forest. Like St. Bernard, I feel that I can go to them and learn everything. I dare not say that like him I feel like the chimaera of the age, lest it suggest a sort of comparison between an unworthy son and so great a Father—and this is a comparison which I cannot afford to make.

Please pray for me to Our Lord that instead of merely writing something I may *be* something, and indeed that I may so fully be what I ought to be that there may be no further necessity for me to write, since the mere fact of being what I ought to be would be more eloquent than many books. Do you ever come down this way? Please do not fail to come and see us if you are ever around Chicago or any of the Middle Western cities which are "near" Gethsemani! This Cistercian house—where as Father Master of Scholastics I am eternally grateful to be able to give my spiritual children nourishment from your wonderful book on St. Bernard—will always welcome you. Consider it your home in this part of the world and come whenever you like. Meanwhile, we will meet before the holy altar of God, and I promise to remember you frequently in my Mass.

Sincerely yours in Christ,
Father Louis [Thomas] Merton
OCSO

LETTERS BETWEEN ÉTIENNE GILSON AND FRANCISQUE GAY (1953)

Archives de l'Institut Marc Sangnier, Paris

July 3, 1953

My dear teacher,
Monsieur Vrin has told me that for unexpected health problems you have had to return to Vermenton from Auxerre. With benefit of almost three years' experience, I would like to add my advice to that of all your friends. Get all of the rest that you have been instructed to get until the improvement already observed is complete and the Faculty gives you complete freedom to return to your activity.

You surely were not too sorry to miss the famous academic meeting. But you have too many friends and admirers who regret your long silence and that on such occasions you no longer offer your judgment on the great problems of the moment.

I could never tell you how much we miss you. Every day, everything that happens brings me new and bitter disappointments. That greatly increase my permanent state of fatigue. I am no longer capable of anything but to mope as I remember the great opportunities that we have not been able to seize.

My publishing house has also caused concerns. I don't know whether I will be able to take even two weeks of vacation. I will be at Dixmont [in Yonne] at least from July 10 to 15, perhaps until July 20, particularly if I am able to convince you to visit us.

How happy I would be if you let me go to get you. We could offer our hospitality to you and your daughter.

On your last trip to France you must have had the feeling that all your friends had "dropped you," and I have so much regretted it that, despite my shyness, I dare to run the risk of appearing indiscreet. It seems to me that if, from the end of 1944 or if from 1945–46, we had known how to give you a good hearing within our movement, perhaps history might not have recorded such a succession of failures.

The MRP has gone bankrupt, not only because of errors in political tactics and strategy, but firstly and above all because, in the great disorder that followed the Liberation, it was incapable of providing our unfortunate country with the thinking, the doctrine, the mystique that would unite a multitude. In all parties, we have had only poor little politicians, who tried to imitate the old radicals.

My dear teacher, please excuse me. Follow the advice of your admirer.

My very best wishes, yours faithfully,
Francisque Gay.
Paris

July 7, 1953

Mr. Ambassador and dear friend,
I want to reassure you about my health. This first warning impressed me, and I immediately began the complete rest that you advise. The result has been excellent. What I have not been able to do is to stop experiencing the anguish caused by the crises of health that proliferate around me. Only work helps me to forget them. I must get back to it without much delay.

I have nothing to complain about regarding the MRP, nothing and no one. I retain all my fondness and loyalty to the Movement, because outside of it there is nothing else. The only thing is that I cannot be of any help or perform any service to it. Moreover, I believe that I could not be useful to any political movement, because I cannot put my confidence in anything but the truth. I believe that to play the card of the truth would in fact have been the highest political skillfulness.

It would have been certain of success. The movement's leaders preferred to be smart alecks—like all the rest. It is not up to me to judge their tactic. It simply is the case that this is a kind of politics to which I am completely unsuited. So everything is all right in this way.

As for journalism, I have involved myself in it only incidentally, provoked by the colossal errors that were committed around 1950 about the true sense of American politics. Only this: to fight, it is necessary to have one's own newspaper. Neglecting oneself is nothing. One must not neglect one's friends. Nowadays, the dice are cast. It is too late to rake back the stakes, and we no longer have any role to play. Germany is going to direct the game on the continent. In America, everything hangs on the duel between McCarthy and Eisenhower. If McCarthy wins, God forbid, we will see a fascism and series of catastrophes that are literally unimagined. Only, what good is it to write about what so many Americans know? There was a moment precisely around 1950, where we could choose our destiny by creating it ourselves. The French did not even want anybody to talk to them about it then. It would be too late to talk to them about it now. I have spent my last days finishing my last books, but not without having the joy in my heart of having been able to know other men as enamored of the truth as I am myself. Those called "men of action" perhaps are right to distrust others, those dreamers they say. We will never settle this conflict, but at least we can recognize and honor and respect each other mutually.

Be assured that I will always always have for you, beside that esteem, my affectionate and grateful friendship,
Étienne Gilson
6 rue Collet, Vermenton (Yonne)

August 5, 1953

My dear Ambassador and Friend,
The voices that kept silence, have, I believe, a common excuse. They could not continue to speak without putting the existence of their works at risk—a great flock, a unique influence in the New World in Jacques Maritain's case—and that with the certainty of not getting anything positive in exchange for this sacrifice. The instance is not peculiar to France. Speech is not freer in other so-called "democratic" countries, with the exception so far in England. It has become a criminal offense to say what every one—among responsible people—knows to be true. Suppose I write again in *Le Monde* to say, or rather repeat, using as supporting evidence that the attacks of *Life* against France, that they express exactly the current opinions

among Republicans on the other side of the Atlantic Ocean. What would happen? In France everyone who has been bought by the dollar would overwhelm me in a new campaign of defamation. In America, I would be forbidden to enter the country, although I receive one or two invitations each month to go there for activities that I believe are useful to the Church and even to France. The only way in which we might have been able to serve would have been as consultants. But never, not even once, even when—through your efforts—I sat in Parliament, did I have any conversation with our leaders. If I had been able to tell them what I thought—and about which I have never believed myself infallible—I would not have written. It is too late now. In the MRP we have never mobilized our troops, the admirable activists that we have in this country; we have never set out in a newspaper the simple, clear, few but immovable principles that would have supported our activity; nor have we carried out through our leaders a specific policy, clearly recognizable as being that of our Movement. To tell the truth I think that our leaders have used the Movement for the objectives of their personal political authority, convinced, and letting us know it, that they were more intelligent by themselves than are all of their troops, while so many activists, whom I have gone to see in north, south, east, and west, had so many things to tell them! No need to be sorry for Maritain or myself. It is for [Victor] Janton, [Barthélémy] Ott, and twenty more that I could mention and who long ago became completely disillusioned by being treated as insignificant, though they were the very substance of the movement. For the moment, the only thing I can see to do is observe the succession of events that are all too foreseeable. France had the initiative and, in what concerns the status of Europe, there was a time when France could, to speak plainly, impose it on the United States. That time is gone. The game is going to be played between the United States and Germany, with only the counterweight of England to effectively delay the catastrophe, maybe even because miracles happen, to avoid it.

I am happy that pre-history keeps you company. Leroy-Gourhan of the Museum of Man is now established at Vermonton, whence he has taken over the excavations of the caves of Arcy-sur-Cure, where you made such a lovely speech to the locals. As for me, I am preparing six lectures on the philosophy of painting, which have been requested by the Washington museum [the National Gallery of Art]. I have published two books in French during the last two years. I have just sent a history of philosophy in the Middle Ages to the American publisher. Lastly, I still have to give courses next year at Toronto. All that allows me not to think to much about my family tragedies. . . .

Most warmly,
Étienne Gilson
6 rue Collet, Vermenton (Yonne)

LETTER FROM ÉTIENNE GILSON TO JULES ROMAINS, JULY 9, 1956

NAF 28403, BNF

My dear colleague and friend,
It has been a great pleasure to receive your *Passengers* . . .[10] For the first time in a long time I am enjoying a bit of leisure in the country, where I have just read the book. Thanks to you, I have had the pleasure of finding myself back in those United States again, which have taken up so many years of my life. And they are certainly the same noble, generous minds that you and I were surrounded with there. I did not know Berle, but I have seen men of action as concerned with ideas as he seems to be. I know Oppenheimer—and Mrs. Oppenheimer, who deserves one or two pages just for herself. He quoted Sanskrit to me too; it is one of his little vanities, but he really knows *some* Sanskrit. And he is truly a great mind.

Only . . . I am not sure that even these great Americans have the words of the most merely temporal life. If the United States possesses the answer to your question, I imagine that it will be given to the world by businessmen, financiers, even politicians, who seem to prepare a future whose formula they do not know themselves. I believe there is an American creative evolution, whose real value cannot be perceived from the meager definitions they give of it. What they do is infinitely more important than what they say. They are *inarticulate*, but they create.

This is the only point on which I feel a bit different about the United States than you. I am less sure than you are about the importance of intellectuals in the view of American public opinion. Nothing is less like the U.S. than a republic of professors. Professors are respected with a shade of amusement, but people seem to think that

10 Jules Romains, *Passagers de cette planète, où allons-nous?* (Paris: Grasset, 1955).

in any case the country should not depend on them for guidance. I agree that the sheer impact of atomic physics has deeply shaken up this indifference, but the Oppenheimer case suggests that the indifference of public opinion in regard to intellectuals remains almost untouched. You note several times, and rightly, that the greatest American universities have freely and courageously maintained their trust in him. That is quite true, but I cannot keep from thinking that precisely this very thing underlines the separation about which I speak. The government has no objection to the great universities' honoring Oppenheimer. Most of the major newspapers say nothing or approve. But no gesture has been made by the politicians (who are so attentive to public opinion) to raise this great mind and great heart from the civic degradation that has been inflicted upon him. He must suffer horribly. I see no concerted effort to rectify the error.

This leads me to doubt the importance of what the great U.S. minds think. European intellectuals are their best audience. All that can change. I share my feelings with you only to give an exact meaning to my remark about the possible (probable??) role of American men of action: Baruch, Ford, Dupont de Nemours, and . . . Truman. If the United States must construct the planet's future, it will rather be, I think, thanks to "creative myths" that are lived, secreted by political, economic, and social action, rather than by the speculative views of the learned.

Enough chatter. Forgive my comments, whose value seems doubtful even to me. One thing is sure in any case: you understand the United States admirably, and you know how to talk about them with perfect tact. You will certainly charm our friends over there.

Cordially yours, my colleague and friend.
Étienne Gilson
6 rue Collet, Vermenton (Yonne)

LETTERS FROM ÉTIENNE GILSON TO JEAN WAHL (1951–1958)

IMEC. The Fonds Jean Wahl contains seven letters from Gilson directed to Jean Wahl (May 12, 1925, February 18, 1932, May 10, 1951, December 9, 1958, December 10, 1958, August 24, 1959, and an undated note). The SMCA archives contain only an unimportant note from Jean Wahl (1959).

May 10, 1951

My dear friend,
I have just finished the correspondence provoked by "the Affair" and naturally the first friends are thanked last. They were at the bottom of the pile. But certainly have no doubt about my gratitude. From the beginning I knew, through our friends Vrin and McKeon, that you were of the few who did not believe that an honorable person could rot in a month. Thank you with all my heart. I still do not understand very well what happened, but the important thing is that it is over. I hope to have the pleasure of meeting you next month at Place de la Sorbonne, where I will go to stock up on philosophical news.

With gratitude and in friendship,
Étienne Gilson
Pontifical Institute of Mediaeval Studies
59 Queen's Park
Toronto 5, Canada

December 9, 1958

Dear colleague and friend,
I emerged from your *Traité de Métaphysique* [Paris: Payot, 1953], with the pleasant impression of having been in your audience at the Sorbonne, and thereby having become a regular in the company you formed long ago with the philosophers. Your students are very lucky to have such a competent guide to introduce them to wisdom or to its study. Your introduction itself is philosophy, which is not praise deserved by all those who pride themselves on introducing others to philosophy.

At the same time I was reading you, I re-read some Montaigne to relax, which I confess, I had not done for a long time, and I thought about how he would have seen your book as a confirmation of his "Apology" [*Essays*, book II, chapter 12]. This is the case precisely because it is excellent and because, despite its excellence, does not lead to any conclusion about which minds like ours, that for the rest are well fashioned to understand each other, might agree. That does not scandalize or distress me. I am only a little surprised that we do not acknowledge how chaotic the situation is. We believe, we pretend to believe or try to persuade ourselves, that the history of metaphysics has meaning, whereas it seems to me to be a slow, fixed whirlwind, the impression of progress depending on the energy with which each of us marks time.

It is very difficult to pass from one philosophy to another. It is not easy to form a chain composed of individual efforts, which become fruitful only when one is isolated and has gone all the way. If I allowed myself a reservation about your method (which you are completely capable of not following, but I am talking about the book) I would say that not once does it allow you to achieve the pure establishment of any metaphysical principle, as if you felt that to do so—whatever the principle—would make the book impossible. It would be necessary to stop and contemplate; the introduction would be over; one would have arrived.

Having practiced a similar method, I have perceived its dangers. We each make our own choice, and yours is that of an idealist. Your points of reference are Plato, Descartes, Kant, and Hegel. What can one say? What can one do? I know them a little, but I am not of their company. Kant in particular only became the destroyer of metaphysics, because he never suspected its nature. One might as well ask a blind man to give an introduction to the perception of colors. His genius is not at issue. I simply say that he used it to construct the philosophy of those who are not concerned with philosophy in so far as it is distinct from science. I have never been able to become interested in it other than for the work's technical perfection and the power of its author's admirable mind. But I have never made contact with any reality or any truth there, other than that of science itself. I would say almost the same thing about Descartes. What you call his "boldness" seems to me rather the naivete of a reckless person who confuses use of a method with "meditation." In a word, I want to reassure you by telling you that since your gods are not mine, all the reservations I can express rather my personal attitude than criticism of yours.

Besides, I scarcely believe in critics. The only thing I am concerned about in what I am writing you is that metaphysics be carried out by individual contemplations. Thinkers say what they see as best they can. They don't prove or demonstrate. Rather, they open up the object of their own vision to the eyes of others. That is all.

In situating myself outside your effort, I will also say (but this time without attaching *any* importance to my remarks) that its efficacy in practice would require a divine metaphysician god. None of us is capable of *comprehending*, as we say, the sequence of great philosophers, and perhaps not even a single one of them. They are at the heart of a region of the mind into which we others hardly penetrate or not at all. No true philosopher philosophizes about philosophy, and if we accompany any of them to the threshold of their sacred retreat, we immediately lose the taste for thinking about this philosopher or any other. Philosophy itself demands the totality of our mind.

The opposite illusion is created by the now fixed practice of teaching philosophy in the schools. No philosopher has ever been able to maintain a teaching career that dealt with philosophy. They all have either refused to teach or else, from Kant to Bergson, spent their time teaching a history of philosophy with or without proper names. It is not always very good history, because for that they need to critique and to link at the same time, which is very different from understanding.

But I could not stop telling you how much your book has stirred up in me. However different you and Brunschvicg are, at the end of the day there is not a huge difference between the two. Thus, I am not surprised by what you said in the chapter where Jacques Maritain and I appear in order to play our little scrap of a role in this great spectacle. It is not that you have identified two doctrines that *contradict each other*. That is not the case at all. But they are alien to each other, and as Leibniz would say, they do not "fit together" with each other. The fact is that each of us on his level—and Jacques Maritain has a philosophical mind far superior to mine—precisely represents personal, original efforts (which is to say that each has its own origin) whose effects cannot be added to, subtracted from, or opposed to each other. I believe that they agree in that they point to the same truth situated beyond the expression of each of them. It would be absurd to reproach you for not having continued to the end of each of these two endeavors. That of Jacques alone would be worth the trouble. But if you had been able to do so—something that the method opposes—you would not have been able to make these two Thomisms fit in the same chapter. I have the greatest admiration for Jacques Maritain, but the atmosphere of his thinking is different from mine. Here is a new subject of amusement for Montaigne! Except that I feel no sympathy for any kind of skepticism. I would prefer to maintain that everything is true rather than to admit that nothing is. Every proposition is true in its sense, order, and place. The hard thing is to discover on which propositions depends the truth of other propositions. It seems to me that the peculiar task of the metaphysician is to find that out, and I would say that of your four heroes, only Plato knew it. Descartes and Kant did not even suspect the nature of the problem. Hegel, who had begun so well, as you yourself have taught me, became more and more a professor and less and less a philosopher in the measure that he taught more. Because he at least ought to have wanted *to teach his own philosophy*. This is the way that one becomes an "author included in the program," but philosophy gets lost on the way.

Claudite jam rivos [Close up the sluices]. . . . I have sent Monsieur Spire something I wrote on Bergson for *Revue de Métaphysique*. I don't know whether it has arrived. It may be that it is no longer useful. I have just received a notice about a congress to be organized in 1959 to commemorate the centenary of the great and very dear Henri Bergson. Another congress! And how is that compatible with your project? A special issue plus "Acts." In any case, if you do not do a special issue, please return my essay. It is absolutely not appropriate for a congress.

I believed that the last indeed ought to be the last. . . .

Thank you again and my warm wishes,
Étienne Gilson
6 rue Collet, Vermenton (Yonne)

P.S. Excuse the disorder of my letter. I never reread a letter, otherwise I would put many in the wastebasket.

December 10, 1958

Dear colleague and friend,
Our letters crossed paths in the mail. I am happy to hear that your project is continuing. It is far and away the most suitable kind of tribute that can be paid to Bergson's memory. Therefore keep my own submission and expect others. If Jacques Maritain, who is more complex and richer than is believed, lets himself go a little, you will receive something interesting from him, perhaps even important.

Would you believe that after having written to you, I went back to the big book? Your *Somme de métaphysique* has at least in common with the other one that it leads to silence. That puts us all in agreement with St. Augustine, *Melius scitur Deus nesciendo*,[11] which

11 Translation: "The best thing that can be known of God is not knowing anything," or "God is known better in ignorance." This is an expression of St. Augustine taken up by Montaigne.

the *Apology of RS* [Raymond Sebond, *Essays*, book II, chapter 12] quotes joining Augustine . . . Tacitus, but our Montaigne here stays on the surface of the problem. Rereading here and there, I thought how curious it is that Heidegger thinks he has discovered this truth (because it is one), that the real metaphysical problem is that of *Sein* (*esse*) beyond that of *Seiende* (*ens*). Perhaps the life of metaphysics is to rediscover this truth to lose it again unceasingly. Even the interpreters of those who discovered it are liable not to find it there.

Good luck with your projects, best Christmas wishes,
Cordially yours,
Étienne Gilson
6 rue Collet, Vermenton (Yonne)

LETTER FROM ÉTIENNE GILSON TO CHARLES JOURNET, JUNE 22, 1961

Archives of the Fondation Journet, Fribourg

In reply to Charles Journet's review of *Le philosophe et la théologie* [*The Philosopher and Theology*] ("Chronique de philosophie," *Nova et vetera* 36, no. 2 [April–June 1961]: 141–157), Gilson sent the theologian a letter dated June 22, 1961. To situate the debate, we quote a long passage from Journet's review.

Selection from the review by Charles Journet:
"Étienne Gilson, Christian philosopher"[12]
We will follow the author as he speaks about Christian philosophy; then about Henri Bergson; finally we will gather some quotations from the rich harvest we are offered. . . .

An important part of the Étienne Gilson memoirs is devoted to Bergson, who was "a beloved teacher" for Gilson. The reading of *Deux sources de la morale et de la religion* [*The Two Sources of Morality and Religion*] provokes in him this reflection, which at first sight is somewhat surprising:

> This philosophy of Bergson, so powerless to account for the nature of religion, could have been for Christian philosophers the occasion of a thor-

12 In this passage, all extracts of Étienne Gilson, *Le philosophie et la théologie*, will be taken from the translation by Cécile Gilson, *The Philosopher and Theology* (New York: Random House, 1962).

> oughgoing re-examination of their own philosophy, the prelude to a new era of doctrinal creativeness and enrichment.
>
> The task to be undertaken was not to reform Thomism in the light of the new philosophy. The truth theology lives by is that of the Christian revelation, which is immutable. The Church cannot change her theology every time it pleases some philosopher to propose a new view of the universe. On the contrary, what had to be done was to transform the new philosophy in the light of Thomism. The call was not for an anti-Thomistic revolution by means of the philosophy of Bergson, but rather a revolution within Bergsonism effected by the theology of Saint Thomas Aquinas. The undertaking had become a legitimate one from the moment Bergson himself openly crossed the border between the two territories, and, leaving that of philosophy, entered the domain of religion. But there was no one to undertake the task, so that we shall never know exactly what the result would have been. In this case, however, it is not philosophy that failed theology; all the philosophical materials required for such an undertaking were there, collected, ordered, and made ready for use by the genius of Bergson. Only, when the time came to purify and to order them in the light of theology, we discovered that wisdom had forgotten her time-honored function of guiding star. More simply, perhaps, she was busy elsewhere. At any rate, she was not interested. (Étienne Gilson, *The Philosopher and Theology*, 110–11)

Let us try to sift through Gilson's thinking. He had no illusions about the incompatibility of theology and Bergson's philosophy. At Strasbourg around 1920, when Bergson suggested that he orient his research toward philosophy of religion, Gilson saw the matter in Bergson's perspective—but another perspective was possible—and he immediately defended himself.

> What a proposal! Philosophy and religion together, all at once, for a young apprentice still in the process of getting acquainted with his own theology.... In the seconds of silence that followed, two ideas flashed through my mind: religious life at the most advanced point of creative evolution; the institutions and dogmas of Christianity left behind by this spiritual energy as its material by-products. Obviously this would not do. Catholicism would always refuse to recognize itself under this simplified scheme. I could not hesitate on the answer to give: "Why would you not undertake such a piece of research yourself? It requires no lesser a philosopher than you." Bergson answered with a smile, slightly lingering on the last words: "Descartes did not very much like to publish his thoughts in matters of morals and religion. He wanted to preserve his peace of mind. . . ." We

> laughed. We had understood each other. The offer of this perilous mission was not renewed. (*The Philosopher and Theology*, 166–67)

> That the philosophy of Bergson remained to the end a naturalism can scarcely be doubted. In this religion of the *élan vital*, whatever transcends the order of nature still belongs within nature. (*The Philosopher and Theology*, 167–68)

> Far from seeing in *The Two Sources* the point of Bergson's nearest approach to Christianity, I am rather inclined to see in this work the symbol of the inability of his philosophy to reach the level of the Christian religion. (*The Philosopher and Theology*, 168)

Accordingly, however severe a critic was an instant ago, how could he reproach the theologians for not having been able to transform the new philosophy in the light of Thomism? What could the critic expect of them? He reproaches them for only having proposed to Bergson "the static God of Aristotle" instead of presenting to him "the Pure Act of Being, the I AM of Scripture and the God of Thomism, Who transcends the finite categories of the static and the dynamic, the immobile and the mobile, the ready-made and the self-making, in short, the being and the becoming, in order to extract from the new philosophy the precious nugget of gold it contained" (*The Philosopher and Theology*, 169).

Are there grounds for the reproach? It seems to me that on the Thomist side, we find at least a philosopher and at least a theologian—Gilson names him—who were exempt from the beginning.[13] But that is unimportant here. What Gilson intends to establish is what he calls "Bergson's revenge." It is twofold: it concerns the concept of intelligence and that of being and God.

E. G. thinks that by the term "intelligence," Bergson really only meant the process of reason. His critique would oblige the neo-Scholastic to emerge from their lazy rationalism to rediscover the true concept of intelligence[14]

13 At bottom, Gilson complains about all the members of the Thomist school, whom he labels *essentialists*, and whom he accuses of having forgotten the *existential* character that the word *being* has in St. Thomas.

14 Here, consider the praise of Fr. Rousselot. [Translator's note: Pierre Rousselot, SJ, was born in 1878, and killed in action in 1915 during World War I. Regarded as the founder of transcendental Thomism, his most imortant works were *L'Intellectualism de Saint Thomas* (Paris: Alcan, 1908) and *Pour l'histoire du problème de l'amour au Moyen Âge* (Münster: Aschendorff, 1907). They have been translated, respectively, as *Intelligence: Sense of Being, Faculty of God*, trans.

and "speak of an intellectual intuition conceived as able to fulfill all the operations attributed by Bergson to intuition" (*The Philosopher and Theology*, 171).

Moreover, the premonitions of truth contained in Bergsonism invite our minds to rediscover *the God of St. Thomas*, whose absolute transcendence in the order of being posits once and for all beyond any conceivable limit:

> It is an error to see this event as a contamination of Thomism by Bergsonism. On the contrary, it was a decontamination of schoolroom Thomism disfigured and robbed of its efficacy by the proliferation of adventitious theologies. Bergson did not convert us to Bergsonism, nor did he convert us to Thomism, nor still did he induce us to bergsonify Saint Thomas; rather, by sobering our minds of the aftermath of an excess of abstraction, he enabled us to hear in the words of Saint Thomas some essential truths of Christian philosophy to which his own doctrine was attuned. The philosophy of Bergson has made it easier for us to approach the authentic God of Saint Thomas." (*The Philosopher and Theology*, 172)

Something bothered us, let us acknowledge, in this lively and well grounded exposition: when the author, starting from the fact that in Bergson's philosophy there are only two types of knowledge, *intelligence*, referred to the reasoning of scholars, and *intuition*, related to instinct, brusquely concludes: "It is not enough to say that Bergson had no faith. He never suspected the meaning of the word in a Christian theology" (*The Philosopher and Theology*, 162). Let us stop speaking about Bergson's philosophy. Let us talk about Bergson. He would therefore have been ignorant, he would have "never suspected" Pascal's third order, the order of the heart. He would not have situated *metaphysical* intuition, which as a philosopher he employed, on any level except that of mystical intuition, which he attributed only to saints, whom he envied. We are morally certain that this was not the case. Cf. [Journet], "Autour d'Henri Bergson" in *Nova et vetera* 33, no. 4 (1958): 262–78. The last sentence of this study even tried to answer in advance the question posed by E. G. on p. 178: "I have often wondered how those who were hoping for it, could visualize what would have been for Bergson the day after his conversion" (*The Philosopher and Theology*, 162).

Andrew Tallon (Milwaukee, WI: Marquette University Press, 1998); and as *The Problem of Love in the Middle Ages: A Historical Consideration*, trans. Alan Vincelette (Milwaukee, WI: Marquette University Press, 2002).]

Letter from Étienne Gilson to Charles Journet, June 22, 1961

June 22, 1961

Sir and dear theologian,

I found your *Nova et Vetera* article when I returned from the Academy, where we voted on the Grand Prix of French Literature. It was given to our friend Jacques Maritain. I hope he will excuse us. Even if someone does not need it for himself, it is easy to find good causes to help with a million. Especially if we want to honor ourselves by honoring him.

I am very grateful for your kind article, in which you clarify many issues that become simpler in your usual lucidity.

The word that shocked you was not used by mistake. I simply thought that there would be no interest, or benefit for anyone, in provoking a controversy that is both too late and premature. Time will clarify all that, and one should look forward. It is especially necessary not to divide our forces. At least I have forbidden myself to do so, and I hope to continue in the future.

Incidentally, I read what you wrote about Fr. Teilhard de Chardin with great interest. I have never been able to convince myself to take his thinking seriously. This is a sure indication that I am not qualified to judge it. Two years ago I went to Fribourg for the first time in my life, but it was at a date when the universities are empty. At least for now I have the pleasure of being able to picture the land where you live.

Please accept my expression of thanks and esteem,

Étienne Gilson
6 rue Collet, Vermenton (Yonne), France

Appendix B: Sources

ARCHIVES

Archives in Canada

Saint Michael's College Archives (University of Toronto): Kelly Library [SMCA]

"Gilson Collection," located in the library of the *Pontifical Institute of Mediaeval Studies*. Works and offprints of Étienne Gilson; dedicated works.

"Fonds Gilson" [FG], in the Archives Division: author's personal archives, manuscripts, courses, lectures, rough drafts, correspondence received, family photographs, memorabilia, diaries. There are fifteen feet of archive shelves. The collection has a great wealth of material; it was carefully organized by Gilson himself.

Archives of the University of Montreal: Gaudry Pavilion

Fonds de l'Institut Scientifique Franco-Canadien, directed by Étienne Gilson starting in December 1937. Fonds P12. 1926–1972.

Archives in the United States

University of Chicago Archives: The Joseph Regenstein Library, Special Collections, University of Chicago.

Richard McKeon Collection: box 36, folder 11 (correspondence with Gilson 1925–1955).

Mortimer J. Adler Collection: correspondence (1937–1938, 1968).

Harvard University Archives, Widener Library

Ralph Barton Perry Collection; Edward K. Rand Collection; Papers of the Green Family; Scott Milross Buchanan Papers; William Ernest Hocking Papers; James Bryant Conant Presidential Files; Abbott Lawrence Lowell Presidential Files. The collection has been reproduced and is available in the Gilson Collection in Toronto.

Thomas Merton Center, Bellarmine University, Louisville, Kentucky

Correspondence between Thomas Merton, Dan Walsh, and Étienne Gilson. Gilson's letters date from November 30, 1949 (to Dan Walsh); November 4, 1951; September 25, 1954; November 22, 1962; and June 17, 1968 (to Thomas Merton).

Archives of Notre Dame University, South Bend, Indiana, Hesburgh Library [UNDA]

Several Files: correspondence, Institute of Mediaeval Studies, Congregation of the Holy Cross, Astrik Gabriel, lectures given in 1934–1937, 1947, 1950.

Archives in Belgium

Fonds Maurice Blondel, Catholic University of Louvain

The Fonds Maurice Blondel contain works dedicated by Gilson (*Introduction à l'étude de Saint Augustin*, 1929; *L'esprit de la philosophie médiévale*, 1932); correspondence (an undated letter from EG to MB; a letter from EG to MB of April 29, 1928; a letter from EG to MB of August 28, 1929; a letter from EG to MB of March 21, 1931; a letter from MB to EG, of May 8, 1928); and several archival dossiers: on "The Concept of Christian Philosophy"—Reflections of Étienne Gilson / Société Française de Philosophie, March 21, 1931; manuscript about

"Catholic Philosophy, Current Aspects of the Problem" in reply to the text of Gilson and Émile Bréhier.

Archives in Italy

Archives of the Congregation for Catholic Education, Rome

University of Toronto. Busta 1929–1934. Institute of Mediaeval Studies. Request for Canonical Approval. Newspaper articles; Fr. Chenu's letter supporting canonical recognition (December 10, 1932); Étienne Gilson's letter of June 23, 1934.

Work files of the Congregation of Seminaries and Universities.

Archives in Switzerland

Archives of the Cardinal Charles Journet Foundation: Université de Fribourg

Étienne Gilson's letter to Charles Journet, June 22, 1961.

Archives of the Albertinum Convent, Fribourg

Fr. Geiger Collection: eight letters of Étienne Gilson (1950–1965).

Archives in France

Archives nationales, Pierrefitte-sur-Seine

Archives de la Présidence de la République—Général de Gaulle: AG/5(1)/1177: correspondence between Étienne Gilson and General de Gaulle (November 18, 1959; May 26, 1960; June 27, 1960; March 28, 1963; April 14, 1963; April 21, 1963; April 23, 1964; May 5, 1970).

F ^{17}. Dossier 13618. Archives of section V of EPHE [École pratique des hautes études]. Report on the work of the section (1886). Organization (1885–1923). Recommendation of the assembly of the section that the diplomas should entitle students to the same privileges as the diplomas of section IV (1901). Creation of courses: candidacies (1885–1921). Free courses, temporary lectures, candidacies, proposals authorizations (1887–1933). Personnel: nominations, promotions, wages. Students: nominations (1889–1932). Advertisements (1915–1928).

F ^{41}. Dossier 28: "Commissariat général à l'Information. Section Amérique du Nord. 1939"

Fonds André Colin: 681 AP 10—dossier 8 (MRP—national organization). André Colin was the secretary general of the MRP (1945–1955); served as deputy and senator for the MRP. Report by André Colin (no date), of the March 1950 meeting; Gilson, Étienne, "Les bases doctrinales du MRP et notre conception de la démocratie" (April 5, 1948, mimeographed document).

Fonds Culture Radio France: 20000392/11. Dossier on the preparation for and broadcast of a colloquium with Étienne Gilson, Paul Guth, and Francine Leullier, "Permanence de l'Académie," May–June 1952.

Fonds Louis Madelin: 355 AP 3. Correspondence, two letters from May and June 1946.

Fonds Charles Maurras: 576 AP 183. A number of handwritten notes, particularly on various manuscripts, particularly Joseph de Maistre, de Bonald, Louis Veuillot, Felicité de Lamennais, Auguste-Joseph-Alphonse Gratry, Romano Guardini, several ecclesiastics, Frédéric Ozanam, Étienne Gilson, and others. In Gilson's case there is a simple mention of the title *Pour un ordre catholique*.

Fonds Gustave Cohen: 59 AP 3. Correspondence, two notes, 1925.

Archives du Ministère des Affaires étrangères, La Courneuve

Fonds "Service des Œuvres françaises à l'étranger." The Service des Œuvres françaises à l'étranger [SOFE] was founded at the end of World War I following the reorganization of the French Propaganda Service. It was established by the decree of January 15, 1920. From 1920 to 1940, it was headed successively by Albert Milhaud, Jean Giraudoux, Paul-Émile Naggiar, Fernand Pila, and Jean Marx. The archives cover the period 1912–1940.

Fonds 417QO: Dossier 416, North America. General file, 1932–1940. United States and Canada; Dossier 417, Reports of the French consuls at Montreal and Vancouver on French activities in Canada, 1936–1940.

Fonds 420QO: Canada Series B, 1922–1940. Dossier 2: General Dossier, grants for activities, Franco-Canadian relations; French consular organization in Canada; tours of duty; preservation of the French language; declarations and commemorations (1922–1930); Dossier 3: Same for 1931–1940; Dossier 5: Religious issues; Canadian religious organization, grants, oblates, Institute of Mediaeval Studies in Ottawa (1924–1940); Dossier 6: education, general file; grants to Canadian francophones; relations between French and Canadian universities;

Dossier 15: Institut scientifique franco-canadien (July 1926–February 1932).

Collection for United Nations—International Organizations (372QO). Dossiers 3–7: San Francisco Conference (February–June 1945); French participation; procedure; correspondence of private persons with the delegation; general dossiers; Security Council, French viewpoint; mechanism of pacts; speeches; mandates; guardianship of non-autonomous territories; Naggiar report: preliminary conversations among the representatives of the five great powers.

Papers of Paul-Émile Naggiar (199PAAP). Dossiers 4–11: Consulate General in Montréal. Dossier 47: report, Naggiar adjunct delegate to the United Nations San Francisco Conference, February–July 1945. Correspondence received, instructions from the French government, reports, notes. Economic and social problems, naval mission.

Senate Archives

Manuscript of Gilson's lecture of February 11, 1948, entitled "Notre Démocratie," and directed to the MRP parliamentary group.

Bibliothèque nationale de France. Manuscript Department, Paris

Fonds Msgr. André Combes: NAF 28257, correspondence (sixty-seven letters, 1931–1963).

Fonds Stanislas Fumet: NAF 28171, correspondence (four letters, 1960–1973).

Fonds Lucien Laberthonnière: NAF 28025, correspondence with Étienne and Thérèse Gilson (April 12, 1906, July 28, 1912–December 1914, twelve letters rediscovered). Le Fonds Laberthonnière has been very tentatively classified into 195 groups; the correspondence is classified by important correspondents (Blondel, von Hügel, Mercier); and for miscellaneous letters by year (1901–1932, around eighty groups). We have consulted: 4–5, 34–43, 52–53, 68–71, 76–77, 159–161 ("Thomism" and "Scholasticism").

Fonds Claude Lévi-Strauss: NAF 28150 (letter of January 3, 1973).

Fonds Gabriel Marcel: NAF 28349, correspondence (twelve letters exchanged between 1928–1972; manuscript of a lecture by Étienne Gilson on Gabriel Marcel, given at the UNESCO in December 1946 and published with the title "Un exemple," 5 pages, 1947).

Fonds Jules Romains: NAF 28403, correspondence (three letters: October 14; 1946, January 7, 1950; July 9, 1956).

Bibliothèque nationale et universitaire de Strasbourg

Fonds Maritain: correspondence, dedicated works.

Institut national de l'audiovisuel

Digitalized—accessible from the BNF—François Mitterrand Building

The inventories of the INA Television Archives make no mention d'Étienne Gilson. The INA Radio Archives, by contrast, contain many broadcasts in which Étienne Gilson speaks about political and cultural issues. He participated in some twenty radio broadcasts between 1940 and 1973, notably at the time of his election to the French Academy, and at the time of the broadcasts in honor of Paul Claudel (January 3, 1969); Henri Bergson (November 16, 1957; February 11, 1966; May 11, 1967; May 13, 1967); Jacques Maritain (November 15, 1967).

Two broadcasts were devoted to Gilson: January 17, 1953 ("Permanence de l'Académie," with Paul Guth, Francine Leullier, and Georges Godebert); December 28, 1979, with Jean-Luc Marion, on France-Culture.

1940, "Étienne Gilson discusses the film director Robert Flaherty."

December 30, 1946, "Émission pour le Canada. Festival de France," with Étienne Gilson, Paul Claudel, and Madeleine Renaud.

May 5, 1947, "Allocution d'Étienne Gilson au Cercle Inter-Allié," "Archives politiques de mai 1947," on Petrarch.

January 5, 1948, "Perspectives intellectuelles," with Étienne Gilson, Salvador de Madariaga, David Rousset, Carlo Levi, M. Prichett, and others.

April 20, 1948, "Les intellectuels catholiques et les progrès de la science," with Étienne Gilson, Maurice de Broglie, Michel Polonovski, Louis Leprince-Ringuet, Fr. D. Dubarle, on the position of Catholic intellectuals with regard to biological and atomic dangers, within the framework of Catholic Intellectuals Week.

September 20, 1949, "Bilan du troisième festival de Cannes," with Étienne Gilson, Suzanne Borel, Georges Bidault, Jules Romains, and Georges Huisman.

December 28, 1949, "Un demi-siècle d'histoire du monde," with Étienne Gilson, Raymond Aron, Jules Romains, Joseph Paul-Boncour (former

Chief of Government), Georges Bourgin (director of the archives of France).

1949 [date incomplete], "La semaine diplomatique," with a sound track titled "Union française du 31 mars 1950 et autres documents," about the funeral of Madame Étienne Gilson.

November 15, 1967, "Jacques Maritain. Portrait d'un philosophe," with Étienne Gilson, Cardinal Journet, André Frossard, Georges Cattaui, François Mauriac, Julien Green, Stanislas Fumet, Fr. Cottier, Olivier Lacombe, and Henry Bars.

Archives départementales des Yvelines—Musée départemental Maurice Denis, Saint-Germain-en-Laye

Letters of Étienne and Jacqueline Gilson to Maurice Denis (1933–1943)

Bibliothèque municipale de Bordeaux

Service des fonds anciens et patrimoniaux—Département du patrimoine

Fonds P. Augustin-Jean Maydieu: twelve letters from Étienne Gilson, 1937–1948

Bibliothèque et archives du Collège de France, Paris

Fonds Étienne Gilson (16 CDF 156): correspondence, yearbooks, posters of courses, press clippings, biographical notes (1930–1992). Report by Louis Massignon on the creation of a chair of history of medieval philosophy (two copies, four mimeographed pages; faculty assembly of June 15, 1930); Gilson's letter announcing his candidacy (two handwritten letters; December 12 and December 23, 1931); statement of Gilson's qualification for a chair of the history of medieval philosophies (two copies, seven pages printed); statement of Gilson's degrees and publications (seven pages, printed); appointment of Gilson as tenured professor of the Collège de France (March 9, 1932); order establishing Gilson's status (March 23, 1932); missions abroad, to Canada, the United States, and elsewhere.

Fonds "Assemblées des Professeurs": letter from Édouard Le Roy proposing to change Professor Izoulet's chair of Social History to a chair of History of Medieval Philosophy, October 14, 1929 (4 AP 439—minutes of the faculty assembly of November 6, 1929); minutes of the faculty assembly of June 15, 1930 (4 AP 442); letter from Édoard Le Roy proposing to change the chair of Celtic language and literature to a chair of History of Medieval Philosophy, October 12, 1931 (minutes of the faculty assembly of November 15, 1931—4 AP 448); Étienne Gilson's letter supporting Marc Bloch for the creation of a chair of comparative history of European societies, February 18, 1934 (4 AP 461).

Fonds Edmond Faral (58 CDF 10–12): correspondence with Étienne Gilson (1929–1930).

Fonds Louis Massignon (16 CDF 285).

Bibliothèque Interuniversitaire de la Sorbonne, Paris [BIS]

Fonds Léon Chestov: correspondence from Étienne Gilson (two letters, April 4, 1923; March 11, 1936).

Fonds Maurice Pradines: correspondence from Étienne Gilson (eighteen letters, 1928–1948).

Fonds Xavier Léon: correspondence from Étienne Gilson (forty-six letters, 1914–1934).

Archives de l'École pratique des hautes études, Paris

Minutes of the sessions of the Council of the Section of Religious Sciences: Notebook number 2, June 17, 1906 to June 28, 1926 (758 pp.) Notebook number 3, November 7, 1926 to June 21, 1959 (1142 pp.). Gilson's candidacy letter to replace Picavet (July 5, 1921). File for Gilson's incorporation (December 1921).

"Papiers Paul Vignaux": files for preparation of courses and lectures (nine boxes: a Gilson file on "God and being"; files on Henry of Ghent with references to Gilson; a file "Philosophy and Theology of History in different authors—Marrou, Ricoeur, Löwith"; course on "The Place of the Middle Ages in the History of Philosophy," 1961, 22 pp., repeated in 1964, 10 pp., partly published in 1974 in the *Bulletin de la société française de philosophie*).

Centre d'Histoire de Sciences Politiques, Paris [CHSP]

Fonds Jean de Fabrègues: correspondence with Gilson (twelve letters exchanged between 1963–1971); diploma of advanced studies of Jean de Fabrègues, directed by Étienne Gilson; collection of publications (FAB 10, 12, 13, 14).

Fonds Hubert Beuve-Méry: correspondence, articles, "Affaire Gilson," letters from readers, brochures: Association of Anti-Totalitarian

Intellectuals (secretary Jean Le Dantec), "Le neutralisme," Paris, 1953 (BM 133); file "propagande française" in the United States, polemic following the publication of an article by Pierre Emmanuel on "L'Amérique impériale," *Le Monde*, October 25, 1949, reply by Paul Claudel, file of letters from readers (BM 73).

Fonds Gaston Monnerville: letter of Étienne Gilson, November 1948 (GM 69).

Bibliothèque littéraire Jacques Doucet, Paris

Fonds Charles Du Bos: correspondence of Étienne Gilson with Charles Du Bos and Juliette Du Bos (1930–1954, thirty-four letters).

Fonds François Mauriac: correspondence of Étienne Gilson (eight letters, 1945–1969).

Fonds Paul Valéry: two letters from Étienne Gilson (December 19, 1942; May 5, 1944).

Fonds Henri Bergson: two letters from Étienne Gilson (June 5, 1939; October 20, 1939), dedication.

Institut Mémoires de l'édition contemporaine [IMEC], Abby of Saint-Germain-la-Blanche-Herbe

The archives of the IMEC contain more than fifty-five letters from Étienne Gilson to different correspondents. By contrast, the collections Desclée de Brouwer, CCIF, *Esprit*, Claude Tresmontant, and *Les Nouvelles littéraires* contain no documents related to Étienne Gilson.

Fonds Jean et Joseph Baruzi: five letters (1932–1951), course manuscript eighty-four pages long. (These are seven lectures given by Gilson at the Collège de France, "Theologie et classicisme après Petrarch," October-November 1940—with commentaries by Baruzi).

Fonds Noële Boulet: one letter (March 26, 1922).

Fonds Léon Brunschvicg: eleven letters (1916–1939); Étienne Gilson, "Descartes et la métaphysique scolastique," *Revue de l'Université de Bruxelles*, 1924.

Fonds Maurice Halbwachs: assignment at the University of Chicago, 1930; journal, 1923–1944; letter from Maurice to Yvonne Halbwachs, September-December 1930.

Fonds Larousse: a letter from Gilson of February 18, 1938 (originals—LRS 243.9); a letter to Gilson about a translation into English of his article devoted to Gabriel Marcel (May 22, 1959, LRS S2.01).

Fonds Emmanuel Levinas: a letter, private.

Fonds Lucien Lévy-Bruhl: thirteen letters (1915–1930), eight of which were written during the war.

Fonds Emmanuel Mounier: two letters (May 11, 1931; February 7, 1947); undated notes from reading Gilson's book *Le thomisme*, 1923, two pages (MNR 2.D5-04-02).

Fonds J. Paulhan: three letters from Gilson; three copies of letters from Paulhan (December 1962–January 1963).

Fonds J.-C. Renard: one letter (June 21, 1971).

Fonds Pierre Seghers: one letter (February 1973).

Fonds Jean Wahl: seven letters (1925–1959).

Centre d'Études et Musée Edmond-Michelet, Brive

4 EM 967: 1968. Profession of faith of Pope Paul VI. Letter of fidelity addressed to the Pope by Edmond Michelet, François Mauriac, and Étienne Gilson, published in *Le Monde*, December 18, 1968: newspaper article, newspapers, correspondence, controversy about the "letter of the mandarins."

Archives du Centre Alexandre Koyré (CNRS – UMR 8560), Paris

Letters from Étienne Gilson, Henri Gouhier, Raymond Aron, and Emmanuel Levinas to Alexandre Koyré (years 1931–1934 principally). Review in Russian of a work by Gilson, 1925. The correspondence concerns the management of the journal *Recherches philosophiques*, edited, beginning in 1931, by Alexandre Koyré and Albert Spaïer.

Archives de l'Archevêché de Paris [AHAP]

Fonds Petit Séminaire Notre-Dame-des-Champs (years 1840-1900): série 1 H. Documentation on students, outcomes, notes, exercises, and so forth. 1 H 12 17: rhetoric notebooks, Gilson's rhetoric grades; 1 H 12 33: honors notebook for the second year class (year 1900-1901); 1 H 12 35: honors notebook for the rhetoric class; 1 H 12 43: minutes Teachers Council (1901–1908).

Fonds Cardinal Suhard: 1 D 14-13 (files on the composition and reception of the pastoral letter *Essor ou déclin de l'Église*, 1947).

Bulletin de l'*Association fraternelles des anciens élèves de Notre-Dame-des-Champs*, 1875–1950.

Notices: Fr. André Gilson, Fr. Lucien Paulet.

Archives de la Province dominicaine de France, Le Saulchoir, Paris [APDF]

The archives of headquarters of the éditions du Cerf are in the process of reorganization. Consequently, it is difficult to give precise sections of the files, distributed among several collections.

Fonds of éditions du Cerf: correspondence, documentation for *Sept*, work files.

Fonds *Sept*: 1934–1937, correspondence.

Fonds of Fr. Marie-Vincent Bernadot: diary, correspondence.

Fonds of Fr. Pierre Boisselot: Notes on the history of Cerf (1929–1940), composed in 1943, at Saint-Alban-Leysse.

Fonds of Fr. Marie-Dominique Chenu: correspondence.

Fonds of Fr. Yves Congar: Delos correspondence; statement on Gilson (1947); file listing correspondence with Gilson (six letters exchanged from 1932 to 1959), scattered correspondence during the nineteen-sixties.

Fonds of Fr. Augustin-Jean Maydieu: file "Exchanges with a view to resumption of *Vie intellectuelle* after the Liberation," May 1944, eleven page letter from Étienne Gilson to Fr. Maydieu, typewritten, titled "Conversation with an Absent Friend," dated May 28, 1944.

Archives de la Librairie philosophique Joseph Vrin

Dossiers of reviews and newspaper articles. Dossier "The Gilson Affair."

Dossier of newspaper articles at the time of Gilson's death.

Dossier for the Institut Scientifique Franco-Canadien, covering the years 1930–1950.

Aspects of the Princeton bi-centenary; propaganda during 1939–1940; Conseil de la République.

Correspondence (Chenu, Pegis, Montpetit, McCorkell, Phelan, and Jean Marx).

Copies of correspondence (Mauriac, Koyré, and Gouhier).

Unpublished article "La France contre Pétain."

Some photographs (Gilson with Paul VI).

Maison de Robert Schuman, Scy-Chazelles

Letter of Étienne Gilson to Robert Schuman, August 29, 1949.

Institut Marc Sangnier, Paris

Correspondence between Étienne Gilson and Francisque Gay (twenty-one letters, 1919–1960).

Archives of the Benedictine Abbey of la-Pierre-qui-Vire, Yonne [APQV]

Letters of Étienne Gilson to Fr. Irénée, OSB (sixteen letters, 1942–1946).

PUBLISHED SOURCES

Annuals, Journals, Newspapers

America (New York)

Annuaire de l'École pratique des hautes études (Paris)

Annuaire du Collège de France (Paris)

Aspects de la France (Paris)

Bulletin de la Société française de philosophie (Paris)

Commonweal (New York)

Esprit (Paris)

Foi et vie (Paris)

Harvard Alumni Bulletin (Cambridge, Massachusetts)

Action Française (Paris)

L'Aube (Paris)

L'Européen (Paris)

L'Osservatore Romano (Rome)

La Croix (Paris)

La Documentation catholique (Paris)

La France catholique (Paris)

La Vie catholique (Paris)

La Vie intellectuelle (Paris)

Le Figaro (Paris)

Le Monde (Paris)

Le Temps (Paris)

Les Nouvelles littéraires (Paris)

New Blackfriars (Oxford)

Revue de la Croix-Rouge (Genève)

Revue trimestrielle canadienne (Montreal)

Seminarium (Rome)

Sept (Paris)

The Nation (New York)

University of Toronto Monthly (Toronto)

Published Correspondence

Étienne Gilson—Karl Barth

Letter of Étienne Gilson to Karl Barth, January 15, 1946. Published in Hommage et reconnaissance. Recueil de travaux publiés à l'occasion du soixantième anniversaire de Karl Barth, Cahiers théologiques de l'actualité protestante. Paris and Neuchâtel: Delachaux et Niestlé, 1946, 41–42.

Étienne Gilson—Albert Béguin

Letter from Étienne Gilson to Albert Béguin, dated March 11, 1951. Published in "Journal à plusieurs voix." *Esprit* 19, no. 178 (April 1951): 596–99.

Letter from Étienne Gilson to Albert Béguin, dated March 19, 1951. Published in *Esprit* 19, no. 178 (April 1951), 593–96, in the context of the Gilson Affair.

Étienne Gilson—Marc Bloch

Eight letters published as an appendix of the volume *Correspondance Marc Bloch—Lucien Febvre*, vol. 2, 459–64. Paris: Fayard, 2003.

Étienne Gilson—Maurice Blondel

Long, Fiachra. "The Blondel—Gilson Correspondence through Foucault's Mirror." *Philosophy Today*, 1991, 351–61. Partial publication of letters of Étienne Gilson to Maurice Blondel, April 29, 1928; August 28, 1929; March 21, 1931.

Étienne Gilson—Père André Boulet, SM

Chiron, Yves, ed. "Une lettre inédite d'Étienne Gilson sur Teilhard de Chardin et la crise de l'Église," letter from Étienne Gilson directed to Fr. André Boulet, May 12, 1969. *Aletheia, Lettre d'informations religieuses*, 2004, 1–2.

Étienne Gilson—Marie-Dominique Chenu, OP

Murphy, Francesca A., ed. "Correspondance entre Étienne Gilson et Marie-Dominique Chenu: Un choix de lettres (1923–1969)." *Revue thomiste*, Toulouse, 105 (2005): 25–87. Thirty-four letters are published here, of more than sixty listed by the editor—to which the letters of Fr. Chenu located in the archives of Librairie Vrin should be added.

Étienne Gilson—Thomas Deman, OP

"Étienne Gilson—Thomas Deman, OP, Lettres inédites." Edited by B. Hodel, OP, and F.-X. Putallaz. *Nova et vetera* (Fribourg) 87 (2012): 447–68.

Étienne Gilson—Charles Du Bos

Cahier Charles Du Bos, 1964, no. 9, 36.

Étienne Gilson—Henri Gouhier

Prouvost, Géry, ed. "Lettres à Henri Gouhier choisies et présentées." *Revue thomiste* 94 (July–September 1994): 460–78.

Fafara, Richard, ed. and trans. *The Malebranche Moment: Selections from the Letters of Étienne Gilson and Henri Gouhier (1929–1936)*. Milwaukee, WI: Marquette University Press, 2007.

Étienne Gilson—Georges Kalinowski

Kalinowski, Georges. "Fragment de trois lettres d'Étienne Gilson," dated January 12 and 24, 1964; August 14, 1965. In *L'impossible métaphysique*, 243–48. Paris: Beauchesne, 1981.

Étienne Gilson—Michel Labourdette, OP

Donneaud, Henry, ed. "Correspondance Étienne Gilson—Michel Labourdette." *Revue thomiste* 94 (1994): 479–529.

Étienne Gilson—Henri de Lubac, SJ

de Lubac, Henri, ed. *Lettres de M. Étienne Gilson adressées au P. de Lubac et commentées par celui-ci.* Paris: Cerf, 1986; rev. ed., 2013. English translation by Mary Emily Hamilton, *Letters of Étienne Gilson to Henri de Lubac, with Commentary by Henri de Lubac* (San Francisco: Ignatius Press, 1988).

Prévotat, Jacques, ed. *Lettres de Monsieur Étienne Gilson au Père de Lubac et commentées par celui-ci: Correspondance 1956–1975.* Œuvres complètes du Cardinal Henri de Lubac 47. Paris: Cerf, 2013. This is a new larger edition of letters written by Fr. de Lubac.

Étienne Gilson—Jacques Maritain

Etienne Gilson and Jacques Maritain. *Correspondance 1923–1971: Deux approches de l'être.* Edited by Géry Prouvost. Paris: Vrin, 1991.

Mougel, René, ed. "Deux lettres retrouvées d'Étienne Gilson." *Cahiers Jacques Maritain*, no. 37. Kolbsheim: "Association des amis de Jacques Maritain," 1998.

Étienne Gilson—Thomas Merton

Merton, Thomas. *The School of Charity: The Letters of Thomas Merton on Religious Renewal and Spiritual Direction.* New York: Farrar, Straus & Giroux, 1990; repr. 2011. The volume includes two letters from Thomas Merton to Étienne Gilson, November 12, 1951, and October 11, 1962.

Letter from Thomas Merton to Étienne Gilson, November 12, 1951. *Nunc*, Paris, November 2004, 30–31.

Étienne Gilson—Bruno Nardi

Dronke, Peter, ed. *Etienne Gilson's Letters to Bruno Nardi.* Florence: Edizioni del Galluzo, 1998. 21 pp.

Étienne Gilson—Augusto Del Noce

Borghesi, Massimo, ed. *Caro collega ed amico, Lettere di Etienne Gilson ad Augusto Del Noce (1964–1969).* Sienna: Cantagalli, 2008. 167 pp.

Published in French as *Cher collègue et ami: Lettres d'Étienne Gilson à Augusto Del Noce, 1964–1969*. Paris: Parole et silence, 2011. 112 pp.

Étienne Gilson—Paul VI

Letter from Étienne Gilson to Paul VI. Published in *L'Osservatore Romano*, August 24, 1968, p. 4, column 2; in *La France catholique*, August 30, 1968.

Letter from Paul VI to Étienne Gilson, April 8, 1975. Published in *L'Osservatore Romano*, September 11, 1975, and reproduced in *La Documentation catholique* 72, October 5, cols. 812–13. The complete text is available on the Vatican website.

Étienne Gilson—Fernand Van Steenberghen

Van Steenberghen, Fernand, ed. "Correspondance avec Étienne Gilson." *Revue philosophique de Louvain* 87, no. 4 (1989): 612–25.

Maurice Blondel—Lucien Laberthonnière

Correspondance philosophique, présentée par Claude Tresmontant. Paris: Seuil, 1961.

Maurice Blondel—Auguste Valensin

Correspondance (1899–1912), extraits de la correspondence (1912–1947), with notes by Henri de Lubac. Paris: Aubier, 1965.

Gabriel Marcel—Gaston Fessard

Correspondance (1934–1971). Presentation and notes by Henri de Lubac, Marie Rougier, and Michel Sales. Paris: Beauchesne, 1985.

Jacques Maritain—Charles Journet

Correspondance Journet—Maritain. 6 vols. Fribourg: Saint-Augustin, 1997–2008. This edition includes one thousand nine hundred and eight letters indexed and published.

Jacques Maritain—Emmanuel Mounier

Correspondance. 1929–1949. Edited, annotated, and presented by Sylvain Guéna. Paris: Desclée de Brouwer, 2016. Complete edition of the two hundred letters exchanged.

Jacques Maritain—Yves Simon

Correspondance Jacques Maritain—Yves Simon. Edited by Florian Michel. 2 vols. Paris: CLD, 2008 and 2012. Includes eight hundred letters exchanged between 1927 and 1961.

Pierre Teilhard de Chardin—Auguste Valensin, Henri de Lubac, Bruno de Solages, André Ravier

Lettres intimes de Teilhard de Chardin à Auguste Valensin, Bruno de Solages, Henri de Lubac, André Ravier: 1919–1955. Introduction and notes by Henri de Lubac. Paris: Aubier-Montaigne, 1974.

Bibliography

Gilson's World: Books and Articles

Armogathe, Jean-Robert, ed. *Histoire générale du christianisme*. 2 vols. Paris: PUF, 2010.

Aron, Raymond. *Mémoires: Édition intégrale inédite*. Collection Bouquins. Paris: Robert Laffont, 2010. First edition, 1983.

Auzepy-Chavagnac, Véronique. *Jean de Fabrègues et la jeune droite catholique: Aux origines de la Révolution nationale*. Lille: Presses Universitaires du Septentrion, 2002.

Avon, Dominique. *Les Frères prêcheurs en Orient: Les dominicains du Caire (années 1910–années 1960)*. Paris: Cerf, 2005.

———. "Une polémique catholique sur les origines d'Islam. Autour des travaux de Hanna Zacharias." In Fourcade and Avon, *Mélanges offerts à Gérard Cholvy*, 203–37.

Azouvi, François. *La gloire de Bergson: Essai sur le magistère philosophique*. Paris: Gallimard, 2007.

Barbier de la Serre, René. "Pour un ordre catholique." *Sept*, January 25, 1935, 3.

Bataillon, Marcel. "Le problème de l'incroyance au XVI siècle d'après Lucien Febvre." *Mélanges d'histoire sociale*, no. 5 (1944): 5–26.

Bédarida, François. "Les intellectuels catholiques et le Vatican en 1952–1953: Un épisode inédit." In *Mélanges offerts à M. le doyen André Latreille*, 242–52. Lyon: Audin, 1972.

Benda, Julien. *La trahison des clercs*. Paris: Grasset, 1927.

Bloch, Marc, and Lucien Febvre. *Correspondance*. Vol. 1, *1928–1933*; Vol. 2, *1934–1937*. Paris: Fayard, 1994, 2003.

Blondel, Maurice. *Itinéraire philosophique*. Paris: Spes, 1928.

———. *Le problème de la philosophie catholique*. Paris: Bloud et Gay, 1932.

Bonino, Serge-Thomas, ed. *Saint Thomas au XXe siècle: Actes du colloque du Centenaire de la Revue thomiste*. Paris: Éditions Saint-Paul, 1994.

Boulnois, Olivier, ed. *Paul Vignaux: Citoyen et philosophe (1904–1987)*. Turnhout: Brepols, 2013.

Boureau, Alain. "Des politiques tirées de l'Écriture: Byzance et l'Occident." *Annales, Histoire, Sciences Sociales*, 55, no. 4 (July-August 2000): 879–87.

Bouyer, Louis. *Le métier de théologien: Entretiens avec Georges Daix*. Paris: éd. France Empire, 1979; Ad Solem, 2005.

———. *Mémoires*. Afterword and notes by Jean Duchesne. Paris: Cerf, 2014. English translation by Anne Englund Nash, *Memoirs* (San Francisco: Ignatius Press, 2015).

Bréhier, Émile. "Y-a-t-il une philosophie chrétienne?" *Revue de métaphysique et de morale* 38 (1931): 133–62.

Brito, Emilio. "La 'philosophie chrétienne' a-t-elle un avenir?" *Revue théologique de Louvain* 36, no. 4 (2005): 508–38.

Cahiers Jacques Maritain, periodical, first issue September 1980. Meudon: Association des Amis de Jacques Maritain.

Calmette, Arthur. *L'OCM. Organisation civile et militaire: Histoire d'un mouvement de résistance de 1940 à 1946*. Paris: PUF, 1961.

Camus, Albert. *Carnets II: Janvier 1942–mars 1951*. Paris: Gallimard, 1964.

Les Carnets du cardinal Alfred Baudrillart, 1932–1935. Paris: Cerf, 2003.

Charle, Christophe, and Christine Delangle. "La campagne électorale de Lucien Febvre au Collège de France (1929–1932): Lettres à Edmond Faral." *Histoire de l'éducation* 34 (1987): 49–69.

Chenaux, Philippe. *Une Europe vaticane? Entre le Plan Marshall et les Traités de Rome*. Brussels: Editions Ciaco, 1990.

———. "La seconde vague thomiste." In Colin, *Intellectuels chrétiens et esprit des années 1920*, 139–67.

———. *Entre Maurras et Maritain: Une génération intellectuelle catholique (1920–1930)*. Paris: Cerf, 1999.

———. *De la chrétienté à l'Europe: Les catholiques et l'idée européenne au XXe siècle*. Paris: CLD, 2007.

Chenu, Marie-Dominique. *Un École de théologie: Le Saulchoir*. Kain-Lez-Tournai, Belgium: Le Saulchoir, 1937; re-published Paris: Cerf, 1985, with studies by Giuseppe Alberigo, Étienne Fouilloux, Jean Ladrière, and Jean-Pierre Jossua. [Cited page numbers refer to the 1985 reprint.]

———. *Un concile pour notre temps*. Paris: Cerf, 1961.

Chestov, Léon. *Athènes et Jérusalem: Un essai de philosophie religieuse*. Paris: Vrin, 1938.

Colin, Pierre, ed. *Intellectuels chrétiens et Esprit des années 1920*. Paris: Cerf, 1997.

Colum, Padraic. "The Light of Medieval Thought." *The New York Times*, January 29, 1939.

Compagnon, Antoine. "Paul Hazard transatlantique." Lecture at the Collège de France, May 19, 2016, presented during the colloquium, "Histoire et historiens des idées: Figures, méthodes. problèmes," May 18–20, 2016.

Compagnon, Antoine, and Philippe Roger. "Biographies, modes d'emploi." *Critique*, nos. 781–82, June-July 2012, 879–87.

Congar, Yves. "*Civitas Dei* et *Ecclesia* in St. Augustine." *Revue des études augustiniennes* 3 (1957): 3–14.

Coutrot, Aline. *Un courant de la pensée catholique: L'hebdomadaire "Sept" (mars 1934–août 1937)*. Preface by René Rédmond. Rencontres 61. Paris: Cerf, 1961. New edition: *Sept. Un journal, un combat, mars 1934–août 1937* (Paris: Éditions Cana, 1982).

Cowell, Frank R. "Planning the Organisation of UNESCO, 1942–1946: A Personal Record." *Cahiers d'histoire mondiale, Journal of World History, Cuadernos de Historia Mundial* 10, no. 1 (1966): 210–34. Republished in *What UNESCO for the Future? Forum of Reflection* (Paris: UNESCO, 2006), appendix, i–xxxi.

Daguet, François. *Du politique chez Thomas d'Aquin*. Paris: Vrin, 2015.

Decaris, Germaine, and Pierre Mac-Orlan. *Paul Gilson*. Poètes d'aujourd'hui. Paris: Pierre Seghers, 1959.

Della Sudda, Magali. "La suppression de l'hebdomadaire dominicain *Sept*: Immixtion du Vatican dans les affaires françaises (1936–1937)?" *Vingtième Siècle. Revue d'histoire* 4, no. 104 (October–December 2009): 29–44.

de Lubac, Henri. *Le mystère du surnaturel*. Paris: Aubier, 1965.

———. *Mémoire sur l'occasion de mes écrits*. Collection Œuvres complètes du Cardinal Henri de Lubac 33. Paris: Cerf, 2006.

de Lubac, Henri, and Jacques Maritain. *Correspondance et rencontre*. Paris: Cerf, 2012.

Du Bos, Charles. *Journal*. Vol. 9. Paris: Édition de la Colombe, 1961.

Duby, Georges. "Encore un histoire de philosophie." *Annales* 12, no. 4 (1957): 674–75.

Dulong, Claude. *Notice sur la vie et les travaux de Jean Laloy (1912–1994)*. Paris: Palais de l'Institute, Gauthier-Villars, 1996.

Duployé, Pie. *La littérature dans le Royaume de Dieu*. Paris: Bibliothèque de l'homme d'action, 1962.

Dupront, Alphonse. *Le mythe de croisade*. Paris: Gallimard, NRF, 1997.

Durand, Jean-Dominique, ed. *Histoire et théologie: Actes de la Journée de l'association française d'histoire religieuse contemporaine*. Paris: Beauchesne, 1994.

———. *L'Europe de la Démocratie chrétienne*. Brussels: Éditions complexes, 1995.

Eck, Hélène. "Poète et directeur: Paul Gilson." *Cahiers de l'histoire de la radiodiffusion*, no. 36 (1993): 61–68.

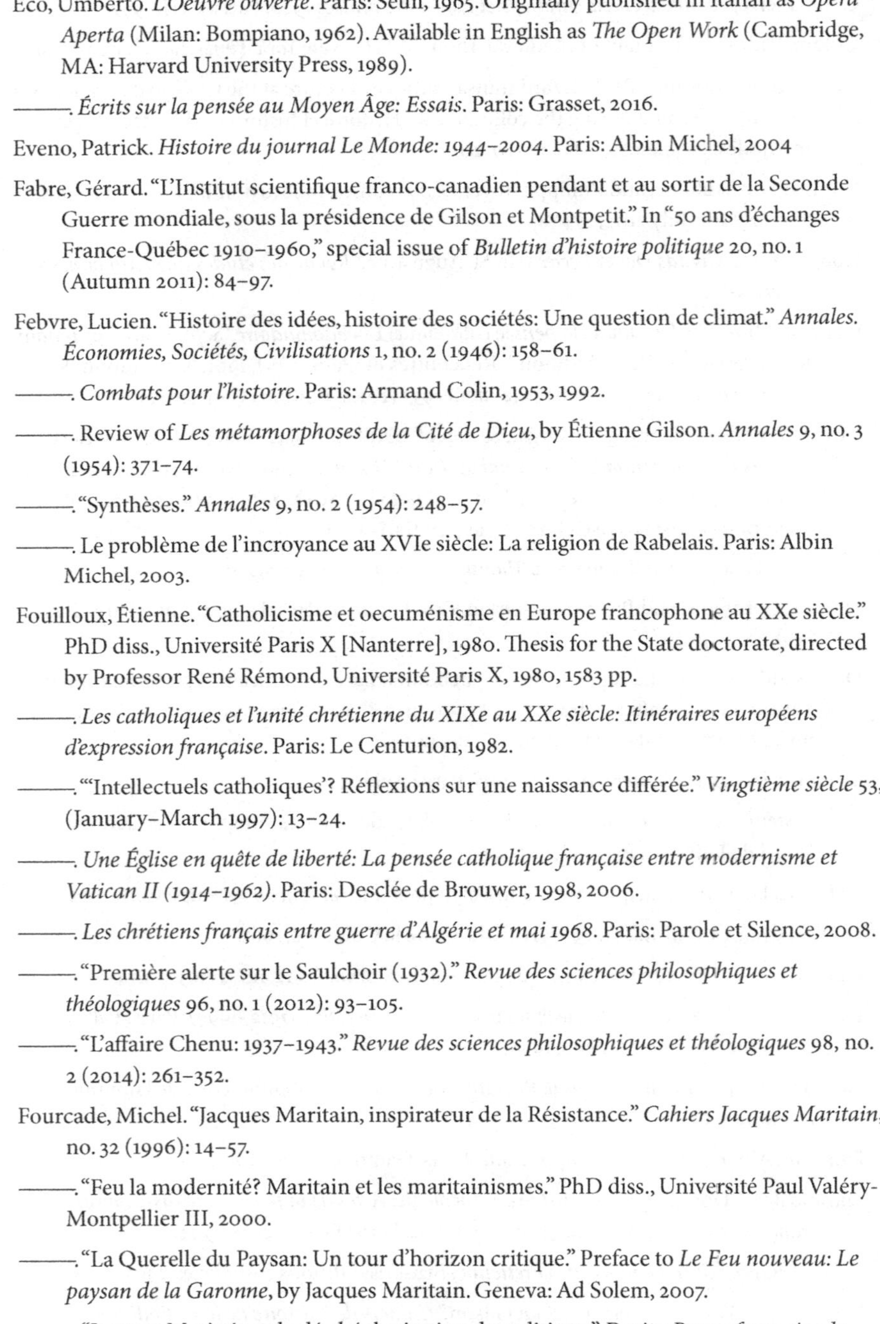

Eco, Umberto. *L'Oeuvre ouverte*. Paris: Seuil, 1965. Originally published in Italian as *Opera Aperta* (Milan: Bompiano, 1962). Available in English as *The Open Work* (Cambridge, MA: Harvard University Press, 1989).

———. *Écrits sur la pensée au Moyen Âge: Essais*. Paris: Grasset, 2016.

Eveno, Patrick. *Histoire du journal Le Monde: 1944–2004*. Paris: Albin Michel, 2004

Fabre, Gérard. "L'Institut scientifique franco-canadien pendant et au sortir de la Seconde Guerre mondiale, sous la présidence de Gilson et Montpetit." In "50 ans d'échanges France-Québec 1910–1960," special issue of *Bulletin d'histoire politique* 20, no. 1 (Autumn 2011): 84–97.

Febvre, Lucien. "Histoire des idées, histoire des sociétés: Une question de climat." *Annales. Économies, Sociétés, Civilisations* 1, no. 2 (1946): 158–61.

———. *Combats pour l'histoire*. Paris: Armand Colin, 1953, 1992.

———. Review of *Les métamorphoses de la Cité de Dieu*, by Étienne Gilson. *Annales* 9, no. 3 (1954): 371–74.

———. "Synthèses." *Annales* 9, no. 2 (1954): 248–57.

———. Le problème de l'incroyance au XVIe siècle: La religion de Rabelais. Paris: Albin Michel, 2003.

Fouilloux, Étienne. "Catholicisme et oecuménisme en Europe francophone au XXe siècle." PhD diss., Université Paris X [Nanterre], 1980. Thesis for the State doctorate, directed by Professor René Rémond, Université Paris X, 1980, 1583 pp.

———. *Les catholiques et l'unité chrétienne du XIXe au XXe siècle: Itinéraires européens d'expression française*. Paris: Le Centurion, 1982.

———. "'Intellectuels catholiques'? Réflexions sur une naissance différée." *Vingtième siècle* 53, (January–March 1997): 13–24.

———. *Une Église en quête de liberté: La pensée catholique française entre modernisme et Vatican II (1914–1962)*. Paris: Desclée de Brouwer, 1998, 2006.

———. *Les chrétiens français entre guerre d'Algérie et mai 1968*. Paris: Parole et Silence, 2008.

———. "Première alerte sur le Saulchoir (1932)." *Revue des sciences philosophiques et théologiques* 96, no. 1 (2012): 93–105.

———. "L'affaire Chenu: 1937–1943." *Revue des sciences philosophiques et théologiques* 98, no. 2 (2014): 261–352.

Fourcade, Michel. "Jacques Maritain, inspirateur de la Résistance." *Cahiers Jacques Maritain*, no. 32 (1996): 14–57.

———. "Feu la modernité? Maritain et les maritainismes." PhD diss., Université Paul Valéry-Montpellier III, 2000.

———. "La Querelle du Paysan: Un tour d'horizon critique." Preface to *Le Feu nouveau: Le paysan de la Garonne*, by Jacques Maritain. Geneva: Ad Solem, 2007.

———. "Jacques Maritain et la dé-théologisation du politique." *Droits: Revue française de théorie, de philosophie et de culture juridiques* 58, no. 2 (2013): 81–100.

———. "Vatican II dans l'histoire de la sécularisation." *Droits. Revue française de théorie, de philosophie et de culture juridiques* 61 (2016): 53–70.

Fourcade, Michel, and Dominique Avon. *Mélanges offerts à Gérard Cholvy*. Montpellier: Publications Université Paul-Valéry, 2004.

Fournier, Marcel. *Marcel Mauss*. Paris: Fayard, 1994.

———. "L'élection de Marcel Mauss au Collège de France." *Genèses* 22 (1996): 160–65.

Fumet, Stanislas. *Histoire de Dieu dans ma vie*. Paris: Fayard-Mame, 1978; Paris: Cerf, 2002.

Garrigou-Lagrange, Reginald. "La nouvelle théologie, où va-t-elle?" *Angelicum* 23, no. 3-4 (1946): 126–45.

Germain, Marie-Odile, ed. *Stanislas Fumet ou la Présence au temps*. Paris: Cerf, 1999.

Gilman, Richard. *Faith, Sex, Mystery: A Memoir*. New York: Simon & Shuster, 1986.

Gilson, Paul. *Le roi des rois*. Paris: Denoël et Steele, 1935. 42 pp.

Grémion, Pierre. "Preuves dans le Paris de guerre froide." *Vingtième siècle* 13, no. 1 (1987): 63–82.

Guérend, Jean-Pierre. *Cardinal Emmanuel Suhard: Archevêque de Paris (1940–1949)*. Paris: Cerf, 2011.

Gugelot, Frédéric. *La conversion des intellectuels au catholicisme en France 1885–1935*. Paris: CNRS, 1998.

Guiraud, Jean. "La croisée des chemins." *La Croix*, January 23, 1935, 1–2.

———. "La collaboration des catholiques à l'enseignement laïque," *La Croix*, January 29, 1935, 1.

———. "L'humanisme, terrain d'entente?" *La Croix*, February 1, 1935, 1.

Halbwachs, Maurice. "Ma campagne au Collège de France." *Revue d'histoire des sciences humaines* 1 (1999): 189–229.

Hazard, Paul. "Six professeurs français à l'Université Columbia." *Revue des deux mondes*, October 1923, 623–33.

Hubert, Bernard, ed. *Jacques Maritain en Europe: La reception de sa pensée; Actes du colloque sur la réception de la pensée de Jacques Maritain dans divers pays d'Europe les 18 et 19 novembre 1993 à l'Institut catholique de Toulouse*. Paris: Beauchesne, 1996.

Hürten, Heinz. *Waldemar Gurian, Ein Zeuge der Krise unserer Welt in der ersten Hälfte des 20. Jahhunderts*. Mainz: Matthias-Grünwald-Verlag, 1972.

Husserl, Edmund. *Méditations cartésiennes*. Translated by Gabrielle Peiffer and Emmanuel Lévinas. Paris: Vrin, 1947; repr. 1992.

Journet, Charles. "Chronique de philosophie." *Nova et vetera* 36, no. 2 (1961): 141–57.

Joutard, Geneviève and Philippe. *De la francophilie en Amérique: Ces Américains qui aiment la France*. Arles: Actes Sud, 2006.

Julliard, Jacques, and Michel Winock. *Dictionnaire des intellectuels français: Les personnes, les lieux, les moments*. Paris: Seuil, 1996, 2002.

Kalinowski, Jerzy, and Stefan Swieżawski. *La philosophie à l'heure du concile*. Paris: Société d'Éditions internationales, 1965.

Koyré, Alexandre. *De la mystique à la science: Cours, conférences et documents, 1922–1962*. Paris: EHESS, 2016.

Langlois, Claude. "La naissance de l'intellectuel catholique." In Colin, *Intellectuels chrétiens et Esprit des années 1920*, 213–33.

Latour, Geneviève. *Le Théâtre, reflet de la IVe République: Événements, politique, société, idées*. Paris: Bibliothèque Historique de la Ville de Paris et l'Association de la régie théâtrale, 1995.

Laurence, William L. "'Non-Racial Truth' Called Liberator." *The New York Times*, September 3, 1936, 15.

Le Goff, Jacques. "Au Moyen Âge: Temps de l'Église et temps du marchand." *Annales* 15, no. 3 (1960): 417–33.

Lemon, James. *Toronto Since 1918: An Illustrated History*. Toronto: Lorimer Publishers, 1985.

Leymarie, Michel, and Jean-François Sirinelli, eds. *L'histoire des intellectuels aujourd'hui*. Paris: PUF, 2003.

Libera, Alain de. *Penser au Moyen Âge*. Paris: Seuil, 1991.

———. *La querelle des universaux: De Platon à la fin du Moyen Âge*. Paris: Seuil, 1996, 2014.

———. *Où va la philosophie médièvale? Leçons inaugurales*. Paris: Fayard-Collège de France, 2014.

———. *L'invention du sujet modern, Cours du Collège de France 2013–2014*, Paris: Vrin, 2015.

Loubet del Bayle, Jean-Louis. *Les non-conformistes des années 30: Une tentative de renouvellement de la pensée politique française*. Paris: Seuil, 1969; repr. 2001.

Lustiger, Jean-Marie. *Le choix de Dieu: Entretiens avec Jean-Louis Missika et Dominique Wolton*. Paris: De Fallois, 1987.

Madiran, Jean. "Un témoignage chrétien: Le philosophe Gilson et la théologie." *Itinéraires: Chroniques et documents*, no. 44, June 1960, 46–67.

———. *Chroniques philosophiques*. Paris: Difralivre, 1992.

Manaranche, Louis. "L'engagement politique et spirituel de Stanislas Fumet (1944–1983)." Master's thesis, Université Paris 4 Sorbonne, 2012.

Marion, Jean-Luc. *Dieu sans l'être*. Paris: Fayard, 1982; Paris: PUF, 1991. Translated into English as *God without Being* (Chicago: University of Chicago Press, 1991).

Maritain, Jacques. "Grandeur et misère de la métaphysique." *Chroniques de la "Roseau d'or,"* December 1925. A revised version became the introduction to *Distinguir pour unir, ou les Degrés du savoir*.

———. *Degrés du savoir*. Paris: Desclée de Brouwer, 1932. English translation by Bernard Wall and Margot Adamson, *Degrees of Knowledge* (London: Geoffrey Bless, 1937).

———. *Christianisme et démocratie*. New York: Éditions de la Maison française, 1943.

———. *Carnets de notes*. Paris: Desclée de Brouwer, 1965.

———. *Le Paysan de la Garonne*. Paris: Desclée de Brouwer, 1966. There is a new edition prepared by Michel Fourcade, *Le Feu nouveau: Le Paysan de la Garonne* (Geneva: Ad Solem, 2007).

———. *Oeuvres complètes*. 16 vols. Fribourg, Switzerland: Éditions Universitaires, and Paris: Editions Saint-Paul, 1982.

———. "Carnets de notes." Edited by Dominique et René Mougel. Years 1925–1927, 1928, 1929, and 1930. *Cahiers Jacques Maritain* (Kolbsheim), vols. 67–71, 2014–2016.

Maritain, Jacques and Raïssa. *Œuvres complètes*. 17 vols. Fribourg: Éditions Universitaires, 1986–1999.

Maurel, Chloé. "L'UNESCO de 1945 à 1974." PhD diss., University of Paris 1, Pantheon-Sorbonne, 2005. Published as *Histoire de l'UNESCO: Les trente premières années; 1945–1974* (Paris: L'Harmattan, 2010).

Mauriac, François. *Bloc-notes. 1952–1970*. 5 vols. Paris: Point-Seuil, 1993.

———. *La paix des cimes: Chroniques, 1948–1955*. Paris: Bartillat, 2000, 2009.

Mauss, Marcel. "Un inédit: La leçon inaugurale de Marcel Mauss au Collège de France." Presented by J. F. Bert. *Terrain* 59 (September 2012): 138–51.

Mayeur, Jean-Marie, ed. *L'histoire religieuse de la France, XIX–XXe siècles: Problèmes et méthodes*, Paris: Beauchesne, 1975.

———. *Des partis catholiques à la Démocratie chrétienne, XIXe–XXe siècles*. Paris: Armand Colin, 1980.

Merton, Thomas. *La nuit privée d'étoiles*. Paris: Albin Michel, 1951. Originally published in English as *The Seven Storey Mountain*. New York: Harcourt, Brace & Company, 1948.

Michel, Florian. "Entre tradition et traduction: Philosophes, philologues et théologiens dans un débat conciliaire." *Revue de l'histoire de l'Église de France*, no. 229 (July-December 2006), 435–75.

———. "Intégrisme catholique et politique." *Études* (September 2009), 211–22.

———. "Jacques Maritain pendant la drôle de guerre: Notes et documents." *Cahiers Jacques Maritain* 59 (December 2009): 4–57.

———. *Traduire la lturgie: Essai d'histoire*, Paris: CLD, 2013.

———. "Les universités pontificales, un lieu de gouvernance pour le Saint-Siège? Perspectives comparatistes entre la France, les États Unis et le Canada dans l'entre-deux-guerres." In *Le gouvernement pontifical sous Pie XI. Pratiques romaines et gestion de l'université*, edited by Laura Pettinaroli, 757–73. Rome: École Française de Rome, 2013.

———. "La chrétienté, nom commun à l'époque contemporaine." In *La chrétienté dans l'histoire: Une notion mouvante*. Edited by Nicole Lemaitre, 47–67. Paris: Parole et silence, 2014.

———. "la gestion de conflits et la governance ecclésiale au temps de la réforme liturgique (1963-1975)" in Vincent Petit, Christian Sorrel, Bruno Dumons, eds., Liturgie et société XIXe–XXe siècles, 205-23.

———. "L'Affirmation transnationale de la culture catholique française (années 1920–années 1960)." *Revue historique* 3, no. 679 (July 2016): 605–27

Monod, Jean-Claude. *La querelle de la sécularisation: Théologie politique et philosophies de l'histoire de Hegel à Blumenberg*. Paris: Vrin, 2002

Montini, Giovanni Battista. *Discorsi e scritti milanese (1954–1963)*. Brescia: Istituto Paolo VI, 1997.

Mounier, Emmanuel. *Carnets de route*. Vol. 2, *Les certitudes difficiles*. Collection Esprit. Paris: Seuil, 1951.

———. *Feu de la Chrétienté*. Paris: Seuil, 1951.

———. *Œuvres complètes*. Vol. 4, *Recueils posthumes. Correspondance*. Paris: Seuil, 1963.

———. *Scritti Fucini (1925–1933)*. Brescia: Istituto Paolo VI, 2004.

Naud, André. "Le cardinal Léger au concile et la conduite de l'intelligence chrétienne." In *L'Église canadienne et Vatican II*, 237–63. Quebec: Fides, 1997.

Nord, Philip. *France's New Deal: From the Thirties to the Postwar Period Era*. Princeton, NJ: Princeton University Press, 2010.

Papini, Roberto. *L'internationale démocrate-chrétienne (1925–1986)*. Paris: Cerf, 1988.

Paupert, Jean-Marie. *Vieillards de chrétienté et Chrétiens de l'an 2000*. Paris: Grasset, 1967.

Pelletier, Denis. *La crise catholique: Religion, société, politique en France (1965–1978)*. Paris: Payot, 2002.

Perrin, Luc. *Paris à l'heure de Vatican II*. Paris: Éditions de l'Atelier, 1997.

Perrin, Marie-Thérèse. *Laberthonnière et ses amis: Dossiers de correspondance (1905–1916)*. Paris: Beauchesne, 1975.

Petit, Vincent, Christian Sorrel, and Bruno Dumons, eds. "La gestion de conflit et la gouvernance ecclésiale au temps de la réforme liturgique (1963–1975)." In *Liturgie et société XIXe–XXe siècles*, 205–23. Rennes: Presses Universitaires de Rennes, 2016.

Piketty, Guillaume. "Bouquins." In *Dictionnaire de la France Libre*, 1096–98. Paris: Robert Lafont, 2010.

Pomeyrols, Catherine. "La formation des intellectuels québécois dans l'entre deux guerres." PhD diss., Université Bordeaux Montaigne, January 1994.

Poulat, Émile. *Intégrisme et catholicisme intégral*. Paris: Casterman, 1969.

Prévotat, Jacques. "Théologiens laïcs des années trente." In *La Foi à l'épreuve du XXe siècle*, 49–69. Les Quatre Fleuves 17. Paris: Beauchesne, 1983.

———. *Les catholiques et l'Action Française: Histoire d'une condemnation*. Paris: Fayard, 2001.

Ratzinger, Joseph. *La théologie de l'histoire de saint Bonaventure*. Translated into French by Robert Givord. Paris, PUF, 1988. Translated into English by Zachary Hayes as

The Theology of History in St. Bonaventure (Chicago: Franciscan Herald Press, 1971 and 1989). Originally published as *Die Geschichtstheologie des Heiligen Bonaventura* (Münich: Verlag Schnell et Steiner, 1959).

Rémond, René. *Les catholiques dans la France des années 1930*. Paris: Cana, 1979.

Rémond, René, Jacques Julliard, Daniel Lindenberg. "L'histoire des intellectuels catholiques." Interview of René Remond. *Mil neuf cent*, Cahiers George Sorel 13 (1995): 14–24.

Roger, Philippe. *L'ennemi américain: Généalogie de l'antiaméricanisme français*. Paris: Seuil, 2002.

Romains, Jules. *Passagers de cette planète, où allons-nous?* Paris: Grasset, 1955.

Roncalli, Angelo G. *Journal de France, I, 1945–48*. Introduction and notes by Étienne Fouilloux. Paris: Cerf, 2006.

Roume, Charles. *Origines et formation de la communauté des prêtres de Saint Basile: Contribution à l'histoire religieuse de Vivarais*. Privas, France: Volle, 1965.

Rousseaux, André. "L'aventure de Étienne Gilson." *Le Figaro littéraire*, July 16, 1960.

Saunders, Frances Stonor. *Qui mène la danse? La CIA et la guerre froide culturelle*. Paris: Denoël, 2003.

Suhard, Cardinal Emmanuel. *Essor ou déclin de l'Église: Lettre pastorale, Carême de l'an de grâce 1947*. Paris: Éditions A. Lahure, 1962.

Serry, Hervé. *Naissance de l'intellectuel catholique*. Paris: La Découverte, 2004.

Sevegrand, Martine. *Temps présent: Une aventure chrétienne (1937–1992)*. Vol. 1, *Un hebdomadaire (1937–1947)*. Paris: Éditions du temps présent, 2007.

Siegfried, André. *Les États-Unis aujourd'hui*. Paris: Armand Colin, 1927.

———. *Le Canada: Puissance internationale*. Paris: Armand Colin, 1937, 2014.

Simon, Yves. *La campagne d'Éthiopie et la pensée politique française*. 2nd ed. Paris: Desclée de Brouwer, 1937.

Souday, Paul. "Les Livres." *Le Temps*, January 21, 1926, 3, col. 6.

St. Onge, Ruth Ellen, *The Étienne Gilson Collection*, Toronto: PIMS, 2012.

Sutton, Michael. *Charles Maurras et les catholiques français, 1890–1914: Nationalisme et positivisme*. Paris: Beauchesne, 1994.

"Thèse de M. Étienne Gilson, agrégé de philosophie." *Revue de métaphysique et de morale* 21, no. 3 (May 1913): 24–32.

Thümmler, Illen. *Katholischer Publizist und amerikanischer Politikwisssenschaftler. Ein Intellektuelle Biographie Waldermar Gurians*. Baden-Baden: Nomos-Verlag, 2011.

Toupin-Guyot, Claire. "Entre morale et politique: Le Centre catholique des intellectuels français face à la décolonisation (1952–1966)." *Vingtième Siècle. Revue d'histoire* 63 (July–September 1999): 75–86.

———. *Les intellectuels catholiques dans la société française: Le Centre catholique des intellectuels français, 1941–1976*. Preface by René Rémond. Rennes: Presses universitaires de Rennes, 2002.

Tranvouez, Yvon. *Catholiques et communistes: La crise du progressisme chrétien 1950–1955*. Paris: Éditions du Cerf, 2000.

Tronchet, Guillaume. "Savoirs en diplomatie: Une histoire sociale et transnationale de la politique universitaire internationale de la France (années 1870–années 1930)." PhD diss., Université Paris 1 Panthéon-Sorbonne, 2014.

Tuc, P. "Politique d'abord." *L'Action Française*, January 26, 1935.

Valéry, Paul. *Fragments des mémoires d'un poème*. Paris: Grasset, 1938.

———. *Eupalinos, L'âme et la danse, Dialogue de l'arbre*. Paris: Gallimard, 1944.

Vecsey, George. "John Cardinal Wright Dies at 70: Top-Ranking American in Vatican." *The New York Times*, August 12, 1979, 32.

Vignaux, Paul. Sur la place du Moyen Âge en histoire de la philosophie." In *Bulletin de la Société française de philosophie. Séance du samedi 24 novembre 1973*, 1–29. Paris: Armand Colin, 1974.

———. "Introduction autobiographique." In *Philosophie au Moyen Âge*, 39–87. Paris: Vrin, 2004; 1st ed., 1987.

———. *Philosophie au Moyen Âge*. Paris: Vrin, 2004.

———. La philosophie franciscaine et autres documents inédits." In Boulnois, *Paul Vignaux: Citoyen et philosophe (1904–1987)*, 129–40.

Virgoulay, René. *Philosophie et théologie chez Maurice Blondel*. Paris: Cerf, 2002.

Winock, Michel. "Les générations intellectuelles." In "Les générations," special issue, *Vingtième Siècle. Revue d'histoire* 22 (April–June, 1989): 17–38.

———. *Esprit: Des intellectuels dans la cité (1930–1950)*. Paris: Seuil, 1996.

———. "Histoire d'historiens." *Critique*, June-July, 2012, no. 781–782, 511–23.

Books and Articles about Étienne Gilson

Arbib, Dan, and Francesco Marrone, eds. *Gilson et Descartes à l'occasion du centenaire de La liberté chez Descartes et la théologie*. Examina philosophica, "I quaderni di Alvearium" 2. ClioEdu, Lecce: 2015.

"Autour d'Étienne Gilson." Special issue of *Revue thomiste* 94 (1994).

Bastien, Hermas. "L'Institut scientifique franco-canadien." *L'Action universitaire* 6, no. 5 (April 1940): 5.

Bonino, Serge-Thomas. "Historiographie de l'école thomiste: Le cas Gilson." In *Saint Thomas au XXe siècle: Actes du colloque du Centenaire de la Revue thomiste*, ed. S.-T. Boninio, 299–313. Paris: Éditions Saint-Paul, 1994.

Chenaux, Philippe. "Étienne Gilson." In *Dictionnaire des intellectuels français*. Paris: Seuil, 2002.

de Libera, Alain. "Les études de la Philosophie Médiévale en France d'Étienne Gilson à nos jours." In *Gli Studi di filosofia medievale fra Ottocento e Novecento, Contributo a un bilancio storiografico* Atti del convegno internazionale, Roma, 21–23 settembre 1989, edited by Ruedi Imbach and Alfonso Maierù, 21–50. Rome: Edizioni di Storia e Letteratura, 1991.

de Lubac, Henri. *Letters of Étienne Gilson to Henri de Lubac*, with commentary by Henri de Lubac. Translated by Mary Emily Hamilton. San Francisco: Ignatius Press, 1988.

Dewan, Lawrence. "Étienne Gilson." In *Penseurs et apôtres du XXe siècle*, 170–82. Saint-Laurent: Fides, 2001.

Donneaud, Henry. "Étienne Gilson et Maurice Blondel dans le débat sur la philosophie chrétienne (1931–1933)." *Revue thomiste* 99, no. 3, 1999, 497–516.

Doz, André. "Étienne Gilson, historien de la philosophie médiévale." In *Dire le Moyen Âge hier et aujourd'hui*, edited by Michel Perrin, 211–20. Paris: PUF, 1990.

"Etienne Gilson Anniversary Studies." Special issue of *Mediaeval Studies* 20 (1958).

Étienne Gilson et nous, la philosophie et son histoire, actualités de la pensée d'Étienne Gilson, 28–29 mai 1979. Paris: Vrin, 1980.

An Etienne Gilson Tribute, presented by His North-American Students with a Response by Étienne Gilson. Milwaukee, WI: Marquette University Press, 1959.

Gouhier, Henri. "Discours de réception de M. Henri Gouhier, avec éloge d'Étienne Gilson." Appeared in *Le Monde*, November 23, 1979.

———. "Étienne Gilson historien et philosophe." In *Études sur l'histoire des idées en France depuis le XVIIe siècle*, 159–70. Paris: Vrin, 1980.

———. *Étienne Gilson, trois essais: Bergson, la philosophie chrétienne, l'art*. Paris: Vrin, 1993.

Guiraud, Jean, editorial, *La Croix*, January 23, 1935.

Humbrecht, Thierry-Dominique. "Étienne Gilson et la politique." *Revue thomiste* 104, no. 2 (2014): 227–87.

Jacques, Francis. "Relire Étienne Gilson." Chapter 1 of *La croyance, le savoir et la foi*. Chaire Etienne Gilson. Paris: PUF, 2005.

Jeauneau, Édouard. Translatio studii, *The Transmission of Learning, a Gilsonian Theme*. The Etienne Gilson Series 18. Toronto: PIMS, 1994.

Kuklick, Bruce. *A History of Philosophy in America, 1720–2000*. Oxford: Clarendon Press, 2001.

Madiran, Jean. "Pour saluer Gilson." Chapter 1 in *Gilson: Chroniques philosophiques*, Paris: Difralivre, 1992.

Maritain, Jacques. "Antimoderne." In *Oeuvres complètes*, vol. 2. Fribourg: Éditions universitaires, 1987.

Maritain, Jacques, et al. *Étienne Gilson, Philosophe de la Chrétienté*. Paris: Cerf, 1949.

Maurer, Armand. "The Legacy of Etienne Gilson." In *One Hundred Years of Thomism: Aeterni Patris and Afterwards; A Symposium*, edited by Victor Brezick, 28–44. Houston: University of St. Thomas, Center for Thomistic Studies, 1981.

Michel, Florian. "Étienne Gilson et *Les Tribulations de Sophie*: Une théologie sans philosophe?" In *Un nouvel âge de la théologie? 1965–1980, Colloque de Montpellier, juin 2007*, edited by Dominique Avon and Michel Fourcade, 45–67. Paris: Karthala, 2009.

———. "Le Moyen Âge au Nouveau Monde: L'enjeu culturel des 'Mediaeval Studies.'" *Archives des Sciences sociales des religions* 149 (January–March 2010): 9–32.

———. *La pensée catholique en Amérique du Nord: Réseaux intellectuels et échanges culturels entre l'Europe, le Canada et les États-Unis (années 1929–1960)*. Paris: Desclée de Brouwer, 2010.

———. *Traduire la liturgie. Essai d'histoire*. Paris: CLD, 2013.

Mounier, Emmanuel. Review of *Pour un ordre catholique*, by Étienne Gilson. *Esprit* 3, no. 30 (March 1935): 959–64.

Murphy, Francesca. *Art and Intellect in the Philosophy of Étienne Gilson*. Columbia: Missouri University Press, 2004.

Paix et droit, organ de l'alliance isarélite universelle, Paris, March 1933, 7 (contains Gilson's condemnation of Nazism).

Prévotat, Jacques. "Étienne Gilson est-il un chrétien modéré?" In *Les "chrétiens modérés" en France et en Europe (1870–1960)*, edited by Jacques Prévotat and Jean Vavasseur-Desperriers, 433–53. Villeneuve d'Ascq: Presses Universitaires du Septentrion, 2013.

Redpath, Peter A. *A Thomistic Tapestry: Essays in Memory of Étienne Gilson*. Value Inquiry Book Series 142. Amsterdam: Rodopi, 2003.

Schmitz, Kenneth. *What Has Clio to do with Athena? Etienne Gilson, Historian and Philosopher*. The Etienne Gilson Series 10. Toronto: PIMS, 1987.

Shestov, Lev. *Athènes et Jérusalem: Essai de philosophie religieuse*. Paris: Vrin, 1938.

Shook, Laurence. "Étienne Henry Gilson (1884–1978)." *Mediaeval Studies* 41 (1979): vii–xv.

———. *Étienne Gilson*. Toronto: PIMS, 1984.

Souday, Paul. "Dans la tranchée." *Le Temps*, May 8, 1916, 1.

———. "Un esthéticien en captivité." *Le Temps*, June 8, 1917, 1.

Temple, Frédéric-Jacques. *Paul Gilson: Hommage et contribution bio-bibliographique*. Lausanne: Éditions le Front Littéraire, 1983.

Thiry, André. "Le philosophe et la théologie." *Nouvelle revue théologique* 84, no. 4 (1962): 337–64.

Vallery-Radot, Louis Pasteur. "Réponse au discours de réception d'Étienne Gilson." May 29, 1947. https://www.academie-francaise.fr/reponse-au-discours-de-reception-detienne-gilson.

Van Riet, Georges. "Le philosophe et la théologie." *Revue philosophique de Louvain* 58 (1960): 308–13.

Vignaux, Paul. "Témoignage sur une jeunesse étudiante (1925–1932)." In *Crise de notre temps et réflexion chrétienne (de 1930 à 1975)*, by Henri-Irené Marrou, 107–8. Paris: Beauchesne, 1978.

———. "Étienne Gilson." In *Encyclopedia Universalis*. Paris: CFL-Encyclopaedia Britannica, 1979.

Weigel, George. "Ways of Thinking and Believing, *The Philosopher and Theology* by Étienne Gilson." *The New York Times*, July 22, 1962.

Wenin, Christian. "Actualité de la pensée d'Étienne Gilson (Paris, 28–29 mai, 1979)." *Revue Philosophique de Louvain* 78, no. 40 (1980): 590–94.

On the "Gilson Affair"

"L'affaire Gilson et la presse parisienne." *Le Monde*, March 15, 1951.

["Amicus"]. "Les néo-thomistes se mettent à l'abri." *Aspects de la France*, February 16, 1951, 4.

Bataillon, Marcel. "À propos de l'honorariat conféré par le Collège de France à M. Étienne Gilson." *Le Monde*, January 2, 1957.

Béguin, Albert. "L'affaire Gilson." *Esprit* 19, no. 178 (April 1951): 590–93.

Bernus, Pierre. *Journal de Genève*. January 27, 1950.

Beuve-Mery, Hubert. "Un procès manqué: l'Affaire Gilson." *Le Monde*, March 10, 1951, 1, 3.

Boegner, Henri. "L'affaire Gilson n'est pas close." *Aspects de la France*, March 16, 1951, 4.

Borne, Étienne. "Le cas Gilson." *Centre d'informations catholiques*. Paris, February 1951, 15 pp.

———. "Feu l'affaire Gilson." *L'Aube*, Sunday Supplement, March 17–18, 1951, 1, 5.

———. "Mission et démission des intellectuels." *Terre humaine*, April 1951.

Boutang, Pierre. "Thomiste discuté, MRP indiscutable." *Aspects de la France*, February 2, 1951, 1, 4.

———. "Au temps où le fuyard donnait des leçons de résistance." *Aspects de la France*, February 9, 1951, 6.

———. "Le fuyard Gilson." *Aspects de la France*, March 2, 1951, 4.

Brisson, Pierre. "M. Étienne Gilson rompt le silence." *Le Figaro littéraire*, February 17, 1951.

Carité, Maurice. "Calomniateurs au pilori." *L'Aube*, March 8, 1951, 1.

Corbett, James. "Une lettre de M. James Corbett." *Le Monde*, April 14, 1951.

"Le cas du fuyard Gilson." *Aspects de la France*, February 9, 1951, 1, 6.

De Corte, Marcel. "Nouvelles réponses à notre enquête." *Aspects de la France*, February 16, 1951, 4.

["Fabrice"]. "France, ton Collège fout le camp!" *Aspects de la France*, February 9, 1951, 6.

Fontaine, André. "L'Affaire Gilson." *Le Monde*, September 22, 1978.

Gelis, M. G. "L'Affaire Étienne Gilson et la querelle du neutralisme." *Journal de Neuchâtel*, February 28, 1951, 1, 9.

"The Gilson Controversy." *Commonweal*, May 18, 1951, 134.

Gilson, Étienne. "M. Étienne Gilson rompt le silence. Lettre à Pierre Brisson." *Le Figaro littéraire*, February 17, 1951.

———. "Une lettre de M. Étienne Gilson." *Le Monde*, February 22, 1951.

———. "M. Étienne Gilson répond à M. Waldemar Gurian." *Le Monde*, March 8, 1951.

———. "Lettre à Albert Béguin." *Esprit* 19, no. 178 (April 1951): 593–96.

———. "Letter from Étienne Gilson to Henri Gouhier, October 31, 1932." *Revue thomiste* 94 (1994): 471.

Gurian, Waldemar. "Europe and the United States: An Open Letter to Étienne Gilson." *Commonweal*, December 15, 1950, 250–51.

———. "Lettre ouverte à Étienne Gilson champion du neutralisme." *Le Figaro littéraire*, January 27, 1951.

———. "Une lettre de M. Waldemar Gurian." *Le Monde*, March 5, 1951.

———. "Une nouvelle lettre de M. Waldemar Gurian." *Le Monde*, March 10, 1951.

———. "Lettre de M. Waldemar Gurian." *Le Figaro littéraire*, March 24, 1951.

———. "Une nouvelle lettre de M. Waldemar Gurian." *Le Monde*, April 23, 1951.

Halévy, Daniel. "La réponse de M. Daniel Halévy." *Aspects de la France*, February 9, 1951, 6.

"Justice rendue à M. Étienne Gilson." *Combat*, December 28, 1956, 1, 7.

Marcel, Gabriel. "La réponse de M. Gabriel Marcel." *Aspects de la France*, February 9, 1951, 6.

———. *Rome n'est plus dans Rome*. Paris: *La Table ronde*, 1951.

Mauriac, François. "Les amarres rompues." *Le Figaro*, February 20–21, 1951.

———. "Le même peuple." *Le Figaro*, March 14, 1951.

Paulhan, Jean. "Nouvelles réponses à notre enquête." *Aspects de la France*, February 16, 1951, 4.

Phelan, Gerald. "Une lettre du Président de l'Institut médiéval de l'Université Notre Dame." *Le Monde*, March 8, 1951.

"Quand Gilson fou de rage insulte son parrain." *Aspects de la France*, March 23, 1951, 4.

Rémy, Colonel. "Nouvelles réponses à notre enquête." *Aspects de la France*, February 16, 1951, 4.

[Salleron, Louis]. "Le point de vue de l'homme de la rue." *Carrefour*, February 13, 1951.

Soutou, Georges-Henri. *La paix de 50 ans*. Paris: Fayard, 2001.

Treno, R. "M. Étienne Gilson a sa cabane au Canada." *Le canard enchainé*, January 31, 1951.

Vallery-Radot, Pasteur. "L'Académie devrait exclure M. Gilson." Interview by Pierre Louis Berthaud. *Carrefour*, February 20, 1951.

Vaussard, Maurice. "En marge de l'affaire Gilson." *L'Aube*, April 14–15, 1951, 1, 4.

GILSON: IN MEMORIAM

Borne, Étienne. "Stature d'Étienne Gilson." *La Croix*, September 22, 1978.

d'Alverny, Marie-Thérèse. "Nécrologie. Étienne Gilson." *Cahiers de civilisation médiévale* 22, no. 88 (December 1979): 425–35.

Fabrègues, Jean de. "Un regard sur la terre et le ciel: La mort d'Étienne Gilson." *Le Monde*, September 22, 1978, 1, 23.

Gandillac, Maurice de. "Étienne Gilson le précurseur." *Nouvelles littéraires*, September 28, 1978.

Guitton, Jean. "Étienne Gilson est mort, une sorte de lion de la pensée." *Le Figaro*, September 21, 1978.

Habert, O. "Notes sur les études médiévales." *La Vie catholique*, October 25, 1924, 9–10.

Lacroix, Jean. "Un grand existant." *Le Monde*, September 22, 1978, 23.

———. "De Gilson à Jean d'Ormesson et retour." *Commentaire*, no. 13, 1981, 148–50.

Marion, Jean-Luc. "Le découvreur d'un continent." *Le Monde*, October 7, 1978.

———. "Gilson fondateur." In *La pensée catholique en Amérique du Nord: Réseaux intellectuels et échanges culturels entre l'Europe, le Canada et les États-Unis (années 1929–1960)*, 97–115. Paris: Desclée de Brouwer, 2010.

———. "Étienne Gilson, nouvel Alcuin d'une nouvelle Chrétienté?" *L'Amitié Charles Péguy* 143–44 (July–December 2013): 419–40.

Rupp, Jean. "Gilson tel que je l'ai connu." *L'Homme nouveau*, March 4, 1979.

Schumann, Maurice. "Discours prononcé à l'occasion de la mort de MM. Étienne Gilson et Jean Guéhenno." *Séance de l'Académie du 28 septembre 1978* [Session of the Académie française, September 28, 1978]. Paris: Firmin-Didot, 1978.

Shook, Laurence. "Etienne Henry Gilson (1884–1978)." *Mediaeval Studies* (Toronto) 41, (1979): vii–xv.

Soisson, Jean-Pierre. "Étienne Gilson, un homme simple." *L'Yonne républicaine*, September 22, 1978.

Souday, Paul. "Dans la tranchée." *Le Temps*, May 8, 1916, 1.

———. "Sur Flaubert." *Le Temps*, June 26, 1916, 1.

———. "Un esthéticien en captivité." *Le Temps*, June 8, 1917, 1.

Vignaux, Paul. "Étienne Gilson." *Annuaire de l'École pratique des hautes études* 77 (1978–1979): 27–37.

———. "Étienne Gilson." *Encyclopedia Universalis*, May 1979, 591–92.

———. "Étienne Gilson." *Revue de métaphysique et de morale* 84, no. 3 (1979): 289–95.

Books by Étienne Gilson

[The complete bibliography of Étienne Gilson's books, articles, reviews, and lectures includes some eight hundred entries. See Margaret McGrath, *Étienne Gilson, A Bibliography* (Toronto: PIMS, 1982), 124 pp.]

Index scolastico-cartésien. Paris: Alcan, 1913.

La liberté chez Descartes et la théologie. Paris: Alcan, 1913. English translation by James Colbert, *Theology and the Cartesian Doctrine of Freedom* (South Bend, IN: St. Augustine's Press, 2019).

Le thomisme: Introduction au système de saint Thomas d'Aquin. Strasbourg: Vix, 1919; 2nd ed., Paris: Vrin, 1922; 3rd ed., 1927; 4th ed., 1942; 5th ed., 1945; 6th ed., 1965.

Études de philosophie médiévale. Strasbourg: Université de Strasbourg, 1921. English translation by James Colbert, *Studies in Medieval Philosophy* (Eugene, OR: Cascade Books, 2019).

La philosophie au Moyen Âge. Paris: Payot, 1922; 1930; 2nd ed. 1944. Page numbers refer to the 1944 edition.

La philosophie de saint Bonaventure. Paris: Vrin, 1924; 2nd ed. 1943; 3rd ed. 1953. English translation by Dom Illtyd Trethowan and Frank J. Sheed, *The Philosophy of St. Bonaventure* (Paterson, NJ: St. Anthony Guild Press: 1965).

Saint Thomas d'Aquin. Paris: Gabalda, 1925.

Introduction à l'étude de saint Augustin. Paris: Vrin, 1929; 2nd ed. 1943; 3rd ed. 1949; 4th ed. 1969. English translation by L. E. M. Lynch, *The Christian Philosophy of Saint Augustine* (New York: Random House, 1960).

Les idées et les lettres. Paris: Vrin, 1932.

L'esprit de la philosophie médiévale, Paris: Vrin, 1932, 2nd. ed. 1944; 1969. Translated to English by A.H.C. Downs, *The Spirit of Mediaeval Philosophy*, Sheed and Ward, London, 1936; New York: Charles Scribner's Sons, 1940.

Pour un ordre catholique. Paris: Desclée de Brouwer, 1934; republished, Paris: Parole et Silence, 2013.

La théologie mystique de saint Bernard. Paris: Vrin, 1934; 2nd ed. 1947; 3rd ed. 1969. English translation by A. H. Downes, *The Mystical Theology of Saint Bernard* (New York: Sheed and Ward, 1940).

Le réalisme méthodique. Paris: Téqui, 1935, 1937, 2007. English translation by Philip Trower, *Methodical Realism* (Front Royal, Va.: Christendom Press, 1990).

Christianisme et philosophie, Paris: Vrin, 1936; English translation by Ralph McDonald, CSB, *Christianity and Philosophy* (New York: Sheed & Ward, 1939, for the Institute of Mediaeval Studies.

Medieval Universalism and Its Present Value. Cambridge, MA: Harvard University Press, 1937.

Héloïse et Abélard. Paris: Vrin, 1938; 2nd ed. 1948; 3rd ed. 1964. English translation by Laurence K. Shook, *Heloise and Abelard* (Chicago: Regnery, 1951).

Reason and Revelation in the Middle Ages. New York: Scribners, 1938.

Réalisme thomiste et critique de la connaissance. Paris: Vrin, 1939. English translation by Max Wauck, *Thomist Realism and Critique of Knowledge* (San Francisco: Ignatius Press, 1986).

Dante et la philosophie. Paris: Vrin, 1939; 2nd ed. 1953; 3rd ed. 1972. English translation by Leo R. Ward, *Dante and Philosophy* (Gloucester, MA: Peter Smith, 1968).

God and Philosophy. New Haven, CT: Yale University Press, 1941. Translated into French by a monk of Fontgombault as *Dieu et la philosophie* (Fontgombault, France: Petrus a Stella, 2013).

History of Philosophy and Philosophical Education. Aquinas Lecture 1947. Milwaukee, WI: Marquette University Press, 1948.

L'Être et l'essence. Paris: Vrin, 1948; 2nd ed. 1962. Not a translation, but an equivalent in English is *Being and Some Philosophers* (Toronto: PIMS, 1949).

L'École des muses. Paris, Vrin, 1951. English translation by Maisie Ward, *Choir of Muses* (New York and London: Sheed & Ward, 1953).

Les métamorphoses de la Cité de Dieu, Paris: Vrin, 1952, 2005. English translation by James Colbert, *Metamorphoses of the City of God*, (Washington DC: The Catholic University of America Press, 2020).

Jean Duns Scot. Introduction à ses positions fondamentales. Paris: Vrin, 1952. English translation by James Colbert, *John Duns Scotus, Introduction to His Fundamental Positions* (London: T&T Clark, 2019).

Painting and Reality. Mellon Lectures, The Bollingen Foundation, Washington, 1957. New York: Pantheon Books, 1957. Published in French as *Peinture et réalité* (Paris, Vrin, 1958; 1972).

Introduction à la philosophie chrétienne. Paris: Vrin, 1960; 2nd ed. 2007, with introduction by Thierry-Dominique Humbrecht, OP. English translation by Armand Maurer, *Christian Philosophy: An Introduction* (Toronto: PIMS, 1993).

Saint Thomas, textes sur la morale. Paris: Vrin, 1998.

Le philosophe et la théologie, Paris: Fayard, 1960. English translation by Cécile Gilson, *The Philosopher and Theology* (New York: Random House, 1962).

Introduction aux arts du beau, Paris: Vrin, 1963. English translation *The Arts of the Beautiful*. New York: Charles Scribner's Sons, 1965; reissued by Dalkey Archive, Providence: Rhode Island, 2000.

Linguistique et philosophie: Essais sur les constantes philosophiques du langage. Paris: Vrin, 1965. English translation by John Lyon, *Linguistics and Philosophy: An Essay on the Philosophical Constants of Language* (Notre Dame, IN: Notre Dame University Press, 1988).

Les tribulations de Sophie, Paris: Vrin, 1967. English translation by James G. Colbert, *The Tribulations of Sophia*, South Bend, IN: St. Augustine's Press, 2021.

La société de masse et sa culture. Paris: Vrin, 1967. English translation by James G. Colbert, *Mass Society and Its Culture and Three Essays Concerning Étienne Gilson on Bergson, Christian Philosophy, and Art* (Eugene, OR: Cascade Books, 2023).

D'Aristote à Darwin et retour: Essai sur quelques constantes de biophilosophie. Paris: Vrin, 1971. English translation by John Lyon, *From Aristotle to Darwin and Back Again* (Notre Dame, IN: University of Notre Dame Press, 1984; reissued, San Francisco: Ignatius Press, 2009).

L'athéisme difficile. Paris: Vrin, 1979.

Saint Thomas: Textes sur la morale. Paris: Vrin, 1998.

Oeuvres complètes. Vol. 1, *Un philosophe dans la cité 1908–1943*. Introduction, presentation of texts, and notes by Florian Michel. Paris: Vrin, 2019.

Oeuvres complètes. Vol. 2, *Un philosophe dans la cité 1944–1973*. Introduction, presentation of texts, and notes by Florian Michel. Paris: Vrin, 2023., Paris: Vrin, 2023.

Journal Articles by Gilson

1916 "Art et métaphysique," *Revue de métaphysique et de morale* 23, no. 1 (January 1916): 243–67.

"Du Fondement des jugements esthétiques." *Revue philosophique de la France et de l'étranger* 83 (January–June 1917): 525–46.

1924 "Rabelais franciscain." *Revue d'histoire franciscaine*, no. 3 (January 1927): 257–87.

1925 "L'humanisme de saint Thomas." In *Atti del quinto congresso Internazionale di filosofia, Napoli 5-9 maggio, 1924*, edited by Guido del Valle, 976–89. Naples: Società Anonima Editrice, 1925.

1926 "Le VIe Congrès international de philosophie, Harvard University, Cambridge, USA, 13–17 septrembre 1926." *Revue de métaphysique et de morale* 33, no. 4 (1926): 509–44.

1931 "La tradition française et la chrétienté." *Vigile*, cahier 1 (1931): 53–87.

1932 "Examen de conscience." *Vigile*, cahier 2 (1932): 85–99.

Letter from Étienne Gilson to Henri Gouhier, October 31, 1932, *Revue thomiste* 94, 1994.

1934 "Liberalisme et neutralité," November 9, 1934

1936 "La corporation médicale dans un ordre social-chrétien." *Cahiers Laënnec* 2, no. 1 (January 1936): 1–15 [stenographer's notes of a lecture given March 11, 1935, at the Laënnec Conference].

1940 "L'Europe et la paix." *Revue trimestrielle canadienne* 26, no. 101 (March 1940): 27–43.

1942 "Sagesse et société." *Témoignages*, no. 1 (1942): 39–54.

1945 "L'esprit de chrétienté." *La Vie intellectuelle*, February 1945, 18–36.

"Jacques Maritain au Vatican." *La Vie intellectuelle*, March 1945, 36–38.

"Pour une éducation nationale." *La Vie intellectuelle*, April 1945, 116–32.

"Le thomisme et les philosophies existentielles." *La Vie intellectuelle*, June 1945, 144–55.

1946 "Monde moderne, monde chrétien: Pas d'illusions rétrospectives." *Esprit* 14, no. 125 (1946): 192–96.

"Une aristocratie de l'homme moyen." *Esprit* 14, no. 127 (1946): 672–82.

"Un gomor de manne." *La Vie intellectuelle*, November 1946, 6–19.

1948 "L'État, l'Université, et les universités." *Politique*, no. 5 (1948): 673–90.

"Le domaine public payant." *La Revue. Littérature, histoire, arts et sciences des deuxmondes*, no. 1 (May 1948): 31–45.

1949 "Le catholique et la politique." *Culture catholique. Présence de la Pensée chrétienne*, no. 1 (June 1949): 119–28.

"Les terreurs de l'an deux mille." *La Revue* 2 (1949): 193–206; and *Revue de l'Université d'Ottawa* 19 (January–March 1949): 67–81.

"Compagnons de route." In *Étienne Gilson: Philosophe de la chrétienté*, 275–95. Paris: Cerf, 1949.

1950 "Artists and Saints: *In memorian* C. F. Ramuz." *Measure* 1 (1950): 48–59.

1951 "Les recherches historico-critiques et l'avenir de la scholastique." In *Scholastica ratione historico-critica instauranda*, edited by Carol Balič, 40-48. Rome: Pontificium Atheneum Antonianum, 1951.

1955 "Révélation et unité des hommes." *La Vie intellectuelle*, February 1955, 6–24.

1956 "Cité des hommes et cité de Dieu." *La documentation catholique* 53, cols. 1437–47.

1970 "Prophètes de malheur." *Revue des deux mondes*, January 1970, 10–22.

"Hommage à François Mauriac: Pour le tombeau de François Mauriac." *Revue des deux mondes*, October 1970, 128–46.

1974 "Charles Du Bos et les théologiens." *Cahiers Charles du Bos*, no. 19 (May 1974): 3–16.

Newspaper and Periodical Articles by Gilson

1923 "Le bilan religieux du XIXe siècle français." *Foi et vie*, no. 21, December 16, 1923, 1107–1202.

1924 Letter to the Editor. "Pour travailler tranquille." *La Vie catholique en France et à l'étranger*, November 1, 1924, 2.

1925 "Une heure avec Étienne Gilson." *Les nouvelles littéraires*, January 3, 1925, 1–2. Conversation with Frédéric Lefèvre, republished in Lefèvre, *Une heure avec. . ., Third Series*, 63–79. Paris: Librairie Gallimard, 1925.

1927 "The University Will Lead the Way. St Michael's College Will Establish a Department of Mediaeval Philosophy." *University of Toronto Monthly*, March, 1927, 253–54.

"St. Michael's Establishes Institute of Mediaeval Studies." *University of Toronto Monthly*, December 19, 1927, 119–21.

"Why not?" *St Michael's College Yearbook*, 32–33.

1928 "The Ethics of Higher Studies." *Harvard Alumni Bulletin*, October 27, 1927, 127–13. Republished as the first selection in *A Gilson Reader*, edited by Anton C. Pegis, 24–30 (Garden City, NY: Image Book, 1957). It was also partly reproduced with the same title in *Bulletin of the American Association of University Professors* 14, no. 3 (March 1928): 208–10. It was published again in 1965 with the title "Education and Higher Learning" in *The Norton Reader: An Anthology of Expository Prose*, edited by Arthur M. Eastman, 213–25 (New York: Norton, 1965).

1929 "Mediaevalism in Toronto." *Commonweal* 9, no. 26, May 1, 1929, 738–740.

"Autour de Julien Benda: La mare aux clercs." *L'Européen*, May 29, 1929, 4.

"Vues prises de Marbourg." *L'Européen*, June 19, 1929, 1–2.

"Métaphysique de la réfutation, autour de Benda." *L'Européen*, July 10, 1929, 4.

"Adieux à Monsieur Teste." *L'Européen*, October 23, 1929, 1–2.

"Vues prises Marbourg." *L'Européen*, December 18, 1929, 1; *Bulletin mensuel de la chambre de commerce de Montréal*, January 1930, 5–8.

1930 "Lettre ouverte à M. Teste en faveur de Blaise Pascal." L'*Européen*, January 29, 1930, 1–2.

"Autour de Jacob Boehme." *L'Européen*, February 5, 1930, 5.

"Giovanni Papini et saint Augustin," *L'Européen*, March 5, 1930, 5 .

1934 "En marge de Chamfort." *Sept*, no. 1, March 3, 1934.

"La démocratie en danger." *Sept*, no. 2, March 10, 1934.

"Chesterton, Le Moyen Âge et la Réforme." *Sept*, March 17, 1934.

"L'État sans philosophie." *Sept*, no. 5, March 31, 1934, 2.

"La croisée des chemins." *Sept*, April 14, 1934, 2.

"Intermède soviétique." *Sept*, May 19, 1934, 2.

"Un document sur le problème scolaire." *Sept*, May 19, 1934, 4.

"Entre la tour d'ivoire et la tour de Babel." Editorial. *Sept*, no. 14, June 2, 1934, 1.

"Pour un ordre catholique." *Sept*, no. 15, June 9, 1934, 2. Reproduced with the title, "L'ordre catholique et la France," in *Pour un ordre catholique*, 100–107

"Le crime de Dante." *Sept*, no. 15, June 9, 1934, 9

"Le curé de Galapian." *Sept*, no. 19, July 7, 1934, 2 .

"Notre courrier." *Sept*, no. 19, July 7, 1934, 35.

"Superstition des diplômes," *Sept*, no. 25, August 18, 2 .

"À quel prix collaborer?" *Sept*, no. 33, October 12, 1934, 3.

"Quand Israël demande un roi." *Sept*, no. 35, October 26, 1934, 3.

"Libéralisme et neutralité." *Sept*, no. 37, November 9, 1934, 3.

"Laïcité et laïcisme." *Sept*, no. 39, November 23, 1934, 3.

"Laïcisme et libre-pensée." *Sept*, no. 41, December 7, 1934, 3.

"L'Église et la liberté." *Sept*, no. 43, December 21, 1934, 3.

1935 "The Layman and Society." *New Blackfriars* 16, no. 182 (1935): 377.

"Ordre catholique et unité nationale." *Sept*, no. 47, January 18, 1935, 3.

"Action catholique ou action politique." *Sept*, no. 49, February 1, 1935, 3.

"Les vrais problèmes." *Sept*, no. 50, February 8, 1935, 3.

"Anatole France et saint Augustin." *Sept*, no. 52, February 22, 1935, 4.

"Le trésor de l'Église de France." *Sept*, no. 54, March 8, 1935, 4.

"Le devoir du laïque." *Sept*, no. 57, March 29, 1935, 4.

"La France et le paganisme." *Sept*, no. 62, May 3, 1935, 6.

"Pour éclairer *La nouvelle lanterne*." *Sept*, no. 68, June 14, 1935, 4.

"Par-delà le Sillon et l'Action Française." *Sept*, no. 69, June 21, 1935, 4.

"Action politique et action catholique." *Sept*, no. 70, June 28, 1935, 4.

"En marge de l'Action Française." *Sept*, no. 71, July 5, 1935, 4.

"La parole que nous attendons." *Sept*, no. 73, July 19, 1935, 4.

"Les catholiques et les partis nationaux." *Sept*, no. 74, July 26, 1935, 4

"Les catholiques et l'action sociale." *Sept*, no. 75, August 2, 1935, 4.

"Qui est Mammon?" *Sept*, no. 76, August 9, 1935, 4.

"Action catholique et action politique." *Sept*, no. 77, August 16, 1935, 4.

1936 "Notre position." *Sept*, February 14, 1936.

"The Catholic Mind." *New Blackfriars* 17, no. 195 (1936): 408–16.

"The Truth Shall Make You Free." Editorial. *The Nation* 143 (September 12, 1936): 294.

1939 "Mon ami Lévy-Bruhl, philosophe, sociologue." *Les nouvelles littéraires*, March 18, 1939, 1.

"Le *Traité des passions* de Descartes inspira-t-il *Phèdre* de Racine?" *Les nouvelles littéraires*, April 15, 1939, 1 .

"Érasme, citoyen du monde." *Les nouvelles littéraires*, May 6, 1939, 1–2.

"Sapho a-t-elle lu Descartes?" *Les nouvelles littéraires*, May 27, 1939, 6.

"Henri Heine a-t-il prévu Hitler?" *Les nouvelles littéraires*, July 1, 1939, 1–2.

"Ce que nous devons à Henri Bergson." *Les nouvelles littéraires*, September 2, 1939, 1–3.

1940 "A French View of the War." *America*, no. 62, February 3, 1940, 452–56.

"Ligne Maginot et ligne Domitien." *L'Indépendant de Woonsocket*, March 28 1940, 1.

"Étienne Gilson à Woonsocket." *L'Indépendant de Woonsocket*, March 20, 1940, 1.

"La France dans le conflit actuel: Causerie de M. Étienne Gilson, philosophe français, à l'occasion d'une visite officielle au Bureau général." *L'Union: Organe officiel de l'Union Saint-Jean Baptiste* 40, no. 4 (April 15, 1940): 1–2.

1945 "L'équilibre canadien." *Chroniques de France* 9 (1945): 17–20.

"Instruire ou éduquer?" *Le Monde*, January 9, 1945, 1–2.

"Hitler fera-t-il notre révolution ?" *Hebdomadaire du temps présent*, January 12, 1945, 1, 8.

"La circulaire 45 ou: comment l'on se propose de pervertir la vérité." *Hebdomadaire du temps présent*, March 2, 1945, 1.

"La révolution par l'amitié redressera la Cité." *Hebdomadaire du temps présent*, March 9, 1945, 3.

"Le schisme national." *Hebdomadaire du temps présent*, March 30, 1945, 1.

"L'éducation des Nations Unies." *Le Monde*, October 28–29, 1945, 1.

"Provincialisme ou coopération." *Le Monde*, November 7, 1945, 1.

"L'université mondiale." *Le Monde*, November 10, 1945, 1.

"L'équivoque de Londres." *Le Monde*, November 21, 1945, 1.

"UNESCO et ses membres." *Le Monde*, December 5, 1945, 1.

1946 "Enseigner la France." *Le Monde*, January 1, 1946, 1.

"Entre deux centenaires (d'Abélard à Saint Bernard)," *Le Monde*, February 12, 3.

"Un pape américain." *Le Monde*, February 24–25, 1946, 1.

"Le drapeau des Nations Unies (symbole des quatre libertés)." *Le Monde*, March 7, 1946, 3.

"Le baromètre américain." *Le Monde*, April 10, 1946, 1–2.

"Naissance du canadien." *Le Monde*, March 15, 1946, 1–2.

"Ravitaillement canadien." *Le Monde*, May 19–20, 1946, 1.

"Une erreur franco-américaine." *Le Monde*, June 12, 1946, 3.

"Le catholicisme aux États-Unis." *Le Monde*, July 3, 1946, 3.

"Exportations intellectuelles." *Le Monde*, July 5, 1946, 3.

"Le Canada et la paix." *Le Monde*, July 31, 1946, 1.

"Le Vatican et les nationalisations." *Le Monde*, August 8, 1946, 1–2.

"Les pionniers intellectuels." *Le Monde*, December 4, 1946, 1.

"L'UNESCO et sa philosophie." *Le Monde*, December 20, 1946, 1.

"Qui n'a rien appris?" *Le Monde*, December 31, 1946, 1.

"Staline et la métaphysique." *Le Monde*, literary supplement, September 28, 1946, 11.

"Une spiritualité littéraire." *Le Monde*, literary supplement, November 20, 1946, 11.

1947 "Justice politique et justice sociale." *Relations* 7, no. 73 (October 1947): 304–5.

"L'arbre canadien." *Le Monde*, January 6–7, 1947, 1–2.

"Le point de vue de Moscou." *Le Monde*, January 9, 1947, 1–2.

"Le point de vue de Poughkeepsie." *Le Monde*, January 19–20, 1947, 1.

"Au pays des caméléons." *Le Monde*, January 23, 1947, 1.

"Philosophical movements in France." *Listener*, no. 37, February 6, 1947, 251.

"En lisant Staline." *L'Aube*, February 12, 1947, 1.

"La maison à l'envers." *Le Monde*, March 21, 1947, 1.

"Depuis le XVIIIe siècle, le Canada a sa littérature originale." *Le Monde*, April 26, 1947, 11.

"Le point de vue de Cleveland." *Le Monde*, May 21, 1947, 1–2.

"Le point de vue d'Arminius." *Le Monde*, May 27, 1947, 1.

"Le sans-parti." *L'Aube*, May 28, 1947, 1.

"Ceux qui ne votent jamais." *L'Aube*, June 5, 1947, 1, 4.

"Avons-nous des universités?" *Le Monde*, June 17, 1947, 1.

"Le clerc devant l'urne." *L'Aube*, June 25, 1947, 1.

"Les finances et l'Université." *L'Aube*, July 18, 1947, 1–4.

"L'Université et son recteur." *Le Monde*, July 20–21, 1947, 1–2.

"Misère de la science française." *L'Aube*, July 22, 1947, 1, 4.

"Le point de vue du Vatican aux Semaines sociales en France." *Le Monde*, July 31, 1947, 1.

"History and Prophecy." *Commonweal*, no. 46, August 29, 1947, 473–78.

"Le système et l'esprit." *Politique* 4, no. 27 (October 1947): 673–77.

1948 "La poutre et la paille." *Le Monde*, January 6, 1948, 1.

"Une réforme bicéphale." *L'Aube*, January 8, 1948, 1, 4.

"Le parlement et les partis (avant la rentrée des chambres)." *Le Monde*, January 24, 1948, 1.

"Avertissement à l'esprit." *Le Monde*, February 4, 1948, 1–2.

"Démocrates allemands ou une conversion nécessaire." *Le Monde*, February 14, 1948, 1–2.

"Le parlement et les lapins." *Le Monde*, February 23, 1948, 3.

"Le domaine public." *Le Monde*, February 26, 1948, 1–2 .

"À propos du domaine public. Une lettre de M. Gérard Bauer." *Le Monde*, March 3, 1948, 3

"Les héritiers du roi Salomon." *Le Monde*, March 4, 1948, 1–2.

"La poésie impure." *Le Figaro littéraire*, March 27, 1948, 1–3.

"L'incident des écoles libres." *L'Aube*, April 1, 1948, 1, 4.

"Pour la culture européenne." *Le Monde*, April 1, 1948, 1.

"Les Français en Ontario." *Le Monde*, April 14, 1948, 3.

"Notre democratie." *L'Aube*, April 26–30, May 2–5

"Le congrès de l'Europe." *Le Monde*, May 5, 1948, 1–2.

"Carence de Bacchus." *Le Monde*, May 7, 1948, 3.

"Un lever de rideau." *Le Monde*, June 10, 1948, 3.

"Gouvernement et parlement." *Le Monde*, July 28, 1948, 3.

"Le droit d'enseigner." *L'Aube*, August 14, 1948, 2.

"Vacances parlementaires." *Le Monde*, August 16, 1948, 3.

"L'assemblée des Trente." *Le Monde*, August 21, 1948, 1.

"L'encombrement parlementaire." *L'Aube*, August 24, 1948, 2

"Monopole et neutralité." *L'Aube*, August 28, 1948, 2.

"Le plus pressé." *Le Monde*, August 31, 1948, 1.

"Soigner la chute." *Le Monde*, September 6, 1948, 1.

"Perplexités parlementaires." *Le Monde*, September 11, 1948, 1–2.

"1=3." *Le Monde*, September 16, 1948, 1.

"Le pédagogue incompétent." *L'Aube*, September 18, 1948, 2.

"La planche vermoulue." *Le Monde*, September 18, 1948, 1.

"Métamorphoses de l'empire." *Le Monde*, October 30, 1948, 1–2.

"L'empire vu du Canada." *Le Monde*, November 18, 1948, 1–2.

"Le Canada et la guerre." *Le Monde*, December 2, 1948, 1.

"Un nouvel isolationnisme." *Le Monde*, December 11, 1948, 1–2.

"Les États-Unis et les problèmes de l'Europe Occidentale, un peuple juste." *Le Monde*, December 25, 1948, 3.

1949 "Le Vatican et le communisme." *Le Monde*, February 5, 1949, 1–2.

"Cendrillon." *Le Monde*, February 20–21, 1949, 1–2.

"L'alternative." *Le Monde*, March 2, 1949, 1–2.

"L'équivoque." *Le Monde*, March 6–7, 1949, 1–2.

"Le pacte et le Sénat américain." *Le Monde*, March 26, 1949, 1.

"Le communisme et la paix." *Le Monde*, April 8, 1949, 1–2.

"Les États-Unis et l'Allemagne." *Le Monde*, April 22, 1949, 1–2.

"Un pacificateur." *Le Monde*, May 12, 1949, 1–2.

"Que devient le pacte atlantique?" *Le Monde*, July 6, 1949, 1–2.

"Le millénaire de Cluny." *Le Monde*, July 10–11, 1949, 1–2.

"Pour la paix religieuse." *Le Monde*, July 20, 1949, 1–2.

"Encore le baccalauréat." *Le Monde*, August 4, 1949, 3.

"Un avertissement perdu." *Le Monde*, August 20, 1949, 1.

"Une découverte russe." *Le Monde*, August 26, 1949, 3.

"Un avertissement solennel." *Le Monde*, September 2, 1949, 1–2.

"L'Amérique et nos colonies." *Le Monde*, October 18–19, 1949, 1.

"Un verdict américain." *Le Monde*, October 20, 1949, 1.

"Évolution canadienne." *Le Monde*, October 27, 1949, 3.

"Le coup polonais." *L'Aube*," November 29, 1949, 1.

"Le réarmement allemand." *Le Monde*, November 30, 1949, 1.

"Un canadien d'expression française, M. Édouard Monpetit, correspondant de l'Institut." *Le Monde*, December 1, 1949, 6.

1950 "Un drame de l'amitié, Charles du Bos et André Gide." *Esprit* 18, no. 171 (September 1950): 415–19.

"Un hétérodoxe." *Le Monde*, January 7, 1950, 1.

"L'ombre de la servitude." *Le Monde*, January 12, 1950, 1.

"1940–1950." *Le Monde*, January 14, 1950, 1.

"La plaie." *Le Monde*, January 21, 1950, 1–3.

"La plainte." *Le Monde*, January 25, 1950, 6.

"En marge des négociations atlantiques: 1. Défaitisme et neutralité." *Le Monde*, April 28, 1950, 1–2.

"En marge des négociations atlantiques: 2. La neutralité vers l'Est." *Le Monde*, April 29, 1950, 1–3.

"En marge des négociations atlantiques: 3. La neutralité vers l'Ouest." *Le Monde*, April 30, 1950, 1–2.

"Des différentes notions de la neutralité." *Le Monde*, May 20, 1950, 2

"L'avenir du Commonwealth." *Le Monde*, June 21, 1950, 1

"Neutrality for France?" *Bulletin of the Atomic Scientists* 6, no. 7 (July 1950): 203–5.

"Le temps de la décision." *Le Monde*, July 13, 1950, 1.

"Au pays de Descartes." *Le Monde*, July 21, 1950, 1.

"Dans l'étau des faits." *Le Monde*, August 6–7, 1950, 1.

"Sur un manifeste." *Le Monde*, August 11, 1950, 1.

"Un appel américain." *Le Monde*, August 17, 1950, 1.

"Le labyrinthe." *Le Monde*, August 24, 1950, 1–2.

"L'homme de Strasbourg." *Le Monde*, August 27, 1950, 1–2.

"Querelles de mots." *Le Monde*, August 30, 1950, 1–2.

"L'appel du Bec." *Revue de la pensée française*, no. 9 (September 1950): 14–17.

"Un échec." *Le Monde*, September 7, 1950, 4.

"Épilogue." *Le Monde*, September 29, 1950, 1–2.

1951 "The Right to be Neutral." *The Nation*, no. 172, 435.

"Cloisonnement cellulaire." *Le Monde*, February 14, 1950, 1.

"Une lettre de M. Étienne Gilson." *Le Monde*, February 22, 1951, 1, 4.

"M. Étienne Gilson répond à M. Waldemar Gurian." *Le Monde*, March 8, 1951, 4.

"Lettre à Albert Béguin." *Esprit* 19, no. 178 (April 1951): 593–96.

1952 "Le salut de la France au Canada." *France-Amérique Magazine. Revue mensuelle des nations américaines*, Special issue on "le Nouveau Canada," no. 7–9, 1952, 192–96.

"Hommage à l'Université Laval." *Revue des Deux Mondes*, November 1, 1952, 16–19.

"À propos de l'Université de Laval." *Le Monde*, November 14, 1952, 7.

1953 "Le jubilé de Louis de Broglie." *Le Monde*, January 8, 1953, 5.

1954 "Avenir d'une tradition." *Le Monde*, September 11, 1954, 2.

1957 "Le centenaire d'Auguste Comte." *Le Monde*, September 4, 1957.

1958 "Un philosophe singulier: À propos de Gabriel Marcel." *Nouvelles Littéraires*, June 19, 1958, 1, 7.

1959 "L'Allemagne et l'Europe." *Le Monde*, June 27, 1959, 1.

"Preparation for Examinations." *Basilian Teacher*, no. 3, 1959, 208–12.

1962 "L'itinéraire d'Henri Bergson." *Nouvelles littéraires*, January 25, 1962, 1, 9.

1963 "Souvenirs du Père." *La France catholique*, June 7, 1963, 1–2.

1965 "Suis-je schismatique?" *La France catholique*, July 2, 1965, 1

"Une vie déromancée. Auguste Comte." *Les Nouvelles littéraires*, July 8, 1965, 7

1966 "*Sicut et Nos*: Sur le Notre Père." *La France catholique*, February 18, 1966.

"L'absence du Millénaire." *Les Nouvelles littéraires*, August 25, 1966, 1–10.

"Comme un diable dans un bénitier, Huysmans à Lourdes." *Les Nouvelles littéraires*, September 22, 1966, 9.

1968 "Des laïcs disent au pape leur confiance." *La France Catholique*, December 20, 1968, 1.

Courses, Talks, Lectures, Interviews, and Addresses

1908 "Discours d'ouverture." *Distribution solennelle des prix*, Lycée Lalande, Imprimerie générale, Bourg-en-Bresse, July 30, 1908, 7–14

1911 "Discours." *Distribution solennelle des prix*, Lycée Descartes, Tours, October 1911, 32–36

1922 "Enquête sur la situation actuelle des enfants en Ukraine et dans les régions de la Volga: Enquête pour le Comité français de secours aux enfants, 15 août–15 septembre 1922." *Revue de la Croix-Rouge*, October 1922.

1926 Participation in the discussion: "Les conditions d'existence de l'enseignement supérieur de la philosophie," February 13, 1926; published in *Bulletin de la Société française de philosophie*, no. 26, 1–28; see in particular 24–25 for two brief contributions by Gilson. The discussion was led by Léon Brunschvicg, with written or oral contributions by numerous colleagues (Maurice Blondel, Célestin Bouglé, Jean Wahl, M. M. Belot, Bourdon, Carteron, Davy, Parodi, Rivaud, Léon Robin, Georges Lyon, André Lalande, Étienne Gilson.)

1931 "Exposé des titres pour une chaire d'histoire de la philosophie au Moyen Âge au Collège de France, Paris."

1932 "Professor Gilson's Lecture to the Students in the Study Hall." December 13, 1932, Saint Michael's College, Toronto, 10 pp.

1934 "Discours de M. Étienne Gilson." *Association fraternelle des anciens élèves de Notre-Dame-des-Champs*, 16–21. Paris: Louis de Soye, 1934.

1940 "Le français et la philosophie." Broadcast by the Montreal radio station CKAC on March 30, 1940, for la Société du Bon Parler Français, published in *L'action universitaire* 6, no. 8 (April 1940): 5–6.

1946 Participation in the discussion: "Can UNESCO Educate for World Understanding?" The University of Chicago Round Table, December 1.

"Le monde va-t-il vers un nouveau Moyen Âge? Entretien avec Paul Guth." *Le Littéraire*, Paris, December 28, 1946, 1, 3.

1947 "Les données chrétiennes de la politique nationale" [title of the course in manuscript, SMCA]; "Les forces religieuses et la vie politique par Étienne Gilson de l'Académie française. Professeur au Collège de France" [title of the published courses]. René Grousset, Étienne Gilson, André Siegfried, Louis Massignon, André Latreille, *Les forces religieuses et la vie politique*, 3 vols., collection: Les cours de droit (Université de Paris, Institut d'études politiques, 1947), 2:84–141.

Discours de réception à l'Académie française, 3–10. Paris: Firmin-Didot, 1947.

Notre démocratie. Paris, SERP, 1948. 30 pp.

"Les intellectuels dans la chrétienté." Lecture given April 12, 1947, during the first Congress of the Pax Romana, at Palazetto Venezia, Rome. Published in *Travaux et documents*, May-June 1947, 3–15; republished in *Les Intellectuels dans la Chrétienté* (Geneva: Pax Romana / Mouvement International des Intellectuels Catholiques, 1948), 159–78.

"Letter from Étienne Gilson to Louis-Pasteur Vallery-Radot, Reply to the reception speech by Étienne Gilson, May 9, 1947, complete text available on the Académie française website: https://www.academie-francaise.fr

Proposition de Résolution tendant à demander aux bouillères des bassins d'Aquintane, des Cévennes et de la Loire à donner à bail aux associations des parents d'élèves les locaux des ancienens écoles privés des mines, Conseil de la République, 1re législature, sessions de 1946–47, annexe no. 482 séance du 30 juillet 1947, 505. [Proposal to require the coal mines of the Aquitaine, Cévennes, and Loire basins to transfer immediately to the parents of students the buildings of former private schools of the mines, Conseil de la République, first legislative term, 1946–1947, appendix no. 482, session of July 30, 1947, 505.]

Proposition de Résolution tendant à inviter le Gouvernement à régulariser dans les plus brefs délais la situation des fonctionnaires détachés de leur adminsisration d'origine dans autres administrations, Conseil de la République, 1re législature, sessions de 1946–1947, annexe no. 974, séance du 30 décembre 1947, 767 [Proposal to request the government to normalize as quickly as possible the status of civil servants reassigned from their entity to another entity, Conseil de la République, first legislative term 1946–1947, appendix no. 974, session of December 30, 1947, 767.]

"Rapport tendant à inviter le gouvernement à créer des cours de droit d'outre-mer dans les facultés de la métropole qui n'en possèdent pas encore, Conseil de la République, 1re législature, annexe no. 485, séance du 30 juillet 1947, 507 [Report made on behalf of the National Education Commission to request the gouvernement to create courses on overseas law in any metropolitan law faculties that do not have them already, Consei de la République, first legislative term, 1946–1947, appendix no. 485, session of July 30, 1847, 507.]

"Raport fait au nom de la commission de l'Éducation tendant à inviter le gouvernement à prendre d'urgence les mesures nécessairse pour converver ou restituer à leur usage normal d'écoles publiques laïques les bâtiments scolaires acquis régulièrement," Conseil de la République, Ire législature, annexe no. 902, séance du 17 decembre 692–93 [Report submitted on behalf of the National Education Committee to take necessary measures to preserve or restore duly acquired school buildings of secular public schools to their normal use." Conseil de la République, First Legislative Term, appendix no. 902, session of December 17, 1947].

1948 Étienne Gilson's speech at the Congress of Europe, The Hague, May 8. Document available online at www.cvce.eu/en.

"The Task of the Democratic State." Paper presented at National Summer Conference of the Young Liberal Federation of Canada, McMaster University, Hamilton, Ontario, September 1 to 5, 1947. Published in *Canada Looks Ahead: A Series of Addresses and Papers Presented at the National Summer Conference of the Young Liberal Federation of Canada*, 78–91 (Ottawa: Tower Books, 1948).

"Culture et civilisation." In *Les cents ans de l'Institut canadien de Québec: Compte rendu des fêtes du centenaire en septembre 1948*, edited by Alphonse Desilets, 76–84. Québec: L'Institut Canadien de Québec, 1948.

"La question de l'enseignement libre en France." *La Documentation catholique* 45, September 12, 1948, 1163–69.

"Les intellectuels et la paix." In *Les intellectuels devant la charité du Christ*, 218–29. Paris: De Flore, 1948.

1949 "Situation des philosophes actuels devant la foi." Semaine des intellectuels catholiques de 1949, session Monday, May 9. Étienne Gilson presided with Étienne Borne, Henri Gouhier, and Aimé Forest. Published in *Foi en Jésus-Christ et monde d'aujourd'hui*, 34–55. Paris: De Flore, 1949.

1950 "La liberté politique et les partis." Unpublished lecture of Étienne Gilson, January 18, 1950.

1951 "La sagesse et le temps." *Lumière et vie: Revue de formation doctrinale chrétienne*, December 1951, 77–92.

1952 "Dogmatism and tolerance." *International Journal* 8, no. 1 (Winter 1952/1953): 7–16; published separately with the title *Dogmatism and Tolerance: An Address to the Students and Faculty of Rutgers University Given at the Voorhees Chapel of the New Jersey College for Women on December the 12th, 1951*. New Brunswick, NJ: Rutgers University Press, 1952.

"The breakdown of morals and Christian Education." Saint Michael's College, Toronto, 16 pp. "A Lecture in the Adult Education Program of Saint Michael's College, University of Toronto." Rochester, NY: St. John Fisher College, 1960. Also available at SMCA.

"Religious Wisdom and Scientific Knowledge." In *Christianity in an Age of Science*, 15–22. Toronto: Canadian Broadcasting Corporation, CBC Publications Branch, 1952.

1953 "The Eminence of Teaching." In *The McAuley Lectures: Truth and the Philosophy of Teaching*, 5–15. West Hartford, CT: Saint Joseph College, 1953.

Thomas Aquinas and our Colleagues. The Aquinas Foundation Lecture. Princeton, NJ: Princeton University Press, 1953.

1954 "*École à la croisée des chemins*. Lecture given at the Collège Jean-de-Brébeuf, April 25, 1954. Montréal: Collège Jean-de-Brébeuf, 1954. 32 pp.

1955 "The Role of Science in Catholic Education." In *Disputed Questions in Education*, vol. 2, 5–16. New York: Doubleday, 1955.

1956 "The Place of History in Catholic Education." Given as a lecture on October 7, 1955, at the Diocesan Teachers Institute, Diocese of Cleveland, Ohio. Published in *Disputed Questions in Education*, vol. 3. New York: Doubleday, 1956. 27 pp.

1959 "Philosophie du plagiat." Session of Monday, November 9, 1959. *Bulletin de l'Académie royale de Belgique*, Brussels, 556–72, offprint Brussels: Palais de académies, 1959.

1961 "L'unité spirituelle de l'Europe du Moyen Âge à l'heure actuelle." In *L'unification européenne: Réalité et problèmes; Atti del V Convegno di Cultura Europeana*, 21–24. Bolzano, 1961.

1963 "Réflexion sur l'éducation philosophique." Lecture given at the first Sémaine de philosophie at the University of Montreal, March 19, 1963. Recovered from a recording in SMCA and published in the journal *Conférence*, no. 26 (August 27, 2008): 611–31.

1965 "Allocution de M. Étienne Gilson, prononcée lors de la messe célébrée à New York à la mémoire de M. Henri Daniel-Rops, le 13 novembre 1965." 3–5. Paris: Institut, Firmin-Didot, 1965, available on line at the website of the Acadèmie francaise.

1967 "Hommage public à Henri Bergson: Allocution de M. Étienne Gilson." Ceremony at the Pantheon, Thursday, May 11, 1967. Published as a pamphlet, Paris: Firmin-Didot, 1967.

1969 "Paul Claudel, poète catholique." Delivered at the colloquium, December 13, 1968 at l'Institut catholique de Paris. Published in *La pensée religieuse de Claudel*, ed. Centre catholique des intellectuels français, 31–44. Recherches et débats. Paris: Desclée de Brouwer, 1969. Published in *France catholique*, December 20, 1968, 3; and in *Nouvelles de l'Institut catholique de Paris*, January 1969, 9–23.

1970 "Discours prononcé à l'occasion du 150e anniversaire de l'Académie de Savoie. Chambéry. Séance solennelle publique du vendredi 8 mai 1970." Paris, L'Institut, Firmin-Didot, 1970.

"Propos sur le bonheur: Séance publique annuelle tenue le jeudi 17 décembre 1970," 3–12. Paris: L'Institut, Firmin-Didot.

1973 "Propos sur l'Académie: Séance publique annuelle tenue le jeudi 14 décembre 1972," 3–11. Paris: L'Institut, Firmin-Didot.

"Cinquantième anniversaire de la mort de Pierre Loti. Inauguration du Musée Pierre Loti à Rochefort-sur-Mer. Discours prononcé le 8 avril 1973 à Rochefort-sur-Mer." Paris: Firmin-Didot, 1973. 8 pp.

Reviews, Prefaces, Letters, Forewords, and Introductions

1919 Review of two works by Alfred Loisy, *La discipline intellectuelle* et *La paix des nations et la religion de l'avenir* (Paris, 1919). *Revue philosophique de la France et de l'étranger*, no. 88 (1919): 129–31.

Review of Gonzague Truc, *Le retour à la scolastique* (Paris, 1919). *Revue philosophique de la France et de l'étranger*, no. 88 (1919): 322–24.

1921 Review of three works: Agostino Gemelli, *Le dottrine moderne della delinquenza* (Milan, 1920); Agostino Gemelli, *Religione e scienze* (Milan, 1920); and Francesco Olgiati, *Carlo Marx* (Milan, 1920). *Revue philosophique de la France et de l'étranger*, no. 92 (1921): 298–99.

1926 Letter from Étienne Gilson to Henri Gouhier. December 30, Archives Madame Gouhier, Paris.

1932 Preface to *À la mémoire du Dr. Henry Gilson (1857–1932)*, 7–15. Liège: G. Thone, 1932.

1935 Letter from Étienne Gilson to Henri Gouhier, July 4, Archives Gouhier.

1946 "L'hémisphère occidental." Preface to *Romanciers américains contemporains*, xi–xiv. Paris: Librairie Didier, 1946.

1946 "Lettre d'Étienne Gilson." *Hommage et reconnaissance: Recueil de travaux publiés à l'occasion du soixantième anniversaire de Karl Barth*, 41–42. Cahiers théologiques de l'actualité protestante. Paris and Neuchâtel: Delachaux et Niestlé, 1946.

1947 "Le mouvement et le Parti, Mouvement Républicain Populaire." Foreword to *Vers une démocratie nouvelle*, 7–12. Paris: SERP, 1947.

"Un exemple." Preface to *Existentialisme chrétien: Gabriel Marcel*, 1–9. Paris: Plon, 1947.

Preface to *Le grand mystère, de la cellule à l'homme: Essai sur le problème sexuel*, by Dr. Pierre Vallery-Radot, 7–10. Paris: Éditions Paul Dupont, 1947.

Preface to *Les églises de Paris, la rive gauche*, 3–8. Paris: Cerf, 1947.

1948 "Une sagesse rédemptrice." Preface to *Jacques Maritain: Son oeuvre philosophique*, 3–5. Bibliothèque de la Revue thomiste. Paris: Desclée de Brouwer, 1948.

Preface to *Canada: réalités d'hier et d'aujourd'hui*, by Jean Bruchési, 7–13. Montreal: Édition Variétés, 1948.

1950 Preface to *Jean-Baptiste Muard, fondateur de la Pierre-qui-Vire*, by Dom Denis Huerre, 5–10. Saint Léger Vauban: Abbaye de la Pierre-qui-Vire, 1950.

Preface to *Soyons neutres*, by Jacques Nantet, 7–10. Lyon: Éditions LAC, 1950.

1954 Preface to *L'abbaye de Reigny*, by Abbé Marcel Terre, 3–4. Semur-en-Auxois: Imprimerie générale, 1954.

Introduction to *The Church Speaks to the Modern World: The Social Teachings of Leo XIII*, 1–28. Garden City, NY: Image Books, 1954.

1955 Introduction to *A Grammar of Assent*, by J. H. Newman, 7–21. Garden City, NY: Image Books, 1955.

1959 Preface to *Charles Du Bos: Choix de textes*, 9–15. Paris: Éditions du Vieux Colombier, 1959 (texts assembled by initiative of Madame Du Bos, Étienne Gilson, Jean Mouton, and Jean Rounault, and prepared by Gilson, Mouton, and Rounault).

1964 Foreword to *The Poetics of Space*, by Gaston Bachelard, vii–x. New York: Orion Press, 1964.

Index of Names

Index of Terms